The Potter's Dictionary

OF MATERIALS AND TECHNIQUES

The Potter's Dictionary

OF MATERIALS AND TECHNIQUES

FRANK HAMER

Pitman Publishing, London
Watson-Guptill Publications, New York

First published 1975 in Great Britain by Pitman Publishing,
39 Parker Street, Kingsway, London WC2B 5PB

Published simultaneously in the United States by Watson-Guptill Publications,
a division of Billboard Publications, Inc., One Astor Plaza, New York, N.Y.10036

Library of Congress Cataloging in Publication Data
Hamer, Frank
    The potter's dictionary of materials and techniques
    Bibliography: p.
    1. Pottery craft—Dictionaries. 2. Ceramic materials—Dictionaries.
    I. Title.
TT919.5.H35 1975   738.1'03   74–703

U.S. ISBN 0–8230–4210–3
U.K. ISBN 0–273–31465–3

First printing 1975

Printed in Great Britain
at the University Printing House, Cambridge.

G.3355:13

To Janet

PREFACE

This book is for individual potters, teachers and students. It turns a magnifying glass on to the fundamentals, e.g. why clay is plastic and what happens in the firing; it explains how the information was first discovered and how the vocabulary is used.

As a teacher, lecturer and potter I have often been called upon to explain words, phrases and phenomena of pottery and ceramics. There is an increasing interest in the 'fascinating world of the clay crystal' and an awareness that an understanding of technology helps one to be creative as well as to solve problems.

The book can be used for detailed study or for quick reference to a word or process. It is laid out as an index of key words and phrases which give immediate access to short articles. Each article specializes under its own heading and related articles are cross referenced. These allow the reader to find his own path through the information from his starting point. Non-technical language is used and numerous illustrations augment the text.

I am indebted to many people for information. Eleven authors are acknowledged but more must take credit. Their work has influenced mine but this book also contains original research and, I hope, some fresh observations.

Acknowledgement is made to my wife Janet for innumerable re-readings of script, for constructive criticism and help with drawing, photographing, checking and testing; to other readers: Michael Casson, Brian de Graaf, Avis Loshak, Frances Tasker and Ian Herbert; to numerous friends who gave help, criticism and information which is incorporated in the text: Rollo Charles, Sydney Clark, John Davey, Derek Emms, Emlyn Evans, Harry Fraser, Sybil Hollingdrake, Peggy Isaac, David Leach, John Lewis, Kay Jenkins, Mary Hughes, Peter Hughes, Colin Pearson, Brian Pugh, Roy Purnell, Gordon Slinn, Colin Skene, Harry Stringer, Alun Williams and those whose names have been inadvertently omitted; to all potters whose work is reproduced and to the owners of the pots; to previous friends, teachers and authors who have given me information which has become part of my experience and been incorporated in the book. Authors of books frequently in use are M. Cardew, A. E. Dodd, B. Leach, H. N. Holmes, C. W. Parmelee, D. Rhodes, A. B. Searle, K. Shaw, F. Singer, A. Wedgwood, W. E. Worrall; to the organizations, manufacturers, etc. who assisted with information or photographs: Australian High Commission, William Boulton Ltd, Borax Consolidated Ltd, British Standards Institution, Bullers Ltd, Canadian Department of Consumer Affairs, Canadian High Commission, Cardiff College of Art, Craftsmen Potters Association, Edwards and Jones Ltd, Gosling and Gatensbury Ltd, Gwent Pipe and Firebrick Co. Ltd, Harrison Mayer Ltd, Metrication Board, National Museum of Wales, New Zealand High Commission, Edward Orton Junior Ceramic Foundation, Podmore and Sons Ltd, South Wales Potters, United States Information Service, Watts Blake Bearne and Co. Ltd, Wengers Ltd.

Ponthir   FRANK HAMER
January 1975

CONTENTS

Preface   vii

Standard Abbreviations   x

Alphabetical Entries   1

Appendix of Tables

Standard abbreviations	327
Atomic weights of common elements	327
Simplified ultimate analyses of some common materials	328
Table of Harrison pyrometric cones	329
Table of Harrison pyrometric cones (computer numbers)	330
Table of Orton pyrometric cones	330
Table of Seger pyrometric cones	331
Conversion scales	332
Tables concerning densities and contents of suspensions	333
Table of elements	334
List of capacity equivalents	334
Pint weight equivalents	335
List of weight equivalents	335

List of length equivalents	335
Capacity factors	335
Density factors	335
Dry weight factors	335
Table of oxide effect on surface tension	336
Table of thermal expansion and contraction	336
Table of acceptable limits for unity formulae of glazes	336
Mohs' Scale of hardness	336
Effective ranges of glaze oxides	337
Table of mineral constants	338
Table of incandescence	344
Conversion of temperatures	345
List of temperature equivalents	345
Valency table	345
Percentage reckoner	346
Atomic to visible particle sizes compared with wavelengths of electromagnetic radiation	347
Periodic table of elements	348
Potter's periodic table	348

Bibliography   349

Standard abbreviations

At No	Atomic number		cm	centimetre(s)
AW	Atomic weight		cub	cubic
BS	British Standard		cwt	hundredweight(s) avoirdupois
°C	Degrees centigrade or Celsius		fl oz	fluid ounce(s)
CF	Conversion factor		ft	foot (feet)
D	Density		gall	gallon(s)
EMC	Equilibrium moisture content		gm	gram(s) also written g
°F	Degrees Fahrenheit		imp	imperial measure (UK)
H	Hardness on Mohs' Scale		in	inch(es)
I/G	Inglaze colour		kg	kilo(s) or kilogram(s)
°K	Degrees Kelvin		l	litre(s)
MF	Molecular formula		lb	pound(s) avoirdupois
MP	Melting point		m	metre(s)
MW	Molecular weight		ml	millilitre(s)
O/E	Onglaze enamel			(synonymous with cc)
O/G	Onglaze colour		mm	millimetre(s)
SG	Specific gravity		oz	ounce(s) avoirdupois
°TW	Degrees Twaddell		oz pt	ounces per pint
U/G	Underglaze colour			(correctly weight of one pint in ounces)
UK	United Kingdom		pt	pint(s)
	(imperial capacity measure)		qt	quart(s)
US/USA	United States of America		wt	weight
	(capacity measure)		yd	yard(s)
avdp	avoirdupois			
cc	cubic centimetre(s) also written cm^3			
	(synonymous with ml)			

A

Absorbent. Capable of sucking in water etc by capillary action. Absorbency in biscuit ware is made use of in the glazing process. For tests of absorbency, see **Porosity.**

Absorption is not to be confused with adsorption which involves the collection of molecules of water from the moisture in the atmosphere. See **Adsorption.**

Accelerator. Catalyst. A substance that speeds up a chemical action. In mixing plaster of Paris the setting time can be decreased by adding an already crystalline substance such as common salt, gypsum or previously set plaster. This starts the chemical action which in this case is a crystal growth and is noticeable as setting. One per cent of set plaster will decrease the setting time of a fresh plaster from about 25 to 15 minutes and the time available between mixing and commencement of setting will be decreased from about 7 to 2 minutes.

Acid. To the potter there are acid solutions used in slips and slops, acidic compounds used in bodies and glazes, and acidic gases liberated during firing. An acid is a chemical compound which liberates protons, the positive electrical charges at the centre of atoms. Acids go into solution with non-acidic compounds from which solution new compounds, called salts, may be precipitated. The process may be immediate, e.g.

$$2HCl + Na_2O \longrightarrow H_2O + 2NaCl$$

hydrochloric acid — soda — water — sodium chloride

(strong acid) + (strong alkali) $\longrightarrow$ (salt solution)

Or it may be slow and require heat, e.g.

$$SiO_2 + CaO \xrightarrow{1100°C} CaO.SiO_2 \text{ or } CaSiO_3$$

silica — calcia — calcium silicate

(acid) + (alkali) + (heat) $\longrightarrow$ (molten solution which may crystallize upon cooling)

The acid destroys the other compound and itself in a process of neutralization. The non-acidic compounds are alkalis and amphoteric substances.

A common household acid is vinegar. The sting in its taste is the attack by the positive electrical charges of the hydrogen ions seeking neutralization. Acidic solutions, like vinegar, are used to flocculate slips.

Slips that have become too watery and will not settle have probably become so because the water is too alkaline. They can be made to thicken and eventually settle by the addition of vinegar to neutralize the alkali. The acid encourages the clay particles to form box-like structures which link together and become larger particles. The larger particles then sediment. The box-like structure is called 'card-house structure'.

The same structure is used to create the opposite effect in glaze slops composed of non-clay materials. Here a small amount of extremely fine clay is added to the glaze slop and flocculated by an acid. It is usual to use bentonite, about 1% of the recipe, for the clay and calcium chloride for the acid. Flocculated bentonite gives an extremely open, jelly-like structure which noticeably stiffens the glaze, thereby holding the non-clay materials like flint and whiting. It does not prevent their settling but inhibits this for long enough to facilitate the glazing process. See **Flocculation** and **Fluidity.**

The potter, who is familiar with silica as the hard rock called quartz or as a white insoluble flint powder, does not think of it as an acid or as a possible solution. Molten glazes are, however, solutions and silica is included in these. It can also exist as a solution with water at room temperature. The solution is silicic acid (H_2SiO_3 or $H_2O.SiO_2$). It can be prepared but not by merely mixing silica and water. Silicic acid is a weak acid but its existence shows the acidic tendency of silica.

Another glass-former, boric oxide is well-known in solution form as boric or boracic acid (H_3BO_3 or $3H_2O.B_2O_3$). This is a very weak acid and is used as a mild antiseptic. The potter would happily accept boric oxide as an acid when he might not accept silica as one. Yet silica has a stronger acid potential than boric oxide.

One must accept the idea of talking about some oxides as acids although they are not acidic solutions in the form in which they are handled. The classification of silica as an acid and of some other oxides as acids under certain circumstances is an important way of assessing their potential in bodies and glazes. During firing they are neutralized by alkalis (fluxes) and other non-acidic oxides to form solutions (glasses). The most stable glazes contain at least twice as many acidic molecules as alkaline ones. See **Acidic oxides** and **Periodic table.**

Flue gases and gases from clay and glaze materials are often potentially acidic. Electric kilns without flues fill the kiln room atmosphere with sulphur dioxide and trioxide, chlorine and fluorine which combine with the atmosphere to form acids. These acids attack the kiln's metal framework and over a period of years the fluorine will etch the workshop windows until they are like frosted glass. This is obviously an unhealthy atmosphere for the potter.

Acidic oxides. Oxides displaying acidic properties in ceramic fusions. They are silica (SiO_2) and phosphorus pentoxide (P_2O_5).

A number of other oxides, which are mostly dioxides, display some acidic properties in ceramic fusions. However they also display amphoteric properties which make it difficult to assess the unity formulae in which they appear. Those with strong acidic properties are:

> boric oxide (B_2O_3)
> titania (TiO_2)
> tin oxide (SnO_2)
> zirconia (ZrO_2)
> ceria (CeO_2)
> vanadium oxide (V_2O_5)
> germania (GeO_2)

Those with slight acidic properties are:

> antimony oxide (Sb_2O_3)
> arsenic oxide (As_2O_3)
> praseodymium oxide (PrO_2)

Two other oxides display acidic properties in the raw state but change their oxidation during firing to become alkaline in character. They are:

> manganese dioxide (MnO_2)
> lead dioxide (PbO_2)

Manganese dioxide becomes manganous oxide (MnO) at 1080°C (1976°F). Lead dioxide is part of the lead compound called red lead (Pb_3O_4). It becomes lead oxide (PbO) at 600°C (1112°F).

Adhesive. Binder. Glue. Any substance added to a glaze to make it remain on the pot before firing. By hardening a friable glaze, it acts as a binder and makes the ware easier to handle in the kiln setting. Adhesives are sometimes put on to a biscuited pot, especially a hard biscuit, to provide a key for the glaze, which will also contain some adhesive.

Any paste or glue will work. Some smell more than others before and during the firing. Gelatinous glues may have the effect of temporarily thickening a glaze slop for the hour or two after being added. Polymer adhesives also give flocculatory effects. See **Flocculation** and **Suspender**. Cellulose pastes and resin gums often give deflocculatory effects.

Adit. Name given to the clay layers, especially when mining or quarrying ball clays.

Adsorption. The action whereby a substance, such as water, is attracted to and concentrated on the surface of a solid. This is an electrostatic action, and results from the atomic charges. It should not be confused with absorption, which is the taking of water into spaces by capillary and gravitational action, as with a sponge. Adsorption comes into the potter's vocabulary with the attraction of water to fully-dried clay, for a description of which see **Readsorption**. The electrostatic charges involved are described under **Double layer theory**.

Agate ware. A decorative ware made from partially blended dark and light clays which give striations. The effect is sometimes created with surface slips. The name comes from the semi-precious agate stone, a form of crypto-crystalline quartz with striated markings.

The photograph shows 'petaloid' ware, a form of solid agate made by Harry Horlock Stringer.

Ageing. Souring. Maturing. The storing of clay in plastic state to improve workability. See **Workability**. Ageing is used as a synonym for souring although a difference can be inferred. Clay can be aged in damp rooms, in airtight bins or by wrapping in polythene sheets. The intention is to keep the clay damp. A warm atmosphere is acceptable if humid, but frost should be avoided at this stage because it brings the water out of the clay leaving it difficult to deal with by hand methods of wedging and kneading. Weathering is an earlier stage of clay conditioning which uses frost.

Ageing involves the slow penetration of water between clay particles giving a net result of more particles of smaller size. This means a higher plasticity. When the clay is put to age, there should be extra water available in the clay. If this is not done the clay cannot age properly and may be too stiff to use after ageing. It is an easier process to dewater a clay slightly by kneading on an absorbent surface than it is to add water and mix this in.

Another action during ageing is the slow compression of the clay particles. A stack of clay is compressed slightly under its own weight. Particles which are closer together have more strength. They are held together by suction with the seal of water. Providing there is water between the particles, the full plasticity will be maintained. The compressed clay has increased workability.

Compression can be achieved without ageing by vigorous wedging. A good pugmill will also compress the clay but the ideal simulation is a de-airing pugmill. The use of a vacuum causes air pockets to explode and subsequent pugging from the vacuumed state packs the particles together. Once through a de-airing pugmill is said to equal two months of ageing.

Ageing is also used to give clay a rest. Clays which have been overworked, thrown on the wheel, passed through a pugmill with worn blades or cut about in a mixer, become tired. Like the potter, they require a rest. There is no question here of increasing plasticity. It is a matter of regaining strength in the clay by general compression and thereby regaining workability. The same effect is achieved by de-airing the clay. Contrary to popular opinion, plasticity is not increased by de-airing, but workability is; and this is noticeable to the potter.

Ageing is a physical action. Souring is slightly different: it involves organic action. Bacteria in the clay break down the organic matter and multiply. In so doing they create a colloidal gel through the water which is between the clay particles. This gel has the property of plasticity which adds to that of the clay. The clay turns a blue-grey colour inside and begins to smell. This is why it is called souring.

A clay which smells like rotting vegetation is therefore prized. Portions are added to other clays to spread the growth. A clay kept especially for handles should always smell. It will be the same clay as the body clay but will have extra plasticity/workability. A gardener's soil disinfectant which encourages bacteria can be added to clays to promote this action. It should be added in a much-diluted form or else it will kill the bacteria.

The organic matter, upon decomposition, releases amino acid which slightly flocculates the clay giving the particles a more pronounced polarity. Slight re-arrangement of particles may take place which provides larger spaces for water. There may be some action here which counteracts that of compression but the overall result of a clay's increased water capacity is likely to be an extended workability range. A small amount of extra water, added first, should be available.

De-airing can simulate ageing but it cannot simulate souring. In fact it often seems to produce a very dense plastic clay which does not sour readily. The more open clays produced by the dough mixing method appear to sour more readily. If both processes are used, the clay should be soured first and de-aired afterwards.

Alabaster. Calcium sulphate. Gypsum. $CaSO_4 . 2H_2O$. See **Gypsum**.

Albany slip. A slip glaze made from Albany clay alone or modified with feldspar and other fluxes. The clay is an alluvial deposit of the Hudson River in the vicinity of Albany in New York State.

When used as a glaze it produces a series of rich yellows, blacks and browns over a wide range of temperature from 1100°C to 1300°C (2012°F to 2372°F). It was first developed when the early American potters followed the European practice of refining the body clay to make a glaze.

In Britain, the mud from many of the larger tidal rivers gives similar effects. It can be modified with feldspar, wood ash etc, and gives mostly tenmoku-type slip-glazes for stoneware.

Albarello. The Spanish and Italian decorated drug jar of the 13th to 18th centuries. The best examples are maiolica, about 15 inches high and 6 inches wide. They

are of interesting proportions: often a slightly concave cylinder with smaller neck and foot. Liquid drugs were kept in bottles also referred to as albarellos.

Albite. Soda feldspar. $Na_2O.Al_2O_3.6SiO_2$. The second common form of feldspar, the most common being orthoclase (potash feldspar). Albite is used, as is orthoclase, for a body and glaze flux, but being soda-based it gives slightly different results. It is sometimes called white feldspar to differentiate it from orthoclase which is often pinkish, but the term is not specific enough to be used other than between potters in one workshop.

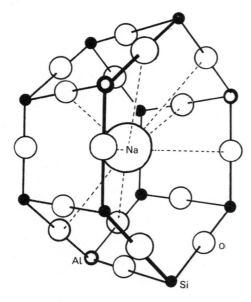

The photograph shows a large, almost pure, albite crystal about 2 inches across. Potter's albite is rarely so pure but contains some of the other feldspars and therefore potash and calcia are present amounting to perhaps 4% of the whole.

The drawing shows the lattice structure of albite. Oxygen tetrahedra centred on three silicon atoms and one aluminium atom create four-sided rings which link to give crooked chains. The chains are cross-linked by the tetrahedra to give a honeycomb of holes. Sodium atoms occupy the holes in eight-fold co-ordination. The structure is very similar to that of anorthite, the diagram for which is represented in a complementary way.

It is often possible to substitute albite for orthoclase or cornish stone in bodies and glazes without causing large changes in the result. There must be differences, however slight, because, both chemically and physically, albite is unique. The qualities of albite (soda feldspar) are most easily understood in a comparison with orthoclase (potash feldspar).

The alkaline properties of soda are different from those of potash and therefore slightly different colour responses occur when albite is used in place of orthoclase. The blue from cobalt oxide is slightly more purple and the green from copper oxide tends more towards blue.

As a flux, soda is more powerful than potash but its range is much shorter. Soda starts its fluxing action about 800°C (1472°F) and begins to volatilize at 1200°C (2192°F). Potash starts to flux at 750°C (1382°F) and has no upper limit. However, since soda is a more powerful flux, albite has a melting point of approximately 1170°C (2138°F) which is lower than orthoclase's 1200°C (2192°F). Albite is therefore useful in the middle range of 900°C to 1200°C (1652°F to 2192°F) as a body and glaze material, and in combination with orthoclase, it assists glaze fluidity without detracting from the overall stability. Above 1200°C, glazes with a high proportion of ablite are prone to bubbling due to volatile soda. See **Soda in glazes**.

Soda has a higher coefficient of expansion than potash. Glazes containing albite instead of orthoclase are more likely to craze. They craze because they contract more than the body in cooling. Some adjustment of contraction can be made by simple substitution of albite for orthoclase and *vice versa* in body and glaze recipes. See **Glaze fit**.

The soda content of albite tends to be slightly soluble and for this reason albite is often dry ground instead of being ground in water. Prolonged maturation of glaze slops containing albite and clay may involve deflocculation of the clay content by the soluble soda in the albite. It is often preferable to purchase a water-ground albite if available. It is also finer.

Alkali. The opposite of acid. Potters call the glaze and body fluxes their alkalis. These are the non-colouring metal oxides which react with the acids in the presence of heat to produce silicates (glasses). The so-called strong alkalis are:

lithia (Li$_2$O)
soda (Na$_2$O)
potash (K$_2$O)

which are soluble in water. The weaker alkalis are partly referred to as alkaline earths or by the more general name of bases. They are:

beryllia (BeO)
magnesia (MgO)
calcia (CaO)
zinc oxide (ZnO)
strontia (SrO)
cadmium oxide (CdO)
baria (BaO)
lead oxide (PbO)
bismuth oxide (Bi$_2$O$_3$)

They are not necessarily weaker in ceramic fusions but are less actively soluble in water. They do not give the same bright colour response in glazes as the strong alkalis. The alkalis are described in relation to the other oxides, amphoteric and acidic, in the section on the Periodic table.

The terms alkali and alkaline oxide are used in this book when describing all the above oxides. The chemist's terms 'base' and 'basic oxide' are avoided because, to the potter, a 'base' is more often part of a pot and 'basic' has the more general meaning of fundamental.

Alkalis release negatively-charged hydroxyl ions (OH$^-$) when dissolved in water. They have a sting and are corrosive in a similar way to acids whilst being neutralized by the substances they meet. The soluble alkalis, soda ash and sodium silicate, are used to de-flocculate clay for slip casting. See **Deflocculant**.

Alkaline glazes. Glazes have a high content of alkalis. They still contain acidic oxides which form the glass but are usually low in the amphoteric oxides. For this reason they are usually runny. The alkalis present are the stronger alkalis: lithia, soda, potash and baria.

Soda and potash have high rates of expansion and contraction. Glazes which contain a high proportion of these oxides, especially soda, are likely to craze. Also these glazes are brittle and can be impractical without the more stabilizing effects of lead oxide and boric oxide. Lead oxide unfortunately modifies the interesting colours obtainable, but small amounts of boric oxide can be used in alkaline glazes to give elasticity. As explained under **Glaze fit**, boric oxide also has the effect of decreasing the rate of expansion and thus correcting some of the worst crazing. Some crazing seems inevitable if the best colours are to be obtained. Some of the best known colours are: turquoise blue from copper, pink from cobalt, and blue from iron. They are

amongst the brightest and purest of pottery colours.

Alkaline glazes were used effectively on early Egyptian pottery and modelling and on Persian pottery and tiles. The bright sunlight of the area demanded a brightly-coloured ware. Some examples of these wares

have been strongly weathered and the glazes have disintegrated. This serves as a reminder that alkaline glazes tend to be unstable. Whilst copper oxide can give a good colour, its poisonous nature in unstable glazes must be overcome if alkaline glazes are to be used on functional wares.

Alluvial. Material deposited by a river. Clay is often an alluvial deposit. It has been removed by rainwater from its place of origin where it would have been called a primary or residual clay. It settles when the river runs slowly enough, e.g. on a flood plain or in a lake. It is now called a secondary or alluvial clay. In the process of being moved the clay is ground finer, is sorted by particle size and picks up impurities. Hence alluvial clays are usually more plastic, stickier, darker in colour and less refractory than residual clays.

Alumina. Corundum. Aluminium oxide, trioxide or sesquioxide. Al$_2$O$_3$. An important oxide in ceramics: it is second only to silica in importance. It is combined with silica in the clay crystal and it is alumina's presence that causes a flat crystal and thereby gives clay its plasticity. In glazes alumina is an intermediate oxide and serves to stabilize the combination of fluxes and glass-formers. It affects the stiffness of the molten glaze: too little and the glaze is too runny; too much and the surface remains pinholed or cratered. It is rarely necessary to introduce pure alumina into a body or glaze. It is usually possible to introduce sufficient in compound minerals like china clay and feldspar.

Alumina occurs naturally as the crystalline mineral corundum. Large crystals, tinged by traces of chromium, cobalt, copper and iron are the precious stones ruby and sapphire. The alumina spinels are also gem stones. The pure crystal of alumina is second only to diamond in hardness of natural minerals. It is number 9 on Mohs' Scale. Impure corundum which is greatly stained by iron is called emery and is used as an abrasive. Alumina occurs in hydrated form as bauxite, gibbsite and diaspore. These are easier to crush but become the hard crystal alumina upon calcination. From these can be produced a white powdered alumina and these are also the source of the metal aluminium which is important in light-weight alloys.

Igneous rocks invariably contain alumina. All the feldspars and feldspathoids are alumino-silicates in which alumina is combined with silica. This combination results in a slight off-balance of the overall electrical charge which is stabilized by the attraction of another element and the creation of an alkaline content such as potash or soda. Clay results from the decomposition of igneous rocks and the kaolinite (clay) crystal is an alumino-silicate with the balance of charges equated by hydrogen.

Alumina is an amphoteric oxide. It is capable of acting as an alkali or an acid or as a link between the two extremes. The interaction of alkali/acid with heat loosens the solid state structure thus resulting in ceramic fusion. At very high temperatures alumina acts as a flux. The melting point of silica can be lowered from 1710°C (3110°F) to 1545°C (2813°F) by the addition of 10% alumina. Alumina's own high melting point of 2050°C (3722°F) severely limits its activity as a flux at normal ceramic temperatures. It is usual therefore to consider alumina as an anti-flux. The term 'anti-flux' is to be preferred to 'acid' because alumina is not a glass-former.

In most cases the amount of alumina in a body or glaze can be controlled by the use of alumino-silicates. The mineral with the highest alumina content is china clay, followed by the ball clays, feldspars and cornish stones. When pure alumina is introduced it is for a special purpose.

ALUMINA IN BODIES. In bodies, powdered alumina acts as a refractory opener. It cuts down the drying shrinkage on the raw clay and makes the body able to withstand a higher temperature during firing. Its use is restricted by its price. It is a little more effective than silica (flint or quartz) but is more expensive. However in some vitrified bodies it may be preferred to silica on account of its different rate of thermal expansion.

In cases where a higher alumina chemical content is required in a body, the obvious long-term alteration would be in the choice of a more aluminous clay with a grog of similar material.

ALUMINA IN GLAZES. In glazes, the function of alumina is to act as an intermediate oxide linking the alkaline and acidic oxides in stable glasses. Most glazes contain between 5% and 15% alumina and this is easily dissolved in the glaze. Amounts in excess of this, up to perhaps 25% of the glaze, separate from the molten mass during cooling to give crystalline opacity and a matt surface. Recrystallization of alumina happens quickly. Time is only a small factor in consideration of alumina matts. The usual consideration is of the alumina : silica molecular ratio. Proportions of 1:5 and downwards (1:4, 1:3) will result in crystalline glazes.

Alumina matts are not difficult to produce. The average transparent glaze can be matted by the addition of alumina powder. Alternatively the adjustment of a recipe towards the inclusion of more china clay, possibly in calcined form, or of more feldspar, will bring about a matting of the glaze surface and opacity due to crystallization.

Alumina matts can be very beautiful but they can also be very greyish, of poor opacity, pin-holed and crawled. They can be improved in opacity and whiteness by a small amount of zirconia. The crystal quality can be improved by the use of alkaline matting agents like calcia, magnesia and zinc oxide but the addition of these is not an automatic improvement because their fluxing action might give the opposite result from the one required. The amount of agent required must be established by tests.

In reverse consideration, the fluxing action of zinc oxide can be restrained by the use of alumina. Zinc matts can easily be very runny glazes because zinc oxide is an active flux. Alumina helps to hold the glaze during fusion although it is the combination of free silica with the zinc oxide which produces the matting crystals. A safe balance is found in the use of a calcined mixture of china-clay and zinc oxide in equal amounts by weight. This matting agent provides alumina stability and crystals together with zinc silicate crystals but the effect is not as exciting as zinc silicate crystals alone.

Alumina matts show the action of alumina as an anti-flux. Increasing the amount of alumina in a glaze raises the melting point. This effect is very useful and can be achieved simply by the addition of alumina (or alumina hydrate) powder. Alternatively the proportion of the china clay or feldspar in the glaze recipe can be increased.

When the glaze finally melts, the alumina will be dissolved in the molten glass, but as mentioned above, some alumina might crystallize out of solution during cooling. If crystallization is an undesirable side effect one should add silica as flint or quartz. Silica is only half as effective as alumina in its power to raise a melting point but it is cheaper and results in increased shine and transparency. A balance of alumina and silica is usually required and china clay is therefore used.

silicon

oxygen

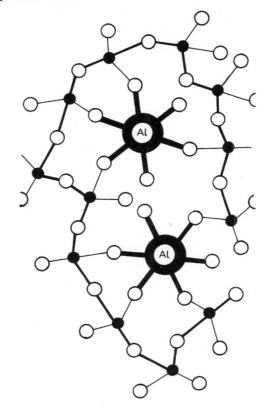

Whilst some slight opacity and matting of surface might be undesirable, a third effect of an increase in alumina is a stiffening of the glaze. This cannot be achieved in any similar way and is therefore an important reason for alumina's use.

Alumina stiffens the molten glaze by hindering the loosening of silica's molecular chains. It introduces itself into these chains and by the six-fold co-ordination of aluminium it becomes widely involved. This is shown by the two diagrams: a loose silica chain and a chain stiffened by alumina.

Glazes containing little or no alumina are very runny. They melt quickly and run down the side of the pot. When cool, they often craze, are subject to attack by culinary acids and scratch easily. The solubility of lead is decreased by the presence of alumina which is fully involved in the fused glaze.

The usual pottery practice is to introduce alumina by approximately 10% of china clay. This will give nearly 4% alumina to the glaze. If more alumina is required, more china clay can be added or substituted for some flint, quartz or feldspar until a balance has been found. Glazes can rarely absorb more than 25% china clay and this amount gives a crystalline matt. In this case the total alumina content of the glaze will be around 20%. Of this, 10% will have been provided by the china clay and 10% by the feldspars.

Lastly the undesirable effects of too much alumina are a glaze's over-stiffness and over-stressed surface tension. Over-stiffness means that the glaze cannot smooth over once the surface has been broken. Craters resulting from gassing therefore show as pinholes in the finished glaze. See **Run**. Coupling this with the extra surface tension of the viscous glaze results in the glaze crawling back from any breaks in the surface which might have occurred before firing. See **Crawling**.

Amakusa. See **Cornish stone.**

Amblygonite. Lithium alumino-fluophosphate. Li. AlF.PO$_4$. A lithium ore which has had some experimental use as a glaze material. It is an active flux and gives phosphoric opacity but can only be used in limited amounts because it causes blistering. It requires oxidation.

Amorphous. Having no definite form, that is, noncrystalline. Glazes are called amorphous glasses when they have not had time to crystallize on cooling.

One of the characteristics of amorphous solids is that they do not have definite melting points. Instead they have softening, melting or maturing ranges over which they slowly soften and eventually become liquid. Crystalline solids have a definite melting point below which they are solid and above which they are liquid.

A glaze is complex and contains many different substances which have different crystalline states. The melting range of a glaze is dictated by the different melting points of the constituents and their interaction on one another in eutectic combinations. The glaze becomes a liquid which on cooling becomes an amorphous solid.

Amphoteric. Intermediate. Capable of acting as either an acid or an alkali according to whichever opposite is presented. In glazes the amphoteric substances are important as a bridge or link between the acidic glass-formers and the alkaline fluxes. They act as stabilizers sometimes giving valuable stiffening to the glaze and, if in excess of what can be dissolved, they often create crystals. The potter's most important amphoteric substance is alumina. See **Alumina.**

There are many oxides which in a wide use show amphoteric properties. However, in ceramic use they tend to act as either acid or alkali. They are listed and described under **Periodic table.** The important ones are boric oxide, ferric oxide and chromium oxide which are sesquioxides (R_2O_3), and the opacifiers titania, zirconia and stannic oxide which are dioxides (RO_2).

Analysis. A method of describing a substance by its different parts. An analysis is made in two ways: qualitative, which determines only the nature of the parts present, and quantitative, which determines also the amount of each part present. The latter gives a percentage composition of the substance, but may group similar parts together for convenience.

An analysis provided by a supplier of potter's materials is always a convenient combination of qualitative and quantitative analyses and should be understood as such. This convention assists in making comparisons between different materials.

There are three main types of analysis. They describe the chemical content, the mineral content and the physical properties of a substance. The chemical content is given by chemical, ultimate and fired analyses of which the ultimate is the most useful to the potter. The mineral content is given by rational and proximate analyses which assist in appreciating the properties of the raw material. The physical properties listed in a mechanical analysis are those of grain and particle sizes.

Analyses assist assessment of a material in different ways but do not obviate the necessity for practical tests. In order to contrast the information given by the different analyses, an imaginary 'clay-like' material has been taken as an example. Six analyses are given of this sample material and comments made upon each analysis. The items and numbers are simplified to clarify the examples. The analyses are: chemical, ultimate, fired; rational, proximate; mechanical.

CHEMICAL ANALYSIS. Analysis of a material expressed in single elements or convenient compounds. For example an analysis of limestone could express the calcium carbonate as $CaCO_3$, as CaO and CO_2, or as Ca, C and O. The material to be analysed may be merely a mixture, e.g. iron oxide and silica, or may be a complex compound, e.g. cornish stone.

To be of value to the potter, the chemical analysis needs to be quantitative and preferably expressed as oxides. It then becomes, for his purpose, the same as an ultimate analysis and the potter is able to read this as compounds which give the material its fired character.

The items in a chemical analysis are usually listed in the order of abundance and the list often concludes with items which have been traced but not isolated or measured.

The following comparative example of a chemical analysis is given in single elements. The same sample given as oxides is seen under Ultimate Analysis (see below). This chemical analysis shows that the material does not contain the elements sulphur, fluorine and chlorine which could give gassing troubles.

Oxygen	51
Silicon	26
Aluminium	12
Iron	5·5
Potassium	2·5
Calcium	1
Hydrogen	0·75
Carbon	0·25
Titanium	
Magnesium	
Manganese	
Sodium	

ULTIMATE ANALYSIS. A type of chemical analysis expressed as proportions of metal and non-metal oxides that are involved in the ceramic fusion. Elements and oxides which do not enter the fusion may be grouped together as volatiles, sometimes called 'H_2O etc' or 'loss on ignition'. The oxides listed do not necessarily exist in the material but are arrived at from a previous analysis.

For example if the mineral cryolite Na_3AlF_6 is used in a glaze, the bonds between the three elements sodium, aluminium and fluorine are replaced with bonds to oxygen giving soda and alumina, and liberating the fluorine gas. The oxygen is taken from the kiln atmosphere and therefore enters the calculation as an extra. If 100 grams of cryolite are used, this takes up 22·9 grams of oxygen when it decomposes. Thus 100 grams of cryolite produces 44·3 grams of soda, 24·3 grams of alumina and liberates 54·3 grams of fluorine. This is a total of 122·9 grams. The potter is not interested in the amount of fluorine, provided that he can expel it from the kiln. His ultimate analysis would therefore read: Na_2O 44·3%, Al_2O_3 24·3%, loss 31·4%.

The word loss is quite literal. This represents a loss of weight for which he has paid. The others represent what is used. The ultimate analysis, therefore, is of use to the potter in comparing the cost of one material with another because it tells him what he will eventually put into the fusion.

Most books on ceramic calculations use the system of a conversion factor. This will be seen to coincide with the ultimate analysis after taking into account the acquired oxides. For example, the conversion factors for soda and alumina in cryolite are 0·443 and 0·243 respectively. These factors are multiplied by the weight of cryolite to discover the weight of oxides obtained.

The comparative example of an ultimate analysis shows how it can help in estimating the value as a glaze material.

SiO_2	59
TiO_2	1
Al_2O_3	19
Fe_2O_3	9
CaO	1
MgO	0·5
Na_2O	0·5
K_2O	2
Loss	8

In comparison with a feldspar, it is relatively high in alumina and low in silica. It will therefore be fairly refractory. The iron oxide content indicates that, when fused, it will be dark in colour. There are no details about volatiles. For these one must refer to the chemical analysis.

FIRED ANALYSIS. A type of chemical analysis in which all elements have been converted into ceramic oxides. Volatiles are discounted and the remainder is recalculated as a percentage. This analysis is used for calcined materials.

The comparative example of a fired analysis would be:

SiO_2	64·1
TiO_2	1·1
Al_2O_3	20·6
Fe_2O_3	9·7
CaO	1·1
MgO	0·6
Na_2O	0·6
K_2O	2·2

RATIONAL ANALYSIS. Analysis of a material expressed as proportions of theoretically pure kaolinite (called clay substance), quartz and either feldspar or mica. The rational analysis is ascertained by a combination of physical and chemical processes and therefore gives information about the raw material and some indication of its firing behaviour. It does not guarantee that the substances listed are present in the form given. For example, the alumino-silicates not calculable as clay substances are attributed to either feldspar or mica and theoretically combined with discovered bases. The truth is that both feldspar and mica are usually present but analyses containing both would be difficult to compare.

The rational analysis is more useful to the potter than the similar proximate analysis which is calculated entirely by theory from a chemical analysis. The rational analysis is of most use when coupled with a mechanical analysis and an ultimate analysis.

The following is the comparative example:

clay substance	52
feldspar	20
quartz	20

It shows that a large proportion of the material is a true clay substance and therefore the material can be expected to behave as a clay in terms of plasticity and drying shrinkage. Any material with over 45% clay substance on the feldspar basis of analysis or over 30% clay substance on the mica basis can be considered as a clay. Note that this analysis does not include the colouring oxides and free fluxes. For these reference must be made to the ultimate analysis.

PROXIMATE ANALYSIS. Analysis of a material expressed as proportions of kaolinite, feldspar and quartz. It is conceived entirely theoretically from the chemical analysis and is therefore not so accurate an indication of character as is a rational analysis.

The comparative example shows similar amounts to the rational analysis and would be considered in the same way:

kaolinite	49
feldspar	19
quartz	21

MECHANICAL ANALYSIS. Analysis of a material expressed as grain and particle sizes. The sizes may be coarse gradings expressed as mesh size or extremely fine particles measured in microns. When the analysis is all in fine measurements, it is called a particle size analysis.

Often the analysis states only what percentages are above and below a given size but more important are the analyses which define the largest and smallest sizes and the distribution in between. The value of this distribution is seen when choosing between two grogs of apparent similarity. They may both be graded as '60's to dust', meaning that all the material will pass through a 60's mesh. However one may be nearly all dust with a little coarse 60's grade of grog whilst the other contains an even amount of all sizes gradually varying from 60's to dust. These two grogs, apparently the same from description, would give different properties to a throwing clay.

If the mechanical analysis is coupled with a rational analysis, it will give the particle size of the different constituent minerals. For example, the free silica in a rational analysis of a clay is given a mechanical analysis of between 80's and 100's mesh size whilst all the clay substance, feldspar etc is graded finer. In this case it follows that sieving at 100's mesh will remove what is obviously a quartz sand. This is useful information if

9

the clay is to be used both as a body clay and in a glaze. If the clay has to be sieved to remove roots etc, the quartz sand can be left in for texture and throwing character by using a sieve coarser than 80's. For the glaze, which may not require this amount of silica, the sand can be removed by sieving at 100's mesh or finer.

The comparative example gives a mechanical analysis for the material as a whole. This is expressed as percentages of material which are composed of particles of equivalent spherical diameter less than the given sizes.

0·1	1·0	10	25	50	100	microns
2	26	45	60	80	87	per cent

Retained by 100's mesh: 10%

From it one can deduce that although by the rational analysis the material appears to be a clay, this material is rather coarse. Only 26% of the material is of particle size below one micron and most potting clays would have between 30 and 70%. Also there is little ultrafine material below 0·1 micron. Most potting clays would have 10 to 30% of their material below this size. The 10% retained by 100's mesh is contrastingly low. The material would be easy to process for glazes and it could probably be used unprocessed in bodies.

Anatase. TiO_2. Natural titanium dioxide. Anatase is one of the three oxide ores of titanium. The other two are rutile and brookite. They are chemically alike but different in crystal form.

Anatase crystals appear to be brown, bluish and black but they are free from the iron impurity which colours rutile. Anatase is a source of white titanium dioxide. See **Titania**.

Andesine. One of the plagioclase feldspars. It is mostly soda feldspar but contains up to 49% lime feldspar.

Anhydrite. Natural calcium sulphate. $CaSO_4$. See **Calcium sulphate.**

Anhydrous. Without water. The term usually implies that there existed some water chemically combined in the crystal structure, as in kaolinite, borax and aluminium hydroxide. The term anhydration is sometimes used to describe the ceramic change whereby clay is turned into pot by the removal of bound water.

Anorthite. Lime feldspar. $CaO.Al_2O_3.2SiO_2$. One of the twelve true feldspars. It is based upon calcia (calcium oxide) which has a high melting point so that this feldspar has a melting point of 1550°C (2822°F). It could be used in glazes to introduce calcia, alumina and silica but these can be more profitably introduced separately when their amounts can be adjusted.

Anorthite crystals are part of the devitrification occurring in lime matts. The lattice is a series of

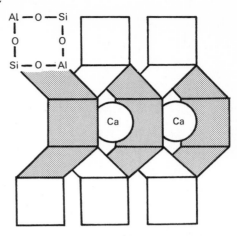

squarish rings each composed of oxygen tetrahedra. Half of the tetrahedra are built around aluminium and half around silicon. The rings form crooked chains. Between these chains are large holes which can accommodate calcium in eight-fold co-ordination as in other feldspars.

Anorthoclase. Soda orthoclase. Soda microcline. $NaKO.Al_2O_3.6SiO_2$. A feldspar which is chemically halfway between albite and orthoclase. There are two crystal structures. See **Feldspars, types of**. The term anorthoclase is also used for any variable feldspar which cannot be considered 90% albite or orthoclase, and in this sense is synonymous with the potter's term 'mixed feldspar'.

Anti-flux. A term used throughout this book to express the action of minerals or oxides in glazes and bodies. An anti-flux obviously does not act as a flux but hinders the fluxing action. Most refractory minerals hinder fluxing in the early stages of fusion but these are not described as anti-fluxes. Rather, the term has been reserved for action which deserves special consideration, e.g. calcia which is a strong flux above 1100°C (2012°F) but hinders fusion before this temperature is reached. Although it is chemically alkaline and will become part of the molten glass at temperatures below 1100°C, its inclusion in a glaze does little to improve fusion or lower the melting temperature. Small amounts (up to 1%) might have some fluxing action, as indeed all impurities would have, by virtue of the phenomenon called interaction. However, larger amounts could be correctly called anti-flux. Their inclusion at these lower temperatures is often to provide a more stable glass.

Similar effects will be experienced with magnesia, baria and zinc oxide. Each of these is a strong flux in its own temperature range.

Other anti-fluxes are the acidic opacifiers: tin oxide, zirconia, ceria and titania. In very small amounts up to 1% they could give some fluxing by interaction but their normal action is against the fusion which they do not fully enter.

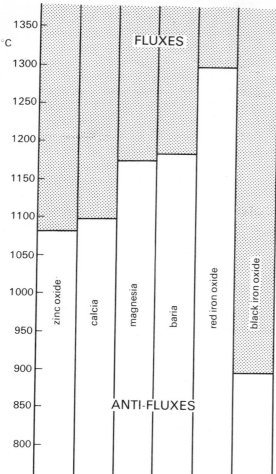

Amphoteric oxides also exhibit anti-flux properties. This is as one would expect of an oxide behaving as either alkali, acid or both. Arsenic oxide, antimony oxide, bismuth oxide, chromium oxide, red iron oxide and alumina each inhibit fusion when present in certain amounts at certain temperatures and in relation to other oxides.

As a general rule it could be said that amphoteric oxides act as anti-fluxes when more powerful fluxes are present. The presence of alkali causes the amphoteric oxide to present itself as the opposite, that is, as an acid or anti-flux. In the absence of powerful alkaline fluxes, the amphoteric oxides present themselves as alkalis towards the acidic silica. However, they usually require temperatures higher than the alkaline fluxes.

The case of the amphoteric red iron oxide is particularly interesting. Because it is such a common oxide and present in large amounts, its influence has been studied and the effects are often very noticeable. It should be remembered that red iron oxide is susceptible to even slight reduction which changes it partially to black iron oxide, a distinct flux. See **Iron oxide.**

The atomic structure of red iron oxide is similar to that of alumina. However it is less compact and there-fore it is more susceptible to the effects of heat and interaction. It melts at a lower temperature than alumina and acts as a flux towards silica at temperatures over 1300°C (2372°F). Therefore below this temperature it must be regarded as an anti-flux.

However its presence in a glaze often seems to cause fusion. This is not because it acts as a flux but because it presents itself as an acid towards the alkaline fluxes. In such cases it is quite easily fused by strong alkalis. Glazes which contain an excess of alkali, for example lime matt glazes, are noticeably affected by the addition of red iron oxide which forms a solution with the alkali. Eutectic relationships are relevant here and the alkali/red iron oxide solutions in relation to alkali/silica solutions causes increased fusion.

Antimonate of lead. Naples yellow. $Pb_3(SbO_4)_2$. This is a creamish yellow paint pigment which can be used to introduce antimony oxide into lead glazes and 5% of antimonate of lead will give a bright yellow colour. The ultimate formula can be considered $3PbO . Sb_2O_5$. The acidic antimony pentoxide (Sb_2O_5) becomes the amphoteric antimony trioxide (Sb_2O_3) and liberates oxygen when it melts and dissolves in the lead silicate. This occurs as soon as the lead silicate fuses.

Antimony oxide. Antimonious oxide. Antimony Trioxide. Stibium sesquioxide. Sb_2O_3. An oxide with various properties which depend upon its combination with other oxides. Antimony is a metalloid, that is, it behaves sometimes as a non-metal and sometimes as a metal. The oxide therefore has some properties which belong to the non-metal oxides and some properties which belong to the metal oxides. It is a glass-former. It is also a modifier and opacifier, as are many amphoteric substances, and it is a colouring oxide.

Antimony occurs freely in nature but is usually mined as the ore stibnite (Sb_2S_3). China, Mexico and the USA are the main sources. The ore is roasted to oxidation or first melted and then oxidized. It is used in lead alloys and as a paint colourant. Antimony compounds are poisonous.

In glazes which are rich in lead, 1% of antimony oxide will give a bright yellow colour. In a slip to be covered with a lead glaze, at least 8% of antimony oxide is required to give a yellow. It is more usual to introduce the antimony oxide into a glaze already combined with the lead oxide as antimonate of lead. Five per cent will be required and the glaze must also contain lead. The combination of lead and antimony oxides is sometimes referred to by its paint colour of Naples yellow. The addition of small amounts of iron oxide will make the colour more orange.

In leadless glazes, antimony oxide gives an opacity because it does not dissolve. At least 10% is required. The result is not particularly exciting and is therefore considered an expensive way of producing an opaque glaze. Its redeeming quality is that it can sometimes

11

modify or mellow an otherwise harsh colour.

There is a tendency for antimony oxide to volatilize at stoneware temperatures.

Anvil. A pebble or piece of wood used to beat pot walls. The anvil is used inside the pot, a beater or paddle is used outside. The process compresses the clay, thins the pot wall and enlarges the pot. To assist the clay to stretch without cracking, the anvil is often 'pecked', that is, it has its surface covered with small chipped holes. See also **Paddle and anvil**.

Apatite. $3Ca_3(PO_4)_2 \cdot Ca(Cl,F)_2$. Natural calcium phosphate and fluoride/chloride of igneous origin. The ultimate formula varies between $9CaO \cdot P_2O_5$ and $3CaO \cdot P_2O_5$. It is a source of calcium phosphate for bodies and glazes but the fluorine and chlorine often cause trouble. Bone ash is a better source.

Appendage. A piece of clay, paper, card or any other material, including wax resist, which assists the potter to do the job in hand but is not part of the pot and is not a tool. For example, when coating the inside of globular pots which have no neck, it is difficult to pour out the excess slip or glaze without spilling some over the out-side. A coil of clay put round the rim, with a spout quickly modelled on it, solves this problem. The clay is removed immediately after use. Also pieces of card or paper are used to direct poured glaze on to the correct part of a pot and to protect other parts. In these cases the card is often held in place with some clay. Again, in modelling figures where complications of weight distort the work during drying, and also during firing of some soft paste porcelains, a prop of clay is used as an appendage.

Applied ornament. Usually refers to clay pieces which are added to pottery as decoration and therefore have no part in the functional forms of the pottery. See **Sprigging**. The term is also used for transfer printed decoration.

The photograph shows a detail of applied ornament on a pot by Bernard Rooke.

Aquamanile. A medieval water server in the form of an animal. They were used at table for hand rinsing. Some 13th-century English examples are in the form of knights in armour on horseback.

Arabian lustre. A transmutation lustre.

Argonite. $CaCO_3$. See **Calcite**.

Arenaceous rocks. Arenite. Sandstones. Rocks composed of layers of previously existing sand in which the grains have been cemented together by siliceous, calcareous or ferruginous solutions. Drifts of sand from these rocks occur in rivers and lakes of the locality and sometimes provide a source of opener giving interesting textures.

Argentite. Silver ore. Silver sulphide. Ag_2S.

Argillaceous rocks. Mudstones. Rocks composed of sedimented and compressed material of very fine particle size. Argillaceous rocks often contain a proportion of clay. The ground rock is not likely to constitute as a clay but may be useful in glazes. See also **Albany slip.**

Ark. Storage tank for clay or glaze slips. The slip is prevented from settling by continuous mechanical stirring. The ark shown is at Cardiff College of Art.

Arsenic oxide. Arsenious oxide. Arsenic trioxide. Arsenious acid. White arsenic. As_2O_3. A glass-forming oxide which is often present in small quantities in glazes. It is rarely deliberately introduced by potters but is occasionally used for its amphoteric properties as a modifier. In small quantities it is capable of absorbing unwanted colouring in transparent glazes. However, it does not itself easily dissolve, and may give opacity at low temperatures. Arsenic compounds are poisonous.

Asbestos. Calcium magnesium silicate. $CaMg_3(SiO_3)_4$. Asbestos occurs as a mineral in South Africa and Canada. It is mixed with Portland cement to make cement boards. These boards are slightly absorbent and are used by many potters as work boards and wheel-head bats.

The term asbestos is also loosely given to some other fibrous silicates with similar insulatory properties. Because they are fully oxidized, they will not burn and because they are fibrous, they do not shatter.

Asbolite. Asbolan. Cobalt ore containing manganese and iron impurities. It was the source of underglaze blue for Chinese porcelain. It is the only cobalt ore that is an oxide and safe to use. The other cobalt ores contain arsenic.

Ashes. The non-combustible remains of animal (bone) and vegetable matter used by the potter as a source of body and glaze fluxes. The commonest uses are of bone ash in bone china body and vegetable and wood ashes in stoneware ash glazes. See also **Bone ash** and **Wood ash.**

The ashes provide fluxing and other oxides. The main ones concerned are calcia, phosphorus pentoxide, potash, soda, alumina, silica and many trace oxides. Although the original matter is organic (that is, with carbon being the most important element and hydrogen, nitrogen and sulphur also involved) the potter is seeking the inorganic content. Thus from a large bulk of wood the potter collects a relatively small amount of ash.

Even so, the ash is only a half-way stage between the original matter and the required oxides. Vegetable ashes contain carbon, sulphur, fluorine and chlorine. Bone ash contains carbon and fluorine. The burning of the original matter is not intended to, and in fact cannot completely, create a new material composed of required oxides and non-volatile compounds. The burning is a preparation, a controlled calcination, which removes the bulk of unwanted carbon, hydrogen and sulphur, and renders the material to a usable form. The elements involved have reached stable states for dry conditions as oxides, carbonates, sulphates, phosphates, chlorides and fluorides.

Some unwanted compounds can be removed by washing the ash but most will be removed during the firing when the presence of silicates will cause decomposition of the compounds to oxides and volatiles.

The accompanying chart shows how the original elements reach the ceramic fusions as oxides.

It will be seen from the chart that wood and vegetable

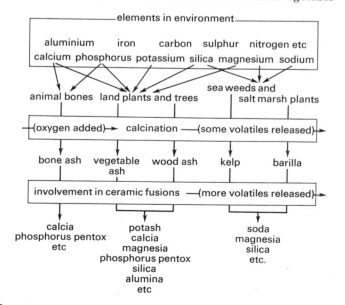

ashes are the most complex. A few contain sufficient silica to fuse to a glass alone, but the majority of ashes contain mostly fluxing oxides. Wood and vegetable ashes are therefore considered as fluxes, especially for glazes. They also introduce colouring and crystallizers which give textures.

Many wood ashes contain a large proportion of monovalent oxides which give strong fluxing action at stoneware temperatures. If sufficient ash is used, and it is the glaze's only flux, it creates the decorative effect known as stringing. This is seen in the photograph of a stoneware jar by William Marshall.

Two example recipes are given for wood ash glazes to be fired at 1250°C (2282°F). The first is to go on biscuit:

feldspar	50
china clay	10
quartz	10
wood ash	30

The second recipe is for a slip glaze and contains a second (divalent) flux (calcia) to stabilize the fusion:

feldspar	30
ball clay	30
wood ash	30
whiting	10

Astbury, John and son Thomas. Early 18th-century Staffordshire potters who incorporated into their work various ideas which developed English earthenware. Starting with the precision of red stoneware, John Astbury used coloured sprigging, including some freely executed work, and covered this with the traditional lead glaze. The use of white clays for sprigging led the Astburys to make white ware and to add flint to the clay to make a denser body when fired. See **Creamware**.

Atmosphere. Air surrounding pottery during forming, drying and firing. A potter working with nature, rather than under controlled factory conditions, watches the weather to judge the drying qualities of the atmosphere and estimates the pressure and wind for the firing. See **Drying**. Kiln atmosphere is dealt with under **Oxidation** and **Reduction**.

Atom. The smallest part of an element that can take part in a chemical combination or reaction. In a chemical formula, one atom of an element is represented by the chemical symbol. In a compound containing more than one atom of the same element the number of the atoms appears large before, or in small type, below and after the chemical symbol. For use, see **Formula, chemical**.

An atom consists of a positively charged nucleus at the centre, with orbiting negatively charged electrons. The number of electrons determines the identity of the atom as an element and the number is called its atomic number. The electrons are in layers or shells of distinct numbers. The power of an atom to combine with other different atoms depends upon whether its outer electron layer is filled or only partly filled. This power is called an atom's valency. See **Valency**.

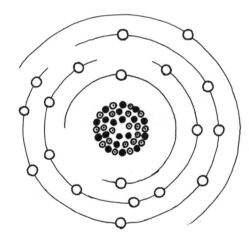

The first diagram shows a theoretical potassium atom. At the centre is the nucleus of 19 protons of positive charge with 20 neutrons which are electrically neutral. Around this nucleus revolve 19 electrons of negative charge. The atomic number of potassium is 19, the same as the number of electrons. The atomic weight of potassium is 39 which is the number of protons and neutrons in the nucleus. The electrons are of negligible weight. Potassium is an active element because it is willing to part with the single outer electron. The other orbits of electrons are complete and not easily disturbed. Having parted with this electron, the atom has an excess of positive protons and is attracted to a negatively-charged atom, probably the one to which it has given its negatively-charged electron.

The second diagram shows how potassium quickly reacts with oxygen to form potassium oxide (potash).

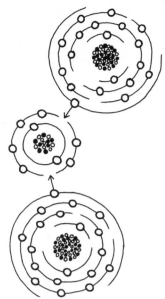

Pottery painted with contemporary scenes had earlier been popular in the Mycenaean period, 1600 to 1100 B.C., but had become outmoded by the introduction of the geometric style at the beginning of the Classical Iron Age. Interest in pictorial decoration, especially mural painting, was revived by trade with Egypt and western Asia. Attic pottery then developed through distinct stages known as Black-figure, Red-figure and White Ground, each style using greater control of painted detail than the preceding one.

Two atoms of potassium are required, each providing one electron, to complete the outer orbit of 8 electrons on the oxygen atom. Therefore in one molecule of potash there are two atoms of potassium and one atom of oxygen and the chemical formula is K_2O.

Atomic number. The number of electrons orbiting the nucleus of an atom. It is also the number of protons inside the nucleus. Atomic numbers are used to put the different elements in an order from which can be deduced the probable properties of the elements. See **Periodic table**.

Atomic weight. The average weight of an atom of a specified element. The weight is expressed as a number of atomic mass units. These were originally based upon the idea that hydrogen was 1 and oxygen was 16 times this weight. The international system is now based upon an accepted weight for the carbon 12 isotope.

Atomic weights are used to calculate molecular weights. In turn, these are used to discover the effective number of molecules which will enter a ceramic fusion from a given recipe. See **Formula, unity**.

Attic pottery. Athenian pottery produced during the classical period, 700 to 400 B.C. The only rival pottery of the time was made at Corinth. The forms are expressions of intellect rather than of use of plastic media. In the most admired pieces, the potter showed complete control creating severe shapes on which detailed scenes were skilfully painted. It was the painter who signed the work and this ware is the earliest known signed pottery. At the same time there were productions with freer interpretations of form and decoration. These were mostly for export. The decoration of Attic pottery is invaluable as historical documentation of costume, rituals and legends.

The slips for the decoration were finely levigated and had additions of iron oxide and fluxes. They vitrified during firing, and were sometimes reduced to produce the darkest lustrous effects. Glazes were not used.

Aventurine glazes. Aventurine is a feldspar containing tiny haematite crystals that catch the light and give it sparkle. Aventurine glazes contain tiny crystals usually associated with iron or other colouring oxide. These crystals catch the light and sparkle with varying colour. The crystals are not large enough to be seen individually. They are the beginnings of crystallization, which takes place on cooling when there is more colouring oxide than will remain dissolved in the glaze.

For aventurine effects, lead glazes, low in alumina, are popular. Tests should be made with increasing amounts of colouring oxide to find the correct addition. Too little will not give any crystals. Too much will give crystals which make the glaze opaque and matt. The speed of cooling also influences the crystal growth. Some aventurine glazes contain as much as 30% red iron oxide. See also **Devitrification**, **Galena** and **Crystalline glazes**.

Azurite. Natural basic copper carbonate. $2CuCO_3$. $Cu(OH)_2$. A weathered ore of copper which is easily identified by its bright turquoise-blue colour. It occurs with malachite (the green ore) and can be found amongst the wash-out from mines. See **Malachite** and **Copper ores**.

B

Bag. Bag wall. The wall which divides the combustion space from the pot space in a kiln. Its purpose is to deflect the flame as it enters the chamber and thereby stop the creation of a hot spot amongst the pots nearest the heat source.

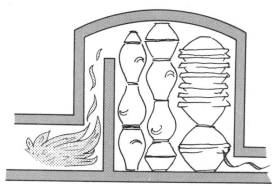

Baiting. Periodic kiln stoking.

Ball clay. Blue clay. A highly plastic clay, usually light in colour, which is the basis of many potting bodies. Alone, it tends to be too fine and slippery for use, but additions of sand, grog and coarser and less-plastic clays actually improve workability. Ball clay is a general term for many clays. It comes from the practice of digging the clay out of the open pits in convenient blocks of about 25 lbs, called balls. These clays are always plastic, are mostly cream and vitrify in the 1100°C to 1200°C (2012°F to 2192°F) range.

Ball clays are usually accepted as once-removed kaolins. They contain a high proportion of kaolinite, the pure clay mineral, but also contain free silica, potash, soda, calcia and magnesia as feldspar or associated cations. The presence of these fluxes brings down the vitrification range of the kaolinite to 1100°C to 1200°C. A few ball clays will withstand 1300°C (2372°F) and a few actually deform before 1100°C (2012°F).

Fortunately few ball clays have collected iron oxide and titania as impurities and therefore most are cream burning.

Mention should be made of blue and black ball clays which colours describe the raw clay. This is no indication of the fired colour. The blue and dark grey colours are due to the presence of carbonaceous matter. The black ball clays were once considered to be more plastic than the white. It is true that some carbonaceous matter improves plasticity. All ball clays, however, contain some carbon. It is usually less than 1% which

gives no difficulties in the firing. Some contain as much as 3% which must be carefully burned out during the firing. See **Black core**. Ball clays, excellent in other respects, have been reported with 10% carbonaceous matter. Such clays must be difficult to fire but may be acceptable for high temperature blends which can be soaked and remain 'open' at 750°C (1382°F) to burn out the carbon.

Ball clays have extremely fine particles, many of colloidal size. This accounts for their plasticity. It also means that suspensions of ball clay settle very slowly, if at all. Ball clay slurries are also difficult to dry off to plastic consistency. As the water moves out from between the particles, these are pulled together to form a waterproof layer through which further water cannot pass. Without admixtures of other coarser materials and the use of excessive doping, it is impossible to filter-press a ball clay. Ball clays are therefore sold 'plastic as dug' or in dry powder state. The powder state is often airfloated to allow heavy foreign particles to fall out, a process similar to winnowing but involving the collection of the lightest material.

The fine particle size and purity of the clay content means that ball clays respond well to treatment with deflocculants and flocculants. Ball clays are an important addition to casting slips to provide fluidity with bulk and green strength.

Plastic ball clays contain a large percentage of moisture which is necessary to surround all the particles. Water can account for 25 to 35% of the weight of a plastic ball clay. This is a considerable bulk to eliminate in drying so it is not surprising that ball clays contract about 10% (linear) in drying from plastic to dry. They also shrink a further 10 to 15% (linear) in firing to vitrification.

The British ball clays are located in the south-west of England and are said to have originated with the

17

granites of the south-west peninsular. They were deposited in their present locations in the Cainozoic Era some 30 to 70 million years ago. In one pit there are a number of very different ball clays in overlapping seams or veins. They are documented by number and by general names like 'top', 'rough' or 'brook's bottom', which become their specific trading names.

The photograph shows the strata of an open-cast ball clay pit and mechanical extraction. Both pits are owned by Watts, Blake, Bearne and Co Ltd, of South Devon, who supplied the photographs.

Ball clays are often described as aluminous or siliceous. Aluminous ball clays contain 30 to 40% alumina. Siliceous ball clays contain 60 to 80% silica. A comparison of a group of ball clay analyses will show a wide variety of chemical composition. The following ultimate analysis shows the ranges:

$$SiO_2 \quad 40\text{–}80\%$$
$$TiO_2 \quad 2\%$$
$$Al_2O_3 \quad 15\text{–}40\%$$
$$Fe_2O_3 \quad 6\%$$
$$MgO \quad 1\%$$
$$CaO \quad 1\%$$
$$K_2O \quad 3\%$$
$$Na_2O \quad 1\%$$
$$Loss \quad 5\text{–}10\%$$

Ball clays are often included in glazes to assist suspension of the slop and provide adhesion before firing. They introduce alumina and silica as does china clay but they are not so white. Whilst an ultimate analysis is desirable when calculating a glaze's unity formula, the following unity formulae for ball clays will be found reasonably accurate for small amounts. See also **Particle size**.

Average ball clay: MW. 387
$Al_2O_3 . 4SiO_2 . 2H_2O. 0\cdot1K_2O$
Aluminous ball clay: MW. 267
$Al_2O_3 . 2SiO_2 . 2H_2O. 0\cdot1K_2O$
Siliceous ball clay: MW. 696
$Al_2O_3 . 9SiO_2 . 2H_2O. 0\cdot2K_2O$

Ball mill. Pebble mill. A grinding mill used for the fine grinding of glaze and colour minerals. The balls are natural or manufactured pebbles which fall onto one another and thus grind the materials.

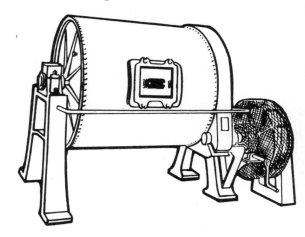

The drawing shows the ball mill manufactured by William Boulton Ltd.

The mill consists of a steel drum which rotates about a horizontal axis. It is lined with stone, porcelain or steel plates and is charged and emptied through a sealing door in the side. The mill, containing a charge of minerals, pebbles, airspace and usually water, is rotated at a critical speed which tumbles the pebbles in a continuous cascade. The drum may be up to 8 feet in diameter.

Small mills employ a porcelain jar instead of a steel drum. See **Jar mill**.

Barilla. The ash from burnt glasswart marsh plants. It was used as a source of soda for glass-making during the 18th century. Sea plants yield sodium carbonate upon being burnt. The sodium is derived from the sodium salts in the sea. Land plants yield potassium carbonate and calcium phosphate. See **Sodium carbonate**.

Baria. Baryta. Barium oxide. BaO. An auxiliary flux in earthenware frits and high-temperature stoneware glazes. It is usually introduced for its crystallizing properties which give excellent satin matts. Barium compounds should be treated with care because they are poisonous. Baria is soluble in water and is introduced into glazes via a frit or in barium carbonate.

Baria does not occur as a mineral. It is an unstable oxide which reacts with moisture. The minerals of barium are barytes (barium sulphate), witherite (barium carbonate) and barytocalcite (carbonate with calcium). The metal barium quickly tarnishes in the air. It melts at 850°C (1562°F) but the melting point of baria is 1923°C (3493°F). The oxide is refractory and enters fusion by virtue of its instability and hence interaction with silica. Its instability is one of attraction rather than dispersion so it is resistant to reduction. Its bond with other compounds is strong once formed. Its bond with carbon dioxide in the compound barium carbonate ($BaCO_3$) is so strong that the carbonate does not decompose with heat alone but requires some reduction. See **Barium carbonate**. Potters have been known to use barium sulphate in paste glazes. It is not to be recommended because the sulphate is a soluble poison and sulphurous fumes are released during firing.

Baria is the heaviest of all the divalent oxides used as fluxes, and as such it is often considered a high-temperature substitute for lead oxide. It has similar properties of body attack and high shine, but it cannot be used as the only flux, as can lead oxide.

Baria's fluxing action is dependent upon its method of introduction into the glaze and the other glaze constituents. Like magnesia, calcia, zinc oxide and strontia, the other divalent oxides, baria is proportionately most active by interaction and when it is only a small percentage of the total glaze. Increased amounts give no advantage for its use; calcia gives more dependable results. However, there is an optimum point at which it forms beautiful small crystals which give a satin-like matt surface. It is for this matt surface that baria is usually required.

The fluxing action of baria is unusual. It will act as a flux for all temperatures, providing it is incorporated in a frit with soda and potash. Such frits need first to have been fused above 1200°C (2192°F) in the active range of baria. Without this close association, baria is limited to temperatures above 1175°C (2147°F). Below 1175°C it retains its crystalline form and opacifies the glaze. This is a popular use of baria and amounts of up to 20% barium carbonate in the recipe give opacity through crystals with various amounts of matt surface. At the higher temperatures the crystalline matt is still possible with 10% and over of barium carbonate.

Although baria gives some alkaline colour responses, it has some amphoteric tendencies in glazes. Baria is able to remain crystalline in the presence of the fusion between soda, potash and silica. If silica alone were present it would try to go into solution. Similarly in the presence of the more fusible glass-former boric oxide, the baria is dissolved. Matts therefore should not contain boric oxide but may use potash, soda and calcia as their fluxes.

Barium carbonate. $BaCO_3$. A barium compound occurring as the mineral witherite. Barium carbonate is also prepared from the mineral barytes by precipitation. Both are used in glaze recipes to introduce the oxide, baria. In glaze slops the precipitated carbonate is preferable because it is lighter and more easily suspended. It is also introduced into slips to combat the scum which occurs on unglazed ware.

In glazes barium carbonate is used because it is relatively insoluble whereas the desired baria reacts with water. It is intended that, during firing, the car-

bonate decomposes to become the required baria and carbon dioxide. Barium carbonate is the most difficult of the carbonates to decompose. It is strangely necessary to use some reduction in order to deprive the carbonate of some of its oxygen. Thus deprived, an unstable compound is produced which breaks down, releasing the desired baria. The equation is:

$$BaCO_3 \;+\; CO \xrightarrow{900°C} BaCO_2 + CO_2\uparrow$$
$$\text{(stable)} \quad \text{carbon} \qquad\qquad \text{(unstable)}$$
$$\text{monoxide} \qquad\qquad\qquad \hookrightarrow BaO + CO\uparrow$$
$$\text{baria}$$

The temperature required for this decomposition is at least 900°C (1652°F). The reduction therefore comes after the usual period of oxidation of carbonaceous matter. Reduction need not be heavy but temperature alone will not suffice to effect the change. If the carbonate is not decomposed, it becomes involved in the melt as an opacifier with anti-flux properties. This gives matt effects but not the matt effects associated with the oxide, baria. In prolonged firings the carbonate will slowly dissolve and decompose. The small silky crystals promoted by baria will then appear upon cooling if the balance of the glaze is conducive to their growth.

Barium carbonate is varyingly reported as soluble and insoluble. It can be accepted as insoluble in pure water and hence can be used in glaze batches. However, glaze slops that contain a flocculant to deter sedimentation are slightly acidic. Some barium carbonate will become soluble in such a suspension as it exchanges its acid radical with the flocculant. The previously soluble flocculant will be precipitated as the insoluble carbonate. For example:

$$CaCl_2 \;+\; BaCO_3 \longrightarrow BaCl_2 + CaCO_3\downarrow$$
$$\text{calcium} \quad\; \text{barium} \qquad\quad \text{barium} \quad\; \text{calcium}$$
$$\text{chloride} \quad \text{carbonate} \qquad \text{chloride} \;\; \text{carbonate}$$
$$\text{(soluble)} \;\; \text{(insoluble)} \qquad \text{(soluble)} \;\text{(precipitate)}$$

The barium chloride will continue the action of the flocculant though weaker than the calcium chloride. Only a small amount of barium carbonate is involved and providing water is not syphoned off, the compound will produce baria in the final glaze. The calcium will act as a flux. The amount is too small to be noticed.

This same process of anionic radical exchange is used with clay for two different reasons: to get rid of scum on unglazed fired ware and to prepare clays which are to be used for casting slips.

Soluble calcium salts, and to a lesser extent magnesium salts, crystallize on the surface of ware during drying. If these crystals are broken by handling, the finger-prints show after firing either as white prints or as dark over-fluxed prints. This is called scum. The commonest salt is calcium sulphate and this can be rendered insoluble by the addition of barium carbonate. See **Scum**. The radical exchange equation is:

$$CaSO_4 + BaCO_3 \longrightarrow BaSO_4 + CaCO_3 \downarrow$$

| calcium | barium | barium | calcium |
| sulphate | carbonate | sulphate | carbonate |

The barium sulphate remains in solution but it does not cause scum.

Clays which are to be used for making casting slips must not contain natural flocculants that act against the required action of the deflocculants. Clays which contain calcium sulphate, which is a strong flocculant, are therefore difficult to make into casting slips. The addition of barium carbonate effects the exchange previously described. The resulting calcium carbonate is insoluble and barium sulphate is a less active flocculant. Clays which are intended for use in casting slips are often treated in this way so that deflocculation can take place without interference from soluble salts. The weak action of barium sulphate can be neutralized by the sodium deflocculants. See **Deflocculation** and **Casting slips**.

Barium compounds. To introduce baria into bodies and glazes it is usual to use barium carbonate. However, the soluble barium sulphate has been used in paste bodies and paste glazes. The compounds used by the potter are:

baria	BaO
barium carbonate	$BaCO_3$ (mineral: witherite)
barium sulphate	$BaSO_4$ (mineral: barytes)

Bars. Holdcroft's Bars. Pyroscopes compounded from glaze minerals and graded to soften at different temperatures. They are 2 inches long and are supported horizontally by their ends in a refractory cradle so that they can sag after subjection to the appropriate heat-work. They are placed in the kiln so that they can be seen during the firing.

Bars are an alternative to cones and like cones are produced with different compositions so that a series of bars can be used to indicate progressive amounts of heat-work.

They were originally manufactured by the Holdcroft Company but are now produced by Harrison Mayer Ltd who also make pyrometric cones.

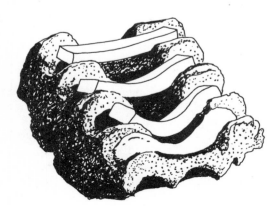

Barytes. Barite. Calk or calk-stone. Barium sulphate. $BaSO_4$. The commonest and most important barium mineral. It is found associated with lead ore and in veins of calcite and fluorspar where it can be identified by its weight. It is much heavier than the two other 'spars' and is known as 'heavy spar'. It is variously coloured and crystalline. Sometimes there are large flat crystals which form rosettes and are known in America as desert roses.

Josiah Wedgwood was probably the first to realize the potential of baria as a body and glaze constituent. In 1775 after some ten thousand trials, he successfully produced his Jasper ware which was 40% barytes.

Barytocalcite. $BaCO_3 . CaCO_3$. Double carbonate of barium and calcium. This is an idealized mineral found in association with lead ores. In practice it is a variable replacement of barium by calcium and given local names like alstonite $((Ba,Ca)CO_3)$.

Basalt. A basic (alkaline), extrusive, igneous rock, that is, one which contains between 45 and 55% silica contained in plagioclase feldspars and mafic minerals. There is no free silica. Basalt originated as a flowing lava

sheet which, as it cooled, contracted into compact masses often in hexagonal columns as in the illustration.

Basalt is very hard, heavy, of fine crystalline texture and a dark grey colour from its iron content. It melts to a fluid glass between 1150°C and 1250°C (2102°F and 2282°F) mainly because of its calcia content. It requires further feldspar and free silica to turn it into a practical glaze which will always be dark in colour. See also **Mafic minerals**.

Basalt is very difficult to grind but powder can sometimes be obtained from road-metal quarries. Alternatively, chips of basalt can be used for decorative effects when melted on to tiles fired horizontally.

Basalt ware. A black unglazed stoneware originated by Josiah Wedgwood. In this ware approximately 50% of clay is vitrified and coloured by 50% of iron and manganese oxides. See also **Black**.

Base. Alkali. A chemistry term for a substance which is the opposite of an acid and reacts to neutralize the acid and form a salt. Bases are metal oxides and they are listed under alkali. The term 'base' is often avoided in this book in favour of 'alkali' which, although strictly narrower than the term base, is less open to confusion. A base to a potter is more often a part of a pot.

Similarly the term 'basic' is avoided in its scientific sense and the term 'alkaline' used instead to denote compounds which have more than the 'average balance' of alkali to acid. Basic often means fundamental or a starting point for further work to the potter considering glaze recipes.

Bat. Batt. Batten. A common word with many meanings in the pottery. It implies a flat surface and is used for kiln shelf, pot board, detachable wheel head and pot beater. Shelves are mentioned under **Refractory**. Beaters are described under **Paddle and anvil**.

Pot boards are made from any suitable material which is slightly porous. Plain wood, chipboard and asbestos are popular. Dense substances like glazed tiles or painted boards do not allow the base of a pot to dry and are one of the causes of base cracks. Wheel-head bats need not be porous if they are only a means to throwing and moving pots. If pots are allowed to dry on the bats then the bats should be slightly porous. Chipboard and asbestos, both thin hard and thick porous, plaster and even fired clay, are used. Plywood and plain wood tend to warp. This upsets most potters although some throwers seem to revel in the eccentricity. If pots are left on the bat to dry they should first be separated from the bat by a wire otherwise base cracks may occur in drying or later in the firing.

Most potters use round wheel-head bats and stick these to the wheel head with soft clay or locate them by means of studs in the wheel head and corresponding holes in the bats. A central stud and one other has been

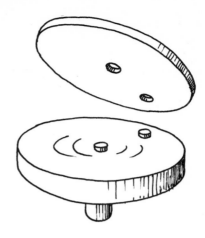

found to be the best method. Alternatively, square bats can be located within a framework of similar material glued or otherwise fastened to the wheel head. Special cup-heads with extractor or lifting devices are also available.

Also illustrated is a bat of fired clay. It is held in both hands by its loop handle and used for batting out sheets of clay for press-moulding.

Bat wash. A slurry of refractory material used to prevent kiln furniture from fusing together or pots fusing to shelves or to their lids when fired in position. The ideal wash is one which is not affected by interaction with shelves, furniture or the ware during firing. It should also be relatively cheap and should be easy to make up into a wash which stays put during setting, and lastly it should easily wash off the foot rims, lids etc of the finished ware.

Flint is popular, but above 1250°C (2282°F) especially with reduced bodies, it tends to fuse to the ware. It is also a possible source of silica dust and is to be avoided for this reason. See **Silicosis**. Alumina, zircon (zirconium silicate) and sillimanite are also popular, but expensive. A mixture of alumina hydrate two parts, china clay one part will be found excellent for most purposes both oxidized and reduced. Salt glaze does not always need a wash, depending upon the body temperature. If one is used, any combination of alumina and silica is avoided and pure alumina or pure silica is used. Also lime washes of whiting and water are used for salt glaze and in some cases a few thicknesses of newspaper on the kiln shelf gives sufficient lime (calcia) to prevent the pots from sticking.

Batch. Mill batch. Charge. Body batch or glaze batch refers to the materials weighed out to a recipe for that particular mixing.

Bauxite. Alumina hydrate. $Al_2O_3.2H_2O$. Mineral source of aluminium and alumina. It is used as a bat wash etc both raw and calcined and is sometimes added to glazes to give mattness. Variations of hydration are called diaspore ($Al_2O_3.H_2O$) and gibbsite ($Al_2O_3.3H_2O$).

Beading. Excessive crawling in which the glaze rolls back on itself to form a series of globules on an otherwise bare pot. See **Crawling**.

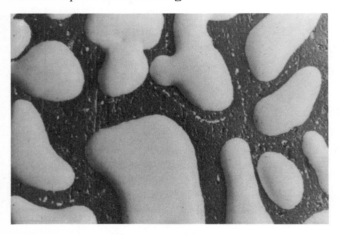

Beating. See **Paddle and anvil**.

Bell beaker. An early type of Bronze Age pot. The Beaker Folk were bronze traders who traded throughout the western sea approaches of Europe from 2000 B.C. It has been suggested that they also traded in beer and that their beakers were the first beer mugs.

The beakers have a small, flat base, swelled body and conical top which is as wide or wider than the rest of the pot. Some of the beakers have handles. They hold from

one to four pints. The term bell beaker is reserved for the pots of the original traders. The pots of the later settlers are simply called beakers. The illustrations show a beaker and part of the corded decoration.

Bellarmine. Grey beard or Bartmanner. A saltglazed beer bottle with a relief bearded face on the neck. All sizes were made from about 6 inches to 24 inches. Bellarmines originated at Cologne in the mid-16th century and were made in the Rhineland, in Flanders and in London up to the end of the 17th century. It is said that the face was modelled deliberately to insult Cardinal Bellarmine but this is not so. Bottles with modelled faces, like jugs with faces, were made long before the Cardinal lived. The name was a nickname to describe the bottle and insult the Cardinal, though a likeness may have been attempted on later work. It is possible that the first Bellarmines made in Britain were made by John Dwight.

Bentonite. A highly plastic clay originating in the decomposition of volcanic ash. It is extremely fine and can be dispersed widely through bodies and glazes, in which it is used to impart plasticity and an ability to keep a glaze slop in suspension. Up to 2% can be safely

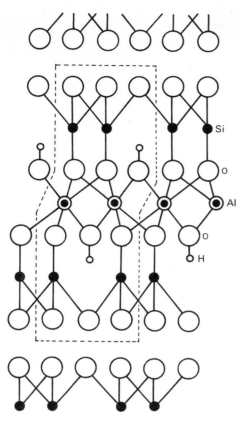

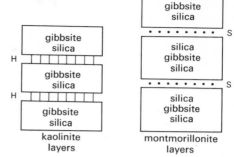

added to all bodies and will improve plasticity. Up to 1% can be safely added to glazes and the slop water made slightly acidic by a few drops of calcium chloride solution.

Decomposition of igneous rocks under different humidities and pressures resulted in the formation of different silicates. The most important to the potter is kaolinite of the kaolinite group. Kaolinite is the mineral crystal of clay. Next in importance is probably the feldspar group with free silica (quartz). Not often mentioned is the montmorillonite group which has a structure similar to kaolinite and produces mixtures of high plasticity. Bentonite is one of the montmorillonites and is often called a clay, although strictly it is not one.

It is usually accepted that bentonite decomposed from volcanic ash and occasionally from lava. Kaolinites and montmorillonites occur in the same decompositions but there is always an overwhelming dominance by one or the other. Most of the world's bentonite comes from Central North America near Fort Benton but there are deposits in other parts of the world.

The difference between a kaolinite and a montmorillonite is in the molecular structure. Both have layers but in kaolinite the repetition unit is gibbsite-silica and in the montmorillonite it is silica-gibbsite-silica. See following diagram.

In kaolinite the layers are held together by weak hydroxyl bonds from the gibbsite of one layer to the silica of the next, (H in diagram). In montmorillonite there are no hydroxyl bonds available on the outside of the layers. The outsides are composed of the oxygen atoms of the silica. The layers therefore have no hold on one another and can slide past one another. This gives the montmorillonite mineral, bentonite, its greasy feel. Bentonite is used as a lubricant in well drilling. Its swelling properties, described next, are useful to seal off wet porous rocks which are encountered.

Because there is no bond between the layers it is possible for water to enter and divide the particles. This happens when bentonite is put into water. The particles of bentonite separate to colloidal size and in some cases almost down to molecular units. The result is that bentonite can absorb a vast amount of water. 10 lbs of bentonite can accommodate 25 lbs of water and still not be liquid. Compare this with ball clay, 10 lbs of which with 14 lbs of water makes an average slip. Bentonite swells and produces not a clay but a greasy mass with obvious lubricating properties. Bentonite is one of the minerals in fuller's earth which is used for cleansing by absorption of grease, dye etc.

The idealized bentonite would have the formula $Al_2O_3 . 4SiO_2 . H_2O$. Usually some of the silicon has been replaced by aluminium. This leaves a deficiency in positive charge. The deficiency is made up by the presence of sodium or calcium cations on the surface of the layers. These provide exceptionally weak bonds joining the layers, (S in diagram). Sodium cations actually keep the layers at a wide distance apart which helps water to penetrate quickly. The best bentonites for pottery purposes are therefore sodium bentonites. The calcium bentonites can be converted into sodium bentonites by cation exchange.

The sodium bentonites are obviously deflocculated and provide excellent lubricants to improve plasticity of clays. The addition of up to 6% of bentonite to a clay of low plasticity will improve plasticity but it does not necessarily improve the workability range. See **Workability range**. Stoneware bodies can be prepared from refined fireclays by the addition of 2 to 3% bentonite. If this is added at blunging stage, then it will assist in the flow properties for sieving and levigation. However it will increase the time required for settling.

Porcelain bodies which contain little other plastic material and are to be used for throwing, require 6% of bentonite. A perfectly white quality of bentonite may be required.

Bentonite has a high cation exchange capacity. This means that it reacts dramatically to the presence of acids and alkalis. The presence of an acid induces strong polarity in the particles producing a flocculated or card-house structure. This is useful in glaze slops to inhibit the tendency of larger and heavier particles, like flint and lead frit, to settle out of suspension. One or 2% of the recipe is sufficient bentonite and this can be flocculated with a few drops of calcium chloride solution. It is best to add the bentonite to the water first and mix thoroughly. Then add the calcium chloride, mix, and add the other materials of the batch.

Beryllia. Beryllium oxide. Glucinum oxide. BeO. One of the alkaline oxides which acts as a high-temperature flux. It has been used in some porcelain glazes and as an opacifier and modifier at lower temperatures. Alone, it is a refractory with a melting point at around 2500°C (4532°F). It is practically insoluble in water but is poisonous. As a flux it must rank as one of the most expensive, costing 50 times as much as calcia which is more effective.

Beryllia is found only in beryl, the mineral silicate ($3BeO . Al_2O_3 . 6SiO_2$) of igneous origin. Beryl stained with chromium is called emerald. A bluish variety is called aquamarine.

Bi. Di. A term used in chemical nomenclature to indicate a combination with two atoms or two molecules. For example, titanium dioxide (TiO_2) has two atoms of oxygen: lead bisilicate ($PbO . 2SiO_2$) has two molecules of silica.

Bianco sopra bianco. (White on white.) Italian name for a style of maiolica which was further used on Bristol Delft. The colour of the common white tin glaze had degenerated to a dirty colour by the use of cheaper ingredients. Cobalt oxide had been used to enliven the white effect but this only resulted in a pale greenish blue for the commonest wares. By making particularly white and opaque glaze and painting this onto the standard white glaze an effective light decoration was achieved and was used successfully on plate borders. In an attempt to enhance the effect, the background glaze was further darkened, and the charm and delicacy of the style was thus lost.

Bisc, bisque. Hard biscuit. Unglazed fired pottery. The words bisc and bisque are used to imply the industrial method of a high temperature firing of the unglazed ware to be followed by a lower temperature glaze firing. The individual potter uses it in relation to raku pots which are separately biscuited to a temperature higher than that to which the raku glaze is fired.

The advantages of bisc firing are:
1. the ware is harder and easier to handle for glazing.
2. firing cracks are likely to show and money and

time are thus saved in not glaze firing these pieces.
3. any warpage arising from shrinkage can be controlled by setting the pieces in sand during bisc firing.
4. shrinkage is complete and the glaze firing can be more economically set.

The disadvantage is that with coarse clays it is difficult to get a sufficiently thick layer of glaze to adhere to the ware because the porosity of the ware is very low. In this context, most clays used by individual potters would be considered coarse because the comparison is with industrial clays.

Biscuit. To fire ware unglazed in preparation for glazing; also the unglazed fired ware. It is an overall term but individual potters imply the use of a temperature lower than the following glaze firing and use the term bisc or bisque for the industrial method of high-temperature biscuit firings. Meaning literally baked twice, it comes from the 17th-century introduction from France of an extra firing. Previous to this the British potter had used only a single firing of raw glazed ware.

The advantage of biscuit over bisc is that biscuit is more porous and it is therefore relatively easy to get a glaze to adhere to it before firing. If the biscuit ware is very porous it is easy to glaze because it quickly takes in the water of the glaze slop leaving the layer of glaze on the surface of the ware. The more porous the biscuit, the faster it is possible to glaze a batch of pots. The lower the temperature of the biscuit firing, the greater the degree of porosity. The lowest feasible temperature is about 750°C (1382°F) at which point the clay has become pot and has enough physical strength to survive in one piece.

Soft biscuit, besides meaning soft (low) temperature, can be taken literally. Low firing gives physically soft ware which is mechanically weak. As porosity is lost through the increase in temperature, so strength is gained. The pores in the body are filled with melted silicates which on cooling set hard and bind together the particles around the pores. Each clay behaves differently and will have its own temperature at which it is sufficiently strong to be easily handled yet sufficiently porous to be easily glazed.

Potters have their own preferences within the practical temperature range for biscuit firing which is from 850°C to 1000°C (1562°F to 1832°F). Some kilns may even cover this range in temperature differences in parts of the same firing. Potters often use the tongue test to determine how porous the biscuit is. The colour of the ware is some indication but it is confirmed by a quick touch with the tongue which is a very sensitive instrument.

The illustrations show enlarged sections through:
1. very soft biscuit where the clay particles are only sintered;
2. ideal porous biscuit which has the particles fastened together but large pores to give porosity;

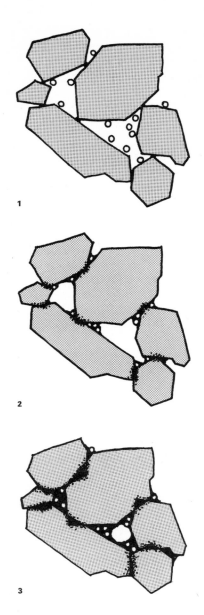

1

2

3

3. dense body where the glassy matrix has almost filled the pores. The progressive breakdown of the clay particle can be seen and the other body constituents assisting this fusion, viz fluxes and free silica, are diagrammatically shown as small circles. Note how the body also shrinks.

For details of biscuit firing, see **Firing**.

Biscuits. Unfired disc setters used under pots to prevent sticking. Being unfired they shrink with the foot rim, thereby saving distortion. They may be made from body clay or refractory clay.

Bismuth oxide. Bi_2O_3. An amphoteric oxide which acts as a flux in ceramic fusions. It is usually introduced in small amounts as a modifier of colourings.

Bismuth occurs as sulphide, oxide and telluride but is mostly recovered from tin, lead and copper ores. It is

a low melting point metal and is used in low melting alloys. Nitrate salts are used in medicine.

The pure metal can be polished like silver. A thin layer deposited on the glaze by reduction gives a mother of pearl lustre. Bismuth nitrate is dissolved in resin and oil for application to glazed ware. The organic materials burn out in the 700°C to 800°C (1292°F to 1472°F) range and leave the pure metal. This lustre medium is used as a carrier for other lustre colours.

Black. When studied critically, a black colour will be seen to be a dark brown, blue or green. Transparent or semi-transparent glazes are easily stained by the addition of the strong colouring oxides which give brown, blue and green.

The fully matured transparent glaze dissolves and uniformly disperses the stain, thus providing a depth of colour which is rich. Transparent shiny glazes give the best black glazes. Opaque tin glazes and crystalline glazes etc can only be a dark grey.

Similarly with bodies and slips, the darkest colour develops with glassiness. Vitrified bodies, like that of the black basalt vase by Colin Pearson illustrated here, are distinctly black, but non-vitrified bodies and slips can only be a dusty dark grey.

A matured transparent glaze covering a black slip always gives a good black colour. The following recipe is for a black slip to go under a transparent glaze at 1120°C (2048°F):

ball clay	76
manganese dioxide	8
red iron oxide	8
cobalt oxide	8

For an unglazed black slip which will vitrify at 1250°C (2282°F), the following recipe can be used:

ball clay or body clay	75
whiting	12
red iron oxide	8
copper oxide	2·5
cobalt oxide	2·5

Colouring oxides can be added to existing glazes to give a black colour. The oxides will give extra fluxing action which should be counteracted by some china clay. Half the weight of the colouring oxides is a suitable starting point for the amount of china clay. The following recipes are balanced with the colouring oxides. The first is for a black shiny glaze for 1120°C to 1150°C (2048°F to 2102°F):

feldspar	30
china clay	15
lead bisilicate	45
manganese dioxide	5
red iron oxide	4
cobalt oxide	1

An alternative colouring is:

manganese dioxide	9
copper oxide	1

Matt crystalline glazes for temperatures below 1150°C (2102°F) are delicate in their balance because the crystals tend to give a light colour and produce a grey. The following recipe gives a black crystalline glaze when fired to 1120°C (2048°F) and cooled slowly:

feldspar	14
nepheline syenite	14
china clay	13
quartz	6
lead carbonate	40
whiting	5
red iron oxide	4
manganese dioxide	4

The next recipe is for 1200°C (2192°F). This glaze has a fine crystalline surface with some separation of oxide as speckles:

feldspar	50
china clay	15
flint	5
whiting	15
cobalt oxide	5
manganese dioxide	5
red iron oxide	5

See also **Tea-dust**.

Nickel and chromium oxides are often used in the production of calcined black stains. They may also be used in glazes without calcination and help to produce neutral blacks. Two examples of colouring to be added to existing glazes are given:

nickel oxide	2	1
red iron oxide	5	6
cobalt oxide	5	3
manganese dioxide	2	–
chromium oxide	1	5

Black core. Blue core. The dark grey centre which

shows in the section of some fired bodies. It is caused by local reduction. The black colour is black iron oxide possibly with some carbon. In ivory and cream bodies the colour is a pale grey often lighter in colour than the oxidized surround.

Black core occurs when the carbon inside the body has not been successfully burnt out. All clays contain some carbonaceous matter. This oxidizes to give carbon dioxide at temperatures above 750°C (1382°F). Oxygen enters the pores of the body, combines with the carbon and escapes as a gas. If insufficient oxygen is present in the kiln atmosphere, then the carbon cannot burn (oxidize). However at this temperature it is exceedingly greedy for oxygen and will achieve oxidation by taking oxygen from any red iron oxide which may be present. The result is black iron oxide. The equation is:

$$2Fe_2O_3 + C \longrightarrow 4FeO + CO_2\uparrow$$

red iron oxide	carbon	black iron oxide	carbon dioxide

At 900°C (1652°F) the black iron oxide becomes an active flux and is immediately involved in the early stages of vitrification. Later oxidation will be unable to reoxidize this black iron oxide which is combined in a melt. The vitrification continues through the firing and is one cause of premature breakdown.

The lack of sufficient oxygen between 750°C and 900°C by an unclean atmosphere or by too rapid a firing can lead to breakdown, bloating etc at higher temperatures. See **Breakdown**. Black core is often a fault arising in the biscuit firing that does not show itself until the glaze firing.

Black-figure ware. Early classical Greek pottery which was decorated with a partially reduced ferruginous slip. The figures were painted in solid black upon a lighter ground. Red and white slips were sometimes added and details were drawn on by sgraffito through the black slip. See **Attic pottery**.

Black-hard clay. Any type or colour of clay at the stage between leatherhard and white-hard. It is the stage at which clay looks its darkest colour with the edges just beginning to look whitish. With earthenware clays and some stoneware clays most of the shrinkage has now taken place. Any drying cracks are likely to have formed already, even if they are not visible, and further drying can be relatively quick. Alternatively this is the ideal stage for the application of slip glazes composed of wood ash and clay. Stoneware clays are usually stronger at this stage than when white-hard. The slight wetting received in glazing only strengthens the clay further, yet drying can be swift after glazing. See also **Drying**.

Blacksmith's scale. Iron spangles. Finery cinder. Fe_3O_4. The lustrous blue flakes produced when hot iron is hammered. It is a source of speckles for clays and glazes because it does not immediately dissolve during the firing. See **Iron oxide, types**.

Blakeley's tuning fork. This is a device similar to Steger's bending bar for measuring the stress between body and glaze.

Blistering. Unwanted gassing of a glaze resulting in bubbles and the craters of burst bubbles. Blistering occurs where the glaze has not had time to smooth out before it sets.

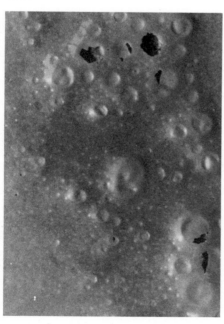

The bubbles are gases originating in the glaze or in the body beneath. See **Bloating**. With the rise in temperature and its attendant interactions, many gases are liberated, e.g. sulphur dioxide from crocus martis above 900°C (1652°F), oxygen from manganese dioxide at 1080°C (1976°F) and fluorine from cornish stone above 1150°C (2102°F). Also some constituents begin to boil and volatilize, e.g. lead oxide above 1150°C and soda above 1200°C (2192°F).

To overcome blistering: cut down the amount of offending material, alter the firing cycle and alter the viscosity of the molten glaze.

It is sometimes possible to replace glaze materials with more practical ones though often with some loss of character. Feldspars can often be substituted for cornish stone, iron oxides for crocus martis, etc.

The firing cycle can be altered to include a slower maturing of the glaze towards top temperature. Possibly a slightly lower top temperature but a longer firing may smooth out the glaze. The introduction of oxygen in the later stages often helps to clear gases out of the chamber and clean up glazes. A soaking at top temperature or, better still, an extended cooling down the first 50°C or 100°C (90°F or 180°F) allows the bubbles to escape and the glaze to heal over.

A stiff glaze often traps bubbles in it giving it a frosted opacity. See **Stiff glazes**. The stiffness when molten is called a glaze's viscosity. It is possible to alter this viscosity by adjustment of the glaze recipe. A glaze which is fluid allows the bubbles to escape quickly and also heals over the scars. See **Viscosity of molten glazes** and **Surface tension**. It should be remembered that bubbles try to rise vertically. They take longer to escape from overhanging surfaces near the base of swelling forms and from inside foot rims. A slightly thinner glaze layer may be necessary.

Bloating. The unwanted blistering of the body caused by trapped gases. The defect occurs in stoneware and between body and slip in slipware.

During firing, many gases are liberated from the body. Most of these escape through the body pores and if necessary through the molten glaze. If the body pores are blocked by a stiff fusion of body-glaze layer or by a stiff vitrifying slip, the gases cannot escape. They then

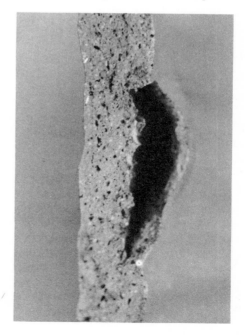

build up pockets of gas behind a 'plastic' barrier which is distorted to accommodate the gas bubble.

The gases involved are carbon monoxide and dioxide which escape from 700°C to 900°C (1292°F to 1652°F); sulphur in various oxidations from 700°C to 1150°C (1292°F to 2102°F) and fluorine from 700°C to 1300°C (1292°F to 2372°F).

The greatest trouble arises from carbon which has not been completely burnt out at biscuit stage. If there is only one 'through' firing then the biscuiting part of this may have been rushed. The result is carbon still trapped in the body and unable to oxidize because sealed from the outside atmosphere. See **Black core** and **Firing, biscuit**. This carbon eventually oxidizes by taking oxygen from iron oxide. The reduced iron oxide acts as a body flux, the body is softened by over-vitrification and the carbon oxides create bloats.

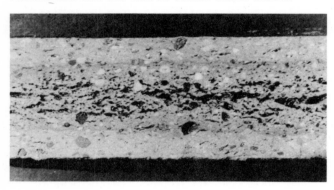

This defect is emphasized in stoneware where the body is intentionally reaching vitrification. In earthenware, with the exception of slipware described later, the gases usually manage to escape from the still porous body and the worst effect from black core is a blistering or milder pin-holing of the glaze.

Sometimes a clay contains so much gas that it cannot be fired satisfactorily. Gases which are liberated after the body has become vitreous are obviously difficult to disperse. The only answer lies in the lower temperatures for the firing which do not involve vitrification and gassing.

Bloating in slipware can be overcome by using vitreous slips on one side of the body only. It may even be necessary to leave one side unglazed. This was common with some 17th- and 18th-century English slipware which was raw glazed. The soft-firing lead glaze fused before the carbon had burnt out of the body. In a few examples which are glazed all over, some interesting reduced colourings were sealed. These have re-oxidized around the craze lines. There is also unfortunately some bloating.

Blue. This colour has always been popular on pottery and was one of the earliest colours used in glazes. It was achieved in early Egyptian and Persian wares by cobalt oxide in lead glazes and copper oxide in high-alkaline glazes.

Cobalt oxide usually gives a blue colour in glazes and bodies. The blue varies in hue according to the predominance of lead oxide or boric oxide. Lead oxide gives an inky blue with a slightly greenish tint. Boric oxide and alkaline glazes give purply blues of the royal blue and willow blue type. Cobalt oxide is very dependable and can be used at high temperatures. It bleeds slightly into the glaze as it forms the cobalt silicate colourant. To overcome the bleeding, a more permanent stain is used which is prepared as cobalt aluminate and known as matt blue. This must be produced prior to addition to the glaze.

An even more dependable stain, which again must be prepared first as a colourant, is produced by a combination of vanadium trioxide and zirconium silicate.

The copper oxide blue is only obtainable under special conditions in glazes which are not particularly stable or highly practical. The blue is the result of copper silicate in combination with an alkali-silicate (using lithia, soda, potash and/or calcia). The presence of magnesia, lead oxide, boric oxide or alumina kills the pure blue colour.

See **Cobalt oxide**, **Vanadium stains** and **Alkaline glazes**.

Blue and white. A term implying white porcelain with painted blue decoration. It usually refers to Chinese porcelain which had been perfected to a white translucence by the 13th-century and was painted with cobalt blue. The Mongolian Yuan Dynasty (1280–1368) is famous for the introduction of a particularly pure cobalt ore from Persia.

The Chinese porcelains were later copied in Europe and are also called 'blue and white'.

Blue core. See **Black core**.

Blunge. To mix materials and water thoroughly. Blunging is done in an octagonal or hexagonal tank with a central vertical shaft. On this shaft are fastened radial blades or paddles. These are set at an angle so that, when the shaft rotates, the blades force the mixture downwards. The resulting creamy slurry is run out of the tank by a tap at the bottom. It can then be sieved, settled etc.

The drawing shows the principle of the blunger and the photograph a 12-inch octagonal blunger manufactured by Gosling and Gatensbury Ltd and marketed by Harrison Mayer Ltd.

A recent development is centrifugal blunging which uses a small, high-speed impellor at the base of the tank. The drawing shows the highly-efficient impellor made by Edwards and Jones Ltd.

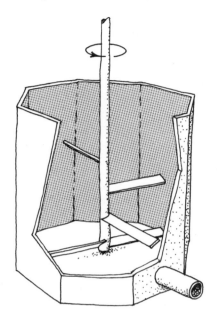

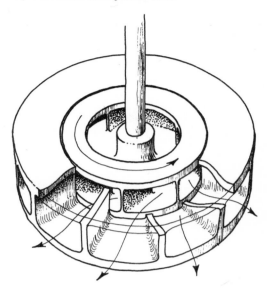

Blunging by hand. The act of thoroughly mixing a slip or slop without a machine. Small amounts, such as a bucketful, are left to soak and then are most quickly dealt with by the hand. Larger amounts need either a paddle, which is a flattened stick, or a dolly, which is a perforated disc set on the end of a stick. The underside of the disc has a few sharp dowels protruding which break up the solids as the dolly is raised and lowered. The holes flush the mixture to mix it. Electric motors and even the power drill having a long rod with a loop at the end have mostly rendered hand blunging obsolete.

Blurred outline. Bleeding. Some colouring oxides, such as copper, manganese and to a lesser extent cobalt, are easily dissolved in glazes. If these oxides are used

for decoration, the area of colour inevitably bleeds into the glaze with the effect known as blurred outline.

Boccaro. Unglazed red stoneware originally from 17th-century China. Now used as a name for any vitrified red clay ware especially when such ware is domestic pottery and has at least some unglazed parts, often with relief decoration. The photograph is of a tiny Chinese teapot.

Body. (1) The clay part of a pot as opposed to any additional parts such as slips, glazes and colours. Since the clay ceases to be clay and becomes ceramic during firing the term 'body' is a useful one, in contrast to glaze, in the discussion of actions taking place during firing or in discussing the final result.

Body. (2) A clay for a special purpose. It is created by blending different clays or by adding to clays other minerals, such as feldspar and flint, in order to produce a desired workability or finished result. A body is the result of man's technology. A clay is the natural product, though possibly simply processed to make it homogeneous.

Body constituents. The different materials used in compounding and blending pottery bodies. They can be classified as clays, fluxes, hardeners and openers. Natural clays often contain fluxes, hardeners and openers. Some of these may be undesirable and may be removed during preparation.

Instead of starting with a natural stoneware clay which has the properties required, one may create a blend with a ball clay for plasticity and raw strength, a china clay for whiteness and refractoriness, and a fireclay for refractoriness and texture. To this clay blend will be added the fluxes, hardeners and openers.

The fluxes used in bodies are feldspathoids such as cornish stone, feldspar and nepheline syenite, or in the soft maturing bodies may be fluxes such as lead oxide, boric oxide and calcia. The fluxes themselves melt and flux the free silica in the body to produce a molten glass which fills the interstitial spaces. On cooling the larger particles are thus cemented together by a glassy matrix.

The hardeners are the free silicas which may be added as flint, quartz, silica sand and cristobalite. Silica is hard but is fluxed during the firing and then gives its hardness to the resulting glass.

The openers are used to give texture and workability. They are grog, fireclay, and organic matter such as sawdust, cereal husks, chopped straw and cow dung.

In the preparation of a body it is usual to blunge the clays, fluxes and hardeners together, the proportions being determined by dry weight. The blunged slurry is sieved and dried to plasticity by filterpress or drying troughs. The openers are usually added at the wedging and kneading stage or at the pug mill, the proportions being determined by dry weight of opener to plastic weight of clay. The use of clay mixers which mix dry powders together with water to a plastic state without the intermediate state of slurry has meant that openers can be added from the start. In these cases the proportions are dry weight of opener and dry weight of clay. If working from someone else's recipe for a body it is advisable to discover how the proportions, especially of openers, are calculated against the other constituents.

Body-glaze layer. Intermediate layer. Interface. The part of a fired pot where the glaze meets the body. It is seen in section as a gradation from body to glaze. Sometimes it is darker than either the body or the glaze. This layer is more strongly defined in stoneware and porcelain where the higher temperature and longer firing give greater opportunities for interaction to take place.

The layer begins to form as soon as the fluxes in either body or glaze begin to melt with the silicates. If the melt is soft enough it will envelop not only adjacent particles in its own substance but also in the neighbouring one of body or glaze. As the glaze becomes molten some of it will soak into the body if the body is sufficiently porous. It will immediately begin to flux the body surrounding the cavities which it has entered.

The body-glaze layer often contains more alumina than the glaze because it has more clay in it, and therefore on cooling it forms crystals. These crystals are often the place where other crystals start their growth in a crystalline glaze. Thus a prolonged soaking during

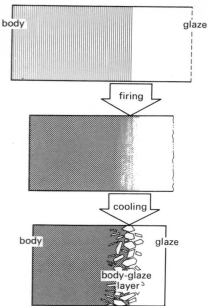

firing can help to produce crystals although the crystals only form during the cooling.

A thick body-glaze layer acts as a cushion to absorb the stress between body and glaze. The deliberate formation of this layer is some insurance against crazing, and to a lesser extent, shivering. Such a layer would be termed a buffer layer.

A thick body-glaze layer develops in porcelain. Here it can be twice the thickness of the glaze remaining as pure glaze. Thus a strong compression of the glaze can be cushioned and the overall strength of a glazed piece of porcelain can be double that of its unglazed counterpart.

Bog ore. A general name covering a variety of ores which are the result of precipitation. Lakes, marshes and other areas of land-locked water often contain iron in solution. The iron is precipitated as the end product of a series of reactions which starts with the decomposition of vegetable matter. The precipitate is at first the colloidal state iron hydroxide ($Fe(OH)_3$ or Fe_2O_3 . $3H_2O$) and later the ore limonite ($2Fe_2O_3$. $3H_2O$). Pure deposits can be won as rich ores.

Sand and other silt often become involved in the deposition resulting in sedimentary rocks called ironstones. These sometimes contain sufficient iron to be worth recovery. Others provide horizon markers in coal mining and have descriptive names like 'black band' and 'clay ironstone'. They often weather quickly to a crumbly state and are useful as glaze constituents. See **Iron oxide**.

Boiling point. Normally means the boiling point of water at 100°C or 212°F. However all liquids have a boiling point. Glazes, in their liquid state during firing, boil periodically as the different compounds, which are mostly oxides, reach their individual boiling points. At a certain temperature, as an oxide boils it becomes vapour in the same way that water becomes steam. It does not require much liquid to make a lot of vapour and create a lot of bubbles which froth the glaze.

All glazes boil during melting, or more correctly some constituent of the glaze boils. This results in bubbles which spoil the smooth surface of the glaze. The vapour must be cleared by a higher temperature and/or a prolonged firing otherwise the bubbles may be trapped in the glaze. If they do get to the surface and burst, the resulting crater also needs time to heal before the glaze stiffens and sets. Materials which are likely to give trouble are previously fritted to a higher temperature than the one at which they will be used.

Bole. A fine red clay occurring in the countries of the eastern Mediterranean. It is used as a pigment and in the compounding of enamel colours. It is relatively pure as a clay, approximating kaolinite plus iron oxide.

Bone ash. Ground calcined bones, usually cattle bones. It is one source of calcium phosphate; others are phosphorite and apatite. It is used as a flux in bodies where the calcia does the fluxing and the phosphorus pentoxide acts as a glass-former in the melt and also checks over-rapid fusion. Its stiff glassy character is seen combined with that of feldspar in bone china. Bone china contains 45 to 50% of bone ash. A small amount of carbon remains in bone ash when calcination is controlled and this carbon assists the raw plasticity of the body.

A typical analysis of bone ash would be calcia 55%, phosphorus pentoxide 40% with the remainder composed of fluorine, silica and alkaline oxides. An acceptable formula for bone ash is $Ca_3(PO_4)_2$ ultimately $3CaO . P_2O_5$ which proportion could vary to $13CaO . 4P_2O_5$.

Bone ash is used in glazes as an opacifier. In spite of its large percentage of calcia its fluxing action is checked somewhat by the phosphorus pentoxide which produces a stiff melt. It can be used to assist tin oxide so that less tin oxide is required, especially where a less shiny surface is acceptable. However bone ash can be a cause of crawling and blistering. Small amounts are said to assist the formation of a good chun glaze by introducing phosphorus. The quality of depth in Sung glazes is attributed to phosphorus and could have come from bone ash.

Bone china. A British porcelain in which the body is first fired to translucent state without a glaze. The glaze firing is at a lower temperature. For the bisc firing, the body is supported in powdered alumina to inhibit warping.

The ware was developed in the 18th century to meet the demand for a white translucent ware which arose with the importation of Oriental porcelain.

Calcined ox bones are used to provide a viscous body flux. A typical bone china body is composed of:

china clay 25
feldspar 25
bone ash 50

This body is very short when plastic and fragile when dry. It is most suitable for slip-casting but with plasticizer (bentonite 6%) can be press-moulded. It is bisc fired to 1280°C (2336°F) and glaze fired below 1080°C (1976°F).

Bone-dry clay. Clay which has been dried beyond the naturally dry state which it reaches in the air. Dry clay contains water equal with the atmosphere but bone-dry clay has had this water removed. To achieve the bone-dry state, the clay is heated to over 100°C (212°F), the boiling point of water. In the early stages of a firing, this is called water smoking. See **Drying**.

If bone-dry clay is allowed to cool it will take up moisture from the atmosphere by a process of adsorption and capillary action. A slight expansion will take place which sometimes leads to unequal sizes of adjacent parts, stress and cracks. See **Readsorption**.

Boracite. Stassfurtite. Borate and chlorate of magnesium. $6MgO.MgCl_2.8B_2O_3$. A complex and variable mineral of magnesium and boron which is used in frits. It occurs associated with gypsum, rock salt and anhydrite in Germany.

Boracitis. A word concocted by J. W. Mellor in the early 1930's to describe the unwanted action of boric oxide. Additions of small amounts of boric oxide to a glaze have beneficial effects as an anti-craze. This is described under **Glaze fit**. However, there is an optimum amount for this benefit and this amount is different for each glaze recipe. Above this point further additions of boric oxide have the opposite effect and can cause crazing. The effect is due to the loss of elasticity in the glaze. An elastic glaze has the capacity to absorb the stress between body and glaze which a more brittle glaze cannot achieve.

Borate. Boric oxide (oxide of boron) in combination with other elements. Boric oxide (B_2O_3) which is used in pottery glazes rarely occurs alone in nature. The boron minerals are called borates and the important ones are: borax, boric acid, boracite, colemanite and ulexite. These are separately indexed in this book.

The combinations of boric oxide with water, soda, calcia etc are various. Their individual structures have not yet been fully explained with the result that borate nomenclature is still tentative. Different ceramic chemists use different names and arrangements of chemical symbols to emphasise the consideration involved in the absence of proof of lattice structure. Where possible, the system used for borates follows the system used for other compounds in this book. The oxides are often separate for ease of reading: a method not acceptable to many chemists because it implies that separate molecules exist, which of course they do not in a compound. The names given are those commonly in use by potters and are often the more visually descriptive names of minerals rather than the scientific names of chemicals. Chemical names are appropriately used in reference to oxides which are involved in fusions where they are no longer the original mineral.

The following is an explanation of some of the borate nomenclature:

1. Borax is usually written as $Na_2B_4O_7.10H_2O$ which implies that there is a sodium, boron and oxygen lattice into which water, as hydrogen and oxygen, is integrated. Potters prefer to see it written as $Na_2O.2B_2O_3.10H_2O$. They ignore the water which they know will burn out during firing and see the borax as soda and boric oxide thereby viewing its potential in a glaze.

2. Borax is referred to as sodium pyroborate because of its volcanic origin. Other names arise from its chemical formula: sodium tetraborate refers to the four atoms of boron per molecule ($Na_2B_4O_7$); sodium diborate refers to the two boric oxide molecules ($Na_2O.2B_2O_3$). The term 'hydrated', that is, with water of crystallization, is often added.

3. $NaBO_2$ is called sodium monoborate because there is one atom of boron per molecule. It is also called sodium metaborate which means simply that the sodium is with boron and implies a sense of change. If the formula is multiplied by two, one achieves: $2NaBO_2 = Na_2O.B_2O_3$ which is referred to as sodium orthoborate because there is a straight or equal balance of molecules, soda: boric oxide.

4. BO_2H is called metaboric acid. The 'meta' here implies the halfway position between boric acid and boric oxide. See **Boric acid**.

5. B_2O_3 which is usually called boric oxide is occasionally called boron trioxide or boron sesquioxide.

6. Some other borate minerals are:

kernite
$$Na_2B_4O_7.4H_2O = Na_2O.2B_2O_3.4H_2O$$
pandermite
$$Ca_4B_{10}O_{19}.7H_2O = 4CaO.5B_2O_3.7H_2O$$
boracite
$$Mg_6Cl_2B_{14}O_{26} = 5MgO.7B_2O_3.MgCl_2$$

Borax. Tincal. Hydrated borate of sodium. $Na_2B_4O_7.10H_2O$ or $Na_2O.2B_2O_3.10H_2O$. A crystalline mineral which is the source of boric oxide with soda. It is used in making low-melting glaze frits without lead oxide. Borax occurs naturally as a precipitate from lakes and marshes in California. Tincal is the name for Asian borax. Lower phases of hydration are also found and have the mineral names rasorite and kernite with the formula $Na_2O.2B_2O_3.4H_2O$.

Borax is the chief source of boric oxide for glazes but because it is soluble in water it is necessary to introduce it into the glaze batch in a fritted form. Strictly speaking, once the borax has been dehydrated and incorporated in a frit it is no longer borax but a complex of sodium metaborate and boric oxide with silicates. However the term borax frit is used to indicate its origin and is obviously less cumbersome than any alternative.

Borax decomposes upon heating to form sodium metaborate, boric oxide and water:

$$Na_2B_4O_7.10H_2O \rightarrow 2NaBO_2.B_2O_3 + 10H_2O \uparrow$$

The sodium metaborate/boric oxide combination is also written $Na_2O.2B_2O_3$ and is therefore referred to as sodium diborate. This end product has a melting point of 741°C (1366°F) when it is known as fused borax. For clarification of the nomenclature, see **Borate**. The simplest borax frit has the formula $Na_2O.2B_2O_3$. $3SiO_2$ and is useful in the glaze range 900°C to 1100°C (1652°F to 2012°F) over which it is itself maturing. See **Boric oxide** for use in glazes.

Borax frit. A frit made from borax and silica (or silicate). The borax provides soda and boric oxide. The soda is a flux; the boric oxide is a flux and a glass-former. Both flux the silica at a low temperature to produce a molten glass. This is shattered with water and ground to a powder. If a silicate is used there will be alumina present also.

There are many possible unity formulae for borax frits. The simplest is:

$$Na_2O.2B_2O_3.3SiO_2$$

Borax frits are used with feldspars and clays to compound leadless glazes. The frit melts in the 850°C to 1000°C (1562°F to 1832°F) range thus originating the fusion of the glaze. Pure borax cannot be used in a glaze slop because it is soluble in water. In fritted form it is insoluble. See **Boric oxide** for use in glazes.

If borax frit is being prepared for use in a lead (low sol) glaze, it is never fritted with the lead oxide. Lead silicate must be prepared separately from the borax frit in order to render the lead oxide insoluble. See **Low sol** and **Double fritting**.

Boric acid. Boracic acid. Orthoboric acid. Sassoline. $B(OH)_3$ or H_3BO_3 or $B_2O_3.3H_2O$. A boron mineral occurring as waxy white crystals around some Italian hot springs. It is also manufactured from borax and is used as a mild acid antiseptic for the eyes. Its use in pottery is in the preparation of boro-silicate frits.

Boric acid is soluble in water and therefore must be fritted with silicates before it can be used in a glaze slop. When subjected to heat during the fritting process, the boric acid decomposes to boric oxide (B_2O_3) and water (H_2O). The equation is:

$$2B(OH)_3 \xrightarrow{100°C} 2BO_2H + 2H_2O \uparrow \xrightarrow{200°C}$$
$$2B_2O_3 + 3H_2O \uparrow$$

Time, as well as temperature, is an important factor in this dehydration process.

Boric oxide. Boron trioxide. B_2O_3. A glass-forming oxide which is one of the most useful of glaze constituents. It melts at a low temperature and is therefore suitable for low-temperature glazes where it acts both as a glass-former and a flux. It rarely occurs alone in nature but is available as a series of borates in combination with water, soda, calcia and magnesia. These minerals are mostly soluble in water and hence they are incorporated in frits before being used in glazes. Boric oxide itself is hygroscopic and freely soluble in water. See **Borate**.

In glaze theory it is considered that there is a molecule of boric oxide (B_2O_3) and that this becomes linked in endless chains with itself and silica (SiO_2). To achieve the boric oxide chain one must melt the crystals of boric oxide. Melting begins at 300°C (572°F) when the crystals start to break down. The molecule B_2O_3 goes through a series of divisions into sub-oxides with partial melting until full fusion is reached at 700°C (1292°F). A useful glass is now formed from the chains or boric oxide and this does not recrystallize on cooling. It is an amorphous substance and as such has no melting point but a melting range. Remelting will be in the range 570°C to 600°C (1058°F to 1112°F), which enables boric oxide to be used as a low-temperature flux (alkali) as well as a glass-former (acid).

Boric oxide frits and glazes were developed as an alternative to lead glazes to overcome lead poisoning. It is possible to make glazes melting as low as 750°C (1382°F). However boric oxide is also extremely useful in combination with lead silicates. In fully fused glazes it decreases the solubility of the lead oxide and it extends the firing range of lead silicates. It assists the glaze balance and is well known as an anti-craze. See **Glaze fit**. Lead oxide increases the elasticity of boric oxide glazes and the combination of the two produces a range of finishes and colours. As a generalization, the boric oxide gives harsher colours than lead oxide.

Boric oxide is a glass-former and therefore works in a similar way to silica in the glaze. It provides part of the glass network into which are incorporated the other oxides. One of its greatest merits is its low melting point and it is often used for this property. Its theoretical introduction into glazes is simple. It can be substituted for some of the silica on a molecular basis. See **Equivalent**. Small amounts (0·1 equivalents) make appreciable differences in the melting point of the glaze. With matt glazes it is better to substitute the boric oxide for some of the alumina. However the low melting point of boric oxide makes the theoretical consideration of matts difficult. Once the boric oxide has melted it naturally assists other actions and therefore has some interaction with the alkalis which would cause the crystalline matt.

33

BORIC OXIDE AND RECIPE ADJUSTMENTS. Boric oxide is a glass-former (acid) but also acts as a flux (alkali). Its sesquioxide formula tells us that it is indeed amphoteric and will act accordingly. Potters often have difficulty in putting it into its proper place in unity formulae. Its correct place is with the amphoteric oxides but one must realize that if the equivalents of boric oxide exceed 0·05 it is difficult to relate the formula to others which contain none.

In most glaze adjustments the boric oxide to be added will be part of a frit. It will be necessary to know the unity formula of the frit if one is to calculate from formula to new recipe. If one is making one's own frit, it is better to keep the frit recipe and formula simple. If the soluble parts are rendered insoluble and the frit is soft enough to grind there is no advantage in fritting more than is necessary of the glaze recipe. See **Frit**. Some frits of very simple unity formula, e.g. Na_2O. $2B_2O_3 . 3SiO_2$, are available commercially for potters who wish to work by calculation, but what starts as an intention of simple substitution can become complex when related to compound minerals in the recipe for the glaze batch. See also **Formula, unity** and **Calculations**.

Most potters regard theoretical substitution as difficult and prefer the simple addition of a frit. In this case the frit should be chosen with regard to the composition of the glaze. Assuming that the glaze is as required except that it needs to be softened slightly, one would choose a frit containing the same oxides as the glaze. If the glaze is a limestone, clay and soda feldspar glaze it is the simplest course to introduce a frit which also contains calcia, soda and alumina as well as the boric oxide and silica. The introductory tests should be done with a mixture of the glaze and frit at one end of a line blend and the straight glaze at the other. If in doubt as to the choice of frit one should first try the most popular standard frit available. It is likely that this has been developed for general occasions which one's own case will fit. If the original glaze has no especial merit, then the addition of any frit will probably bring some interest.

BORIC OXIDE AND NEW RECIPES. One often starts with someone else's glaze recipe and adjusts this empirically to one's own potting. The word frit alone in a recipe has little value and could mean a material melting at 750°C or 1100°C. In the absence of detail as to which frit to use, start by using a frit in a line blend. Boric oxide frits are various and are manufactured for most situations. The manufacturer's advice should be sought as to which frit will be suitable for the temperature range, colour, clay etc.

For temperatures up to 1150°C (2102°F), a line blend is easily prepared. Most frits within their suggested temperature ranges begin to look like glazes with the addition of 10% china clay. If this is taken as one end of a line blend and the other end is 90% feldspar with 10%

of china clay, then a suitable glaze requiring minor balancing by silica and whiting should be possible.

For temperatures above 1150°C (2102°F), it is better to start without the boric oxide frit and introduce this only as necessary to improve glaze surface, shine, colour, range, balance and anti-craze.

Borocalcite. See **Colemanite** and **Calcium borate**.

Bottle. The examples shown are by: Paul Brown, Ken Jones, Janet Leach, Frank Vining, Harry Stringer, and Haverfordwest Pottery.

Boulder clay. A clay of glacial origin containing boulders. Some of the boulders are massive whilst others are only small pebbles. Sometimes there are more boulders than there is clay but some deposits are workable as clay and provide a fairly uniform and smooth clay. It is a fusible clay suitable for soft-fired earthenware.

During its transportation the clay was ground, split and weathered. It also gathered impurities which were equally fine. It settled in lakes dammed by ice or was washed out of melting glaciers at the end of the last glacial period.

Because it is full of impurities of similar size to the clay, it cannot be purified by sieving. The impurities make it vitrify at approximately 1100°C (2012°F) and melt by 1300°C (2372°F). It is therefore suitable for low temperatures as a body or higher temperatures as a fusible slip, possibly with the addition of some wood ash or soft frit.

Bowl. The examples shown are by: Harry and May Davis, Poterie de Digan, Janet Hamer, Helen Pincombe, Paul Philp, Lucie Rie.

Boxing. Putting cups or bowls together rim to rim for drying and firing. Bowls are often boxed and also stacked foot to foot as in the following illustration.

Boxing is done to cut down drying warpage. The pots are placed together at cheesehard state. The drying is slowed down because the insides and the rims are protected. In a soft biscuit firing the rims of boxed pots are held firmly which prevents warpage. Boxing is also used in stoneware glaze firings when the pot rims are

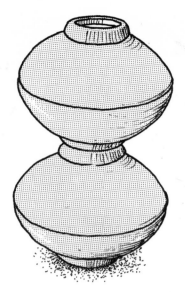

left unglazed. Cups and bowls with handles are less likely to be pulled out of true by the handle weight if they are boxed.

Brass. A class of alloys incorporating copper and zinc. Brass filings are used by potters to speckle clays and glazes. After oxidation the zinc oxide becomes a powerful flux and the copper oxide a strong stain.

Breakdown. The actions of decomposition, disintegration and deformation, especially when they are undesirable. The commonest use is to describe the deformation of bodies caused by over-fluxing. The special case of breakdown caused by iron oxide is treated under a sub-heading.

Clays deform when they are over-fired. They collapse and might even melt to a glass. At this point the silica and silicates of the clay have been successfully fluxed by alkaline oxides. The alkaline oxides could be present in the feldspar, in the sand, in chalk or limestone flour, and in the salts. Throughout a firing, from the completion of the ceramic change at 600°C (1112°F), the body fluxes are working on the silicates. The action is desirable. It causes vitrification which is the creation of glassy parts within the body. These weld the whole together into the strong structure of the finished product. See **Vitrification.** The process becomes breakdown when it has developed too far. Here the glassy parts completely surround the solid parts so that the solid parts have lost frictional contact. Under the force of gravity or the force of gases, the solid parts slide past one another and the desired form is lost.

The natural body fluxes are potash, soda, calcia, magnesia and iron oxide. Potash and soda start their action around 600°C (1112°F) and the work they do progresses steadily. They are ideal fluxes because with them the maturing range is long and progressive so that a slight under or over firing is not ruinous. A good clay for earthenware and stoneware will contain in the region of 1 to 3% of potash and soda. Depending upon the kaolinite content of the clay, this is sufficient to vitrify the clay in the range 1000°C to 1300°C (1832°F to 2372°F).

Calcia and magnesia are active only above 1100°C (2012°F) and 1170°C (2138°F) respectively. Their actions are then such that coupled with the previous action of potash and soda they produce a very rapid vitrification. The action is so quick that it is difficult to fire such a body with accuracy. It is soon overfired with resulting breakdown. The calcia and magnesia content is rarely more than 1% but some brick shales, brick marls and estuarine muds contain up to 4% of magnesia which causes a very rapid breakdown at around 1200°C (2192°F).

It will be seen that clays containing more than 1% of calcia or magnesia, coupled with aluminium content below 25% are likely to be unsuitable for temperatures above 1100°C (2012°F). These are therefore the earthenware potting clays. This statement ignores prepared earthenware bodies for the industrial high bisc and low glost method.

The clays which are low in calcia and magnesia, and those which contain over 25% of alumina are the stoneware clays.

BREAKDOWN DUE TO IRON OXIDE. Iron oxide presents a special case. Its presence in a clay can result in premature breakdown.

All clays contain some iron oxide. In china clay it is only 0·1% but most ball clays and fireclays contain 2% and red clays contain 5 to 8%. The critical amount is around 1·5%, above which the iron oxide must be regarded as a possible fluxing force.

If the iron oxide were all red iron oxide (Fe_2O_3), there would be no fluxing action from it. Red iron oxide is a refractory amphoteric oxide with no fluxing action in the presence of stronger fluxes like potash and soda. On the other hand if the iron oxide were all black iron oxide (FeO), there would be strong fluxing action from 900°C (1652°F) upwards. Black iron oxide is an alkaline flux.

The state of red iron oxide or black iron oxide is established by the atmosphere inside the kiln. An atmosphere with surplus oxygen, called an oxidizing atmosphere, will give oxygen to the iron oxide to create the red state:

$$2FeO + O \longrightarrow Fe_2O_3$$

Whereas an atmosphere short of oxygen, called a reducing atmosphere, will take oxygen from the iron oxide to create the black state:

$$Fe_2O_3 + \underset{\substack{\text{carbon} \\ \text{monoxide}}}{CO} \longrightarrow 2FeO + \underset{\substack{\text{carbon} \\ \text{dioxide}}}{CO_2}$$

Black iron oxide (FeO) is greedy for oxygen, but it is not so greedy as carbon monoxide (CO). If there is a limited amount of oxygen available, the carbon monoxide will claim it. Thus by controlling the kiln atmosphere one controls the iron oxide content of the body and establishes either the red or the black state. One also thus controls whether the iron oxide will act as a flux or not.

By reduction, therefore, one can perhaps double the body fluxes. The following is an example analysis of a stoneware clay. Note how the fluxes total either 2·5% or 4·5% according to whether one uses an oxidized or a reduced firing.

Alumina	28%
Silica	57
Iron oxide	2
Calcia and magnesia	0·5 } 2·5 } 4·5
Potash and soda	2
Loss on firing	10·5

Clays suitable for oxidized firing are rarely suitable for reduced firing. The exceptions are the white bodies with less than 0·5% iron oxide content.

Iron oxide is an acceptable flux if used intentionally. It requires the presence of some calcia or magnesia to give elasticity to vitrification. Iron oxide, with only potash and soda, tends to give brittle glasses and hence brittle bodies.

Breakdown occurs with the unintentional use of iron oxide as a flux. At any temperature above 900°C (1652°F) it will not be possible to reoxidize a reduced iron oxide. Above 900°C the black iron oxide acts as a flux and at least half of it will be involved in a melt. One cannot expect it to change to red iron oxide and undo the fluxing action it has achieved. Therefore in bodies which have been reduced, one can only expect about half of the iron oxide to be still available for return to red iron oxide by oxidation.

For the production of a fully oxidized ware, like red stoneware, it is necessary to fire slowly with deliberate oxidation of the atmosphere by the provision of clean air passage through the kiln. The danger of accidental reduction then comes from impurities in the clay. All clays contain impurities which are burnt out in the firing. Carbonaceous matter is burnt out by oxidation before 900°C. Sulphur is oxidized between 900°C and 1150°C (1652°F and 2102°F). Oxygen enters the pores of the body, and combines with the sulphur in the action of burning or oxidation. The new compound is sulphur monoxide. This is a gas. The gas escapes through the pores into the kiln atmosphere where it takes up more oxygen to become sulphur dioxide. The sulphur dioxide escapes from the kiln through a flue or cracks round the door etc. One can smell these gases in the workshop atmosphere, especially from an electric kiln without a flue.

If the body has become semi-vitrified before this burning out period, then the oxidation is impeded. The sulphur, excited by the heat, turns to other sources of oxygen. Iron oxide is a ready source because it can be persuaded to part with some oxygen as has been previously explained. Hot sulphur is as effective as carbon monoxide. The result is a sulphur gas, monoxide or dioxide, and black iron oxide. A simplified equation would be:

$$2Fe_2O_3 + S \xrightarrow{900°C} 4FeO + SO_2 \uparrow$$

red iron oxide — sulphur — black iron oxide — sulphur dioxide

The newly-formed black iron oxide acts as a flux and produces molten glass which fills the pores in the body. The sulphur gases cannot escape because the pores are blocked. Yet as the sulphur gas is formed there is rapid expansion from the solid state. The result is bloating which is a bubble of gas pushing aside the sealed and softened body in an attempt to escape.

Once started, this action accelerates. It is assisted at temperatures over 1100°C (2012°F) by calcia, if this is present. Bloated bodies are often a black, cellular froth within. The black is reduced iron oxide.

Black core is another factor often assisting this premature breakdown. If the body has a black core this contains reduced iron oxide due to insufficient oxidation between 750°C and 900°C (1382°F and 1652°F). At 900°C the reduced iron (black iron oxide) acts as an unintentional flux.

It is difficult, if not actually impossible, to keep a body so completely oxidized that there is no formation of black iron oxide at all. The red bodies which burn to the brightest colour are the ones containing very little carbon and sulphur.

Bristol (England). Famous for Bristol delft from about 1650 to 1750 and for Bristol glazes when zinc oxide was introduced to replace the poisonous lead oxide in the 19th century. Bristol glazes were developed for all temperatures from 1150°C to 1300°C (2102°F to 2372°F). Zinc oxide is an active flux above 1100°C (2012°F) and can also be used to produce opaque and

crystalline effects. Many of the early Bristol glazes were of this type. See **Zinc oxide**.

The photograph is of a Bristol-glazed jug by Janet Hamer using the following recipe for 1250°C (2282°F). This recipe gives a similar result to the old Bristol stoneware but suffers from the usual defect of zinc glazes in that it easily crawls if applied too thickly.

Feldspar	65
China clay	9
Flint	3
Whiting	8
Zinc oxide	10
Titanium dioxide	5

Brongniart, Alexandre. (1770 to 1847). Director of the Sèvres porcelain factory from 1800 to 1847. He was an eminent geologist and mineralogist who turned potter and thereby brought to pottery the scientific reasoning which was developing at the close of the 18th century. He complemented the work of English potters like Whieldon and Wedgwood who moved towards the scientific approach in pottery making from the simpler rule-of-thumb approach. Brongniart is known as the father of ceramic chemistry and is best known for the Brongniart formula for converting slop measure to dry weight. See **Formula, Brongniart's**.

Bronze. A class of alloys incorporating copper and usually tin or aluminium. Bronze filings can be used for speckle staining. Bronze lustre is obtained by the reduced firing of chromium and lead compounds.

Bronze Age pottery. Pottery made during the periods when metals were first used. Bronze (copper and tin) was important but gold and copper were also worked. Iron was not used until later because it required a higher temperature to soften the ore. The change to iron occurred with the development of more efficient furnaces and naturally coincides with improved pottery kilns.

The earliest Bronze Age was in Egypt starting perhaps 5000 B.C. and spreading through the eastern Mediterranean and eastern Europe from 2600 B.C. In western Europe and eastern Asia the era is from about 2000 B.C. and in all places lasted about 1500 years. The Ages typify a period of expanding trade, agriculture and stock rearing.

Bronze Age pottery of the eastern regions, from Greece to the Far East, shows a diversity and multiplicity of forms. In the Mediterranean area, the decoration was painted. See **Crete** and **Mycenaean**. The pots are free and expressive of life, but towards the late Bronze Age one can see that they were influenced by bronze objects.

The Western potters permutated well-tried forms which were few in number. They were able to keep a more plastic expression in their work and were not influenced by bronze objects. The decoration is textural

patterning, sometimes scratched but mostly impressed. The pot shown above is a drinking beaker from south Wales, c. 1600 B.C. The decoration is produced by a notched rocker tool. See also **Bell beaker, Cinerary urn** and **Pygmy cup**.

Brookite. TiO_2. Natural titanium dioxide. Brookite is one of the three oxide ores of titanium. The other two are rutile and anatase. They are chemically alike but individual in their crystal structure.

Brookite crystals appear to be coloured but are colourless within and are the source of the white titanium dioxide. See **Titania**.

Brown. Brown colours are easily achieved in bodies and glazes by additions of iron oxide and manganese oxide either alone or in combination. The browns can be modified with zinc oxide and nickel oxide.

Iron oxide gives colours ranging from yellow through reddish browns and rusts to dark browns and blacks. Manganese oxide gives colours from gingery orange to purply brown. In glazes, some very rich, deep, reddish browns can be obtained which sometimes contain metallic speckle at the surface, by a combination of the two oxides. See **Iron oxide** and **Manganese dioxide**.

Brown mouth. The dark rim of a pot resulting from the iron in the body showing through the glaze. If the glaze is fairly liquid during firing it tends to leave a thinner layer on the rim. The iron oxide of a dark body-glaze layer will then force its way through the thin layer of glaze to the surface. The term brown mouth is especially used to describe the Chinese Kuan ware of the Sung dynasty.

Buffer layer. Glaze-body interface. Glaze-body interlayer. Engobe layer. A controlled body-glaze layer. In certain circumstances it may be desirable to encourage the development of the body-glaze layer to create resistance to crazing or shivering or to improve colour and crystallization. The deliberately created layer is a buffer layer. The interlayer absorbs the stress between body and glaze. Normally a longer firing at the same temperature, called soaking, will do this but may be undesirable because of its effect upon the body as a whole. See **Body-glaze layer**. The only way is to create the body-glaze layer artificially or at least assist its formation by a wash of soft flux on the biscuit before the glaze is applied, or more popularly by an engobe attached to the raw ware.

The engobe would be approximately half body and half glaze and not necessarily the same body and glaze. As with normal slips, the opportunity to introduce a colour should not be missed. Also the use of a white buffer layer assists the formation of clean colours, especially iron colours in stoneware. The white surface reflects the heat back into the glaze and fuses it more whilst protecting the body slightly. At the same time it is fusing the two together as a body-glaze layer, which it is intended to do, and introducing clean or white crystals into the iron layer of the glaze to give good rust colours on cooling. A buffer layer of this type is very useful on the rims of dark coloured stonewares producing not only a good colour but also preventing the thinner rim from becoming over-vitrified and too brittle. Some buffer engobes are more refractory than the body and may be desirable in cases similar to the one just quoted.

In testing different buffer layers one must remember to note the difference in body-glaze layer and body breakdown as well as colour differences. If the body and glaze are not fitting properly so that crazing or shivering is occurring, the buffer layer can be used to act as a cushion for the stress. The normal buffer engobe is a 50/50 mix of body and glaze. Free silica in the form

of sand is often removed or alternatively it is carefully studied in test sections to see that it is becoming involved in the melt. If it does not become involved but remains as crystalline silica, it is subject to the silica inversions and could cause more difficulties.

Buller's rings. Firing trial rings. Pyroscopes compounded from minerals which interact upon one another over a wide temperature range producing a progressive shrinkage. They were introduced in 1910 by Bullers Ltd of Hanley. The ring is really a flat disc about 2½ inches in diameter with a convenient hole in the middle by which it can be easily withdrawn from

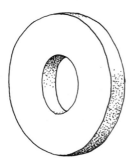

the kiln on the end of a hooked rod. The diameter is measured on a special gauge which relates the shrinkage which has taken place to a temperature. Rings are effective for the range 960°C to 1400°C (1760°F to 2552°F) and can be withdrawn and the heat-work calculated as a temperature at any time during a firing. They are not returned to the kiln. New ones are withdrawn for each reading that is required.

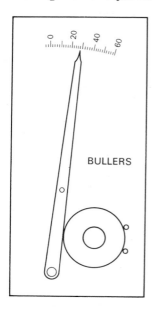

Unlike cones and bars, the rings are not in themselves related to temperatures. Cones and bars are selected for specific points in a firing and only give indication when this point is reached. Rings can be removed at any time and indicate what is happening. They help the fireman to take correct action during the firing and are especially useful with tunnel kilns. Cones and bars indicate end points of firings and are useful for post-firing diagnosis.

Bung. A pile of saggars. In the kiln, saggars are stacked vertically one on top of another, the top one often having a lid. The rim of each saggar has a wad or snake of refractory clay to give a firm seating, seal the saggar if necessary and provide a soft joint which will split apart easily after the firing. Bungs are arranged with varying gaps between them to direct the flames through the kiln.

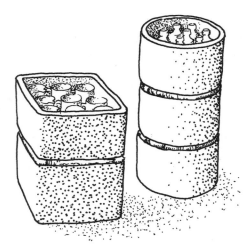

Burning off. A casual term for the removal of bound water in the ceramic change.

Burning out. The removal of unwanted matter by heat in the kiln. Some colours are applied to glazes with gums and oils. These are not part of the final colour required but merely convenient carriers for the colour when it is applied. The gum etc is burnt out before the colour melts to form its ceramic state. Also in many clay and glaze materials there is unwanted

carbon, sulphur and fluorine. This is burnt out by oxidation at temperatures above red heat. If not burnt out, these unwanted materials would damage the body, glaze or colour with bloating, bubbling, blistering and discolouration. See also **Hardening on**.

Burnishing. Polishing leatherhard clay by rubbing with a hard object like a smooth pebble, the back of a spoon or a strip of spring steel. Pinched and coiled pots are often burnished. Thrown pots can be burnished after turning by reversing the spin of the wheel and laying flat the torn roughness created by the turning tool. For decorative purposes and to give a hard and dense coating on unglazed ware, fine slips can be painted over coarse clays and burnished when leatherhard.

The photograph shows a contemporary west African pot which is burnished in traditional manner.

Butterfly. A particular type of glaze crawl in which a piece of glaze leaves its place and folds back on itself to give a double thickness next to a bald patch. See **Crawling**.

Bytownite. One of the plagioclase feldspars. It is mostly lime feldspar but contains up to 25% soda feldspar.

C

Cadmium. Cd. A metal, the sulphide of which is a common orange and yellow pigment in paints and ceramics. The oxide (CdO) also occurs in glazes but is not deliberately introduced although its presence has some modifying effect upon colours.

Cadmium sulphide (CdS) gives brilliant yellows. In combination with cadmium selenide (CdSe) a range of oranges and bright reds is possible. These colours are fugitive. The selenium volatilizes easily so that the firing must be rapid. Also the colour must be protected from the effects of oxidation by a suitably reducing atmosphere. Coloured glazes are made but most use is in on-glaze colours.

Cake. A slab of clay, usually from the filter-press as in the photograph.

Calamine. Mining name for zinc ores especially zinc carbonate.

Calcia. Calcium oxide. Lime. CaO. A readily available and extremely useful body and glaze material. It is used as a filler in low-temperature bodies and glazes; and as a flux in high-temperature glazes. Large amounts encourage crystalline growth during cooling.

The pure oxide, calcia (CaO), is also called quicklime. It reacts with water combining with it to produce calcium hydroxide, called slaked lime, (Ca(OH)$_2$). Calcia is therefore introduced into bodies and glazes in the insoluble form of the carbonate (CaCO$_3$) and the borate (Ca(BO$_2$)$_2$). See **Calcium carbonate** and **Calcium borate**.

Calcia is often introduced into bodies, but whether it is introduced or is already present, it is necessary to involve it in part of the fusion. If calcia is not involved

somehow in a silicate, a glassy part of the body, it remains as the very absorbent quicklime. This can happen with very low-fired porous bodies which naturally absorb moisture from the air. The quicklime does so with attendant swelling which is enough to cause flaking or even complete shattering of a finished piece of work.

Yet calcia which is involved in the fusion brings to a body some noteworthy properties. Calcia has a high rate of contraction which is valuable in earthenwares to prevent crazing of the glaze. Malms or true marls contain up to 20% calcia which accounts for their successful use for maiolica ware fired at 1050°C (1922°F). Calcia also prevents warping and gives whiteness. It is introduced into some low-temperature pressing bodies for these reasons.

However calcia cannot be used in vitreous bodies or those to be fired above 1100°C (2012°F). Above 1100°C, calcia becomes an active flux and is therefore not practical in bodies. The rapid fluxing action makes the body mature too rapidly. It is therefore difficult to successfully fire because a kiln will contain too many pieces that are under-mature and too many that are overfired and distorted. Clays naturally high in calcia do not make good stoneware bodies and are therefore used mostly in the 1000°C to 1080°C range (1832°F to 1976°F).

Again, in glazes, the actions of calcia can be divided into low and high temperature by the 1100°C (2012°F) mark. Below 1100°C it is not active as a flux although small amounts sometimes give some interaction. Generally it will be found to be an anti-flux but one whose action is not strong. It readily involves itself in glassy fusions with soda, potash and lead oxide, and brings to glazes a hardness and acid resistance that is worth its introduction. It helps to involve lead oxide and thereby reduces solubility. It also stabilizes the soda-silica combination. Up to 10% can often be absorbed in earthenware glazes with little loss of shine and great improvement in durability. It may make lead glazes more susceptible to crazing but it increases the craze resistance of glazes which are high in soda and potash.

Large amounts of calcia, perhaps as much as 35%, in soft earthenware glazes encourage the growth of crystals. See **Lime matt**. Calcia in boric oxide glazes also encourages the formation of calcium borate devitrification giving a decorative flushing or milkiness to the glaze without upsetting the high shine of the boric oxide glaze. The amount of calcia here need not be larger than 5% in some glazes.

Calcia begins its fluxing action at 1100°C (2012°F)

and from then upwards it is an active and practical flux for all glazes at all temperatures and atmospheres. Its own melting point is 2570°C (4658°F) and with silica alone, whose melting point is 1710°C (3110°F), it cannot produce a molten glass below 1400°C (2552°F). However, in combination with or in interaction with other fluxes, the calcia can produce fluid melts. A typical recipe for a transparent stoneware glaze for 1250°C (2282°F) which uses calcia as the main flux in interaction with potash and soda is:

mixed feldspar	50
china clay	15
quartz	15
calcium carbonate	20

An important point about calcia is its stable structure during a firing. The melting point of the metal calcium is 852°C (1566°F) but the melting point of the oxide is 2570°C (4658°F). The ions of calcium and oxygen make a strong bond, each in six-fold co-ordination as shown in the drawing.

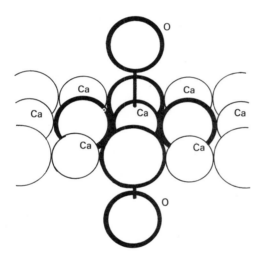

In interaction with other oxides, and especially over 1100°C (2012°F), these bonds can be loosened. Hence its fluxing action, but it is impossible to completely separate the calcium from the oxygen by reduction below 2200°C (3992°F). Calcia is therefore suitable for all glazes and is unaffected by deliberately or accidentally reducing atmospheres. There are in fact no difficulties in its use but there is one remaining property that should be taken into consideration.

Calcia is a bleach whose effect is sometimes surprising. Where the colouring oxide is small in amount, the result can be interestingly alkaline with copper blues and cobalt mauves. This happens in lime matts. However calcia cannot cope with strong colours.

With oxidized iron oxide (red iron oxide) a bleaching effect is noticeable. Up to 3% of iron oxide is bleached to a yellow in lime matts. Here the iron oxide presents itself as an alternative to silica because there is a surfeit of calcia. Instead of calcium silicate ($CaO.SiO_2$) a

spinel type of combination which could be called calcium ferrate ($CaO.Fe_2O_3$) is formed.

Reduced iron oxide (black iron oxide) is not affected because calcia cannot combine with it. It is unlikely to be available either, because, as soon as oxidized iron oxide becomes reduced iron oxide it is an active flux and combines with the silica. Its fluxing action can take place at 900°C (1652°F) which is long before calcia becomes active.

Oxidation and reduction therefore have an effect upon iron glazes in which the main flux is calcia, not because the calcia is changed but because in one case it links with iron oxide (red), and in the other the iron oxide (black) is already committed and not available. For this reason calcia is an excellent flux for reduced iron glazes like the clean-coloured celadons and blue-black tenmokus; but it is not a suitable flux for oxidized tenmoku because the crystals of calcium ferrate cloud the colour of the iron dissolved in the silicate.

Calcine. To purify by the action of heat, from the use of the word to describe the burning of lime (calx). The potter uses the term to describe the preparation of a material by heat, usually in the region of 700°C (1292°F). For example, the calcination of china clay produces an alumino-silicate for use in glazes and bodies which has the same ultimate chemical content as china clay but is without the properties of a clay.

Calcining is not the same as fritting which involves fusion and the creation of new and complex compounds. Calcining is essentially a purifying process.

Calcining can be done on a small scale by putting the material in a pot for the biscuit firing. The sintered mass is then crushed in a mortar and sieved if necessary.

Calcite. Calcspar. $CaCO_3$. Crystalline calcium carbonate occurring in many forms as spar crystals, stalactites, chalk, marble etc. As clean crystals it occurs as white veins and pockets in limestones and is often mistaken for quartz. However it is much softer than quartz and can be scratched with a penknife, which quartz cannot. Being soft it is easily ground for use as calcium carbonate in glazes.

Nail-head spar, dog-tooth spar and Iceland spar are

different varieties of the calcite crystal. Aragonite is chemically identical but of a different crystal structure.

Calcium borate. $Ca(BO_2)_2$. The anhydrous state of borocalcite. See **Colemanite**. Calcium borate is the theoretical combination of one molecule each of calcia and boric oxide ($CaO.B_2O_3$). In reality, colemanite is a much more variable structure.

Calcium borate crystals occur as partial devitrification in some glazes and create attractive blue flushes. See **Clair-de-lune** and **Chun**.

Calcium carbonate. Carbonate of lime. $CaCO_3$. A stable and insoluble (in water) compound of calcium which is used to introduce the oxide calcia (CaO) into bodies and glazes.

Calcium carbonate is the chemical name. The potter's materials which are almost pure calcium carbonate are whiting, limestone, marble and chalk.

Calcium carbonate decomposes by 825°C (1517°F) to give calcia and carbon dioxide. The carbon dioxide escapes without difficulty leaving the calcia in the body or glaze.

$$CaCO_3 \xrightarrow{825°C} CaO + CO_2 \uparrow$$

Calcium chloride. $CaCl_2$. A highly soluble and deliquescent crystalline compound. It is used to flocculate clay suspensions.

A few drops of a concentrated solution of calcium chloride are sufficient to flocculate up to 5 oz of bentonite. This expands the bentonite in a box-like jelly structure which holds non-clay minerals and inhibits their sedimentation. See **Flocculation**.

Calcium fluoride. Fluorspar. Blue John. CaF_2. See **Fluorspar**.

Calcium minerals. The element calcium accounts for approximately 4% of the earth's crust but it does not occur as a native metal. It is always combined with other elements in compounds of which there are many. Calcium is essential to animal life as the constituent of bones, shells and teeth.

The most common of the calcium compounds is calcium carbonate which the potter uses as a source of calcia for his glazes. A list of the calcium compounds used in ceramics follows:

calcia	CaO
calcium carbonate	$CaCO_3$
calcium chloride	$CaCl_2$
calcium fluoride	CaF_2
calcium phosphate	$Ca_3(PO_4)_2$
calcium sulphate, anhydrite	$CaSO_4$
calcium sulphate, gypsum	$CaSO_4.2H_2O$
calcium borate	$Ca(BO_2)_2$
dolomite	$CaMg(CO_3)_2$
wollastonite	$CaSiO_3$

Calcium phosphate. Tricalcium phosphate. $Ca_3(PO_4)_2$, ultimately $3CaO.P_2O_5$. Phosphorus pentoxide is combined with calcia in its occurrence in rocks, the soil, plants and animals. It is introduced as calcium phosphate into bodies and glazes from apatite, phosphorite, vegetable ashes and bone ash. Small amounts in glazes give flushes or cloudy opacity. Larger amounts give opacity, a dull surface and blisters. In bodies, calcium phosphate gives controlled vitrification as in bone china. See **Bone ash, Phosphorus pentoxide** and **Colloid, glaze**.

Calcium sulphate. Anhydrite. $CaSO_4$. The anhydrous state of gypsum which is found as a salt in Germany. It is soluble in water and is used as a flocculant to prevent the rapid settling of glaze slops. See **Flocculation** and **Gypsum**.

Calculations. Most of the calculations which the potter is called upon to do depend upon straightforward addition, subtraction, multiplication and division of known numbers. The numbers are obtained from recipes, by weighing or by looking them up in the appropriate lists as in the Tables of this book. Often the numbers are inserted into a formula, as for example when converting °C to °F. Some formulae are given under Formula in this book. Three examples are worked here along with examples involving the unity formulae of glazes which require a series of stages. For the use of unity formulae see **Formula, unity**.

EXAMPLE OF TEMPERATURE CONVERSION. In this example the temperature equivalent in °F is required for 900°C. The formula for converting from centigrade to Fahrenheit is:

$$\frac{°C \times 9}{5} + 32 = °F$$

therefore:

$$900°C = \frac{900 \times 9}{5} + 32 = 1620 + 32$$

$$= 1652°F.$$

A list of comparable temperatures °C and °F is given in the **Tables** of this book.

EXAMPLE OF FINDING A MOLECULAR WEIGHT. In this example the molecular weight is required for albite feldspar. The chemical formula is:

$$Na_2O.Al_2O_3.6SiO_2$$

The first step is to find the atomic weight of each of the elements involved. These are given under **Element** and again in the **Tables**. The small numbers below the formula refer to the number of atoms of the preceding element. The large number 6 indicates that the whole of the molecule SiO_2 is present six times. See **Formula, chemical**.

$Na_2O = (23 \times 2) + 16 = 62$

$Al_2O_3 = (27 \times 2) + (16 \times 3) = 102$

$6SiO_2 = 6 \times (28\cdot1 + (16 \times 2)) = \dfrac{360\cdot6}{524\cdot6}$

The molecular weight for albite is therefore 524·6. A list of the molecular weights of common minerals is given in the **Tables** of this book.

EXAMPLE OF CONVERSION OF PERCENTAGE GLAZE RECIPE TO BATCH RECIPE. Given the percentage recipe:

borax frit	75
feldspar	15
china clay	10

calculate the actual weights required to make ten UK gallons of glaze slop at 29 oz to the UK pint. Twenty-nine oz pt is typical for leadless glazes.

The total amount of dry material is discovered by using Brongniart's formula. This states that the dry weight content per pint is equal to the apparent dry weight multiplied by the specific gravity divided by the specific gravity minus one.

$$(\text{oz pt} - 20) \times \frac{SG}{SG - 1}$$

The formula is explained under **Formula, Brongniart's**. The specific gravity of the glaze materials approximates 2·5 and this is a typical average for most of the leadless materials. See **Tables**. Therefore the dry weight for ten gallons of glaze slop will be:

$$10 \times 8 \times (29 - 20) \times \frac{2\cdot5}{1\cdot5} = 1200 \text{ oz}$$

and the weight of the water will be:

$$(10 \times 8 \times 29) - 1200 = 1120 \text{ oz}$$
$$= 7 \text{ UK gallons}$$

The total weight of 1200 oz is achieved by multiplying the percentage amounts in the recipe by 1200 and dividing by 100 (the total of the recipe numbers).

$$\text{borax frit} \quad \frac{75 \times 1200}{100} = 900 \text{ oz}$$

$$\text{feldspar} \quad \frac{15 \times 1200}{100} = 180 \text{ oz}$$

$$\text{china clay} \quad \frac{10 \times 1200}{100} = 120 \text{ oz}$$
$$\overline{1200}$$

The batch recipe for ten gallons of glaze slop now reads:

borax frit	56 lbs	4 oz
feldspar	11 lbs	4 oz
china clay	7 lbs	8 oz
water	7 gallons	

Most potters will have discovered that with leadless glazes and slips, approximately equal weights of dry material and water gives a workable slip and that a percentage recipe taken in ounces gives approximately $\frac{3}{4}$ gallon of slip.

EXAMPLE OF FINDING THE UNITY FORMULA OF A GLAZE. To find the unity formula one starts with the glaze recipe and uses either the chemical formula for each material or an ultimate analysis of each material to discover which oxides are entering the glaze fusion and in what proportional amount. Both methods are shown.

Given the glaze recipe:

albite	35
lead monosilicate	57
wollastonite	8
	100

METHOD 1. *Stage 1*. Ascertain the chemical formula and molecular weight of each material. See **Tables**.

albite $Na_2O.Al_2O_3.6SiO_2$	MW 524·6
lead monosilicate $PbO.SiO_2$	MW 283·3
wollastonite $CaO.SiO_2$	MW 116·2

Note that the chemical formulae have been separated into the constituent oxides which are to be considered as entering the fusion. If there are volatiles, e.g. CO_2, these are also listed separately.

Stage 2. Divide the recipe amount by the appropriate molecular weight. This gives the number of molecules of each oxide which is present in the glaze, or at least gives a series of numbers which proportionately represent this.

$$35 \div 524\cdot6 = 0\cdot0667$$
$$57 \div 283\cdot3 = 0\cdot2012$$
$$8 \div 116\cdot2 = 0\cdot0685$$

The resulting numbers tend to be small decimals. This can be avoided by appropriately inflating the recipe numbers by multiplying each by 10,000 and the molecular weight by 10. Decimal places are then ignored and the numbers are more manageable.

$$350\,000 \div 5246 = 67$$
$$570\,000 \div 2833 = 201$$
$$80\,000 \div 1162 = 69$$

Stage 3. These numbers represent the number of molecules of each material. The number of molecules of each oxide is discovered by reference to the chemical formulae. Only albite with its six molecules of SiO_2 requires special care. All the others become straightforwardly interpreted. Thus:

albite provides 67 Na_2O, 67 Al_2O_3 and 6 × 67 SiO_2
lead monosilicate provides 201 PbO and 201 SiO_2
wollastonite provides 69 CaO and 69 SiO_2

45

When this is written in the usual layout it becomes:

$$
\begin{array}{l}
67 \ Na_2O \\
201 \ PbO \quad 67 \ Al_2O_3 \quad 672 \ SiO_2 \\
69 \ CaO \\
\hline
337
\end{array}
$$

The RO group of oxides is totalled (337) and all the numbers are divided by this figure to bring the RO group to unity and the other groups into proportion. This is the unity formula:

$$
\left.\begin{array}{l}
0\cdot199 \ Na_2O \\
0\cdot593 \ PbO \\
0\cdot205 \ CaO
\end{array}\right\} 0\cdot199 \ Al_2O_3 \quad 1\cdot994 \ SiO_2
$$

$$0\cdot997$$

METHOD 2. *Stage 1*. Ascertain, from the suppliers, the ultimate percentage analysis for each material. If there are volatiles which are lost in the firing, these are included at this stage.

$$
\begin{array}{lll}
\text{albite:} & SiO_2 & 66 \\
& Al_2O_3 & 21 \\
& Na_2O & 9 \\
& K_2O & 3 \\
& CaO & 1 \\
\\
\text{lead monosilicate:} & SiO_2 & 21 \\
& PbO & 79 \\
\\
\text{wollastonite:} & SiO_2 & 50 \\
& CaO & 49 \\
& Al_2O_3 & 1
\end{array}
$$

Stage 2. Multiply each item by the appropriate number (amount) in the recipe. Volatiles can now be ignored.

$$
\begin{array}{lrcl}
SiO_2 & 66 \times 35 & = & 2310 \\
Al_2O_3 & 21 \times 35 & = & 735 \\
Na_2O & 9 \times 35 & = & 315 \\
K_2O & 3 \times 35 & = & 105 \\
CaO & 1 \times 35 & = & 35 \\
SiO_2 & 21 \times 57 & = & 1197 \\
PbO & 79 \times 57 & = & 4503 \\
SiO_2 & 50 \times 8 & = & 400 \\
CaO & 49 \times 8 & = & 392 \\
Al_2O_3 & 1 \times 8 & = & 8
\end{array}
$$

Stage 3. Repeated amounts are totalled and the amounts are divided by their respective molecular weights:

$$
\begin{array}{lr}
SiO_2 & 2310 \\
& 1197 \\
& 400 \\
\hline
& 3907 \div 60\cdot1 = 65\cdot0
\end{array}
$$

$$
\begin{array}{lr}
Al_2O_3 & 735 \\
& 8 \\
\hline
& 743 \div 102\cdot0 = 7\cdot3 \\
Na_2O & 315 \div 62\cdot0 = 5\cdot1 \\
K_2O & 105 \div 94\cdot2 = 1\cdot1 \\
CaO & 35 \\
& 392 \\
\hline
& 427 \div 56\cdot1 = 7\cdot6 \\
PbO & 4503 \div 223\cdot2 = 20\cdot2
\end{array}
$$

Stage 4. When this information is put together in the usual layout it becomes:

$$
\begin{array}{ll}
5\cdot1 & Na_2O \\
1\cdot1 & K_2O \quad 7\cdot3 \ Al_2O_3 \quad 65\cdot0 \ SiO_2 \\
20\cdot2 & PbO \\
7\cdot6 & CaO \\
\hline
34\cdot0
\end{array}
$$

Stage 5. The RO group of oxides is totalled (34) and all the numbers are divided by this figure to bring the RO group to unity and the other groups into proportion. This is the unity formula:

$$
\left.\begin{array}{l}
0\cdot150 \ Na_2O \\
0\cdot032 \ K_2O \\
0\cdot594 \ PbO \\
0\cdot224 \ CaO
\end{array}\right\} 0\cdot214 \ Al_2O_3 \quad 1\cdot911 \ SiO_2
$$

$$1\cdot000$$

There is a noticeable difference in the two unity formulae produced by these two methods. The first method is easier and sufficiently accurate for most cases. The second method is more accurate but takes longer to do. It is necessary when a material has no chemical formula that can be used. For example, ball clay and wood ash could only be converted by the use of an ultimate analysis.

METHOD 3. The time taken in doing these calculations can be shortened by the use of logarithms or a slide rule. The Rapid Glaze Calculator designed by Colin Pearson and Dennis Healing is an invaluable aid in this respect, and obviates the necessity of understanding the reasoning behind each stage. The same recipe converted to unity formula by this calculator gives:

$$
\left.\begin{array}{l}
0\cdot2 \ Na_2O \\
0\cdot6 \ PbO \\
0\cdot2 \ CaO
\end{array}\right\} 0\cdot2 \ Al_2O_3 \quad 2\cdot0 \ SiO_2
$$

EXAMPLE OF CONVERTING A UNITY FORMULA INTO A RECIPE. In this calculation, one starts with a unity formula and by use of chemical formulae and

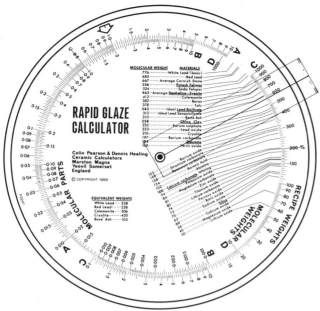

molecular weights one projects a recipe of desired materials. The materials chosen must contain suitable oxides in suitable proportions.

Given the unity formula:

$$
\left.\begin{array}{l}
0\cdot3\ K_2O \\
0\cdot1\ MgO \\
0\cdot6\ CaO
\end{array}\right\}0\cdot4\ Al_2O_3 \quad 4\cdot0\ SiO_2
$$

$$1\cdot0$$

Stage 1. Suitable materials are chosen which will give the appropriate oxides. They are written so that the proportions of their constituent oxides can be seen:

orthoclase = $K_2O.Al_2O_3.6SiO_2$
dolomite   = $CaO.MgO.2CO_2$
whiting   = $CaO.CO_2$
china clay = $Al_2O_3.2SiO_2.2H_2O$
flint   = SiO_2

Stage 2. The amounts of molecules in the unity formula are satisfied by amounts (molecules) of the desired glaze materials:

	K_2O	MgO	CaO	Al_2O_3	SiO_2
0·3 orthoclase =	0·3			0·3	1·8
0·1 dolomite =		0·1	0·1		
0·5 whiting =			0·5		
0·1 china clay =				0·1	0·2
2·0 flint =					2·0
	0·3	0·1	0·6	0·4	4·0

Stage 3. The molecular amounts of materials are converted to actual comparable weights by multiplying each one by its own molecular weight:

orthoclase	0·3 × 556·8 =	167·04
dolomite	0·1 × 184·4 =	18·44
whiting	0·5 × 100·1 =	50·05
china clay	0·1 × 258·2 =	25·82
flint	2·0 × 60·1 =	120·20
		381·55

Stage 4. To bring this recipe to a comparable percentage, each amount is multiplied by 100 and divided by the total (381·55). The percentage recipe reads:

orthoclase	43·8
dolomite	4·8
whiting	13·1
china clay	6·8
flint	31·5
	100·0

Cane clay. A refined fireclay often sandy in texture but less refractory than fireclay. The fired colour is that of cane or straw.

Cane clay was used for relief modelled pottery in the late 18th and early 19th centuries. Its pastry colour was effectively used to produce lidded serving pots which imitated pies when flour was taxed in the early 19th century.

Carbon. Carbon is present in most clays and even when only one or two per cent of the clay, it gives the clay a grey colour. This colouration is removed by careful firing in the oxidation period. See **Firing**. If the carbon is not removed it may cause discolouration of the ware or possibly bloating. See **Black core**. Surface clays tend to contain carbon introduced by the roots of plants. Clays which were once surface clays, like fireclays and some ball clays, contain a high percentage of carbon.

Carbon sometimes builds up on pots in the early stages of a firing by wood, coal, oil and gas. This is caused by incomplete combustion and is called sooting. The carbon later burns effectively producing heat, if sufficient oxygen can enter the kiln above 700°C (1292°F). Carbon not oxidized in this way can discolour glazes. Soft leadless glazes are quickly spoilt once they begin to melt.

Carolina stone. See **Cornish stone**.

Casserole. A lidded, oven-cooking dish for meat and vegetable stews. It is intended as oven-to-table ware, that is, for cooking in and serving from.

The following examples are casseroles by: Janet Hamer, John Leach, Harry Stringer.

Cassiterite. Tin stone. SnO_2. The ore of tin which is a crude form of the tin oxide known to potters as a white opacifier. The ore contains impurities of arsenic, bismuth, copper, iron and zinc. It occurs in igneous acid rocks often within quartz veins. The crushed raw ore

and also the tin-containing slurry from tin mines has been used by potters in glazes and as a decorating pigment.

Casting slip. A clay and water suspension used in the process of slip-casting. The suspension is poured into porous moulds and poured out again when a sufficient layer of clay has adhered to the sides. The resulting hollow form is dried, fettled and fired etc.

There are 5 requirements of a casting slip:

1. it should contain all the ingredients to form a good pottery body when fired.

2. it must be sufficiently fluid to pour into the moulds and fill all details.

3. it must be capable of taking an accurate impression of the mould.

4. it must be reasonably permeable so that as a layer of clay builds up on the wall of the mould, more water can pass through it to increase the thickness.

5. the newly-formed cast, although still wet, must remain firm until it has hardened sufficiently to keep its form as a clay.

The requirements are met as follows:

1. The casting slip will contain many minerals. At least two clays will be used to give a more controllable balance. There may be feldspathic minerals to act as viscous fluxes, flint or quartz for whiteness and hardness, sand or grog for texture and hardness, and cristobalite for glaze fit. It is necessary that a precise sequence is followed in the preparation of a slip in order to get the desired end result. An example sequence is described later.

2. Fluidity can be achieved by a watery slip but this gives difficulties in the amount of water to be absorbed by the moulds. The usual practice is to use deflocculants which enable a fluid slip to have high density. See **Fluidity** and **Deflocculation**. A pint of deflocculated slip will weigh 34 to 38 oz and still be fluid. An equally fluid slip made without the aid of deflocculants could not contain this weight of materials and would only weigh 29 oz to the pint.

3. It is pointless to have a fluid slip if it is mostly composed of coarse particles. The majority of the slip should pass a 120's sieve. It may permissibly then contain some grog or other coarse material which should not be coarser than 60's. Too coarse a material will settle during casting giving a non-uniform composition.

4. Most natural clays are permeable. However when deflocculated these same clays become impermeable. See **Flocculation**. A balance must be chosen between deflocculation and natural state to allow sufficient permeability. Permeability of the slip is assisted by the non-clay ingredients of the recipe. Pitchers made specially from a flocculated body are sometimes added for this purpose. A permeable body also means that the casts can dry out quickly. There is an advantage in workshop space saved if production is large.

5. Suspensions 'set' slightly when allowed to rest.

The phenomenon is a property of all clay suspensions and of some other suspensions. See **Thixotropy**. The property is destroyed by some deflocculants but not by others. A balance of two deflocculants must therefore be used.

PREPARATION OF CASTING SLIP. It will be seen that a casting slip is a compromise of many factors. Whilst scientific in approach, the workshop practice is inevitably one of trial and error, assessment and adjustment. To discover the ideal slip for one's own production, one must decide first upon the quality of the finished ware and establish the body recipe. A test amount of a few pounds should be mixed as a thick creamy slip of known amounts of dry materials and water. For convenience, the coarse materials like grogs can be omitted at this stage.

The slip is progressively deflocculated with a combined deflocculant made from:

sodium silicate 140°TW	1 fluid oz
sodium carbonate	1 oz
hot water	2 fluid oz

The amount of this combined deflocculant, which is added at each step of the test, should be accurately measured with a burette. At each addition of the decided amount of deflocculant, the whole slip is very thoroughly stirred. It is then poured through a funnel and the time taken for this operation is measured. A watch or clock with a second hand is necessary. The funnel should hold all the slip at once. It can be successfully made from an inverted plastic bottle with the base removed. It is also possible to measure the deflocculant without a burette by using a small, deep-bowled measuring spoon.

The results of the test show as seconds taken to drain the funnel related to the progressive additions of deflocculant.

It is not necessary to plot a graph unless the steps taken have been too large. In this case a graph will help to locate the optimum point more accurately. See **Deflocculant**. It should be pointed out that one will not make use of full deflocculation because this would destroy the permeability and make casting impossible. Again a graph will help to locate a suitable point of deflocculation which will give latitude for slight inaccuracies of measurement.

The amounts must now be recalculated as a batch recipe. The deflocculant amounts can be calculated by taking the amount of solution used to get the desired effect as a fraction of the amount of solution at the beginning. The amount of deflocculant materials is this same fraction of their starting amounts.

There follows a description of the preparation of a batch of casting slip. It is a light-coloured body to fire to 1000°C (1832°F) biscuit and 1200°C (2192°F) glaze. It illustrates a typical approach to the amounts used and the process involved. The batch recipe is:

china clay	20 lbs
ball clay	40 lbs
cornish stone	25 lbs
flint	10 lbs
whiting	5 lbs
grog 60's/dust	40 lbs
distinguishing stain	2 oz
sodium silicate 140°TW	2 fluid oz
sodium carbonate	2 oz
water	4 UK gallons plus

Approximately half the water is put into a blunger and approximately a quarter of the clay is added. This is blunged for a few minutes whilst the sodium silicate and sodium carbonate are dissolved in very hot water. About a quarter of this solution is added to the mixture and blunged for about five minutes. The remaining water is now added together with the distinguishing stain which has been mixed with hot water and passed through a fine sieve (120's to 200's). The remainder of the clay and the deflocculant solution are added and blunging continued for about half-an-hour. The slip should now be extremely fluid.

The cornish stone, flint and whiting are now added and the whole slip blunged for another half-an-hour. It is now sieved through a 120's mesh. There remains the grog to be added. This should be separately screened if possible to regulate its size. It is added to the slip and if possible blunged in thoroughly by use again of the blunger or by hand blunging. At this point it may be found necessary to readjust the fluidity of the slip by adding still more water. The amount required may be small or it may be a couple of pints. The types of ball clay and grog will affect this.

Industrially it is normal practice to work to an accurate pint weight. In small workshops it is safer to err on the side of fluidity and compensate for this by additional casting time. The above slip should make up at approximately 34 oz to the pint.

It may be necessary to adjust future batches for density and deflocculation. It is difficult to rebalance existing slips except by adding water. The use of slips, their troubles and remedies is dealt with under **Slip casting**.

ADJUSTMENT OF CASTING SLIP. A number of defects arise in cast ware which require diagnosis and corrective measures. The assessments should be read in conjunction with the articles on **Deflocculation, Thixotropy** and **Fluidity**. Adjustment amounts are often quite small. Faults and adjustments required are summarized below:

1. Wreathing or livering which is a rippled or uneven surface on the inside of the cast and roping which is when this unevenness is in raised lines:

The slip has insufficient thixotropy. The sodium silicate should be reduced and if necessary the sodium carbonate increased to maintain a working fluidity. Swilling the remaining slip around the mould before draining may help to overcome the trouble.

2. Cast buckles:

The cast has been removed from the mould too early.

3. Cast warps:
   i. The cast has been removed from the mould too late.
   ii. The cast has freed itself from one side of the mould but remained attached to the other, possibly due to the angle at which the mould was resting.
   iii. The drying has not been uniform.

4. Cast is flabby and distorts when handled:
   i. Casting time has been too long owing to a wet mould or a slip which contains too much water and insufficient sodium silicate.
   ii. Equally, of course, if the slip has been deflocculated to its maximum, it produces an impervious layer during casting which also increases casting time and gives flabby casts. In this case, decrease both deflocculants.

5. Pinholes in the surface of the cast on the mould side:
   i. The slip has insufficient fluidity and/or contains air bubbles. The water and/or the deflocculants should be increased.
   ii. The slip was not poured into the mould with sufficient force to 'wet' the mould wall. The whirler should be spun faster.

6. Check marks which are horizontal lines on the ware:

The slip was poured into the mould too slowly and probably with a pause. The mould must be filled quickly.

7. Cast is brittle at leatherhard and dry stages:

The thixotropy is too low so that the cast does not 'set' properly. The dry strength is too great which makes the cast brittle. In both cases the sodium silicate should be decreased.

8. Flashing or casting spot which is a discolouration on the finished ware:

The discolouration is due to an area of different composition and is where the slip first hit the mould. At this point, if the mould is very porous, a thin slip breaks up into clay and non-clay particles. The pressure of the slip hitting the mould should be reduced by introducing the slip through a pipe. The fluidity of the slip should be decreased by decreasing the amount of deflocculant used, especially the sodium silicate.

Castor ware. Romano-British pottery made at Castor, Northamptonshire. The colour varies from a yellowish grey to a slate blue and is the finest of the Romano-British wares. It was not glazed; decoration was added in the form of freely and elaborately trailed white slip depicting figures, animals and scenes.

Catalyst. A substance which assists a chemical or a physical change to take place in another substance. It may speed up the rate of change or enable the change to take place more easily but after the change the catalyst itself is unchanged. Calcia, magnesia, potash, soda, alumina and ferric oxide act as catalysts assisting the conversion of the quartz phase of silica into the cristobalite phase.

Catenary. A curve made by a chain hanging from two fixed points. It is the result of the balance of stresses over the whole length. When this line is inverted and used for arches, all the thrust comes within the base. A kiln which is itself a catenary arch has therefore no need of buttresses or angle iron support across its arch.

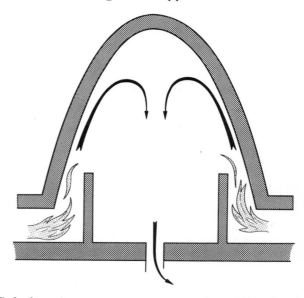

Celadon. A grey-green stoneware glaze. The glaze is a feldspathic type usually fairly stiff and applied thickly. The colour is derived from iron oxide which in the reducing firing has been turned to the black ferrous oxide. Celadon ware was of Chinese origin and covers the Yueh, northern celadon, and Lung-Ch'uan. These are

the grey-green dark-coloured and thickly-glazed wares. When these wares first arrived in Europe they were grouped together as celadons. The name was derived from Céladon, a shepherd in the 17th-century French play *L'Astrée* who wore grey-green ribbons and cloak. Today many potters emulate the pale bluish green porcelain known as Ying-Ch'ing and count this also as a celadon. See **Iron oxide in glazes**.

The photograph shows a porcelain celadon bowl by David Leach.

Celestine. Celestite. Strontium sulphate $SrSO_4$. The slightly soluble strontium mineral associated with clay shales and salt deposits.

Celsian. Barium feldspar. $BaO.Al_2O_3.2SiO_2$. One of the true feldspars. See **Feldspar, types of**. It is very rare and available only as hand-picked specimens.

Celsius. °C. Degrees Celsius are the same as degrees centigrade. They are named after Auders Celsius, the 18th-century Swedish astronomer, who introduced the centigrade thermometer in 1742. A century later, Lord Kelvin took the principle of the centigrade scale and extended it to an absolute scale beyond the temperatures associated with water. See **Kelvin**.

Centigrade. °C. Degrees Centigrade are units for the measurement of temperature. The centigrade scale referred to throughout this book is the proportionate extension upwards of the Celsius scale in which the freezing point of water is 0°C and the boiling point of water is 100°C.

Ceramic change. The change from clay to pot, upon which the whole pottery industry is founded. Clay can be dried and reconstituted to plastic state *ad infinitum* but once it has been subjected to 600°C (1112°F) it is no longer clay but a hard material which cannot be disintegrated and dispersed by water. The ceramic change involves the removal of hydroxyl groups (OH) from the clay lattice and water (H_2O) from the adsorbed layer attached to the broken ends of the lattice. Chemically these two items are expressed as water in the acceptable formula for clay which is $Al_2O_3.2SiO_2.2H_2O$. The removal of the two molecules of water in the formula leaves a bonded alumino silicate which is often referred to as metakaolin. See **Clay, the crystal structure of; Firing** and **Water, (bound)**.

The ceramic change is a slow process. First the attached water molecules are sheared from their positions at the ends of the clay lattice. Secondly, the hydroxyl groups within the lattice are loosened and removed. These immediately become water vapour. The bound water thus released in the ceramic change can amount to 14% of the weight of dry clay. It is not surprising, therefore, that this water can be seen as water vapour escaping from the vents of muffle kilns. These vents have previously dried after the removal of the pore water during the water-smoking period.

The first stage of the ceramic process approximates 450°C to 550°C (842°F to 1022°F) although with some fireclays it begins about 100°C (180°F) earlier. The second stage takes over at 550°C and lasts till 700°C (1292°F). The whole presents a steady process of water liberation starting gradually at a point somewhere between 350°C (662°F) and 450°C (842°F) and increasing to a maximum at 600°C (1112°F) after which there is a rapid decrease in liberation trailing off to 700°C (1292°F).

The ceramic change presents little danger from explosion by steam pressure because the pores of the body are open. As the heat enters the body, the water which seals the passages is released to the outside.

Ceramics. Keramics. Clay products made permanent by heat (the ceramic change); also the study of this subject. The word comes from the Greek *keramos* meaning potter's clay and the ware made from it but it is used to describe non-clay refractories which are changed or formed by heat and also many silicate products. It is often used by the individual potter when he feels that the name 'pottery' is too limiting a description of his work.

Ceramics became a subject of study during the late 19th century when courses were established in many European countries to train chemists and engineers specifically for the pottery industry. Previously the chemists and engineers had first gained their knowledge in other spheres and had then been employed by the potteries.

Prior to the college courses, the only scientific pottery training had been at Wedgwood's and Sèvres, which were two of the earliest potteries to be organized with scientific control.

The early use of the word ceramics to describe a subject of study was entirely biased towards technology. At the present time, ceramics describes the whole range of pottery and claywork with equal emphasis also given to the skills of designing and making.

Ceramist. One who works with clay and glazes in an objective way.

The word was coined in the late 19th century to describe the chemists and mineralogists who were employed by the clayworking industries. They worked to put pottery-making on a scientific basis rather than the traditional reliance upon the skilled judgments of master potters.

In the broader sense in which the word is now used, it describes a potter who gives precedence to technical achievement and subordinates intellectual and subjective expressions.

In the 1960's the further name 'ceramicist' was coined to describe the individual potter.

Ceria. Cerium dioxide. CeO_2. One of the lanthanide oxides in the amphoteric area of the periodic table. It is an acidic anti-flux with properties similar to tin oxide. It is very refractory and does not dissolve easily. It therefore remains as an opacifier in glazes fired below 1000°C (1832°F). At higher temperatures it begins to dissolve. It is a suitable substitute for tin oxide at low temperatures.

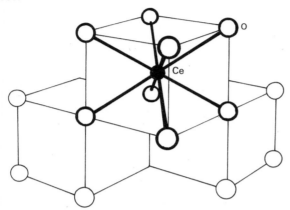

Ceria gives yellow colours in combination with titania. In slow-maturing glazes the two oxides can be added to the glaze and will satisfactorily combine. Approximately 3% of ceria is required with 5% of titania. The colour will withstand high temperatures.

Ceria is used as a stabilizer in the production of yellow stains using vanadium and antimony oxides.

Chalk. Calcium carbonate. $CaCO_3$. The softest of the limestones. It was deposited as a calcareous mud and hence is extremely fine in texture. It varies in colour with impurities of iron. It is a source of calcia in glazes. See **Limestone** and **Calcium carbonate**.

French chalk is not chalk in the same sense. This is talc: magnesium silicate.

Chamotte. French name for grog. Ground-fired fire-clay or other refractory clay. Through its use in Scandinavia, the term chamotte ware or chamotte has come to mean artistic wares produced in a coarsely grogged clay especially one containing a lot of plastic fireclay. It is a more romantic name than the English equivalent of saggar-marl ware. See **Grog**.

The photograph is of chamotte ware by Leighton Clark.

Charging. Packing a kiln or filling a blunger or grinding mill. A charge is a measured amount of material to be put into the mill etc.

Chattering. The rhythmic rippling which appears when turning. It occurs when the clay is too hard or too soft, or is not uniformly leatherhard. Blunt and unsuitable turning tools also cause chattering. A tool that is too flexible on a hard clay or one that is too stiff on a soft clay sets up a series of waves which become accentuated.

It is possible to use chattering as a decorative feature, in which case it is deliberately encouraged to occur. This can be done effectively when turning plaster of Paris plate moulds.

To overcome chattering the tool should be resharpened and held at a new angle to cut across the chatter. Alternatively, reverse the wheel and use a loop or smaller, pointed tool to cut a series of lines through the chatter before attempting to cut away the whole surface.

Cheesehard. The stage at which the clay has dried sufficiently from its plastic state to be carefully handled without deformation. It is the softest stage at which a pot can be shaved or turned on a wheel or lathe. The next stage in this setting up or stiffening is leatherhard when enough water has dried out for the clay particles to touch one another and the form is almost rigid. Nearly all drying shrinkage has taken place by the leatherhard stage.

Chemical symbol. A shorthand way of writing the name of an element by using the initial letter or two letters of its English or Latin name. The symbol represents the element, e.g. Si means silicon. The symbol is also used to denote one atom of an element when it appears in a compound. For example, SiO_2, which is silicon dioxide, usually called silica, has one atom of silicon to every two atoms of oxygen. The symbols are standardized and accepted internationally. See **Tables** and **Formula, chemical**.

Chequer. The pierced floor of a kiln through which the flames reach the chamber. The chequer pattern results from the use of standardized bricks supported by other bricks on end to give flues underneath the floor.

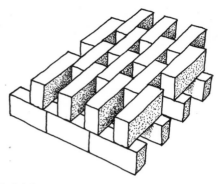

China. British porcelains and white earthenwares are often loosely called 'china'. The term comes from the habit of naming imports by their country of origin. Chinese porcelain was 'china' and so also were its European imitations and derivatives. Today china has a specific meaning amongst potters and implies a translucent white body covered with a glaze fired at a lower temperature than the body.

A development dating from the 18th century is bone china which uses calcined ox bones to provide a viscous flux for the body. See **Bone ash**. A 20th-century development is translucent china or non-bone china which uses mineral fluxes in a similar way to the soft paste porcelains.

China clay. Kaolin. The purest natural clay. Its composition is approximately equal to the mineral kaolinite and it is therefore given the same chemical formula of $Al_2O_3 . 2SiO_2 . 2H_2O$. It is used in bodies to give whiteness, to clarify colours and to control vitrification. In glazes it gives fluidity control at slop stage, viscosity control during the molten stage and adds stability to the final glaze.

China clay is an essential ingredient in making porcelain body and bone china body. See **Porcelain** and **Bone china**.

During the 17th century, Europe was searched for white clays with which to make porcelain. The imported Chinese porcelain had created the demand for a European product. Suitable clays were eventually discovered in France and later in England and Czechoslovakia. They were called kaolins like the Chinese clays but whilst of similar chemical composition they had different physical properties. Unlike the Eastern kaolins, Western kaolins are not very plastic. Some American kaolins are of sedimentary origin and have a little more plasticity.

China clay contains very little iron oxide and titania. Therefore it is white in its raw state and remains white through the firing. It is used for whiteware bodies and is indispensable for translucent white porcelain. Its whiteness also helps to clarify the colour of other clays, red and buff clays for example, which are improved by the addition of some china clay. Many prepared red bodies have this addition.

China clay is high in alumina and average in silica content. It is therefore a refractory clay. Its relatively large crystals melt slowly giving it a long maturing range. It is vitrified by 1770°C (3218°F) at which point it deforms. It was used as a standard of refractoriness by Dr Hermann Seger and became cone number 35. In bodies it is used to introduce controlled vitrification, as in porcelain. It is also used as a refractory for heat treatment furnaces. In glazes it is used to introduce alumina and silica to control glaze viscosity during firing and give stability to the final structure.

China clay has large crystals in relation to other clays like red earthenware and ball clays. There is therefore a relatively low total surface area to the particles and it requires little water to bring the dry clay to plastic consistency. In some cases as little as 15% moisture content is sufficient. The resulting plasticity is poor. As the water dries out of the plastic clay, the contraction is naturally small compared with more plastic clays. In some cases it is as little as 2% linear contraction plastic to dry. Similarly, firing shrinkage is low, but this is to be expected when the clay is fired to a point which is a long way below vitrification. These properties are of use in blending bodies.

China clay originated as granite which decomposed to clay, quartz, mica and feldspar. See **Clay origin**. Most china clays are won from their original position as granites and are called primary clays. Secondary china clays have been washed away from these locations and deposited as sediments. In the process they have often been subjected to a process of natural levigation, which allows the heavier particles of quartz, mica and feldspar to settle out and the finer particles, which are mostly clay, to be carried further before settling.

China clays which are still *in situ* are won by being washed from the parent rock with power hoses. The slurry is levigated and settled in a series of channels with riffles as traps for the heavier particles.

Many new methods which are less wasteful of space and china clay are being introduced to separate the sand and mica from the clay. The eventual pure clay slurry is filter-pressed and usually dried and pulverized. The three photographs are of automatic washing out, hydrocyclones and filter-press at the works owned by Watts, Blake, Bearne and Co Ltd of Newton Abbot, England.

The kaolinite content, that is, the idealized clay mineral content of the decomposed granite, is as low as 25%. The 'by-products' are therefore commercially important. The eventual clay claimed might account for 32% of the original rock. The by-products will be 50% quartz sand and 10% mica. The remainder is soluble salts. The china clay will contain approximately 88% kaolinite and 12% mica and quartz.

An ultimate analysis, typical of a china clay is:

SiO_2	46·6
Al_2O_3	38·3
TiO_2	0·1
Fe_2O_3	0·4
CaO	0·3
MgO	0·3
Na_2O	0·3
K_2O	0·7
Loss	13·0

China stone. A pure white cornish stone used in bone china recipes. About 25% is used with 25% of china clay and 50% of bone ash. See **Cornish stone**.

Chromite. $FeO.Cr_2O_3$. Natural chrome iron ore occurring in ultrabasic igneous rocks and the source of chromium oxide for paints, dyes and ceramics. The oxidized form, $Fe_2O_3.Cr_2O_3$, is called iron chromate and is used as a grey colourant in ceramics.

Chromium oxide. Chromium (III) oxide. Chromic oxide. Chrome oxide. Chromium sesquioxide. Cr_2O_3. The only stable oxide of the metal chromium. It is purchased as a prepared green powder which has a strong staining power in glazes giving mainly greens (up to 2%) but also reds under special conditions. It can be used at all temperatures but above 1200°C (2192°F) some of the oxide will volatilize.

Chromium oxide is found in combination with iron oxide in the ore chromite. The metal chromium is used with iron (ferro-chrome) to produce steels. The compounds of chromium are used in paint pigments, dyes and ceramic colours. The oxidized form of chromite, called iron chromate, gives an opaque grey colour in ceramics. Brushwork under glazes can be interesting where the chromium oxide remains stable and opaque, and the iron oxide bleeds into the glaze.

Chromium oxide is an amphoteric oxide and therefore plays different roles in ceramic fusions, depending upon the circumstances presented. It is not easily dissolved in fusion and often gives the appearance of an opaque pigment dispersed in the glaze. Apparently it is slow to act as either a flux or an acid but small amounts (up to 1%) can be dissolved in most glazes. In these cases the chromium oxide is probably fulfilling a linking role partially combined with the fluxes and partially with the acids. It gives a green colour known as chrome green which is not a single hue but a range. It will be appreciated that the particular action which the chromium oxide is fulfilling determines its colour and therefore the properties of the other oxides are important. Calcia, zinc oxide, baria, lead oxide, boric oxide and zirconia give significant differences.

Chromium oxide acts as an acid and dissolves more easily in combination with the strong flux lead oxide. It then gives reds and oranges known as chrome reds or chrome coral pinks. Zinc oxide acting amphoterically in lead glazes extends the chrome orange colour.

Chromium oxide acts as a flux and dissolves in combination with the acidic tin oxide. Here it gives a crimson pink colour known as chrome-tin pink. The colours from chromium oxide can be tantalizingly variable. Consistent results will only be obtained by separate preparation of the colouring as a stain.

CHROME GREEN. Chromium oxide gives greens

under most conditions. Amounts up to 1% disperse and dissolve fairly easily and give greens of a drab colour in leadless glazes and yellowish greens in lead glazes. Amounts up to a maximum of 3% give opacity and greyish green colours. The oxide powder is often quite a rich blue-green colour but it is impossible to keep this colour in glazes without the assistance of cobalt oxide. Chromium oxide can also be used to stain slips and bodies. Amounts up to 5% give different grey greens.

CHROME PEACOCK GREEN. The drabness of many greens can be enlivened by the addition of cobalt oxide. Both chromium and cobalt are strong oxides. Only 1% of each is required to give a bright colour. Boric oxide, or boric oxide and soda, glazes give the best results. This is a useful addition to the colouring range for potters who use alkaline frit glazes.

CHROME RED. Small amounts of chromium oxide dissolve well and give a bright red colour below 900°C (1652°F) in combination with lead oxide and silica. The presence of alumina detracts from the quality of red and therefore it is not easy to produce a satisfactory glaze for pottery. However, it is easy to produce exciting red and orange glasses for filling hollows in horizontally-fired tiles. The firing needs to be fully oxidized to achieve the red colour. These glazes are not suitable for raku because they blacken if reduced.

Prepared lead silicates give excellent colours with very little or preferably without feldspar, clay and minerals containing alumina. Chromium oxide is introduced as potassium dichromate which provides a stabilizing extra flux, potash, to carry the chromium oxide into finer dispersion. Potassium dichromate is soluble in water, therefore only the required amount of water should be added to the glaze. It is also poisonous. A suitable recipe is:

lead bisilicate	90
china clay	5
potassium dichromate	5

CHROME ORANGE. The red colour from lead oxide and chromium oxide becomes orange and then yellow with firings of approximately 950°C (1742°F) and 1050°C (1922°F), although duration of firing is another very important factor. The orange colour can be extended in the temperature range upwards and maintained even in glazes containing alumina by the presence of zinc oxide and iron oxide. It should be noted that these oxides are also amphoteric oxides. The colour is not quite the same orange but is rather harsh in colour and distinctly opaque. It relies upon the brown of the zinc and chromium oxides being heightened by a clean red iron oxide. The following recipe is an example for the 1100°C to 1150°C (2012°F to 2102°F) range:

feldspar	30
china clay	10
flint	5
whiting	6
lead bisilicate	40
chromium oxide	2
zinc oxide	5
red iron oxide	2

CHROME-TIN PINK. Chromium oxide also produces reds in combination with tin oxide. Here the chromium oxide acts as a flux and enters a loose structure of the normally inert tin oxide. There is therefore no temperature limit with this combination. The resulting colour is a harsh crimson.

Only a small amount of chromium oxide is required. The maximum is 0·5% and less than 0·1% will give results. The amount of tin oxide can vary from 4 to 10% with equal results. The best soft pinks are obtainable with lime matt glazes containing less than 5% of tin oxide and less than 0·1% of chromium oxide. The example recipe is for a glaze firing at 1200°C (2192°F). At this temperature the chromium oxide becomes volatile and some will travel to adjacent pots in the kiln. It is impossible to keep other tin oxide glazes in the same firing from becoming flashed with pink. The original glaze does not seem to be thereby depleted in colour.

cornish stone	48
china clay	14
flint	5
whiting	28
tin oxide	5
chromium oxide	0·1

Chuck. Chum. A thrown and/or turned clay form which is centred and stuck onto the wheelhead where it is used to hold a pot for turning. The chuck should be in a fairly soft cheesehard condition in which it is slightly sticky and thus grips the pot.

When not in use, a chuck is stored to keep it in cheesehard state. Wrapping it in polythene to exclude the air is excellent.

Some potters use a plaster chuck which sits in a cuphead.

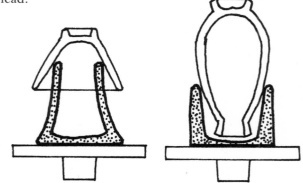

Chun. A pale blue, opalescent stoneware glaze named after a town in northern China where it was first made in the 11th century. The chun glaze is related to the celadon glaze, being a feldspathic glaze on a buff body and fired in a reducing atmosphere.

The beauty of the chun glaze lies in its fine visual texture and opalescent colour. It looks its best on simple forms. It sometimes incorporates patches of purple as on the illustrated plate by Derek Emms.

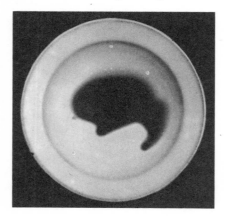

The blue opalescence is caused by scattered light. White light entering the glaze is diffused by suspended particles of colloidal size. The violet to blue light is scattered back to the observer but the other light waves (green, yellow, orange, red) pass through the glaze and are absorbed by the dark-coloured body. For maximum effect, the glaze must be applied thickly. Where the glaze is thinner, on rims for example, the colour seen is that of the body beneath and the glaze is virtually transparent because insufficient blue light is scattered.

The particles which scatter the short-wave violet to blue light are smaller than can be seen with the naked eye. See **Colloid**.

In chun glazes, these particles are nuclei of crystals and have been attributed, by different researchers, to phosphorus pentoxide, black iron oxide, calcium borate, titania, silica, and devitrification of alumino silicate from the body-glaze layer. Reduction helps to keep the phosphorus pentoxide isolated. It is also essential to incorporate the iron oxide in ferrous silicate nuclei which remain separate from the surrounding glass. The low alumina content of many chun glazes preserves these nuclei. Many wood ashes contain phosphorus and iron, and chun glazes are associated with wood ash and feldspar glazes. The calcium borate and titania nuclei usually produce long streaked flushes rather than the short-grained flushes. These occur with or without reduction. See **Clair-de-lune flush**.

Chuns are obviously obtainable in various ways. Any form of incipient devitrification which remains within a transparent and colourless glaze will give scattering of light and look bluish. The difficulty is in controlling the situation and producing the correct amount of devitrification to give a chun. An underfired chun is usually semi-matt, dull and not blue because there is too much crystallization. An overfired chun is transparent and glassy because the isolated particles become fully involved in the melt. See **Crystalline glazes**.

The red splashes are due to heavily reduced copper of colloidal size. The amount of copper required is very small and can be successfully added as a thin wash of copper slip on the raw ware. Three per cent of copper carbonate in the slip is adequate.

One of the chun glaze recipes used by Derek Emms is:

feldspar	43
china clay	1
quartz	30
whiting	20
talc	4
colemanite	1
black iron oxide	1

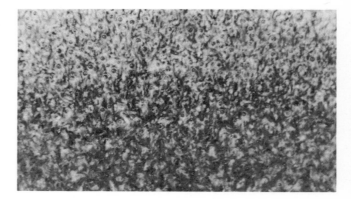

The enlarged detail of this glaze shows that its opacity is partially caused by minute bubbles as well as the flush streaks. The lower half of the photograph is part of a red-purple splash.

Cider jar. A storage jar for cider with a draw-off tap. The example shown is by Ray Finch.

Cinerary urn. A pot used for burial of cremated remains or part of the remains. Sometimes it was inverted over the remains and may have been part of a ritual of transporting them. Cinerary urns are found throughout the world and are usually associated with the first large communities. Prior to this the more isolated villages and nomadic groups used inhumation and later peoples tended to have religious beliefs which inhibited cremation.

Clair-de-lune flush. A 19th-century romantic term used to describe the pale blue striations found in Chinese stoneware glazes and emulated by softer glazes in western Europe. The striations are chains of crystal nuclei which have isolated themselves from the molten glaze.

Cinerary urns vary in size from the pygmy cups, only 2 inches tall, to enlarged food vessels 20 inches tall. Many Western cultures from Bronze Age to Roman used this method of burial but the best pottery examples come from the Middle Bronze Age of South Wales, Britain, 1400–1000 B.C. The one illustrated shows the typical collar and decoration of pecked bands.

Cistercian ware. Sixteenth-century earthenware, some of which was made by the Cistercian monks. It is thinly potted ware of deep red clay with a dark shiny glaze containing iron and manganese oxides. Most pieces are multi-handled small mugs, the forerunners of the tygs of the next two centuries.

Ferrous oxide in high alkaline and low alumina glazes, phosphorus pentoxide in stoneware glazes and calcium borate in hard and soft glazes are some of the sources of flushes. See also **Chun** and **Calcium borate**. The photograph shows an enlargement of a calcium borate flush.

Clam. Clam up. Clem. Clag. To smear clay slurry over kiln brickwork, especially the wicket, which is rebuilt for each firing. The words clam and clay have the same origin in the Greek word *gloios* meaning a sticky substance.

Clay. Hydrated silicate of aluminium. A heavy, damp, plastic material that 'sets' upon drying and can be changed by heat into a hard, waterproof material.

There is the idealized clay mineral called kaolinite which is always considered to be of chemical purity though of variably-sized crystals; and there is the clay which all potters know as their fundamental material which seems to bear little relationship to an idealized substance but is a variable, responsive material.

The properties of clay upon which pottery depends are the workability which allows forming and retention of form; and the property of ceramic change to a new material by heat.

Clay is used for other things as well as pottery. Ceramically it is used for bricks, tiles, sanitary ware, electrical insulators and heat insulators. It is also used in cosmetics and as a filler in rubber and paper.

Clay is here covered under the following sub-headings:

ORIGIN OF CLAY; TYPES OF CLAY; CHEMISTRY OF CLAY; PHYSICS OF CLAY; THE CRYSTAL STRUCTURE OF CLAY; CLAY IN GLAZES. For clay and heat: see **Firing**. For clay preparation: see **Preparation of clay**.

ORIGIN OF CLAY. Clay is a mineral with a crystal structure, but the individual crystals are too tiny to be seen with the naked eye or even through a powerful magnifying glass. Most people would describe clay as a mud, deposited by rivers in lakes and the sea. However, before it can be thus transported it originates as a pure mineral in decomposed igneous rocks. The decomposed rock is no longer the hard igneous rock of the original but is a soft disintegrating rock which, if exposed, is weathered and washes away. During transportation by a river, or by ice or sea, the clay is ground, picks up impurities, loses associated minerals and is finally settled into areas of similar particle size. See **Levigation**. The result is a clay stratum of progressive variation from fine to coarse with possible change of colour and composition also. This is a typical clay bank. Sedimentary clays rarely show a uniformity over a wide area. This is why blending of different clays is necessary to keep a constant product.

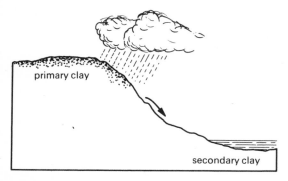

Clays which occur in their place of origin are called primary clays. They are the end product of a chain of reactions and are therefore also called residual clays.

The only common examples are china clay and bentonite. Clays which have been transported from their place of origin and settled elsewhere are called secondary clays or sedimentary clays. Ball clays, red marls and stoneware clays are of this type. See also **Kaolinite** and **Disordered kaolinite**.

All present clays therefore originated in the same way as deep-seated igneous or metamorphic rocks. Hot magma was pushed up from below. It did not reach the surface and therefore cooled slowly in large masses. These were often domes of rock, created where the magma was trapped, preventing further upward movement. These domes are the granite bosses which form upland areas today, like Dartmoor. Whilst cooling and still in a thermoplastic state, the future clays were subjected to hypogenic action. That is, a recreative action from below. This consisted of hot gases including carbon dioxide, water, boron and fluorine.

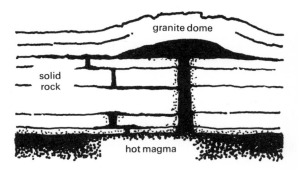

By a series of substitutions, the gases were able to decompose a potentially hard rock into a soft one which included clay. The hard rock included the mineral feldspar which by hydrolization becomes clay, silica and a salt. The accommodation of hydroxyl ions within the feldspar forms alumina into a sheet. By later substitutions and accommodations to this sheet a laminar crystal results. The clay (kaolinite) crystal is just such a crystal. Highly siliceous rocks like granite have an end product of clay (kaolinite), quartz, mica and other silicates. The kaolinite is not likely to be more than 25%.

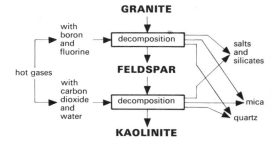

The sheet structure of alumina, however, is capable of being the basis of more minerals than kaolinite. The end result is dependent upon the original rock composition and the humidity and pressure etc of the hypogenic action. Montmorillonites, micas and chlorites are silicate minerals of similar plate-like structure to kaolinite. However only the montmorillonite mineral called bentonite resembles clay in its plasticity. The other minerals exist as impurites in clay and give to a clay some of its individuality.

Simplified origin of clays

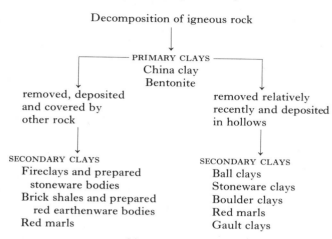

TYPES OF CLAY. Clay can be classified in many ways and each classification can be sub-divided again and again. For example, one of the sedimentary clays is ball clay which can be further classified by the area from which it comes. In each area, it will be found that there are a number of pits and each pit might contain ten or twenty differentiated clays lying in seams or veins, and as isolated pockets. The following divisions are offered as a guide to clay nomenclature and are therefore given the general name of types.

1. *Primary clays*, also called residual clays, are clays which can be mined from the position in which they decomposed from the parent rock. The most important primary clay is china clay which decomposed from feldspar and succeeded in remaining free from colouring impurity. Its attraction is its whiteness. The second important primary clay is bentonite. Apart from bentonite, the primary clays tend to be relatively large in particle size and hence low in plasticity. See **China clay**.

2. *Secondary clays*, also called sedimentary clays, are clays which have been deposited in their present position by the action of water or ice. This category covers most clays. In their removal from parent rock or previous residence, these clays were subjected to abrasion, frost action, leaching and other weathering. Inevitably these break up the particles producing finer clays and hence more plastic ones. Secondary clays are more plastic than primary clays. Most secondary clays contain impurities of which iron is the most common giving a grey, cream or brown colour. They have also collected organic matter which may also give a darkened colour and cause the clays to smell. See **Disordered kaolinite**.

3. *Plastic clay* is a classification of a property which can be possessed by any clay. It assumes better than average plasticity. Some clays, notably ball clays, are highly plastic and are used as additions to clays low in plasticity. All clays can have their plasticity improved by high-speed blunging, adding plasticizers, and de-aired pugging. Plastic clays are also called long clays and fat clays. They are strong clays and withstand vigorous handling during forming. Naturally plastic clays are also strong at cheesehard and raw state, and usually after firing if fired correctly. Ball clays and most red clays are plastic clays.

4. *Short clays*, also called lean clays, are non-plastic clays or, more correctly, clays of low plasticity. Clays with large particles are naturally low in plasticity and require treatment to improve it. Clays which contain a large proportion of non-plastic material, like sand, are also naturally short. Short clays have no strength in the forming process and usually little at cheesehard and dry state, although this property does not follow automatically. They may or may not be strong after firing. Fireclays and specially prepared bodies for pressing are often short clays.

5. *Shales* are previously sedimented clays which have been subjected to pressure. The clay particles orientate themselves to resist this pressure by lying across its path. The result is a compacted clay with a tendency to break into small flat flakes. Shales subjected to extremes of pressure with heat produce slates. Shales weather and are removed into nearby deposits often as highly plastic clays which show their earlier quality. Such shales can be crushed and blunged to produce excellent plastic clays. Fireclays and brick clays are often shales in deposit state.

6. *Refractory clays* are those which will withstand a high temperature without deformation. Their use is in making fire bricks, kiln furniture etc, and blending with other clays to improve firing behaviour. They are often the purer clays containing little iron but it does not follow that all light-coloured clays are refractory. China clay, fireclay and prepared crank mixtures are refractory clays. Fireclays and crank mixtures are often added to bodies for the textural effects they give as well as their refractory properties.

7. *Fusible clays* are the opposite of refractory clays. They will not withstand high temperatures but break down with heat and melt before 1300°C (2372°F). They are almost invariably dark-coloured, either black or brown, but some cream ball clays are fusible. They are used as clays for low temperatures because they are often highly plastic. They have become plastic by repeated removals but have also collected impurities in the form of fluxes. They are also used alone or with wood ash as slip glazes for stoneware. Some red marls, gault clay and most estuarine muds are fusible clays.

8. *White clays* are usually prepared bodies which

include china clay for whiteness and some ball clay for strength and plasticity. Other additions are flint, feldspar, plasticizer and cobalt stain to bleach any tendency to look cream.

9. *Grey clays* usually contain iron oxide in reduced state. They often contain a high percentage of organic matter which keeps the iron oxide reduced and gives a black colour by its carbon. Grey clays burn pink or cream-white. Many fireclays and ball clays are grey in the raw state.

10. *Red clays* are not bright red but a rust red from red iron oxide. Natural clays can contain up to 8% of iron oxide but even 2% will give a strong colour. The iron oxide and other collected impurities cause red clays to vitrify before 1200°C (2192°F).

11. *Coloured clays*. Natural clays fire to white, cream and brown, but clays can be stained with metal oxides and prepared stains to give other colours. The colour at raw stage is not necessarily the colour developed after firing when the colouring material has formed silicates. See **Oxides, colouring**.

12. *Raku clays* have the capacity to withstand thermal shock. Almost every clay can be made into a raku clay by suitable additions of grog, sand, etc. See **Raku clay, Fireclay** and **Crank mixture**.

13. *Earthenware clays* are many and various. All clays can be used for making earthenware in the sense that, for earthenware, the clay is fired to provide a strong product which is porous and is covered by a waterproof skin of glaze, therefore giving the best opportunity for the full expression of free, rich and varied forms.

Red earthenware clays are the red clays mentioned above. In Britain, these are the red clays of a pleasant, fine, sandy texture and are amenable to forming by any process: throwing, turning, pressing, slabbing and coiling. They are the least inhibited by specific requirements and can be used in combined forming techniques. When glazed, their colour can be used to add richness, especially with glazes which contain lead oxide. See **Red clay**.

Buff earthenware clays are used for tin-glazed ware. Traditionally the true marls are used and these fire to a soft pink or an ochre buff. Stoneware clays and coloured ball clays are also used but they lack the capacity to put a compression onto the glaze. See **Marl**. Some buff clays are also used for slipware. White earthenware clays are prepared bodies blended from china clay, ball clay, flint, feldspar etc. They are usually produced for a specific forming process and are given sufficient plasticity for this process but with most emphasis given to whiteness and fired durability. For this ware, the system of high biscuit firing followed by lower glaze firing was perfected. See **Creamware**, **Bisc** and **Glost**.

14. *Stoneware clays* are those which mature slowly during the firing. It is therefore possible to fire them to the dense state of stoneware without undue deformation. See **Vitrifiable clay**. Natural stoneware clays are related to ball clays but contain more impurities of sand and colouring. Fireclays of the plastic variety are often used or added to ball clays to produce stoneware bodies. See **Stoneware clay, Fireclay, Underclay, Crank mixture**.

15. *Porcelain clays* are usually specially prepared bodies. A few plastic kaolins exist like the hua shih of the original Chinese porcelain but Western clays tend to be very short when they are sufficiently pure and white. A porcelain clay is rarely textured. If grogged it will be with its own body. See **Pitchers**. The translucency of fired porcelain is obtained by the almost total vitrification of the body. Unlike stoneware, a porcelain body is homogenous. It does not contain particles of various sizes like grog and sand. It is therefore able to vitrify completely and high fired porcelain integrates with the glaze to produce a thick bodyglaze layer. See **Porcelain, China clay** and **Bone china**.

CHEMISTRY OF CLAY. The potter accepts clay as a medium of many properties. The chemist sees clay as a complex mixture and combination of minerals. The chemist gives an analysis of clay in two ways. One way separates the oxides, lists them and possibly gives amounts. The other tries to give some idea of the clay's properties by grouping the oxides as clay content, feldspar, mica etc. See also **Analysis, chemical and rational**. For example, a boulder clay could be analysed as:

alumina	23
silica	62
iron oxide	1
calcia and magnesia	3
potash and soda	2
loss on firing	9

Or it could be given the analysis:

clay content	50
feldspar	15
free silica	29
plus	
iron oxide	1
limestone	5

The clay content is the theoretical clay which is based upon the clay crystal structure with the formula $Al_2O_3 . 2SiO_2 . 2H_2O$. This gives theoretical clay a composition of:

alumina	39·5
silica	46·5
water	14·0

It will be noticed that there is a theoretical 14% of water. This is in the form of hydroxyl groups (OH) in the gibbsite layer and therefore many chemists prefer to describe the clay crystal by the formula $Al_2Si_2O_5(OH)_4$. They also call it hydrated aluminium silicate.

Clay contains water in the crystal structure called bound water; water in the holes between the particles called pore water; and water to allow the particles to slide past one another called water of plasticity. See **Water**.

A hundred pounds of clay in dry state contains 14 lb of bound water. This is over 11 pints of water (UK measure) which is locked in the crystal and present as hydroxyl groups (OH). During the firing, these groups are released and become water which in turn becomes steam. The steam escapes slowly over a period starting around 450°C (842°F) intensifying up to 600°C (1112°F) and tailing off to 700°C (1292°F). The bound water can escape as steam without causing trouble because the pores of the clay are open at this temperature. It is very unlikely that any pot would burst from the escape of this water although 11 pints of water give 370 cubic feet of steam. With muffle kilns the water vapour will be seen escaping from the kiln at this temperature.

Dry clay also contains pore water. This remains in the pores and does not dry out because there is water in the atmosphere. This pore water could equal another 11 pints in 100 lb of 'dry' clay.

Plastic clay contains more water still. This is the water of plasticity. In extreme cases this water of plasticity could account for 30% of the weight of plastic clay but 20 to 25% is more normal. Plastic clay based upon the theoretical clay would have the formula:

$$Al_2O_3 . 2SiO_2 . 2H_2O . 2H_2O . 5H_2O.$$

And a percentage analysis of:

alumina	26
silica	30·5
bound water	9·25
pore water	9·25
plasticity water	25

Seen thus, it is not surprising that there is shrinkage from plastic state to fired body.

The following are analyses of typical clays. They give percentage amounts of oxides after the ceramic change and therefore do not include water.

	China clay	Fireclay
Alumina	44	41
Silica	53	55·5
Iron oxide	1	2·3
Calcia/magnesia	1	0·7
Potash/soda	1	0·5

	Ball clay	Stoneware clay
Alumina	37·5	32
Silica	56·5	63
Iron oxide	2	2·2
Calcia/magnesia	0·5	0·6
Potash/soda	3·5	2·2

	Brick shale	True marl	Etruria marl
Alumina	26·5	15	21·5
Silica	62	64	65·5
Iron oxide	6·5	4	9·5
Calcia/magnesia	3·5	14	1·5
Potash/soda	1·5	3	2

PHYSICS OF CLAY. The physics of clay is concerned with the size and shape of the clay crystal and resulting agglomerate particles; and the effects arising from these. The effects concern plasticity and shrinkage.

The shape and form of the clay crystal are dependent upon its lattice structure previously described. Each sheet of aluminium silicate structure contains thousands of atoms. Thousands of sheets, layered on one another produce a clay crystal. The layers do not fit over one another in exact repetition but are slightly displaced since there is no reason for exact location. However the overall crystal has a roughly hexagonal appearance and is of course flattish, fig. 1.

Fig. 1 represents an average-sized clay crystal. The true size is about 0·5 micron across. This diagram is therefore 100 000 times too large. On the same scale, the smallest clay crystals are like the solid hexagon in fig. 1 and the largest crystals about the size of this page. China clay and some fireclays have the large crystals. Ball clay has the smallest crystals.

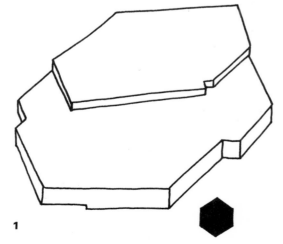

1

These crystals must not be confused with clay dust or grains. These crystals are so small that they are invisible to the naked eye. Many hundreds of particles make up a grain of clay dust. In comparison with the clay crystal in fig. 1, a hole in a 60's mesh sieve would be a square with sides as long as a lawn tennis court.

Because of the electrostatic forces of attraction and the compression that clays at rest have undergone, the larger grains are often replicas of the smaller crystals. That is, they are flattish and roughly hexagonal. Therefore whether one is considering the largest grains or the smallest crystals, the theory remains the same. Variation will be by amount of effect. In the explanation of strength, plasticity etc which follows, the word particle is used to describe the individual pieces of clay involved.

Water is the lubricant between the particles. Fig. 2. If there is plenty of water, the particles can slide past one another without difficulty. In such a case, there is little friction. A very soft, wet, plastic clay is in this state. When there is less water between the particles, there is some stickiness, like a wet pack of cards. In this case, the friction gives strength. A stiff plastic clay is in this state. As the water dries out of clay, the particles are brought closer together. The clay object becomes a solid. See also **Adsorption, Drying** and **Water** for an explanation of water involvement.

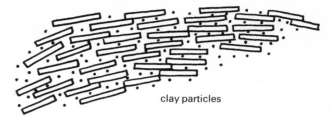

clay particles

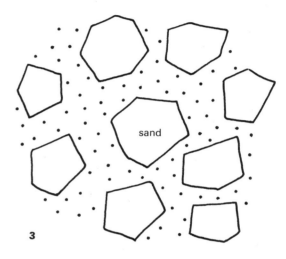

3

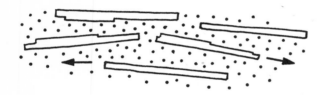

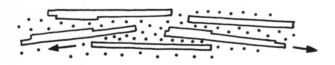

2

The water gives plasticity because the particles are able to hold onto one another. The contrast of a plastic material like clay and a non-plastic one like sand is shown in fig. 3. The clay particles can hold onto one another by suction. The water between the particles gives the necessary seal.

Fine clays are more plastic than coarse ones. This refers literally to the particle size. As will be seen by reference to fig. 4, for the same amount of overall movement, two adjacent coarse particles must slide further past each other. The fine clay is shaped by a

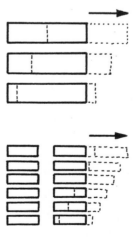

4

total of small adjustments. Fig. 5 shows that the fine clay will also contract more than the coarse clay during drying. The fine clay also contains more water. See also **Plasticity** and **Workability**.

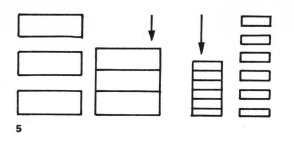

5

Fig. 6 shows why fine clays are stronger than coarse clays. In an equal bend, the fine clay has less displacement to accommodate per particle, than has the coarse clay.

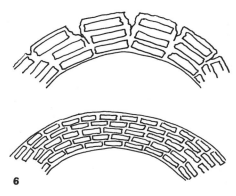

6

Fig. 7 shows how a clay will shrink more in one direction than in the other providing that all the clay particles are lying flat upon one another. In fig. 7 they are stacked in neat rows but the effect is the same if they are stacked brickwise. If we assume that the gaps which the water fills are of equal width, there are 6 gaps in the height and only 2 in the width of fig. 7. As the water dries out, there must be more shrinkage in the height than the width. This situation arises in pots.

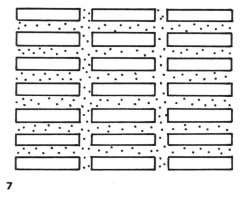

7

Clay particles position themselves with their flat faces opposing the direction of pressure. An extreme example of this is seen in compressed clays which have become shales. However in all potting use, the particles are being asked to rearrange their relative positions. Rolling and press moulding lays the particles flat along the clay sheet. This gives strength. In kneading clay, the particles are placed concentrically. This gives a circular strength which is useful on the wheel and is

further added to by the centring process. During opening of the clay in throwing, the base of the pot is compressed. This lays the particles flat across the base giving strength. It also makes the larger drying shrinkage through the thickness of the base rather than across the base. The firing shrinkage also follows this course. A compressed base is less likely to crack than an uncompressed one. The uncompressed one often tears apart in what is called an S crack. See **Crack**. Many other minor idiosyncrasies are explained by understanding which way compression was applied. For example, lids which are thrown upside down often shrink more than the pots they were measured to fit.

The angle of compression is important. In throwing one might expect the particles to line up in the pot wall parallel to the sides of the wall as in fig. 8. However, the clay was lifted to this position and therefore the pressure was upwards as well as inwards. The outer hand was also probably below the inner one putting a diagonal pressure upon the particles as in fig. 9.

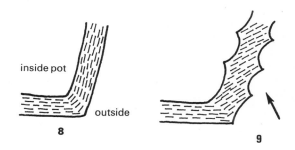

inside pot

outside

8

9

In throwing, the hands describe a slow spiral up a pot in a clockwise direction—clockwise seen from above on an anti-clockwise wheel. The particles will follow this course which coincides with the throwing rings. The line of greatest shrinkage therefore becomes a steep twist at right angles to the throwing rings. Fig. 10. A quickly thrown pot will have more twist shrinkage than one thrown slowly with very close throwing rings.

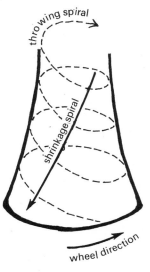

throwing spiral

shrinkage spiral

10

wheel direction

This shrinkage is responsible for the twisting in the firing of thrown teapot spouts and tall pots. The twist follows the direction of the throwing spiral, taking the pot further on in a clockwise direction. This is often baffling to the beginner who expects the twist to be in the opposite direction as if it were associated with regaining a position once held as if by elasticity. This it is not.

The properties of clay described as plasticity and strength which give to clay its workability character, are further described under **Plasticity** and **Workability**. Clays can be improved in workability by blunging, ageing, souring and de-airing which divide the clay grains into smaller particles and improve the lubrication between particles. The processes are described under **Ageing, Blunging** and **De-airing**.

THE CRYSTAL STRUCTURE OF CLAY. Oxygen is the commonest element in the earth's crust, in the sea, and in the atmosphere. It is not surprising to learn that oxygen is the linking force in clay. The clay crystal is composed of alternate layers of silica and gibbsite. Each layer has oxygen as its major constituent forming the structure. Each silica layer is fastened to a gibbsite layer by oxygen links. The combined silica-gibbsite layer is attached to others by hydroxyl bonds to form crystals. This is the kaolinite or clay crystal.

The structure is in sheets and can therefore be conveniently represented by a series of two-dimensional diagrams. As an indication of scale, 16 million of these diagrams side by side would equal one inch. Fig. 1 shows the silica layer. This is an hexagonal structure which is not exactly regular. There is slight variation in the silicon-oxygen-silicon link which is not a straight link but is more often an angle. Each oxygen atom requires links with two silicon atoms. The hexagonal structure allows this and promotes a sheet structure which can continue indefinitely on all sides but cannot extend from the oxygen atoms above or below. In this respect it is like the diagram which is flat on the page. However, each silicon atom requires links with 4 oxygen atoms and in this sheet there are links with only 3. There is also not yet sufficient oxygen to give the common silica formula of SiO_2.

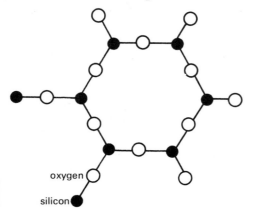

1

oxygen
silicon

Fig. 2 shows how each silicon atom obtains its fourth oxygen atom. This is positioned above each silicon atom thus forming a little three-sided pyramid out of the 4 oxygen atoms with the silicon atom fitting snugly inside.

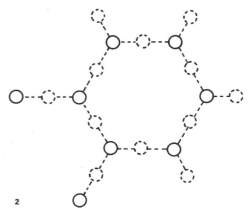

2

The original layer shown in fig. 1 is now shown in dotted outline. There are now too many oxygen atoms to give the common formula SiO_2. This is because the top layer of oxygen atoms shown in fig. 2 are as yet not attached to the requisite number of other atoms (their valencies are unsatisfied). The mineral silica known as quartz would result if the unsatisfied atoms of oxygen were to link up with more silicon and so on upwards. However this possibility is inhibited in clay by the presence of aluminium which forms the next layer called the gibbsite layer. The silica of figs. 1 and 2 is also called the Si_2O_5 layer and the tetrahedral layer.

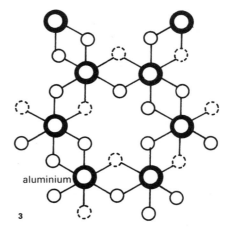

aluminium

3

Fig. 3 shows the strictly regular gibbsite layer. The presence of aluminium in six-fold co-ordination with oxygen (links with 6 oxygen atoms) makes a stiff and regular lattice. Part of this lattice is composed of the oxygen atoms from fig. 2, here shown as dotted outlines. Their valencies are now satisfied by a link with silicon below and two weaker links to aluminium atoms above. The other oxygen atoms of this gibbsite layer have their unsatisfied valencies occupied by a hydrogen atom each. The total atoms in the composite sheet represented by figs. 1, 2 and 3 are $Al_8Si_8O_{36}H_{16}$ which when rationalized gives $Al_2O_3.2SiO_2.2H_2O$.

The gibbsite layer is sometimes called the octohedral layer, because the six oxygen atoms surrounding each aluminium atom, when considered in terms of packing together, form a three-dimensional figure which has eight sides. The gibbsite layer is rigid. The silica layer is not rigid. If it were, it would not be able to fit exactly into the gibbsite layer. The slight flexibility of the hexagonal structure allows it to adjust to the requirements of the layer above.

The hydrogen atoms of the gibbsite layer do not form a rigid bond but are able to oscillate in their attachment between these oxygen atoms and other oxygen atoms in an adjacent layer. The adjacent layer is another composite sheet above of identical make-up. The hydrogen oscillation holds the two layers together by what is called the hydroxyl bond.

A clay crystal is therefore a pile of alternate silica and gibbsite layers held together by common oxygen atoms and hydroxyl bonds. Because of the third dimension of the crystal lattice it is impossible to produce a simplified side view which corresponds exactly with the plans of figs. 1, 2 and 3. However, a simplified diagram can be drawn which fulfils the conditions of valency as ex-

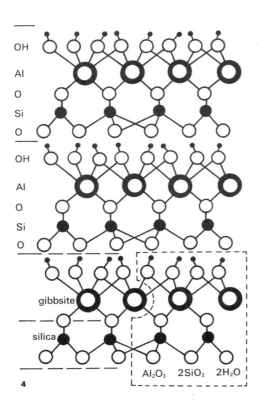

pressed in the sheet structure. This is done by superimposition as in fig. 4. This figure shows the silica and gibbsite layers linked by oxygen atoms and the composite layers held by hydroxyl bonds.

CLAY IN GLAZES. Clay is often included in a glaze recipe to provide glaze slop suspension, adhesion to the pot and stiffening to the maturing glaze.

Clay in the glaze slop settles slowly. If the water is acidic, and it is usual to add some calcium chloride to make it so, then the clay is flocculated and produces an open mesh of particles. This mesh hinders the settling of non-clay minerals like flint and feldspar which would otherwise settle quickly. See **Calcium chloride**.

Dry glaze on pottery awaiting the firing is in powder form. Clay in the glaze helps to bind this together giving it strength. About 10% of china clay is usual in a glaze and serves this purpose as well as others. Glazes without clay are very friable.

Pure clay is alumina and silica. In the glaze, silica provides glass and the alumina provides a stiffening. Clay is high in alumina and therefore glazes containing 20% and more of china clay tend to be stiff matt glazes. See **Alumina** and **China clay**.

Clays are chemically similar to glazes. Both are alumino-silicates but glazes melt because they contain fluxes in sufficient quantity to engage all the silica in fusion. A few clays, notably estuarine muds, contain an abundance of flux. These clays can be used as clay for pot-making providing the firing does not exceed about 1050°C (1922°F). However they are more often used as glazes, either alone as slip glazes, or as the main glaze constituent tempered with flint and/or wood ash. Most estuarine muds show this property and examples of these clays are the Albany slip of the United States and Nottingham marl of Great Britain.

Clobbering. The practice of adding extra decoration to someone else's pottery with or without permission. It was done mainly in the 18th and 19th centuries to increase market value of the ware. Some antiques are given a face lift in this way. The term is obviously not intended to be complimentary.

Cobalt carbonate. $CoCO_3$. A compound of cobalt which is used for colouring slips and glazes. Upon heating to the region of 800°C (1472°F) it decomposes into cobaltous oxide and carbon dioxide.

$$CoCO_3 \xrightarrow{800°C} CoO + CO_2 \uparrow$$
$$100\% \qquad 63\% \quad 37\%$$

Because the carbonate is only 63% effective blue stain (CoO) it is easier to use than the more concentrated cobalt oxides, black and grey. It is a lighter powder and can be spread more evenly through the glaze thus avoiding the tendency to specking which is common with cobalt oxide.

The release of the carbon dioxide gas is automatic and without incident except where very low-melting glazes or fluxes are used, e.g. raku glazes and enamel colours. Here the gas may cause some blistering. It should be noted that the oxides also may cause blistering. This difficulty can be avoided by previous calcination and fusion.

Cobalt carbonate may be added to glazes in amounts up to 1·5% and gives shades of blue. See also **Cobalt oxide**.

Cobalt oxide. CoO. CoO_2. Co_2O_3. Co_3O_4. A general name for a number of compounds of cobalt and oxygen which have been used as blue stains for pottery for nearly two thousand years. Cobalt oxide is an extremely strong ceramic stain. In fact it is the most powerful colouring oxide. Less than one per cent dispersed throughout a glaze is sufficient to give a very strong blue. The blue varies from a violet to a greeny blue according to the other oxides present. Most potters find its strong colour too pure and monotonous and therefore modify it with other colouring oxides such as iron and manganese to give a softer slate blue. Other blue stains are now commercially prepared without cobalt oxide but the ease with which the cobalt oxide gives blue ensures its continuing use. It is not poisonous and it is chemically stable at room temperature and during firing. It is unaffected by oxidation or reduction and is not volatile even at 1400°C (2552°F). It can therefore be easily stored and handled, and it can be used effectively over the entire range of pottery-making.

Cobalt is a metal which occurs as ores in combination with nickel, arsenic, sulphur and manganese. The most rewarding deposits are in Canada and southern Africa. The oxide is extracted from the ore by roasting or as a by-product recovered from nickel ore. The purest oxide marketed contains traces of nickel and iron oxides. It is not advisable to attempt to roast one's own ore or to use raw crushed ore because of the arsenic and sulphur content. Cobalt is also a trace element in vegetables and an important vitamin (B12) in stock-rearing. Cobalt metal is used in steel and chromium alloys. Cobalt salts are used as driers and the oxides are used in paint pigments and pottery stains.

Cobalt oxide is usually purchased as cobalto-cobaltic oxide (cobaltosic oxide, Co_3O_4) which is black. This is a stable form at room temperature which liberates its excess oxygen during firing above 800°C (1472°F) to form cobaltous oxide (CoO). Cobaltous oxide is the stable form at higher temperatures and the one which combines with the silicates and borates to give a blue colour. Other convenient forms are cobaltic oxide (Co_2O_3) which is grey but contains only 90% effective stain against the 93% of the black oxide, and cobalt carbonate ($CoCO_3$) which is mauve in colour and is only 63% effective stain content. The acidic cobalt dioxide (CoO_2) also exists but is not marketed for pottery use because the other forms are sufficiently stable for storage and are convenient in use. Cobalt oxide is also marketed as silicates, alumino-silicates and aluminates for use as glaze and body stains, and in underglaze colours etc.

Cobaltous oxide is a powerful glaze flux, equalling the strong alkaline oxides potash and soda. It is therefore very active in a glaze and dissolves readily in most glazes, especially high alkaline and boric glazes, although it has a high melting point alone (2860°C or 5180°F). As it dissolves in the glaze it diffuses over an area. It is therefore impossible to keep a hard edge to underglaze painting in cobalt oxide. The edge will inevitably bleed slightly into the surrounding glaze.

Cobalt oxide is a very powerful colourant and only a small amount is needed to stain a glaze. This small amount would eventually spread throughout the glaze but in most firings there is insufficient time for this to occur and the result is that the glaze appears patchy or speckled around the separate particles of cobalt oxide. A deliberate speckle is easily obtained by adding the cobalt oxide to the already sieved glaze and stirring it in without further sieving. To avoid a speckle one must grind the colour with part of the glaze and sieve the whole glaze at least twice through a fine mesh (120's). Alternatively, the use of cobalt carbonate helps to spread the colour because it is a less powerful colourant for its bulk than is cobalt oxide.

To obtain a blue glaze one has merely to add cobalt oxide to the recipe. A strong blue will be obtained by only 0·5% if the glaze is one that fuses fully, e.g. a transparent earthenware glaze. Even 0·05% (one two-thousandth part of the glaze) is perceptible in transparent and semi-transparent glazes. Glazes which are opaque tend to require more colourant because only the colour at the surface of the glaze is seen. Opaque tin glazes are fully stained to a deep blue by 1% cobalt oxide. Crystalline glazes, especially barium matts, are capable of absorbing as much as 10% cobalt oxide before the colour becomes blackened. Too much cobalt oxide gives an unpleasant inky blackness in all glazes. Excesses of cobalt oxide appear on the glaze surface as metallic patches. The effect is misleadingly known as 'ironing'. The following recipe contains its limit of cobalt oxide. It is a crystalline barium matt glaze for use in combination with vitrifying slips and other matt glazes at 1200°C (2192°F):

feldspar	50
china clay	10
soft borax frit	10
barium carbonate	20
magnesium carbonate	4
cobalt oxide	6

Slips and bodies require more stain than glazes. Approximately 5% cobalt oxide in a slip gives the same intensity of blue as 1% in a tin glaze. However 10% is still the limit. This gives a very deep blue which is almost black and is partly due to the fusion of the slip and partly to the fact that the cobalt oxide is not forming a full silicate. This is the same as the 'ironing' of the glaze. This proportion of oxide gives enough fluxing to render the slip almost a glaze at temperatures above 1200°C (2192°F). It should be noted that it is not cobalt oxide itself that is blue. In fact the cobaltous oxide (CoO), if isolated, would be found to be a red crystal! Any attempt to get a red powder at room temperature is thwarted by the occurrence of the black and grey of the other cobalt oxides. Attempts to get a red crystal in the glaze are thwarted by the active combining of the cobalt oxide to form silicates. The blue is the colour of cobalt silicate which is the combination of cobalt oxide and silica occurring during the firing. For this reason a cobalt blue slip or body appears grey in the raw state and changes to blue during the firing.

It is possible to use a very weak stain to counteract the tendency of some white clays to appear cream coloured. The cream colour is due to traces of iron oxide which the cobalt oxide over-rides with its opposite colouring. If too much iron is present the result is a muddy colour. Only about one part of cobalt oxide in 20,000 parts of clay is required but the total used represents the largest use of cobalt in the ceramic industry. Traces of cobalt oxide are also used in low solubility glazes to counteract yellowish tinges.

It is possible to produce a variety of blues from cobalt oxide as can be seen by any collection of Chinese blue and white porcelain. All are typically cobalt blues but they range from a purple-blue to a green-blue. The fluxing oxides in a glaze determine the character of a glaze's surface shine, transparency etc. They similarly affect the colouring. With a lead glaze the cobalt oxide gives a middle blue. This blue is brightened by the strong alkalis, potash and soda, and given a purplish overtone with a particularly interesting feeling of depth. Boric oxide has a similar effect. The purple tinge can be further extended in high alkaline glazes where magnesia is present but only a very small amount of cobalt oxide is needed. This gives some delightful soft mauve colours. It is possible to get these colours in crystalline stoneware glazes by overlapping a cobalt-stained glaze by a white crystalline glaze. The underneath glaze should contain some magnesia as talc or

dolomite, approximately 10%, and cobalt oxide, approximately 0·1%. The upper glaze may be a dolomite matt or a lime matt with approximately 5% of tin oxide. The tin oxide helps to keep the colour clean.

If a glaze is very high in alumina, then the cobalt colour may be tinged greenish like weak Prussian or Chinese blue. The colour is due to the establishment of some cobalt aluminate, but is dependent upon the fluxes present as well as the alumina. It is easier to obtain this colour by introducing cobalt aluminate in the first place because cobalt oxide, if given the option, will form cobalt silicate which is the purplish blue. The greenish tinge can be more easily established by the presence of zinc oxide but the colour is not very clean. The purest of the non-purple blues is achieved by the use of a crystalline matt glaze which does not contain free silica. It should also be without lead oxide and boric oxide and be as low as possible in the high alkaline fluxes. The main flux and crystallizer should be calcia. A small amount of zinc may be used and the presence of tin oxide helps to keep a clean colour.

The strong blue is not to everyone's liking. After the first excitement of the pure colour many potters modify it with other colouring oxides. Iron oxide, manganese oxide and nickel oxide give subtle slate greys. Zinc oxide gives greys and greens. Uranium oxide gives greens and blacks. Bright modifications are obtained in high alkaline glazes with copper oxide and chromium oxide giving turquoises and peacock blues.

As with all colourings, consistent results are best obtained by first calcining the colourant separately. However cobalt is probably the most dependable colour that the individual potter will use and only the extreme variations will require separate preparation as a stain.

Coffee pot. The tall pot with long spout originated as a metal object in south-west Asia. The tall pot successfully allows the grounds to settle but with today's methods of coffee-making which involve straining or filtering there is less need for the tall pot. The spout

67

which is long and narrow gives more precise control of the flow although it should be noted that the absence of the strainer, which one associates with the teapot, can cause too fast a flow into the spout resulting in edge turbulence at the outflow.

The coffee pot presents a challenge to the potter to harmoniously combine specific functional parts. See also **Spout**, **Lid, Handle** and **Teapot**. Examples shown for comparison are a late 19th-century pot by Doulton of Lambeth, and contemporary pots by Michael Cardew, Michael Casson, Janet Hamer and a coffee jug by the Leach Pottery, St Ives, England.

Coiling. Hand-building a pot using 'snakes' of plastic clay. The term is extended to cover many techniques in which the 'snake' varies from a thin strip to a large thick sausage which is squashed and added with a pinching technique. Each coil is usually integrated with the previous one so that its separate identity as a coil is lost.

Only rarely are coils left showing the method of construction and then it is as a decorative feature. Coiling is usually done from the base upwards to the rim but wide bowls are often coiled upside down starting at the rim. Either way, the process is one of organic construction and the feeling of steady growth and expansion is expressed. The photograph on page 69 is of a coiled pot by Helen Pincombe.

Pre-Columbian American pottery and West African pottery are usually quoted as good examples of coiling. Historically, most Neolithic and Bronze Age peoples

produced good coiled pottery and continued to do so for large storage jars when the wheel became used for smaller repeat items. Western Asia, the Mediterranean and northern China can provide some excellent examples.

Some potters use a turntable of some kind on which to build the pot whilst they remain in one place but others prefer to walk around the pot as coils are added and the pot is scraped and shaped. Combinations of coiling and throwing, or coiling and turning are used and give their own particular qualities.

Tools used in coiling are simple, being coarse combs; hard scrapers of metal, plastic or natural shells and seed pods; and beaters and pebbles used in a paddle and anvil technique.

Most clays are suitable for coiling. Coarse clays are popular because their texture can be fully exploited. Coarse clays with some fine highly plastic content coil well and dry quickly and uniformly. Sandy and short clays can be made suitable for coiling by the liberal addition of bentonite but it may also be necessary to use some slurry to help one coil to join to the next. The more plastic clays can be worked in soft plastic state without use of water or slurry.

Colemanite. Borocalcite. Hydrated calcium borate. Priceite. Pandermite. $2CaO.3B_2O_3.5H_2O$. A variable, crystalline mineral providing calcium and boric oxide in relatively insoluble form. It occurs in the western USA associated with ulexite which is similar but contains soda. Colemanite is variable from $CaO.2B_2O_3.6H_2O$ to $2CaO.3B_2O_3.5H_2O$. The mineral pandermite which comes from Turkey is $4CaO.5B_2O_3.7H_2O$. Colemanite is a useful means of introducing boric oxide into a glaze without recourse to fritting. About 10% of the glaze recipe is the usual limit for colemanite and this amount actually improves the brilliance of colour and the gloss.

Colemanite is a powerful flux in glazes. It introduces calcia which begins its action at 1100°C (2012°F) and boric oxide which begins to fuse at red heat (600°C or 1112°F). It is especially useful in low- and middle-temperature glazes where its fluxing action begins at

approximately 900°C (1652°F). In glazes for the 1000°C to 1100°C (1832°F to 2012°F) range it gives some opacity. Above 1100°C the colemanite becomes a very active flux giving bright shiny glazes.

One advantage of colemanite is in the production of leadless glazes without using commercial or self-made frit. However, an important use is in combination with lead to form low-sol glazes which are craze-resistant. These glazes can have an attractive bright shine and a longer maturing range than simple lead glazes or leadless glazes.

In stoneware glazes, the introduction of colemanite instead of calcium carbonate will render the glaze more fusible at the same temperature or will lower the melting point of the glaze.

In coloured stoneware glazes, the two distinct fluxing actions of boric oxide and calcia produce a time lapse between a first fusion and a second or final fusion. Between these two there is time for the glaze to smooth itself out at the surface. The second fusion breaks this surface in a characteristic mottling. The effect is most striking on semi-matt glazes but shiny glazes also may still retain some of this texture.

Boric oxide has a low coefficient of expansion. If boric oxide is introduced into the glaze, the whole glaze will contract less upon cooling after firing. This glaze is therefore less likely to craze. Colemanite is therefore used in small amounts to balance a glaze and at the same time to correct slight crazing. See **Glaze fit**.

Colemanite is often used in small amounts for three reasons. Firstly, it is used only as a balancing flux and not the main flux. Secondly, although small additions brighten the gloss and improve colours generally, large amounts tend to give a dull opacity. Thirdly, the water content of colemanite must escape from the glaze and large amounts of water vapour tend to loosen the unfired glaze and thereby cause crawling when the glaze melts. The water may not be completely released until 800°C (1472°F).

Colemanite is the only mineral which contains boric oxide in insoluble form and is therefore valuable for introducing boric oxide, along with calcia, into raw glazes. In all other cases, boric oxide is obtained from soluble minerals which must be fritted before being introduced into the glaze slop. Even so, some colemanite will be found to be slightly soluble and the calcia, possibly assisted by the boric oxide will act as a deflocculant on clay and clay content minerals in the glaze slop. The glaze will then be thinner than required and will not settle sufficiently to have the extra water syphoned off. This will happen only with glazes which are stored and is no worse than similar trouble with wood ashes. It can be countered by the use of calcium chloride solution or vinegar.

The name borocalcite is often used for calcium borate $(Ca(BO_2)_2)$. This crystalline combination of boric oxide and calcia sometimes occurs as devitrification in glazes. It can be responsible for some attractive blue flushes, especially in glazes covering dark bodies. See **Clair-de-lune flush** and **Chun**.

Colloid. Colloidal particles are those of a finely divided substance when these are dispersed throughout another substance. Colloidal particles exhibit characteristics which are not associated with the same substance in bulk form. For example:

1. What is really a transparent substance can produce a milky blue opalescence in a glaze.

2. A substance that is normally $2\frac{1}{2}$ times as heavy as water produces a suspension in water that will not settle.

The finely divided particles are called the dispersed phase or discontinuous phase. The substance through which they are dispersed is called the dispersion medium or continuous phase. Both phases together are called a colloid. A colloid is halfway between a suspension, such as a glaze slop, and a true solution.

The degree of fineness involved is from 10^{-4} cm to 10^{-7} cm (0·0001 cm to 0·0000001 cm). This includes particles smaller than the wave-lengths of visible light. Therefore they cannot be seen separately with the naked eye even with the help of a magnifying glass but require an ultramicroscope or an electron microscope to identify them. Though one colloidal particle is invisible to the naked eye the collective qualities of many particles give a visual effect.

COLLOIDAL CLAY. All particles of a substance tend to have the same predominant electrical charge resident on the surface. The particles thus repel one another if dispersed in a liquid.

The finest clay particles are of this type and in some very plastic ball clays may account for 30% of the bulk. Slips made from such clays do not settle completely. The particles move around in the water repelled by one another and moved by the water molecules, which are also in motion. The force is from all sides and is sufficient to counteract gravity. Warming a slip will help to settle it by increasing the motion and causing some collision of particles. Particles which have collided become one larger particle. A larger particle is not able to move as far with the same force and if it is large enough, the force of gravity has the greater exertion and it will sink. The activity of colloidal particles in a liquid is known as Brownian movement.

Suitable electrolytes disturb the shells of electrical charges surrounding the particles with the result that the particles no longer repel one another. They are therefore able to aggregate or produce flocs. Thus a clay slip which will not settle can be persuaded to settle by the addition of a small amount of acid. The acid is referred to as a flocculant. Calcium chloride is a popular flocculant but vinegar will also work. Unlike with a deflocculant, it is not possible to add too much flocculant. However, an excess beyond the amount required for the result is wasted or may have undesir-

able side effects with other materials. The settling is called sedimentation. The aggregation of particles is called flocculation. See **Flocculation** and **Deflocculation**.

GLAZE COLLOIDS. Another colloid which the potter encounters is that of particles dispersed in a finished glaze which give a colour effect.

These colloidal particles may have a colour of their own which is the native colour of the substance. This colour depends upon the ability of the substance to absorb part of the visible light spectrum so that we see the remaining part of the spectrum reflected, and this is the colour which we see.

Colloidal particles may also have a colour which is created by their small size. They may have no colour at all in the bulk state, being transparent, but because the particles are smaller than some light wavelengths, they interfere with some of the light waves and create a coloured effect. This occurs when such particles retain their identity and do not become part of the molten glaze. These can be considered as separate particles in suspension in a liquid even when the glaze has set. The fired glaze is therefore a colloid composed of a dispersed phase of solid or gas in a dispersion medium which is also solid. The particles may be transparent crystals, nuclei of crystals, amorphous solids, or gas, but because they are separate particles they have a surface different from the surrounding glass. This surface bends the light waves with the result that the glaze appears opaque instead of transparent.

Most potters are familiar with opacity due to suspended bubbles which can be seen through a magnifying glass. If the bubbles are of the ultrafine dimension which cannot be distinguished through a magnifying glass the glaze is a colloid. These bubbles collectively disperse the light and give a frosted opacity inside the glaze although the surface of the glaze may be shiny. Sulphur, fluorine and chlorine if not driven off as gases during firing may be present in sulphates, fluorides and chlorides in colloidal state. These are entrapped in the glaze and give an opalescent quality. Carbon also as carbon particles and monoxide gas gives smokey appearances. The glass-former phosphorus pentoxide does not always become part of the random chain of oxides which makes a molten glaze. Instead it remains as isolated particles dispersed in the glaze. When the glaze cools these particles, although transparent, produce a blue opalescence.

The colour seen in the semi-opacity of these glazes is not that of a crystalline solid but is the result of scattered light. The violet and blue light is scattered more than the other colours and therefore a glaze appears semi-opaque and bluish. The red, yellow and green light passes through the glaze. Some of these colours are deflected, so that depending upon the angle of viewing, the glaze appears opalescent and variable. The metals gold, silver and copper as colloids also produce colouring. The colour varies with the particle size. A small amount of the metal is capable of dispersing through a large amount of glaze. Gold and silver produce a wide range of colours but copper colloids tend to be red. The classical Chinese *sang-de-boeuf* is a colloidal copper glaze. Cassius purple colouring is colloidal gold and tin.

The flanged bowl by Derek Emms combines the colloidal copper red, seen here as the darker crescent within the bowl, with the light blue opalescence of nuclei dispersal. See **Chun** and **Sang-de-boeuf**.

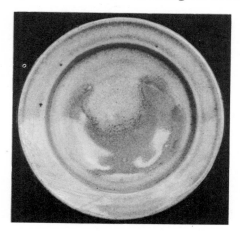

Compound. Chemical compound. Two or more elements so united as to create molecules of an entirely new substance with different characteristics from the constituents. For example, the soft metal aluminium and the gas oxygen unite to form the extremely hard crystal alumina (Al_2O_3) which is used as an abrasive. In order to form a compound, the constituents must be present in determinable numbers of atoms which will form an electrically balanced unit. Therefore a glaze is not a compound although it contains many different compounds.

Compression. Pressure inwards. The state of being pushed to decrease size. Glazes in a state of excessive compression may shiver or flake off. On the other hand if the body exerts some stress of compression on the glaze this acts against any tendency to craze with the periodic expansion and contraction of the body and glaze with heat, or moisture. A glaze can withstand ten times the amount of stress under compression as under tension before rupturing. Some compression is thus desirable providing it is not so great that it causes shivering. Cristobalite is introduced into earthenware bodies to create this stress which is then called the cristobalite squeeze.

Conduction. Transference of heat through solids by the interaction of their atoms and molecules. In the kiln the pottery is heated through its solid mass by conduction, the heat having arrived at its surface by convection and/or radiation.

Cones. Pyrometric Cones. Elongated three-sided pyramids. One to three inches tall, which are placed inside a kiln as a measurement of heat-work.

The cones are made from ceramic minerals and are similar in composition to glazes. With heat the cones soften and eventually bend over. If more heat were applied the cones would melt into a glass. It is the action of bending over, also called collapsing and squatting, which is important. This action can be viewed from outside the kiln through a spyhole and thereby the potter has knowledge of what heat-work is taking place inside the kiln. Because the cones are made from ceramic minerals their actions relate directly to pottery, but they are used by workers in other heat-treatment fields.

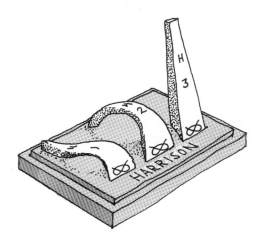

By having cones of different compositions, it is possible to have cones which collapse with different amounts of heat-work. Each cone is given a number corresponding to a temperature at which it will collapse through heat-work if that temperature is arrived at through a specified cycle. Cones are therefore more accurate than electric pyrometers which measure only temperature without relation to time. For example, a Harrison cone 6 which is given the temperature of 1200°C (2192°F) would collapse at about 1185°C (2165°F) if fired extremely slowly taking, for instance, 3 days. Prolonged soaking would give a more marked difference. Correspondingly the cone would be able to survive to a temperature in the region of 1220°C (2228°F) before collapsing if the firing were rapid, say 3 hours. Bodies and glazes would be affected in a similar way so the cone 6 would be a better indicator than an electric pyrometer. Conversely it is more accurate to refer to a glaze as a cone 8 glaze than as a 1250°C (2282°F) glaze. The glaze materials are related much more closely to a cone composition than they are to an abstract temperature. The only disadvantage in this is the difference in cones number 8 from different manufacturers.

For example, cones number 8 are available as follows. The squatting temperatures are those quoted by the manufacturers. A more complete list is in the **Tables** of this book where it will be noted that the rate of temperature rise is also quoted.

Type of cone	°C	°F
Standard Seger	1280	2336
Miniature Seger	1295	2363
Standard Harrison	1250	2280
Small Harrison	1250	2280
Large Orton	1263	2305
Small Orton	1300	2372

ORIGIN AND TYPES OF CONE. The form of the pyrometric cone was adopted by Dr Hermann Seger in 1885, for use in testing the refractoriness of materials. The idea of pyrometric cones had been used previously at Sèvres. Seger's cone was $2\frac{1}{4}$ inches high and the base was a triangle with $\frac{1}{2}$-inch sides. The effects of heat penetrating a cone obviously meet first within the narrow upper part of the cone and fusion progresses down the cone. A cone therefore bends slowly and gives time to study the effects.

Dr Seger followed the experiments on natural materials with compounded ones and devized a series of cones based upon a progression in the unity formula he had invented. The cones were given numbers and each was linked in a relative way with a given temperature. However Dr Seger was not concerned with making cones which would collapse at predetermined temperatures. He was interested in producing an accurate scale of refractoriness against which natural materials could be measured. This method of describing refractoriness is still used. A material is given a cone number rather than a temperature to describe the limit of its ability to withstand heat.

Dr Seger took his formula for feldspar as a starting point. This was $K_2O.Al_2O_3.6SiO_2$. He altered the alkaline oxide to include calcia and by reducing the potash content he was able to alter the alumina:silica ratio to 1:10. It is worth noting that this ratio is a common one in glazes. The alumina equivalent was now 0·6 molecules and the silica 6 molecules. This cone was therefore given the number 6 and corresponded to the slow maturing point of feldspar at 1200°C (2192°F) or a quicker firing to 1250°C (2282°F).

By adding 0·1 molecule of alumina and 1 molecule of silica at each step the progression of cones was numbered upwards in ones. Each step was subsequently found to relate approximately to 25°C (45°F). Dr Seger next worked downwards progressively to number 1 with additions of iron oxide and, later still, alterations were made to the alkaline oxides. To denote the change of alkaline oxide, the cones were given the suffix A with the number.

Later still, someone else extended the range below 1A and the numbers given were 01A, 02A etc. These numbers therefore increase down the temperature scale whereas Seger's numbers increased up the scale.

Also they do not refer to any molecular equivalents within the recipes but are merely numbers.

Different composition, different cone sizes and some different sections have been tried since the original series was produced. The original recipes have been altered to produce a more consistent step between the numbers and to achieve exact temperatures at end points after specified temperature increases. Specified increases vary from 20°C (36°F) per hour to 600°C (1080°F) per hour.

The types of cone at present available are Orton cones made in the USA, Seger cones made in West Berlin and Harrison cones made in the UK. Harrison cones were previously known as Staffordshire and British Standard cones. It should be noted that the suffix used on Harrison cones is not used in the same way as on the original Seger scale. The A and B suffixed numbers provide a separate scale of cones for the 950°C to 1310°C (1740°F to 2390°F) range. This scale conveniently overlaps the normal scale so that the combined scales provide a finer degree of indication approximately every 10°C (18°F). Miniature cones approximately 1 inch in height are available and are very useful in small kilns where space is limited.

CONES IN USE. Because a cone measures the heatwork rather than a temperature, it is a more accurate indicator of the completion of a firing than is an electric pyrometer. To make full use of a cone, it should be set at a slight angle into a base socket. A piece of refractory clay is excellent and holds a cone securely. The cone should be set at an angle of about 70° from the horizontal which ensures that it will collapse in that direction only. This is useful in a tight packing of pots when one can predict that it will collapse into a space and not touch a pot. Harrison and Seger cones should be set with the impressed number on the side that will be on top when the cones have collapsed. Orton cones are set to collapse over a side leaving the number on one of the two outside faces. The correct angle is 82° from the horizontal. After the firing it should be possible to read the cone number should there be any doubt as to the temperature reached.

Cones should be placed in the kiln thoughtfully if they are to be accurately used. Placing close to a spyhole during one firing and then deeply in the kiln for the next will not give consistent firings. The same position should be sought every time. Cones are not easy to see above 1200°C (2192°F) but silhouetting them against a space helps. In muffle kilns this is easy but where they are to be sheltered from the action of flames by a refractory box they cannot be so placed and are difficult to see. A mental note should be made of what the cone looks like in position. This will help in discerning it when the kiln is hot. Sometimes it is necessary to use a place close to the spyhole. Providing this is consistently done, the firings should be the same. Spyholes which are above halfway, in most kilns, tend to have hot air coming out of them. This may be a disadvantage for viewing but it prevents the cones from being chilled by the entry of cold air.

The cone is more important than a pot. To misposition the cone in order to get a pot in the kiln could result in spoiling the whole firing.

Cones are also used as a check on different parts of the kiln to assess what has happened. These cones are not visible during the firing but are recovered on drawing the kiln. Rings are also used for this purpose.

It is common practice when firing by visible cones to set three cones next to one another. One cone will be the one for the correct firing temperature and the others will be the consecutive ones above and below this. Thus there is a warning of about 20°C (36°F) when the first cone collapses and the potter knows that he must watch the second or firing cone in order to be accurate. The third cone should remain standing as proof that the kiln was not overfired. Cones that have not collapsed cannot be used again because they have been subjected to an amount of heat-work and would not be accurate.

If the spyhole gives a limited view, which happens in many small kilns, the three cones should be set in a piece of fireclay to collapse alternately opposite ways. See illustration. They are set so that they are all along

the line of sight through the spyhole. The softest cone is nearest the spyhole and a note should be made of which way the cones are expected to collapse.

Opinions vary amongst potters about the setting and use of cones. Some start the cone vertical whilst others start it at about 50°. Starting the cone in an already inclined position precipitates the end point. A variation of 10°C (18°F) could occur in extreme settings. Setting vertically can mean that when a cone does collapse it goes very quickly. This can be a nuisance because one may miss it. Some potters count the cone as down when it is pointing horizontally like a crooked finger whilst others wait until the tip is bent over and is level with the base. It seems sensible to count the end point of the cone as the latter because this will give a longer time in which to view the bending.

Consistency of use is however more important than method. Where more than one person is setting and firing a kiln, an agreed method in detail will be required to maintain consistency. In laboratory work the angle of setting and the length of cone which protrudes from the mount are carefully measured. The Orton Foundation has done much research in this field and has introduced the self-supporting cone to overcome some of these variables.

Continuous kiln. A kiln in which the fire never goes out. The other type of kiln is the intermittent kiln.

The first type of continuous kiln was presumably one used for raku but here there is intermittent setting and stoking. The first truly continuous kiln was the tunnel kiln at Vincennes in use for enamel firing for the second half of the 18th century. Since then tunnel kilns have been developed for all ceramic processes and are naturally economical but are efficient only for a continuous production. The ware passes on trucks or a moving hearth through the tunnel, the centre section of which is at the top temperature and of course remains so. An air movement from exit end to entry end is used. The air which cools the ware becomes preheated for the burning. The hot fumes from the burning preheat the ware entering.

The illustration of the tunnel kiln is diagrammatic only. A kiln would have many more than five trucks to be efficient.

The term continuous kiln is also used for kilns used for brick burning. See plan. In these the bricks are set in a continuous chamber or in a series of chambers linked together to form continuity. The fire is moved on from one section to the next. Again, exhaust gases

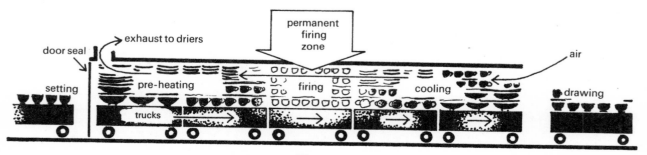

are used to preheat the ware etc. There is always one section being fired whilst the others are cooling, being drawn, set and preheated. These kilns are usually two straight chambers linked by rounded ends. The flues are down the centre and around the outside and are linked to a tall chimney. The fuel enters the burning

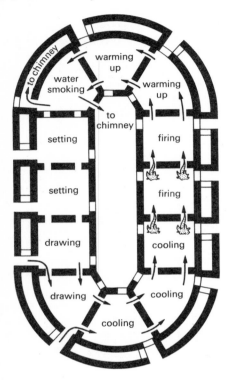

chambers from above. Kilns like this have been continuously firing for decades and any structural repairs are carried out during a cool phase after drawing. There are many variations on the four main types called Hoffmann, Belgian, Staffordshire and Lancashire kilns.

Contraction. Decrease in size due to temperature change. In pottery, this means a decrease in size with a drop in temperature, and it is important in the understanding of glaze fit and ovenware. Each mineral, clay, feldspar etc and each oxide involved in ceramics has its own rate of contraction. The overall result is proportionately cumulative and therefore the contraction rate of a piece of pottery can be altered by altering its chemical composition. See **Glaze fit**.

Contraction is exactly reversible by a reversal of the temperature change. The reversed result is called expansion. Contraction should not be confused with shrinkage which is usually assessed as a one-way decrease in size, starting with the drying of clay and bodies and ending with vitrification in the firing.

Convection. Transference of heat by moving air. In the kiln the convection agents are the flames or hot gases which move from the heat source and transfer their heat to objects against which they impinge.

Conversion factor. CF. A number used to discover the amount of oxide that will enter a fusion from a raw material. For example, the CF for cupric oxide (CuO) is 1·0 because all the material enters the fusion as CuO. Therefore 100 grams of cupric oxide would ultimately put into a glaze $100 \times 1·0 = 100$ grams of CuO.

However, the CF for cuprous oxide (Cu_2O) is 1·11 because this takes up oxygen during firing to increase its bulk and becomes CuO to enter the fusion. Therefore 100 grams of cuprous oxide would become $100 \times 1·11 = 111$ grams of CuO.

Compare this with copper carbonate ($CuCO_3$) the CF of which is 0·645 because there is a loss of carbon dioxide during firing. Therefore 100 grams of copper carbonate would become $100 \times 0·645 = 64·5$ grams of CuO.

There may be other reasons for wanting to use Cu_2O or $CuCO_3$ but assuming that the only reason is to get CuO to enter the fusion, then by using the CF it is possible to discover the most economical. If all three cost the same then Cu_2O is obviously the best value.

A list of conversion factors appears in the **Tables** in this book.

Copper carbonate. $CuCO_3$. (Also the basic carbonate $CuCO_3.Cu(OH)_2$.) A useful source of copper oxide for staining bodies and glazes. See **Copper oxide**.

The formulae of decomposition are:

$$CuCO_3.Cu(OH)_2 \xrightarrow{200°C} CuCO_3 + CuO + H_2O \uparrow$$

$$CuCO_3 \xrightarrow{500°C} CuO + CO_2$$

The conversion factor of copper carbonate is 0·645. This means that only $\frac{2}{3}$ of the copper carbonate becomes a staining oxide. The carbonate is therefore a less powerful stain than the oxide and more carbonate than oxide is needed to get equal staining power. The carbonate is therefore able to disperse through a body or glaze more uniformly than the oxide and is used where the slight speckle of the oxide is unwanted. This property is useful in brushwork decoration. To convert a copper oxide amount in a recipe to a copper carbonate amount, multiply by $1\frac{1}{2}$.

Copper lustre. A layer of metallic copper on the surface of the glaze. The effect is produced by heavy reduction of copper oxide in the glaze. There must be sufficient copper oxide in the glaze layer at the surface to present a full film of metal. The amount is upwards of 2%; sometimes as much as 8% is needed.

These glazes are usually soft and are fired oxidized to between 900°C and 1000°C (1652°F and 1832°F). The reduction takes place upon cooling. It needs to be intense but intermittent with periods when the kiln atmosphere is allowed to clear. The reduction and clearing in 5- to 15-minute cycles continue until the glaze has set around the dull red heat. This is easily achieved in small electric kilns by introducing slivers of wood through the spy-hole. The kiln has been switched off before reduction begins so there is little damage to the electric elements. The following glaze fired to 960°C (1760°F) gives good lustres both full copper and ruby. The ruby lustre requires less reduction and can be achieved with less copper carbonate. See **Ruby lustre**.

china clay	10
soft alkaline frit	70
lead bisilicate	16
copper carbonate	3
bentonite	1

There is also the copper lustre produced by transferring copper from a refractory paste on to the glaze surface. See **Transmutation**.

Copper ores. There are over ten workable copper ores in which the copper is combined with oxygen, sulphur, carbon and the metals iron, lead, tin and zinc. The oxide and carbonate ores are the result of weathering during deposition or exposure of a lode.

The oxide ores are tenorite and cuprite. Tenorite is cupric oxide and is a black colour. Cuprite is cuprous oxide and is a deep red colour.

The carbonate ores are malachite and azurite. Malachite is a bright emerald green colour and azurite is a bright turquoise blue.

Cuprite, malachite and azurite are easily distinguished in rock exposures and as small pieces amongst the wash-out debris of old mines. Tenorite, being black, is not easily found and has usually disintegrated. All are easily crushed by hand pestle and mortar, and provide colourant for glaze and brushwork.

The chemical formulae are:

tenorite	CuO	black
cuprite	Cu_2O	deep red
malachite	$CuCO_3.Cu(OH)_2$	bright green
azurite	$2CuCO_3.Cu(OH)_2$	bright blue

Copper oxides. Cupric oxide (CuO) and cuprous oxide (Cu_2O). Both oxides are strong colouring oxides in ceramic fusions. In the average oxidized glaze, 2% copper oxide gives a strong green and 5% gives a metallic black surface. In bodies the colour varies from fawn to green depending upon the amount of vitrification. Five per cent copper oxide in a slip is equivalent in colour to 2% in a glaze.

The metal copper occurs as native copper, but mostly it is combined with oxygen, carbon, sulphur and the metals iron, lead, tin and zinc. There are over ten workable copper ores of which the oxide and carbonate ores are the most beautiful and also useful to the potter. See **Copper ores**. Copper is used in electrical conductors, wires, terminals etc; as roofing; for pipes and boilers; and in the alloys brass, bronze, bell metal etc.

These metals are easily oxidized before or during a firing. Metal filings will give strong speckle stains to bodies and glazes. Potters' merchants market the two copper oxides and copper carbonate.

Copper was the first metal to be worked by man. Copper was known in Egypt in 3000 B.C. Copper oxide was used in early glazes giving the turquoise of Egyptian faience, the green-blue of Islamic pottery and the greens of Chinese lead-glazed tombware, glazed Roman cups and of English medieval jugs.

Cupric oxide (CuO) is black and is marketed and known as black copper oxide. Cuprous oxide (Cu_2O) is a deep red, sometimes a dull and brownish colour. It is known as red copper oxide and copper sub-oxide. Copper carbonate ($CuCO_3$) is pale green: the basic carbonate is a deeper green. They are both called green copper carbonate and sometimes erroneously green copper oxide.

All the above oxidize to black copper oxide and give a green colour when dissolved in glass. Amounts up to 2% give increasingly strong greens. Five per cent gives a black which so fills the glaze that the surface is metallic. The black copper oxide will often come off the surface onto the fingers when a black copper glaze is touched. Since this oxide is soluble in fruit juices, glazes strongly stained by copper oxide should not be used for food because the copper is poisonous.

The colour of the green varies according to the flux or combination of fluxes in the glaze. Rich grass greens varying from bluish to yellowish occur with the main fluxes: calcia, boric oxide, potash, magnesia and baria. In matt glazes from the last two the colour is brownish. Turquoise blues are possible with soda and lithia whilst lead oxide gives soft apple greens. Combinations with iron oxide give excellent yellow-greens and with cobalt oxide, blue-greens. When copper oxide is present in extremely small amounts, bright yellows sometimes occur. The colour is fickle and not easy to reproduce.

Copper oxide dissolves readily in the molten glaze. It is therefore not easy to contain it within a decorative motif. The copper oxide from a slip or from brushwork will bleed into the surrounding glaze. The effect can be very decorative but it can be a surprise if unexpected. In spite of the ease with which the copper oxide dissolves and spreads, the black copper oxide is still a strong stain and the particles tend to give a speckled colour in all but the most runny glazes. Copper carbonate, which is less powerful in colouring, is used to overcome this speckle.

COPPER OXIDE IN REDUCTION. Copper oxide is very susceptible to changes in the kiln atmosphere. It is easily reduced from black to red state. The oxygen is withdrawn from the black copper oxide by the oxygen-greedy carbon monoxide. See **Reduction**. The equation is:

$$2CuO + CO \longrightarrow Cu_2O + CO_2 \uparrow$$

A green glaze can thereby be turned into a red glaze. The red colour tends to be brownish or purplish and rather opaque if there is 1% or more of copper oxide in the glaze.

The brightest reds are achieved by the reduction of glazes which in the oxidized state would be hardly coloured by the copper oxide. The amount involved is less than 0·5%. These bright reds, called flambé and *sang-de-boeuf*, are the result of colloidal copper. See **Colloid**. The copper oxide is subjected to complete reduction to metal state:

$$Cu_2O + CO \longrightarrow Cu_2 + CO_2 \uparrow$$

The third type of copper oxide glaze is the lustre. See **Copper lustre**.

Copper sub-oxide. Copper (I) oxide. Cuprous oxide. Cu_2O. Red copper oxide. The term sub-oxide is used to denote the fact that a deliberate reduction of the oxygen content has been made from the state of highest oxidation.

Cornish stone. Cornwall stone. China stone. Carolina stone. Pegmatite. Graven. Gowen. Manx stone. Meldon stone. Growan. Petuntse. Amakusa. D.F. stone. A feldspathoid which is used as a flux in bodies and as a major constituent in glazes. It contains feldspar, quartz, kaolinite, mica and a small percentage of fluorspar. It melts in the range 1150°C to 1300°C (2102°F to 2372°F) to a stiff glass which is opaque with suspended fine bubbles. It is often used as a substitute for feldspar because it introduces a number of alkalis: potash, soda, calcia and magnesia, which give additional properties.

A few Swedish feldspathoids approximate the composition of cornish stone and are used as substitutes when the original is unobtainable.

Cornish stone is not a single mineral like potash feldspar or whiting and thus it cannot be given a chemical formula. It is a crushed igneous rock with similar properties to those of feldspar but varying greatly in actual composition. Hence its many names, some of which are linked with a single quarry source. It can be described as a complex and variable alumino-silicate closely related to the feldspars and considered by many potters as a mixed feldspar with impurities. Cornish stone is important in that however variable it may be, it is almost free from iron and thus is nearly white. The purple variety of cornish stone is coloured by fluorspar but this burns to white (colourless) also.

Cornish stone originated as an igneous rock of the acidic type, like granite, or possibly as a sedimentary silicate rock which underwent granitization. The result in either case was a crystalline rock containing feldspar, mica and free quartz with often some fluorspar. The slow decomposition (kaolinization) of this rock has started when it is considered to be cornish stone and it is therefore slightly softer and easier to grind than a feldspar.

Such a complex and variable material as cornish stone cannot be given a single unity formula. Each specimen can be given an analysis from which a formula can be calculated. An acceptable unity formula follows but it must be understood that this can only be accurate for one specimen, the analysis for which is also given.

$$\left.\begin{array}{l} 0·42\ Na_2O \\ 0·25\ K_2O \\ 0·31\ CaO \\ 0·02\ MgO \end{array}\right\} 0·92\ Al_2O_3 \quad 7·6\ SiO_2$$

SiO_2	72·92	K_2O	3·83
TiO_2	0·02	CaO	2·08
Al_2O_3	14·95	MgO	0·09
Fe_2O_3	0·05	CaF_2	1·07
Na_2O	4·13	Loss	0·86

The foregoing specimen would be considered a 'hard purple' variety with similar properties in a fusion to those of a soda feldspar. It melts over the range 1180°C to 1240°C (2156°F to 2264°F). To show the wide range of cornish stone, a unity formula for a 'soft white' specimen is also given. Notice that the alumina and silica contents are very high, making this a harder material to melt and correspondingly stiffer. It melts over the range 1250°C to 1350°C (2282°F to 2462°F).

$$\left.\begin{array}{l} 0·07\ Na_2O \\ 0·49\ K_2O \\ 0·36\ CaO \\ 0·08\ MgO \end{array}\right\} 1·7\ Al_2O_3 \quad 12·0\ SiO_2$$

Sample unity formulae are sometimes given with alumina unity, a method reserved for clays and body materials to establish comparison with kaolinite. If a sample formula has $1·0\ Al_2O_3$, it is wise to total the alkalis as a check on which unity has been used.

The varieties of cornish stone are due to the different parent rocks and to progressive stages of decomposition whereby the feldspathic content becomes clay mineral (kaolinite) and quartz. During this process, the alkaline (fluxing) content becomes soluble and is washed away. The fluorspar, which gives the purplish colour, is also dissolved and removed. In the early stages of decomposition, the rock is hard and purplish in colour. It contains more feldspar, and thus more flux, and it will melt at a lower temperature than the rock in its later stages of decomposition. As the rock decomposes, it becomes physically softer and whiter but its melting point becomes higher (harder). Thus the anomaly, which is mentioned under Hard (2), is that hard purple cornish stone is softer (melts at a lower temperature) than soft white cornish stone. The hard purple is therefore the stronger flux for bodies and is easier to melt in glazes.

The side effects from the release of fluorine gas from purple stones are deterioration of kiln linings, etc and harmful gas in the workshop. See **Fluorspar**. Suppliers

76

of cornish stone now process some by flotation to re-move the fluorspar and also the ferreous micas. The defluorinated cornish stone is known as D.F. stone.

Cornish stone is partly kaolinized and contains 5 to 12% kaolinite. It therefore responds to flocculation and deflocculation when in a glaze slop and assists glaze grip before firing. However the clay-like property can also cause pre-firing cracks which give crawling. This occurs with a glaze which already contains a high pro-portion of clay in the recipe.

Paradoxically, cornish stone is sometimes sub-stituted for some feldspar in a glaze recipe to cure crawling. Here its property in molten state is required. Although similarly stiff in molten state to a pure feld-spar, cornish stone has not the same high surface ten-sion because of the interaction of its more numerous alkalis. This wide spread of alkalis ensures a gradual maturity and a wetting action when molten.

Costrel bottle. A bottle with lugs near the neck by which it can be slung on a thong, carried by the fingers, or held for drinking. It originated in post-classical Greece, was also used in Persia and the form had reached China by the 6th century. There are various forms; some are tall, some fat, some flattened and some barrel shaped. They were used by travellers and harvesters until recent times. See also **Pilgrim flask**.

Cottle. Cockle. Cockling. Expendable wall of card, plastic or clay to contain poured plaster until it has set.

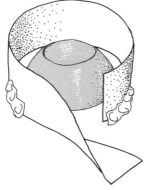

Cow's lip. The genuine lip of a cow, cured and used as a piece of leather by press moulders. The rubber kidney has rendered the cow's lip almost obsolete.

Crack. (1) To make the first opening of a kiln after firing. As the kiln cools it is clammed up at red heat to give uniform cooling over the dunting period. It is cracked when dunting and other thermal shock hazards are passed.

Crack. (2) An unwanted break in a piece of pottery. It should always be remembered that cracks are caused by physical stress and that some stress is always present in a pot resulting from the expansion, contraction and shrinkage the pot has experienced. Cracks occur when the stress is greater than the pot can withstand.

General points in the analysis of any crack are as follows:

1. The position of the crack on the pot is related to the form of the pot. The design of the pot controls the form and therefore the stresses. A badly designed pot, with awkward angles etc of unequal section, is likely to crack although it may be made from ideal materials. A well-designed pot made from infamously awkward materials may survive. Two pots which are similar but not identical may be on each side of an unknown safety line. One may crack; the other remain sound.

2. If one takes liberties in pottery-making, one must expect differing results. Potters talk about good-natured clays and well-disposed glazes but this only emphasises that they can be otherwise. A variation in body, form, method of making, method and speed of drying, firing temperature, firing cycles, slip or glaze will result in a variation of product. The variety may include a crack.

3. Cracks in raw ware arise from faults in the making of the pots, and these can be overcome however diffi-cult the clay may be to deal with. The design, that is, the form, is all important and achieving the design means working with the clay and not against its nature. Uni-form consistency of clay, before and after making, uniform thicknesses and uniform drying are the ideal principles.

4. In finished ware one should look where the crack started to understand when it happened. The wider end of the crack was the starting point. If the crack started at the rim, the fault is likely to have been some-where at the raw stage. If in the base, the crack usually occurred in the firing and could be caused by the materials, the type of firing and the type of setting used.

5. The edges and faces of the crack are another indication of when the crack occurred. Frayed edges and rough faces on the two sides show that the crack occurred relatively slowly and probably at the making and drying stages even though it may be that the crack did not show until after firing. A glaze on such a crack will be seen to have rolled back from the edge and rounded itself. On the other hand, if the edge of the crack is sharp and the faces of the crack are smooth,

the crack is a kiln crack. If glaze around the crack has smoothed itself and is rounded at the edge, the crack must have occurred early in the firing and the glaze during fusion crawled back from the edge. If the glaze is sharp-edged, the crack must have occurred after the glaze had set during the later stages of cooling.

6. Whether a crack is hairline or wide is a matter of amount of stress. A differentiation should not be so much in width as in whether there is sideways displacement as well as parting. Fine dunts may be undiscernible but are discovered by touch when the finger catches upon an edge. In this case there is a displacement. Displacements are usually firing cracks. Cracks which are partings without displacement, even if apparently happening in the glaze firing, are usually from an earlier process, e.g. a biscuit dunt or a drying crack.

The illustrations show typical cracks and a brief comment is made on the causes. The reader is often referred to other items in the book for details.

CRACK A. The crack is at right angles to the rim and is wider at the rim and peters out below.

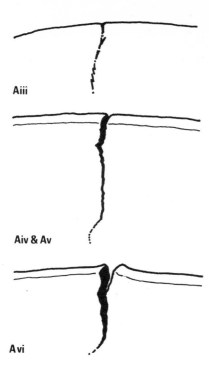

Aiii

Aiv & Av

Avi

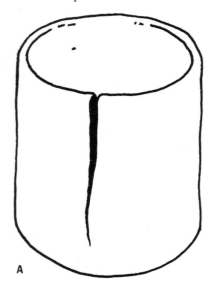

A

Crack A in raw ware :

1. The design is poor giving a structurally weak pot. Probably the rim is too thin to contain the stresses in the remainder of the pot.

2. Method of working was incorrect for the clay used. Probably the drying was too rapid and unequal.

3. If the crack is in newly-thrown clay and shows whilst still on the wheel or soon after removing, it is likely to be insufficiently prepared clay or possibly tired clay or over-short clay. If the clay has had extra sand or grog added this may have made the clay too short for the type of throwing used. This crack has the appearance of a fibrous tear. Illustration A iii.

4. If the crack is in the rim of a plate or dish, especially a press-moulded dish, the clay was probably over-wet unequally in some way. Also the drying which fol-

lowed was too rapid for the clay to equalize its moisture content. Illustration A iv.

5. If a slip coating has been poured or brushed inside the dish it was done when the dish was too dry. Illustration A v.

6. If a slip coating was used and the dish was too damp then some distortion will have taken place. Illustration A vi.

7. If the crack is hairline, it could be that the pot has been waiting for firing over a period which involved dry weather followed by wet weather. The resulting crack is a result of readsorption and the phenomenon is described under **Readsorption** in this book.

Crack A in biscuit and glazed ware :

8. The crack is probably the development of one that was latent at the raw stage. The stress at the raw stage may have ruptured the clay without visible signs at the surface. Such cracks are called latent or dormant cracks and no matter how careful the firing they are forced to develop. Mishandling of raw ware when packing a biscuit kiln may have induced cracks, but the cause should first be sought as poor design, rapid drying, unequal drying, incorrect method and readsorption.

9. Stress in the raw ware which could be successfully contained by careful drying and firing may have been over-emphasised by too rapid a firing in the early stages of biscuit.

CRACK B. The crack is at right angles to the rim but is wider below the rim and almost undiscernible at the rim. It starts at the base or some other feature.

Crack B in raw ware :

1. Very rare but could result from a thin base and unequal drying.

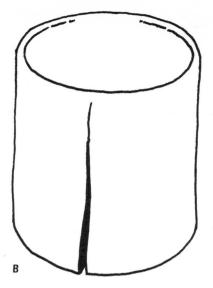

B

Crack B in biscuit ware and glazed ware :

2. The crack is a cooling dunt caused by the crystalline silica in the body. The crystalline silica undergoes an inversion or change of crystal structure. This is accompanied by a change in size which proportionately affects the body of the pot but not the glaze. Stress within the body, or between body and glaze, may be sufficient to rupture the pot. See **Dunting, cooling dunts**.

CRACK C. The crack is at right angles to the rim and the sides are almost parallel. The crack originates at a star-shattering in the base. See crack F.

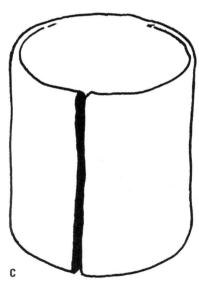

C

Crack C in raw ware :

1. The wall and the base are unequal in thickness, with the base probably too thin for the pot. It is also likely that the base was left too wet after throwing and that drying followed immediately and was too rapid. This could occur where a wet pot was left on a very absorbent surface.

Crack C in biscuit ware :

2. The crack is a development of one that already existed at the raw stage.

Crack C in glazed ware :

3. This type of crack is most common on glazed ware and is a cooling dunt caused by a thick glaze layer inside the pot. It does not matter that the glaze is crazed and therefore one would expect it not to force the pot body apart. There existed a point during cooling when the glaze was too large for the pot surrounding it. It is most likely to occur where the pot is glazed inside only and the base is thinner than the walls.

CRACK D. The crack is clean and sharp-edged. It divides the pot into two almost equal pieces. It is common on stoneware and porcelain bowls, especially re-fires, where it is discovered on opening the kiln. The parts are unlikely to fit together perfectly because distorted.

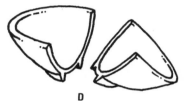

D

Crack D in raw ware :

1. A crack of this sort is virtually impossible because cracks in raw ware tend to avoid the foot rim.

Crack D in biscuit ware :

2. A rare possibility of a cooling dunt caused by a cold draught on an inverted bowl.

Crack D in glazed ware :

3. The clean break through body and glaze shows that the crack took place after the glaze had set. It is classified as a cooling dunt caused by the crystalline silica in the body. The crystalline silica undergoes a change in size and proportionately changes the size of the body. The glaze, which is not crystalline, does not change and stress results. Also, the difference in thermal contraction between body and glaze without consideration of crystalline silica inversions causes stress. See **Dunting, cooling dunts** and **Silica inversions**.

4. In consideration of the above stress between body and glaze there is a factor which exaggerates the danger of a crack occurring. It is the over densification of the body. Overfiring the pot brings the body nearer to its total vitrification point, makes it more brittle and hence, less able to absorb the stress. Refiring pots, even to the same temperature, continues the vitrification process beyond its original point. Already dense ware is forced to be adversely affected and become over-glassy and brittle. During the firing, a bowl is likely to distort and go oval which concentrates the stresses upon cooling.

5. An over-dense body tends to fuse itself to the kiln shelf unless a very efficient bat wash is used. The

foot rim becomes fastened to the shelf upon cooling and, since the shelf is likely to contract less than the pot body, the pot is torn apart starting at the foot.

CRACK E. The crack is a hairline crack which runs across the base in a straight line. It almost invariably continues up the side of the pot at least as far as the thickness of the base. It may continue up both sides of the pot. It is closely related to cracks D and F and occurs on glazed ware only. It is not to be confused with cracks H and G which are more commonly confined to the base.

Crack E in glazed ware :

1. The glaze is obviously too big for the body so that the base of the pot is trying to squeeze the glaze. If the stress is great enough the body ruptures itself. The crack would be classified as a cooling dunt resulting from the different contraction rates of the body and glaze. See **Dunting, cooling dunts, Glaze fit** and **Silica inversions.**

2. If the crack occurs months or even years after the pot has been made, it is likely to be called the result of thermal shock. The cause of the stress is still the difference in contraction rates between body and glaze but not directly attributable to crystalline silica. See **Thermal shock** and **Glaze fit.**

CRACK F. The drawing shows star shattering of the base seen from underneath. The actual pattern of the star varies considerably but there is usually a main crack with subsidiary ones at approximate right angles. There is often a fifth crack making the star as in the example shown.

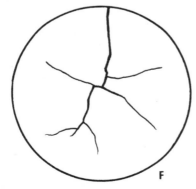

Crack F in raw ware :

1. If the base of a thrown pot is too thin in relation to the walls, it could crack in this way.

2. If the base of a thrown pot was left over-wet and then possibly dried quickly the stress of (1) would be exaggerated.

Crack F in biscuit ware :

3. Cracks in biscuit would be developed from cracks in the raw ware and in this case should have been discernible at raw stage.

Crack F in glazed ware :

4. The star is closely related to cracks D and E. In this case the glaze layer inside is usually thick, even thicker than the base of the pot. The fluxing action of the glaze on the thin base makes the base almost vitrified and hence brittle. In cooling, if the body contracts more than the glaze, even by a small amount, it is too brittle and weak to compress the glaze. The body ruptures and the crack probably continues up the side to the rim as at crack C.

CRACK G. The crack is straight or nearly so. In most cases it is related to crack H. In raw ware and biscuit, it is only a hair crack but in glazed ware there is likely to be some slight sideways displacement as if one side of the crack had curled up and the other side down.

Crack G in raw ware :

1. The crack is the result of unequal drying in some way. For example, the pot was not cut from the wheel-head after throwing but was allowed to dry on the wheel-head or bat. The pot was cut under but not lifted clear from the wheel-head or bat. The pot was lifted clear but was placed on a pot board that was not sufficiently porous to allow the base to dry. These cracks can sometimes be patched at the dry stage by using some very soft and sticky body clay.

Crack G in biscuit ware and glazed ware :

2. The crack is really a drying crack and occurred much earlier although being only a hair crack it was not discovered at the raw stage. In glazed ware the crack sometimes goes the whole way through the base. In this case the glaze will have rolled back from the crack with rounded edges or, if the glaze is very runny, it may have run through the crack and appeared underneath. The crack, if small, can sometimes be patched at biscuit stage with biscuit stopping or pitchers. This is a ground fired body which is mixed with water to form a paste that can be pushed into the crack. The stopping should be allowed to dry before glazing. Stopping of

cracks after biscuit is effective only if the following glaze firing is at a lower temperature than or only slightly more than the biscuit temperature.

CRACK H. This base crack is known as an S crack because it often forms an S across the base. The two illustrations show the crack as seen from (a) inside the pot and (b) underneath. It occurs in thrown ware. The crack, if seen without the glaze covering, looks more like a tear than a sudden crack. Where there is a glaze, it may or may not have flowed into or away from the crack, dependent upon the properties of the glaze and shrinkage cycle of the clay. In these cracks the glaze is no indication. The character of the crack itself is sufficient evidence.

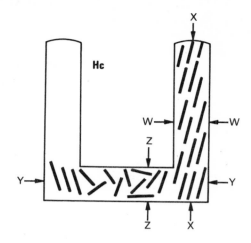

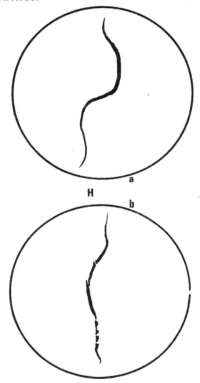

Crack H in raw ware, biscuit ware and glazed ware. The cause is the same throughout. It is the unequal shrinkage of the clay in the base and walls of the pot. Shrinkage starts as the clay dries and continues as the pot fires and is matured or vitrified. The shrinkage is equal in all directions only when the clay particles are haphazardly mixed. This does not happen in a pot. The clay particles are disc-like plates which align themselves across the pressure. There is always some pressure in a pot wall caused by the fingers inside and out. The clay shrinks proportionately to the gaps between the particles and therefore if the particles are all lying in one direction there will be a concentration of the shrinkage. In the diagram H(c) the clay particles are vastly enlarged in a section of a pot to show how there are as many gaps between particles through the wall of a pot as in its height. In this exaggerated case the shrinkage on the pot wall

thickness (w) would equal the shrinkage in height (x). The slight angle of the particles is caused by the lifting action of the throwing. See **Clay, physics**.

No harm comes to the pot wall by this shrinkage, in fact, it is strengthened. The base should be similarly subjected to pressure across its thickness resulting in the alignment of particles in a flat way across the base. However in the diagram the base has not been subjected to sufficient pressure. The particles are haphazardly arranged and show only a slight tendency to alignment from the pressure received at the opening up stage of throwing. This pressure has only emphasized an arrangement of the particles vertically because the pressure was outwards from the centre. Shrinkage on this base will be greater at y than at z. The result will be an S crack.

To overcome the S cracks requires a change of throwing technique to include a compression of the base. The term compression is used in this sense. Some potters beat the bases of the pots as soon as the pots can be inverted but this is likely to be too late for most clays. Although damaging to modern wheel bearings, the age-old custom of throwing the clay down hard onto the wheel head may help. Holes in wheel-head bats are a place where pressure can be lost and can be a starting point for an S crack. Most trouble is experienced when throwing many pots from one lump. It is very difficult to compress the base sufficiently. A technique has to be developed whereby pressure downwards inside the pot is met by a pressure upwards from a squeezing action of the other hand. These pots should be turned when fairly soft and the base beaten before turning.

With large flat plates and dishes it may be necessary to beat the inside of the base with a stone, piece of wood or the hand before finishing the throwing. Also running the fingers towards the centre as well as outwards helps. Traditionally the thrown oven dishes were often made oval by cutting a leaf-shaped piece from the base and pushing the joint together. Extra clay was stuck onto the join and beaten into place. The extra compression thus gained improved the strength of the base and overcame the S cracks. Also by cutting across the base, the centripetal base stress was hindered from development in the thermal shocks of use. An oval dish has the stresses connected with only the lesser width but has the stability of the greater width. See also cracks I and K.

CRACK I. The crack is a hairline around the base seen from the underside but probably invisible inside. At its worst it forms a complete circle and the base falls out. However this is more common with crack J which is slightly different and more drastic. Crack I appears on ovenware, both glazed and unglazed, and is often noticed because it has stained. It will be seen to extend itself slowly with further use of the piece of pottery.

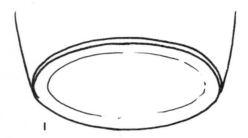

Crack I in fairly dense ware both glazed and unglazed. The crack is caused by thermal shock. There is probably some difference in thickness between base and wall which results in unequal expansion and contraction. Repeated subjection to the stress in daily oven use extends the weakness. See **Thermal shock.**

CRACK J. The crack is circular, or almost, and has an extension at right angles which goes outwards to the edge of the foot and part way, or all the way, up the side of the pot. The crack occurs quickly with a loud noise, or is discovered on opening the kiln. The circular base piece drops out of the pot. This is most common on plates and dishes.

Crack J in glazed ware. There is stress between body and glaze. The glaze is too large for the body and ruptures the body that is compressing it. See **Dunting, cooling dunts.** It occurs where the glaze is too thick and has collected inside around the base because the base is slightly humped.

CRACK K. There are two hairline cracks seen from underneath. They describe an incomplete oval which would overlap the base. The cracks, or just one of them, appear on ovenware after use.

Crack K in fairly dense ware both glazed and unglazed.

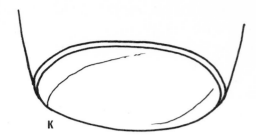

The crack is caused by thermal shock and is similar to crack I. See crack I and **Thermal shock.**

CRACK L. The first illustration shows the underside view of a plate. Haircracks, at first not noticeable, result in rectangular pieces breaking from the rim. In

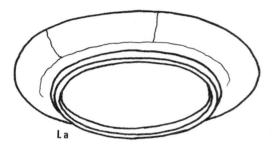

the second illustration the haircracks do not reach the rim but form a set of cracks like brickwork which give that part of the pot a deadness although the rim may still ring when struck.

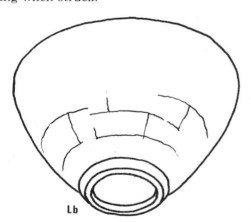

Crack L in biscuit ware:
1. The crack is a dunt caused by cooling the biscuit too quickly or firing it insufficiently to give it strength. See **Dunting, biscuit dunts.** Plates that are piled one inside the other, not rim to rim, will hold their heat around the foot rims when the outer rims cool. A thin plate on a thick kiln shelf is also unable to cool uniformly.

Crack L in glazed ware:
2. The crack is probably more than a haircrack in a few places and results from a biscuit dunt that was unnoticed at biscuit stage. At biscuit stage some dunts do

not penetrate through the pot. A slip coating could dunt separately from the pot body and *vice versa*.

CRACK M. A sharp-edged crack with sideways displacement. This occurs on glazed ware and is discovered on opening the kiln, soon after and on rare occasions up to a year later. The crack is accompanied by a loud noise as it quickly ruptures the pot. It may not reach the rim.

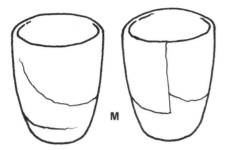

Crack M in glazed ware, especially dense stoneware. There is stress between the body and glaze which cannot be absorbed. The body is compressing the glaze but the glaze is strong and does not flake away as in crack O. The glaze remains as one piece because it is well attached to a dense and finely-grained body. The body therefore ruptures and as it does so there is sideways displacement or strain to accommodate the stress. This displacement ruptures the brittle glaze also. See **Dunting, cooling dunt**. It is likely to happen with stoneware bodies which include cristobalite. See **Silica inversions**.

CRACK N. The cracks are hairlines but, where glazed, are sharp edged and can often be felt before seen because there is a very slight displacement. They appear above, below or along a glaze roll.

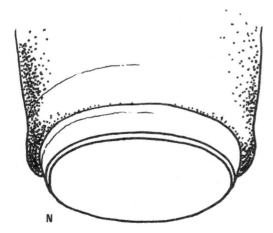

Crack N in glazed ware. The crack is a dunt caused by the difference in expansion/contraction rates of body and glaze. The stress between the body and glaze over most of the pot is satisfactorily absorbed by the body-glaze layer. However at the roll there is an exaggerated stress which is sufficient to cause the dunt. Sometimes

part of the glaze roll will shiver also. See **Dunting, cooling dunt, Glaze fit** and **Shivering**.

CRACK O. This is a crack through the glaze whereby a thin flake of glaze leaves the pot. The flake is sharp edged and if there is a strong body-glaze layer it will have carried with it some of the body. It occurs on rims, edges of handles, relief decoration and throwing marks.

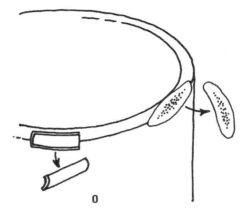

Crack O in glazed ware. There is stress between body and glaze that cannot be absorbed by the body-glaze layer. The flaking is called shivering and shelling and in the case of shelling may have started before the glaze was fired. The lack of bond between body and glaze, or the lack of sufficient body-glaze layer is often caused by over-sponging of rims and edges. Over-sponging takes away the fine clay and leaves behind the sand. If this sand is not fused in the body-glaze layer it presents a weak structure with no elasticity to absorb the stress. See **Shivering** and **Shelling**.

CRACK P. A network of cracks forms a lace-like pattern in the glaze. This is called crazing. It usually develops after the pot is taken from the kiln but in extreme cases occurs during cooling. On opaque glazes it is often difficult to see and only shows if the glaze is misted by condensation or becomes stained.

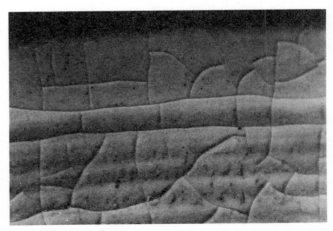

Crazing results when the glaze is under tension and cracks to relieve the stress. See **Crazing** and **Glaze fit**.

CRACK Q. A series of short cracks which divide at the ends to reach into spaces surrounded by other cracks. They occur in slip coatings and are seen at raw stage, biscuit stage and very occasionally through a transparent glaze. They can be one cause of the crawling of the covering glaze. Also glazes which contain a high proportion of clay, e.g. slip glazes and some dolomite glazes, may crack in this way and later crawl during the firing. See **Crawling**. In extreme cases, the slip may peel and lift from the body.

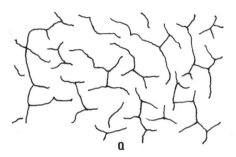

Crack Q in raw ware and biscuit ware. The crack is caused by the drying shrinkage of the clay slip. The slip shrinks more than the clay body which it covers because it is too rich (over-plastic and too fine), applied too thickly, applied when the body was too dry, or dried too quickly. Small cracks rarely show through a glaze. The cracks can be overcome by the addition of some non-plastic material to the slip, e.g. sand, flint, feldspar, pitchers, or by the use of a thinner layer and more controlled drying.

Cracks Q should not be confused with the separate crazing of a slip and with the separate dunting of a slip. The three types of cracks can be identified by their different patterns.

CRACK R. These are defects on finished ware and they are included for completeness. They occur, not necessarily together, on glazed ware.

1. This is a spit-out caused by foreign matter in the body. The object is usually a small stone which decomposes in the firing leaving an unfused spot which is porous. The porous spot absorbs moisture from the air, expands and pushes off a flake of glaze and probably part of the body. This occurs after the pot is taken from the kiln. The foreign matter can sometimes be seen at the biscuit stage and if small can be dug out and the hole stopped with ground biscuited body.

2. The spots are called pin holes. They are small craters left by escaping gases. The glaze is probably stiff and contains a high proportion of alumina. It therefore requires a slightly longer firing to give sufficient time for the glaze to heal over. Alternatively a slightly higher firing may be used but this could result in more pin holes if the higher temperature boils or decomposes one of the glaze constituents. Alteration of the glaze recipe to reduce the alumina content slightly should be considered as a long-term policy.

3. The radiating lines on the glaze surface may be quite tiny or may cover an area $\frac{1}{4}$-inch across. The defect is called crow's feet and occurs on fairly stiff glazes which have difficulty in wetting the body which they cover. Stiff glazes with a strong surface tension do not easily soak into the body or flow into hollows or bridge over large particles. Crow's feet often form around specks of grog and sand on the body surface. Over-sponging, which takes away the fine clay and leaves the coarse clay, sand and grog, is one cause of crow's feet. Under-firing of the glaze is also a cause, because it does not allow the glaze to fuse fully and cover the coarse spot. The use of too much binder in the form of a glue or other organic material on the biscuit or in the glaze can also cause crow's feet. Loss of fine surface by sponging or bad fettling is the usual cause. A reduction in grain size of sand or grog, or the introduction of a ball clay into the body, or a slight extra fusion of the glaze may also be required.

CRACK S. The crack is where a handle joins a pot, either at the top or the bottom. It is called 'springing'. All handles, lugs etc are subject to springing. It originates in the making but may not be seen until after the glaze firing.

Crack S in raw ware, biscuit ware and glazed ware. The handle was incorrectly joined for one or more of the following reasons:

The join was made too wet.

The join was not made wet enough. (Less common than above.)

The join was dried too quickly.

The pot was too dry when the handle was attached.

The handle became too wet during attachment.

The handle clay was too stiff and was subjected to stress during attachment.

The handle was distorted during drying, causing stress.

The handle clay was different from the body clay and was therefore subject to a different shrinkage. A handle which shrinks less than the body of a pot can usually survive better than one which shrinks more.

CRACK T. The crack is a break through the handle other than at the joint. It often occurs in the lower half of a pulled handle as in the illustration. The latent crack occurs during the making but can remain undetected until it shows as two parted ends after the glaze firing.

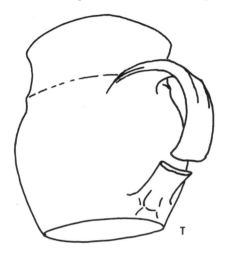

Crack T in raw ware, biscuit ware and glazed ware. There are two possible and related causes. The clay used for the handle was too weak, possibly because it had become tired by being overworked in making the handle. The handle was too thin for the type of clay used.

Crackle. Crackelle. Craquelle. A craze in the glaze used as a decorative feature. On some Chinese porcelains the first long craze lines were filled with a stain before the minor craze lines in between were established. The first cracks are inevitably wide but close as the

stress is eased by further minor cracks. It is thus possible to choose the best time to stain the craze to show the network of lines to its best decorative effect as a crackle.

Crackle is a feature of raku ware. A white glaze shows this to advantage after smoking in sawdust. The example shown is by Pat Collins-Jones.

There is a method known as melt-crackle in which the glaze is first underfired and allowed to craze. Colouring oxides are rubbed into the craze when it achieves a desired pattern, then the pot is refired to fire the glaze to its correct temperature. The craze shows finally as lines which are inlaid stains.

It is possible to produce one crackle network over another by the use of two separate glazes. The two glazes may have completely different patterns of crackle and the effect can be an interesting lacework.

Most potters consider the glaze cracks as a technical fault and call the phenomenon crazing. This is dealt with under **Crazing**.

Crank. A refractory support for plates, tiles etc in glost and enamel firings. By the use of a crank rather than separate shelves, it is possible to more than double the weight of ware in a given kiln space.

With one type of crank, the plates and tiles rest upon projections (pins) which support the ware close to its edge. Thus this type is not suitable for maturing bodies which would sag. In the other type of crank, the crank is built from a series of separate chairs, tables or thin shelves which support each plate by its base.

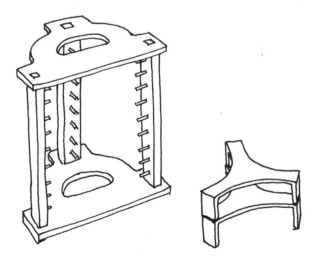

CRANK MIXTURE. Fireclay or other refractory clay used for making cranks. It is well grogged and sometimes sanded. It is finer in texture than sagger marl and chamotte clay, and is often used as the basis of raku bodies and coarse stoneware bodies.

Crawling. Creeping. Rolling. Ruckling. Beading. The glaze defect characterized by the way the glaze parts and rolls back on itself leaving a bald patch of body. The defect may happen on a part of a pot such as an edge or where a pre-firing crack in the glaze occurred. Or it may happen in small patches all over a pot, or on the part where there is a slip. Sometimes it is very decorative although unwanted. If the glaze rolls itself into separate globules it is called beading. See **Beading**. The photograph shows a semi-opaque glaze which has crawled over a black slip to produce an interesting, if unintentional effect.

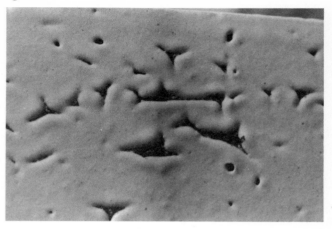

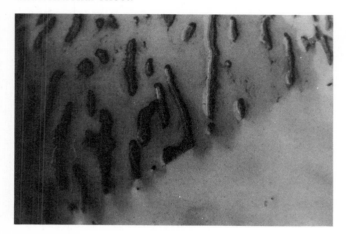

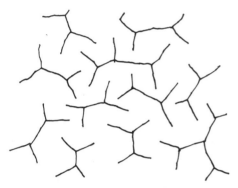

Glazes which crawl have a high surface tension and are viscous when molten. A high alumina content makes a glaze viscous. Tin oxide and other opacifiers tend to increase surface tension and thus encourage crawling. Zinc oxide is a particular culprit because it causes pre-firing shrinkage and pulls a glaze together during fusion. See **Surface tension**.

Glazes crawl away from a pre-firing crack in the glaze layer which occurs at a sharp edge, on a throwing ring and where slip or other decoration meets plain pot, etc. The crack is often caused by the shrinkage of the glaze. When the glaze dries after application it is liable to shrink slightly, especially if it contains some clay. Over a uniform area the cracks will be many and small, such cracks may 'heal' during fusion. But on a variable surface, the shrinkage is liable to concentrate into larger areas pulling open a wide single crack. This can be seen where the glaze is thick, for example, around a handle joint.

To cure crawling, it may be necessary to alter a glaze recipe. A glaze which contains a high proportion of clay can be altered in a few ways: some of the clay can be replaced by feldspar; some can be calcined to render it non-plastic; and some or all can be replaced by a clay of low shrinkage. Some china clays are available which have a low shrinkage from wet to dry. This type should be used. With reference to calcining, zinc oxide gives far less trouble if it is calcined with some of the china clay before adding both to the glaze batch.

The second photograph shows another enlarged detail of crawling. This example was caused by pre-firing shrinkage of a dolomite glaze containing 25% of china clay. The typical lines of crawling due to shrinkage are simplified in the accompanying drawing.

A pre-firing crack is the commonest cause of crawling but another cause is greasy and dusty biscuit which prevents the glaze from adhering properly before firing. Also the over-grinding of a glaze can make it too fluffy to adhere properly to the biscuit. Similarly the firing of ware which is still wet from glazing causes steam from the body to lift and loosen the glaze. The loosened glaze, like the glaze over dust or grease, crawls when it melts. This crawling is also called lifting. When a viscous glaze melts, it prefers to stick to itself rather than wet the body and stick to that. As a general rule, lead glazes are more wetting in their fusion than leadless glazes and are therefore less likely to crawl.

Crawling occurs on all types of ware and is not a particular fault of earthenware or stoneware. It is common with Bristol glazes, celadons and borocalcite glazes. With Bristol glazes it is the zinc oxide content which causes the crawling. With celadons it is the high alumina content. Chinese Sung celadons are often crawled and this may also be due to the prolonged grinding the potters are reputed to have given their celadon glazes. Borocalcite glazes lack sufficient fluxes of the low surface tension type. See **Surface tension**. Sometimes a glaze begins to crawl when it has previously been satisfactory. Firing of wet ware should first be considered as the cause. The second possibility is that a thicker layer of glaze is being used. The glaze slop may have thickened by evaporation or use. Alternatively, the biscuit ware may be slightly underfired. This gives a more absorbent biscuit which not only takes a thicker layer of glaze but dries it too quickly to allow it to become compact. An immediate remedy may be to thin the glaze slop and add a little gum to hold the glaze firmly. A third possible cause is that the biscuit has become dusty or has been overhandled and become greasy.

Crazing. Crackle. Craquelle. The glaze defect characterized by a network of fine cracks. The effect can be decorative and if deliberate is called crackle. However it is usually considered undesirable and a fault.

On earthenware, the glaze is intended to be an impervious layer to cover an absorbent body. If the glaze crazes, it no longer fulfils this function. Crazed earthenware which has been in use for a number of years will have absorbed dirt with the moisture so that the craze lines show distinctly. On tableware this is unpleasant and probably unhygienic. On true stoneware the crazing does not present such a hazard. The body itself is impervious and the glaze's function is to present a smooth hygienic and decorative surface.

Crazes are cracks in the glaze. They occur because the glaze contracts more than the body as the pot cools after firing. If the glaze is unable to sustain the tension that thereby comes upon it, it cracks. The first cracks that occur are usually long ones which often spiral upwards on a pot or go straight across a plate. If these

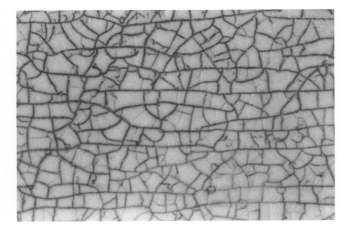

cracks were inspected through a lens they would be seen to be wide. Even so, stress still exists between body and glaze which is eased by further crazing of the areas between the first long cracks. The long cracks are called primary crazing.

The filling in of an area with smaller cracks to form a host of little squares and/or triangles is called secondary crazing. When secondary crazing has taken place, close inspection of the primary cracks will show that they have closed considerably. At the time when the primary crazing has taken place, it is possible to rub colouring into the cracks to give a decorative effect. This was done with Chinese crackle celadons.

Crazing may take place during the cooling in the kiln but most glazes come from the kiln craze-free. The

stresses which will cause the crazing exist but are contained by the strength and elasticity of the glaze. However these stresses become exaggerated by the expansion and contraction during everyday use until they result in crazing. This may take many years. Earthenware bodies are porous and absorb moisture from the air. As they do so they expand permanently. The glaze does not expand but crazes to accommodate the tension put upon it. This is another reason for the crazing on earthenware and other porous bodies.

To counteract this expansion through moisture it is usual to arrange for the body to be too small for the glaze. The glaze is then under compression and not tension. This allows the body to expand later without causing tension in the glaze. The device employs the cristobalite squeeze and is described under **Cristobalite** and **Silica inversions**. Crazing often occurs on ovenware because of the unequal heating and cooling of glaze and body. This is detailed under **Thermal shock**.

The correction of crazing is theoretically simple but not always so in practice. It is explained in detail under **Glaze fit**. A glaze or a body can be altered in composition thereby altering its rate of expansion and contraction. Harmony of body and glaze can be achieved but only at one temperature. The various temperatures of a day, of a pot's use as tableware and especially of its use as ovenware invariably create stresses. These stresses, if not absorbed by the resilience of body and glaze, result in crazing, or its opposite, shivering. Shivering is the worse because it ruins the pot and is dangerous on table and kitchen ware. Most potters therefore are content if their wares craze occasionally.

A glaze can be made more elastic by the addition of lead oxide and/or boric oxide. Glazes based upon the alkalis soda and potash, and to less extent calcia, are brittle and likely to contract a large amount. Alkaline glazes are notorious for crazing because their oxides, potash and soda, have a high rate of contraction. Boric oxide has an extremely low rate of contraction and amounts of up to 15% in the glaze will have beneficial effect in countering crazing. This is approximate. The amount is different for each glaze. More than 15% may have the opposite effect because the glaze's resilience is lowered by large amounts of boric oxide. The effect has been called boracitis.

Glazes often craze if they are underfired or overfired. In the former case it is because there is insufficient body-glaze layer forming. This layer absorbs the stress between the body and the glaze. Improvements in craze resistance can be achieved by facilitating the growth of a body-glaze layer as described under **Buffer layer**.

Where a glaze is overfired and then crazes it is because the overfiring affected the body more than the glaze. This happens on stoneware where body and glaze mature together. The crystalline silica in the body becomes fused silica and in this form it has a much lower rate of contraction. The glaze still has the same rate of contraction and therefore in proportion it contracts more when overfired than when correctly fired.

This phenomenon explains the apparent anomaly in the statement that to cure crazing one adds silica to the glaze, or the body, or both. In the case of the glaze the extra silica fuses in the melt. In this state it has a low contraction rate. Alumina is also effective in small amounts and therefore china clay is often added to glazes to counteract crazing. In the case of the body the extra silica is intended to remain crystalline, a form in which it has a high rate of contraction. Sand is often used for stonewares but flint is used for earthenwares with the additional possibility of creating cristobalite. Cristobalite squeeze has already been mentioned.

Crazing is a common fault which is simple to understand but difficult to eradicate. In earthenware the answer would lie in the balanced use of lead oxide and boric oxide in the glaze and possibly cristobalite in the body. If the earthenware body is biscuited at a higher temperature than the glaze will be fired, then this temperature greatly affects craze resistance. Underfiring biscuit will cause crazing. Overfiring of noncristobalite bodies may also cause crazing by fusing the previously crystalline free silica.

In dense stoneware, cristobalite may lead to the worse faults of shivering and dunting, and the temperatures used may be too high for lead which has a practical upper limit of about 1250°C (2282°F). Therefore a pure silica sand in the body, boric oxide in the glaze or an adjustment of the glaze oxides will be necessary. The glaze oxides to be considered first would be boric oxide to replace silica, additional silica possibly with some alumina, or the replacement of soda by potash or potash by calcia, baria, lithia etc.

Creamware. Cream-coloured earthenware. The forerunner of today's English white earthenware. It was developed in the early 18th century by the Astburys, and later perfected by Whieldon and Wedgwood. Creamware was possible because of the increasing use of china and ball clays, and cornish stone from southwest England. A typical recipe shows their importance:

china clay	25
ball clay	25
flint	35
cornish stone	15

The photograph shows an example of scratch-blue creamware by W and T Taylor, Greenhead Pottery, c 1760.

It was on creamware that the method of using a glaze slop was perfected. This was possibly introduced into southern England with the making of delft in the 17th century and was taken up by the slipware potters of northern England in the early 18th century. At first galena was mixed with water but later flint was added and lead oxide replaced the galena. By 1750 a balanced

glaze slop was in use which gave a uniform layer of glaze when fired. At the same time plaster of Paris was replacing gypsum and biscuit as a mould material. When, in 1760, the idea of biscuiting ware before glazing was introduced, the foundations of the mass-production industry had been laid.

Creeping. See **Crawling**.

Crete. The Mediterranean island which had a highly-developed Bronze Age known as the Minoan Civilization. From 2600 B.C. a series of distinctive pottery styles developed with robust forms and decorative painting. The decoration was based upon flowers and sea creatures and was the most exuberant of any Bronze Age pottery. The pottery decoration was contemporary with but not the same as mural painting. The two need to be seen as a whole. The pottery decoration was purely a decorative treatment and owed nothing to a religious significance. The climax of the pottery decoration was about 1900 B.C.; after this, more expression went into mural painting. Eventually the forms and the decoration became rigid and the freedom was lost. This coincided with the Iron Age and this rigidity reflects the stricter qualities of both the material, iron, and the people who worked it.

Cristobalite. Silica. SiO_2. One of the primary phases of silica which are important to the ceramist. The others are quartz, tridymite and silica glass. See **Silica phases**. These four phases are chemically identical but are physically different in their molecular structures. They therefore exhibit different physical properties. It is for its unique expansion rate that cristobalite is used in ceramics. Cristobalite bodies have anti-craze properties.

Cristobalite does not expand at a constant rate when heated from room temperature. In the first 200°C (360°F) it expands approximately 0·7% volumetrically. Then at 226°C (439°F) it suddenly expands by 3%. Following this, a slow rate of expansion is continued.

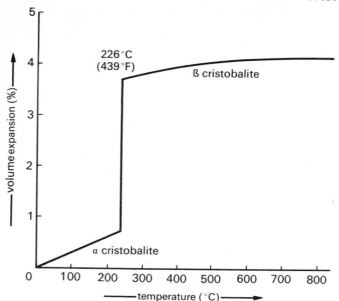

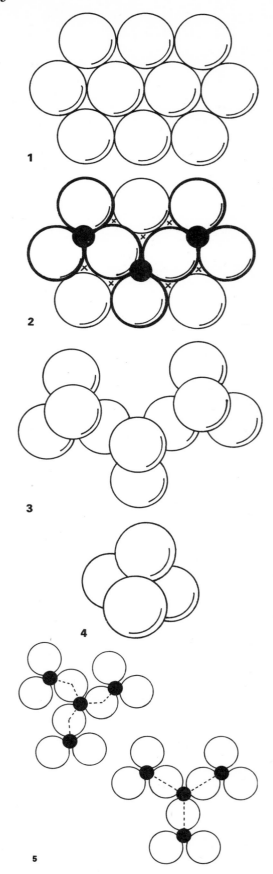

The expansion curve is shown in the accompanying graph.

PHYSICS OF CRISTOBALITE. Cristobalite is a crystalline solid. The sudden expansion is caused by a straightening of the Si-O-Si bonds of the crystal lattice. The silica lattice, whilst maintaining the valency commitments of its atoms, is capable of some nine regular variations. Of these, quartz, cristobalite and tridymite are important to the potter. They are each capable of a slightly collapsed version and a very straight, extended version. These give the two forms alpha and beta and account for the size change which takes place.

If oxygen atoms are packed together they can be most economically packed in a regular way as in fig. 1. In silica, each oxygen atom is attached to two silicon atoms and this is achieved by placing silicon atoms in the hollows formed by three adjacent oxygen atoms. Such sites are marked with large dots in fig. 2. The sites marked X cannot be occupied because the oxygen atoms drawn in thicker line are already satisfied in their valencies by the silicon atoms already inserted.

However, although the oxygen atoms may be satisfied, the silicon atoms are not. They require four oxygen atoms each to satisfy their valency requirements. These extra oxygens fit one on top of each silicon as in fig. 3. The building brick of silica is therefore a tetrahedron formed by four oxygen atoms surrounding one silicon atom. Fig. 4. See also **Crystal**, which includes drawings of the single tetrahedron.

The silicon atom is slightly too large for the space left inside the four oxygen atoms. The silicon therefore pushes the oxygen atoms slightly apart. This gives space in the lattice for minor adjustments like those of the alpha to beta forms. These occur by a collapsing or straightening of a line drawn through the silicon-oxygen-silicon bonds as in fig. 5.

This accounts for the inversions but there is also

space for larger adjustments as can be seen from fig. 3 which is obviously more open as a lattice than is the tight packing of fig. 1.

If this is visualized as a three-dimensional structure one can imagine how the individual tetrahedra, whilst retaining their identity and with comparable links with other tetrahedra, can be placed in different relationships to one another. An obvious one is that in which alternate tetrahedra of a chain are inverted as in fig. 6.

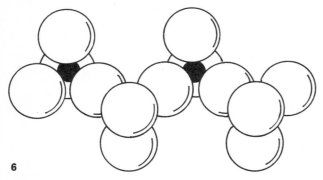

6

Many possibilities apparent in a flat diagram cancel one another out when viewed from other angles. However some nine variations are possible of which fig. 6 represents cristobalite in contrast to fig. 3 which is quartz. The individual way in which each can collapse as an alpha form accounts for its different behaviour at inversion.

CRISTOBALITE IN BODIES. One of the defects of glazed earthenware is crazing. Crazing occurs when the glaze contraction is greater than that of the body. The accompanying graph shows comparative cooling curves for a glaze and two bodies during the last stages of cooling. The temperature is indicated across the graph cooling from left to right. Note that this is the opposite of the previous graph. Contraction is indicated down the graph so that the glaze shown by the heavy line (G) contracts by the amount from A to G (approximately 0·9%) in cooling from 400°C (752°F).

Cristobalite's 3% firing expansion is sudden and it is

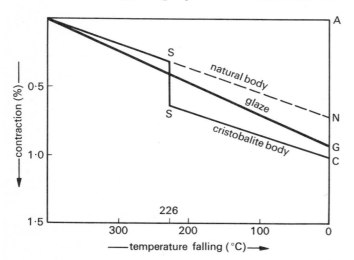

exactly reversible. That is, during cooling, the cristobalite suddenly contracts by this amount. If cristobalite is present in a pottery body, the whole body will suddenly contract at this temperature in proportion to the amount of cristobalite it contains. This is a valuable characteristic because by giving a body this extra contraction, crazing of the glaze can be overcome.

A natural earthenware body contracts only by the amount from A to N (approximately 0·7%) and is therefore larger than its covering glaze. The result is crazing of the glaze.

If 10% cristobalite is present in the body, the body will contract by the amount A to C (approximately 1%). This is more than the glaze which is thereby compressed by the body and unable to craze.

The compression, which occurs at 226°C (439°F), is shown at SS on the graph. This is known as the cristobalite squeeze and it is invaluable as an anti-craze measure. It can, however, be over-accentuated, resulting in the opposite of crazing which is shivering. See **Crazing** and **Shivering**. Fortunately a glaze can withstand about ten times the amount of stress under compression before it shivers than the amount of stress it can withstand under tension before it crazes.

The stress which is created between the body and glaze by the cristobalite squeeze can have a marked effect upon the overall strength of the pottery object. It is possible to double a pot's resistance to physical knocks, as well as to create so much compression that a pot is at a tense point where the slightest knock shatters it. The optimum amount can only be discovered by tests. Such tests are beyond the means of the individual potter who, if he wishes to incorporate cristobalite into his body, should do so by a series of simple tests containing 1%, 2%, 3% etc of cristobalite. The effect can be judged by the crazing of a thick layer of glaze. The maximum addition of cristobalite is unlikely to exceed 10%. Some loss of plasticity and the opening effect of a non-plastic refractory material are to be expected.

The amount of cristobalite required cannot be calculated from the amount of crazing. The experiences of one potter in terms of percentage additions of cristobalite are not directly transferable to another potter's work unless it is identical. The presence of some cristobalite in a body encourages the conversion of other silica to cristobalite phase. The presence of other free silica, of other catalysts and the temperatures involved all play a part. Refiring a piece of pottery encourages the conversion of further cristobalite which upsets the balance of glaze compression and makes the ware extremely brittle. Before the mechanics of the cristobalite squeeze were understood, potters introduced talc into the clay. It had been empirically discovered that this addition inhibited crazing. The magnesia in the talc encourages the conversion of quartz to cristobalite. See **Silica conversion**.

Cristobalite, with or without attendant catalysts and compensatory body fluxes, can be purchased in fine-grain and fine-powder forms. It is preferable to add the cristobalite to the clay at the blunging stage but it can be satisfactorily added along with sand, grog etc at the plastic stage, providing that it is thoroughly mixed into the clay. Like all fine powders it tends to cling to itself thus making it difficult to thoroughly disperse it.

The sudden contraction of the cristobalite squeeze creates a stress within a piece of pottery as well as between its body and glaze. Earthenware bodies which are 'open' and hence resilient can withstand this stress but dense stoneware cannot. The sudden contraction can be disastrous to stoneware. See **Dunting, cooling dunts**.

The cristobalite squeeze occurring at 226°C (439°F) is within the range of a domestic oven. Cristobalite is therefore undesirable in ovenware. To overcome the sudden contraction and yet exert compression upon the glaze is a problem that has been overcome industrially by the use of tridymite in combination with cristobalite.

The combined cristobalite/tridymite is often referred to as disordered cristobalite. Powders purchased as cristobalite are sometimes of this order and give a smoother contraction of slightly less amount but over a temperature range of some 100°C (180°F). Tridymite is unlikely to form in pottery bodies because it takes longer to convert from quartz than does cristobalite. See also the description of cristobalite and tridymite in **Silica inversions**.

CRISTOBALITE IN GLAZES. There is no advantage whatsoever in using cristobalite rather than quartz, flint or sand in a glaze. All are silica and chemically identical. Their physical differences disappear once their lattice structures are destroyed by the molten state.

Critical moisture content. The water content of a clay, paste or other suspension, where this water fills all the hollows between the particles yet leaves the particles in contact. The critical moisture content is usually considered in relation to clay or suspensions as they dry out. It is the point at which a glaze slop 'sets' on the ware and the point at which plastic clay becomes a solid. In normal usage the point of critical moisture content for a clay is the same as the leather-hard stage.

Crocus martis. Anhydrous ferrous sulphate. Calcined copperas. $FeSO_4$. A cheap iron salt used for colouring glazes. It is soluble in water and in the glaze, giving soft yellows in lead glazes and greenish colours in boric glazes, (3%–6%).

If heated alone it does not fully decompose until approximately 1200°C (2192°F) when it forms red iron oxide, sulphur trioxide and sulphur dioxide:

$$2FeSO_4 \longrightarrow Fe_2O_3 + SO_3 \uparrow + SO_2 \uparrow$$

Partially decomposed crocus martis is often used to obviate the possible problem of solubility in the glaze slop. Its further decomposition only takes place during the later activity of glaze melting and it therefore produces a speckle. The partially decomposed crocus martis is a dark purple-brown and can be obtained by calcining at approximately 900°C (1652°F). It has a theoretical formula of $FeO.Fe_2O_3.FeSO_4$.

Cross draught kiln. Horizontal kiln. A kiln in which the hot gases travel through the ware across the chamber from a pierced bag wall to exit flues in the opposite wall.

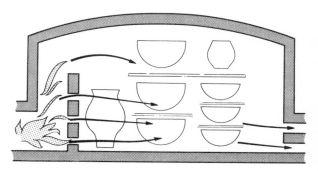

Cryolite. Fluoride of aluminium and sodium. Na_3AlF_6. A natural mineral associated with granites. It is used in the preparation of vitreous enamels and occasionally in frits and glazes. Cryolite, albite and nepheline are the only native sodium compounds that are insoluble in water.

Cryptocrystalline. Composed of exceedingly fine crystals which are not detectable with the naked eye or normal magnification. The crystals may be no more than the nuclei of crystals with each structure only a few molecules in size. However the fact that they are crystals may be important as starting points for crystal growth or, in the case of flint, important because subject to inversions.

Crystal. The concentration of many identical molecular units in regular three-dimensional pattern. See also **Lattice structure**.

The atoms which form simple molecules and the molecules (radicals) which form complex molecules group themselves in balanced ways dictated by their electrical charges and their physical sizes. A compact group produces a 'cell' which is the unit of the whole structure. Many units together give a crystal whose form is directly related to the cell.

The illustrations show a quartz crystal whose six-sided column (fig. 1) is composed of units which have triangular sides (fig. 2). The unit 'cell' is a tetrahedron which is a three-sided pyramid standing on a triangular base (fig. 3). This is the silica tetrahedron (SiO_4) (figs. 4 and 5) which becomes SiO_2 when each oxygen is linked to another silicon. See **Silica structure**.

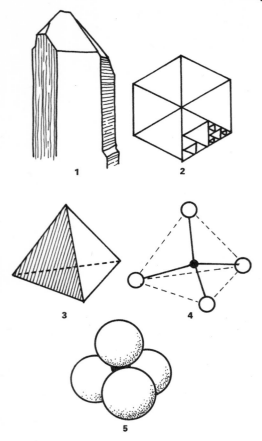

In a crystal, one set of bonds will always be weaker than the rest and this set will form planes through the solid. A crystal splits most readily along these planes of cleavage producing pieces which are smaller versions of the original.

Crystalline solids tend to melt suddenly at a given temperature. Here all the links of one type are released. See also **Amorphous**, which describes non-crystalline solids.

The crystals in crystal glazes are built up from units which separate from the molten glass upon cooling. They are usually complex crystals like calcium silicate, magnesium silicate and various titanates.

Crystalline glazes. Glazes which contain crystals within the amorphous (glassy) matrix of the glaze. The glaze itself is not entirely composed of crystals. The crystals give opacity, colour and surface texture as smooth and rough matts. The crystals grow during cooling by isolation of the essential oxides from the surrounding fluid glaze. The process is known as devitrification and is given encouragement by holding the kiln temperature around 800°C (1472°F).

Crystalline glazes contain crystals within the glaze and on the surface. The crystals which are within the glaze are of both the flat and the needle variety. They sometimes grow from the body-glaze layer but there is a limited space for such crystals to grow and they tend

to be small. These crystals include iron sulphate in galena glazes; iron oxide in aventurine glazes; iron oxide in oxidized tenmokus; zirconium silicate in white opaque glazes; and calcium phosphate and calcium borate in chun glazes.

Surface crystals are again of both flat and needle variety when small. They include calcium silicate, calcium magnesium silicate, magnesium silicate, iron oxide and calcium silicon titanate. Large flat crystals can form at the surface under suitable conditions. These crystals are often zinc silicate and zinc titanate. For information about the crystalline minerals involved, see **Diopside, Enstatite, Ilmenite, Titanite, Willemite** and **Wollastonite**.

Crystals grow more readily in glazes which have low viscosity. Such glazes are more thoroughly dispersed and during the building of the crystal present little resistance to the growth of a perfect lattice. Alumina stiffens glazes and is therefore kept to a minimum. The resulting fluid runny glazes are eminently suitable for tiles which are fired horizontally but less suitable for tall pots. The fine-grained alumina matt is one obvious exception. See **Alumina in glazes** and **Run (1)**.

It is necessary to 'seed' the process of crystal growth by introducing suitable crystal nuclei into the glaze. Titania is one of the most popular seeds. Ilmenite, zirconium silicate, zinc oxide, calcia, magnesia and calcium phosphate are also effective and the different silicas from different sources like wood ashes often retain their identities throughout the firing to provide starting points for devitrification upon cooling. The seeds and the crystals which grow upon them give rise to some specific names for some crystalline glazes. See **Chun, Dolomite matt, Lime matt, Magnesium matt, Satin matt** and **Zinc oxide, crystallizer**.

The chemistry of crystalline glazes is interesting. Assume first that a molten glaze is a completely fluid mixture of individual molecules of silica, alumina, soda, potash, lead oxide, calcia, magnesia, zinc oxide, titania etc. Upon cooling, these molecules link together in random fashion to form chains. This gives the amorphous substance called glass.

There are inevitably some unsatisfied valencies within a glass which, if given the opportunity are satisfied by orientation of the molecules into more regular chains. If the cooling is done slowly, the molecules seek to establish patterns of bonds which completely satisfy their valency requirements. Such bonding produces a regular structure or lattice which is the framework of a crystal. See **Crystal** and **Lattice structure**.

Each oxide has a temperature range in which it is is able to loosen the bonds between its molecules and re-establish similar bonds with identical molecules or completely new bonds with the molecules of different oxides. The range extends from an oxide's melting point downwards. The lower end of the range is determined by the other oxide present.

From the melting point upwards, the molecules free

themselves completely from bonding to produce a liquid.

For example, silica has a melting point of 1710°C (3110°F) yet in the presence of alumina it can be persuaded to melt as low as 1545°C (2813°F). With both calcia and alumina, the melting point of silica is depressed still more to around 1200°C (2192°F). The lowest point at which silica can be persuaded to melt is 510°C (950°F) in the presence of lead oxide. This is, of course, the phenomenon of eutectic mixtures and fluxing actions, but seen in reverse, the silica will not freeze (set solid) until these temperatures are reached upon cooling.

At a specific temperature therefore a combination of two or more oxides can freeze by forming the necessary molecular bonds. In coming from a hot to a cooler state they are often said to be precipitated because the melt can no longer hold them in solution (dispersed state). As they are precipitated, time is necessary for the orientation of molecules to take place so that the frozen precipitate has a regular structure, that is, it is crystalline. It is worth remembering that the crystals may or may not include the colouring oxide present in the glaze. Crystallization is a selective process so that white crystals within a coloured matrix are possible as in the photograph of a crystalline glaze by Theo Whalley.

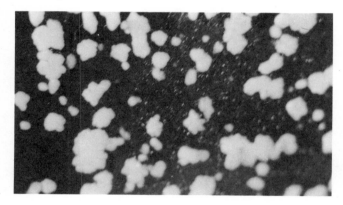

At a given temperature therefore there are crystals which are able to form and also potential crystals awaiting suitable conditions but still in fluid state. Many mixtures will never crystallize. They form the glassy matrix of the glaze which freezes quickly and is therefore unable to crystallize.

The isolation within the molten glaze of some of its constituents upsets the balance of the rest. Some of the remaining oxides are no longer able to stay in solution because the oxides whose close presence enabled them to be liquid have been removed by crystallization. These second precipitated oxides combine as larger molecules themselves; anchor themselves onto the first crystal to form; form crystals with another oxide; and/or form bonds in random fashion with the nearest available molecules of other oxides. The removal of the second stage of oxides hastens the isolation of

others with the net result that the glaze sets quickly. The setting of the matrix precludes the full development of the original crystals which engendered the whole action.

In contrast to the above, plutonic igneous rocks are often completely crystalline and consequently one might academically consider it possible to render a glaze completely crystalline if a comparable cooling time of perhaps 20 years were used. However plutonic rocks are subjected to extreme pressures and although the last mineral to crystallize in them is often silica it remains sufficiently plastic to allow orientation of its molecules into crystalline state. At atmospheric pressures the isolated silica would set immediately to an amorphous glass.

The setting of a matrix of a crystalline glaze will therefore occur whether the temperature is falling, steady or even rising. It is brought about by the creation of the particular combination of oxides which sets at this temperature. Naturally this combination is likely to set more quickly if the temperature is falling and more quickly still if the temperature is falling rapidly. Thus both temperature and time do affect the setting of a crystalline glaze and affect the amount of crystallization that is able to take place. A tightly packed kiln will cool more slowly than one openly set and will give different results. Pots near the door or walls of the kiln will be different from ones in the middle of the kiln. A single pot may come out with its glaze having crystallized on one side but not on the other. The photograph shows such a pot in which a lime matt has developed on one side but quick cooling has prevented it on the other where instead, a transparent and shiny glaze has resulted.

If the cooling rate cannot be controlled a refiring of the glaze through the crystallization temperature can be used. The graph shows how a refire, drawn in solid line, gives more than double the time within the crystallization range. The dotted line shows the normal cooling from the glaze firing. Putting a pot in with a soft biscuit firing often has the result of forming crystals, sometimes with colour, that did not previously exist. Crystals will grow whether the temperature is falling, rising or steady providing the conditions are suitable, that is, the

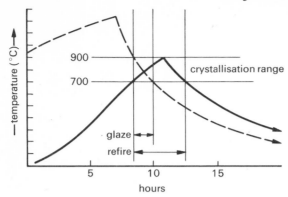

glaze is not too viscous and the necessary oxides are present.

Out of a fluid mixture of perhaps ten different oxides, a crystalline combination like calcium silicate can isolate itself. But it is impossible to establish an exact temperature and time scale for a particular crystal which can be used under all circumstances. Although it is known that isolated calcium silicate has a freezing point of 1545°C (2813°F) the growth of this crystal in a glaze is dependent upon the composition of the melt from which it is precipitated. Thus a separate cooling graph must be established for each glaze if the maximum crystal growth is to be achieved in each case.

Different titanate crystals have been proved to grow in glazes at various temperatures between 1300°C and 500°C (2372°F and 932°F). Fortunately most glaze crystals are isolated in the narrower range between 900°C and 700°C (1652°F and 1292°F). This is well below the melting points of many of the crystalline minerals involved and results in the sudden creation of many small crystals. Lime matts, which rely upon calcium silicate, have small crystals giving a fine grain. The growth of large crystals is dependent upon the opportunity for orientation of molecules over a wide area. A combination of zinc silicate and lead titanate is precipitated nearer to their melting points and therefore presents this opportunity and results in large crystals up to 3 inches across.

Lastly the process of seeding requires explanation. Crystals grow much more rapidly if they have a starting point of sympathetic construction. Mullite in the body-glaze layer often starts in-glaze crystals but for other glazes suitable nuclei are introduced via the glaze recipe. These are refractory particles, often of colloidal size and possibly consisting of only a small group of identical molecules. Being refractory they do not enter the fusion of the glaze because their own molecular bonds are not broken by the heat. If seeded glazes are over-fired they cannot satisfactorily crystallize upon cooling because their seeds have been broken up and dispersed through the melt. Although it is true that crystals grow more easily from a thoroughly dispersed molten glaze, it is necessary to have the seeds in isolated existence. The required dispersed melt is achieved by

making the glaze of low viscosity which usually means low in alumina content.

Seeding of high-temperature glazes can be done with titania or ilmenite to foster titanate crystals; calcium phosphate and zirconium silicate to foster calcium borate and calcium silicate crystals; and different sources of silica for silicate crystals. One per cent is often sufficient seed but the glaze must contain suitable oxides.

For low-temperature glazes more seed is required because it must also provide the eventual crystal oxides. Titania up to 15% or titania 3% with up to 18% of zinc oxide give the fine-grained satin matts.

Crystalline silica. Silica in crystalline form in contrast to silica glass. The distinction occurs in consideration of dunting where crystalline silica, whether quartz or cristobalite in crystal structure, is subject to inversion (change of size). Silica glass is not subject to inversion. See **Silica inversions**. In these considerations, the crystalline silica which exists in a body as flint, quartz, sand or cristobalite is referred to as free silica.

Cullet. Broken glass bought as pieces or powder and useful for melting into hollows on decorative plates and tiles. Cullet is cheaper than glaze and enamel but its composition is not guaranteed. It is not intended to be used as a glaze and therefore contains little stiffening or stabilizer.

Culm clay. Clay from the culm measures of the carboniferous system. Culm is a coal which contains too many impurities of clay and limestone to be acceptable as coal for burning. Culm clay was the seat-earth for the vegetation and can be regarded as a type of fireclay. It is very variable containing much quartz sand and is often sandwiched between two layers of gritstone showing a progressive change from one grit to the other via soft crumbly grit, shale, a black coal layer, sand and grit.

Occasionally the culm clay has been weathered and washed out of its deposit, naturally levigated and re-deposited nearby in pockets of workable clay.

Cup and saucer. The idea of a handled cup with retaining saucer is said to have been originated by the Marquise de Pompadour. Its fore-runner was the bowl and stand, a favourite ritualized piece in the Far East.

The examples shown are by Sheila Casson, Janet Hamer, David Leach and the Leach Pottery, St Ives, England.

Cup-head. A wheel-head which has a hollow top into which prepared bats, moulds and chucks can be fitted. The advantage of using a cup-head is that the accessory to be inserted is thereby automatically centred. The accessory is often made from plaster and is cast and turned in the cup-head which it thereby fits perfectly. Sometimes a keyway or natch is included in the design. The jigger and jolley system depends upon the use of a cup-head to centre the moulds. There is need only for one cup-head and one profile which remain on the wheel. The moulds are duplicated.

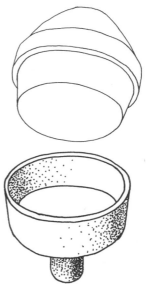

Cupric oxide. Black copper oxide. Copper (II) oxide. CuO. See **Copper oxide**.

Cuprite. Copper sub-oxide ore. Cu_2O. A partially oxidized native copper or copper ore: the result of weathering. It is easily identified by its deep red colour which in samples adulterated by iron might be brownish. It can be crushed and used as a colourant. See **Copper ores**.

Cuprous oxide. Red copper oxide. Cu_2O. See **Copper oxide**.

D

Damper. A device for adjusting the cross-sectional area of the exit flue of a kiln. It is placed at the exit from the kiln chamber where the gases enter the chimney but occasionally it may be part way up the chimney or even at the top of a short chimney. It usually consists of a slab of refractory material held in slots in the brickwork so that it can be slid in or out quite easily from outside the kiln. By closing the damper one cuts down the amount of hot exhaust gases entering the chimney. Theoretically the speed of the gases remains the same because their speed is based upon the temperature difference inside and outside the kiln and the effective height of the chimney. When less gas enters the chimney a pressure is built up within the chamber. This has the effect of baffling or holding the heat within the chamber. At the close of a firing the damper is often completely closed to slow down the rate of cooling.

Dead plaster. Calcined plaster. Plaster which has been overheated during manufacture or accidently afterwards. If all the water of crystallization is driven off the gypsum, there is no crystalline start for a setting action. Dead plaster will therefore not set. Dead plaster is not synonymous with set plaster because set plaster contains hydrated calcium sulphate crystals.

De-airing. The removal of air from plastic clay. This is achieved by a de-airing pugmill which first shreds the clay and then subjects it to a vacuum. Here the air pockets explode and the air is removed. The clay is then re-united and compressed by a pugmill.

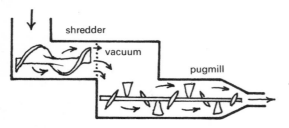

By de-airing it is possible to bring the clay particles into closer contact. In this state they have a greater overall friction although their capacity to slide, that is their plasticity, is neither impaired nor improved. Contrary to popular belief de-airing does not increase plasticity. It increases the strength of the clay which thereby improves its 'workability'. See **Workability**.

Deflocculation. The action of dispersing the fine clay particles in a slip so that the slip becomes more fluid.

Slips used in casting are deflocculated and can thereby have a high density, that is, they can contain a high proportion of clay, whilst remaining fluid enough to be poured.

Deflocculation is achieved by adding, to the suspension water, suitable soluble alkalis called deflocculants. These exchange their ions (charged atoms) with those of the clay particles so that the clay particles are all of similar powerful electrostatic charge. See **Zeta potential**. In this state they repel one another and are unable to aggregate. No matter how closely they are packed together they prefer to slide past one another and avoid contact. The repulsion acts as an effective lubricant.

Thus a slip can be created which contains a large proportion of clay and only a small proportion of water. A pound of plastic clay can be converted into a fluid slip with less than a tenth of a pint of water plus suitable deflocculants. Without the deflocculants it would require half a pint of water to reach the same fluidity.

The exact amounts of deflocculant can only be established by trials. See **Casting slips**. The type and amount is dependent upon the type of clay. The following recipe for a casting slip is included as a guide to the amounts involved:

plastic red clay	25 lbs
water	2 pints
sodium carbonate	1 oz
sodium silicate 75°TW	$1\frac{1}{2}$ fluid ozs

Details of deflocculants and their actions are given later. In general terms, deflocculation involves the build-up of electrostatic charges on the clay particles. Each particle has two layers: the inner layer is negative and the outer layer is positive. See **Double layer theory**. When strong enough, the outer layer has the ability to repel identical layers on other particles as in the diagram.

The principle of deflocculation is to replace the small-charge ions, in these layers, with stronger ones and, if possible, increase their number. The whole character of a clay is thereby changed. One possible equation for this action is:

$$\left.\begin{array}{c} Ca \\ Mg \end{array}\right\} \begin{array}{c} \text{ions} \\ \text{on} \\ \text{clay} \end{array} + 2Na_2CO_3 \longrightarrow 4Na \left\{\begin{array}{c} \text{ions} \quad CaCO_3 \downarrow \\ \text{on} + \\ \text{clay} \quad MgCO_3 \downarrow \end{array}\right.$$

Here sodium carbonate, which is soluble, is used to effect an ionic exchange. The calcium and the magnesium ions take the carbonate radical and are precipitated

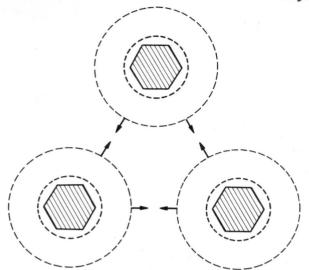

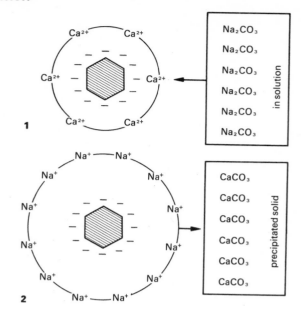

$$Ca\,(clay) + Na_2CO_3 \longrightarrow Na(clay)Na + CaCO_3 \downarrow$$

as insoluble compounds of calcium carbonate and magnesium carbonate.

Deflocculation involves **Deflocculants, Fluidity, Thixotropy, Forces of attraction, Double layer theory** and **Zeta potential** which are separately indexed.

DEFLOCCULANT. Deflocculent. A soluble material which is added to clay suspensions (slips) to increase fluidity. Increased fluidity without loss of bulk is advantageous in the slip-casting process. The deflocculant creates fluidity by increasing the electrostatic forces of repulsion which the clay particles possess so that they repel one another. Thus the particles refuse to aggregate and prefer to slide past one another even though the number of particles suspended in the water is great. The particles are said to be in dispersed state or a state of deflocculation. See also **Fluidity**.

Deflocculants are of two types: the alkali cation type and the polyanion type. It is usual practice to use one of each type in combination because although their action in creating fluidity is the same they give different side effects. The most important side effect is that upon thixotropy.

The alkali cation type of deflocculant promotes cation exchange between itself and the clay particle. The new cation increases the zeta potential of the particle. For example, sodium carbonate replaces each calcium cation on the clay particle with two sodium cations. It similarly replaces magnesium cations. The displaced calcium cation takes up the carbonate radical to become calcium carbonate. This is precipitated because it is insoluble and so it becomes suspended particles of solid matter in the slip.

The clay particle thus realizes an outer layer of sodium cations which have a large 'stand-off distance'. Figs. 1 and 2 show this action in diagrammatic form. The repulsive force is strong and able to repel like particles. See **Zeta potential** and **Double layer theory**. The equation is:

Examples of the alkali cation type of deflocculant are sodium carbonate, potassium carbonate, sodium hydroxide and sodium oxalate.

There is obviously a limit to the defloculatory effect which can be achieved by cation exchanges. The full effect is achieved when all the exchangeable cations have been replaced by those of greater 'stand-off distance'. At this state a slip is fully deflocculated because the zeta potential of the clay has reached its greatest possible value. The addition of more alkali cation now has an opposite or flocculatory effect. Additional cations crowd into the double layer system filling the theoretical gap which is the stand-off distance. The zeta potential is therefore reduced. This overcrowding caused by adding too much alkali deflocculant is called salting-out or over-doping.

The polyanion deflocculant achieves similar defloculatory results but in a slightly different way. The polyanion type provides cations for the outer layer as does the alkali cation deflocculant but it also enters the inner layer. Here the polyanion half of the deflocculant replaces the anions on the clay particles. This is an anion exchange and is effective in defloculatory terms because polyanions of multiple negative charge replace simple hydroxyl groups of single negative charge. The overall result is that the negative charge is increased and therefore there are additional sites for cations in the outer layer. The charge of the outer layer is thus stronger and the zeta potential value is higher. The exchanges are diagrammatized in figs. 3 and 4.

Examples of the polyanion type of deflocculant are sodium silicate, sodium poly-phosphate, sodium polyacrylate and sodium tannate.

Again, there must be a limit to the defloculatory effect which can be achieved. However, the effect of

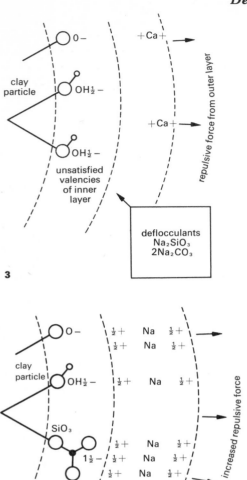

exchange. Any precipitates from these two are harmless in the suspension and fired ceramic.

Sodium carbonate gives effective progressive deflocculation but with little effect upon thixotropy. Sodium silicate gives equally progressive deflocculation with attendant decrease in thixotropic effect. Some thixotropy is required in casting slips and therefore a balance of the two deflocculants is required. See **Casting slips** and **Thixotropy**.

Deflocculatory materials can only act when there is sufficient water for them to go into solution and thereby release their ions for exchange. Also they can only produce a result when the solid in suspension is of colloidal size. Thus clays, especially the fine clays like ball clays and bentonite, give good results, but other minerals like feldspar are hardly affected. Some specially ground materials intended for fine dispersion give some favourable reaction. An example is prepared zirconium silicate. Coarse materials like flint show no reaction to deflocculants but some to flocculants. Thus the suspension must be a colloidal suspension for deflocculation and the deflocculant a solution, although it may be weighed and calculated as a solid.

Dehydration. The removal of water. The term is usually reserved for the removal of chemically combined water in such minerals as kaolinite, borax and aluminium hydroxide. The manufacture of plaster of Paris involves a semi-dehydration of gypsum.

Dehydroxylation. The process whereby the bound water is removed by heat between 450°C and 600°C (842°F and 1112°F). It is described under **Bound water**.

Delft. Faience. Maiolica. Tin-enamelled ware. Tin-glazed earthenware produced at Delft in the Netherlands. This ware was first made by Italian potters working in Delft in the mid-16th century. Although incorporating Gothic and Renaissance decoration its greatest influence was from Oriental porcelain which it sometimes copied. Thus delft is often thought of as blue decoration on a white glaze although red-brown, yellow and green were also used.

It is possible that the Italian potters moved on to England soon after settling in Delft but production in England cannot be proven before 1630. English delft never reached the perfection of the Dutch in thinness of potting and quality of glaze. However the English delft had its own qualities. It divorced itself from imitating Oriental and Continental wares and gained a freedom of overall decoration which is artistically equal to any other tin-glazed ware. Only in some of the early Spanish maiolica is there an equivalent freedom and feeling for pattern. English delft was an important artistic expression and a practical ware. The commemorative plate shown here is dated 1680.

In England delft was made at Lambeth, Bristol and

over-doping is not so drastic. Once the optimum effect has been reached, further additions of polyanion deflocculants serve only to crowd the double layer with anions. This crowding does little to reduce the effectiveness of the cation outer layer so that the result may be negligible in terms of the zeta potential unless a great excess is added. There is certainly not the drastic effect of over-doping experienced with alkali cation deflocculants. In fact there often appears the additional phenomenon of 'protection' whereby the crowding of the double layer by anions prevents the over-crowding by cations. Crowding by excess anion deflocculant therefore provides some protection against over-doping.

A balance of two deflocculants should therefore give full control of deflocculation. The potter's choice for casting slips is usually sodium carbonate for cation exchange and sodium silicate for cation and anion

Liverpool. It enjoyed a steady vogue for 150 years until the development of creamware. See also **Galleyware** and **Lambeth**.

Devitrification. The crystallization of a glaze upon cooling. Transparent shiny glazes contain no crystals and are referred to as supercooled liquids. However if glazes are cooled very slowly, crystals begin to form and the resulting glaze is clouded with crystals and the surface often appears matt. This is called devitrification and it may happen that it only occurs on part of a pot. It is avoided for transparent shiny glazes by cooling them as quickly as possible down to their freezing points. Conversely glazes intended to be crystalline are cooled slowly and also contain oxides which encourage crystal growth such as calcia, titania and zinc oxide. The blue flushes of some chun glazes are partial devitrification. See **Chun**.

It would seem natural to expect crystals of different silicates to grow at different temperatures during cooling. Zinc oxide having acted as a flux to melt the glaze combines with the free silica in the glaze to form zinc silicate crystals at approximately 1000°C (1832°F) during cooling. Calcia behaves similarly and forms calcium silicate crystals at approximately 700°C

(1292°F). If both are present, one will undoubtedly influence the other so that it would be difficult to isolate the two results. In the complexity of a glaze magma are many fluxes capable of combining with silica to form silicate crystals and with boric oxide to form borates under certain conditions. These conditions may be fulfilled especially when encouraged by other crystals. See **Crystalline glazes**.

The formation of crystals, notably alumino-silicates, encourages other combinations by isolating those combinations and providing edges of crystals upon which the new combinations can grow. This probably encourages combinations to crystallize which would not otherwise have done so. If devitrification is occurring where it is not wanted and a quicker cooling is not possible the crystallizing agents calcia, titania, magnesia, zinc oxide, manganous oxide and the iron oxides will have to be replaced partly or totally by other oxides.

Once crystals have started to grow they continue to grow as the glaze cools until the glaze becomes too stiff to allow the different silicates and borates to isolate themselves within the glaze. This lowest point is therefore dependent upon the general maturing range of the particular glaze and can be as low as 500°C (932°F) even for glazes that have been melted at 1200°C (2192°F). Because of the complex nature of a glaze, the devitrification can occur anywhere between 1050°C and 500°C (1922°F and 932°F). It is usual to hold the temperature somewhere between 850°C and 700°C (1562°F and 1292°F) or at least to slow down the rate of cooling to encourage crystal growth. Holding the temperature in this range gives most glazes the chance to crystallize. See also **Lag**.

Dewatering. Taking water out of clay or slip. This is done by leaving the clay, slurry etc outside in pits to dry in the sun and wind; by putting the clay on to an absorbent surface such as plaster, asbestos or bricks sometimes heated from below; or by filter-pressing which is forcing the slurry into pervious cloth bags. The illustration shows a plaster drying trough and a soft biscuit one. See also **Filter-pressing**.

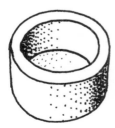

D.F. stone. See **Cornish stone**.

Diaspore. $Al_2O_3 . H_2O$. Alumina hydrate of pure form. It is whiter and harder than the other aluminium ores.

Diatoms. Inshore plankton whose cell walls are silica. They are simple creatures usually with spines. They are the normal diet of many sea creatures but in some places their carcases have been deposited as reefs. These rocks are almost pure silica and are composed of empty silica cells. Pieces cut from these rocks make excellent high-temperature insulation bricks. Where impurities of calcia and iron oxide are found with the diatoms this is called diatomaceous earth. This material is also an excellent insulation because of its cellular structure but is limited to temperatures up to about 900°C (1652°F).

Dinas rock. A pure silica gritstone or quartzite quarried in South Wales and used as a source of silica for making refractory silica bricks.

Diopside. Calcium magnesium silicate. $CaMg(SiO_3)_2$. A non-aluminous pyroxene which occurs in igneous rocks. The crystals grow as long needles and it is possible for this same mineral to precipitate itself from dolomite glazes. See **Dolomite matt** and **Crystalline glazes**. Chains of SiO_3 molecules form sheets when held together by Ca and Mg ions in eight-fold and six-fold co-ordination.

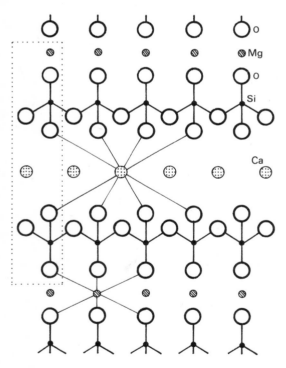

Dioxide. An oxide combining two atoms of oxygen with one atom of the other element. For example, silica is silicon dioxide in which one molecule is made up of one atom of silicon and two atoms of oxygen. The chemical formula is SiO_2. See also **Oxide**.

Disordered kaolinite. The clay crystal which has been subjected to isomorphous substitution. The composition therefore no longer meets the formula Al_2O_3.

$2SiO_2 . 2H_2O$. Instead, some of the aluminium and possibly also the silicon sites in the molecular structure have been occupied by iron and magnesium. There may also be some unsatisfied valencies existing because the stacking of the gibbsite and silica layers is not ideal.

The disordered kaolinite crystal is therefore distorted and is not able to attach closely to other similar crystals. The net result is a weakness, not only within the crystal itself but in the build-up of particles and grains. Unlike the ordered kaolinite which forms almost perfectly shaped large grains, the disordered kaolinite forms grains of random aggregation. During weathering water can more readily infiltrate the random aggregation and break this down into a very fine and hence very plastic clay.

Disordered kaolinites, when weathered and transported, therefore become the fine and plastic secondary clays, e.g. ball clays, stoneware clays and some low-grade fireclays. Ordered kaolinites on the other hand resist break-up of crystal and become low-plasticity secondary kaolins and high-grade fireclays. They also remain refractory unless they have collected impurities. These impurities are external to the clay crystal which remains refractory whereas the disordered kaolinite crystal actually contains some fluxes in its structure and could never be as refractory as pure kaolinite. See **Kaolinite** and also **Clay, origin**.

Distinguishing stain. Organic stain. Burnaway colour. A colour used to stain bodies and glazes for identification before firing. The colour is due to a combination of carbon, hydrogen and oxygen and therefore burns away completely during the firing. Usual colours are pink, blue and blue-green.

Divalent oxides. Divalent fluxes. The oxides of the elements in Group II of the Periodic table. They are:

beryllia	BeO
magnesia	MgO
calcia	CaO
zinc oxide	ZnO
strontia	SrO
baria	BaO

They are referred to in this book collectively with the other fluxes as the alkaline oxides. Zinc oxide and baria display some slight amphoteric properties.

A characteristic of the group is that the fluxing action must be in collaboration with at least one other oxide. That is, whilst each is a flux, it cannot give a satisfactory glaze alone with alumina and silica. Its action is only practical in interaction with other fluxes.

A second characteristic is that each oxide has a minimum temperature at which it acts as a flux. Below this temperature its action is neutral or even anti-flux.

Details are given under each oxide and they are collectively compared under **Viscosity, Surface tension, Glaze fit** and **Periodic table**.

Dod box. Dog box. This operates on the same principle as a wad box but is used for making dods which are strips of clay for handles. The handle section is created by the specially shaped hole or die in the bottom of the box. Dod boxes are also used for making strips for coiled pottery.

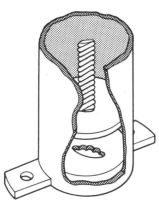

The drawing shows a cut-away view of the box with a dod plate in position. The photographs are of the dod box made by Gosling and Gatensbury Ltd and supplied by Harrison Mayer Ltd; and of a dod handle on a 19th-century Lambeth salt-glazed jug.

Dog ears. Dog's teeth. The torn edge on a slug of clay emerging from a pug mill. The ears are the result of a partial blockage or an insufficiently polished nozzle especially on square sections. If the nozzle is clean, it can be taken as an indication of insufficient plasticity in the clay. Otherwise, dog ears are not an indication of clay condition but of the condition of the pug mill.

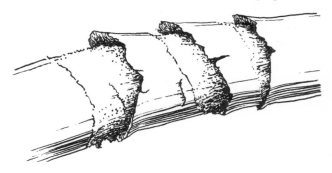

Dolomite. Dolomite limestone. Magnesian limestone. $CaMg(CO_3)_2$ or $CaCO_3.MgCO_3$. The double carbonate of calcium and magnesium which is a single crystal structure and not a mixture of the two carbonate crystals. Dolomite exists as a rock which forms complete strata and it is also present in areas of normal limestone where magnesium has been able to substitute itself for some of the calcium during deposition in the sea. Dolomite is used to introduce calcia and magnesia into glazes.

The dolomitization is not always completed up to the maximum of equal molecules in any sample of rock. The proportions of the ideal dolomite mineral are 54% $CaCO_3$ and 46% $MgCO_3$. There is usually more calcium carbonate and less magnesium carbonate. There is usually also some ferrous carbonate which makes it a buff colour and makes glazes cream coloured. Partially dolomitized limestones are often called dolomitic limestones.

Its value in glazes is as a high-temperature flux and crystallizer. It does not reach its full power as a flux until 1170°C (2138°F). If the glaze contains a high percentage of dolomite, the crystalline mineral diopside is formed during cooling, giving the popular crystalline effect. See **Dolomite matt**.

Dolomite matt. A matt-surfaced glaze achieved by the creation of crystals of calcium and magnesium silicates. Dolomite is the double carbonate of calcium and magnesium which decomposes to become calcia (CaO) and magnesia (MgO) in the firing. These act as fluxes creating the silicates which devitrify upon cooling. The pot illustrated is by Frank Vining.

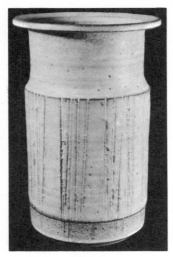

Dolomite matts are deservedly popular because they give variable effects, taking some colouring from the body where thin and producing oatmeal mottlings in brown and black. Where thick they look buttery and unctuous. They are usually cream but vary from buff to white according to the quality of the dolomite used. They are particularly suitable for reduced stoneware. Reduction has no effect whatever upon the calcia and magnesia but reduces the small iron oxide content giving more fluxing power and turning the colour more grey. The additional breakdown of the body in reduction results in a thicker body-glaze layer and hence more texturing of the glaze, to be blacker.

Some matting can be achieved at temperatures below 1100°C (2012°F) but the effect is usually like an unglazed slip. It would not be considered a dolomite matt by most potters who see this as essentially a high-temperature glaze. The fluxing action of dolomite is not effected below 1170°C (2138°F).

During the firing, the dolomite decomposes. This is a slow process starting with the loosening of the molecular bonds at 350°C (662°F) when the magnesia, if isolated, would be released. However, the complexity of the structure keeps it together until approximately 500°C (932°F) when the structure becomes too loose to remain. The carbon dioxide is then released and the process is complete by 800°C (1472°F). There remains then calcia, magnesia and a small percentage of ferrous oxide, which reoxidizes to ferric oxide if fusion of the glaze has not begun.

$$CaMg(CO_3)_2 + FeCO_3 \xrightarrow{800°C} CaO + MgO + FeO + 3CO_2 \uparrow$$

Dolomite matt glazes are often fairly viscous during fusion because there is more than adequate dolomite to flux the silica present. The extra flux can only inhibit fusion although it is involved in the melt. The glaze is therefore a solution with excess alkali which encourages crystallization upon cooling. The calcia and magnesia seek free silica to form diopside crystals

$(CaMg(SiO_3)_2)$. See **Diopside**. It is possible that some alumina is actually isolated which causes separate crystals of alumina. Other crystals involved are enstatite, wollastonite and anorthite. See **Crystalline glazes**.

The following recipes are dolomite matt glazes. In the first one, fusion at 1200°C (2192°F) is made possible by the inclusion of a small amount of lead bisilicate in the recipe.

feldspar	48
china clay	23
whiting	6
dolomite	15
lead bisilicate	8

In the second recipe, which is for 1250°C (2282°F), the amount of whiting is very high. This gives a very viscous glaze which will smooth out on vertical surfaces but not on horizontal ones. For horizontal surfaces the whiting should be decreased to 10 parts and the potash feldspar increased to 30.

feldspar potash	20
feldspar soda	20
china clay	20
whiting	20
dolomite	20

Double dipping. A glazing action whereby the inside and outside of a pot are glazed in one action without glazing the base. A sharp jerk upwards, after dipping the pot, rim first, into the glaze, splashes the inside of the pot provided that the rim does not come out of the glaze.

Double fritting. The process of making two separate frits which are destined for the same glaze. The frits are usually a lead silicate and a boro-silicate. At the glaze slop stage there is usually some additional china clay and feldspar.

The advantage of using two frits over using a single combined frit are:

1. By separating the lead silicate from boric oxide, soda and potash, the solubility of the lead content can be effectively decreased to a point where it presents little hazard as a poison. See **Lead poisoning**. The principle of double fritting was discovered as early as 1899 by Prof Almstrom of Sweden, but was not fully developed until the 1920's when Dr Petrik of Germany explained how the frits could be commercially produced and effectively used. See **Low sol**.

2. Blends between two different frits produce a range of effects equivalent to a large number of single frits. Standardization of these two frits assists the frit manufacturer to establish efficient fritting plants.

3. Two frits can achieve a wider maturing range than one frit. The fusion is also more uniform. Adjustments to the range are easily achieved by adjusting frit amount rather than altering the frit composition.

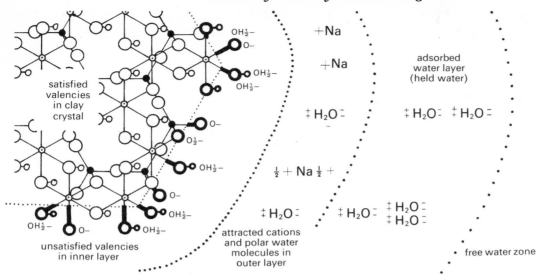

satisfied valencies in clay crystal

OH½–
O–
OH½–
OH½–
O–
O½–
OH½–
O–
OH½–
OH½–
O–
OH½–

+Na

+Na

‡H₂O⁼

½+Na½+

‡H₂O⁼

adsorbed water layer (held water)

‡H₂O⁼ ‡H₂O⁼

‡H₂O⁼ ‡H₂O⁼
‡H₂O⁼

unsatisfied valencies in inner layer

attracted cations and polar water molecules in outer layer

free water zone

Double layer theory. Theory which explains the electrostatic charges on colloidal clay particles whereby particles repel one another and do not sediment in a suspension. The theory concerns the ends of the atomic lattice of the clay crystal. See **Clay, crystal structure**.

The clay crystal is a continuous sheet in which atoms satisfy the valency requirements of the adjacent atoms on both sides. It follows that at the edge of the crystal there are unsatisfied valencies. This is called the 'broken bond theory' and it is accepted that the end atoms are oxygens and hydroxyl groups (O^{2-} and OH^-). The unsatisfied charge is therefore negative. This is the inner layer. See diagram.

The outer layer of the double layer has therefore a positive charge. See diagram. It is composed of sodium, potassium, calcium and magnesium cations ($Na^+ K^+ Ca^{2+} Mg^{2+}$) and also water molecules. This is the anchorage of the adsorbed water layer. See **Adsorption**. The water molecules, although electrically neutral with the two negative charges of the oxygen satisfied by the positive charges from two hydrogen atoms, have a polarity like a small magnet. They orientate themselves towards the clay, positive pole inwards.

Whilst the outer layer contains different elements, clays tend to have outer layers which have a dominant element. Most natural clays are calcium dominant. The dominant element gives a character to the clay in terms of plasticity and behaviour in suspension. The reason is that the cations of these different elements have different 'stand-off distances'. Their character is measured as the latent energy they possess for repulsion of like charges. See **Zeta potential**.

However, the cations composing the layers can be quickly replaced by others of different character. This is done by introducing suitable cations into the suspension water. The process is called cation exchange and occurs in the deflocculation of casting slips. See **Fluidity, Deflocculant** and **Casting slips**.

Down-draught kiln. A kiln in which the hot gases, after rising upwards on entering the chamber, are drawn downwards through the ware before escaping through holes in the floor or floor level flues. In order to effect sufficient draw a tall chimney is usually required. A down-draught kiln is more efficient than an up-draught one because the hot gases travel twice as far within the chamber. Also more uniform heating of the chamber, more control of the firing cycle and more control of the kiln atmosphere are possible.

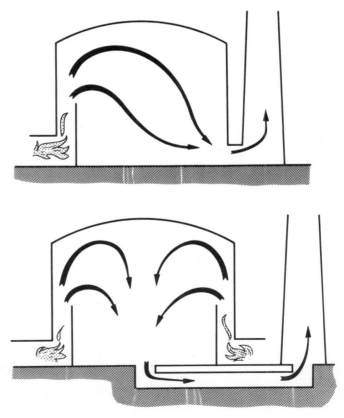

Draw. (1) To unpack a kiln.

Draw. (2) The energy exerted by a chimney on the kiln gases.

Drift. Mining term for a tunnel which has to be at a steep angle in order to follow the seam. Used in coal, fireclay and ball clay mining. A horizontal tunnel is called a level.

Dry clay. Clay which has dried completely and is therefore as dry as the surrounding air. The workshop test for a dry pot is to put it to the cheek. The dry pot feels as warm as the air but the pot which is still drying feels cold.

Because the atmosphere contains moisture, dry clay will always contain some moisture by virtue of the effects of adsorption and capillary condensation. See **Adsorption**. Therefore the early stages of a firing are taken slowly in what is called the pre-heating or water-smoking period. See also **Drying,** in which the term bone-dry clay is used for clay which has reached 120°C (248°F) in an artificial drying situation.

Drying. The removal of moisture. In pottery this usually means the drying of wet clay or newly-glazed ware. Technically, drying is the establishment of equilibrium moisture content between object and air. Wet clay dries by wetting the air around it. When the air holds as much water as the clay, the drying ceases.

Clay can therefore only dry out up to a point which is determined by the atmosphere. If taken beyond this point by applied heat, which creates its own special localized atmosphere, the clay will take up moisture from the atmosphere when the heat is removed. See **Readsorption**.

Three factors are involved in drying: temperature, which encourages evaporation; humidity of surrounding air, whether this is the general atmosphere or a controlled one; and the movement of the air past the surface, thereby replacing saturated air with drier air. In simple terms, the conditions which are good for drying washing out of doors are good for drying pots, whether these conditions are natural or created in the workshop. When barometric pressure is high, the atmosphere can hold more water than when pressure is low. Warm, dry and breezy weather is more effective than cool, damp and still weather. The most effective conditions could cause unequal drying out at rims and handles. This results in warpage and cracking and must be avoided by sheltering the pots or slowing down the drying rate. Pots will need to be turned around and over to even out the effects of sun and wind.

The easiest way to understand the theory of drying and to relate this to pot-making is to consider it as two stages. The first stage is the removal of the water of plasticity and the second stage is the removal of the pore water. See **Water**. The leatherhard state is the dividing point.

The enlarged sections, figs. 1 to 5 show the stages in detail. Figs. 1 to 3 are the first stage and figs. 3 to 5 are the second stage.

Fig. 1 is a clay slip or slurry. The clay particles are suspended in water and can move freely. Fig. 2 is plastic clay. Here, the particles are much closer together and there is therefore some friction caused by the suction seal of water between particles. See **Plasticity**. However the particles can be moved past one another using the water as lubricant. In contrast, fig. 3 shows leatherhard clay in which the particles have physical contact and friction.

At this point it should be realized that each clay particle has a surrounding layer of water which is firmly attached. In the diagrams, this is shown as a solid thick line. This is part of the bound water content. The water is held there by the hydroxyl groups and unsatisfied valencies of the clay crystal structure. See **Double layer theory**. In comparison with the clay crystal, it is a very thin layer—a few molecules in thickness. On the finest clay particle this would mean about a hundredth of the diameter. Yet this layer provides a lubricated cushion. In leatherhard clay, as shown in fig. 3, these cushions are touching and thus provide a 'solid' state. The anchorage is by molecular attraction but there is still sufficient 'loose' water on the outside of the layer to act as a lubricant. Leatherhard clay can be reshaped by strong pressure without rupturing the whole piece of clay.

Clay can only dry where the water can evaporate at the surface. The clay surface is shown at the top of the diagrams. Water migrates from the centre of the clay through the pores (P) to the surface (S). See figs. 2 and 3. As the gaps between the particles close, it becomes increasingly difficult for the water to migrate. It can do so only by a system of substitutions along the bound water layers or by circuitous routes via pores that are still linked. The drying process therefore slows down considerably.

The rate of drying can be shown by a graph as fig. 6. Here it is assumed that the drying conditions are constant, i.e. a constant temperature, humidity and air

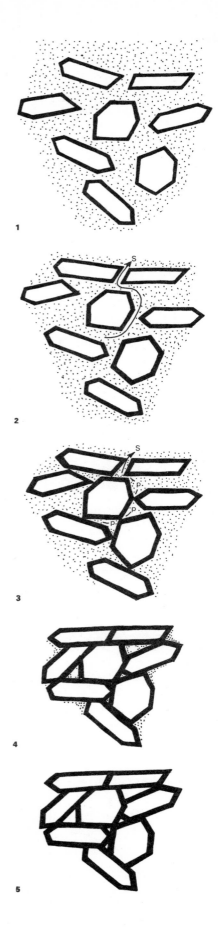

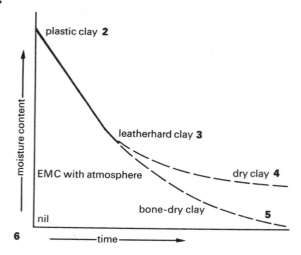

flow. The rate of drying is constant from plastic state to almost leatherhard state, but the escape of the water is hindered as the particles come closer together. The leatherhard stage is a distinct turning point which is reached in about a third of the total drying-out time and at a point when about half the water has evaporated. The dotted lines show the possible variation of drying out dependent upon the humidity of the air around.

Fig. 4 represents air-dried clay. This is the furthest dry state possible in the open air. The tiniest pores are still filled with water but the large pores have drained and contain only a meniscus of water held by capillary action. The bound layer of water around each clay particle is theoretically reduced to its minimum. This is seen where two particles 'touch'. The particles now share the same layer and it is only two or three molecules thick. The whole mass of clay is now solid and cannot be reshaped without rupturing the bonds between the particles and thus breaking the clay.

Fig. 5 represents bone-dry clay. This state occurs in the early stages of firing, after the water-smoking period, and is considered as existing from 120°C (248°F) up to the ceramic change at 600°C (1112°F). See **Firing**. In bone-dry clay, the pore water has gone but the bound water remains to be eventually driven off in the ceramic change. The pore water must be driven off carefully because there are few passages through which it can escape to the surface. See **Water smoking**. Happenings above 120°C (248°F) are described under **Firing** and the diagrams used are a continuation of those used for **Drying**.

An important effect of drying is shrinkage. Shrinkage, or rather unequal shrinkage, is responsible for drying cracks and warping. See **Cracks** and **Clay, physics**. A clay's behaviour is shown diagrammatically by a drying-shrinkage graph. Fig. 7 is a typical graph related to the figs. 1 to 5. The vertical axis of the graph represents, in cubic centimetres, the volume which 100 grams of dry clay becomes at different water contents. The water contents are represented on the horizontal axis and the numbers here refer, in grams, to a weight

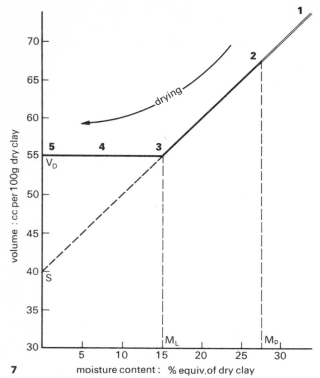

7

of water which is combined with the theoretical 100 grams of dry clay. This is usually described as percentage moisture content but it should be understood that the figures here do not correspond to the description of a plastic clay as 20% water. The 20% water of plastic clay is compared with the weight of the plastic clay as a whole and not the dry clay content only. For an explanation of the two methods of percentage expression see later in connection with fig. 8.

Reading this graph in relation to the figs. 1 to 5 one finds that fig. 1, which represents slip, relates to a point somewhere in the top right-hand corner of the graph. An exact position would be determined by the water content. Fig. 2, which is plastic clay, comes further down the line and fig. 3, which is leatherhard clay, further still. These three points are in a straight line which slopes at 45° since 1 gram of water is 1 cubic centimetre in volume. As the moisture content of the clay decreases in grams, so the volume of the clay decreases by an equal number of cubic centimetres. From these first three points one might expect the final dry solid piece of clay to be point S on the graph, but of course, at leatherhard state the particles are touching and so the overall volume of the clay decreases very little from that point to the bone-dry state (fig. 5).

One finds therefore that most drying-shrinkage graphs have angular 'curves' and that the line from V_D (the dry volume) to the point of moisture content M_L (leatherhard moisture content) is often horizontal or nearly so. The danger period for shrinkage cracks is therefore from plastic state to leatherhard state and not from leatherhard to dry state.

Each clay is individual in physical behaviour so suppliers often quote the figures for points V_D, S, M_L and M_P. To make comparisons one can draw graphs using the information supplied, starting at point S and drawing the 45° line. The leatherhard state is directly above point M_L. The leatherhard point is joined by a straight line to point V_D.

Fig. 8 is a diagrammatic representation of the water content of different clays. The amounts are true only for the actual clays tested but serve as a guide to similar clays. Plastic clay is taken as 100%. For example, plastic ball clay is approximately 80% dry clay content and 20% water, by weight. The water content of leatherhard clay is shown by horizontal shading. The weight of the clay after the ceramic change is included to link with the articles on **Firing, Ceramic change** and **Water**.

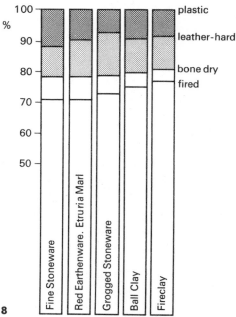

8

Formulae for discovering percentage content of water in clay etc are as follows. If percentage contents are required, it is first necessary to discover the water content of a sample piece of plastic clay by weighing the sample when plastic and when thoroughly dry. Weight of plastic clay minus weight of dry clay = weight of water content.

Dry basis method for percentage:

$$\frac{\text{weight of water}}{\text{weight of dry clay}} \times 100 = \% \text{ moisture content.}$$

Plastic basis method for percentage:

$$\frac{\text{weight of water}}{\text{weight of plastic clay}} \times 100 = \% \text{ moisture content.}$$

For example if a piece of plastic clay which weighs 12 lb is composed of 9 lb of dry clay and 3 lb of water, the resulting percentage contents are: $33\frac{1}{3}\%$ on the dry basis and 25% on the plastic basis.

The basis chosen is dependent upon the approach one is making. If one is concerned with dry clay and is adding an amount of water to this one would consider the dry clay as 100% and add to this a further percentage of water. For example a recipe for a slip would be expressed as a percentage recipe and the water to be added would be expressed as a further percentage weight above the 100% of the recipe. On the other hand if one were starting with a plastic clay and one wished to know how much of it was water, then one would express the water as a percentage of the whole.

Dunk. Tunk. To dip or plunge into liquid. Raku pots are often dunked into water to seal special effects. Dunking also causes quick crazing. Stained water or tea may be used to colour the first crazed pattern. Dunking is sometimes used as an empirical thermal shock test for ovenware.

Dunting. Cracking of pottery caused by stresses which form during firing and cooling. The resulting crack is called a dunt. See also **Crack**.

The main causes of dunting are the two silica inversions which take place at 573°C and 226°C (1063°F and 439°F). Differential contraction of body and glaze, without the action of a silica inversion, also causes stress which could result in dunting. All pots have stresses within them and most pots are strong enough to contain them. The few pots that crack do so because a number of factors come together: excessive stress, poor design (weak form and wrong material) and perhaps imprudent firing.

Some pots are already cracked when the kiln is opened whilst others crack a month or more later. Both are cases of dunting. If however a pot, such as a teacup, cracks in use, there will be other factors involved and such cracks are said to be caused by thermal shock. See **Thermal shock**.

The following dunts can be differentiated: biscuit dunts, firing dunts and cooling dunts. See also **Silica inversions** and **Glaze fit**.

BISCUIT DUNTS. Biscuit ware may dunt during cooling because the quartz and cristobalite inversions cause sudden decreases in body size. A very soft biscuit firing, e.g. 800°C (1472°F), may not sufficiently vitrify the body to give it strength to withstand the sudden change.

Biscuit dunts are hair cracks, almost invisible and easily overlooked. They are concentric with the pot and vertical, often looking like brickwork. The hair cracks show when the pot is being glazed. When the pot is taken out of the glaze slop and is still wet, the cracks will show lighter in colour because they have taken more glaze. Badly dunted pots disintegrate when being taken from the kiln or sometimes when being glazed, however a mild dunting of a single hair crack could pass unnoticed. Unfortunately, such a dunt usually opens during the glaze firing.

Slips sometimes dunt separately from the body. This happens when the slip and body are not matched in their vitrification range. If the slip is more refractory and more siliceous, the slip will dunt. A common example is the use of a siliceous ball clay as a white slip on a red body. Again a brickwork net of lines will show at the glazing stage. The cure is to add some flux or glaze to the slip.

The dunting cracks in a slip should not be confused with a network of crazing cracks which is the result of poor fit. Crazing cracks are more usual when the slip is over-fluxed. Crazing cracks are irregular squares, pentagons and hexagons whereas dunting cracks are rectangles following the lines of the pot. Dunted slip does little harm, except for the uneven glaze application, but it is an indication that dunting conditions were present and that the slip and body are not fully compatible.

To avoid biscuit dunts, a number of cumulative measures can be employed.

1. A slightly higher biscuit temperature will strengthen the ware by extra vitrification. It will also leave less free crystalline silica in the body.

2. A slower rate of cooling will allow a pot to adjust itself slowly to the change in size. The fastest contemplated rate should be a uniform 100°C/hr from 600°C (180°F/hr from 1112°F).

3. A decrease in the free silica in the body will decrease the amount of sudden contraction. Free silica may be quartz, flint, sand or cristobalite.

4. An increase in the amount of body flux will strengthen the ware by extra vitrification. It will also convert free silica (crystalline silica) into silica glass which is not subject to inversion.

The problem is similar to that of **Cooling dunts** which should be read in conjunction with the above.

FIRING DUNTS. Cristobalite and quartz inversions may cause dunts during the warming-up period of a glaze firing. Such dunts are rare. The inversions give the body a sudden increase in size, which, if not allowed to happen uniformly throughout a pot, would cause stress between two parts of the pot. This happens if the firing is too rapid.

In practice most biscuit ware, which is what the body is at this stage, is strong enough to withstand the stress over the temporary period until all the pot has had its cristobalite or quartz inverted. Refires suffer if made from bodies which are fine and dense and contain cristobalite as an anticraze. Cracks which occur during firing can be distinguished from those which happen during cooling because the glaze crawls away from the crack or fuses with rounded edges on the crack.

Firing cracks, as opposed to cooling cracks, are usually the result of previous cracks which open further. They could be biscuit dunts but they could equally be other cracks which started before the biscuit and remained undetected after the biscuit firing. They could be the result of unequal structure, drying stress, mishandling, or readsorption at the raw stage. These cracks occur no matter what precautions are taken with the glaze firing although they are often blamed on the glaze firing. They are described simply as firing cracks. See **Crack**.

Firing dunts may be ring cracks concentric with the pot or vertical cracks from the rim possibly spiralling around the pot. The pot often falls in pieces, the pieces jumping apart. It should be repeated that firing dunts are rare. They can be overcome by the following measures:

1. A slower rate of firing over the dunting points allows a pot to expand as a unit as the silica inverts.

2. A slightly higher biscuit firing will give a stronger biscuit to withstand the stress.

3. A reduction of the free silica in the body will reduce the sudden expansion proportionately.

COOLING DUNTS. The most common time for dunting to take place is during the cooling after a glaze firing or after a high-temperature firing of unglazed stoneware. The immediate period after taking pots from the kiln and before they are put into use is also included.

Cooling dunts are long, clean, body cracks with sharp edges. If the ware is glazed, then the glaze obviously cracks with the body and since the glaze is set when the crack takes place, it too has very sharp edges. There is often some sideways displacement (strain) which makes the dunt detectable by touch although it may not be immediately visible. The cracks are vertical ones, horizontal ones (ring cracks) and spiral ones which may or may not reach the rim. See also **Crack**.

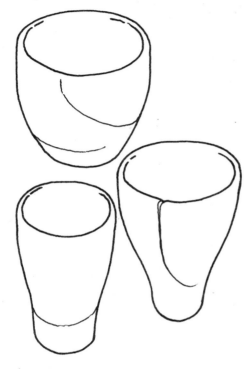

For the purposes of explanation, three types of cooling dunt are discussed: two which occur in the kiln and are discovered upon opening; and one which occurs one or two months after the pots are taken from the kiln. The first two types of dunt occur with glazed and unglazed ware. The third type occurs only with glazed ware. The types are very closely related and look the same.

The first type of cooling dunt is the result of the quartz inversion which occurs at 573°C (1063°F). Here the free silica (quartz phase) undergoes a sudden contraction. See **Silica phases** and **Silica inversions**. At this point, the body contracts proportionally to the amount of free silica (quartz) which it contains. The ideal cooling would allow the whole pot to reach this dunting point at one moment so that it could contract as a whole. In practice it is difficult to arrange this and a pot must undergo the stress of having one part contracting before another. If the body contains much free silica, the contraction will be great. The stress between two parts of a pot will also be great and it is at this stage that dunting may take place. Even the usually safe descent of 200°C/hr (360°F/hr) may not be slow enough for a large pot.

A tall pot on a thick shelf will cool quicker in its upper part than near the base. The thick shelf on which it stands will hold the heat and keep the base of the pot hot whilst the rest cools. At dunting point, when the free silica changes its size, the upper part of the pot contracts but the base does not. The result is a ring crack around the pot about an inch up from the foot.

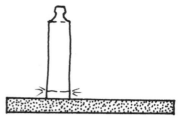

Similarly, a wide bowl is fortunate if it can contract as a whole. If one side cools before the other, cracks occur at the intermediate points. These cracks run from the rim downwards then curve towards the cooler side. A piece of the bowl may even break away completely. It will be seen that uniform cooling is important and for this reason all draughts are excluded from a kiln during cooling below 600°C (1112°F).

The second type of cooling dunt is the result of the cristobalite inversion which takes place at 226°C (439°F). This concerns free silica of the cristobalite phase. See **Silica phases** and **Silica inversions**. All the points relevant to quartz inversions are applicable to cristobalite inversions and of the two types of dunt, the cristobalite one is the one to be feared. A potter is unlikely to open a kiln, except a raku kiln, above 573°C (1063°F) but there is a natural eagerness to open a kiln at about 250°C (482°F) when the glazes can be seen. In fact, the drawing of some wares, ovenware for instance, could actually begin at this temperature but it could be disastrous for dense wares containing cristobalite.

Some potters cool their kilns quickly from top temperature to 1000°C (clear red heat, 1832°F), but they then clam up all cracks and vents to provide a slow cooling thereafter. The kilns are not opened until the ware is cool enough to handle with bare hands. An initial quick cooling is important with stoneware because it hinders the formation of cristobalite. The silica conversion of quartz to cristobalite takes place above 1100°C (2012°F) and whilst some cristobalite in the body is useful as an anticraze it is possible to get too

much. Dense stonewares are susceptible to cristobalite dunting. Earthenware bodies, which are porous and more elastic, can absorb a larger amount of cristobalite movement.

The third type of cooling dunt is the one which occurs after the pot is taken from the kiln. The pot remains whole, for perhaps six or eight weeks, then suddenly rips apart, possibly with a loud report and probably during a particularly cold night. This type of dunt is caused by stress between body and glaze, which stress may have originated with a silica inversion but may be the result of unequal body and glaze contractions.

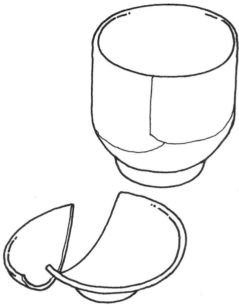

At 573°C (1063°F) by far the majority of glazes are still plastic. This means that any stress set up between body and glaze by the quartz inversion in the body could be absorbed by the plasticity of the glaze. A dunt caused by body-glaze stress arising from quartz inversion is therefore unlikely.

However, at 226°C (439°F) the glaze has set and the cristobalite inversion in the body must create a stress between body and glaze. This phenomenon is known as the cristobalite squeeze and is encouraged as an anti-craze measure. See **Cristobalite in bodies**. Excessive stress which cannot be contained results in a dunt known as a cristobalite dunt.

The name cristobalite dunt is often used to describe a dunt which occurs after the pot is removed from the kiln. It should be realized however that a similar stress can occur without the assistance of a cristobalite inversion simply by the different contraction rates of body and glaze. See **Contraction**.

The stress which causes these dunts is in the form of a compression on the glaze. That is, the body is squeezing the glaze because it, the body, has contracted more than the glaze during the cooling. Considered another way, the glaze is putting a tension onto the body. That is, the glaze is stretching the body because it, the glaze, has contracted less than the body during the cooling. If the body is stronger than the glaze, it will shed the glaze. See **Shivering**. But if the glaze is strong and the body weaker by being perhaps brittle, the body is torn apart as a dunt. When this occurs, the covering glaze invariably goes with it.

Poor resistance to stress is accentuated by certain construction features. For example:

1. A thick layer of glaze on the inside of a pot and only a thin layer or no glaze at all on the outside forces all the stress one way. The dunt is usually a spiral.

2. If the outside glaze stops short of the foot, especially in a thickened roll, the stress produces a ring crack.

3. If the inside glaze has run down and produced a pool inside the pot, the tension on the body creates a split across the base of the pot. This crack may carry on up to the rim of the pot on one side or the pot may crack into halves. Such cracks in bases are often difficult to see and inside a bowl, a crack may look very similar to a single craze line. However it can often be felt as a sharp edge by the fingers in a way that a craze cannot. This is because, in releasing the stress, the strain has resulted in a misalignment of the edges.

4. Often in combination with number 3, the unequal thickness of the body accentuates the stress on the thinnest parts. If the pot is thick-walled with a thin base and the glaze has run down into a pool as in number 3, there is a high risk of a dunt occurring.

5. A thin brittle body is not strong enough to exert compression upon a thick glassy glaze. Overfiring often causes the body to be brittle and the glaze to be glassy.

6. A thin, open and weak body like an underfired fireclay, is not strong enough to exert compression upon a glaze. This might happen if the wrong body were used or a porous body normally kept for ovenware were used for thinly-potted tableware with a thick glaze.

Cooling dunts can be overcome by a number of measures, some of which seem contradictory and cannot be used together. It is not easy to decide which preventative action to take and some experimental testing may be necessary.

1. Slowing down the rate of cooling at the dunting points will help large pots to survive the silica inversions, but it will not remove a stress which exists between body and glaze. If the pots dunt after being taken from the kiln, other measures must be taken to remove the stress.

2. If the stress is diagnosed as between body and glaze, the glaze can be altered to make it contract more. See **Glaze fit**. Alternatively the body can be made to contract less.

3. If cristobalite is part of the body recipe, this should be drastically reduced or left out altogether.

4. The firing and cooling cycle can be altered to reduce the amount of time that the pots withstand temperatures above 1100°C (2012°F). The top temperature remains the same and, as far as possible, the glaze fusion remains the same. However, the heat has less time to penetrate the body and therefore less quartz is converted into cristobalite. Time is an important factor in silica conversion. This method is effective with medium and coarse stoneware and ovenware.

5. The amount of sand, quartz and flint should also be lessened. The less free silica that there is in a body, the less proportionately will be the overall contraction. This is important with glazed ware.

6. The addition of more flux to the body will decrease the free silica by incorporating some of it into the molten parts of the vitrification. Feldspar and cornish stone are the usual body fluxes but the usual glaze fluxes are effective with the exception of calcia and magnesia which act as catalysts. See **Silica conversion**.

7. A slightly higher firing or a slightly extended soaking will involve more of the free silica in glassy vitrification. It will then no longer be crystalline and thus not subject to inversion. This is the method to use with fine stoneware and porcelain. Here the free silica is extremely fine and vitrification helps to give translucency. It is not always effective with coarse sandy stoneware bodies which resist involvement.

8. In contrast with number 7, if the body is too brittle because it is too dense and glassy, a lowering of the top firing temperature will give strength and a capacity to absorb the stress. This method is used with sandy bodies. See **Vitrification** and **Thermal shock**.

Dunting points. Inversion points. The temperatures at which the silica inversions take place. They are 573°C (1063°F) for quartz and 226°C (439°F) for cristobalite. These are given as exact temperatures because this is the way in which the potter thinks of the action as taking place. They are the usually accepted dunting points but the ceramic physicist has proved that under differing circumstances the quartz inversion may vary between 550°C and 575°C (1022°F and 1067°F) and the cristobalite inversion between 220°C and 260°C (428°F and 500°F). Quartz and cristobalite dunting points are also called the upper and lower dunting points respectively. See **Silica inversions**.

The upper dunting point is the one at which most biscuit dunts occur. The lower dunting point is the one at which most of the dunts to glazed ware occur. A slow cooling past these points is necessary with most pottery.

Dwight, John. The first English potter to experiment systematically on a scientific basis. In 1671 he started to produce salt-glazed stoneware and in 1674 founded his famous Fulham Pottery. He made both brown and white salt-glaze, some of which was translucent where thin, but he laid no claim to it as a porcelain. He experimented with soft-paste porcelain and red porcelain or red stoneware.

E

Earthenware. Pottery made of a porous body which is waterproofed, if necessary, by a covering glaze. The simplest division of all pottery is into earthenware and stoneware. A criterion for this division is the porosity of the body. If the fired body has a porosity of more than 5%, then it is earthenware.

Many potters add to this criterion of porosity a consideration of the temperature at which the glaze is fired. The softer temperatures below 1100°C (2012°F), which are associated with earthenware glazes, allow a wider range of colour and a particular quality of visual shine and texture. They usually contain lead oxide and/or boric oxide. By considering only the porosity of the body, one ignores the glaze which is probably more important since most earthenware is almost completely glazed. It is also in the glaze that differences between earthenware and stoneware are first apparent. The physical hardness or softness of the glaze is also a possible criterion and so is the presence or otherwise of a well-formed body-glaze layer. See **Hard** and **Stoneware**.

The following are earthenwares:

Raku: porous body and soft glaze.

Slipware: mostly porous body with little integration of body, slip and glaze; soft glaze.

Maiolica, Majolica and Faience: porous body and soft glaze.

Creamware: porous body in spite of possible high bisc temperature; soft glaze.

The following are earthenwares by quality:

Bone and non-bone china: soft glaze although covering a non-porous body.

Soft paste porcelain: soft glaze and use of soft temperatures for firing.

Red stoneware: soft glazes integrating with a dense body at soft or medium temperatures.

The widest range of working methods is used for earthenware: throwing, hand-building, pressing, slabbing, jigger/jolley and slip-casting. No one clay is sufficiently versatile to be used for them all. Earthenware clays are therefore many and various. They are chosen for their colour and their workability. When buying prepared clays or bodies one should ascertain for what making method they are intended. See **Workability**, **Plasticity** and **Clay, types**.

Element. Chemical element. A substance which is so pure that it contains only atoms of the same atomic number. For example if all the atoms in a substance are of atomic number 29, then the substance is the element

copper. The following list gives elements which the potter is likely to use and includes their chemical symbols, valencies and atomic weights correct to one decimal place.

Element	Symbol	AW	Valency
aluminium	Al	27·0	3
antimony	Sb	121·8	3
arsenic	As	74·9	3
barium	Ba	137·3	2
beryllium	Be	9·0	2
bismuth	Bi	209·0	3
boron	B	10·8	3
cadmium	Cd	112·4	2
calcium	Ca	40·1	2
carbon	C	12·0	2 and 4
cerium	Ce	140·1	4
chlorine	Cl	35·5	1
chromium	Cr	52·0	3
cobalt	Co	58·9	2 and 3
copper	Cu	63·5	1 and 2
fluorine	F	19·0	1
germanium	Ge	72·6	4
gold	Au	197·0	—
hydrogen	H	1·0	1
iron	Fe	55·8	2 and 3
lead	Pb	207·2	2 and 4
lithium	Li	6·9	1
magnesium	Mg	24·3	2
manganese	Mn	54·9	2, 3 and 4
nickel	Ni	58·7	2 and 4
nitrogen	N	14·0	3
oxygen	O	16·0	2
phosphorus	P	31·0	3 and 5
platinum	Pt	195·1	—
potassium	K	39·1	1
praseodymium	Pr	140·9	4
selenium	Se	79·0	—
silicon	Si	28·1	4
silver	Ag	107·9	—
sodium	Na	23·0	1
strontium	Sr	87·6	2
sulphur	S	32·1	2 and 4
tin	Sn	118·7	4
titanium	Ti	47·9	4
uranium	U	238·0	3, 4 and 5
vanadium	V	50·9	2, 3, 4 and 5
zinc	Zn	65·4	2
zirconium	Zr	91·2	4

Elephant's ear. A close-textured, natural, springy sponge shaped roughly like an elephant's ear. It is flattish and about 5 inches across. It is used in press-moulding where its springy character is useful for forcing the clay against the mould without scratching the surface.

Elers (Ehlers) brothers, John and David. Dutch potters who settled in England in 1688 and produced a red stoneware, first in London, then at Bradwell Wood in Staffordshire. They used the Staffordshire red clay and washed and levigated it to obtain a fine body. This was thrown and turned to a thin section. It was burnished and had sprigging from engraved brass and copper moulds applied to it. Tableware was popular in Boccaro style, the dense body firing to a rich red brown and being unglazed.

Elutriation. The separation of fine clay from a mass of coarse clay by use of the property of fine clay to remain in suspension in water when larger particles, such as sand and stones, will sink. Elutriation uses a mechanical device to move the slurry, sometimes upwards against gravity. The finest particles can be moved the furthest distance. Proportionately coarser ones fall out on the way. Elutriation differs from levigation which uses gravity to move the slurry slowly past settling riffles. In sedimentation and settling the slurry is not moved at all but is allowed to stand still in bins or tanks.

Enamel. Onglaze enamel. Metal enamel. Glass enamel. Vitreous enamel. Porcelain enamel. A soft-melting glass used to decorate pottery, metal and glass. The material is similar in all cases and like other ceramic glazes is composed of fluxes and alumino-silicates. Soda, potash and boric oxide are the main fluxes with some lead oxide in glass and onglaze enamels. The colours are the usual metal oxides.

Potters mostly use the onglaze enamels but some of the other types give interesting results when melted as pools on tiles and into hollowed areas on decorative dishes etc. In using other than onglaze enamels, one should remember that enamels for metal often contain minerals which may volatilize and cause blisters in the longer duration of a pottery firing. See also **Cullet**.

The terms onglaze enamel and onglaze colour are used for pottery enamels. These are abbreviated to O/E and O/G. See **Onglaze**.

Metal enamel is used for decorative metalwork cloisonné mostly on copper. Glass enamel is used for decorating glassware. Vitreous enamel and the rather misleading name porcelain enamel are names for the glaze coatings given to sheet ironware and cast ironware.

Encaustic. A method of decoration whereby coloured clays are inlaid in the body clay. The inlaid pieces are made to fill cut-out lines and shapes or are rolled onto the surface. See **Rolled inlay**. The encaustic method was used by the Cistercian monks to produce paving tiles. It provided a decoration which was permanent even when the covering glaze had worn away.

Engobe. A term of wide meaning often interchangeable with slip but including other materials. An engobe is used to cover a clay, produce a buffer layer and give a different surface, texture and colour. It is applied by brush, dip, spray etc.

Clay slips and glaze slops are essentially fluid forms. An engobe can be in a jelly form or a stiff form. It is often halfway between a clay and a glaze in composition and contains materials which are normally considered glaze materials. It therefore fires to a more vitreous state than the body which it covers. However, since it does not fuse to a glassy state, it cannot be called a glaze. And since it can be composed entirely of non-clay materials, it cannot be called a slip. The term engobe is often the only one that is suitable.

Enstatite. Magnesium silicate. $MgO.SiO_2$. The simplest and purest of the pyroxene minerals. It is a crystalline precipitate in intermediate and basic igneous rocks. The crystal growth is quickly established because in basic rocks there is no lack of suitable alkaline oxides in with the silica melt. This crystal growth occurs in cooling glazes which are similarly high in magnesia. See **Magnesian matts** and **Crystalline glazes**.

For example, if a glaze contains talc for the purpose of a flux, it is likely to recrystallize as enstatite upon cooling, giving an opacity and mattness. The stage formulae would be:

$$3MgO.4SiO_2.H_2O \xrightarrow[1652°F]{900°C} \text{decomposes to give:}$$

$$\underset{\text{talc}}{}$$

$$\underset{\substack{\text{free} \\ \text{magnesia}}}{3MgO} + \underset{\substack{\text{free} \\ \text{silica}}}{4SiO_2} + \underset{\text{water}}{H_2O \uparrow} \xrightarrow[2156°F]{1180°C}$$

At 1180°C (2156°F) the magnesia and silica are involved in a ceramic fusion. During cooling, some of the magnesia and silica devitrify to give:

$$\underset{\text{enstatite}}{3(MgO.SiO_2)} + \underset{\substack{\text{free silica involved} \\ \text{in other fusion.}}}{SiO_2}$$

The diagram shows the lattice of enstatite in which continuous SiO_3 silica chains have alternate units inverted. Two silica chains are drawn. The Mg^{2+} ions are in six-fold co-ordination, each regularizing one silica chain and linking it to one other. Thus a sheet type of structure is formed with emphasis upon the long needles of the thereby straightened silica chains.

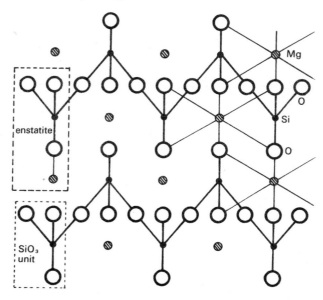

Epsom salts. Epsom salts are sometimes used to thicken a glaze slop that is too thin. This is a rule-of-thumb procedure used when one cannot wait for the glaze to settle and have its water syphoned away. Only a small amount of epsom salts is required. The action is that of flocculation. Other flocculants are plaster of Paris and calcium chloride. See **Magnesium sulphate**.

Equation. Chemical equation which shows in symbol or formula form what is happening in a chemical action. For example:

$$CaMg(CO_3)_2 \longrightarrow CaO + MgO + 2CO_2 \uparrow$$

The two sides of an equation should balance in number of atoms represented.

Equivalent. Equivalent number of molecules. The term is used when referring to the substitution of one compound for another when the calculation of amount is done on the basis of the unity formula.

For example, supposing one wished to increase the amount of soda feldspar in a glaze recipe at the expense of the potash feldspar. This may be necessary to overcome shivering. A straightforward substitution, weight for weight, is the usual approach of the potter and is sufficiently accurate in most cases. However, if the glaze is carefully balanced, as may happen with a dolomite matt, it may be necessary to do the substitution on the basis of the number of molecules involved. This is called an equivalent substitution. Soda feldspar and potash feldspars have different molecular weights and therefore a weight for weight substitution would involve a different number of molecules.

For the purpose of this example, the dolomite recipe from dolomite matt will be used. The recipe is:

potash feldspar	20
soda feldspar	20
china clay	20
whiting	20
dolomite	20

The unity formula is:

$$\left.\begin{array}{l} 0.073\ K_2O \\ 0.077\ Na_2O \\ 0.222\ MgO \\ 0.628\ CaO \end{array}\right\} 0.309\ Al_2O_3 \quad 1.218\ SiO_2$$

The adjusted unity formula substituting 0.05 equivalents of soda for potash is:

$$\left.\begin{array}{l} 0.023\ K_2O \\ 0.127\ Na_2O \\ 0.222\ MgO \\ 0.628\ CaO \end{array}\right\} 0.309\ Al_2O_3 \quad 1.218\ SiO_2$$

And the percentage recipe calculated from this new unity formula is:

potash feldspar	6.26
soda feldspar	33.05
china clay	20.23
whiting	20.23
dolomite	20.23

A potash molecule is heavier than a soda molecule. In order to get the same number of molecules, the soda feldspar has only needed to be increased by 13.05%

whereas the potash feldspar has been decreased by 13·74%. To keep the whole recipe in percentage form, the other items have been increased. It must be realized that the overall proportion of molecules $RO:R_2O_3:RO_2$ has remained the same throughout.

Eutectic mixture. The proportioned mixture of two or more substances which melts at the lowest possible temperature. This temperature is called the eutectic point.

For example, lead oxide melts at 880°C (1616°F) and silica at 1710°C (3110°F). It would be reasonable to expect that a 50/50 mixture by weight would melt at the halfway point of 1295°C (2363°F). However such is the interaction of these two materials that this mixture would probably melt at about 800°C (1472°F). This temperature is lower than the melting points of the constituents and it is by no means the eutectic point or lowest possible melting point for lead oxide and silica combinations. The lowest melting point is achieved by the eutectic mixture approximating 90% lead oxide and 10% silica with a melting point at 510°C (950°F).

Another example is that of alumina and silica melting at 2050°C and 1710°C respectively (3722°F and 3110°F). Both these substances are considered highly refractory and are often added to glazes to raise the melting point, that is, to stiffen a glaze which melts too much. Yet alumina and silica have a fluxing power on each other so that a 50/50 mix melts at about 1750°C (3182°F) instead of an expected halfway of about 1880°C (3416°F). The eutectic mixture is 10% alumina and 90% silica melting at 1545°C (2813°F), which again is lower than the melting point of either constituent.

All alkaline oxides react with silica to produce melting points lower than one could calculate by a straight-line graph. Thus in graph 1, the dotted line shows the straight line between the two melting points of imaginary alkaline oxide RO and silica. Along this straight line one might expect to find the melting points of the mixtures as they range in proportion from 100% RO at the left-hand side to 100% silica at the right-hand side. However, in reality, the melting points lie on the continuous line at the lower temperatures. The point E is the eutectic point and, in this imaginary example, the eutectic mixture is 60% alkaline oxide and 40% silica.

Graph 1 shows that if one starts with 100% silica at the right-hand side of the graph and progressively adds the alkaline oxide, and at the same time decreases the silica, the mixtures melt at progressively lower temperatures until point E is reached. After point E the addition of more alkaline oxide, with decreasing percentage of silica, results in mixtures which melt at progressively higher temperatures. Since most glazes are typical of the right-hand side of this graph whereby an increase in alkaline oxide results in more fusion, alkaline oxides are generally termed fluxes. However, if one considers the left-hand side of the graph one will realize that the increasing amounts of silica are having a fluxing action upon the alkaline oxide.

Some alkaline oxides have very low melting points to begin with, so that mixtures with silica cannot melt below the temperature of the pure oxide. Strictly speaking, there is no eutectic mixture and no eutectic point. Graph 2 shows this using the same graph framework as graph 1. There still occurs an optimum point marked E on the graph which most people agree upon calling a eutectic point. Graph 3 shows a more complex line with three eutectic points (E) and two reverse eutectic points (R). Some alkaline oxides, notably lead oxide and copper oxide, give graphs like this. Potash,

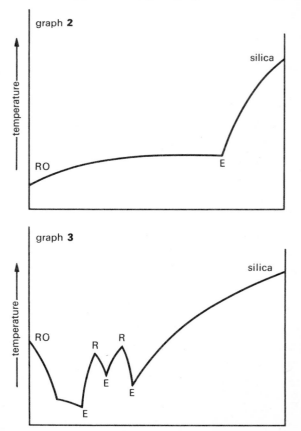

graph **2**

graph **1**

graph **3**

soda and lithia give graphs like graph 2, and the high melting oxides of magnesia, calcia, zinc oxide and manganous oxide give graphs like graph 1.

Eutectic mixtures in glazes are not a simple matter of one oxide with silica but a case of each oxide reacting with every other. The most obvious reactions are those of alkali with acid, e.g. soda with silica. The reaction is usually considered the simple effect of a flux attacking a silica. This is an over-simplification. It is equally true that the silica attacks the flux as was earlier proven. Also in mixtures of amphoteric oxide and acid there will be a reaction because the amphoteric oxide presents an alkaline property. Similarly in a mixture of amphoteric oxide and alkali there will be a reaction because the amphoteric oxide presents an acidic property.

All oxides are excited in the presence of heat and in the presence of other oxides the excitement is multiplied. The increased intramolecular vibration results in fluidity, that is, melting. Therefore some effect must result from a mixture of any two oxides, even two acids, e.g. silica and phosphorus pentoxide, or from a mixture of two alkalis, e.g. potash and soda. However the most significant results will be those with strong alkali and strong acid. Only silica need be considered as the acid but there are many alkaline oxides and each one is different in its effectiveness as a glaze flux.

As a glaze is heated the simplest eutectic combinations will melt first. Once fluid, they will soak into the surrounding material and discover other combinations or oxides with which to produce more complex eutectics. This continues until the whole mass is molten. If the process is stopped before the end point, it will be found that some parts have completely melted producing a glass but within this glass are specks of unmelted material. The effect may be a desirable opaque glaze but the end point, where all the eutectic combinations have occurred, would be a transparent, if coloured, glass.

It is relatively easy to understand the graphs 1, 2 and 3, but, as has just been stated, a glaze is much more complex. In glaze reasoning one would usually be faced with substances which within themselves contain potential eutectic combinations, e.g. cornish stone, feldspar, flint and dolomite. These eutectic mixtures may combine to form more complex ones involving 3, 4, 5, 6, 7, 8 etc, individual oxides. Involved combinations cannot be represented on graphs like 1, 2, and 3. A graph for three constituents is plotted as in graph 4. Here point P represents 70% silica, 20% RO(A) and 10% RO(B). This is arrived at by counting across the graph from a flat side towards an apex. At an apex 100% is represented for the ingredient there named. There is no room on this graph for a temperature scale but only for the various mixtures. The temperature of the melting points of the various mixtures is therefore plotted as a series of lines linking mixtures with the same melting temperatures.

In this example graph the temperatures are 700°C,

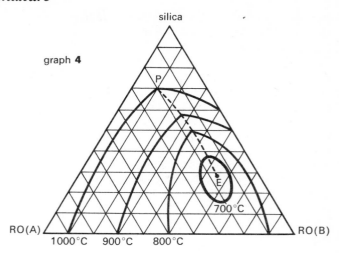

800°C, 900°C and 1000°C. The eutectic mixture appears at a point E. However it can happen that no point E exists, because within the enclosed line linking the lowest temperatures, the mixtures melt at higher temperatures. In this case the most practical mixture for glazes is the one containing the most silica. In fact it is usual to find, as in graph 4, that there is a point or angle on each temperature line. Joining these points gives what is known as the eutectic axis.

If four constituents are involved, the graph becomes three-dimensional. The fourth constituent would be at the apex of a pyramid based on graph 4. The reading of such graphs is obviously difficult, so most ceramists would standardize one constituent and plot a series of graphs like graph 4, or else standardize two constituents and plot a series of graphs like graphs 1, 2 and 3. All this work is beyond most individuals and requires the resources of a factory. Simple methods of testing in refractory test blocks, where the mixture is packed into A and seen to run and melt into B, or where the mixture is made into a bar C, which sags when melting, can only be done a few per firing without a special test kiln which has a good viewing system.

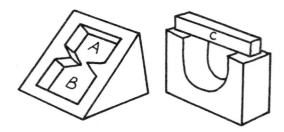

Rather than consider different temperatures, most potters have a series of test mixtures in the kiln fired to the same temperature. The three-sided graph can be used to plot areas which have similar results, e.g. matt rough, matt smooth, shiny, bubbled. Such results are obviously the outcome of eutectic fusion, or lack of it, but the graph could not necessarily be used to position a point E. Graphs like 4 can be plotted for any three

115

materials such as clay, wood ash and feldspar as well as pure oxides as illustrated here.

Individual potters need not make exhaustive eutectic tests. It is sufficient to understand the theory behind eutectic mixtures and apply this theory to workshop situations. It is possible to draw the graph 5 which is purely theoretical, yet sufficiently typical, to enable one to understand any glaze. The line represents all the possible mixtures of flux and silica. Here flux means all the alkaline oxides present in a glaze. An increase in flux assumes a decrease in silica and *vice versa* because the graph represents a ratio of the two at a constant total weight.

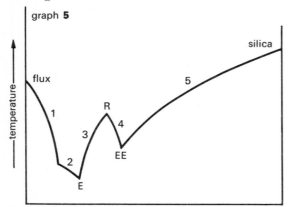

graph **5**

General observations would be that glazes having mixtures between flux and E would tend to be matt-surfaced due to crystallization. Between E and EE glazes would be shiny, and from EE to silica the glazes would get progressively duller.

Normally one would expect that an increase in flux would result in the glaze melting more easily. This is true for most glazes, such as maiolica and transparents, both earthenware and stoneware, and is represented on the graph by Area 5. It takes quite large changes of amounts to make appreciable changes in the glaze. This is shown by the shallow angle of the line of the graph. The difference between 40% and 50% of silica may not be discernible in some glazes.

If minute changes of less than 1% affect the glaze then it is probably in Area 3. This is a steep part of the graph and here only slight variations of the flux : silica ratio will result in very different fusion temperatures and hence results at a given temperature.

If the glaze happens to coincide with the point E or EE then any alteration as increase in flux or silica will result in a glaze fusing less at a given temperature. When tests prove this, and one is not satisfied with the glaze, one is in a very bewildering position. One must introduce yet another eutectic mixture, or near eutectic mixture, which is different from all those present. This needs to be very soft: certainly softer than the glaze by 300°C to 400°C (540°F to 720°F), otherwise it may be found not to give sufficient reaction. Simple frits like lead monosilicate are likely to be more effective than complex ones. If the results are still not satisfactory there must exist another eutectic point for the glaze which has not yet been discovered.

If the glaze is at position R, an increase in either flux or silica results in over-fusion. Results tend to be disastrous as well as disappointing. Sometimes increases in flux in the Area 3 can be satisfactory. Area 4 is unlikely to be satisfactory because it contains the unstable bright, shiny glazes. The best solution is to attempt to step across into Area 5.

Glazes from Area 5 are more usable and satisfactory, giving practically the same visual result and with more silica are composed of more stable silicates. Lastly, Areas 1 & 2 are the matt glazes. Area 1 is too steep a graph to be practical and contains too little silica to be a stable hard glaze when set. Area 2 contains the lime matts, alumina matts and zinc matts, in both earthenware and stoneware, and the stoneware dolomite matts. The point to note is that an increase in flux does not produce an increase in fusibility. If one wants such a glaze to melt more one has to decrease the flux content. This is an unusual approach for a potter who has previously only dealt with the more conventional glazes from Areas 5 and 3.

Expansion. Increase in size due to temperature change. In pottery one is concerned with rates of expansion as a means of calculating the expansion and contraction of bodies and glazes. See **Glaze fit**. Each constituent oxide of a body and glaze has its own rate of expansion.

For comparison, a few examples are given of volumetric expansion resulting from a rise in temperature from room temperature to 600°C (1112°F). They are based upon the observations of Winkelmann and Schott.

silica glass	(SiO_2)	0·5%
alumina	(Al_2O_3)	2·9%
lead oxide	(PbO)	1·7%
calcia	(CaO)	2·9%
soda	(Na_2O)	5·8%
potash	(K_2O)	4·3%

F

Fahrenheit. °F. Degrees Fahrenheit. The Fahrenheit scale is a scale of temperature measurement which is an extension of the thermometer scale 32°F to 212°F for the freezing point to boiling point of water. The scale is named after Gabriel Fahrenheit, the early 18th-century physicist.

Faience. Earthenware with colourful decoration or colourful glazes. Faience was the term originally given to wares from Faenza in northern Italy. These were tin-glazed wares of the maiolica type. However as the popularity of tin-glaze earthenware spread through Europe its character changed. Modelled decoration, as used on stoneware, was included with glazes which were more fluid than the maiolica glazes. This is the style that is now considered faience, that is, plain and modelled surfaces covered with shiny and matt glazes often blended together. Besides tin oxide, titanium dioxide and rutile are much used.

The name faience is used by archaeologists to describe tin-glazed wares from Egypt and south-west Asia. Also any glazed pottery, pottery ornaments and small beads, as yet unclassified, and which were made throughout Europe during the Bronze and Iron Ages are collectively referred to as faience. The photograph shows a turquoise tin-glazed bottle from Persia.

Fat clay. Long clay. Plastic clay. Clay of high plasticity. The term is reserved for clays which have more than ample plasticity for the requirements of the work in hand. These clays are often added to other clays to im-prove workability. Ball clays, for example, are fat clays. See **Plasticity**.

Feather combing. A slipware pattern of feathered shapes produced by combing through a series of trailed lines. One colour, traditionally white, is trailed across a ground slip of contrasting colour which covers a slab of clay. The trailed slip is made to sink into the ground slip by knocking the board on which the clay slab rests. A bristle, bullrush or feather is then combed across the lines to give the feathering.

The partially dried slab of clay was pressed over a mould to produce the boar's head dish or oven bottom dish as shown here in this 19th-century example.

Feldspar. Fieldspar. Felspar. A group of minerals used in proportions of up to 25% as flux in bodies and up to 100% in glazes. Feldspars contain alkalis plus silica and alumina and are therefore natural frits or glazes. In fact, they have cooled and crystallized from a molten magma. They contain alkalis, notably potash and soda, which if alone are soluble, but when combined with alumina and silica in feldspars, these alkalis are reasonably insoluble. The value of feldspar is thus seen as an opportunity to introduce alkalis into a body or glaze without recourse to fritting.

Feldspars begin to soften at about 1150°C (2102°F) but because of their high alumina content do not run, even at 1300°C (2372°F). The photograph shows test

blocks of feldspar fused at 1250°C (2282°F). Feldspars make very stiff glasses containing innumerable small bubbles giving a milky opacity. They can be converted to usable glazes by the addition of more flux and silica. For example, a simple glaze for 1250°C (2282°F) is feldspar 70, flint 12, whiting 18.

Some feldspars show signs of plasticity like clay and similarly react to flocculation. This quality is too small however to be of use in getting a feldspathic glaze to grip to ware before firing. A binder should be included in the recipe. Clay is to be preferred because it will help the slop suspension.

Feldspar has a high surface tension during fusion so that too much feldspar in a glaze can result in crawling. The crawling starts because the glaze is reluctant to grip the body before firing.

The commonest feldspar is orthoclase, so that if no other type of feldspar is indicated in recipes it can be assumed that orthoclase is intended. Albite is the second commonest feldspar.

Crystalline rocks can often be approximately identified as feldspars and feldspathoids by their general properties of cleavage into angular pieces with hexagonal tendencies, a grained appearance on the surfaces, polarized reflections at the broken edges and, with orthoclase, a pinkish colour. The accompanying photographs show the comparison between normal pieces of broken feldspar and a selected specimen of a twinned crystal of orthoclase. See also **Albite** and **Orthoclase**.

TYPES OF FELDSPAR. There are 12 types of true feldspar and many other feldspathic materials called feldspathoids. The important feldspars are orthoclase, albite and anorthite, and these are separately indexed in this book. The 12 true feldspars can be separately identified by chemical composition and crystal structure and will correspond to idealized formulae, though this is only possible in carefully selected specimens. Feldspar quarried in bulk cannot be so pure but always contains some admixture of another feldspar and traces of other minerals. Thus orthoclase will contain a small amount of soda and possibly calcia. Calculations using the theoretical formula will therefore not be so accurate as ones using the percentage analysis. See **Calculations, finding the unity formula**.

The chart shows the relationship of feldspars to one another.

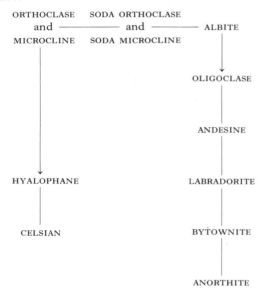

The three across the top are called the alkaline feldspars. At the left-hand side is the most common feldspar called orthoclase. Microcline is chemically identical to orthoclase but its crystal structure is different. Orthoclase and microcline are the potash feldspars and have the chemical formula $K_2O . Al_2O_3 . 6SiO_2$. Albite at the right-hand side is the soda feldspar with the formula $Na_2O . Al_2O_3 . 6SiO_2$. Between is a combination of the potash and soda feldspars called perthites or soda-potash feldspars. There are two, called soda orthoclase and soda microcline. They are chemically alike but different in crystal structure and have the formula $NaKO . Al_2O_3 . 6SiO_2$.

Below albite are listed four feldspars in a chain leading to a fifth one called anorthite. Anorthite has the formula $CaO . Al_2O_3 . 2SiO_2$ and is therefore called lime feldspar. The feldspars in between albite and anorthite are progressive stages in the replacement of Na and Si by Ca and Al. The whole group of six feldspars from albite to anorthite is known as the plagioclase feldspars.

A similar progression at the left-hand side of the chart has only two stages in which K and Si are replaced by Ba and Al to give celsian with the formula $BaO.Al_2O_3.2SiO_2$. Hyalophane and celsian are called barium feldspars.

Feldspathic glaze. A glaze which contains a high percentage (50–100%) of feldspar. For example, a feldspathic glaze for 1250°C (2282°F) is:

feldspar 66
flint 10
whiting 23

The term is also used for a glaze which, whilst containing less than 50% feldspar, is compounded of minerals which create an artificial feldspar. Such glazes use one or two fluxes only and have a high proportion of alumina. The alumina:silica ratio may be as high as 1:6 as in the common feldspars. For example, another feldspathic glaze for 1250°C (2282°F) is:

feldspar 45
china clay 20
flint 20
whiting 15

Feldspathic glazes are usually stoneware and are stiff glazes with a milkiness due to minute bubbles. They tend to crawl because they have a high surface tension when molten and tend to craze when cool because their alkalis have a high coefficient of expansion and contraction. The photograph shows a globule of feldspathic glaze made opaque by thousands of bubbles.

Feldspathoids. Feldspathic minerals. Feldsparic minerals. Feldspar is such an important mineral to the potter that it has given its name to a whole family of minerals which are not true feldspars at all. These are more correctly called feldspathic minerals or feldspathoids.

Feldspathoids have similar properties to feldspars: they are alumino-silicates with various alkaline oxides and they are crystalline. They melt between 1100°C and 1300°C (2012°F and 2372°F) and are useful in glazes. However they cannot be considered as true minerals because they do not conform to unified chemical formulae.

Feldspathoids are therefore not single chemical compounds with regular lattice structures. They are a mixture of different compounds whose lattices partially link in random fashion. They are therefore more easily weathered than the true feldspars, often contain soluble substances and are often easier to fuse because of their variety of alkaline oxides. Any formula given for a feldspathoid is necessarily complex and more in the nature of an analysis.

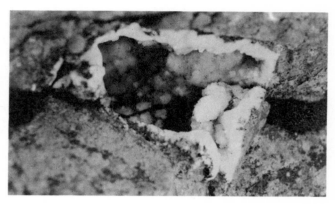

The commonest feldspathic minerals are cornish stone and nepheline syenite. Others are riebeckite, granite, nepheline, leucite, sodalite, petalite, lepidolite and spodumene. The photograph shows a cavity in basalt filled with zeolithic feldspathoids.

Ferreous. Containing iron in any form. This term includes both ferriferous and ferruginous.

Ferric oxide. Red iron oxide. Fe_2O_3. The most stable state of iron oxide derived from oxide ores and rust. It is a red or red-brown coloured crystal which is soft and easily crushed to an exceptionally fine powder. As such it is used to colour clays and glazes. It is insoluble in water but soluble in high-temperature glazes etc. See **Iron oxide**.

Many potters prefer to use the term red iron oxide for the raw mineral and reserve the term ferric oxide for the theoretical oxide involved in ceramic fusion.

Ferriferous. Capable of yielding iron or iron oxide. For example the iron ores contain iron which can be extracted. Red and brown clays also contain iron but it is not possible to isolate the iron and therefore these are called ferruginous.

Ferrosic oxide. Ferroso-ferric oxide. Tri-iron tetroxide. Tri-ferric tetroxide. Magnetic iron oxide. Fe_3O_4. Product of the ore magnetite and known by potters as a coarse, black, metallic-lustred powder which is insoluble in water but has some solubility in high-temperature glazes. See **Iron oxide, types**.

Ferrous oxide. Black iron oxide. FeO. The monoxide of iron produced by reduction of ferric oxide. It is a black powder which is insoluble in water but very soluble in glazes up to saturation point (about 8%). See **Iron oxide**.

Ferrous titanate. See **Ilmenite**.

Ferruginous. Containing red iron oxide. For example, the red and brown clays are ferruginous clays. The term is often used to signify the colour as well as the origin of the colour.

Fettling. The trimming away of excess clay either at leatherhard or dry state. This may be large amounts turned off by shaving on a wheel or lathe or small seam marks from casting which are scraped off with a knife held at right angles to the surface.

Fictile. A general description of those clays suitable for potting or of work made by the potter. It comes from the Latin *fingere*, to form, and *fictilia*, pottery.

Filler. A non-plastic addition to a clay or body. Its functions are:
  1. to open the clay for texture and/or workability (grog and sand);
  2. to control drying shrinkage and firing shrinkage (grog, sand, pitchers and whiting);
  3. to change the fired state for reasons of porosity, glaze fit or whiteness (flint, quartz, feldspar, whiting and calcined china clay).

The grain size of a filler is an important consideration if it is to fulfil its function properly. In relation to the three functions above, the following observations can be made:
  1. The smallest grain size will usually be 120's mesh for grog and 80's mesh for sand. Some very fine openers kill plasticity without assisting a clay's workability. See **Preparation of clay, control of grain size**.
  2. Drying shrinkage is proportional to the amount and fineness of the clay content. Fillers therefore proportionately reduce shrinkage but different grain sizes give different speeds of drying according to the sealing effect of the clay content. As a general rule, medium grogs etc in the 60's to 100's range tend to give the faster drying when compared weight for weight with coarser or finer material.

Firing shrinkage is dependent upon the chemical nature of the filler as well as its grain size. Whiting and some pitchers are only effective as refractory fillers up to defined temperatures. Quartz and flint fillers are often finely ground (smaller than 200's mesh). As fine grains they do not present a refractory property in bodies but become involved in the molten phases. As such, they could accelerate vitrification and subsequent shrinkage. See **Grain size**.
  3. Similarly, a body's densification, its ultimate porosity and expansion rate for glaze fit purposes are dependent upon whether the filler is involved in the glassy parts of the body. In this context silica needs particular assessment because it can present three different phases each with distinctly different character: quartz phase as a refractory, cristobalite phase giving anti-craze properties and amorphous phase giving glassy and apparently fluxing results. See **Silica phases and conversion, Cristobalite** and **Grain size**.

Filter-pressing. Mechanized dewatering whereby a prepared slip is turned into plastic clay. The slip is pumped at pressure into pervious cloth bags formed from two sheets clamped together at the edges. The cakes of clay are removed by unbolting the frames. The photograph shows the press at Cardiff College of Art, Wales.

Vacuum filtering and centrifugal filtering are also done. See also **Dewatering**.

Finger combing. Wet combing. The most direct form of sgraffito, whereby freshly applied slip or glaze is removed by the stroking action of the fingertips. The beauty of this method is the feeling of freedom it imparts to the decoration which is enlivened by the thickening of the colour where it is displaced alongside the track of the finger. The plate by Pat Culpin shows finger-combed slipware.

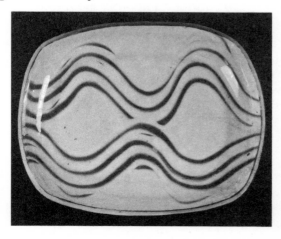

Fireclay. Clay associated with the coal measures of the Carboniferous System of sedimentary rocks. A few deposits are residual clays similar to china clay. Fireclays are often refractory clays and are used for firebricks. The name fireclays gives this impression but there are fireclays which vitrify below 1300°C (2372°F). These are used for drainage pipes, building bricks, sanitary ware and stoneware. Grog is usually fired and ground fireclay.

Fireclays can be divided into the compressed rock fireclays and the underclays. The rock fireclays are both solid rocks and shales. The rock fireclays must be crushed in a mill before they can be wetted and pugged or even blunged. They are often mined rather than quarried and come to the surface as hard lumps which take twenty or thirty years to weather to a plastic clay. In contrast, the underclays have often remained damp. They are more obviously clays when won and can often be blunged without previous milling. They weather quickly, surprisingly quickly for their clay particle size, and produce plastic clays suitable for ovenware.

All fireclays are the seat earths of vegetation which grew during the Carboniferous Period over 280 million years ago. The underclays were the soil for the coal forests and this is why an underclay is found immediately under a coal seam. The coal forest vegetation has taken from the soil much of the potassium and other soluble salts. It may also have taken some silica but it has not taken alumina. Hence these clays are high in alumina and are refractory. The rock fireclays tend to be less refractory than the underclays. All contain organic impurities, some as much as 3% carbon and others actual carbonaceous matter as old root hairs etc. They also contain free quartz, which may be large visible grains; mica; iron pyrites; iron carbonate (siderite) and calcium carbonate (calcite).

The presence of impurities which are volatile, e.g. the carbon in the organic impurities, the sulphur in the pyrites, the carbon dioxide in the carbonates, dictates a careful firing of these clays if the impurities are not to be trapped. Trapped carbon and sulphur cause the most trouble. Even a relatively small amount like 0·5% of the dry clay is sufficient to cause a black core with attendant problems at higher temperatures. See **Black core**. The carbon dioxide usually escapes without difficulty from the carbonates and also the bound water presents no difficulty. With fireclays more than with other clays, the bound water escapes over a long period of the firing starting around 350°C (662°F) and continuing up to 600°C (1112°F). This fact and the general coarseness and quick-drying nature of these clays often lead potters to think that they can withstand any treatment.

The fired colour of fireclays is pale buff. Some are nearly white. All tend to be speckled with iron particles which originally were pyrites. Well-weathered fireclays have often had the pyrites decomposed to carbonate and fire to a more uniform pink colour. Fireclays associated with iron ore deposits are often red-burning and are used for making bricks.

Fireclays are various in chemical composition. It is usual to quote a fireclay by its alumina content and to relate this, with some justification, to a point of refractoriness. Whether a clay deforms at a low temperature or a high temperature is dependent equally on the amount of alkali present but it is true to say that a fireclay containing 40% alumina is unlikely to melt easily. Fireclays contain between 10% and 40% of alumina, between 40% and 80% of silica. Compare this with china clay, which contains 38% alumina and 46% silica.

Some fireclays are as refractory as china clay and are able to withstand 1700°C (3092°F) without deformation and probably melt around 1800°C (3272°F). In Britain these are the Scottish fireclays. It has been suggested that nearly all the fireclays originated in the north of the British Isles and were transported southwards. In so doing the impurities were collected. Certainly there seems to be some progression in the amount of impurities from north to south and a resultant drop in refractoriness.

It will be understood that it is impossible to give an accurate chemical formula for fireclay. In calculations one should correctly work from an analysis. However for the small amounts which may be contained in a glaze, and for quick calculations, the formula $Al_2O_3 . 4SiO_2 . 2H_2O$ will be found reasonable. The aluminous fireclays of Scotland approximate the formula for china clay: $Al_2O_3 . 2SiO_2 . 2H_2O$. With increasing free silica and proportionate decrease of alumina in the more southerly ones, an acceptable formula for south Wales fireclay is $Al_2O_3 . 5SiO_2 . 2H_2O$.

Firing. The process of conversion from clay to pot. It involves heat of at least 600°C (1112°F). Clay disintegrates in water but is changed by firing into a stone-like material, unaffected by water, and in some cases impervious to water. The change is called the ceramic change. Other changes occur during the firing, e.g. organic matter is burned away, the colour changes, a layer of glass is fused onto the surface.

The decorative effects which are used in pottery often require separate firings. The first firing converts the clay to pot. It is called the biscuit firing. Subsequent firings involve colour, perhaps underglaze colour, glaze, on-glaze colour, lustre and are named after these purposes. They will vary in temperature, speed of temperature rise and fall, and in atmosphere (oxidation and reduction). However it is often possible to achieve a number of results from one firing. It is only the sophistication of potting methods, occurring in the last 300 years, that has resulted in the general practice of separate firings for biscuit, glaze and colours. Prior to this, the general practice was a single firing, although the use of subsequent firings for different effects was known to early potters around the Mediterranean. See **Biscuit,**

Through firing, Onglaze, Lustre, Oxidation and **Reduction**.

The stages of a biscuit firing are:

Water smoking
Decomposition of vegetable matter
Ceramic change
Burning out or oxidation of carbon and sulphur
Progressive vitrification

This achieves a strong and porous material: strong so that it may be handled and porous so that it may be glazed. A summarized description is given in the next section and references made to other articles.

The stages of a glaze firing are:

Drying out
Start of glaze fusion
Continuation of vitrification of body
Integration of body and glaze
Completion of glaze fusion

The cooling which follows involves the growth of crystals within the body-glaze layer, in the glassy parts of the body and possibly in the glaze. The individual actions of the different glaze constituents are given under these materials. A summarized general description is given in the section following the summary of the biscuit firing.

BISCUIT FIRING. The progression is described under headings taken from the accompanying chart, fig. 1. The sectional diagrams showing clay particles are a continuation of those used in the article on **Drying**.

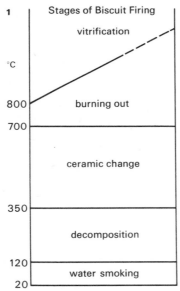

1 Stages of Biscuit Firing

°C

vitrification	
800	burning out
700	
	ceramic change
350	
	decomposition
120	
20	water smoking

Water smoking. The remainder of the pore water, which has been unable to dry out because of atmospheric humidity and pressure, is now driven out by heat. The action takes place between room temperature (20°C or 68°F) (fig. 2) and boiling point of water (100°C or 212°F). It is usually considered to be com-

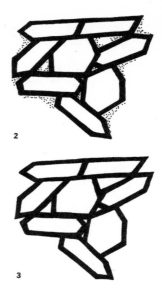

pleted by 120°C (248°F) (fig. 3). This period of a firing must be taken cautiously. Two hours is usual for general ware up to an inch in thickness. Thicker ware will require proportionately longer. Too rapid a rise in temperature will cause steam pressure to build up and possibly shatter the clay. The water-smoking period is over when the kiln vents are dry. During water smoking there will be water vapour escaping from the chamber. This can be seen or, if not visible, can be detected by condensation onto a cold glazed surface held near the vent. See **Water smoking, Drying** and **Water**.

Decomposition. Many clays contain vegetable matter which breaks down at approx 200°C (392°F). This is the same action as the compost heap and with surface clays the effects can very occasionally be detected by smell. This is not a burning process. The burning out of carbon comes later. This part of the firing can be taken quickly because there are no changes to cause trouble. Even the presence of cristobalite makes no difference at this dry clay stage although the cristobalite dunting point is passed. There is a very slight expansion of the ware over this period. It rarely amounts to more than 1% linear and, since the kiln props and shelves have similar expansion, it is unlikely to cause trouble. However, large pots set close to the kiln arch have been known to break their rims against the roof. In such cases the kiln structure is probably expanding inwards to meet the pots and it is advisable to leave about ¾-inch clearance between pot and kiln arch.

Ceramic change. The bound water which is part of the crystal structure of clay is driven off at this stage (fig. 4). The result is a change from clay to pottery body known as the ceramic change. This action begins very gently between 350°C and 450°C (662°F and 842°F) and increases to a maximum at 600°C (1112°F), after which the action quickly fades away before 700°C (1292°F). There is little danger from the escaping steam and the firing can be taken quickly. Water

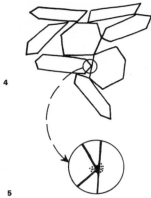

vapour will be seen escaping from kiln vents which have been dry during the decomposition stage.

Dunting point (573°C, 1063°F) is passed during this period, but the open texture of the body enables adjustments of size to be made without rupture.

Theoretically the now thoroughly dried particles are only just touching, as shown in fig. 4. However the body retains its form and does not collapse as a pile of dust, because the particles are fastened to each other by a process called sintering. This is not fusion in the vitrification sense but a welding of similar particles at points of extremely small contact as shown in fig. 5. It is as if a vibration at these points creates an incandescence of sufficient heat to fuse the tips together.

The strength created by sintering is sufficient to hold a pot in one piece whilst allowing adjustments of size caused by the silica inversion. Dunting is therefore very unlikely to happen. However there is insufficient strength to allow a pot to be held for glazing and so it is necessary to take the firing to a higher temperature. A partial vitrification is necessary to give a satisfactory biscuit ware and it is also necessary to burn out the carbon and some of the sulphur content from the body.

There is a very slight shrinkage over the period of ceramic change.

Burning out. Carbon and sulphur are present in clays and remain to be burnt out by the process sometimes called oxidation. They combine with oxygen to form monoxide, dioxide and trioxide gases (CO. CO_2. SO. SO_2. SO_3). This process requires at least the dull red heat of 700°C (1292°F) and reaches its climax around 800°C (1472°F). Most of the carbon has been burnt out by 900°C (1652°F) but some sulphur lingers until 1100°C or 1150°C (2012°F or 2102°F).

It is essential that this process is thoroughly completed. With thick pieces of work this may take a number of hours. Some potters slow down the rate of firing or try to hold the temperature steady at 800°C (1472°F) for a couple of hours. With normal potting clays made into tableware, the thickness is not great and the usual hour taken from 750°C to 850°C (1382°F to 1562°F) is satisfactory. Surface clays and present day estuarine muds require more care because they contain a lot of carbon and sulphur respectively.

These volatiles cause trouble at a later stage if they are not removed from the body. The vitrification of the body begins at 800°C (1472°F) and, from this point, the body progressively loses its pervious nature. A body will bloat if the outer part becomes impervious by the action of heat whilst there is gas attempting to escape from the inner part. The impervious outer part is soft and glassy by vitrification. Bloating usually occurs at the upper temperatures of a stoneware firing and is often a sign of overfiring of the body. However, the causes of premature bloating lie with a hurried burning-out period in the biscuit firing. At biscuit stage the fault is not visible on the outside of the body, but, in broken section, a black core will be found. See **Black core, Breakdown** and **Bloating**.

Clearly, different clays require different treatments because the amounts of carbon and sulphur vary from clay to clay. The coarser clays, like fireclays and brick shales, often contain a lot of carbon which takes a few hours to burn out in spite of the open texture of these bodies.

A problem arises in the through firing of these clays, that is, when firing these clays with glazes in one firing. The glaze must not melt before the burning out is completed or else the outer pores of the body will be sealed. Some fine slips can cause trouble in this way and it is noticeable that on much of the traditional slipware, which was once-fired with soft lead glazes, the pieces are slipped and glazed on one side only. Plates and dishes are glazed top side only and jugs etc were glazed inside and just over the rim. Potters with less troublesome clays were able to decorate and glaze all over but this achievement was limited to a few localities.

During the burning-out period there will be no change in body size. Any slight expansion is countered by the sintering and incipient vitrification.

Vitrification. This begins at 800°C (1472°F) when the soda and potash within the body start to flux the free silica. Vitrification progresses throughout the firing, filling the pores between the alumino-silicate (original clay) particles and eventually involving these also. The body shrinks during vitrification. See figs. 6, 7 and 8 which show the effects of vitrification but do not show the original fluxes and free silica. For simplicity these have been omitted from all the diagrams.

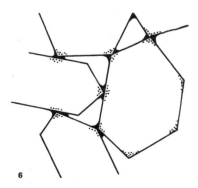

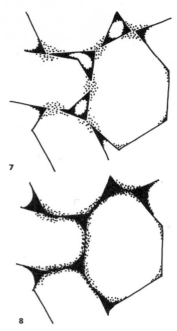

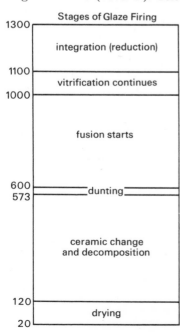

Vitrification strengthens the final product by welding the particles together with glass. If the firing were to continue, then the vitrification would be completed to the point where the whole body melts to a glass.

Above 1000°C (1832°F), the fused alumino-silicate is able to form mullite. Mullite crystals are long needles which considerably strengthen the final body. See **Mullite**.

The temperature chosen for a biscuit firing depends upon the balance required of the properties of strength and porosity. See **Biscuit**. Strength is also required to withstand the shock of the silica inversion during cooling. See **Dunting, biscuit dunts**.

Cooling. During cooling, the biscuit contracts at a regular rate except for the sudden contractions occasioned by the quartz and cristobalite inversions. The glassy parts of the body set solid, possibly with crystals, binding the whole into a strong unit.

GLAZE FIRING. There are two types of glaze firing: the one in which glaze and body mature together; and the one in which the body is already matured and only the glaze is affected. Both types have advantages and disadvantages.

An example of the first type is porcelain. With porcelain, the body matures and becomes translucent during the glaze firing. At the same time the glaze matures and together body and glaze create a thick body-glaze layer which is often thicker, in section, than the pure glaze layer.

An example of the second type is raku. Here the body is already fired to a temperature equal to or higher than the glaze firing. It is therefore unaffected by the heat of the glaze firing but the glaze changes completely. There are obvious advantages in this. The biscuited ware can be inspected with the knowledge that it will retain its biscuit properties of soundness and shape through the glaze firing. Delicate ware is easier to handle. With the English industrial earthenware method, the differences in temperature between biscuit and glaze are marked. The biscuit temperature may be in excess of 1250°C and the glaze below 1080°C (2282°F and 1976°F respectively). The terms bisc and glost are used for these firings to indicate this temperature difference. See **Bisc** and **Glost firing**.

The disadvantage of a glost firing is that there is little body-glaze layer established. Glaze fit must therefore be accurate. Without it, the glaze readily crazes or flakes.

Returning to the first type in which body and glaze mature together one can see that the advantage is in the establishment of a sound body-glaze layer. The integrated ware has a soundness which can be related in terms of strength in comparison with unglazed ware. For example, a piece of glazed porcelain can be twice as strong as its unglazed counterpart. The strength lies in the integrated bonding of body and glaze with the slight compression of the glaze by the body. Integration also gives integrated colour, a fact made full use of in reduced stoneware. Earthenware, although not reaching the vitrified state of stoneware, can still make use of this integration if the biscuit firing is around 950°C (1742°F) and the glaze firing around 1100°C (2012°F).

The disadvantage of this combined maturation is the possible over-fluxing effect which the glaze can have on the body. Over-fluxing results in warping, or worse still, bloating and deformation.

The combined maturation can occur in a glaze firing which follows a soft biscuit or in the firing of a glaze applied to raw ware. See **Raw glazing**. In the following description, it is assumed that there has been a biscuit firing to 1000°C (1832°F). The glaze firing is

Stages of Glaze Firing	
1300	
	integration (reduction)
1100	
	vitrification continues
1000	
	fusion starts
600	dunting
573	
	ceramic change and decomposition
120	
	drying
20	

a stoneware glaze, firing to 1300°C (2372°F). The stages are described under headings taken from the accompanying chart.

Drying. The first 100°C (180°F) of the firing, from room temperature to beyond the boiling point of water, is a drying period. Most glazes are applied as suspensions in water and this water must be driven out of the absorbent biscuit. It must be done slowly. Many potters do it prior to kiln packing by a system of open, slatted shelves and a moving current of warm, dry air. There is an advantage in this when one has to fire the glaze within a tight schedule but a slow warm-up to the glaze firing is acceptable. Too rapid a warm-up will not burst the pots as with raw ware, but it will loosen the glaze from the biscuit. Loose glaze either falls off or crawls when it starts to fuse. The fault is known as wet ware.

Ceramic change and decomposition. A final glaze requires a number of oxides, e.g. silica, alumina, soda and lead oxide. But these oxides do not necessarily appear in the glaze recipe. The recipe includes raw minerals and prepared materials which are also carbonates, sulphates and clays. This use may be for a special effect, ease of handling before firing or for economic and supply reasons. The firing converts these minerals to oxides. Clay is converted to alumino-silicate by the ceramic change between 350°C and 700°C (662°F and 1292°F). Carbonates and hydrates decompose at various temperatures up to 900°C (1652°F). Each compound has its own decomposition temperature. Sulphates often require the presence of other minerals to assist their decomposition. See **Ceramic change** and the individual mineral concerned.

Dunting. The biscuited body is subjected to a sudden expansion because of its crystalline silica content. This occurs at 573°C (1063°F). A temperature rise which is too rapid could create a large temperature difference across a pot causing a stress which results in a crack. See **Dunting, firing dunts.**

Fusion starts. Some fusion starts at 600°C (1112°F) with soda and potash. Also the earthenware glaze fluxes, lead oxide and boric oxide, start their work here. By 1000°C (1832°F) most earthenware glazes are semi-molten but stoneware glazes, although bonded like a biscuited body, are rarely as vitrified as the body at this point.

Vitrification continues. Up to the biscuit temperature, the body is unchanged. But from that temperature upwards, the arrested vitrification continues. It is here that the body fusion actually assists the slow fusion of the glaze. But whilst the body makes a slow but steady maturation towards the final temperature, the glaze makes an increasingly rapid one. The glaze fluxes start their action at different temperatures, and therefore as the temperature rises, more fluxes become involved in active fusion. Calcia, zinc oxide and magnesia are notable examples. See **Fluxing action** and **Viscosity of molten glazes**.

Integration. During the later stages of firing, the body and glaze flux each other to produce a body-glaze layer. This is the period of the active glaze fluxes. It is the period when the glaze truly melts to a glass. As the glaze melts, it is very susceptible to changes of atmosphere. Reduction is most effective at this point. Once the glaze has fused, it is difficult for reduction to effect a change. See **Reduction** and **Oxidation**.

Cooling. At the top temperature of the firing, there are a number of crystals growing or establishing nuclei for later growth. These are in the body-glaze layer. Upon cooling, the crystals grow thus establishing a firm bond between body and glaze. Cooling is part of the firing 'cycle' and its rate affects glaze shine, colour and mattness by allowing or hindering reoxidation and the formation of crystals.

Even the relatively refractory stoneware glazes do not set solid until about 500°C (932°F). Crystals are able to grow during cooling down to about 700°C (1292°F), after which, the glaze slowly sets, becoming stiffer and stiffer. The final colour is not reached until below 150°C (302°F).

During cooling from 1300°C (2372°F) to room temperature, a body and a glaze contract about 3% volumetrically. If a glaze contracts more than the body, it is put under tension and might break to accommodate the stress. This is called crazing. If a glaze contracts less than the body, shivering might result. See **Glaze fit**.

Two temperatures at which trouble can occur are the dunting points of 573°C and 226°C (1063°F and 439°F). Here the free crystalline silica in the body is subjected to a sudden decrease in size. Wide bowls and thin pots on thick shelves are prone to cracking if the temperature-fall rate is too rapid. The 226°C (439°F) decrease in size is unusual in stoneware but often present in earthenware where it helps to compress the glaze and prevent later crazing. See **Cristobalite** and **Glaze fit**.

Firing cycle. The time and actions of firing and cooling pottery. The term is used in relation to graphs or other information about the rate of temperature rise and fall. The word cycle implies that it is repeated but it is really only a part of the larger kiln cycle which also includes packing, drawing, cleaning up and sorting the ware.

First red. Description of the incandescent glow of the pots in a kiln. The temperature is about 600°C (1112°F) and is an indication that dunting point 573°C (1063°F) has been passed and that the ceramic change is almost complete. Where open flames are concerned or electric elements may be glowing, the first red is about 500°C (932°F).

Fishout. Draw-out test. Trial. Draw ring. Any object taken out of the kiln during firing to determine what is happening within. Buller's rings and Watkin's recorders are fishouts. Loops of clay are often used and glazed appropriately. These are easily withdrawn by a hooked rod. The effects of glaze fusion and especially reduction can thus be considered during firing and appropriate action taken. Note that there is a danger in using a metal rod for fishouts from an electric kiln.

Fit. See **Glaze fit**.

Flaking. See **Shelling**.

Flambé. Rouge flambé. Iridescent red glaze produced by transmutation of colloidal copper into a relatively transparent glaze.

Flameproof ware. Fireproof ware. Ware capable of withstanding the extreme thermal shock of direct flame contact. Ovenware withstands a temperature of about 300°C (572°F) all over. To be flameproof a pot must withstand 500°C or 600°C (1112°F) in direct contact at one point only. Another part of the pot may be quite cool. Extremes of heat expansion must take place and very few bodies are capable of absorbing the difference.

Primitive cooking pots are sometimes flameproof. The globular form of these pots is strong and resilient to thermal shock. The extra flameproof quality can be attributed to careful selection of materials, empirically discovered, which contain a high proportion of micaceous sand. Also an extremely low firing was used which achieved the ceramic change but did not flux any free silica to form a glassy matrix. The body particles are held together by sintering of the particles which leaves the mass extremely elastic.

Some high-fired porcelains are also flameproof. They have achieved a state where they contain negligible crystalline silica. Free silica has been fused and so rendered of low expansion rate. See **Table of thermal expansion**. These porcelains are almost glasses but do not contain any of the oxides of high expansion rate which have low resistance to thermal shock. They are fired at over 1400°C (2552°F) which is necessary to vitrify the extremely pure form of china clay which is used.

Some medieval cooking pots were used on the fire but it is unlikely that they withstood the flames or direct contact with the hottest parts of the fire. For cooking there is sufficient heat if the pot is near to the fire or amongst the hot ashes. Today it is occasionally possible to make a soft-fired redware which is capable of withstanding a gentle flame.

Since the making of the first cordierite body by Felix Singer in 1926, many ceramists have tried to produce a commercial cordierite body. Cordierite is a magnesium alumino-silicate of low expansion and cordierite bodies withstand flames. The difficulty lies in producing a sufficiently plastic body which is free from catalysts that upset the equilibrium of the cordierite.

Flashing. The interesting or annoying colouration and fusion which occurs when volatiles settle on pots and produce unexpected ceramic combinations during the firing. Firing by wood produces fine ash which settles on pots and gives flashing. The reducing action of a flame can also increase the fusion of a pot on one side giving a scorched appearance. Salt-glazing is deliberate flashing.

The volatiles involved are soda, lead oxide, boric oxide and to a lesser extent baria, zinc oxide and potash. These oxides produce shiny glaze surfaces by fluxing unglazed parts. The effect is often an attractive toasted colour.

Some colouring oxides are also prone to volatilization which thereby distributes colour to other glazes in the same kiln. Small amounts can give surprising results on what was intended to be a pure white ware. The oxides concerned are chromium oxide, copper oxide, cobalt oxide and manganous oxide.

Deliberate colour flashing is sometimes done by placing pots in a sagger. The required volatiles are painted onto the inside walls of the sagger and a lid used to almost seal the atmosphere inside. Alternatively, calcium chloride or common salt (sodium chloride) is placed in a dish with the pots in a completely sealed sagger. The chlorine gas combines with the colouring oxides which have been painted onto the ware. These become volatile chlorides for a brief spell and cause a flashing of the colour around the original decoration. This effect is also termed flowing and is to be seen around painted decorations on salt-glazed ware.

Flashing is also the name given to discolouration patches which occur on slip-cast ware. See **Casting slip, adjustment of**.

Flint. SiO_2. Cryptocrystalline native silica. Flint is almost pure silica containing less than 5% impurity in the form of calcium carbonate. It is prepared by washing, calcining and grinding. The calcination turns the flint from its native dark colour to white. Thus flint is purchased as a white powder for introduction into bodies and glazes. In bodies it gives a whiteness, hardness, and a resistance to crazing. In glazes it provides extra silica when needed and is often used to balance the silica amount when adjustments are made for purposes of glaze fit. See also **Silica**.

Thomas Astbury was the first potter to add flint to his clay to produce a white body. This was in the early 18th century. By the end of the century the addition of some flint was standard practice and flint was also used in glazes. Flint's properties as an anti-craze, when added to both body and glaze, had also been discovered.

Flint occurs as hard nodules in chalk and as chert nodules in limestone. It varies in colour from light to dark brown and black. Its exceedingly fine crystalline grain gives it a glassy character so that it fractures conchoidally. It is related to the semi-precious chalcedonies. See **Quartz**.

The structure of native flint involves 3% or 4% of water and 3% or 4% of calcium carbonate. The water is locked within the cavities of the irregularly joined micro-crystals. It is likely that some water is involved in the structure as hydroxyl groups and its presence prevented the full crystallization of the silica when it was dissolved from its original place in the carcases of diatoms and siliceous sponges and redeposited in the chalk cavities.

Raw flint is hard and therefore difficult to grind. However calcination renders the flint crumbly and brittle. The water within the flint is removed by calcination at around red heat and sometimes the hot flints are dropped into water to shatter them into smaller pieces preparatory to grinding them in a ball mill. Calcination breaks the existing weak bonds between the micro-crystals enabling grinding to break down the flint into an exceedingly fine powder. The photograph shows a raw and a calcined flint pebble.

Grinding was originally done in open stone mills—sometimes dry. The flint dust was a severe silicosis hazard. Grinding is now undertaken in closed ball mills and the powder is always kept wet. It is sold with sufficient water, often 5% to 10%, to prevent its dispersal as dust. Flint powder should preferably be stored wet and allowance made for its moisture content if it is measured by weight. It is the almost invisible fine particles which cause silicosis. See **Silicosis**.

Flint is introduced into bodies to provide a non-plastic and refractory addition; to give whiteness; and to produce anti-craze properties produced by the cristobalite squeeze. See **Cristobalite**. For earthenware bodies, it is preferred to quartz or sand as the silica addition because it more readily converts to cristobalite during the firing. It does so because of its cryptocrystalline nature and intimate involvement with the catalyst calcia. See **Silica conversion**. Earthenware bodies can contain up to 50% of flint.

Flint is not used for stoneware because of conversion. For stoneware the coarser grained sand and quartz is used.

Flint is almost interchangeable with quartz in glaze recipes. It is often a matter of personal choice. Theoretically flint should melt more readily because of its calcia content. However it does not always appear to do so, probably because other factors are involved owing to the presence of the other glaze constituents. The two types of silica, flint and quartz, are sometimes used to deliberately introduce two types of silica nuclei for chun and other crystalline effects. Alternatively a mixture of flint and quartz is often found to provide extra fusion in a glaze when substituted for the single type.

Flocculation. The action of altering the physical properties of fine particles in a suspension so that they no longer repel one another but aggregate into larger particles, called flocs, and settle by gravity. The action is most noticeable with the colloidal particles of clay but other minerals are subject to the effect if the particles are sufficiently fine.

Flocculation is used by the potter:

1. to settle fine suspensions;

2. to make a suspension more permeable so that it dries quickly;

3. to thicken slips for use on clay, and glazes for use on hard biscuit;

4. to thicken glaze slops in a way that keeps the coarser minerals in suspension.

All particles, whether fine or coarse, have mutual attraction. See **Forces of attraction**. The attractive pull increases as the distance between two particles decreases. Exceedingly fine particles in suspension are pulled together and held together by these forces. The flocs thus formed settle under gravity. The deliberate acceleration of this process is called flocculation.

Acting against this tendency to flocculate are the electrostatic charges of the particles. If these are stronger than the forces of attraction, the particles will repel one another. It is then possible for extremely fine particles to overcome the downward pull of gravity completely and suspensions like this will never settle. These are called colloidal suspensions. The deliberate establishment of this state is called deflocculation.

127

Flocculation is achieved by reducing the overall electrostatic charge of the particles so that the mutual forces of attraction can take over from the forces of repulsion. When the overriding repulsive charge is reduced it is found that extremely fine particles, e.g. those of colloidal size, often exhibit polarity like magnets. They therefore attract one another in a distinct pattern which completes the magnetic field. The most important example of this is the clay particle which is a flat hexagonal crystal. The edges of the crystal have a dominant positive charge and the faces have a dominant negative charge. Clay flocs therefore follow a magnetic pattern which will appear as in fig. 1 if seen edgewise. The structure is known as 'card-house structure'.

For greater scientific detail relating to flocculation see **Flocculants, Viscosity, Fluidity, Forces of attraction, Double layer theory** and **Zeta potential**.

The general details of the potters' use of flocculation are as follows:

1. Colour pigments are often ground in excess water with the intention of settling the slop to a usable paste. If the suspension will not settle, the use of a flocculant may be necessary. Dilute hydrochloric acid is often used but vinegar or calcium chloride work equally well in most cases.

2. Clay suspensions which are slow to settle often produce slippery, dense sediments. The clay particles are tightly packed together in what is called a 'card-stack structure'. Here the plates lie flat upon one another. As the water dries from this structure on the outside of the clay it pulls the plates together thus presenting an impermeable layer through which the remaining water cannot pass. See fig. 2. This occurs against porous surfaces like drying troughs, against pervious surfaces like filter cloths used in filter-pressing, against clay in slip coating, against biscuit in glazing, and against the air in normal drying of slip and glaze coatings. See **Dewatering**.

The problem presented by this is one of slips and glazes that will not dry on pots and of slurry that cannot

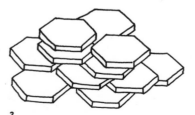

be dried to plastic clay. The solution is flocculation by a small amount of vinegar or calcium chloride.

The flocculant encourages polarity in the particles, which as previously explained are platelike with negative charges on the faces and positive charges on the edges. The structure produced is therefore one of 'card-house' as opposed to 'card-stack'. See figs. 1 and 3. Card-house structure is full of pores through which water can pass.

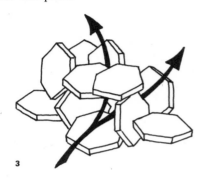

3. Clay slips and glaze slops are sometimes too fluid to give a coating of sufficient thickness. If the suspension contains a high proportion of clay, as occurs with a slip and a slip-glaze, the trouble often arises from soluble salts in the water. These may be in the water supply as water softeners or in the case of the glaze may have dissolved out of a wood ash or other glaze material. The net result is deflocculation and the solution to the problem is flocculation with vinegar or calcium chloride.

In the case of a glaze, the problem may be one of over-fired biscuit which cannot absorb sufficient water. Flocculation will provide a more viscous and bulkier slop which will give a thicker layer. Magnesium sulphate (epsom salts) and calcium sulphate (plaster of Paris) give satisfactory results with glazes containing some colloidal clay, e.g. ball clay and bentonite. See **Magnesium sulphate**. Glazes which contain very small amounts of colloidal clay, e.g. fritted glazes containing china clay but no ball clay or bentonite, do not respond so well. They can sometimes be temporarily flocculated by the use of gelatine and polymer adhesives. Gelatine should be dissolved in hot water and added until the desired viscosity is reached. The effect will last a few hours. With polymer adhesives, the effect lasts a few days. Over-doping with these organic acids, especially gelatine, may lead to problems of glaze creep in the warming-up stage of the firing.

4. Glazes which contain a high proportion of non-clay materials, like frits and flint, have a tendency to settle rapidly. If the water contains soluble salts there is also the added nuisance of the sediment's setting to a hard layer in the bottom of the tub. To keep the glaze in suspension, a clay is often included in the recipe. Approximately 10% of china clay is popular. A ball clay works even better but may discolour the glaze. A small amount of bentonite, even 1%, gives noticeable results.

This clay content is flocculated to make its power more effective.

It may seem strange that clay which will not settle is flocculated to make it do so and yet to keep a glaze in suspension, the clay content is also flocculated. The difference is one of clay amount. Within the glaze slop there needs to be sufficient flocculated clay structure to hold the heavier particles. The open structure around the particles creates flocs which are of lower density than the particles alone. The flocs of clay and other materials therefore sediment more slowly than the other materials would do without the clay's help. Flocculation does not prevent sedimentation but it slows it down.

The flocculated clay in the glaze increases its bulk in an open card-house structure. Bentonites swell to twenty or thirty times their dry volume and produce a viscous jelly-like structure which is highly effective in the holding of non-clay particles and the slowing down of their sedimentation. Bentonites are usually flocculated with calcium chloride. One per cent of bentonite in a glaze recipe is sufficient to keep the remainder in suspension during glazing operations.

FLOCCULANT. Flocculent. A soluble material which is added to a suspension to increase the viscosity. Flocculants are usually considered as acids.

Increasing amounts of flocculant have progressively more flocculatory effect but an optimum point is reached after which further increases have no effect. There is no reverse effect as there is with the use of deflocculants. The amount of flocculant required is very small. The optimum effect is usually achieved by amounts of flocculant in the region of 1% of the amount of colloidal matter involved. In practical terms this means that a few drops of concentrated calcium chloride solution are sufficient to flocculate about 4 gallons of glaze slop containing about 5 oz of bentonite.

Flocculants are acids or salts which act as acids. They release free, positively-charged ions (cations) into the suspension water. These cations do two things: first they neutralize free anions in the water. These anions are negatively-charged ions which have encouraged cations of large repulsion to exist around the colloidal particles. Secondly those not involved in the neutralization replace the cations of large repulsion. The substituting cations have a lower repulsive charge. The replaced cations take up the radical of the flocculant to become new compounds either in solution or in precipitated form.

For example, a deflocculated clay of strong electrostatic charge (Na_2 clay) is suspended in water which is alkaline. The water is alkaline in character because it contains free hydroxyl anions (OH). They are free because they are not combined with cations but serve to create a negative force which balances some of the sodium cations on the clay. To this suspension is added hydrochloric acid (HCl) as a flocculant.

$$Na_2(clay) + OH^- + HCl \longrightarrow$$

The hydrochloric dissociates in the water to become hydrogen cations and chlorine anions.

$$Na_2(clay) + OH^- + H^+ + Cl^- \longrightarrow$$

The hydrogen cation combines with the hydroxyl anion to form water (H_2O). This decreases the pressure on the clay to maintain all its original sodium cations. Some therefore are able to combine with the chlorine anions to form sodium chloride (NaCl).

$$Na_2(clay) + H_2O + NaCl$$

The sodium chloride solution is weak and can do nothing to effect any reversal of the equation. The clay particle is left with a much weaker charge and the suspension is less deflocculated.

A second example shows the action of the flocculant calcium chloride ($CaCl_2$). This effects a cation exchange with the clay to give a clay with calcium cations and sodium chloride in solution.

$$Na_2(clay) + CaCl_2 \rightleftharpoons Ca(clay) + 2NaCl$$

This is a reversible equation but it is weighted in the direction left to right because calcium is of higher valency than sodium. To reverse the equation would require a far higher concentration of sodium chloride than occurs here.

Flocculants are acids or salts which act as acids. The following are flocculants:

Inorganic acids:
hydrochloric acid (HCl)
Salts of divalent cations:
calcium chloride ($CaCl_2$)
calcium hydroxide ($Ca(OH)_2$)
calcium sulphate ($CaSO_4$)
magnesium sulphate ($MgSO_4.7H_2O$)
magnesium chloride ($MgCl_2.6H_2O$)
Organic and amino-acids:
vinegar
gelatine
polymer adhesives

Vinegar is an effective flocculant but its effect is not permanent. The treated suspension will slowly return to its original fluidity over a couple of weeks. Gelatine and polymer adhesives create structures through a glaze slop that encourages the clay particles to adopt similar structures. They act as fillers rather than flocculants. Again the effect does not last. The gelatine structure breaks down in a few hours. The polymer adhesives last a few days. Gelatine and the adhesives also give a binding effect which is useful with friable glazes.

Flotation. Separation by density. A process whereby two materials, one heavier and one lighter than water, can be separated from a mixture. The mixture of the materials is put into water and stirred. The heavier material sinks, the lighter material floats. Flotation is used in the separation of wood ash from charcoal. The charcoal floats for a while until waterlogged. Industrially, the process of flotation is used to separate very fine particles from coarse particles. The fine particles are floated away in a foam caused by rapid agitation and assisted by suitable chemicals.

Flow. Run.

Fluidity. The property of a liquid to be able to flow or move freely without the hindrance of friction. The friction involved is between adjacent particles or molecules within the liquid. The term is used to describe slips, e.g. deflocculated casting slips that pour freely; and to describe glazes which melt to very runny glasses. The opposite of fluidity is viscosity.

It is normal technical practice to speak of slips and other suspensions in terms of fluidity but to speak of molten glazes in terms of viscosity. Therefore a stiff slip will be described as of low fluidity but a stiff molten glaze will be described as of high viscosity.

Fluidity is measured first as viscosity. That is, the amount of drag which neighbouring particles or molecules impose on one another. The unit of measurement for viscosity is the poise. Values given for viscosity are then recast as values of fluidity and are measured as rhe.

$$\text{rhe} = \frac{1}{\text{poise}}$$

A freely-flowing suspension like a glaze slop with a viscosity of 2 poise has a rating of $\frac{1}{2}$ rhe or 0·5 rhe. A stiff slip might reach a rating of 0·002 rhe which is very low fluidity. Water has a fluidity of 100 rhe.

FLUIDITY OF SLIP AND GLAZE SUSPENSION. Plastic clay and wet powdered glaze materials have high viscosities because their particles drag upon one another. Their viscosities will be in the order of a million times that of water. Therefore when water is added it provides a lubricant whereby the particles can more effectively slide past one another. Clay which is soft and easy to push into new forms contains more water than stiff clay. Clay with a large amount of water becomes so soft that it cannot withstand the pull of gravity. At this stage it is a slip. Similarly glaze slops with large amounts of water are 'thin' and easy to stir. Glaze slops made with only a small amount of water are 'thick' and paste-like.

The technician considers all these stages as different fluidities measured in inverse relation to the friction the parts encounter. Thus a runny suspension which has little friction is considered to have a high fluidity.

A number of factors are involved which influence the fluidity of suspensions. They are: the particle size and, to a lesser extent, the particle shape; the particle reaction to electrostatic forces; the density; and the fluidity of the dispersion medium. Since the medium is usually water there are negligible difference in the use of different waters at different temperatures. The factor of density is directly acceptable. Suspensions of high density, that is, heavy suspensions, are less fluid than suspensions of low density. Particle size and the electrostatic forces require fuller consideration.

Particle size. Considering particle size first, one realizes that if the friction is proportionate to the surface area of the particles, then the finer particles present greater total friction. If a lump of material is broken into two pieces it presents two new surfaces as well as the previous surface, whilst the total weight and bulk remain the same. The surface area has been increased by approximately 25%. This increase of surface area continues if the two pieces are further broken and ground to a powder. The eventual surface area is of staggering proportions. A teaspoonful of an ultrafine powder could have a total surface area of twice the area of the pages in this book.

A suspension made from fine materials requires more water to gain the same fluidity as a slop made from coarser materials. This difference is noticeable with different minerals that have been milled to different particle sizes. It is also sometimes noticeable with supposedly similar minerals from different suppliers. It is very noticeable where two clays are involved.

A slip made from ball clay requires almost double the amount of water required to make a slip of similar fluidity from china clay. The ball clay particles average only a fifth of the size of the china clay particles and therefore present a larger total surface area.

Electrostatic forces. Considering electrostatic forces, one is presented with another phenomenon which noticeably influences the fluidity. To understand the phenomenon one must consider the way in which clay particles stack together and relate this to the friction existing between the particles.

The clay particles or crystals are flat hexagonal plates. If these plates lie side by side or on top of one another in a flat way it is possible to fit more in a given volume of water than if the plates are determined to come to rest at angles to each other. These two situations are called 'card-stack structure' and 'card-house structure', figs. 1 and 2.

Small particles tend to attract one another and create larger particles. This effect is a drag upon the movement of a suspension. If the clay particles can be persuaded to repel one another instead of attracting one another, then a more fluid suspension can be created.

By combining the effect of low friction (repulsion) with that of card-stacking it is possible to create a slip of large clay content which is at the same time of high fluidity. Such a slip is required for the slip casting process and is achieved by altering the electrostatic forces. The process is called deflocculation.

By giving strong electrostatic charges to the particles they repel one another and overcome the mutual forces of attraction. These charges are concentrated at the

give a thicker glaze layer on biscuited pieces of low porosity and also hold in suspension the heavy materials like flint and lead bisilicate which would otherwise settle rapidly. The colloidal clay called bentonite is often used for this latter purpose and is flocculated with calcium chloride.

At colloidal size, the friction between particles is mostly electrostatic attraction of unlike charges. However it also includes Van der Waal's force of attraction of like charges, gravitational attraction and physical abrasion.

To achieve a slip of lower fluidity therefore one must reduce the strength of the charges which are repelling the particles. The forces of friction named above can then cause drag between neighbouring particles.

When the strength of the electrostatic charge is reduced it is found that the flat faces of the clay particles have a neutral or slightly negative charge whilst the edges have a positive charge. The edges are therefore attracted to the faces of adjacent particles by the opposite charges as shown in fig. 4. With this lower charge at the edges, there is insufficient repulsion to give the effect of fig. 3.

edges of the plate-like particles and the zone of repulsion is in reality only small. However the effect of the charges is as if the zone were a protective figure-of-eight in section. This is diagrammatized in fig. 3.

The repulsion zones ensure that the particles cannot come into contact and so there is no friction to hinder fluidity. Even in high concentrations of particles, that is, in a slip containing a large amount of clay and a small amount of water, the particles refuse to meet and continue to repel one another. They position themselves in the most economical use of the volume which is the card-stack structure. A slip in this state is said to be deflocculated.

The reverse of the action just described is a combination of high friction (attraction and physical abrasion) and card-house structure. This gives a viscous slip which has an open pore structure. Such a slip is flocculated.

This state is required when it is necessary to dry off the slip to give a plastic clay. The permeability presented by the pores allows the water to be extracted by absorption on a porous surface or by filter pressing. Also a flocculated glaze suspension which contains clay will dry more quickly than an unflocculated one. It will

The decision to have a large or small charge is influenced by electrolytes. These are soluble materials usually referred to as alkalis and acids, although to avoid confusion they are better described as deflocculants and flocculants. Not all alkalis and acids give satisfactory permanent results. The best deflocculants are sodium carbonate and sodium silicate used in combination. The best flocculants are calcium chloride, hydrochloric acid, vinegar, calcium sulphate and magnesium sulphate. The details of cation exchange whereby the charges are altered are given under the articles on **Deflocculation** and **Flocculation**.

Slips of high colloidal content, e.g. ball clays, react dramatically to electrolytes. If fully deflocculated, a slip can be very fluid and it will feel slippery. It will not settle and cannot be dried to a clay because any drying at the surface, whether against an absorbent solid or into the air, forms a compact impermeable layer through which further water cannot escape.

If the same slip is flocculated, the particles attract one another and form flocs. These in turn become aggregates with sufficient weight to sediment under the pull of gravity, providing there is sufficient water in which to settle. The fully flocculated slip will probably be too viscous to move. It will be like a clay but without strength and jelly-like. It will be highly permeable, dry quickly and give a soft and friable dry material. It is important to realize that the process described here is carried out without altering the weight of clay or the amount of water present. The density therefore remains the same.

By the use of some colloidal clays with electrolytes it is possible to adjust the fluidity of slips and glaze suspensions whilst keeping control of the overall density.

FLUIDITY OF MOLTEN GLAZES. It is normal practice to speak of molten glazes in terms of viscosity. More details are therefore given under **Viscosity**. However in trying to understand the phenomenon it is sometimes advantageous to consider it from both points of view. It is here considered as fluidity.

All glaze oxides that increase fusion also increase the fluidity of the molten glaze. Obviously fusion and fluidity are linked. However some glaze fluxes produce more fluid melts than do others. For example, potash produces very fluid melts which are distinctly more runny than those produced with the aid of magnesia, even at magnesia's most active fluxing temperature above 1250°C (2282°F).

It is possible to put the glaze oxides in the order of their action upon fluidity. This order is based upon an ideal balance of molecules of these oxides with the glass-forming silica. At 1250°C (2282°F) the oxide producing the most fluid melt is potash, followed by lithia, boric oxide and soda. Soda volatilizes at this temperature and therefore its action is difficult to assess in relation to the molecules involved. The list continues with baria, calcia, zinc oxide, strontia, magnesia and lead oxide. Again lead oxide cannot be properly assigned a place because its action at this temperature is not constant. A full chart of these oxides and their effects upon fluidity at different temperatures is given under **Viscosity**.

Fluorspar. Fluorite. Calcium fluoride. Blue John. CaF_2. A compound sometimes used in frit preparation. It is not recommended for direct use in glaze recipes. Its main use is as an opacifier in soft enamels for metals where it can be fully involved in the glass structure. The photograph shows a vein of fluorspar through lead ore.

Fluorspar melts at 1330°C (2426°F) but before this temperature it has active fluxing power and yet gives opacity. The fluorine atoms replace oxygen in the silicate chain causing fluid melts at low temperatures. Inevitably however some fluorspar decomposes with the heat of fusion. The calcium atoms then take up oxygen to become calcia and the fluorine is released as a gas.

$$2CaF_2 + O_2 \longrightarrow 2\,CaO + 2F_2 \uparrow$$

Even fluorspar which is incorporated in a silicate frit can decompose, especially if overfired. The escaping fluorine gas causes blistering. This is not easy to clear since the decomposition is a slow and continuous action and not specific to one temperature.

Apart from the nuisance of this blistering, the fluorine gas is a health hazard in the pottery workshop. See **Poison** and **Fumes**. Fluorspar is often present in cornish stones and clays up to perhaps 2% of the whole. It gives the purplish flecks in cornish stone and is here referred to as fluorite. The fluorine gas which is released when these fluorite-containing materials are fired is noticeable in the workshop atmosphere and over a period of years will etch the workshop windows until they are opaque frosted glass. Some cornish stones are marketed as defluorinated (DF). They are cleaner to use and cause less blistering. See also **Cornish stone**.

Flux. An oxide which promotes ceramic fusion by interaction with other oxides. The oxides which are usually referred to as fluxes are the alkaline oxides because they interact with the glass-forming silica. Fluxes are monoxides with chemical formulae in the R_2O and RO group. The acceptable exceptions are the sesquioxides, boric oxide and bismuth oxide. Fluxes are introduced as monoxides, dioxides, carbonates and other compounds. A full list of fluxes follows:

lithia	Li_2O
soda	Na_2O
potash	K_2O
beryllia	BeO
magnesia	MgO
calcia	CaO
zinc oxide	ZnO
strontia	SrO
baria	BaO
lead oxide	PbO
boric oxide	B_2O_3
bismuth oxide	Bi_2O_3
manganous oxide	MnO
ferrous oxide	FeO
cobaltous oxide	CoO
nickel oxide	NiO
cupric oxide	CuO
cuprous oxide	Cu_2O

Fluxing action. Fluxes do not act alike. They have

individual characteristics although as fluxes they have properties in common. Some are active at low temperatures and volatilize at higher temperatures. These are the earthenware fluxes like soda and lead oxide. Others do not start their action until a higher temperature and have no upper limit in their use for pottery. These are the stoneware fluxes like calcia and magnesia. Some act only in the presence of other fluxes by a process of interaction. Details are given under each oxide but assuming some interaction, a chart of activity can be constructed to compare the different useful ranges. See also **Viscosity of molten glazes** and **Surface tension**.

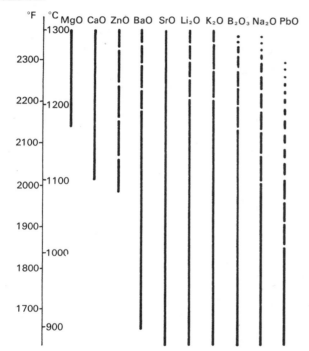

Forces of attraction. Phenomena which cause colloidal clay particles to coagulate. They are referred to collectively in the articles involving fluidity and viscosity as the 'mutual forces of attraction'. They are:

1. The attraction of positive and negative charges which exist as unsatisfied valencies on the broken bonds at the edges of lattices. Colloidal particles sometimes also exhibit a slight 'apparent polarity' which is sufficient to orientate their positions and increase the attraction.

2. Van der Waals' force of attraction, which is caused by the electron movements within the particles. If the movements have rhythmic sympathy, attraction occurs.

3. Gravitational force of each particle which encourages particles in contact or near contact to stay together rather than drift apart.

The overall result of these forces is that colloidal clay particles in suspension tend to be attractive to one another. They thus form flocs which is the first stage of aggregation, sometimes called coagulation. The next

stage is the forming of larger lumps, called aggregates, which are visible to the naked eye. At this stage they come under the pull of gravity and sediment.

The forces of attraction are only small and can be overcome by forces of repulsion. These occur when all the particles possess the same powerful positive charge. Dispersion then takes place instead of coagulation. Suitable electrolytes in the water of suspension will create this condition. See **Double layer theory** and **Zeta potential**.

In consideration of fluidity and viscosity the friction established between particles in suspension, including those of colloidal size, include collision of the particles and the consequent loss of energy through abrasion.

Form. The three-dimensional qualities of a pot or ceramic. These can be analysed as solidarity and weight. The opposite of form is space but both should be considered as positive qualities if good pottery is to be made. This is equally true of food containers and sculptural work.

Formula. A standardized way of expressing involved principles. Ceramists use many different formulae where the individual potter relies upon his skill and judgment. The common formulae which the potter will use are here explained under four areas concerned with:

1. converting one measurement into another: conversion formulae;

2. suspensions (slips and glazes): density formulae;

3. chemical symbols: chemical formula;

4. molecules in ceramic fusions: unity formula.

CONVERSION FORMULA. A simplified framework for calculating a required measurement from known measurements without recourse to the principles involved.

Conversion of dry weights.

To convert from :	into :	multiply by :
ounces	grams	28·35
pounds	kilograms	0·4536
gross cwts (UK)	kilograms	50·803
net cwts (US)	kilograms	45·36
grams	ounces	0·0353
kilograms	pounds	2·2046
kilograms	gross cwts (UK)	0·0196
kilograms	net cwts (US)	0·0221

To convert a batch recipe into a percentage recipe:

$$\% \text{ amount} = \frac{\text{batch item amount} \times 100}{\text{batch recipe total}}$$

For example:

Batch recipe:

frit 14 lb

clay 6 lb

batch recipe total 20

$$\% \text{ of frit} = \frac{14 \times 100}{20} = 70$$

$$\% \text{ of clay} = \frac{6 \times 100}{20} = 30$$

Percentage recipe: frit 70

clay 30

See also calculations for conversion of percentage recipe to batch recipe.

Conversion of capacities.

To convert from :	into :	multiply by :
UK pints	US pints	1·201
UK pints	litres	0·5683
UK fl oz	cc	28·412
US pints	UK pints	0·8327
US pints	litres	0·4732
US fl oz	cc	29·573
litres	UK pints	1·7598
litres	US pints	2·1132

Conversion of densities.

To convert from :	into :	multiply by :
oz pt UK	oz pt US	0·8327
oz pt UK	gm/cc	0·0499
oz pt US	oz pt UK	1·201
oz pt US	gm/cc	0·0599
gm/cc	oz pt UK	20·042
gm/cc	oz pt US	16·705

See also **Density formulae.**

Conversion of temperatures.

See also **Centigrade, Celsius, Fahrenheit, Kelvin** and **Calculations**.

$$^\circ C = \frac{(^\circ F - 32) \times 5}{9}$$

$$^\circ C = ^\circ K - 273$$

$$^\circ F = \frac{^\circ C \times 9}{5} + 32$$

$$^\circ F = \frac{9(^\circ K - 273)}{5} + 32$$

$$^\circ K = ^\circ C + 273$$

$$^\circ K = \frac{5(^\circ F - 32)}{9} + 273$$

DENSITY FORMULAE. These are many and various but all are concerned with suspensions and solutions and the relationships between their weights and capacities.

Density. In order to record the thickness of a slip or glaze in suspension the potter takes note of the weight of a particular capacity. In so doing he is measuring density.

Density is expressed as a mass (weight) per unit volume. For example:

30 ounces per pint

150 grams per 100 cc

1·5 grams per cc

Specific gravity uses these numbers and by relating the weight of the measured capacity of slip to the weight of the same capacity of water is expressed as a single number. For example:

$$30 \text{ oz pt UK becomes } \frac{30}{20} = 1 \cdot 5 \text{ SG}$$

$$\frac{150 \text{ gm slip}}{100 \text{ gm water}} = 1 \cdot 5 \text{ SG}$$

$$\frac{1 \cdot 5 \text{ gm}}{1 \cdot 0 \text{ gm}} = 1 \cdot 5 \text{ SG}$$

The formulae concerned are:

$$\text{Density} = \frac{\text{Weight (Mass)}}{\text{Volume}}$$

$$\text{Volume} = \frac{\text{Weight (Mass)}}{\text{Density}}$$

$$\text{Weight (Mass)} = \text{Volume} \times \text{Density}$$

Density is stated as a mass per unit volume, the two being of comparable nature.

Specific gravity. This is a number which equals grams per cubic centimetre (millilitre). See also the main entry under **Specific gravity**.

A specific gravity number can be converted into ounces per UK pint by multiplying by 20·042 (per US pint by multiplying by 16·705). The formulae can be stated:

$$\text{SG} = \frac{\text{oz pt UK}}{20 \text{ (accurately } 20 \cdot 042)}$$

$$\text{SG} = \frac{\text{oz pt US}}{16 \cdot 705}$$

$$\text{oz pt UK} = \text{SG} \times 20 \cdot 042$$

$$\text{oz pt US} = \text{SG} \times 16 \cdot 705$$

For example, if a slip weighs 152 grams per 100 cubic centimetres, what is the weight of 10 UK gallons in pounds avoirdupois?

$$\text{density} = \frac{152 \text{ gm}}{100 \text{ cc}}$$

$$\text{weight of one pint in ounces} = \frac{152}{100} \times 20 \cdot 042$$

weight of 10 gallons $= \dfrac{152}{100} \times 20{\cdot}042 \times 8 \times 10 =$ 2437 oz $=$ 152 lb 5 oz

Twaddell. Most of the potter's suspensions have specific gravities between 1·0 and 2·0. This gives a very compressed scale of values which must always be expressed with decimal places. To avoid this, the simpler version expressed as ounces per pint is often used or the specific gravity is converted into degrees twaddell. This is an expanded scale whereby the specific gravities between 1·0 and 2·0 are given values between 0 and 200 thus making comparison easier. See **Twaddell**. The formulae are:

$$°TW = (SG - 1) \times 200$$

$$°TW = \left(\frac{\text{oz pt UK}}{20} - 1 \right) \times 200$$

$$°TW = \left(\frac{\text{oz pt US}}{16{\cdot}7} - 1 \right) \times 200$$

$$SG = \frac{°TW}{200} + 1$$

$$\text{oz pt UK} = \left(\frac{°TW}{200} + 1 \right) \times 20$$

$$\text{oz pt US} = \left(\frac{°TW}{200} + 1 \right) \times 16{\cdot}7$$

For example: find the specific gravity in degrees twaddell of a glaze slop weighing 29·5 ounces to the UK pint.

$$°TW = \left(\frac{29{\cdot}5}{20} - 1 \right) \times 200$$

$$= (1{\cdot}475 - 1) \times 200$$

$$= 95°TW$$

Brongniart's formula. A formula for discovering the dry weight content of a slip or slop. The calculation is based upon a standard capacity, often a pint or 100 cc, and its weight in ounces or grams. Larger quantities must be proportionately increased.

If a pint of slip is weighed in ounces, the apparent dry weight is this weight less the weight of a pint of water. However this is not the true weight of the dry content which is related to the specific gravity of the dry material in proportion to that of the water with which it is mixed. The formula is expressed:

weight of dry content

$$= \text{apparent dry weight} \times \frac{\text{specific gravity}}{\text{specific gravity minus one}}$$

For UK capacities where one pint of water weighs 20·042 oz, the formula is as follows. It is assumed that one pint of slip has been weighed in ounces and this is called 'oz pt'.

$$\text{dry wt} = (\text{oz pt} - 20) \times \frac{SG}{SG - 1}$$

For US capacities where one pint of water weighs 16·705 oz, the formula is as follows:

$$\text{dry wt} = (\text{oz pt} - 16{\cdot}7) \times \frac{SG}{SG - 1}$$

For metric capacities where 100 cc of water weigh 100 gm, the formula is as follows. It is assumed that 100 cc of slip have been weighed in grams and this is called 'slip wt'. The weight of the dry content is of course also in grams.

$$\text{dry wt} = (\text{slip wt} - 100) \times \frac{SG}{SG - 1}$$

For example, if one wishes to find the dry weight of materials in 6 UK gallons of stoneware glaze, when for example one pint of glaze weighs 29 oz, the calculation will be:

$$(29 - 20) \times \frac{2{\cdot}5}{2{\cdot}5 - 1} = 9 \times \frac{2{\cdot}5}{1{\cdot}5}$$

$= 15$ oz of dry material per pint of glaze slop.

There are 48 pints of glaze in 6 gallons so the 15 oz is multiplied by 48 and divided by 16 to bring it to pounds.

$$\frac{15}{16} \times 48 = 45 \text{ lb}$$

The amount of water involved is 29 oz minus the dry weight of 15 oz $=$ 14 oz per pint. The total amount is 14 oz $\times$ 48 $=$ 42 lbs.

The calculation is based upon the average specific gravity for stoneware glaze materials which is 2·5. Low sol glazes average about 3·0 and high lead glazes 4·0 Specific gravities are listed in the **Tables**. Another example is given under **Calculations** and comparison pint weights for UK and US capacities under **Tables**.

An extension of the relationships between specific gravities of different slips is afforded by the conversion of slips formula.

If it is necessary to add water to a thick slip in order to make it more fluid, and of a specific pint weight, the amount of water required can be found by the following formulae:

The number of UK pints of water required to be added to each UK pint of thick slip is:

$$\frac{\text{existing oz pt minus required oz pt}}{\text{required oz pt minus 20}}$$

The number of US pints of water required to be added to each US pint of thick slip is:

$$\frac{\text{existing oz pt minus required oz pt}}{\text{required oz pt minus 16·7}}$$

The number of cc of water required to be added to each 100 cc of thick slip is:

$$\frac{\text{existing gm/100 cc minus required gm/100 cc}}{\text{required gm/100 cc minus 100}} \times 100$$

For example, a US pint of slop weighing 25 oz is to be

converted to 23 oz pt. The amount of water required to be added to each pint is:

$$\frac{25-23}{23-16\cdot7} = \frac{2}{6\cdot3} \text{ pints} = \frac{2 \times 16}{6\cdot3} = 5\cdot08 \text{ US fl oz}$$

CHEMICAL FORMULA. A method of representing a chemical compound, a molecule or a radical group by the symbols for the elements. See **Chemical symbol**. By a few letters and numbers a chemical formula states the elements involved and the proportionate number of atoms of each element. It is therefore a useful shorthand in scientific information, and in calculations which involve atoms and molecules.

One molecule of the compound called water is made up of two atoms of hydrogen and one atom of oxygen. The chemical formula for water is therefore HHO or HOH or OHH. When more than one atom of an element is involved the convention is to put a figure below and after the symbol for the element to denote the number of atoms. The usual way to write the formula for water is therefore H_2O.

There is no rule about the order of the symbols but it is usual to put oxygen last and to put other elements in an order which makes sense as a description. This point is mentioned again later.

Formulae are spoken exactly as written. Each letter is pronounced separately. The chemical formula for a molecule of red iron oxide is Fe_2O_3 and this is read as F-E-two-O-three.

When speaking of compounds, a chemical formula represents one molecule of a compound. Thus H_2O stands for one molecule of water and Fe_2O_3 stands for one molecule of red iron oxide. But a formula is also used as a space-saving shorthand in written descriptions and thus H_2O means water, Fe_2O_3 means red iron oxide and MnO_2 is shorthand for manganese dioxide.

The figure which appears below and after a symbol indicates the number of atoms of the preceding element only. Two more conventions exist to indicate that groups of elements are present. They are the use of large figures with full stops and the use of brackets.

For example, in lead bisilicate, there are two molecules of silica, SiO_2, to every one of lead oxide, PbO. The formula is therefore expressed as $PbO.2SiO_2$. It would be acceptable to write it as $PbO.Si_2O_4$ or even to total the oxygen atoms and write $PbSi_2O_5$ but neither explains lead bisilicate quite so graphically as $PbO.2SiO_2$. The large figure 2 which appears before the formula for silica refers to the whole molecule of silica, SiO_2, and not just to the first symbol Si. A full stop is included when it is necessary to indicate where the influence of the large figure ends but if this is at the end of the formula it is often omitted.

Examples with large figures are: $Al_2O_3.2SiO_2$. $2H_2O$ (kaolinite) and $Na_2O.2B_2O_3.10H_2O$ (borax). It will be seen that the figure 1 never appears. The existence of the letter symbol is sufficient to describe the presence of one atom of an element and the letter symbols together describe the presence of one molecule.

Certain groups of elements always appear together but they are not molecules and so cannot be isolated from the rest of the compound by full stops. Nor can they be given a large figure to denote that more than one of the group is present. In such cases brackets are used. For example, copper sulphate is written $CuSO_4$ and the SO_4 group is an important combination although it is not a molecule which can exist by itself. When this group is combined with trivalent iron in ferric sulphate, it becomes necessary to express the conception of two atoms of Fe combined with three groups of SO_4 and this can be done by writing $Fe_2(SO_4)_3$. The brackets enclose the group, in this case the sulphate radical, and the figure 3 below and after the brackets denotes the number of radicals present in the same way that the figure 2 denotes the number of iron atoms present.

Large figures in front of the symbols are reserved for defining a number of molecules. One molecule is separated from another type of molecule in the formula by a full stop. Brackets are used to enclose a radical or other part of a molecule which cannot exist by itself but exists as a convenient expression of a theory.

The chemical formulae as described so far are concerned with the whole numbers of atoms and molecules in strict proportions to one another. All chemical compounds and natural minerals have this property of being combinations of whole atoms and molecules in consistent proportions. It is this fact which enables lattice structures to occur.

When the atoms of two different elements have similar size and valency they sometimes partially replace one another in a mineral. For example, iron can replace calcium in limestone, $CaCO_3$, to produce the mineral siderite, $FeCO_3$. Partial replacements are common and to express this phenomenon the convention of brackets is used around both elements with the elements separated by a comma, e.g. $(Ca,Fe)CO_3$. The comma and brackets therefore mean that both elements are present in an undefined proportion adding up to one atom in relation to the rest of the formula.

A chemical formula which is written on a single line cannot express the three-dimensional lattice structure which is involved in a molecule. For this a structure drawing or a structural formula is used. See **Lattice structure**. However a specific arrangement of the symbols can often be used to imply attachments which are known to exist. For example, there are certain groups of elements which often come together. These are the radicals previously mentioned and are written after the elements to which they are attached. Three common ones are CO_3 (carbonate), NO_3 (nitrate) and SO_4 (sulphate), which occur in $CaCO_3$ (calcium carbonate), KNO_3 (potassium nitrate) and $BaSO_4$ (barium sulphate).

In a similar way, magnetic iron oxide which has the

chemical formula Fe_3O_4 is written as $FeO.Fe_2O_3$ to indicate the theory that one molecule of magnetic iron oxide is a combination of two molecules: FeO and Fe_2O_3. It is true that this division into two oxides, a monoxide and a sesquioxide, makes the whole more easily understood.

Following this practice, it is common amongst potters to divide complex minerals into smaller compounds for convenience. A typical example is that of dolomite which is a single crystal structure created by a double carbonate of calcium and magnesium. The correct chemical formula is $CaMg(CO_3)_2$ which is easier to comprehend if written $CaCO_3.MgCO_3$. Two other examples are kaolinite (pure clay) $Al_2Si_2O_5(OH)_4$ which becomes $Al_2O_3.2SiO_2.2H_2O$ (alumina, silica and water) and orthoclase (feldspar) $K_2Al_2Si_6O_{16}$ which becomes $K_2O.Al_2O_3.6SiO_2$ (potash, alumina and silica).

The expanded formula which the potter uses serves to emphasise the oxides and other compounds with which he is concerned in his considerations of bodies and glazes. The scientist's formula is more concise and often a more accurate description of the relationships between the atoms present.

Molecular formula. A chemical formula which describes a molecule. In the description of molecules the two terms, chemical formula and molecular formula are synonymous. However chemical formulae have a wider use in the description of radicals and groups of atoms which are not stable molecules.

The term molecular formula has also been used for the ceramist's method of describing bodies and glazes. This formula is more correctly called the unity formula and is referred to thus throughout this book. Whilst the unity formula describes proportionate amounts of molecules it does not describe a single molecule of a mineral. The term molecular formula should be correctly reserved for chemical formulae which describe molecules involving atoms in whole numbers.

Structural formula. A convenient diagrammatic representation of a molecule using the chemical symbols

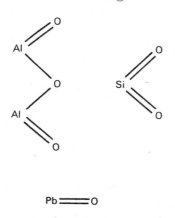

joined by the appropriate number of valency bonds. The examples are of alumina, silica, lead oxide and potash. See also **Lattice structure, Valency** and **Atom**.

UNITY FORMULA. Seger formula. Empirical formula. Ratio of molecules formula. RO formula. R_2O_3 formula. Also misleadingly referred to as molecular formula. A method of setting out in lists the chemical formulae of a glaze or body's constituent oxides. By this method, the balance of alkaline, amphoteric and acidic oxides is quickly assessed, although the composition may be complex. This assists comparison of one glaze or body with another for the purposes of predicting effects and making adjustments.

Whatever materials are used to produce a body or glaze, the result is a combination of oxides. These oxides can be placed in three groups according to their chemical formulae as monoxides, sesquioxides and dioxides. The unity formula uses this grouping and brings the total of molecules of one group to unity, expressing the other two groups in ratio to it.

The unity formula is usually set out as three columns. These are separated by large brackets or vertical lines to imply that there is no especial relationship horizontally except by a group as a whole. For example:

$$\left.\begin{array}{l} 0.5\ CaO \\ 0.3\ MgO \\ 0.2\ K_2O \end{array}\right\} \left.\begin{array}{l} 0.4\ Al_2O_3 \\ 0.1\ Fe_2O_3 \end{array}\right\} \left\{\begin{array}{l} 2.3\ SiO_2 \\ 0.2\ TiO_2 \end{array}\right.$$

unity

Alternatively the oxides are presented as one column divided by horizontal lines:

$$0.5\ CaO$$
$$0.3\ MgO$$
$$0.2\ K_2O$$

$$0.4\ Al_2O_3$$
$$0.1\ Fe_2O_3$$

$$2.3\ SiO_2$$
$$0.2\ TiO_2$$

The unity formula expresses ratios between numbers of molecules. The actual numbers of molecules involved in a glaze are millions of millions. These vast numbers are conveniently scaled down in the unity formula which thereby invariably includes some theoretical fractions of molecules.

The groups are referred to as RO, R_2O_3 and RO_2. R is the symbol which stands for any suitable element capable of fitting the situation. Arising from the actions of the oxides in glazes and bodies, some other names are accorded to the groups in discussion.

RO oxides are monoxides. This group includes R_2O oxides like Na_2O (soda) which are also monoxides.

This group has many names: the RO group, the monoxides, the fluxes, the bases, the basic oxides, the alkalis and the basic metal oxides.

The second group contains the amphoteric oxides which have both alkaline and acidic properties and are sesquioxides. This group has therefore the names: the R_2O_3 group, the sesquioxides and the amphoteric oxides.

The third group has the names: the RO_2 group, the dioxides and the acidic oxides.

Two types of unity formulae are used: unity of the monoxide group and unity of the sesquioxide group.

For glazes and frits the monoxide group is brought to unity as in the example above. This formula is therefore called the RO formula. Unity formulae supplied by manufacturers of frits are invariably of the RO type. The RO formula is used in all the examples here.

For bodies, the sesquioxides are unified and the formula is called the R_2O_3 formula. Suppliers of body materials like clay, cornish stone and other feldspathoids issue unity formulae of the R_2O_3 type.

Two glazes may appear to be very different in recipe form but when their unity formulae have been calculated from these recipes it may be found that they are almost identical. It is possible to calculate back to the recipe from the unity formula and in so doing one is able to compose the recipe of materials which are available. For example, in the above unity formula the MgO would be obtained more easily and cheaply from dolomite than from magnesia, and the SiO_2 would probably be supplied in part by feldspar, part clay and part flint. To calculate a unity formula from a recipe and *vice versa*, see **Calculations**. Alterations to glaze recipes are easier to make at unity formula stage where comparison with other satisfactory glazes can be made on the ratio of the oxide molecules. See **Equivalent**.

Unity formula in use. One unity formula is directly comparable with another unity formula. Once one has established a unity formula for a glaze which behaves well under one's conditions, it is possible to compare other new glazes with it even though the recipe materials are completely different.

For example, supposing the successful glaze has the unity formula:

$$\left.\begin{array}{l} 0.2\ K_2O \\ 0.1\ MgO \\ 0.7\ CaO \end{array}\right\} 0.3\ Al_2O_3 \qquad 3.6\ SiO_2$$

unity

and a new recipe, provided perhaps by a friend, gives the unity formula:

$$\left.\begin{array}{l} 0.2\ K_2O \\ 0.1\ MgO \\ 0.7\ CaO \end{array}\right\} 0.5\ Al_2O_3 \qquad 4.5\ SiO_2$$

unity

By a comparison of the two formulae one can see that the new recipe contains a higher proportion of silica (SiO_2) and will therefore be more refractory, that is, it will require more heat to complete its fusion. It also has a higher proportion of alumina (Al_2O_3) which again is a refractory. In fact, the amount of difference between these two glazes is great. Assuming that the first glaze is fully fused at 1200°C (2192°F), the second glaze will require to be fired in the region of 1280°C (2336°F) to obtain a similar result. The following list relates ratios of fully fused leadless glazes to temperatures. See also the **Table of acceptable limits for unity formulae of glazes** on p. 336.

1000°C (1832°F)	RO:	$0.25\ Al_2O_3 : 2.0\ SiO_2$
1100°C (2012°F)	RO:	$0.30\ Al_2O_3 : 2.5\ SiO_2$
1200°C (2192°F)	RO:	$0.40\ Al_2O_3 : 3.5\ SiO_2$
1300°C (2372°F)	RO:	$0.55\ Al_2O_3 : 5.0\ SiO_2$

Another important point about the two glazes under consideration is the ratio of Al_2O_3 to SiO_2. In the first glaze the ratio is 1:12 but in the second it is 1:9. Compare these with the typical unity formulae above which gradually raise the ratio from 1:8 at 1000°C to 1:9 at 1300°C.

Clearly the first glaze has a higher ratio than average and it will therefore be a very fluid glaze. The second glaze is clearly more viscous than the first. This property can be expected even when it has been melted at the higher temperature. See **Viscosity of molten glazes**. The most viscous glaze would have a ratio of 1:6. This is the ratio of the alkaline feldspars, e.g. orthoclase is $K_2O . Al_2O_3 . 6SiO_2$. Note that because the alkali content in the chemical formula is one molecule, the full formula constitutes a unity formula which is comparable with glazes. Orthoclase is fully fused at 1300°C (2372°F) but it provides an extremely viscous glass. In comparison frits have high ratios in the order of 1:12 and higher.

It should be noted that the foregoing is concerned only with the alumina:silica ratio ($Al_2O_3 : SiO_2$). It cannot be broadened to $R_2O_3 : RO_2$ because this could include other oxides which do not behave in the same way, the most notable example being boric oxide (B_2O_3).

Boric oxide is a glass-former like silica, yet it is a sesquioxide and by its chemical formula would be listed with alumina in a unity formula. To make matters even more complicated it acts as a flux. Unity formulae which contain boric oxide can only be partially compared with others which do not.

The understanding of this and a few other phenomena makes the interpretation of unity formulae a personal technique. Exceptions to the usual behaviour pattern occur with the establishment of eutectic mixtures, with the different fluxing actions of different RO oxides and with the alkali/acid balancing effect of the amphoteric oxides. Each oxide is described separately in this book under its own heading.

Fosted. Frosted. Underfired in one part only. The fosted area shows as a patch on the side of the pot and often looks lighter than the rest of the pot. It occurs where a slight air intake, through a crack or leaking bung hole, chills the pot and prevents its reaching the desired temperature.

Free silica. Silica existing in a clay or body in a separate crystalline or cryptocrystalline state, that is, neither attached to nor involved in a compound like kaolinite or feldspar. Free silica may exist as a fine quartz sand, coarse sand, flint, cristobalite and tridymite. Free silica influences a body's refractoriness, vitrification range and its susceptibility to dunting.

Freezing point. Solidifying point. The temperature at which a liquid becomes a solid. The freezing point is the same as the melting point with crystalline compounds, but with glazes this is not so. Glazes must be considered as supercooled liquids with a softening range. The freezing point will be at the lower limit of the range where the glaze becomes solid. The melting point will be at the top limit of the range. The word freezing is associated with water and ice and therefore the technical term solidifying is perhaps better for glazes.

Frit. Fritt. Part of a glaze recipe that has been melted and reground prior to its inclusion in the glaze slop. For example, in a simple recipe containing litharge, flint and china clay, the litharge and flint could be melted together to form a lead frit. The glaze would chemically remain the same.

First recipe		*Second recipe*	
litharge	50	lead frit	80
flint	30		
china clay	20	china clay	20

The reasons for using the second recipe would be the non-toxicity of the lead content, the absence of silica dust (silicosis hazard) and the probable advantage of a glaze that was easier to fire without blistering.

The purposes of fritting are:

1. To render otherwise soluble minerals insoluble in the glaze slop. For example, the important fluxes of boric oxide, soda and the composite mineral borax are highly soluble in water. Soluble minerals cannot be applied to a pot as an homogeneous material. Some will soak into the pot and some will crystallize on the surface. Solubles also upset the fluidity of the glaze slop. See **Alkali**.

2. To render harmless any injurious substance. The main substance is lead but also antimony, barium, zinc etc are poisonous and silica powders cause silicosis. See **Poison, Lead poisoning** and **Lead frit**.

3. To combine the required minerals and render them less volatile. For example, lead oxide volatilizes less from a molten glaze if it has first been fritted.

4. To give better control over glaze fusion. A frit has a more predictable and uniform rate of fusion than a mixture of minerals. The whole glaze fusion can be accelerated and maturation time decreased. The end result is a shorter glaze firing with less strain on kiln, furniture etc at the top temperature. See also **Grain size**.

5. To prepare the materials which will enter the glaze by ridding them of unwanted volatiles like carbon, sulphur and fluorine. Stiff glazes which are prone to pinholing can be made smooth by fritting part of the glaze. Special low-temperature coloured glazes and enamel colours need to be free from gases which cause blisters.

6. To prepare special colours in the form of stains, which require controlled conditions in the form of heavy reduction or complete absence of alumina etc.

7. To prepare colour stains and coloured glazes which would otherwise result in a speckled effect, when a uniform colouring is required.

8. To incorporate materials that in natural state can give rise to troubles before firing. For example: an excess of raw clay causes shrinkage cracks and peeling; zinc oxide also causes shrinkage cracks which later crawl; magnesium oxide and tin oxide are light powders that make friable glazes.

Commercial frits are made under controlled conditions with testing. Frits are therefore more dependable in chemical composition than many raw materials. Using a frit as part of the glaze gives more consistent results. The batch recipe can also be considerably simplified.

The system of using two frits in a recipe increases the permutations of results from standard frits. The system was developed originally to overcome the solubility of the lead content of lead-borosilicate glazes. See **Low sol** and **Double fritting**.

USE OF FRITS. Frits can be used in any glaze and can also be used as fluxes in bodies, slips and engobes.

When originating a recipe which involves a frit, the best way is to consider the frit as a flux only and not as a glass-former. In this way one will not be satisfied with the result simply because it melts. A frit will always melt, but it is not a suitable glaze alone. It requires other alumino-silicates. For general glazes, like transparent and maiolica, the following method is suggested:

China clay is usually necessary in a glaze to provide alumina and silica and to strengthen the unfired glaze. Start by standardizing the amount at 10%. Flint introduces silica into a glaze. Start by standardizing the amount at 10%, and adjusting this later to balance the

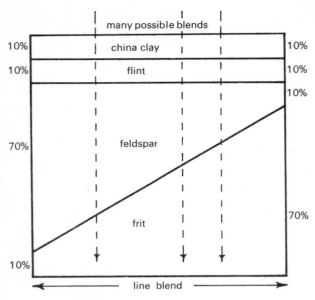

glaze. A line blend is created between feldspar and the chosen frit in the proportions of 70:10 and 10:70. The diagram shows such a line blend. One of the blends is likely to be suitable if the frit has been chosen with consideration of the manufacturer's suggestions. The final balance can be made with adjustments to the china clay and flint with possible additions of whiting. See **Glaze fit**.

The advantages of using a frit have been mentioned with the reasons for fritting. The disadvantages are that the composition is not always known and that a frit settles quickly in the glaze slop because it is inert and homogeneous. If the composition is not known, one could get some unexpected colour responses and problems could arise in the balancing of the glaze. However if the previous blending has been used then sufficient information will probably be available to overcome the disadvantage of not having an analysis.

Manufacturers of frits will often quote a unity formula for a frit and sometimes give a percentage composition of its oxides. These can be used in calculating unity formulae from recipes and *vice versa* only if the molecular weight is also known. If the molecular weight is not supplied it must be proportionately totalled from the unity formula. In calculations involving frits, one must be careful to include only proportional amounts of oxide molecules as they appear in the frit's unity formula.

In requesting information from a frit manufacturer, the specific gravity should also be sought. It is useful in ascertaining dry weights from slop weights by Brongniart's formula.

FRIT MANUFACTURE. Frits are made by intermittent and continuous processes. In both, measured amounts of raw materials are melted together in large crucibles, which are also called kilns and furnaces. The molten frit is run off into water which achieves initial shattering,

after which the frit is ground in water to produce a powder and to wash away the remaining solubles.

The photographs show an intermittent crucible being emptied and a continuous fritting plant for lead bisilicate. Both plants are at the Podmore factory in Stoke-on-Trent, England. The box-like crucible in the background of the continuous process is charged at the far end with raw materials from the floor above. The gas burner can be seen at the near end. A stream of molten frit discharges into a duct and bath of water at the lower end of the dewatering Archimedean screw.

Fritted glaze. A glaze containing frit(s) as its main source of flux. A glaze containing some frit as auxiliary flux would not be called a fritted glaze.

It is rarely necessary to frit a whole glaze except to stabilize a special effect. This occurs with some low-firing coloured glazes, sometimes called enamel glazes, where the glaze must be capable of melting smoothly and quickly.

Generally it would be a disadvantage to frit the whole glaze. To melt and regrind a glaze requires more heat and larger grinding machinery. Also a glaze is physically harder to grind than a soft frit. Lastly an homogeneous, inert mineral, like frit, will quickly settle and set hard in the glaze tub. Unfritted china clay and feldspar are valuable materials for keeping a glaze slop in suspension and helping the unfired glaze to adhere to the pot.

Frog mug. A drinking mug with a modelled frog inside at the bottom. This was an 18th- and 19th-century joke mug for tavern drinking. The idea has recently been revived.

Frost. Air temperature below 32°F and 0°C is considered frost. Any water, physically in the form of liquid, will solidify at this temperature. This includes water in glaze slops, slips, plastic clay and the water still in leatherhard clay and in damp biscuit, e.g. glazed biscuit awaiting firing.

The freezing of slop, slip or plastic clay does no harm providing the whole can be thoroughly mixed again when thawed. This in itself is sufficient nuisance. Leatherhard pots and damp biscuit will sometimes survive and can be completed and fired. However, weaknesses and faults sometimes arise in the finished ware which it is difficult to attribute to causes other than the weakening of the ware by frost action.

When the water freezes it expands. This action is important in the weathering of rocks and the ageing of clays. The particles separated only by a thin film of water are forced further apart so that when thawing takes place a thicker film of water enters. This action is obviously not desirable in pots.

Fuddling mug. A 16th- to 18th-century ale mug. There were also fuddling cups joined in threes, fours and fives with connecting holes. These were part of the same tavern joking as the puzzle jug.

Fuddling mugs and cups were made in slipware, iron-glazed earthenware and galleyware.

Fugitive. Description of colours which are easily lost by incorrect firing. Selenium reds are called fugitive because they quickly volatilize. They require both a quick firing and cooling.

Fumes. The fumes released during the firing of pottery involve water vapour, microscopic carbon in smoke, carbon monoxide and dioxide, sulphur dioxide and trioxide, fluorine and from salt-glazing, chlorine and hydrochloric acid. Some of the glaze oxides also volatilize. They are lead oxide, copper oxide, chromium oxide, antimony oxide, zinc oxide, boric oxide, baria, soda and potash. Cadmium selenide used for red colours also volatilizes.

The fumes which present problems and the greatest hazards are sulphur trioxide, fluorine and lead oxide, especially when these fumes emerge from kiln bung holes directly into the studio or workshop. Sulphur trioxide combines with water vapour to produce sulphuric acid which can be smelt and tasted in the atmosphere. It also corrodes the metal framework of the kiln. Fluorine can also be detected in the atmosphere as a choking gas. It attacks window glass, etching this to a frosted opacity. Lead oxide is not easily detectable but its effect on the human system is cumulative. See **Poison** and **Volatiles**.

Funk. Funk pottery is satirical and joke pottery which uses the normal images of pottery but twists them in a surrealistic, dadaist or other surprise way. Funk also uses clay to produce objects normally of other materials, thereby tripping the viewer into thinking incorrectly about the object which becomes a visual pun. Funk-type objects appear with serious potting throughout history from Chinese imitations of bronzes to the Staffordshire mug with a frog inside. However, funk emerged as a separate North American art form in the 1960's.

Furniture. Moveable kiln fittings which include shelves, shelf supports and the supports for the ware. Furniture is made from refractory materials. See **Refractory**. Saggars and muffles are not furniture.

It is generally accepted that the weight of the furniture often exceeds that of the ware. This means that over half the heat inside the kiln is being used to heat the furniture. There is also the question of weight handling. Consideration should be given to these points although individual potters are not able to incorporate all the specialized furniture which is used by industrial firms. For example, thick shelves bend less and therefore last longer than thin shelves. They can also be used for more varied ware and therefore fewer are needed. Thin shelves however are easier to handle in and out of the kiln and cost less in terms of firing fuel. The saving in fuel and energy may more than offset the cost of frequent replacement.

Shelves may be solid or pierced. Pierced shelves are used in through-flame kilns, especially up-draught, where they act as heat baffles. They are often specially shaped to fit the kiln. See illustration. They are less strong than solid shelves but are more economical because they absorb less heat.

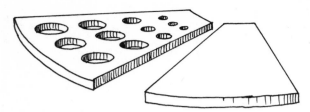

The materials from which shelves are made determine their life and the weight which they will support. Naturally a large shelf which spans a wide space and carries a heavy weight of ware needs to be stronger than a small shelf carrying light ware. Normally a thick shelf is stronger than a thin one and will withstand a high temperature and greater load. Shelves are also called bats.

Shelf supports are called variously props, pillars and castles. Like shelves they have a life dependent upon material and thickness. Cast props are popular and are available in different heights which can be further adjusted by adding castellated tube props on top. Cast props, being thinner, are much weaker than tube props and if used in reduction firings can become very brittle.

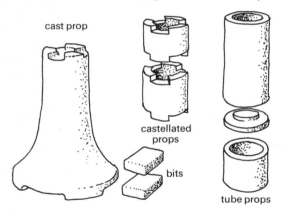

cast prop

castellated props

bits

tube props

Ware supports are used to hold the ware clear of shelves or itself in the firing, thus obtaining uniform

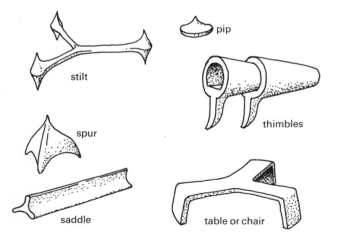

stilt

pip

thimbles

spur

saddle

table or chair

heating and cooling, and preventing glazed ware from sticking together. Ware supports have many names. Some are industrial and trade names whilst others are colloquial ones used at a single pottery. Table, stool, chair, collar, ring and frogs are fairly self-explanatory descriptions. Each gives support over an area especially where it is needed to keep a pot in shape. They are used for dense earthenware, porcelain and sometimes for stoneware. Stilts, pips, pins, thimbles, spurs and saddles give support at a single point and are used for earthenware glaze firing. They set into the glaze and are ground off flush with the glaze surface.

Cranks are frames into which are fitted the expendable pips and pins which support the ware. They are used for flatware, plates and tiles. The pips and pins are easier and cheaper to manufacture than the saddles and thimbles which they have replaced. See **Crank**.

A further part of setting is the use of placing sand, biscuit (pads) and bat wash.

Fusion. Ceramic fusion. The melting of different materials into a homogeneous liquid mass. Fusion requires heat (temperature absorbed over a period of time) and depends upon the interaction of the different materials present.

The factors which affect fusion can be classified as those which hasten the final stage and those which hinder its evolution. The factors which promote fusion are:

1. The material present classified in pottery terms as glass-formers and fluxes. See **Interaction**.
2. The ratio of these materials. See **Eutectic mixture**.
3. A low viscosity in the melt allowing movement of particles and a thorough stirring effect created by escaping bubbles. The low viscosity also allows gases to escape. See **Viscosity of molten glazes**.
4. Opportunity for the melt to move under gravity which allows the different particles to meet one another.
5. Fine particle size which presents a larger surface area to attack by heat and interaction. See **Grain size**.
6. Previous fritting of some or all of the materials. See **Frit**.
7. Prolonged firing which gives more opportunity for maturation. See **Vitrification**.

The factors which hinder fusion are:

1. The materials present as refractories and anti-fluxes. See **Anti-flux**.
2. The ratio of these materials to the other more fusible materials.
3. A high viscosity in the melt which inhibits particle movement and traps escaping gases. See **Viscosity of molten glazes**.
4. Large grain size of the materials. See **Grain size**.
5. A firing of short duration. See **Heat** and **Firing**.

G

Galena. Lead ore. Lead sulphide. Smithum. Blue lead. PbS. The most important ore of lead from which lead is extracted by first roasting to the oxide and then reducing to the metal. Galena is used as a source of lead oxide in glazes. The conversion factor is 0·93. It can therefore be empirically substituted weight by weight for red lead or litharge in a glaze recipe.

Galena glazes must be fired in open chambers or semi-muffles because the sulphur content needs to escape as sulphur gases (sulphur, sulphur monoxide, dioxide, trioxide). These fumes are harmful.

The ground ore is a bluish grey and has an interesting sparkle. This sparkle is said to be retained in galena glazes of the transparent type when they cover dark bodies. However the sparkle in the glaze is more likely to be iron sulphate crystals.

Galena is less poisonous than the oxides and for some time was not subject to the same precautions against lead poisoning. However it is poisonous and precautions should be taken. See **Lead poisoning**.

A typical galena glaze for slipware is:

red body clay	10
white body clay	10
flint	30
galena	50

This is a glaze for raw glazing. It is put on dry raw ware and fired in a rectangular or other down-draught kiln at 950°C (1742°F).

From about the 10th century to the mid-17th century, galena was dusted on to pottery ware through a coarse rag. The dust stuck to the newly thrown wet ware or to a fresh slip coating and fused the upper layer of clay into a glaze during the firing. See also **Lead oxide**.

Galleyware. Gallyware. Galliware. The earlier name for tin-glazed ware of the 16th to 18th centuries. The first exports from Faenza arrived in western Europe by ship (galley) from Venice and became known as galleyware. The name was then transferred to similar pots made in Antwerp, Bristol, Liverpool and Lambeth. After the successful productions at Delft, these wares became known as delftware in the 18th century and it is by this name that we know the ware today. See also **Delft** and **Lambeth** for photographs.

Gault clay. A true marl of the Upper Cretaceous System of sedimentary rocks. It contains a high percentage, as much as 30% in some cases, of calcium carbonate (chalk) in fine particles. This tends to make the clay 'short' for working and it is possible to remove only the larger impurities. However pockets exist of finely divided gault clay which are plastic and can be used for potting. The coarser clays are used for bricks and extruded insulation blocks.

The interesting yellows and buffs associated with gault clay and the fired body are a result of the bleaching of the iron by the calcia. In the soft-fired body, the calcia is not fully involved in silicate fusions and the excess is able to involve itself with the iron oxide.

The high chalk content precludes the use of gault clay as a pottery body for use over 1060°C (1940°F). Gault clay deforms at approximately 1150°C (2120°F) and melts by 1250°C (2282°F). This property makes it a useful constituent in a slip glaze. Usually the iron content makes such a slip very dark. The calcia content which has previously kept the iron light in colour, has become involved in silica fusions. See **Marl** and **Calcia**.

Germania. Germanium dioxide. GeO_2. A glass-forming oxide which is present as a trace in many glazes but is not deliberately introduced.

Gerstley borate. A variety of colemanite which includes soda. It is named after a man who operated a colemanite mine in California.

Gibbsite. $Al_2O_3.3H_2O$. Alumina hydrate of pure white form. It is one of the three hydrates of alumina which are a source of the metal aluminium and alumina for abrasives. It is softer than the other two (bauxite and diaspore) and therefore more easily ground. It is used by potters as a refractory bat wash when it is mixed with some china clay which acts as a binder.

The name gibbsite is used for the aluminium and hydroxyl group layer which occurs in the kaolinite crystal. In this layer, the ultimate composition, also called the average formula, is nearer to $Al_2O_3.2H_2O$ than $Al_2O_3.3H_2O$. However, individual parts (fig. 1) can be seen as $Al_2O_3.3H_2O$ which is also written $Al(OH)_3$ a method which better describes the arrangement of the hydroxyl groups.

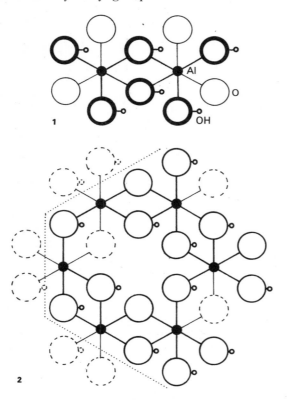

In kaolinite, the layer (fig. 2) is gibbsite in character being weak in structure and inhibited from stronger bonding by the occupancy of the oxygen atoms by the silicon layer. See **Clay, physics**.

The two lattice diagrams (figs. 1 and 2) show the isolation of $Al_2O_3.3H_2O$ and the gibbsite layer with hexagonal structure averaging $3(Al_2O_3.2H_2O)$.

Glass-former. An oxide which is able to retain the amorphous property of its molten state when setting to a solid. Other minerals return to crystalline state as they set or soon afterwards.

Glass-formers are indispensable in pottery. They form the bulk of a glaze and provide the glassy cement which gives strength to the body. The glass-formers, in order of importance are: silica, boric oxide, phosphorus pentoxide, antimony oxide, arsenic oxide, germania and selenium dioxide.

Each glass-former is capable of existing in a crystalline state and it is in this state that it usually occurs in nature. It appears to be white because light is reflected from the crystal facets but it is transparent. If it is heated sufficiently it loses its crystalline nature by melting to a transparent liquid. If cooled very slowly over a period of weeks or even years it returns to crystals, but if cooled quickly over a period of only hours or at most a few days there is insufficient time for the crystals to grow. The liquid state sets as a transparent solid, technically known as a supercooled liquid.

The most important glass-forming oxide is silicon dioxide normally called silica (SiO_2). It is always present in a glaze and is usually by far the largest constituent. It is also the commonest natural oxide constituting 60% of the Earth's crust. It occurs naturally as sand, quartz and flint, and as the semi-precious stones rose quartz, cairngorm and amethyst. All these look glassy when inspected and can be imagined as glazes. See **Quartz** and **Silica**.

The second important glass-forming oxide is boric oxide (B_2O_3). When used in glazes, it is always in combination with silica. It cannot be used without silica because it is soluble in water. Glazes and glasses produced with boric oxide as the main constituent would be soft and soluble.

Native boric oxide is rare. Boric oxide is found combined with other elements in borates of which borax is the most important. See **Boric oxide, Borax** and **Borates**.

The other glass-formers are used in small amounts for special effects. Phosphorus pentoxide retains its individual structure within a glaze and thereby deflects the light giving rise to chun effects. See **Chun**. Antimony oxide does not dissolve in the glaze unless lead oxide is present. It gives opacity in leadless glazes and yellow colours with lead oxide. See **Antimony oxide**. Arsenic oxide is used in the glass industry for clarification of discoloured glass. Germania and selenium dioxide are too rare and unstable to be used on any large scale.

Glaze. A layer of glass which is fused into place on a pottery body. The glaze provides a hygienic covering on pottery because it is smoother than the body it covers and it is non-porous. It is also decorative, providing colour, shine and textural contrast with the body; and it increases the strength of the ware by the creation of a body-glaze layer.

The glaze is first attached to the pottery body in the form of a layer of powder. This powder is composed of glass-forming materials, fluxes and stabilizers. During the firing they all fuse together to form a compact layer of molten material. On cooling, this layer does not separate into its former constituents but remains as the new material, glass.

In order to produce a glaze, there must be present sufficient glass-forming oxides. See **Glass-former**. By far the most important of these is silica and it is introduced into glazes by the minerals quartz (100% silica), flint (95% silica), feldspar (65% silica) and china clay (47% silica).

The glass-forming oxides are fused into a practical glaze by the presence of fluxes and stabilizers. The fluxes are alkaline oxides of which soda, potash, calcia, magnesia and lead oxide are the most important. The most important stabilizer is alumina.

These three groups of oxides: fluxes, stabilizers and glass-formers, are also called the alkaline, amphoteric and acidic oxides. Their relative proportions and the composition of each group give a great variety of possible glazes.

See also **Frit** and **Firing, glaze**.

THE ORIGIN OF GLAZES. Some authorities claim dates as early as 12,000 B.C. for the first glazes. These were on the glazed paste beads which were made in Egypt. The Egyptians discovered glass where sand and sandstones, impregnated with salt, had been fused by a fire. Certainly by 3000 B.C. the Egyptians were using glazes on some of their pottery. These glazes were alkaline copper glazes which were used effectively as decorative coverings. Later, in south-west Asia, glazes were used to give extra strength and durability to bricks, wall tiles and pottery. Around 1500 B.C. glazes were used as practical and hygienic waterproof layers on pottery.

The first Egyptian glaze was a surface fusion of the body which occurred where the soluble salts from the body had crystallized on the surface during drying. In Egypt and south-west Asia, the knowledge of this was used to develop glazes applied as slips. Lead glazes were used to avoid the difficulties which arose with the use of soluble salts but by the 13th century, the solubility of the alkaline fluxes had been successfully overcome by fritting.

Lead glazes were also used in China as early as 200 B.C. Their development ran parallel to the better-known stoneware and porcelain glazes. The high-temperature glazes followed the realization that fine ash from the wood fire had fluxed the pottery surface. The stoneware glazes were composed of wood ashes, clay and feldspathoids. With improvements in kiln construction, higher temperatures were reached and refined porcelains were perfected by the 10th century.

In Europe, lead glazes developed separately from stoneware glazes which were salt-glazes. Lead oxide was used from the 12th to 17th centuries and was applied as a powdered ore which was dusted onto the wet ware or onto a wet clay slip. The method of mixing a glaze and applying it as a liquid coating did not become standard practice in Britain until the 18th century. The practice spread slowly across Europe from the Islamic countries.

It is now usual to apply glazes by dipping or pouring. Spraying and painting are also done industrially and for special effects by individual potters. Some salt-glazing is done by individual potters.

CHEMISTRY OF GLAZES. A glaze is the result of interaction between alkali and acid. When heated, these two are in active opposition and the excitement engendered gives rise to a fluid state—the molten glaze.

The alkalis and acids in glazes are oxides and these are originally solids. The individual oxides would not necessarily create liquids at the temperatures involved in pottery. It is only by interaction that this occurs. Yet the alkalis and acids involved are not violent. Many of the oxides involved one would not associate with the household idea of alkali and acid. It is difficult, for example, to think of silica as an acid, but its reactive properties must be so described in terms of glazes. In the presence of heat, the molecular structure of the oxides vibrates, loosens or even breaks, and under these conditions interaction can take place.

The amount of heat required depends upon the type and amount of the alkalis present. For example, lead oxide, which is an alkali in terms of glaze balance, interacts with silica at temperatures above 500°C (932°F). Lithia (lithium oxide), a stronger alkali in some respects, starts its action at 800°C (1472°F) and magnesia (magnesium oxide) is inert until 1170°C (2138°F) is reached. Details of the other alkaline oxides are given under **Fluxing action**.

The interaction which is necessary for the creation of a glaze can only take place at or above the minimum temperature for the alkali concerned. Time is also required. A higher temperature gives more molecular vibration and is equal to a longer time at a lower temperature. The product of temperature and time is known as heat.

The temperature at which action begins is often described as the melting point of a glaze. However with the necessity of a time consideration and the obvious advantages in the use of a higher temperature to accomplish a full fusion, it is more usual to refer to a range of temperatures rather than a single melting point. The range often extends upwards to the point where the glaze is spoilt by being overfired. This is caused by gassing as some of the oxides become volatile. Thus a glaze is described as maturing rather than melting and is given a lower and upper limit for its use. The difference between these two may be only 10°C (18°F) or it may be 100°C (180°F), depending upon the oxides involved.

Below the maturing temperature range there is no action. Thus the action is checked by cooling and the final glaze is no longer liquid but begins to set. It does not usually set completely at the lower end of the range but tarries in a soft state until approximately 500°C (932°F).

The interaction between alkali and acid in the presence of heat produces fluidity. The degree of fluidity involved depends upon the particular oxides and is referred to in terms of viscosity when discussing glazes. Glazes are made more viscous by the presence of alumina, the most important amphoteric oxide. An amphoteric oxide is half-way between an alkali and an acid, and therefore acts as both. In very small amounts, alumina will rebalance the alkali-acid interaction towards an optimum fusion but in large amounts it has a distinctly stiffening effect. A large amount would be only one-twentieth or one-thirtieth of the glaze.

See also **Anti-flux** and **Eutectic mixture**.

PHYSICS OF GLAZES. Glazes are composed of the molecules of different oxides which are linked together in random chains. Before the firing, these same molecules are linked to identical molecules in a lattice structure. The lattice structure forms a crystal of the oxide concerned and the different oxides which will compose the final glaze are therefore present as different crystals, particles or grains of powdered material.

During the firing, the bonds which hold the molecules together are broken and a fluid state exists in which it is convenient to assume that each molecule is an isolated particle. This is the molten state of the glaze and the action which brings it about is called the fusion. Part of this fusion is a liberation of gases. These effectively stir the mixture of unattached molecules so that upon cooling they are unlikely to re-establish their original bonds.

It is true that if sufficient time is allowed, many of the molecules establish bonds with identical molecules. A preferential selection exists whereby one molecule has affinity with an identical molecule in terms of size and molecular vibration. To some extent this occurs in crystalline glazes, but for most of the molecules an immediate link-up is established with any molecule which offers suitable valency. The atoms which flank an isolated molecule have unsatisfied valencies which can remain so in the excited state of a molten glaze but cannot remain unsatisfied as the glaze cools. The comparatively rapid satisfaction of these valencies gives a series of random chains. The drawings show the constituent oxides and the type of random chain which they produce.

The final glaze partially combines the physical properties of the constituent oxides and partially displays new properties. New properties are those belonging to its amorphous state and include its physical hardness,

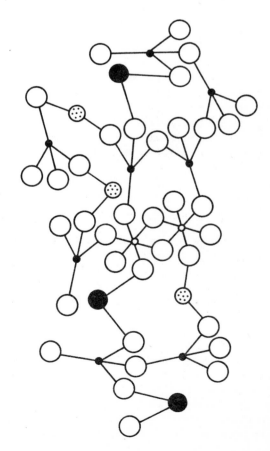

resistance to chemical attack and to abrasion, its colour, transparency, opacity, and its surface texture. The combined properties from the oxides which are displayed by the new state are those of hardness and the overall rate of expansion. The rate of expansion is important if the glaze is to sit harmoniously on a pottery body without defect. See **Glaze fit**.

See also **Devitrification** and **Viscosity of molten glazes**.

GLAZE DEFECTS. Most glaze defects have self-explanatory names. The common defects are separately itemized in this book as: **Blistering, Crawling, Crazing, Devitrification, Flashing, Overfiring, Pinholing, Shivering, Spluttering, Underfiring**.

Glaze fit. In glaze fit one is concerned with achieving a harmony of glaze and pottery body with regard to their thermal expansions and contractions. The suitability of the glaze in terms of colour, texture and thickness is not considered.

A finished pot expands and contracts with the warmth of the day and the cool of the night in common with all other substances, solid, liquid and gas. Pots used as ovenware and food containers are subjected to still more heat and will expand and contract more. The expansion is often sudden so that they are subjected to what is called thermal shock. The body and glaze need to expand and contract together with reasonable harmony. An exact match is impossible and fortunately not necessary. There is a degree of latitude in the harmony of body and glaze expansion and contraction before a defect occurs which spoils the pottery. A defect could show as crazing when the glaze cracks, or as shivering and shelling when the glaze flakes off the body, or as dunting when the body cracks. Glaze fitting is concerned with the adjustment of glaze, and possibly body, composition to achieve the necessary harmony.

The potter is usually concerned with contraction. When the potter opens his kiln and inspects the ware it is after a period of cooling during which the pots have contracted. If they come safely through this period of large contraction he not unreasonably assumes that future small amounts of expansion and contraction will do no harm. In physics it is common practice to talk in terms of expansion and consider contraction as the logical corollary. This practice is followed here.

Nearly all substances expand with heat and contract by the same amount on cooling. Each substance expands and contracts at a different rate but each substance is predictable in that it keeps to its own rate. The glaze is therefore very likely to expand and contract at a different rate from the body. The rate of expansion is a direct result of the composition of a body or a glaze. Each component, usually considered as an oxide, gives to the body or glaze its own expansion rate in direct proportion to the amount present.

For example, if a glaze contains 50% of oxide A which expands a large amount and 50% of oxide B which expands only a little, then the resulting expansion rate is theoretically halfway between these two rates. In practice other factors, e.g. interaction, affect the result so that this statement is only approximately true. By adjusting the percentage composition of a glaze one will undoubtedly influence its expansion rate in a known direction. Alternatively one may substitute another oxide of different expansion rate but very similar glaze behaviour for one of the original oxides. In this way one is able to make substantial alteration to the expansion rate of the glaze with minimum change in the other glaze properties.

Since 1850 research has been carried out to discover the different rates of expansion for different substances including glaze oxides. Published tables give a rate measured as a percentage increase over a rise in temperature of $1°C$. The rate is usually a factor relating to 1% of the oxide in a glaze. Different tables are available which vary according to the way in which the coefficients of expansion were obtained and the tables are named after their originators as English and Turner, Mayer and Havas, Winkelmann and Schott. The table given here is a simplification from various sources and shows the common glaze oxides listed with the greatest expansion rate at the top end, the least at the bottom.

	Fluxes	Amphoteric and acidic oxides	Crystallizers and opacifiers
	Na_2O		
	K_2O		
	CaO		CaO
	BaO		BaO
	PbO		
			TiO_2
	Li_2O		
	ZnO		ZnO
	MgO		MgO
			ZrO_2
			SnO_2
		Al_2O_3	
		SiO_2	
	B_2O_3	B_2O_3	

increasing rate of expansion →

A more detailed table is given in the **Tables** in this book. The actual coefficient numbers rarely concern the individual potter who is more interested in the relationship of one glaze constituent to another. The actual amount measured as a percentage increase is not likely to be of much value to him unless he is trying to compare the expansion rates of two glazes. A potter wishing to make use of these tables of coefficients should ascertain whether they are linear or volumetric, coefficients or factors for calculating coefficients and whether they refer to the temperature range which he is considering.

The problem facing the potter is often one of adjusting an existing glaze to make it fit his standard body. Presumably some defect leads him to this adjustment and the first action is the analysis of the defect. Either the glaze has contracted too much which has resulted in crazing or it has not contracted sufficiently and has resulted in shelling or shivering. A decision can now be made to replace some of the flux for an oxide of different expansion rate.

If the defect is crazing then the new flux must be one which expands less, and hence contracts less, than the previous one. From the table it will be seen that boric oxide (B_2O_3) has the smallest expansion rate. When boric oxide replaces one of the other fluxes, the resulting glaze will contract less and the crazing defect may be cured. Substitution of one oxide for another is usually done on a molecular equivalent basis although the amount to substitute is a matter for judgment and experiment. See **Equivalent**. Such are the different effects of the oxides that the approach is empirical in any case and even the addition of small amounts of a new oxide may have the desired effect. Boric oxide especially is so low in expansion that it has a great reputation as an anti-craze. Additions of small amounts of borax frit to a glaze often cure the crazing and even improve glaze shine and colouring.

In the opposite case of shivering one looks for a flux with a high expansion rate. Lead oxide is popular and has the additional advantage of creating an elastic glaze capable of adapting itself under stress. Alternatively most potters will have noticed how much a soda-based glaze contracts. Alkaline copper blue glazes are notorious for crazing. The introduction of soda feldspar (albite) in place of some or all of the potash feldspar (orthoclase) may be sufficient to cure shivering.

It should be noted there is always some stress between body and glaze. The two cannot lie absolutely side by side without stress. If no stress exists at one temperature there is sufficient difference in their two expansion rates to cause some slight stress in the variations of air temperature. A glaze can successfully contain about ten times the amount of stress when under compression as in tension. It is better therefore that a glaze should be under slight compression.

Glaze fit is a complex subject involving more than is discussed here. The reader is referred to other factors under the headings of **Crazing, Shivering, Thermal shock, Dunting, Body-glaze layer, Buffer layer** and **Interaction**.

The achievement of a good glaze fit is generally considered a matter of glaze adjustment. But where body and glaze are matured together, it may happen that body adjustment is easier. The addition or subtraction of flint, sand or grog may be a simple remedy to a glaze fit problem. If a glaze matures over a shorter range than does its body it is more easily spoilt, than is the body, by under- or over-firing. Alterations to composition often have the effect of moving the range up or down the scale. With a short glaze-range there is little room for this but it may happen that in the body-range there is room for considerable change. See graph.

Glaze-body. The combination layer resulting from the interaction of glaze and body. See **Body-glaze layer** and **Buffer layer**.

Glost firing. Glaze firing. The term has come to us from the industry where a glaze firing at a lower temperature than the biscuit is common practice. Glost implies firing of glaze at a lower temperature than the biscuit which is then called bisque or bisc. See **Bisc**.

Goblet. The two examples are: a stoneware goblet by Haverfordwest Pottery, Wales, and a maiolica one by Alan Caiger-Smith.

148

Gowen. See **Cornish stone**.

Grain size. Particle size. A term used when referring to the fineness or coarseness of materials. The term 'grain size' is usually used for sizes larger than 200's or 300's mesh. This involves the grogs, sands and glaze materials which are handled in dry grain and powder form. The alternative term 'particle size' is more often used when referring to near-colloidal sizes. These involve groups of disordered crystals packed together as in clay suspensions and glaze melts.

Grain sizes are measured in mesh size numbers for the larger sizes from 1 down to 200's or 300's mesh, from which size microns are generally used. A 200's mesh will pass grains of 76 microns (BS 410).

Grain size is relevant in both bodies and glazes.

In glazes, the grain size affects the time required for a complete fusion to take place.

In bodies, the grain size of grogs and other fillers affects the results obtained. Coarse grains give visible and tactile textures but they do not necessarily affect the drying and firing behaviour of the body. Medium grains often alter the drying character of a body by giving a more uniform drying shrinkage over the whole drying period. See **Drying**. Refractory fillers added to bodies as fine grains can give apparently fluxing results.

Specific consideration is given here to the grain sizes of glaze materials and to silica additions to bodies. For a discussion of the difference between china clay and ball clay, see **Particle size**. See also **Filler** and **Preparation of clay** (control of grain size).

Glaze minerals melt by combining two or more oxides to produce a new mineral which is in liquid state. The oxides concerned are usually contained in two different materials, e.g. whiting and china clay. The chemical interaction is only possible where two grains of different minerals can physically touch. The centres of large grains can only melt when the surrounding grain has been removed by melting. Thus large grains are slow to melt because they present a proportionately smaller surface area for contact than do small grains.

If a glaze is to mature quickly, the glaze materials must be finely ground and thoroughly dispersed. Suppliers of glaze materials often mill their products to pass a 200's mesh. Most potters are content if their prepared glaze slops will pass through a 120's mesh. Glazes which use coarse materials like sands and wood ashes require a longer time to mature.

Refractory materials are often fritted with soft materials. The new material thus formed is ground to a fine state in which it melts quickly and smoothly producing immediate homogeneity. In contrast to the original materials, a grain of frit melts when it reaches a determined temperature. At this temperature the bonds between the oxide molecules are weakened and the solid state collapses as a liquid state. The temperature has only to penetrate the grain for this to occur. There is no interaction necessary with grains of other materials.

A frit can be said to 'melt' but glazes composed of different materials are advisedly described as 'maturing'. The grain size in both cases affects the time required.

There is a general test for ground sands and quartz to be added to stoneware bodies. It consists of the feel when rubbed between finger and thumb. There should be sufficient bite for the sand to be felt as granules rather than powder. The dividing line approximates 100's mesh in grain size. For stoneware, especially reduced stoneware involving bodies containing some iron, it is necessary to use a quartz sand of about 80's grade and coarser. Sand which is finer can be completely fused during firing resulting in over-vitrification of the body with consequential deformation of the ware. Quartz sand of coarse grain is regarded as a refractory grog but quartz ground to a fine grain size acts as a body flux.

The effect is not quite so noticeable in oxidized stoneware. It is necessary to use a very fine grain size approaching 300's mesh before the 'fluxing' effect is observed.

There is also a desirable grain size for flint which is added to earthenware bodies. Assuming that the flint is being added to increase the cristobalite content as an anti-craze measure, it must convert to cristobalite and not melt to amorphous phase. The usually quoted optimum size is around 200's mesh. Larger than this can cause internal stresses in the body. The flint is also not as ready to convert. Flint of finer grain size is readily involved in the glassy phases of the body and its crystalline property is lost. See **Cristobalite** and **Silica conversion**.

Granite. A feldspathoid occasionally used in glazes. It originated as molten magma which cooled slowly within the earth and is therefore of large crystalline grain. It is extremely hard, resists weathering and is therefore a difficult material to grind but dust is sometimes available from quarries. It is more refractory in use than pure feldspars and approximates a mixture of feldspar and quartz or one of the more refractory cornish stones. It always contains some iron which gives a greenish tinge when fired. See also **Feldspathoids**.

Granite is related to cornish stone and china clay. These two originated as granite but before setting from molten state the magma was subjected to pneumatolysis, a process of composition alteration by the action of liquids and gases. When cool and solid, the resulting rock was not as resistant to weathering as pure granite. The cornish stones are similar in chemical composition to granite but are much more easily crushed.

Not less than 45% and often as much as 70% of granite is feldspar. Orthoclase accounts for about three-quarters of this with the rest made up of albite or albite and oligoclase. Feldspar gives granite its white sparkle sometimes tinged pink with traces of iron.

Between 20% and 50% of granite is quartz which gives whiteness but also a greyness when the quartz is clear.

Up to 15% of granite is mica, usually black biotite seen as sparkling black specks. There is sometimes a mafic mineral like hornblende also present. The iron in the mica and hornblende gives a grey or greenish colour to the granite and upon melting the iron is usually involved in reduced state giving a greenish tinge.

Granite is more refractory than pure feldspars and most cornish stones. It requires over 1300°C (2372°F) to produce fusion. A molecular formula is not possible for such a complex material but a simplified unity formula would be:

$$\left.\begin{array}{l} 0{\cdot}7 \ K_2O \\ 0{\cdot}2 \ Na_2O \\ 0{\cdot}05 \ MgO \\ 0{\cdot}05 \ CaO \end{array}\right\} \left.1 \text{ to } 1{\cdot}5 \ Al_2O_3 \atop 0{\cdot}1 \ Fe_2O_3\right\} 6 \text{ to } 12 \ SiO_2$$

In the enlarged photograph of a section of granite, the three minerals are clearly visible. The white crystals are feldspar, the mid-tone areas are quartz and the small black pieces are mica.

Graven. See **Cornish stone**.

Green. Greens are produced in ceramics by silicate solutions. If the colouring is not fully fused in a silicate, the tendency is towards grey colours. Glazes can therefore be green but bodies, especially porous bodies, tend to be greyish greens from the same colouring. Copper oxide is the most dependable green stain for the softer temperatures but volatilizes from glazes above 1200°C (2192°F). Chromium oxide produces greyish greens. Both oxides are modified by additions of iron, nickel, vanadium and zinc oxides to produce a wide range of greens. See **Copper oxide** and **Chromium oxide**.

Green ware. Ware which is complete from the making but has not yet dried sufficiently to be ready for firing.

Grog. Chamotte. Ground fired body added to clays to provide a proportion of already fired and often refractory material. Grog provides texture, both tactile and visual, along with bite for better control in forming. Grog is an opener which helps the clay to dry uniformly and because it is already fired it proportionately cuts down the overall shrinkage and hence any tendency to crack or warp. It is usual to consider grog as a body that is more refractory than the clay to which it is added and most grogs are fireclay fired to at least 1300°C (2372°F). The word grog is sometimes used in a less specific way to mean any opener thus embracing sand, quartz etc. See also **Filler**.

Grogs can be considered as either hard or soft. Hard grogs are those which have been previously fired to a temperature above that to which the body is to be fired. The advantage of this is that this grog will not shrink in the firing and hence will work against any tendency to warp. It is useful in the making of tiles and large slab pots. Soft grogs are those which have been fired to temperatures lower than the temperature to which the body will be fired. If a soft biscuit firing is used, a soft grog may even be softer-fired than the biscuit temperature. The advantage of this is that a very porous grog is obtained which can be useful in the tempering of very sticky clays and in quick drying.

If the soft grog is the same body as that to which it is added it is called pitchers. The advantage of using pitchers is that the working character of the body can be altered for various sizes and types of ware, but the fired result is the same. The same glazes and firing schedules can therefore be used.

Grogs are graded by screening and given a dimension, e.g. one-sixteenth inch which means that it will all pass through a hole one-sixteenth inch square. Two numbers such as 40/60 mean that all will pass through a 40's mesh but not a 60's mesh. 60/Dust means that all will pass through a 60's mesh and some particles may be exceedingly small. See also **Analysis, mechanical**.

There are some dark-coloured clays which are still

sufficiently refractory for the potter to use for all the purposes of a hard grog and with the advantage of giving a dark speckle. Coloured pitchers made from dried and ground slips can be added to slips to give colour speckle. This is especially attractive with vitrified slips which burn into matt or other stable glazes.

Growan. See **Cornish stone**.

Gypsum. Hydrated calcium sulphate. Alabaster. $CaSO_4.2H_2O$. The crystalline mineral from which plaster of Paris is prepared. It varies from white to an orange-pink colour. It can be ground and used in glazes as a source of calcia (CaO). The sulphur trioxide is liberated during the firing combining with the atmosphere to form sulphuric acid. See **Acid**.

The decomposition cycle of gypsum is:

$$2(CaSO_4.2H_2O) \xrightarrow{120°-200°C} 2CaSO_4.H_2O + 3H_2O\uparrow$$

$$2CaSO_4.H_2O \xrightarrow{500°C} 2CaSO_4 + H_2O\uparrow$$

$$2CaSO_4 \xrightarrow{1000°-1100°C} 2CaO + 2SO_3\uparrow$$

A large amount of sulphur trioxide is dangerous to health if released into the atmosphere of the workshop. Its passage through an already fusing glaze causes bubbling which may not settle before about 1250°C

(2282°F). Small amounts of gypsum, however, can be used in under slips, engobes or the first glaze of a double layer. Here it will cause bubbling through the covering glaze. If the covering glaze is sufficiently fluid, an oilspot effect can be achieved.

The following is a recipe which uses gypsum to introduce calcia. It is a grey lime matt when fired to 1250°C (2282°F). A slow and fully oxidized firing in an open draught kiln is essential to take away the sulphurous fumes.

cornish stone	35
china clay	10
siliceous fireclay	5
gypsum	50

H

Haematite. Hematite. Martite. Specular iron. Kidney ore. Raddle. General name for a variety of iron ores which are almost pure ferric oxide (Fe_2O_3). The ore is usually black or grey on the outside but red inside giving a red brown powder when ground. Haematite is the source of iron metal and iron oxide for ceramics. The ore is sufficiently pure to be considered 99% Fe_2O_3.

Ferric oxide also exists naturally in hydrated forms, that is, in combination with water. The ores are called limonite and laterite. Haematite was probably of this origin and was subjected to pressure and heat (metamorphism). The precipitate was able to form crystals and in so doing became denser and purer. The hardness varies from H1 to 7.

The softest stones are the raddles and red ochres used by early people for self-decoration. The ore was considered the blood of the mother earth and the same consideration is held in the name haematite—the bloodlike stone. These are easy to grind and use as pottery colours. See **Iron oxide**.

The hardest stones are distinctly crystalline and are called itabirite and specular iron. These are too hard to grind for pottery but are purer forms of ferric oxide.

Handle. The handle is the first part of a pot to be touched by the user. It is therefore a focal point of the pot and is both functional and decorative. It should be so conceived.

There are two types of handle: loop and lug. A loop is formed from a strip or roll of clay which gives a closed space itself or with the pot wall. A lug is a piece of clay attached to the pot and usually modelled in place. Both types perform the same functions of assisting lifting, carrying and directionally controlling the pot.

Lugs are used on small pots or where space around the pot is restricted, as with a casserole. They may pro-

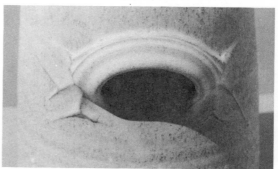

vide only the merest grip or cluster as a friction surface. They are sometimes pierced for decorative effect, practical reasons of firing or use with thongs etc.

The lug handle is the simplest extension of the pot itself and should appear so. It arises from the need for a better finger and thumb grip at the rim or for better side friction. Three casserole handles are shown by John Leach, Haverfordwest Pottery and Janet Hamer.

A loop handle is intended to take the hand or at least

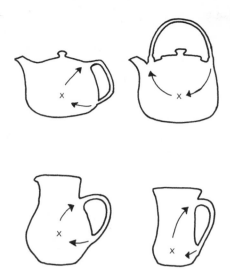

a finger, otherwise a lug is sufficient. The loop makes a rhythm or continuous movement for the eye to follow taking in the weight of the pot in aesthetic appraisal and functional appearance. The theoretically completed loop of the handle should extend inside the pot and encompass the centre of gravity for control.

It is possible to slip-cast a pot with handles attached or create lugs from thrown flanges but for most pots the handles are additions. They are created at a later stage than the bulk of the pot but are a completion of the form. This is so even when the handle is a cane one added after the pot's final firing.

Clay handles are usually added as soon as is practical. Some potters add handles to thrown casseroles, jugs and mugs before cutting them from the wheel. This urgency gives greater unity to the conception. Most potters add clay handles when the pot has stiffened slightly and use a special clay saved for the purpose. This clay has the same composition as the pot clay but has been specially soured and for a longer period. The handle clay is therefore more plastic, capable of greater flexibility in forming and results in a stronger handle.

The strength of a handle is the clay itself. A handle which is weak at the join has not been correctly attached. See **Crack**. The defect can usually be traced to attachment of too soft a handle to too dry a pot or the use of too much water or slip in the process in the mistaken idea that this will effect an automatic weld. Slow drying for the first few hours following attachment is necessary for most clays. This gives the two parts of the join time to adjust their moisture contents, and accommodate the stress they have in relation to one another caused by shrinkage.

Pulled handles are the most popular because they are strong but rolled handles, cut handles and dod-box handles each have an important character. The examples show Michael Casson pulling a jug handle, a cup by Sheila Casson, a 16th-century tyg and a carrying handle on a Persian bottle from the 8th century B.C.

153

Hard (1). Physically hard and difficult to scratch or cut. The hardness of a mineral is classified according to Mohs' scale of hardness which is listed under **Tables**.

Hard (2). Hard, medium and soft are relative terms describing firing temperatures. Hard means at a high temperature, e.g. hard earthenware, hard paste porcelain. The term harder is relative and when used against an example could mean merely 10° or 20° higher in temperature.

In describing glazes, soft means 600°C to 1050°C (1112°F to 1922°F), medium 1050°C to 1200°C (1922°F to 2192°F) and hard 1200°C to 1400°C (2192°F to 2552°F). Hard glazes therefore melt at temperatures above 1200°C (2192°F). They are also physically hard and are not easily abraded. Soft glazes are physically soft and scratch easily.

Hard fluxes are those which work at the higher temperatures but not at the lower ones. Magnesia, for example, does not start its action as a flux until 1160°C (2120°F) and therefore is useful in glazes only above this temperature. Wood ashes are often classified as hard, medium or soft according to the temperatures at which they will act as fluxes. Ashes which contain more silica than flux are classed as hard. Paradoxically hard ashes often come from soft woods.

Cornish stone is also classified as hard or soft but this refers to its physical property. The hard cornish stone is the softer flux.

Hardening on. The fixing of underglaze decoration prior to glazing by a firing in the region of 700°C to 800°C (1292°F to 1472°F). The firing burns out oils and varnishes used as carrying media and fuses the colour slightly by means of soft fluxes so that it adheres to the biscuit surface. See also **Burning out**.

Hare's fur. A variety of tenmoku glaze which has visual qualities resembling a hare's fur. There are two types: one has fine, light-coloured flecks against a dark ground, reminiscent of the hair tips against the fur; the other has the smokey appearance of the soft under-fur.

The hare's fur effect first appeared on Chien bowls during the Sung Dynasty. These glazes were of the smokey grey type in which a lustrous swathe of bluey grey flows down the glaze following the line of gravity. The effect could be due to magnesium sulphate which decomposes after the glaze has melted. The gases disturb the surface and carry with them the magnesium oxide which gives the silky flecks. The bluish colour could be due to manganese oxide in the body or in the clay of the glaze. Occasionally the lustre breaks to a rust colour. The background glaze is a very dark brown. See **Tenmoku**.

Later hare's furs in Northern China had the rust flecks developed into yellow flecks. The flecks are about a quarter of an inch long and run down the glaze in the gravity line. They show the length of movement of the glaze during firing. This is a difficult glaze to reproduce scientifically but the effect sometimes occurs in otherwise black and rust glazes. It could be due to spots of local reduction which encourage the movement to the surface of particles of iron oxide. The effect often appears on slip-glazes made from heterogeneous muds noted for their volatile content. See **Albany slip**.

Harrison pyrometric cones. Cones made by Harrison Mayer of Stoke-on-Trent, England. See **Cones** and **Tables**.

Heat. Energy used by the potter to achieve the necessary chemical and physical changes which convert clay into pot and minerals into glaze. Temperature is a measure of heat but the work to be done in maturing a body and glaze requires more energy than is available at one instant and therefore time must also be considered a factor. Hence the apparently contradictory statement of the kiln burners who fire thick dense wares that 'temperature is not heat'. A potter may talk about achieving 'heat' and 'work done'. The term 'heat-work' is often used, the factors for which are temperature and time.

Heat is the sun's energy which is stored in wood, coal and oil and liberated by fire (oxidation) to be transferred directly or indirectly to the pots in the kiln. The energy can be transferred directly by means of flames composed of excited particles which excite and vibrate the molecules of the pot. Indirectly the energy is transferred possibly first as electricity then as radiant heat from glowing elements or a red-hot sagger wall. The energy is used by the pots in chemical changes and rearrangements of molecules.

Most of these changes are endothermic processes, that is, they absorb more energy than they liberate which is the opposite of the change for example, from wood to wood ash which liberates energy (is exothermic). Thus energy is transferred from fuel to pot effecting a change of state in both.

During the period when a pot is absorbing energy and using it to effect a change of state, the temperature of the pot is theoretically constant. For example, a melting glaze remains at its melting point until all the solid parts become liquid. Then its temperature is able to rise. This is irrespective of the temperature of the surrounding atmosphere in the kiln. The temperature difference between kiln atmosphere and pot serves only to alter the time factor. A greater difference decreases the time required to mature the body or glaze.

The energy absorbed by pots must affect the rate at which the temperature of the kiln can rise. Fluctuations can be discerned on the firing graphs of brick kilns where the ceramic change is endothermic causing a slowing down in the rate of temperature rise. Another cause of fluctuation is the oxidation process which burns out unwanted carbon etc in the body. This is exothermic and if not counteracted would cause an increase in the rate of temperature rise. A similar exothermic process occurs during cooling when glazes crystallize. The temperature of the glaze remains constant or may even increase a little at this point. The release of energy causes what is known as a 'lag' in the cooling curve as drawn on a graph.

The foregoing fluctuations of a firing and cooling curve would be difficult to discern with pottery kilns because the proportion of ware to already-fired kiln furniture and kiln structure is too small. However they are interesting facts necessary to an understanding of the nature of firing.

Hemimorphite. Hydrated zinc silicate. $2ZnO.SiO_2.H_2O$. A variable zinc mineral.

High-temperature glaze. One which matures above 1200°C (2192°F). High-temperature glazes are also called stoneware and porcelain glazes. They make use of the alkaline earth oxides for fluxes and since these can be obtained in insoluble form a glaze can be produced without recourse to fritting. The fluxes are magnesia, calcia, zinc oxide and baria.

Hispano-Moresque ware. Lustred pottery produced during the Moorish occupation of Spain. The occupation lasted from the 8th to the 15th centuries and during this time a great civilization was established, based upon the philosophy of Islam.

One tradition was the making of lustred pottery. According to the teachings of Mohammed the use of precious silver and gold utensils would be a reward in paradise for those who did not seek such things in this life. Lustred pottery was the substitute for the precious metals and was always called gold lustre. The lustre was not gold, however, but a combination of silver and copper. It was painted on to an already-fired tin glaze and fired at a low temperature with reduction. The brush-drawn motifs in lustre were often combined with the maiolica painting in metal oxides giving blue, green and purple. See **Transmutation lustre**.

The Moorish occupation never completely overtook the whole of Spain and there was a fluctuating

uneasiness about the situation. Where the two civilizations of Islamic east and Christian west met there was an interchange of decorative motives. The heraldic symbols of Gothic Europe, including some Christian ornaments, were integrated with the angular patterning and the flowing foliage of Islamic decoration. This evidence of the meeting of two cultures is the true Hispano-Moresque ware.

The potters were both Moors and Spaniards in both the Christian part and the Islamic part of the country and many Moors undoubtedly stayed after Christianity was re-established by the rule of Ferdinand and Isabella in 1492. But without the Islamic influence of the Nasrid court the pottery lost its richness. The lustre became coppery in colour and the decoration became ungainly. This ware can be seen as a separate tradition slowly declining into the 18th century.

Hispano-Moresque ware is important because it brought a new idea into European decoration at the time when it could be incorporated in the Renaissance. See **Maiolica, history**.

Holdcroft's bars. See **Bars**.

Hovel kiln. A term used in Stoke-on-Trent, England, for the type of bottle-neck kiln in which the chimney is an upward extension of the outer wall. The inner oven or beehive chamber is a separate structure. The skeleton bottleneck developed from the hovel kiln by joining the two structures at the base. This restricted the heat loss in the space around the chamber and gave a better draught control thus compensating, to some extent, for the short combustion area.

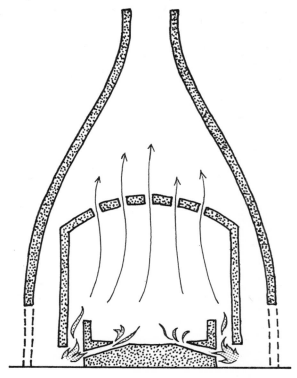

Hua shih. A Chinese plastic kaolin.

Humper. A plate which has distorted, allowing the flat part to rise in unwanted fashion. It is the opposite of a whirler. Humping is accentuated in stoneware and dense earthenware and is usually found on pressed plates and plates which are glazed on the top side only. See also **Whirler**.

Hyalophane. $K_2O . BaO . 2Al_2O_3 . 8SiO_2$. One of the two barium feldspars and halfway between celsian and orthoclase in the group of true feldspars. It is only available as hand-picked specimens but occurs as small percentages of, or traces within, orthoclase. See **Feldspar, types of**.

Hydrate. A compound involving water. Clay is a hydrate because there is water chemically combined in its crystals. This water is called the water of crystallization. Other common hydrates are borax, borocalcite, mica and gypsum. They are called hydrated substances.

The opposites are anhydrous substances which are without water or, more commonly, the term implies that water of crystallization has been removed.

When hydrates are used in a glaze, the water of crystallization is driven off during the first part of the firing. This action starts at 100°C (212°F) and although rapid firings cause exceptions it is usually finished by 500°C (932°F). If the glaze contains a large proportion of one of these substances then there is a large amount of water to escape as steam. If this occurs suddenly, the pressure may lift the glaze free from the pot. Later fusion of the glaze could then result in crawling or in spots of glaze falling from the pot. These are found as small beads of glaze on the kiln shelf and their bald patches are left on the pot. Colemanite, which is nearly 25% water, is especially prone to lifting. It liberates its water at 800°C (1472°F).

The cure for this problem is to fire the kiln slowly over the first 500°C (or more in the case of colemanite) or avoid hydrated substances by introducing fritted ones.

I

Ilmenite. Iron and titanium oxide. Ferrous titanate. $FeTiO_3$ or $FeO.TiO_2$. The ore of titanium and iron. It varies in proportion of iron to titanium. It is difficult to grind and though black in the raw state it gives brown speckles in glazes. It is used in small amounts (up to 1%) to 'seed' crystalline glazes. See **Crystalline glazes**.

The proportion of iron to titanium varies as their atoms occupy, in random fashion, two-thirds of the possible sites within a three-dimensional lattice. Titanium and iron complement one another and present a combined valency of 6 (4 + 2) which allows each to combine with oxygen in six-fold co-ordination.

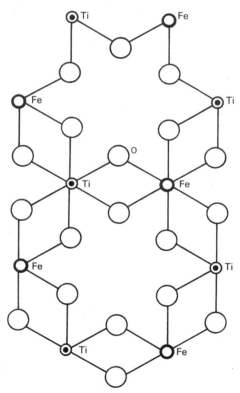

The oxygen is in four-fold co-ordination with titanium and iron in a three-dimensional lattice. One layer only of the lattice is shown in the drawing. There is no TiO_3 unit in the structure and therefore it is more correct to call ilmenite a double oxide rather than a titanate.

Impressed decoration. Decorative motifs stamped directly into the clay by a metal, wooden or biscuit device. The illustration shows a detail of a fine unglazed example of Anglo-Saxon impressed decoration.

Incandescence. The emission of energy as light and heat. The intensity and colour of the light is an indication of the temperature.

As the temperature rises, the first indication of incandescence is called first red and appears at about 600°C (1112°F). With electric kilns there is some illumination of the ware by unshielded glowing elements which at this point are about 250°C (450°F) hotter than the ware. First red in electric kilns therefore appears at about 500°C (932°F). Further temperature rise results in brighter colour passing from red through orange, to yellow and white.

Incandescence	Muffle kilns, etc		Electric kilns	
	°C	°F	°C	°F
blue white	1400	2552		
white	1300	2372	1300	2372
yellow	1250	2282	1200	2192
bright orange	1200	2192	1100	2012
orange	1100	2012	1050	1922
bright red	1050	1922	1000	1832
deep red	900	1652	800	1472
dull red	700	1292	600	1112
first red	600	1112	500	932
black heat	up to		up to	
	550	1022	450	842

Inglaze. I/G. Inglaze colour. Ceramic colours applied on top of an unfired glaze which sink into the glaze and stain it during firing. The colours are pure oxides, prepared stains and strongly coloured glazes.

Inglaze colours are usually applied by brush and the method is described as maiolica painting.

Interaction. Reaction. The influence which two substances have on each other during melting. It is sometimes referred to as breakdown.

It is commonly assumed that there are fluxes and silicas and that the fluxes attack the silicas causing them to melt. This is an over-simplification but is useful in general groupings and differentiation. However it is true to say that the silicas also attack the fluxes and cause them to melt, and that different fluxes attack one another. This is proved by a study of eutectics where it is seen that a small amount of silica helps lead oxide to melt at a lower temperature just as lead oxide helps silica to melt at a lower temperature than it would alone.

Interaction is an embracing term covering all these immeasurable complexities which occur in a body or glaze during firing. It is also used to describe the fluxing action which a glaze and a body have on each other resulting in a body-glaze layer.

Interface. See **Body-glaze layer** and **Buffer layer**.

Intermediate. Has the normal meaning of being between two different things and in pottery is used for glaze temperatures and for chemical properties.

INTERMEDIATE GLAZE. One which matures in the middle temperature range 1000°C to 1200°C (1832°F to 2192°F). This is a wide range. At the lower end the main fluxes are lead oxide and boric oxide. At the upper end the lead oxide can hardly be used because, unless by that temperature it is held in a strong silicate structure, it will volatilize. However, at the upper temperature calcia, zinc oxide and baria can be effectively used.

Intermediate refers therefore to a whole range of glazes of very different structure and there must be no assumption that any one intermediate glaze could be used at all temperatures in the range. As a range it serves to separate those glazes which rely upon the so-called stoneware and porcelain fluxes but have no use for the soft fluxes and those glazes which can only use the soft fluxes.

INTERMEDIATE OXIDE. An oxide of the amphoteric group or one which is so calculated in consideration of a glaze by unity formula. An intermediate oxide is neither acid nor alkali but acts as both and provides a link between these two extremes. Its chemical formula is usually R_2O_3 but some oxides of RO and RO_2 formula exhibit amphoteric properties and may be referred to as intermediate.

INTERMEDIATE ROCK. Igneous rocks are classified according to chemical composition and occurrence. Chemical classification is by the silica content as Acid, Intermediate, Basic and Ultrabasic. Intermediate rocks contain between 55% and 65% silica. Little or none of this silica is present as quartz, i.e. free silica, because it is combined in minerals such as the feldspars and ferromagnesian silicates.

Intermittent kiln. A kiln which is packed with ware, fired and allowed to cool again to withdraw the ware. This is the commonest type of kiln for a small pottery. The other type of kiln is the continuous kiln which requires a continuous flow of standardized production to be efficient and economical.

The disadvantage of the intermittent kiln is seen when one realizes that nearly all the energy put into the kiln as fuel must eventually leave the kiln again as heat before the ware can be withdrawn. In a small studio well over half the energy, whether electricity, oil or gas, will be used to heat the kiln structure. Good insulation in the brickwork, lightweight kiln furniture and a quick firing cycle will help to keep down this waste of heat energy.

The larger the kiln, the more efficient it will be because pot space increases three-dimensionally, whilst the wall increases only two-dimensionally. The same thickness of wall insulation is required for a 1-cubic foot kiln as for a 10-cubic foot kiln if it is insulating the same temperature. Actual figures which take into consideration the thicker structural wall of the larger kiln are 7 cubic feet of wall and door for a 1-cubic foot space and only 30 cubic feet of wall etc for a 10-cubic foot space. The ratio has thus reduced from 1:7 to 1:3 by using a larger kiln.

However, a point is reached, even with the use of down-draughts, under-flues and double chambers, when the fuel used to heat the kiln structure cannot be pushed below 25% of the fuel used. A reasonable estimate can be made for studio gas and electric kilns by weighing the ware from a firing and weighing all the kiln furniture from the same firing. Take the area of walls etc which reached the same temperature as the ware and calculate these as half the weight of standard shelves of the same area. These estimates will be near enough to give an indication of the relative economies of different firings.

The photographs show a 4000-cubic feet round down-draught kiln fired by oil and a Podmore ¾-cubic foot kiln fired by electricity.

Intrusive. A geological term describing igneous rocks which have entered other rocks along a line of weakness. The intrusive rock is liquid or plastic at the time of the intrusion and is probably hot, molten and under great pressure. Quartz veins are intrusions.

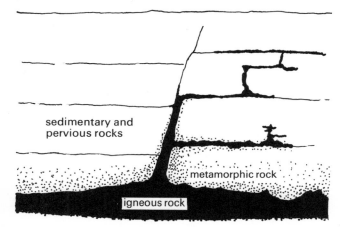

sedimentary and
pervious rocks

metamorphic rock

igneous rock

Inversion. See **Silica inversions**.

Iron Age pottery. Pottery made during the period when people were able to fashion iron articles. The pottery was unglazed. The acceptance of the idea of glazed ware could be considered the end of the period of Iron Age pottery. The term can therefore only be used in relation to Europe and western Asia. In Egypt and the Far East the Bronze Age extended into the period when glazes were used. Around the eastern Mediterranean the period can be considered to extend from 1100 B.C. to A.D. 300 and in western Europe from 500 B.C. to A.D. 600.

Most Iron Age pottery was dense and provided a practical ware for domestic use. Ritual pottery, which had earlier been important, declined as an artistic expression and was superseded by metal artifacts as important objects in burials. This change of attitude released pottery from its ritual role and enabled it to find importance as domestic ware. A faster production of domestic ware was made possible by an increasing

use of the potter's wheel, a fact which characterizes this period.

The Iron Age overlapped and was contemporary with the Roman Empire. The angularity and precision of Roman pottery influenced Iron Age products in many places.

Iron chromate. Ferric chromate. $Fe_2O_3 . Cr_2O_3$ or $FeCrO_3$. A dense compound of iron and chromium oxides obtained from chromic iron ore ($FeCr_2O_4$). It gives opacity and a grey colour in glazes (1–6%) and is also used to give blacks with cobalt and manganese oxides (1–2% of each). It can also be used for underglaze brushwork where the edges can variously bleed with differing colours.

Iron foot. On reduced stonewares, especially celadons, the unglazed foot often reoxidizes during cooling. The iron in the body, with the help of some flashing from the glaze, produces a marked warmth of red brown at this point which is known as iron foot.

Iron ores. The natural mineral in the form of hard rock or soft earth, from which iron can be extracted. Iron very rarely occurs in pure state except in meteorites. Ores are combinations of iron with oxygen, carbon, sulphur and hydrogen. They are of igneous, sedimentary and precipitated origins and like many metal ores have descriptive names. Each has its own character. Some are almost pure iron compounds and therefore are remunerative to win.

Some ore names are: haematite, magnetite, limonite, laterite, marcasite, pyrrhotite, pyrite, siderite, ironstone, kidney ore and bog ore. The more important ores are separately listed in this book. Iron ores are common throughout the world. Some pockets are too small to win commercially whilst others are vast and still untapped. Large deposits occur in Norway, Sweden, Morocco, Brazil, USA and Canada. Small pockets and nodules can often be found which are of the oxide type of ore. These can easily be crushed, especially after weathering, and provide excellent pigments for brushwork and colourants for glazes. See **Iron oxide**.

Iron oxide. $FeO . Fe_2O_3 . Fe_3O_4$. The general name for compounds of iron and oxygen. They are the commonest colourants in individual pottery usually giving yellows, browns, blacks and greys. The different oxides are known by both their English names and their chemical names of Latin origin; e.g. red iron oxide is ferric oxide (Fe_2O_3). Iron oxide is popular because it can give many colour variations. The oxide responds differently to different glaze recipes and kiln atmospheres. Iron oxide is responsible for the brown colour in red-burning clays.

Iron is a metal that is rarely found in a pure natural

159

state. Instead it is combined with oxygen, carbon, sulphur and hydrogen in a variety of ores which constitute the commonest group of ores found throughout the world. The ores are of igneous, sedimentary and precipitated origins, and have various descriptive names like haematite (the blood-like stone) and pyrrhotite (the sceptic's stone). Small pockets of ores can be found in sandstones and limestones, and nodules occur in fireclays. Many ores are soft; they can be crushed by hand, and since these are usually oxide ores they change little in a firing. They can therefore be used without difficulty as colourants for glazes and as pigments for brushwork. A full list is given under **Iron ores**.

Iron and iron oxides occur as important constituents, as impurities and as traces in many substances. There is iron in the human body. Iron stains many minerals including feldspars and clays making them pink and brown. Iron oxide is used as a paint pigment giving yellows and browns in different combinations with other oxides. Some of these combinations are possible in the colouring of glazes.

When iron oxide is present in raw materials it is responsible for a range of colours from yellow through orange and brown to almost black. However, upon heating, the commonest crystal of ferric oxide is formed and this is a red-brown colour. Therefore clays which contain iron become a reddish or pinkish colour after firing to a soft biscuit; even though they may start as yellow ochre, brown or grey clays. When iron oxide enters a fusion it usually becomes brown, sometimes a very dark brown, which is almost black. This is seen in the colour of clays which are fired to densification and in transparent glazes.

IRON OXIDE IN CLAYS. The use of iron oxide in a body or slip is straightforward. The darkest-burning natural clays contain approximately 6% of iron oxide. This gives a rich orange colour after firing to 900°C (1652°F). Higher temperatures to 1100°C (2012°F) give a progressively deeper red turning to brown. Some clays can withstand 1200°C (2192°F) and form a red stoneware. Iron oxide can be added to any clay and will give similar results. To be sure of a uniform colouring it is better to use a red iron oxide and to add this to a clay which is in slip state. The whole should be thoroughly blunged. In slips and bodies to be fired oxidized, with or without a glaze, 5 to 15% of iron oxide will give a range of browns. For reduction, the limit of iron oxide is 10% and this gives a black, unglazed and under suitable glazes.

Speckling of clays can be achieved by the use of coarse iron spangles (magnetic iron oxide). Slips can be speckled with iron filings but these are dangerous in clays because they are sharp. Fireclays contain particles of iron pyrites which are often visible as dark specks in the clay or as light specks in some very dark clays. Finely ground fireclays are added to potting clays to give speckle, amongst other things. Some coarse fireclays contain large pieces (1 to 3 mm diameter) of iron pyrites which form hard cinders at 1000°C (1832°F) and trouble spots above 1200°C (2192°F) when they melt.

Natural clays which contain iron oxide vary in colour from yellow through orange to brown, grey and almost black. The colour is the iron oxide in different forms and combinations. Occasionally manganese oxide is also present giving greys and, when fired, browns. Carbon is present in the blacker clays. Three examples of colour change from clay to oxidized body are given:

1. Some shale clays contain iron as a carbonate which gives a grey colour burning to red.

$$4FeCO_3 + O_2 \xrightarrow[900°C]{450°C \text{ to}} 2Fe_2O_3 + 4CO_2 \uparrow$$
$$\text{ferrous} \qquad\qquad\qquad \text{red iron}$$
$$\text{carbonate} \qquad\qquad\qquad \text{oxide}$$

2. The hydrated form of iron oxide often gives the brightest reds when fired below 1000°C. The iron oxide content is already fully oxidized and therefore gives a pure ferric oxide (Fe_2O_3) when the water of combination is driven off. In some clays the hydrated iron oxide probably exists as a substitution for some of the alumina in the gibbsite layer. Such iron oxide has more protection from local accidental reduction than introduced iron oxide and therefore gives cleaner reds.

$$2Fe_2O_3.3H_2O \xrightarrow{500°C} 2Fe_2O_3 + 3H_2O \uparrow$$
$$\text{hydrated iron} \qquad\qquad \text{red iron}$$
$$\text{oxide} \qquad\qquad\qquad \text{oxide}$$

Hydrated iron oxide gives a yellow colour in clays containing lime. This changes to a bright orange and red with temperatures up to 1050°C. Clays which are high in lime (calcia) content sometimes remain yellow or turn yellow after firing in the 1050°C to 1150°C (1922°F to 2102°F) range. The red iron oxide becomes involved in ferric calcium silicate which is yellow.

$$CaO.Fe_2O_3.SiO_2 + \text{ increasing}$$
$$\text{cream colour} \qquad \text{amounts of}$$
$$SiO_2$$
$$\longrightarrow \text{ yellow colour progressively}$$
$$\text{becoming dirtier and darker}$$
$$\text{to black}$$

The colour occurs at and near the surface of the body where there is the greatest heat and free oxygen. The effect is known as bleached iron. Overfiring causes such clays to deform quickly. Calcia is a strong flux over 1100°C (2012°F) and these clays melt to black glasses at 1250°C (2282°F).

3. Clays which have contained organic matter have often been affected by decomposition. Some of the required oxygen for this decomposition was taken from the iron oxide leaving this in the ferrous state (FeO). These clays look black before firing but burn red.

$$4FeO + O_2 \xrightarrow{900°C} 2Fe_2O_3$$

black iron oxide

red iron oxide

Theoretically it should be possible to achieve the same red colouring whatever the original form of iron oxide. In practice it takes a slow and very deliberate oxidation to achieve full oxidation. The especially difficult case of iron pyrites has already been mentioned but it should also be realized that during the oxidation of the clay between 700°C and 900°C (1292°F and 1652°F) it is difficult to keep the iron oxide fully oxidized. Over 900°C the reduced iron oxide as FeO acts as a flux and is involved in fusion with silicates. Once this occurs it is very difficult to reoxidize it.

The same clays which give reds, oranges and yellows in oxidizing conditions, give greys when fired in reducing atmospheres. These greys can be very decorative, variable and lustrous as used in blue bricks. It is necessary to employ a careful firing which incorporates some oxidation during the early stages. See **Breakdown** and **Black core**. The red iron oxide is easily reduced to black iron oxide around 900°C (1652°F). The exact temperature and cycle are dependent upon the condition of the body. Carbon, which is inside the clay, must first be burnt out so that a black core is not formed. Following this the reduction of the iron oxide can begin before the native fluxes of the clay begin to form silicates with the free silica. Once this fluxing action has started then some of the iron oxide will be involved in the melts. Other iron oxide will be locked in pores which are sealed by molten glass. Both will be difficult to reach with the carbon monoxide. The equation of reduction is:

$$Fe_2O_3 + CO \longrightarrow 2FeO + CO_2 \uparrow$$

red iron oxide | carbon monoxide | black iron oxide | carbon dioxide

Immediately the black iron oxide is formed it will become involved in the melts and there will be little difficulty in keeping it reduced.

IRON OXIDE IN GLAZES. Iron oxide is a fascinating variable; variable, that is, in response to the situation. It can be used to produce a wide range of effects which are the responses to different glaze compositions and firing schedules. Results are broadly predictable but some effects are narrowly balanced so that surprises occur. The surprise element is part of the charm of iron oxide. The properties can be summarized as follows:

1. oxidation gives red iron oxide;
2. reduction gives black iron oxide;
3. neutral atmospheres give a brown iron oxide;
4. the role of iron oxide in the glaze changes with its oxide state;
5. the amount of iron oxide influences the colour;

6. saturated glazes give special effects;
7. over-saturation gives dull glazes;
8. different glazes give different colours from the same oxide;
9. modifiers alter the colour;
10. other colouring oxides can be added.

1. *Oxidation.* The normal state of iron oxide is red iron oxide (Fe_2O_3). In this state the iron has combined with the maximum amount of oxygen and the resulting crystal is red. Pure crystals are scarlet but most red iron oxides contain impurity traces and iron oxides in lesser state of oxidation. They therefore appear red-brown.

Red iron oxide in glazes gives yellows and browns, modified as described later. Average proportions are: up to 4% for yellows; 4% to 6% for tan; 6% to 10% for browns; 10% to 25% for matt dark brown.

2. *Reduction.* Iron oxide is easy to reduce. It responds immediately to carbon monoxide and is willing to release oxygen and become black iron oxide (FeO). The equation is:

$$Fe_2O_3 + CO \longrightarrow 2FeO + CO_2$$

red iron oxide | carbon monoxide | black iron oxide | carbon dioxide

Proportions of black iron oxide and resultant colours are: 1% to 3% for pale to dark grey-green (celadon); 8% for black; 8% to 12% for tenmoku, tessha and kaki.

Once the iron oxide, red and black, is locked in a molten glaze, its oxygen atoms also become involved with other elements, e.g. silicon, aluminium, potassium. These are not as willing to release the oxygen atoms and reshuffle their structures. Oxidation or reduction of iron oxide is therefore more effectively undertaken during the period before and during which the glaze melts. Once a glaze has melted, the reduction or oxidizing atmosphere is only able to affect oxides at the surface of the glaze. To reduce iron oxide in a molten glaze requires a very heavy reduction which also disrupts the chain of gas liberation producing a very bubbled glaze which might not smooth over. The best way is a light reduction throughout the firing with oxidation at the end of firing and during cooling.

The following recipe is for a lightly reduced celadon for 1250°C (2282°F):

potash feldspar	48
china clay	14
flint	18
whiting	18
black iron oxide	2

3. *Neutral brown iron oxide.* Halfway between red and black iron oxide occurs a mixture which has the formula Fe_3O_4. This is simply a mixture and gives a mixed colour of dark brown. This is not a particularly desirable colour and in no way rivals the fully oxidized tans

and browns or the reduced greens and blacks. The mixed oxide occurs in neutral atmospheres and also when oxidation or reduction begins too late to convert all the iron oxide present. Iron oxide in combination with other oxides in fusions is resistant to change.

4. *The two roles of iron oxide.* Black iron oxide is always a flux. Red iron oxide is sometimes a flux but mostly an anti-flux. As iron oxide changes its state of oxidation it also changes its role and since this may happen incidentally as well as deliberately, the results are sometimes unpredictable.

Black iron oxide becomes a glaze flux at temperatures over 900°C (1652°F). Its inclusion in a glaze recipe should therefore be as substitute for another flux. Empirically in lead glazes it can be substituted weight by weight for lead oxide. Or more easily it can be added to existing glazes along with its own weight of silica (quartz or flint). In leadless or low-lead glazes for 1100°C to 1200°C (2012°F to 2192°F) it can be substituted for calcium carbonate, weight by weight, or added with its own weight of silica. Above 1200°C the balance becomes unpredictable. Weight for weight with whiting plus about half its weight in silica is necessary. Alternatively iron oxide can be added along with double its weight in silica. The amounts given are necessarily empirical and in no way intended to be definitive.

In soft glazes it is better to use black iron oxide in the recipe but with hard glazes which begin fusion over 1000°C (1832°F) it is possible to use black or red and reduce to black between 900°C and 1100°C (1652°F and 2012°F).

Red iron oxide should act as an anti-flux in glazes which are kept fully oxidized. The difficulty lies in keeping a glaze fully oxidized. Using a hard biscuit cuts out reduction from the body but the glaze itself contains minerals which decompose and liberate gases. Some of these gases can cause reduction in passing the red iron oxide. The notable example is partial sulphur dioxide liberated between 1100°C and 1200°C (2012°F and 2192°F). Immediately the iron oxide becomes black it will act as a flux and enter fusion. Kiln gases, even in electric kilns, can never be considered exclusively oxidizing.

Different bodies, different kilns and variations of firing cycle, inclusion of various other glazes in the kiln, and even differences of weather and atmospheric pressure will affect the role of the iron oxide. A glaze which is a soft matt tan colour in one firing can become a shiny muddy brown colour in another.

5. *Iron oxide amounts.* Iron oxide is a uniform stain in small amounts and a mottling stain in large amounts when some is undissolved. One per cent will give a slight stain. Approximately 12% is a usual maximum but as much as 25% can be used. Glazes which contain such a high proportion of iron oxide are dark matt glazes in which the surface is dulled by iron oxide crystals.

There is a percentage of iron oxide at which further increases do not serve to stain the glaze by solution but remain as undissolved crystals. These give a mottled effect.

The following table gives the range of iron oxide content for different glazes and suggests the popular percentage which can be taken as a suitable starting point.

	Reduction	
celadon	1% to 6%	(2%)
black tenmoku	4% to 15%	(8%)
kaki	10% to 20%	(12%)

	Oxidation	
amber (lead)	1% to 6%	(4%)
tan (lead)	4% to 10%	(8%)
brown tenmoku	6% to 25%	(12%)
yellow (lime matt)	1% to 4%	(2%)
tan (lime matt)	4% to 8%	(7%)

6. *Saturation with iron oxide.* During firing, iron oxide is dissolved in the glaze. During cooling, some of this iron oxide is precipitated.

The molten glass can absorb more iron oxide in active state, that is, involved in fusion, than can be eventually incorporated in combined state in the cooled glaze. The difference between these two amounts is isolated during cooling and forms its own crystals. This precipitation starts at the surface, which is the first part to cool, and spreads into the glaze partially to embrace other iron oxide as it is isolated.

It is this saturation amount that is responsible for some very beautiful colourings from iron. The best known is the stoneware kaki (rust), which is indexed separately. Also at lower temperatures a metallic rust surface is possible with boric oxide and is used in on-glaze colours. With lead glazes, the iron oxide gives a bright brick red and variations towards maroon.

It is impossible to predict exactly what the two amounts of oxide will be: the amount that will be absorbed when hot and the amount when cold. Each glaze is different and the factors affecting the two saturation amounts are:

(a) the alkali:acid ratio of the glaze;

(b) the iron oxide state; and

(c) the top temperature linked with the type of body.

The diagram shows these three factors in comparable form. Saturation point has been divided into a point for the hot molten glaze (right) and a point for the glaze when set on cooling (left). There is also a point for the metallic surface described in the next section (7) on over-saturation. The diagram rationalizes many different glazes to give five examples and does not try to show limits.

In oxidizing conditions, the red iron oxide is combining with the alkali and therefore if the glaze is high in alkali it will be capable of absorbing a larger amount of iron oxide than a glaze with less alkali. It follows from this that low-temperature glazes, which naturally have a large amount of flux (alkali), are capable of absorbing more iron oxide than high-temperature glazes. The diagram shows this.

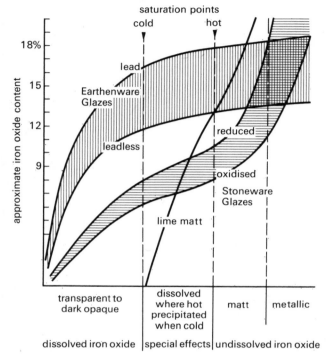

It also shows an interesting comparison between the earthenware glazes and the stoneware lime matt glaze which is also high alkaline. In the latter, amounts of iron oxide up to 8% or 12% give precipitated effects of buffs and oranges whilst more only matts the surface and makes the glaze dark. In some earthenware glazes it is possible to dissolve completely as much as 17% of iron oxide. A slight amount more is dissolved when hot and precipitated on cooling. Too much matts the glaze in an undesirable way. This shows the difficulty of achieving these special effects with earthenware glazes. The aventurine effect is a particular type of precipitated iron oxide which occurs within a very soft lead glaze. Some of these glazes contain as much as 30% red iron oxide.

Reduced and oxidized iron oxides are compared as stoneware glazes of the transparent type. The oxidized iron oxide (Fe_2O_3) is an amphoteric oxide. This means that it can behave as an acid or an alkali. In glazes which are high in alkali it will act as an acid and go into solution with unattached alkaline oxides. In highly-acidic glazes the red iron oxide will act partly as an alkali and form combinations of iron oxide with silica also. Contrasting with this is the reduced iron oxide (FeO). This is always alkaline in character and therefore al-

ways combines with the acid part of the glaze. A general rule is that more iron oxide can be dissolved in a reduced glaze than an oxidized one.

The effect the top temperature has on the amount of iron oxide dissolved is diagrammatized as a difference in percentages at the left-hand side. The two amounts represent the difference between an underfired and an overfired glaze, and show that a higher temperature involves more iron oxide in solution. However, on cooling the amount still held in solution does not vary much. It follows that overfired glazes are more likely to give special effects but here one should also understand what overfiring means. It is overfiring in relation to the body. The body breakdown due to interaction is a necessary part of the process. Most potters are familiar with overfired stonewares which have interesting special effects on bloated bodies. The use of special bodies which help the glaze to overfire without completely disrupting themselves is relevant. White bodies help the development of rust colours by reflection and concentration of heat in the glaze and buffer layers are often used to assist these special effects.

The following recipe is for a rust glaze on white stoneware at 1280°C (2336°F) oxidized:

feldspar	40
china clay	20
flint	10
whiting	15
red iron oxide	15

The following recipe is for a lime matt orange-brown for 1250°C (2282°F) oxidized:

cornish stone	46
china clay	14
tin oxide	5
whiting	28
red iron oxide	7

7. *Over-saturation with iron oxide.* The undissolved iron oxide gives opacity and a matt surface. This iron oxide does not enter the fusion but remains as unattached crystals throughout the firing. It moves through the molten glaze towards the surface where it forms a crystalline skin or matt surface. This surface is dull compared with the precipitated crystals which are cleaner in colour and presumably purer. Its normal colour is a dark and rather dull brown though in lime matt glazes a smokey green-black is possible.

There is a point in over-saturation when the iron oxide gives a metallic surface. Further additions of iron oxide produce a scum and rough surface. The metallic surface is easiest to obtain in reduced stoneware where some lustrous effects are possible. In oxidized stoneware and earthenware there are too many variables to achieve the effect except in small patches.

8. *The effect of the other constituents.* The other glaze oxides might be colourless in the glaze but they present

different properties and hence different colours in combination with the iron oxide. The extreme variations are rare but tendencies are discernible.

In oxidized glazes the red iron oxide turns bluish in combination with soda. Small amounts with boric oxide are also blue. Calcia combinations are yellow. Earthenware glazes high in lead oxide, potash and soda encourage the reddish colour in iron-saturated glazes.

In reduced glazes a saturation of black iron oxide is likely to give black with modifications towards brown if the alumina content is high. Low alumina content, almost amounting to absence, encourages a blue colour in part saturation. The presence of phosphorus pentoxide as a glass-former also encourages the blue.

The other fluxes which are assisting the black iron oxide also modify the colour. Lithia and soda encourage a blue colour. Calcia, baria and potash encourage a green and are useful in celadons to counteract the duller colours given by traces of other modifiers.

9. *Other modifiers.* There are a number of oxides which are colourless and are used to give opacity, or in traces to modify colours. They are zinc oxide, tin oxide, zirconia and titania.

Zinc oxide modifies iron oxide to a series of unpleasant greenish mud colours. Zirconia is a little better. Tin oxide gives some pleasant coffee browns but the best range of yellows and oranges is to be had with titania.

10. *Other colouring oxides.* All colours give what could be described as a visual mix of colour: cobalt oxide adds blue; copper oxide adds green; manganese oxide adds the purplish brown and gives interesting speckles in equal amount with iron oxide.

It is more usual to use iron oxide as a modifier to tone down colours which are too strong like cobalt and copper or to intensify colours like the nickel and chromium orange.

TYPES OF IRON OXIDE. There are three different compounds of iron and oxygen used by the potter. They are red iron oxide, black iron oxide and magnetic iron oxide. They are derived from ores, are precipitated from other iron compounds (before or during calcination or firing) or are altered from other compounds by oxidation and reduction.

Red iron oxide gives yellows, oranges, reds and browns. Black iron oxide gives blacks and greens. Magnetic iron oxide gives black speckles edged with colours derived from the other two oxides. It can exist as separate particles of iron oxide under conditions where the red and black iron oxides would dissolve.

The oxides are described below and their uses are given under **Iron oxide in clays** and **Iron oxide in glazes.**

BLACK IRON OXIDE. Ferrous oxide. Iron monoxide. FeO. The simplest compound of iron and oxygen. It is stable at room temperatures but becomes excited at red heat. This excitement is a loosening of the molecular bonds thereby allowing the black iron oxide to combine with silicates. It will therefore act as an alkaline flux in bodies and glazes. In glazes 1% will give a pale green; 3% a green-grey (celadon); and 8% a black.

The loosening of the bonds also allows the lattice structure to incorporate more oxygen so that the oxide reaches a higher state of oxidation:

$$4FeO + O_2 \longrightarrow 2Fe_2O_3$$
black iron oxide   oxygen   red iron oxide

The process is accelerated by applied heat and although time is a factor, the process of oxidation is inevitable if oxygen is present.

The oxide must therefore be deprived of oxygen if one wishes to keep the black colour of oxide for clays and glazes. Deprivation is achieved by introducing carbon monoxide to give a reducing atmosphere. Iron oxides in any state below full oxidation (Fe_2O_3) are greedy for oxygen but carbon monoxide is even more so! Black iron oxide can be obtained from red by the use of carbon monoxide.

$$Fe_2O_3 + CO \longrightarrow 2FeO + CO_2 \uparrow$$
red iron oxide   carbon monoxide   black iron oxide   carbon dioxide

Further reduction to pure metal requires very heavy reduction and is unlikely to happen in a kiln.

The above equations show complete changes. In practice partial changes occur because time is a factor in the change. Also there may be insufficient oxygen or carbon monoxide to effect a total conversion before the result is sealed by a molten glaze or a temperature fall. The result is the half-way oxide Fe_3O_4 which is dark brown in colour.

$$6FeO + O_2 \longrightarrow 2Fe_3O_4$$
$$6Fe_2O_3 + 2CO \longrightarrow 4Fe_3O_4 + 2CO_2 \uparrow$$

This dark brown iron oxide (Fe_3O_4) is only a theoretical convenience. It is not the same as magnetic iron oxide (Fe_3O_4) because it has not the same crystal structure. It is simply a mixture of the two oxides black and red.

$$FeO + Fe_2O_3 = Fe_3O_4$$

MAGNETIC IRON OXIDE. Ferroso-ferric oxide. Ferrosic oxide. Proto-sesquioxide of iron. Iron scale. Iron spangles. Fe_3O_4. This is a separate crystalline form of iron oxide which is different from the preceding two although at first sight its chemical formula is a simple addition of one molecule of each. The crystal is black and metallic, hard, dense, and resistant to chemical breakdown. The structure is an inverse spinel.

Its action in bodies and glazes is zero until some dissassociation has taken place. This occurs above 1100°C (2012°F) in contact with ceramic fusions.

$$Fe_3O_4 + \text{ceramic fusions}$$
$$\xrightarrow{1100°C} FeO + Fe_2O_3 + \text{ceramic fusions}$$

The action is slow and as it takes place the liberated ferrous and ferric oxides dissolve into the surrounding melt producing bleeding.

The advantage of magnetic iron oxide is its capacity to remain as speckles in a body or glaze. Being hard, it is never in as fine a powder form as red iron oxide and therefore cannot spread itself uniformly. When purchasing magnetic iron oxide it is better to buy the coarse spangles which look like iron filings with a bluish lustre. Here the individual grains are visible. The fine powder which looks like a greyish graphite gives too fine a speckle to be effective except as a pointillist colouring.

It is possible to convert magnetic iron oxide into one of the other forms by oxidation or reduction. The conversion requires at least orange heat, time and a distinctly oxidizing or reducing atmosphere:

$$4Fe_3O_4 + O_2 \xrightarrow{\text{oxidation}} 6Fe_2O_3$$

$$Fe_3O_4 + CO \xrightarrow{\text{reduction}} 3FeO + CO_2 \uparrow$$

The conversions are possible in ceramics at temperatures over 1100°C (2012°F) before glass melts have taken place and the process may be advantageous in producing ferric or ferrous speckling. There is no other advantage in its use as a substitute for red or black iron oxide.

Magnetic iron oxide is found as the ore magnetite and is produced when hot iron is beaten as in wrought iron (iron scales). It should not be confused with the partial reduction of ferric oxide (or the partial oxidation of ferrous oxide) which is given the same theoretical formula: Fe_3O_4.

RED IRON OXIDE. Ferric oxide. Iron sesquioxide. Fe_2O_3. The pure form is a bright red colour. It is crystalline but the crystals are easily broken. Red iron oxide is therefore a fine powder whether ground from ore or precipitated from one of the salts, e.g. ferrous sulphate. This finely divided state enables it to spread uniformly through a slip or glaze as colouring. In glazes 2% gives a yellow and 8% a brown. The fine powder is used as a polishing abrasive by jewellers and is known as rouge. Its fineness also enables it to spread easily in the pottery with the result that it is picked up by fingers and transferred annoyingly to pots and book pages!

Red iron oxide is the stable form of iron oxide and is arrived at in various ways all of which would be called oxidation by the potter. Oxidation is equivalent to burning and some heat is generated although the amount is not likely to have a noticeable effect.

The equations are:

$$FeSO_4 \cdot 7H_2O \xrightarrow{400°C} FeSO_4 + 7H_2O$$
ferrous   crocus   water
sulphate   martis

$$2FeSO_4 \xrightarrow{1200°C} Fe_2O_3 + SO_3 \uparrow + SO_2 \uparrow$$
crocus   red iron   sulphur   sulphur
martis   oxide   trioxide dioxide

$$Fe_2(SO_4)_3 \xrightarrow{1200°C} Fe_2O_3 + 3SO_3 \uparrow$$
ferric   red iron   sulphur
sulphate   oxide   trioxide

$$2Fe(OH)_3 \xrightarrow{500°C} Fe_2O_3 + 3H_2O \uparrow$$
ferric   red iron   water
hydroxide   oxide

Iron pyrites. An ore of iron and sulphur found as an impurity in some clays. See **Pyrite**.

Iron spangles. Iron scale. Blacksmith's scale. Magnetic iron oxide. Fe_3O_4. See **Iron oxide, types**.

Iron spot. Rust spot. Small areas of iron oxide crystallization which occur on the surface of reduced glazes. The reduction draws ferrous oxide from the small nodules of limonite and pyrite in the clay, through the glaze to the surface.

Under reduction the concentration of iron oxide is finely divided producing a smooth surface although its concentration inhibits its complete solution in the glaze. At the surface a small portion of the iron oxide takes up oxygen in a crystallization which gives a sparkle.

The pot by Michael Casson shows iron spots in a stoneware glaze.

J

Jack. Case. Model from which working moulds are made.

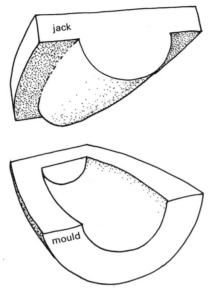

Jar mill. Pot mill. Ball mill. A grinding mill for glazes and colours. The glaze materials are sealed in a porcelain jar with water, grinding media and space. The media is pebbles or specially prepared ceramics, often called balls but not necessarily spherical. Jars are of sizes up to 2 gallons. The jar rotates by resting on driven spindles. The speed of rotation is such that the media falls onto the material continuously, the water providing dispersion of the particles.

The photograph is of the jar mill manufactured by Gosling and Gatensbury Ltd and marketed by Harrison Mayer Ltd. See also **Ball mill**.

Jiggering. Forming a pot by using a spinning mould, usually of plaster, which gives the inside form. Jig-

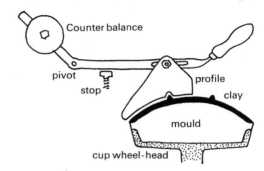

gering is used for plates. The outside of the plate is formed by a metal profile which is fastened to a pivoted arm. This arm is brought down onto the mould and is so adjusted that it leaves the correct clay section.

Joggle. Natch. The hollow and corresponding protrusion used in and on adjacent parts of a plaster mould to ensure correct alignment. The joggle is either cast in the plaster by cutting the hollow in one piece when casting a second up to it or bought as a two-piece plastic attachment which is set into the mould.

Jolleying. Forming a pot by using a spinning mould, usually of plaster, which shapes the outside of the pot. First the fingers and then a metal profile are used to shape the inside of the pot. The metal profile is on a pivoted arm which brings it into action against the clay but is adjusted so that the correct section of clay is given. Jolleying is used for cups and deep bowls.

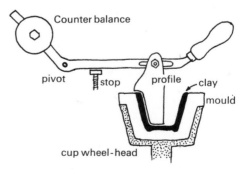

Jug. A container for storing and pouring liquid. Until the 17th century, jugs and mugs were synonymous terms. Both were used for storing, pouring and drinking. The refinement of manners and the development of the pouring spout created the division into two specialized containers. The examples illustrated are by: Ray Finch, Leach Pottery, Janet Hamer, Bernard Leach, David Leach, 16th-century Isnik.

Jutland ware. Peat-fired unglazed pottery which originated in Neolithic times, was perfected early and continued to be made until the mid-20th century. The pots were burnished with a flint pebble and, after firing, soaked in buttermilk to make them non-porous. The pots shown are by Ellen Marie.

K

Kaki. The Japanese for persimmon fruit and following this, the name for the rust colour which results when iron oxide crystals spread as a layer on the surface of stoneware glazes. Further detail is given under **Rust**.

Kalia. Kalium oxide. K_2O. Potassium oxide, more commonly called potash and referred to thus throughout this book. See **Potash**.

Kalium soda. Natrium potash. NaKO. The theoretical combination of potash and soda. $K_2O + Na_2O \longrightarrow 2NaKO$. Its use is in calculations involving feldspathoids where separation of potash and soda is undesirable or impossible.

Kaolin. China clay. $Al_2O_3 . 2SiO_2 . 2H_2O$. The purest clay, approximating closely the idealized clay mineral kaolinite. It contains very little iron impurity and is therefore white. It is a primary clay or a secondary clay moved only a short distance. It has therefore little plasticity but it is popular as a body constituent because of its whiteness. It is high in alumina content and with few alkaline impurities. It is therefore refractory with an assessed melting point over 1770°C (3218°F). It is used in glazes to introduce alumina and silica and to provide bulk in the slop suspension. It is also used as a paper filler and in cosmetics. See **China clay**. The ultimate analysis of a typical specimen is:

SiO_2	46·6
Al_2O_3	38·3
TiO_2	0·1
Fe_2O_3	0·4
CaO	0·3
MgO	0·3
Na_2O	0·3
K_2O	0·7
Loss	13·0

The name 'kaolin' is said to be Chinese for 'High Ridge', which was the district from which the early supplies were obtained. Kaolins are world-wide in distribution but few seem to have a plasticity to equal Chinese kaolins. British kaolins from Cornwall are called china clays; the name kaolin being frowned upon by potters as one used by the uninitiated. In the United States, the word kaolin is correct.

Zettlitz kaolin is the Czechoslovakian kaolin used by Dr Hermann Seger in his study of refractoriness. Kaolins are also mined in France and in the USA in Georgia, Florida and Carolina. The origins of these deposits are various but their ultimate analyses are very similar to that already given.

Kaolinite. $Al_2O_3 . 2SiO_2 . 2H_2O$. The idealized clay mineral. Kaolinite is the correct term for the particular crystal structure which is best represented in the material, china clay. However, all clays with the exception of bentonite, contain kaolinite as their clay constituent. They also, of course, contain many other minerals, e.g. quartz, feldspar and iron oxide.

The term 'kaolinite' is reserved for the description of the pure mineral. The less specific term 'kaolin' is used to describe the material clay. Less pure clays are called simply clays, marls and shales.

The potter uses the formula $Al_2O_3 . 2SiO_2 . 2H_2O$ for kaolinite but this should correctly be written $Al_2Si_2O_5(OH)_4$. This second way is a better description of the structure of the crystal which involves hydroxyl bonds (OH) lacing together an aluminium : silicon : oxygen structure.

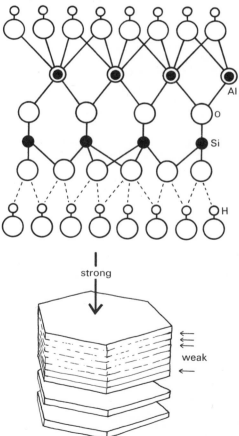

168

The kaolinite crystal has two layers. These are the gibbsite layer of alumina with hydroxyl groups; and the silica layer. These two layers share oxygen atoms and are therefore firmly bonded together. However, the combined gibbsite-silica layer is loosely attached to the next gibbsite-silica layer by alternating hydroxyl bonds. The diagram shows a side-view section through the layers. A sheet structure is developed which is strong in two directions but weak in the third. Kaolinite crystals are therefore flat. They are also hexagonal seen from above. See **Clay, physics of,** and also **Disordered kaolinite**.

Kaolinization. The process of decomposition whereby igneous and metamorphic rocks are changed. The important new mineral which emerges is kaolinite, the pure clay crystal. The term is sometimes broadly used to include any weathering, leaching or chemical change in rocks if it includes the creation of laminar silicates like kaolinite, mica and montmorillonite.

Kelp. The ash from burnt seaweed, especially wracks. It is rich in soda and was used during the 18th and 19th centuries as the flux in glass-making. This source was rendered obsolete by the LeBlanc and Solvay processes of the late 18th and mid-19th centuries which enabled sodium compounds to be manufactured from brine. See **Sodium carbonate**.

Kelvin. °K. Degrees Kelvin are Centigrade measurements of temperature. The Kelvin scale was introduced in 1848 by William Thomson, later Lord Kelvin, professor at Glasgow University. It is an extension of the Celsius thermometer scale which has 100 degrees between the freezing and boiling points of water. However, the Kelvin scale starts at 'absolute zero' and therefore 0°K equals -273°C and the boiling point of water (100°C) is 373°K. Degrees Kelvin are also called degrees Absolute (°Abs). The temperatures throughout this book are referred to as degrees Centigrade with their Fahrenheit equivalents in brackets.

Keuper marl. A superior mudstone of the Triassic Period. It originated as a desert dust. See **Loess clay**. It is not consolidated and so can be reconstituted as a clay for potting. It has a high clay content, a high lime content and a high iron content. It is brown and grey when raw and brown-burning. Low-grade Keuper marls are called foulstones.

Kidney. Press-moulder's kidney. Rubber kidney. A flat kidney-shaped piece of rubber for pressing slabs of clay into or onto moulds. The rubber is about $\frac{1}{4}$-inch thick tapering to a thin edge. There are various shapes and degrees of hardness. As a general rule the larger the work being pressed the harder should be the kidney. Long, very soft kidneys are excellent for small dishes.

Kidney ore. A type of haematite iron ore which looks like a collection of lustrous black bubbles. Although black on the surface it crushes to a brown powder (Fe_2O_3).

Kiln. A structure built to conserve heat. The potter uses the kiln to fire pottery but kilns are used for other purposes. The word kiln is derived from the latin *culina*, a kitchen, as in culinary. Thus, it has to do with cooking. It is pronounced with or without the n and is sometimes mis-spelt 'kill'.

The potter's kiln developed from the open trench system of firing by the addition of a dome of sherds to baffle back the heat. Today's structures are more sophisticated but the principle remains the same. Heat is introduced into the chamber where the pots have been placed. Some heat escapes by radiation and moving air but more heat is introduced than can escape. The temperature in the chamber is thereby raised. Many methods are used to insulate the chamber, e.g. double skin walls, foam refractories and filament fibres as used in space research.

Different kiln types are described briefly under their names.

Kiln cycle. The time and actions surrounding and including the firing of ware. Since all pottery must be fired at least once, the kiln size and efficiency is the ultimate controlling factor in a workshop's output. The amount of clay required at the beginning of the processes has an upper theoretical limit. This limit is easily calculated by assessing the weight of ware per firing multiplied by the number of firings to be done and divided by the number of firings each piece of work undergoes. This is an upper limit irrespective of the number of potters, assistants or students a workshop or school may have.

The kiln cycle is the rhythm of the workshop. At Winchcombe, England, Ray Finch uses the following cycle which illustrates this rhythm. There is a weekly glaze firing and a fortnightly biscuit firing. The kiln is drawn on Monday and the ware sorted etc. The biscuit is dusted and prepared for glazing. The glazes are mixed and glazing takes place on Monday afternoon and Tuesday morning. On Tuesday afternoon and Wednesday morning the kiln is packed and the firing done on the Thursday. The pots are made on Wednesday, Thursday and Friday, and dry out in the kiln shed over the week-end. The wicket is opened on Sunday ready for the drawing on Monday.

Kiss. When two pots touch in the kiln and stick together with their glazes they are said to kiss. The scars left on the pots are called kiss marks. Kissing is usually accepted as the result of sagging shelves or pots rather than careless setting.

Kneading. An action of clay preparation involving the rolling of plastic clay upon itself with stretching and spreading. By kneading, a lump of clay is thoroughly

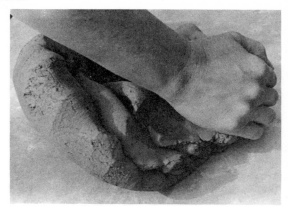

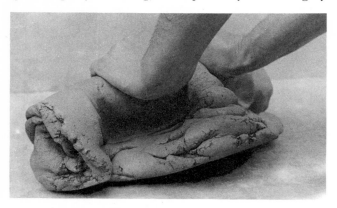

mixed and air bubbles expelled. In this homogeneous condition it is ready for a plastic-forming process which immediately follows. In this way, kneading is a specific preparation and possibly involves a carefully weighed amount of clay. A more general preparation is wedging which often precedes kneading.

Kneading is done on the wedging bench. The desired amount of clay is taken with hands close together and a part of it is pressed against the rest. The action is repeated with a slight progression. Two styles are known. They are ram's head or bull's head kneading which is the European method and the spiral or shell kneading which is Oriental. The reasons for the names should be obvious by reference to the illustrations.

Kochi. Japanese raku ware using a hard-fired biscuit. The hard biscuit has the effect of overcoming some of the disadvantages of soft biscuit such as general softness of finished ware and crazing of glazes. These advantages are at the expense of the control which a soft biscuit gives of the more subtle colourings.

L

Labradorite. One of the plagioclase feldspars. It is mostly lime feldspar but contains up to 49% soda feldspar.

Lag. Temperature lag. The slowing down in the rate of cooling of a glaze caused by crystal growth. During the cooling of a glaze, there are temperatures at which different crystalline solids are precipitated from the molten glass. Crystals appear as new compounds are formed and the creation of new compounds releases new energy in the form of heat. At this point, the temperature of the glaze is maintained or may even increase although the temperature of the surrounding kiln atmosphere continues to fall.

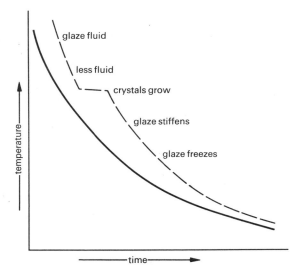

In the graph, the rate of kiln cooling is shown by the continuous line. The dotted line shows the rate for the glaze. The lag shows as a maintained temperature for the glaze. It is obviously too small to be noticeable as an influence upon the temperature curve for the whole kiln, but it is important to realize that by artificially holding this temperature in the kiln then more and larger crystals will grow. See also **Crystalline glazes** and **Devitrification**.

Lambeth. The area of London famous for delftware and salt-glazed ware. It is suggested that the delft was started by Italian potters in 1630, having previously worked in Antwerp. Production lasted for about 130 years until creamware became more popular. The salt-glazed ware was made from the late 17th century into the 20th century.

The first photograph shows a delftware charger made *c.* 1680. The tulip-type motifs set as a spray are typical of the ware and the blue dashes around the rim gave this type of serving plate the name of blue dash charger.

The second photograph shows one example of 19th-century Doulton Lambeth ware. This ware is in the tradition of beer mugs and jugs with sprigged country scenes which were made in Lambeth for 200 years. The pieces were thrown and some were turned. The handles were either dod-box type or modelled greyhounds. Before firing, the pieces were traditionally dipped into Thames mud which gave the characteristic dark brown upper half. See also **Dod-box** and **Sprigging**.

Laterite. Brickstone. A general name given to iron-manganese-aluminium ores in hydrated form. If used without qualification the term laterite is understood to refer to the hydrated iron oxide form with the variable formula: $Fe_2O_3 \cdot 1$ to $3H_2O$. It was formed from an iron substitution into an alumino-silicate followed by the slow leaching of the silica. It could therefore contain up to 50% alumina with a formula of $Fe_2O_3 \cdot Al_2O_3 \cdot 3H_2O$. More than 50% alumina results in the laterite being classified by the more specific term of bauxite. Laterite is found in small deposits around the tropical zone and in parts of western Europe and has been used as a glaze colourant. See **Iron oxide**.

Lattice structure. Lattice. Regular network. The three-dimensional pattern of fixed points on which atoms or molecules are positioned in a crystal. The word lattice signifies that the structure is regular as a repeating pattern and therefore the substance has crystalline character. The word random is used to signify an irregular structure.

Lattices are often drawn as complex scaffoldings with atoms at the intersections. Diagrams showing these openwork structures are deliberately enlarged to make the structure of the lattice more easily understood. It is assumed that in reality the atoms are touching, even conjoined, so that the open structure is only a diagrammatic convenience.

The drawings show three ways of visually explaining the lattice of the gibbsite molecule (here shown as $Al_2O_2(OH)_4$) which is part of the clay crystal. Fig. 1 shows the molecule as it is theoretically imagined but it is impossible to read the structure. Fig. 2 is a slightly expanded version often used for three-dimensional effects and fig. 3 shows the flattened arrangement which enables some, but not all, crystal structures to be diagrammatized two-dimensionally. See also **Network structure**.

Single molecules are often described by what is known as a structural formula. This uses the chemical symbols for the atoms and lines representing valency bonds between them. Fig. 4 shows sodium chloride (NaCl), soda (Na_2O), calcia (CaO), silica (SiO_2), alumina (Al_2O_3), barium sulphate ($BaSO_4$) and ferroso-ferric oxide (Fe_3O_4) which involves one divalent iron atom and two trivalent iron atoms.

Lawn. A fine mesh of wire, natural or man-made fibre. It is used for separating the fine particles of material from coarse particles, the coarse being retained by the lawn. It is usual to lawn materials in a wet state. Unless materials are soluble, it is easier to lawn them in suspension and also this method creates no dust. In practice the word lawn is synonymously used for sieve which is a lawn fastened to a frame or rim.

Lawn prover. A powerful magnifying lens mounted at its focal point over a metal foot. The foot has a hole in it of known measurement so that the number of threads of a lawn can be counted and inspected. Lawn provers are usually foldable and are useful for inspecting glazes and bodies.

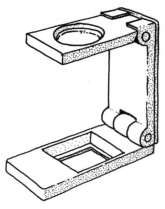

Leach, Bernard (b. 1887) lived in Japan and first studied pottery in traditional workshops there before starting St. Ives Pottery, Cornwall, England, in 1920. His work is the vital link between East and West which gave impetus to the European potters of the early 20th century. He is responsible for bringing to Europe a genuine understanding of the Oriental expression.

European pottery has been influenced by Oriental pottery in a series of impulses since the 17th century. Prior to the arrival of Bernard Leach, the influence had

only inspired technical refinements and superficial copying of decorative motifs. Leach was able to subordinate technique to creative inspirational potting which introduced a better understanding of the Oriental idiom to Europe.

Lead antimonate. See **Antimonate of lead.**

Lead bisilicate. Double silicate of lead. $PbO . 2SiO_2$. A prepared compound in which theoretically one molecule of lead oxide combines with two molecules of silica. The theoretical proportional weights are lead oxide 65%, silica 35%.

Lead bisilicate is the popular lead frit. It is the most versatile of the standard frits and the most practical to manufacture. It can be introduced into almost any glaze in the range 900°C to 1250°C (1652°F to 2282°F) where it will assist with fusion by lengthening the fusion range and smoothing out the glaze surface. Fusion starts at approximately 700°C (650°C with the eutectic mixture) and is complete by 900°C (1292°F to 1652°F). This long range of maturation is important and gives the bisilicate its versatility. For the use of this and other lead frits in glazes, see **Lead frit**.

In the simplest lead bisilicate, the solubility of the lead content could be as high as 8%. However the use of a slight reduction of the silica to 1·9 equivalents produces a eutectic into which 0·1 equivalents of alumina can easily be introduced as a stabilizer. This has the effect of reducing the soluble lead content to below 0·02%. This is the method generally adopted in the manufacture of commercial lead bisilicate. See **Low sol frits** and **Frit manufacture**.

It will be found that various solubility figures are available because different tests have been used. Most tests now favour the use of hydrochloric rather than acetic acid. It is usual to quote a figure for solubility as if it were a percentage of the lead oxide content that was dissolved. Others state it as a percentage of the metal lead, which amounts to the same thing, but sometimes the figure is recast as a percentage of the whole frit which can be misleading. Commercial lead bisilicate is usually produced to be well below 1% solubility of lead oxide and is therefore very satisfactory as a low sol frit.

Lead-borosilicate glazes. The major type of low lead solubility glaze. Prepared low sol glazes are often of the type where the bought powder is a mixture of lead silicate (lead oxide, silica and stabilizers), borosilicate (boric oxide, silica and stabilizers) and other glaze minerals such as china clay and feldspar. The whole fuses to produce a lead oxide-boric oxide-alumina-silica glass with stabilizers. This is shortened to lead-borosilicate.

The use of two frits, lead silicate and borosilicate at the powder stage reduces the solubility of the lead content. A combined frit has too high a solubility of lead but once the whole glaze has been fused there is no danger. The china clay and feldspar in the glaze enable the same frits to be balanced for different glazes. They also provide valuable bulk in the glaze slop to keep the glaze in suspension. See **Lead poisoning, Low sol, Lead frit** and **Double fritting**.

Lead carbonate. Basic lead carbonate. White lead. $2PbCO_3 . Pb(OH)_2$. A source of lead oxide for glazes. See **Lead oxide**. Details for the use of lead carbonate in glazes are given under **White lead**.

Lead frit. Fritted lead. Lead silicate. Plumbic frit. Any prepared mineral that contains lead oxide and silica as the main constituents in fused form. They are usually powders but can be supplied in granule form for self-grinding. A lead frit is only part of a glaze. The least possible addition to it would be 5% of china clay for very soft glazes like those for raku. Usually 10% of china clay and at least 20% of feldspar will be used and for most low sol glazes a borosilicate will also be present. See **Double fritting**.

Lead frits were developed during the first half of the 20th century to combat lead poisoning in the pottery industries. See **Low sol** and **Lead poisoning**. The advantages of using lead frits rather than raw lead compounds and silica are as follows:

1. Fritted lead is easier to suspend in a glaze slop than raw lead. It is also easier to make a glaze which adheres to ware prior to firing by using fritted lead.

2. The glaze slop and materials handled by the potter are far less toxic.

3. The supply of a standard frit is kept chemically constant by the frit manufacturer. It is probable that it is more constant than a supply of raw materials.

4. Frits release fewer volatiles during firing because they have already been fired. The lead content of a frit is also less volatile than raw lead introduced into a glaze.

5. Glaze fusion starts earlier and is more thorough because the frit is often a eutectic mixture. The maturing range of a glaze can thereby be lengthened if required.

6. The frit ensures a more uniform distribution of materials and hence a more uniform fusion.

Lead frits are not crystalline minerals. Their structure is a random one composed of silica chains interlinked with lead oxide. Obviously the composition of lead frits can vary enormously. The amount of lead oxide could be 10% or 90%. In recent years, potters have favoured those with published formulae approximating whole numbers. These are:

lead monosilicate	$PbO . SiO_2$
lead sesquisilicate	$2PbO . 3SiO_2 (PbO . 1 . 5SiO_2)$
lead bisilicate	$PbO . 2SiO_2$

These frits usually contain some stabilizers as trace

amounts of alumina and titania which considerably decrease the lead solubility. Precision potters can consider these and the other variations in calculations but for most purposes the formulae can be taken in their whole number form. Frit manufacturers have welcomed the simplification of supply because they are now using more continuous fritting processes. Trade specifications for frits are established to indicate the limits of composition for these standard lead frits.

The most useful lead frit and the most popular one with frit manufacturers, industrial and individual potters, is lead bisilicate. The solubility of the lead oxide content can be effectively controlled by the use of stabilizers and/or coatings. It can be introduced into any glaze to increase the fusion but in glazes to be fired over 1200°C (2192°F) it could present some problems. Lead oxide begins to volatilize between 1150°C and 1200°C (2102°F and 2192°F). A small amount (under 10%) of lead frit which has been introduced into a stoneware glaze will partially escape in volatile form above 1200°C. It is unlikely to do any damage because the glaze will be sufficiently fluid to allow it to pass. A large amount (over 20%) would seriously disrupt the glaze surface and deplete the flux in the glaze. The result would be a cratered glaze surface. The use of lead frits in stoneware glazes is therefore limited but is valuable for special effects like lizard skin where two similar glazes are required to fuse at different points of the firing.

Below 1200°C (2192°F) there is little difficulty experienced with lead frit. One should consider it as a flux. Consider the glaze as china clay, feldspar or other silicate and add increasing amounts of lead frit as flux until a satisfactory glaze is found. This gives more reliable results than starting with the lead frit, because lead frit alone will give a glaze and comparison of this with other tests is difficult. The whole area can be explored by the use of a blend. See **Line blend**.

For glazes melting over 900°C (1652°F) the best frit is the bisilicate. For glazes below 900°C the sesquisilicate or monosilicate will be needed: they have a lower melting range in glazes. The higher temperature glazes obviously require less flux here considered as lead frit. The higher temperature makes the same amount of flux more active. It also gives a longer time for the action to take place.

The following glazes are given for comparison:

Transparent raku glaze 800°C (1472°F)
lead monosilicate	82
china clay	18

Transparent raku glaze 800°C (1472°F)
lead sesquisilicate	85
china clay	15

Transparent raku glaze 900°C (1652°F)
lead bisilicate	90
china clay	5
flint	5

Opaque raku glaze 900°C (1652°F)

lead monosilicate	75
china clay	15
tin oxide	10

Maiolica glaze 1000°C (1832°F)

lead bisilicate	80
china clay	10
tin oxide	10

Matt maiolica glaze 1100°C (2012°F)

lead bisilicate	60
feldspar	20
china clay	5
flint	5
tin oxide	4
zirconium oxide	3
titanium dioxide	3

Transparent earthenware glaze 1100°C (2012°F)

lead bisilicate	65
feldspar	15
china clay	10
flint	5
whiting	5

Semi-transparent matt stoneware glaze 1200°C (2192°F)

lead bisilicate	20
feldspar	40
china clay	20
whiting	20

Lead monosilicate. Lead metasilicate. $PbO.SiO_2$. A compound in which theoretically one molecule of lead oxide combines with one molecule of silica. The theoretical proportional weights are lead oxide 78·8%, silica 21·2%.

Of the lead content, the solubility can be as high as 30% but this can be reduced to as low as 5% by the use of stabilizing modifiers and to below 1% by the use of coatings. However the monosilicate is still not considered a satisfactory low sol frit for industrial or school use.

Fusion of lead monosilicate is rapid, starting at approximately 700°C (1292°F) and being complete by 800°C (1472°F). It can be used in glazes for the 750°C to 900°C (1382°F to 1652°F) range such as decorative raku. See **Lead frit.**

Lead ore. Lead occurs in many ores and is associated with copper, tin, zinc and iron. The commonest lead ore is the sulphide ore called galena. It is dark blue-grey and occurs as cubic crystals. It is easy to roast and reduce to metal, and for this reason was one of the first metals to be worked. The Ancient Egyptians passed on their skills to the Romans who made full use of lead for pipes, drains etc but they made little use of the Egyptian lead glaze.

The ground ore can be used in glazes. It oxidizes easily but a kiln with flues is necessary to carry away the sulphur. See **Galena**.

Lead orthosilicate. $2PbO.SiO_2$. A compound in which, theoretically, two molecules of lead oxide combine with one molecule of silica. The theoretical proportional weights are lead oxide 88·1%, and silica 11·9%.

Lead orthosilicate is not available as a standard commercial frit because its lead solubility is very high. There is insufficient silica to involve the lead oxide in close fusion with the result that nearly 90% of the lead oxide remains in a soluble form. Lead orthosilicate is sometimes used in the preparation of special colours.

Lead oxide. Plumbous oxide. PbO. An important flux for use at low and medium temperatures. Its action as a flux begins as low as 500°C (932°F) and therefore it can be used for all temperatures up to 1100°C (2012°F) at which temperature it begins to volatilize.

The oxide entering the ceramic fusion is chemically called plumbous oxide (PbO). This is commonly called lead oxide, a simplification which sometimes gives rise to confusion because there are 4 compounds, each of which can correctly be called lead oxide. These are lead monoxide, also called litharge (PbO), lead dioxide (PbO_2), lead trioxide (Pb_2O_3), and lead tetroxide, more commonly called red lead (Pb_3O_4). There is also the basic lead carbonate ($2PbCO_3.Pb(OH)_2$) commonly called white lead and sometimes erroneously white lead oxide. All these lead compounds can be used in glazes but with the exception of the first they all decompose in the early stages of firing to become plumbous oxide (PbO) by 600°C (1112°F). Galena (PbS), the sulphide of lead, is also used in glazes. It decomposes and oxidizes to become plumbous oxide.

The compounds of lead which are useful in pottery are separately indexed and are referred to in the next sections on bodies and glazes.

LEAD OXIDE IN BODIES. It is unusual but perfectly possible to use lead oxide as the flux in low-temperature bodies. Its slow-maturing quality which is noticeable with glazes is however not as noticeable with bodies. It therefore has little advantage over soda, potash and boric oxide except insolubility in water. It has however two disadvantages: its poisonous nature and its cost. It is impossible to keep clay dust out of the atmosphere and impossible to pot without touching the clay.

The following recipe uses a lead frit. It is a low-maturing cream body for 1080°–1100°C (1976°–2012°C). The temperature is critical.

ball clay	60	
china clay	25	by weight
lead monosilicate	15	

Molten lead oxide, when considered as a fluid, is not as searching as boric oxide. A lead glaze does not therefore soak into a body as much as a boric oxide glaze. For this reason, lead glazes do not always adhere to slip-coated ware on the parts which are more refractory, e.g. over a white slip. To assist adhesion, some slipware potters add some of the glaze, or simply a lead oxide to the slip. This encourages the formation of a thin body-glaze layer. See **Buffer layer**.

LEAD OXIDE IN GLAZES. Lead oxide is one of the most useful and versatile glaze fluxes. It gives glazes which are easy to handle: they are simple in recipe form and behave well during firing.

Lead glazes mature gently and are therefore easy to use. They smooth over after gassing and yet are not necessarily over-fluid. They stain readily to a range of rich colours and are distinguished by their soft deep shine.

Lead glazes were probably first used in the Middle East 3000 years ago. Their use spread to the Far East by 500 B.C. and to western Europe by A.D. 100. The Romans, who knew of the method, used lead glazes rarely and the method almost died out in Europe. However, the medieval potters revived them and made expressive use of them and so did the slipware potters up to the 18th century. After this the Mediterranean influences and Oriental standard changed European ideas about glazes and towards the end of the 19th century northern Europe became concerned about the poisonous nature of the raw lead oxide.

To combat lead poisoning, new glazes have been developed in which the solubility of poisonous lead is extremely low. See **Low sol**. Until the 20th century there was no serious alternative glaze for the temperature range up to 1100°C (2012°F). Boric oxide is now used in combination with lead oxide and also in lead-free glazes.

There exist many recipes for simple lead glazes. Many of these have been used for centuries. They are simple because they use lead oxide as the only flux. The silica is provided by flint and clay, the latter also giving alumina and possibly colouring. They are known as the 3:2:1 recipes because when converted from their various measures as bucketsful etc, and considered as dry weights they approximate:

lead compound	3	50%
silica	2	33·3%
clay	1	16·6%

The proportions are varied to suit individual cases but it is possible to see this basis within most lead glazes. Factors giving rise to variation are:

1. Temperature. A higher temperature requires less lead oxide.

2. Body. A porous and refractory body absorbs some of the lead oxide.

3. Type of lead compound. (Litharge, red lead, white lead, galena.)

4. Type of silica. (Flint, quartz and various sands.)

5. Type of clay in the glaze. China clay is the most refractory and provides the most alumina.

6. Glazing conditions. A glaze for raw glazing requires a careful balance of the clay content. Most glazes will adhere to biscuit before firing but with raw ware the required thickness of lead glaze often causes a problem. In some cases the answer lies in increasing the clay content of the glaze. An extreme variation of the 3:2:1 recipe is seen in this successful recipe to be used on red clay, glazed when dry and fired to 1080°C (1976°F). It will be seen that the clay and flint amounts are reversed.

red lead	3
red body clay	2
flint	1

The most logical next step in the development of a lead glaze is the introduction of another flux. This provides more stability in the use of variable materials. A feldspathic mineral, like cornish stone, provides a number of fluxes. It is here introduced as part of the alumino-silicates. This glaze is for decorative ware fired to 1080°C (1976°F). It stains well and is a good basis for enamels and lustres.

red lead	3
china clay	1
cornish stone	1
flint	1

Additions and alterations to the standard recipe, for economic and other reasons, are often possible without apparent loss of quality as colour, shine and fit. However most raw lead glazes contain a high proportion of lead because it provides an elastic glaze which behaves well in the firing and fits more than one body. This final recipe is typical of adjusted recipes but, although apparently complex, the original 3:2:1 can be seen to exist. It is for general purposes at temperatures between 1060°C and 1100°C (1940°F and 2012°F). When stained with red iron oxide 8% and manganese dioxide 8% it gives a metallic black.

white lead	43
whiting	6
flint	8
feldspar	15
nepheline syenite	14
china clay	14

The most important development in lead glazes has been the manufacture of fritted lead to render the lead oxide non-toxic. See **Lead poisoning** and **Low sol**. Part of this development has been the introduction of lead-borosilicate glazes for all purposes where raw lead glazes were previously used. See **Lead-borosilicate glazes** and **Double fritting**. The use of these frits has extended the useful range of lead oxide. Raw lead glazes begin to volatilize above 1100°C (2012°F) but lead oxide as part of a frit is stable up to 1200°C

(2192°F). This is accounted for by the time factor involved in the interlinking of fusion constituents. For the use of lead glazes in the range up to 1200°C and the use of frits see **Lead frit**.

Lead poisoning. Plumbism. Lead and compounds of lead are poisonous in the bloodstream, lungs and digestive system. Lead poisoning has always been a hazard in industries using lead compounds, e.g. the roasting of ores, the use of powdered ores, oxides etc. The greatest danger has been from volatile lead fumes, from dust breathed and from dust which contaminated food.

Symptoms of lead poisoning are lethargy and drowsiness, general abdominal upsets, muscle and joint pains, anaemia and loss of weight. Lead is a cumulative poison. It builds up in the human system until its presence can no longer be accepted. Each person has his own level of absorption before poisoning takes place. Poisoning may be precipitated by other illness in which case it is difficult to diagnose.

Lead poisoning was once a major hazard for the potter and it has been given large publicity. But other poisons are also handled. They are antimony, barium, cadmium, copper, chromium, selenium and zinc which can be equally dangerous handled in bulk. Silicosis is also a potter's hazard. In some cases the mineral handled may not be poisonous but its inclusion in a glaze may precipitate it or alter it in such a way that it becomes a poison in the finished glaze. There are therefore two hazards: the exposure to poisons while making pottery and the risk of contaminating food from finished ware.

Regulations are in force in most countries to protect workers in industry. They include the use of wet materials to inhibit dust, extractor fans from booths for spraying or dusting, the wearing of breathing masks, the use of rubber aprons and other protective clothing, the provision of washing facilities, the isolation of canteen facilities and the prohibition of smoking and eating in the danger areas. Regular medical inspections and workshop inspections are carried out. The use of raw lead glazes is banned or severely restricted. Instead, the lead compounds must be in fritted form and conform to a specification. See **Low sol**.

In Britain, the number of reported cases of lead poisoning in potteries dropped from 432 in 1897 to nil by 1944 as a result of these precautions. Similar restrictions on the use of raw lead and poisonous colours operate in most schools. Most teachers use fritted lead glazes if they use lead compounds at all and also take necessary hygienic precautions. British precautions are in Department of Education and Science memoranda 517 on lead and 2/65 on other poisons.

Individual potters should sensibly protect themselves in a similar way although they are rarely under obligation to do so by law.

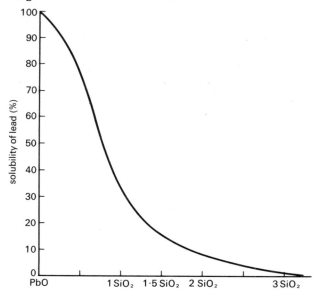

The graph shows the simple combinations of lead oxide and silica (without stabilizers) and relates these by the curve to varying amounts of lead solubility from 100% solubility of pure PbO to 2% solubility of $PbO.3SiO_2$.

There is little danger from lead glazes which have been fully fused. Underfired glazes however are suspect because the lead oxide is probably not fully linked with the silicate chains. In this respect, glazes made from raw lead compounds are more dangerous than those using already fritted lead. In fact the introduction of raw lead to a fritted lead glaze tends to upset the balance. As a general rule, the higher the firing temperature of the glaze, the lower the solubility of the lead content. One would of course expect this since more silica is required for a higher-temperature glaze and this would more easily involve the lead oxide during fusion. Low-temperature glazes like raku, and low-temperature colours like on-glaze enamels are the most dangerous. This is true also for the other poisonous metals which are often used for low-temperature colours, e.g. antimony, cadmium, chromium and selenium. Copper presents a special case. It has been proved to upset the stability of lead glazes and also present a hazard itself when present in metallic effects like copper oxide brushwork.

The amount of poison which can be dissolved from the surface of a fired glaze is usually small but it should be remembered that lead is cumulative and, for a person already sick, even a small dose can be injurious. The poisons are dissolved by strong acids like vinegar and fruit juices, and to a lesser extent by tea, coffee and other drinks. Potters in doubt about their glazes should consult the suppliers of the materials or the local health authority's analyst. The British Standard Specification 4860 states the permissible limits of metal release from glazed ceramic ware. Similar specifications exist in the United States of America.

Lead sesquisilicate. $2PbO.3SiO_2$ or $PbO.1.5SiO_2$. A prepared compound in which theoretically every two molecules of lead oxide combine with three molecules of silica. The theoretical proportional weights are lead oxide 71·25%, silica 28·75%.

The solubility of the lead content is about 12% in the straightforward sesquisilicate. This can be reduced to around 1% by the use of stabilizers, e.g. titania and alumina. It is difficult to get the solubility much lower chemically, but, by using an acid-proof coating on the frit particles, the solubility can be minimalized to below 0·02%. The frit is first ground to 200's mesh and dried. It is then given a silica shell by immersion in hydrolysed ethyl silicate. The resulting coating is hard and will withstand some further grinding as part of a glaze batch. This process was developed and patented by Henry L. Podmore in the 1950's.

Lead sesquisilicate is slightly softer and contains more lead oxide than lead bisilicate. Fusion begins at approximately 700°C (1292°F) and is complete by 850°C (1562°F). Lead sesquisilicate can be used in glazes for the 850°C to 1200°C range (1562°F to 2192°F) and many potters prefer it to the bisilicate. However the sesquisilicate is more volatile at the higher temperatures. Indeed, large amounts are likely to cause over-fluxing and bubbling above 1100°C (2012°F). Its advantage over the bisilicate is seen in the production of bright yellows and brick reds with antimony and iron oxides at temperatures below 1000°C (1832°F). For the use of lead sesquisilicates see **Lead frit**.

Lead titanate. $PbO.TiO_2$. A crystalline mineral which is precipitated from cooling glazes below 1050°C (1922°F). It crystallizes upon titania nuclei and also forms large composite crystals with zinc titanate and zinc silicate. See **Crystalline glazes**.

Leadless glaze. Self-explanatory description with the exception that in Britain a leadless glaze may contain up to 1% lead oxide. It is often used as a synonym for borosilicate glaze because these glazes were developed to replace the poisonous lead glazes. Leadless glazes can also be based upon fritted soda, potash and zinc oxide for the lower temperatures and upon calcia, magnesia and baria for the higher temperatures. If one wishes to imply the absolute absence of lead one should use the term 'lead-free'.

Lean clay. Clay of low plasticity and strength. See **Short clay**.

Leatherhard. The stage, which plastic clay reaches during drying, when the clay particles are just touching and are thereby giving a stability to the clay. The clay is stiff enough to be picked up without distortion yet soft enough to respond to pressure for burnishing. See **Drying**.

Leatherhard state is the ideal state for pots to be turned and have handles attached. Although there may be some aesthetic advantages in working at an earlier (softer) stage.

Drying from leatherhard to bone-dry state causes little stress within the clay. Nearly all of the drying shrinkage has taken place by the leatherhard stage. Most clays decrease in volume by less than 0·5% between leatherhard and bone-dry. A few extremely fine ball clays shrink as much as 2% in volume but they are exceptional. These figures are to be compared with a range of from 10% to 30% volumetric shrinkage from plastic to leatherhard stage.

Lepidolite. Lithium feldspathoid. Lithium mica. Lithium-potassium mica. A natural material used in glazes to introduce lithia, alumina and silica. It is also mined for its 5% lithium content, some of which is prepared as a carbonate for glass and glazes.

Lepidolite is an alumino-silicate with a variable base where lithium replaces potassium and involves variable amounts of fluorine and hydroxyl grouping. Various molecular formulae are acceptable from $(LiKNa)_2(FOH)_2.Al_2O_3.3SiO_2$ to $Li_2F_2.Al_2O_3.3SiO_2$.

Lepidolite has no fixed melting point but matures over a range approximating 1150°C to 1300°C (2012°F to 2372°F). Small amounts of lepidolite can be substituted for other feldspars in glaze recipes with ad-

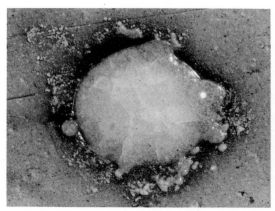

vantageous results for earlier fusion, increased shine and more stable finished glaze. The fluorine content however can cause bubbling and can leave a pitted surface if too much lepidolite is used. It will be noticed that the alumina content is high (over 25%) which results in stiff melts.

The photographs show native lepidolite in fibrous crystal form and lepidolite melted at 1200°C (2192°F) on a test tile.

Levigation. The process of passing a thin slurry through a series of traps where the heavier particles settle and finer particles overflow. The process is used for clays which contain unwanted material like sand which is too fine to be caught in a mesh.

For example, a clay which has been screened through 100's mesh is used for a potting clay. It is desired that the same clay is used in a slip glaze with wood ash, but it is found that the clay contains a fine sand which causes unwanted specking. The first recourse is a finer mesh sieve for the clay to go into the glaze. But if the glaze has already been made up, a finer mesh would probably take out the wood ash also. Levigation and sedimentation are two practical methods. Of the two, levigation gives easier control for small amounts.

A levigation trough is a channel of any convenient length with one open end. Across this channel are placed riffles to act as barriers. The whole can be made of wood or a piece of guttering can be used with riffles made from plastic clay. The suspension must be very fluid with perhaps three or four times the eventual water content. It is run down the trough into a collecting tub. The angle of the trough is adjusted to give the required sedimentation in the traps.

The advantage of this method is that the deposits can be inspected at any time. By gently steepening the angle

of the trough the traps can be emptied of the suspension without losing the sediment. The trough can be sluiced out and the process repeated, usually at a shallower angle, until the unwanted sand etc is removed.

Lid. A hygienic cover which provides a visual focal point and a stimulus for tactile appreciation. A number of appreciation reflexes respond to the way in which a lid sits upon or in its pot. The photographs are of a lidded jampot by Bernard Leach and a lidded storage jar by John Leach.

A lid requires some form of gallery to keep it in place. The gallery can be on the lid, as on the jampot illustrated, which allows the pot to be simpler in the way it finishes at the rim. Or the gallery can be on the pot, as on the storage jar, which gives the lid a look of stability.

A few sections of thrown lids are drawn for comparison. The sunken lid is useful on casseroles and storage jars where height is limited. It is a stable lid for pots which are to be moved. It allows a large serviceable knob which does not protrude inconveniently. The sunken lid which has galleries on both lid and pot is used for teapots and coffee pots to keep the centre of gravity low and thus overcome the problem of the insecure lid during pouring. Locking devices

are possible in a number of ways but rarely seem to be both completely efficient and aesthetically interesting. Most potters rely upon a simple design.

Lifting. A slip and glaze defect in which there is loss of adhesion before firing. Lifting is obvious when pieces of slip or glaze flake off as the raw work is handled. But lifting can occur in the early stages of the firing if the body water is too quickly driven off. The steam pressure lifts the slip or glaze, breaking what adhesion there was. Lifting gives the slip defect of flaking and the glaze defect of crawling and butterfly.

If a slip or glaze has previously been successful but begins to lift, the fault could be that the body was too dry for slip, or too wet for glaze when application was made. The presence of grease or dust on the body, or a different speed of drying effected before or during the firing could cause a previously successful glaze to lift. The photograph shows a stiff glaze which has lifted during firing from a powdery underglaze surface.

The term is sometimes used to describe glazes which leave the pot after firing. However, there are sufficient other words for the various types of this defect described as peeling, shelling, shivering and flaking.

Lime. Calcia. Calcium oxide. CaO. The term calcia is used throughout this book. This is in line with the increasing practice amongst potters to be more specific.

Lime is a term which has wide use to mean different calcium compounds, e.g. gardeners' lime is calcium carbonate and builders' lime is calcium oxide. Quicklime is freshly calcined calcium oxide.

Calcia is an alkaline oxide. It is used as a flux in glazes and is very active above 1100°C (2012°F). Below this temperature it has the opposite effect of inhibiting fusion. Large amounts of calcia have the effect of combining with the silica to produce crystals. These opacify the glaze and give a matt surface. These glazes are called lime matts. See **Lime matt** and **Calcia**.

Lime feldspar. Anorthite. $CaO.Al_2O_3.2SiO_2$. See **Anorthite**.

Lime matt. A matt glaze in which the matt surface is produced by calcium silicate crystals. Lime is calcia.

Calcia is introduced into a glaze by means of whiting, chalk or limestone, which are all calcium carbonate. The carbonate decomposes on heating to 825°C (1517°F) giving calcia and carbon dioxide, which escapes as a gas. To get a matt surface, calcium carbonate is added to a glaze in the proportion of 20% to 30%. Simple transparent glazes and other shiny glazes can be successfully matted. In an earthenware glaze melting below 1100°C (2012°F) the calcia tends to stiffen the glaze and inhibits fusion, and during cooling it forms crystals with the free silica. Although it is an alkaline oxide it does not act as a flux. Above 1100°C however, calcia becomes active as a flux. Therefore in glazes which melt above 1100°C, whether earthenware or stoneware, the calcia added will perform an action as a flux during firing and as a crystal-former during cooling. A typical lime matt recipe for 1250°C (2282°F) is:

cornish stone	50
china clay	15
tin oxide	5
whiting	30

For temperatures in the range of 1200°C (2192°F) and over it is possible to use the calcia as the main flux and the matting agent. In the example recipe, calcia is the main flux, subsidiary fluxes existing in the cornish stone. A little tin oxide has been added to improve whiteness and opacity. This glaze can give alkaline colour responses if a suitably alkaline cornish stone is used.

The correct balance of calcia is sometimes difficult to discover. Up to 15% of calcium carbonate may be correct for a stable semi-transparent glaze. Here the calcia forms nuclei of crystals which give a milky opacity, but the crystals do not extend to the surface. About 20% of calcium carbonate may make the glaze over-fluxed, very runny and transparent. Here the melt is so liquid that the calcium silicate crystals do not have time to grow before a glaze quickly sets. A prolonged cooling could give successful results. About 25%–30% may be the best amount of calcium carbonate and gives a crystal growth that spreads from within outwards to cover the whole surface of the glaze. About 35% may make the glaze very dry-looking and unpleasant. It will look as if it has not fused and is also likely to have lost its adhesion with the pot. It will have peeled back as flakes of loose skin. For a description of crystallization see **Crystalline glazes**.

At the correct amount, there are sufficient crystals to cover the whole surface of the glaze without making it appear too dry. The crystals are mostly wollastonite, with some anorthite. These crystals sparkle with the light as it is reflected from the different crystal facets. The appearance is that of frost and is very attractive. Lime matt glazes are popular for this reason.

It is possible to get a lime matt that is fickle in firing but generally they are very dependable glazes. Careful firing as well as cooling is necessary; they are slow to mature. Too rapid a firing will result in pinholes because the glaze is a stiff one and has not the capacity to flow into craters. If a lime matt which is successful begins to misbehave one should look for a change in firing cycle. Both firing and cooling should be compared with previous firings. The final temperature may also be critical. Overfiring can cause loss of crystals. Similarly extra fusion caused by interaction with a different body, a different slip, or extra reduction could result in loss of crystal growth.

Lime matts are alkaline glazes. They therefore give bright colours with cobalt and copper oxides. The calcia has the effect of bleaching iron oxides so that a range of yellow and green glazes is possible.

On tableware a lime matt has limited application. The crystals form what must be regarded as a rough surface. Whilst attractive, it is not the most practical. Spoons and cutlery scrape the surface with an unpleasant sound. The surface is easily marked by the metal and also stains because of the gaps between the crystals.

Dolomite limestone is a combination of calcium carbonate and magnesium carbonate. Dolomite matt glazes are similar to and are related to lime matts.

Limestone. Stone which is essentially calcium carbonate ($CaCO_3$). It is used by potters to introduce calcia into glazes. It is often more appropriate to use whiting for this purpose. In any case many whitings are crushed limestone.

Limestone occurs widely as a sedimentary rock sometimes of great thickness. The sediments occurred as crystalline precipitates and as shells of sea creatures. Limestones are therefore often highly fossiliferous and whilst mostly grey or buff can be very decorative.

Limestones have many uses. They are used for building stone, road metal, iron ore smelting and for making cement. The potter uses limestone as a source of calcia for glazes.

Although some limestone shales exist which are useful in glazes, most limestone is difficult to grind. Limestone is hard. It stands out in the landscape as cliffs and mountains and this is why it is a good building material and road metal. Where these materials are crushed there is often a surplus of dust which is a possible source for the potter. The dust has been referred to as calcareous rock flour. However, from the potter's point of view, limestone introduces little more than does whiting.

There are many local names like Portland and Bath Stones but the physical types of limestones are:

1. Crystalline limestone which is extremely hard and sometimes called mountain limestone.

2. Fossiliferous limestone which is built up from the shells of sea creatures. The shells vary from a few inches across to ones indistinguishable without a magnifying glass. These limestones often form part of the strata called mountain limestone and are also called shelly limestones.

3. Oolitic limestone is usually softer than the two above and contains some iron giving it a pleasant buff colour. On close inspection it is seen to be composed of spherical particles.

4. Chalk is usually softer than other limestones but it varies enormously. It was deposited as a calcareous mud and therefore the particles are extremely fine. It varies in colour, the purest being white.

5. Marble is crystalline limestone that has had the opportunity to reform its crystals under pressure and heat. It is metamorphic limestone. It is the hardest of the limestones. Some finely textured crystalline limestones are called marbles when they are cut and polished for decorative use.

6. Tufa is crystalline limestone which has been deposited recently. It forms concretions in waterfalls, stalagmites and stalactites. It is not too difficult to grind. Travertine and calc-sinter are similar deposits associated with hot springs.

7. Calcite and aragonite are the pure crystal forms of calcium carbonate. Tufa is composed of tiny calcite crystals. Nailhead spar, dog-tooth spar and Iceland spar are varieties of large calcite crystals. These crystals are softer than the stones and can be ground by hand.

8. Ferruginous limestone is any limestone that is stained by iron. The colourings are often very decorative. The iron is in the form of ferrous carbonate ($FeCO_3$), the iron having replaced some of the calcium. See **Siderite**.

9. Dolomite limestone is a combination of calcium carbonate and magnesium carbonate. It occurs where magnesium has partially replaced calcium in ordinary limestone and where the limestone was deposited under water rich in magnesium salts. See **Dolomite**.

Limonite. $2Fe_2O_3.3H_2O$. The natural hydrated form of iron oxide. The ore is a loose structure which does not form large crystals. It is therefore usually soft and easily crumbled. It varies in colour from a yellow through orange to a dark red-brown. It was originally a bog ore which was precipitated by bacterial action from solution in lakes and therefore is usually relatively pure.

There are large deposits in Scandinavia and North America but small pockets may often be found associated with Carboniferous series rocks. The yellow form, called yellow ochre, is soft and crumbly. The red form contains less water and is called red ochre and raddle. It is harder but can be crushed easily. Hard dark nodules which must be pounded are found associated with fireclays. All forms are useful clay and glaze colourants and the softer forms are often already closely associated and uniformly spread throughout a clay bed. For iron colouring of clay and glazes see **Iron oxide**.

Line blend. A method of determining requirements in practical tests of materials. For example, if one has a black clay and a white clay which are to be blended to produce a predetermined grey, the proportionate blend can be found by a line blend. In this case the obvious way is to start with the white and add increasing amounts of black. A whole series of tests would go into one firing and from them the correct one would be selected. Any convenient number of tests can be decided upon.

It is usual to run a second line blend between two of the tests from the first blend if a fine degree of choice is required. This avoids making the first series unnecessarily long. It is also usual, especially with glazes, to decrease one test ingredient as the other increases. In this way the total bulk remains constant and calculations in percentages are more easily composed. The following two examples should make these points clear:

	A	B	C	D	E	F	G
black clay	0	1	2	3	4	5	6 parts
white clay	6	5	4	3	2	1	0 parts

If the required colour lies between tests C and D a further series might be:

	H(D)	I	J	K	L	M(C)
black clay 2 parts white clay 4 parts	0		1	2	3	4	5 parts
black clay 3 parts white clay 3 parts	5		4	3	2	1	0 parts

This gives four further possible blends to choose from which are known to be in the desired area.

It is important to make line blends from two carefully selected originals. With glazes particularly one has a very wide choice. The two originals should be chosen in order that an estimated best blend based on common sense or pure guess work would lie approximately halfway between the two. Thus the two originals may not be glazes at all. One may be nearly all flux and

the other nearly all silica. Neither of these would melt to a satisfactory glaze. If one is line-blending two glazes in an attempt to get one that melts at 1200°C (2192°F), the obvious originals would be two glazes melting one below and one above this temperature. These glazes would need to be similar in character for a beginning, e.g. both transparents, or both lime matts. This is the normal approach.

Alternatively, one may make a series of empirical tests across areas of glaze types in the hope of a chance winner. Such blends have their uses. They may not give any valuable information on a specific problem but they give the potter experience in fluxing and colouring phenomena which can be used in later choice of originals. Line blends are particularly useful for determining colouring amounts.

Line blends are useful in composing glaze recipes when one is using raw materials for which no easy chemical formulae exist, e.g. wood ash, local clay, local rock, coloured sand. In such cases it is impossible to start with a molecular formula and calculate from this to a suitable recipe. One must work empirically with the materials. One can do this simply by classifying each material as either flux, refractory clay, fusible clay, feldspathic rock, or silica, and consider them as known types for the first test. Alternatively one may wish to discover more about each material first. This may be necessary to discover if any material has a particular colouring value or annoying property. To do this a small specimen of each material is fired on a test tile. This gives some indication of properties and enables a first choice to be made.

It is well to start a series of line blends with only two materials if these are completely unknown. From the first blend, which should contain at least 7 tests, another starting point may be found. From here it may happen that a side blend, as it were at right angles to the first blend, is made. This may be towards a third material or towards another selected blend. By this stage enough information has usually been gained from which to make prediction of further blends.

In the end one usually arrives at two or three possible solutions with very different recipes and one is tempted to try line blends using these recipes but these rarely give conclusive results. It is more profitable to make a series of line blends which cover the area around a predicted best recipe. By doing this one has covered all the possibilities. To decide upon the originals of such a final blend, make the predicted recipe the middle test of the line and increase one ingredient one way and another ingredient the other way. A few blends will be required to fully cover all the possibilities in the area around the predicted recipe.

Lastly, in making glaze tests it is not necessary to weigh out and make each test separately. One only needs to make two originals. These should be made of equal density. It is then sufficiently accurate to make the blends between in spoonfuls of glaze slop. In this way the percentage recipes for each test do not need to be worked out.

Litharge. Massicot. Yellow lead oxide. Lead monoxide. PbO. The raw material nearest to the lead oxide which enters ceramic fusions. It is used in raw lead glaze recipes but great care must be exercised because it is poisonous. See **Lead poisoning**. Its action in glazes is described under **Lead oxide in glazes**. In glaze calculations it is considered to convert exactly weight for weight CF 1·0.

Lithia. Lithium oxide. Li_2O. One of the strong alkaline oxides. It is used as a flux in glazes where it gives similar results to soda. The oxide is soluble in water and is therefore introduced into glaze batches by lithium carbonate or lithium feldspathoids.

There are four natural sources of lithia. They are the three feldspathoids and the fluophosphate: lepidolite, petalite, spodumene and amblygonite. They are all low-yield ores, below 10% yield, which makes lithia an expensive flux. The commerical lithium carbonate is produced from these ores and, of course, these materials can be introduced into glazes. See individual items.

Lithia is an asset to a glaze as an additional flux. Additional, that is, to the number of fluxes; its presence replacing some, but not all, of another alkaline oxide. A diversity of fluxes gives greater interaction with resulting increases in fluidity and gloss. A number of fluxes also usually provides a more stable glaze structure thus giving a more durable glaze.

Lithia is an active flux resembling soda and starts its fluxing action at approximately 800°C (1472°F). It is less volatile than soda above 1200°C (2192°F) and remains an effective flux over the full range of glazes. However, at the higher temperatures, the amount of lithia would normally be decreased in favour of cheaper, but equally effective, fluxes like calcia and magnesia.

The effect that lithia can give, which is different from other stoneware fluxes, is colour response. It gives blues with copper oxide and pinks with cobalt oxide. It is a useful auxiliary flux in the production of the more alkaline lime and barium matts.

Lithium is the lightest metal element with an atomic weight of 6·94. See **Periodic table**. Lithia has a molecular weight of only 29·87 compared with soda 61·97, potash 94·19 and calcia 66·07. This means that in equal weights of these four oxides there is a greater number of molecules of lithia than of soda, potash or calcia. The smaller atom size of lithium gives a compact oxide. See drawing.

Thus a smaller weight of lithia, than other flux, will be required to give an equal number of molecules. Lithia is therefore an economical and effective flux in a glaze on a weight for weight basis.

Expansion and contraction rates for glazes are calculated on the percentage weights of the oxides in the recipe. An oxide like lithia therefore accounts for only a

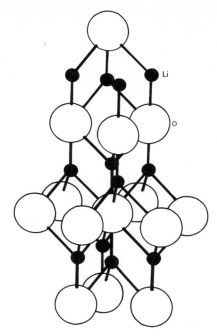

small proportion of this rate compared with soda and potash. When this fact is coupled with the fact that lithia has a lower expansion rate itself than has soda or potash, it will be seen why the inclusion of lithia has such a marked effect upon the expansion and contraction rates of glazes. Lithia is often substituted for some of the soda in order to inhibit crazing. See **Glaze fit**.

The qualities of lithia have long been recognized and it has been used to balance lead-free glazes and produce special bodies and glazes with high resistances to thermal shock. After taking into consideration its economic dispersal in a glaze, it is still more expensive than the other fluxes: about 10 times the cost of calcia and 4 times the cost of baria.

Lithium carbonate. Li_2CO_3. A white crystalline powder, source of the flux lithia for glazes. The carbonate decomposes to become the oxide (lithia) and carbon dioxide during the glaze firing. Only 40% of the carbonate is lithia: the carbon dioxide accounts for 60%. The equation is:

$$Li_2CO_3 \xrightarrow{650°C} Li_2O + CO_2 \uparrow$$

lithium   lithia   carbon
carbonate   dioxide

Lithium carbonate is only slightly soluble in water and is therefore used in preference to lithia which is highly soluble. Lithia's fluxing properties are similar to those of potash and soda, but the much cheaper equivalent compounds of potassium and sodium are still soluble in water. Hence there is an advantage in using lithium carbonate.

Lithium carbonate does not occur as a natural material but is prepared from the lithium ores called lepidolite, petalite, spodumene and amblygonite.

Lithium feldspathoids. These are the three alumino-silicates based upon lithium: lepidolite, petalite and spodumene. They are separately itemized in this book. The lithium feldspathoids occur where lithium has been able to replace sodium and potassium in a residual mica-feldspar. They are mined as low-yield ores for the lithium metal and for the production of lithium carbonate for glass-making. They can also be introduced as feldspathoids into glazes. They are not true minerals because they have variable analyses and chemical formulae. Hence they have no definable melting points but have maturing ranges starting at 1150°C (2102°F) for lepidolite, 1200°C (2192°F) for petalite and 1250°C (2282°F) for spodumene. They are slow to mature.

Lithomarge. A compressed clay which has not yet reached the stage of a shale or slate. The term is sometimes used to describe discoloured china clays.

Livering. A slip-casting fault showing as a rippled or uneven surface on the slip side of a cast. See **Casting slip, adjustment of**.

Liverpool, England. Famous for its production of delft in the late 17th and early 18th centuries and also for the later production of creamware. It was here, in 1755, that John Sadler invented transfer printing after seeing children sticking waste prints onto broken earthenware to make dolls' teasets. The photograph shows a Sadler tile of 1760. Outstanding amongst Liverpool pottery are the large jugs with very pointed spouts and large punch bowls decorated with ships.

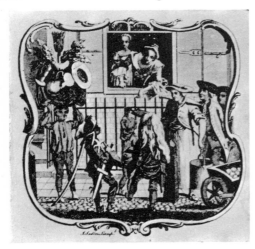

Lizard skin. Snake skin. A mottled glaze effect resembling scales. The effect is often composed of matt and shiny parts as well as parts of different colour and tone. It is a thick glaze and therefore suitable for horizontal surfaces but sometimes the effect can be achieved with stiffish glazes on vertical surfaces.

The effect is achieved by using two glazes of different composition and melting character. These are applied one over the other, the second being applied as

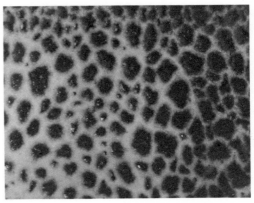

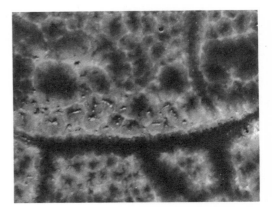

soon as convenient upon the first, and the two are fired together.

The first glaze should sit firmly upon the body without any tendency to flake off. The second glaze tends to pull at the first so the first must not be friable nor yet contain too much clay as binder. A gum or polymer resin binder is useful. Some potters have used a soft firing to bond the first glaze to the body without destroying its absorbency.

The second glaze contains a high proportion of clay. With most glazes 20% to 30% is necessary. This causes the glaze layer to shrink during drying. The second glaze layer thus becomes a series of isolated pieces of glaze. See drawing.

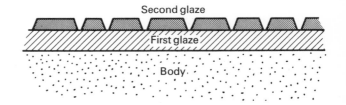

It does not matter which glaze fuses first. It is usually the under one because the second glaze contains more clay. If this is china clay it will be slow to melt and produce a stiff molten state. It is usual also for it to be matt. As the first glaze melts, the pieces of the second glaze sink into it to produce an almost level glaze surface.

Loaf. A raised portion used as a decorative feature in the centre of a plate or bowl.

Loess clay. Aeolian clay. A yellowish calcareous clay of central Europe and Asia. It is a sedimentary clay originally transported by wind across the drier parts of the world during the glacial periods.

Long clay. Clay of high plasticity. See **Fat clay**.

Loving cup. A two-handled cup usually commemorating a wedding and having suitable individual inscription with names and a date. Loving cups were popular in Britain during the 18th and 19th centuries. The example shown is in slipware with the inscription, 'Love's cup in his hand' and is dated T.M. 1768.

Low sol. Low solubility. Description of frits and glazes containing lead oxide where the solubility of the lead oxide is below 5% (British specification). Low sol frits and glazes were developed to overcome the problem of lead poisoning in the pottery industry and to protect users of pottery. See **Lead poisoning**.

Low sol is a general description: it is not specific to one recipe. However it is often used to imply a glaze which is composed of two frits: a lead frit of low solubility and a boro-silicate frit. The method of making a glaze in this way is known as 'double fritting'. For the use of low solubility frits see **Lead frit**.

The acids which break down and absorb ingested lead compounds in the human body are the gastric juices. These approximate an 0.17% hydrochloric acid solution. Tests on frits, glazes and fired glazes therefore use this acid but at the increased strength of 0.25% and at room temperature (20°C or 68°F) for convenience. They involve tests of frits and glaze powders and tests of glazed articles. The lead dissolved is precipitated as lead sulphate, washed, dried and weighed. The soluble content is usually expressed as a percentage of the metal lead or the lead oxide present in the original frit or glaze.

The greatest danger is from finely-ground lead compounds and lead frit powders. A fine glaze powder presents a vastly greater surface area than it does when it is a fused glaze on ware. Fine dust in the atmosphere enters the lungs and the stomach where its soluble lead content is almost completely absorbed. The soluble lead content of a finished glaze is mostly protected within the glaze although the surface is subject to attack by food acids.

Fruit juices such as lemon, orange, grapefruit and apple contain acid. To a lesser extent, other drinks, both beverage and alcohol, contain acid. Many foods contain pickles and vinegar which involve acid. These acidic foods slowly attack the glaze surface and dissolve the soluble part of the lead content. A properly fused glaze presents an acid-proof surface so that in most cases the attack is infinitesimal. Underfired glazes would be slowly attacked, however, and the repeated use of the same vessel over a period of years could involve the user in a lead intake.

It must be remembered that lead is a cumulative poison slowly building up within the human system. There are many recorded cases of lead poisoning, where people have brewed and stored home-made drinks in lead-glazed vessels. With sensible foresight such cases should be rare but they are probably remembered and quoted with a justifiable sense of pride because of the excellent detective work involved that finally established the cause of illness.

Workers in industry are protected by Factory Acts. In Britain the final one forbidding the use of raw lead glazes came into effect in 1949. Similar restrictions on the use of raw lead in British schools etc were made by the Ministry of Education in 1955 with memorandum 517. The highest acceptable level of soluble lead in a glaze powder is 5% oxide content. All the lead oxides, lead carbonate and lead sulphide have solubility above 5%. Lead monosilicate also has too high a soluble lead content to be considered safe, but the other standard lead silicates (sesquisilicate and bisilicate) are considered low sol frits.

To protect the user of glazed pottery, British Standard Specification 4860, part 1 tableware, part 2 cooking ware, (1972) covers the testing of glazed ware and specifies limits for lead and cadmium released by the glazes from different types of vessels. The tests use a 4% solution of acetic acid. Similar specifications exist in British Commonwealth Countries, in some European countries and in the United States of America.

HISTORY OF LOW SOL. The investigation of lead poisoning and an attempt to discover ways of overcoming it were started in Britain in the late 19th century by Sir Thomas Thorpe. He concentrated upon the frits and glazes. See **Thorpe ratio**. Meanwhile, Sir Wilfred Garrett concentrated upon the hygienic conditions in the factories. On the European Continent, regulations sought to protect the user of the pottery rather than the potter and Dr J. Koerner investigated the possibilities of low solubility.

The three researches overlapped and much information was published which was successfully integrated in the work of John Mellor. The German attempt to protect the customer led to the use of lead frits which gave safer glazes even when underfired. This indirectly also protected the glazers. In Britian the development of safer glazes produced frits also. Better milling and storing of glazes cut down on lead dust.

Lead poisoning was a very worrying fact but the problem of producing lead-free glazes seemed insurmountable. The advantages of lead glazes were their viscosity during firing and their accommodating behaviour on finished ware, known as elasticity. Until the mid-1930's, all lead-free glazes tended to run immediately they had melted, and were prone to crazing. The general shine and finish was also unsatisfactory.

The system of double fritting was discovered before 1900 but it seems not to have been commercially viable until the 1920's. It involves the preparation of two frits: one a lead silicate and the other a boro-silicate. These are only brought together when mixed with the remainder of the glaze batch for use. In this way the lead frit can be separately controlled for solubility and a variety of glazes can be compounded from varying proportions of the two frits and other minerals like china clay and feldspar. This method is used in the production of commercial low sol glazes. To ensure further safety in the handling of the glaze or powder before firing, the lead frit is sometimes coated. The coating is an impervious acid-proof layer of silica and the process of coating was pioneered and developed by Podmore and Sons of Stoke-on-Trent, England.

General principles established during these years are still relevant:

1. The solubility of lead decreases with the increase in silica.

2. The solubility of lead decreases noticeably with the presence of alumina, titania, and calcia.

3. Small amounts of titania and alumina are used today to stabilize commercial lead frits.

4. The solubility of lead decreases slightly with the presence of baria, beryllia, zirconia and zinc oxide.

5. The solubility of lead increases with the presence of soda, potash, lithia and boric oxide.

Boric oxide and borax, which contains soda, were important fluxes and glass-formers in the development of lead-free glazes but their undesirable effect upon the solubility of lead in frits and glazes hindered the development of low sol glazes. The problem was solved by double fritting. See **Double fritting**.

LOW SOL FRITS. In the search for suitable lead frits it was found that lead bisilicate ($PbO.2SiO_2$) was the most immediately practical. Whilst lead orthosilicate, monosilicate and sesquisilicate had generally lower melting ranges and were therefore attractive propositions, their lead solubility was too high. Since that time the use of coated frits had enabled the solubility of the sesquisilicate to be lowered appreciably. Trisilicate ($PbO.3SiO_2$) and tetrasilicate ($PbO.4SiO_2$) were also investigated but were found too viscous to pour satisfactorily from the fritting crucible.

Modifications to the lead silicate pivoted round the introduction of alumina which dramatically reduced the lead solubility. It was even found that alumina assisted the melting of the frit. Further tests showed the existence of a eutectic in the region of $PbO.1.9SiO_2$ in which as much as 0.25 molecular equivalents of alumina could be dissolved without affecting the melting range of the frit and with less effect on the fluidity than could normally be expected. Today's lead bisilicates are mostly of this type. They are high in lead oxide content: nearly 65% PbO. They have a smooth melting range, due to the introduction of alumina, and the solubility of the lead content is extremely low. The alumina content is usually below 0.1 equivalents in order to keep viscosity to a minimum. It is also around this point that its optimum power is achieved in its effects upon solubility.

The number of possible lead frits is legion. To simplify the field, the frit manufacturers have concentrated upon the production of a few standard frits. This has been necessary with the building of continuous fritting plants. Lead bisilicate was an obvious choice because there is only a limited application for the use of softer frits, i.e. in the production of special colours. The frits chosen approximate closely to the whole number formulae. They are lead bisilicate ($PbO.2SiO_2$), lead monosilicate ($PbO.SiO_2$) and lead sesquisilicate ($2PbO.3SiO_2$). Trade specifications for these frits are established to indicate the limits of composition, grain size and solubility. Stabilizers are used in the form of alumina and titania, and many frits are silica-coated. However lead monosilicate is rarely considered a low sol frit although some approximations to this formula have solubility below 5%.

The use of low sol frits and glazes, and the controlled manufacture of them has completely irradicated the incidence of lead poisoning in potteries and glaze works. The amount of research involved has also resulted in better glazes. Fritted lead glazes are easier to suspend as slops. In firing they contain less volatile matter and the fritted lead itself is less volatile than raw lead. The glazes mature more uniformly and quicker than raw glazes yet can have wider acceptable ranges. Lastly the crazing characteristic of low sol glazes can be more accurately controlled.

Low-temperature glaze. One which matures in the range up to 1050°C (1922°F). Low-temperature glazes make use of the soft fluxes: lead oxide, boric oxide, soda and potash. With the exception of raw lead glazes it is necessary to employ frits in low-temperature glazes because the fluxing oxides are soluble in water.

Lustres. Metallic surfaces on glazes. The pure metal is deposited on the glaze surface by many different methods but all involve reduction from an oxide or a resinate to the pure metal. The metals used are gold, silver, platinum, copper, bismuth and tin.

The precious metals, gold, silver and platinum are easily reduced. The metal is dissolved in hydro-chloric acid to produce a chloride. The chloride is added to sodium resinate to produce a precipitate which is suspended in oil. The oil medium carries the metal for ease of application. This and the resin burn out in the firing and provide the necessary reduction. An extremely thin layer of metal is thereby deposited on the glaze. The metal does not readily oxidize. Silver sometimes tarnishes and is polished. Commercially prepared lustres are of this type.

Copper gives a deep golden lustre varying to a rich red. The Hispano-Moresque lustres were copper lustres often with some silver. The rich lustre was often mistaken for gold. It was achieved by transferring col-loidal copper from a refractory coating to the glaze surface during a special low-temperature reduction firing. See **Transmutation lustre**.

A copper compound can also be introduced into the glaze mixture or applied to the unfired surface. In both cases the lustre would be called an in-glaze lustre as opposed to the surface lustre of the transmutation method. See **Copper lustre** and **Ruby lustre**.

The photograph is a large bowl by Alan Caiger Smith. It was painted with copper carbonate pigment on the unfired glaze surface. The decoration was there-fore shades of green after its glaze firing but became red to metallic lustre after a special reduction firing to 660°C (1220°F). The detail is of another similar decoration.

All lustres involving copper require reduction. This is usually done with carbon monoxide and the starting

compounds are copper oxide and copper carbonate:

$$CuO + CO \longrightarrow Cu + CO_2 \uparrow$$
$$CuCO_3 + CO \longrightarrow Cu + 2CO_2 \uparrow$$

Some other compounds, e.g. sulphide, require some partial oxidation first before a full reduction can take place.

Bismuth lustre is prepared as a resinate. The bis-muth gives a mother of pearl effect with rainbow iridescence. It is often used as a basis for coloured lustres, the colourings being given by other metals.

Tin lustre is produced in raku. See **Tin lustre**.

Lute. To join together two pieces of clay in leatherhard condition by wetting the seam. The theory is that the two pieces are softened to plastic or softer state so that they produce one piece when brought together with suitable pressure. Slip or slurry is used for fine clays but coarse clays are often more effectively softened with water.

M

Mafic minerals. Ferromagnesian minerals. A complex group of silicates in which iron, magnesium and calcium play important parts. They are mostly dark in colour and alkaline in character. They can sometimes be isolated when they occur as fibrous stars of crystals in small pockets, but mostly they occur as small indistinguishable crystals within basic igneous rocks, e.g. basalt. The remainder of the rock will be a feldspar. Apart from the fibrous pockets they are difficult to grind. Some melt to a black glass at 1250°C (2282°F) but the colour is strong and to make a practical glaze more feldspar and free silica is required. Mafic minerals are sub-divided into: pyroxenes, amphiboles, micas and olivine. A few are marketed in powder form as feldspar variants. See also **Basalt.**

Magnesia. Magnesium oxide. MgO. A constituent of bodies and glazes. At low temperatures it acts as a catalyst in bodies and as an opacifier in glazes. At high temperatures it acts as a flux giving viscous melts which as glazes are opaque and matt. Its action is similar to those of calcia, baria, zinc oxide and strontia but it is not interchangeable for any one of them. For example it gives unique and interesting mauve colours with cobalt oxide.

Magnesia's fluxing action begins at 1170°C (2138°F) from which temperature it is active for all temperatures upwards: it does not volatilize. Prior to 1170°C it is a refractory anti-flux and can be used as an opacifier in earthenware glazes. Its melting point alone is 2800°C (5072°F). However in the presence of other fusions created by soda and potash it can be encouraged at least to enter the fusions although it takes no active part. A small amount will dissolve but most will remain as suspended white refractory particles. See **Magnesian matts.**

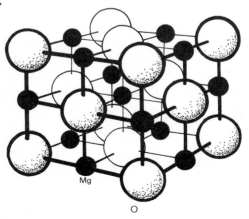

The effect of magnesia as a flux is often most marked in the period from 1190°C to 1230°C (2174°F to 2246°F). When magnesia is included in a glaze as an auxiliary flux it often produces a late fluidity which gives flecks of movement. This is similar to the hare's fur effects. The late fusion is also valuable in producing a mottled and oil-spot effect. In this case the magnesia is included in an underlayer of glaze. The upper layer of glaze fuses first and seals the surface. The under layer begins to melt and boil at a later stage which erupts the lower colouring into the upper surface. The upper layer must be a fluid glaze which quickly heals over.

In stoneware glazes therefore, a small amount of magnesia can be a great help. By virtue of interaction it brings increased fluidity in the later stages of firing but it always brings an increase in surface tension.

The surface tension, however, gives excellent rounded edges to glazes covering modelled surfaces and the finished glaze has a fatty or buttery appearance. It is also valuable in creating a lizard skin effect. Here the tendency to crawl created by the surface tension is used to create pieces of isolated glaze which float in another more fluid glaze.

As a flux alone, magnesia gives viscous melts of high surface tension. These are rarely satisfactory glazes but when magnesia is an auxiliary flux of not more than 0·25 molecular equivalents, it can give a startling amount of increased fluidity. It is also used in very small amounts as an anti-craze. It is substituted for calcia, baria and zinc oxide. See **Glaze fit.**

The surface tension is less noticeable in glazes fired in reduction atmospheres. Reduction also encourages more iron oxide from the body to enter the glaze. The iron oxide stain is a pleasant dark grey and occurs decoratively on edges of throwing rings, handles and modelling. A slightly thinner glaze for oxidized firings will allow the body colouring to burn through and will also overcome some of the problems associated with the high surface tension.

Magnesia is slowly soluble in water forming the slaked hydroxide ($Mg(OH)_2$). It is therefore introduced into glazes by magnesium carbonate ($MgCO_3$) which is less soluble and by dolomite ($CaCO_3.MgCO_3$) and talc ($3MgO.4SiO_2.H_2O$) which are insoluble.

Magnesium is a lightweight metal used in alloys. It is essential to life and its compounds occur in plant growth and are used in medicines. It is a common element occurring in many compounds from which it is extracted, e.g. carnallite ($KCl.MgCl_2.6H_2O$), magnesite ($MgCO_3$), dolomite ($MgCO_3.CaCO_3$) and sea water. It also forms the silicates talc ($3MgO.4SiO_2.H_2O$), serpentine ($3MgO.2SiO_2.2H_2O$), meerschaum ($2MgO.3SiO_2.2H_2O$), olivine ($MgFeO_2.SiO_2$) and asbestos ($3MgO.CaO.4SiO_2$).

Magnesia is introduced into earthenware bodies as a so-called secondary flux. The term flux is here misleading because the desired action is that of a catalyst. At temperatures over 1000°C (1832°F) it assists the conversion of silica from its quartz phase to its cristobalite phase without becoming involved in fusion: the silica remains free and micro-crystalline. It is therefore an effective measure against crazing of the glaze on earthenware and was discovered empirically long before its scientific signification was explained. The magnesia is introduced by talc (magnesium silicate) which is insoluble.

Magnesia is introduced into stoneware bodies to provide a viscous flux. The desired action here is the involvement of free silica in a stiff liquid phase to decrease the amount of crystalline silica, both quartz and cristobalite. Magnesia has a low rate of thermal expansion and by using it to change silica to the non-crystalline phase, bodies can be created which have high resistance to thermal shock. See **Talc.**

Magnesian matts. Matt glazes created by surfeits of magnesia. These glazes are of two types: low temperature and high temperature.

The low-temperature matts employ magnesia as an opacifier and surface modifier. The magnesia is usually introduced as magnesium carbonate in amounts up to 15% of the glaze. This is extra to the normal fluxes. The magnesium carbonate decomposes upon heating to become the highly-refractory magnesia. Some of the magnesia is dissolved by the action of the melt but most of it remains in suspension. The result is a white, opaque and matt glaze, but it is often discoloured and is not as dependable as glazes produced with tin, titanium and zirconium oxides.

The high-temperature matts employ magnesia as a flux, opacifier and surface modifier. More magnesia is present than is necessary for a full fluxing of the silica. Exact amounts can only be established by line blends and will lie between 20% and 30% magnesium carbonate in the batch recipe. The excess, in becoming involved in the molten glaze, creates simple silicates with low amounts of silica. Because there is an excess of alkaline oxides, there is likely to be only from one to three molecules of silica per unit of alkali. Half of these will be involved in the alumino-silicate melt and remain as liquid phase but the simple silicates readily crystallize upon cooling to give opacity and a matt surface. The magnesium silicate crystals, which are of enstatite ($MgO.SiO_2$), possibly stretching to $MgO.2SiO_2$, are often assisted by calcium silicate crystals of wollastonite ($CaO.SiO_2$). There may also be some compounded diopside ($CaO.MgO.2SiO_2$) and isolated alumina (Al_2O_3). See **Enstatite.**

High-temperature magnesian matts are related to alumina matts, lime matts and dolomite glazes. They are capable of giving some interesting colour responses with cobalt and manganese oxides.

Magnesite. $MgCO_3$. A stone, similar to limestone, which is a source of magnesia for glazes. See **Magnesium carbonate.**

Magnesium carbonate. Magnesite. $MgCO_3$. Crushed-ore source of magnesia for glazes. It is obtained from the mineral magnesite and some is prepared by precipitation although the light basic carbonate, described later, is easier to prepare.

The carbonate decomposes at 350°C (662°F) to provide magnesia and carbon dioxide.

$$MgCO_3 \xrightarrow{350°C} MgO + CO_2\uparrow$$

The magnesia is highly refractory and is an opacifier in glazes up to 1170°C (2138°F) when it becomes an active flux. It is then involved in creating silicates which if sufficiently simple will crystallize out upon cooling to give a matt opacity. See **Magnesian matts.**

Light magnesium carbonate or magnesia alba is the basic carbonate ($3MgCO_3.Mg(OH)_2.3H_2O$). It is slowly soluble in water if there is acid content with which to react. Otherwise it is less soluble than the pure carbonate. It is more convenient than the heavier pure carbonate in that it also mixes better in the glaze slop.

Magnesium carbonate is less soluble than magnesia but it must be accepted as slightly soluble. For this reason it cannot be used in clays as a catalyst because it upsets workability. Talc is used instead for this purpose.

The following glaze recipe for a magnesian matt at 1250°C (2282°F) uses light magnesium carbonate. It is typical of the type of glaze that cannot be stored because of the solubility of the magnesium carbonate and the high clay content. The high clay content makes the glaze behave as a slip so that it can be so used on raw clay. Alternatively it gives high pre-fire contraction so that it can be used over shiny dark glazes to give lizard skin effects.

Siliceous ball clay	50
Feldspar	15
Whiting	25
Light magnesium carbonate	10

Magnesium sulphate. $MgSO_4$. Is used in its hydrated form as a glaze flocculant. It is also a stoneware glaze flux. It occurs in many clays and is one source of the annoying scums which occur on unglazed red-burning clays.

Magnesium sulphate occurs naturally in the hydrated form from $MgSO_4.H_2O$ (kieserite) to the more common heptahydrate $MgSO_4.7H_2O$ called epsomite (epsom salts). The chief deposits are in Germany and the United States.

Magnesium sulphate is soluble. In solution with water it creates an acidic (sulphuric acid) reaction with electrolytes. One per cent of a recipe is usually ample magnesium sulphate to keep a glaze flocculated. It is thus used as a substitute for calcium chloride. The effect of the magnesia or magnesium sulphate is unlikely to be seen in the finished glaze because the magnesia content of the fully hydrated sulphate is only 16%.

Sometimes up to 5% of magnesium sulphate is added to an already prepared glaze slop. In this case the effect is that of extreme flocculation, whereby the clay particles in the glaze slop refuse to lie near to one another. Instead they will only rest at angles. The two extremes, deflocculation and flocculation, are shown diagrammatically in figs. 1 and 2. The result is a stiff or thick glaze slop because the clay particles produce a bulky structure with a high degree of internal friction.

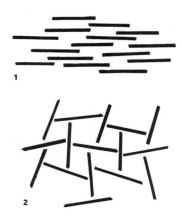

This thickening of the glaze slop is useful when the biscuit has been overfired or one wishes to reglaze previously fired ware. The amount added is usually judged as a couple of teaspoonsful dissolved in warm water and added to the slop until the desired effect is obtained. The amount of magnesia introduced may have a small effect upon the finished glaze. Other rule of thumb methods use calcium sulphate (plaster of Paris), vinegar and gelatine. See also **Flocculation.**

In glaze or body, the magnesium sulphate begins to decompose at 150°C (302°F) when all but one molecular equivalent of water escapes. The remaining water is driven off at approximately 210°C (410°F) to leave the anhydrous magnesium sulphate:

$$MgSO_4 . 7H_2O \xrightarrow{150°C} MgSO_4 . H_2O + 6H_2O\uparrow$$

$$MgSO_4 . H_2O \xrightarrow{210°C} MgSO_4 + H_2O\uparrow$$

In bodies and glazes fired below 1150°C (2102°F) the magnesium sulphate will act as an anti-flux. In glazes it may cause a discolouration resembling smudged pencil marks. Above 1150°C (2102°F) the magnesium sulphate melts and becomes a flux. In both bodies and glazes, amounts greater than 3% of the batch may cause blistering. To overcome these dis-

advantages it is necessary to decompose the sulphate and obtain thereby the oxide form called magnesia. The sulphate is very stable and will not decompose by heat alone but requires an agent. Agents occur in vitreous bodies and molten glazes above 1150°C (2102°F) but here the decomposition causes blistering with the escaping sulphurous gases. Paradoxically the oxidizing process can be achieved in two stages of which the first is reduction. Reduction in the 500°C to 800°C range (932°F to 1472°F) deprives the stable sulphate of its oxygen, leaving it in an unstable state. The unstable state is then oxidized and liberates the sulphur as sulphur trioxide. The equations are:

$$MgSO_4 + 2CO$$
stable   carbon
sulphate   monoxide

$$\xrightarrow{500° \text{ to } 800°C} MgSO_2 + 2CO_2\uparrow$$
unstable   carbon
metasulphate   dioxide gas

$$MgSO_2 + O_2$$
unstable   oxygen
metasulphate

$$\xrightarrow{800°-1000°C} MgO + SO_3\uparrow$$
stable   sulphur
oxide   trioxide gas

Magnesium compounds are present in many clays, especially those originating as marine deposits or associated with salt water or marine rocks like limestones. Clays with magnesium sulphate are often red-burning clays which contain iron oxide. They originally contained iron pyrites which, by weathering, was able to give a sulphate radical to the magnesium and calcium compounds, or exchange it for their carbonate radicals. The sulphur is thus still present in the clay in soluble sulphates. These migrate to the surface of the clay to form crystals as the clay dries. The crystals form a whitish scum which shows as white edges or fingermarks on the fired ware if it is unglazed. See **Scum.**

Magnetite. Loadstone. Lodestone. Magnetic ore. Natural ferroso-ferric oxide (Fe_3O_4). It is a heavy black ore and one of the few that respond to a magnet. It is in crystal or micro-crystalline form and difficult to grind. Hardness on Mohs' Scale: 6. It probably originated as limonite from a bog ore as a laterite. With pressure and/or heat it became metamorphosed and was able to crystallize. It is found in metamorphic and igneous rocks.

Magnetite is an excellent ceramic colourant. Ground magnetite tends to be in large particles when compared with limonite. It therefore produces a speckled effect in bodies and glazes. It is sold under various names such as black magnetic oxide, magnetic iron oxide etc. See **Iron oxide, types of.**

Maiolica. Decorated tin-glazed earthenware. Maiolica is traditionally soft-fired with a lead glaze made opaque by tin oxide.

The low temperature, originally dictated by the type of clay and some of the colours used, was responsible for a delicate suffusion of colours which allowed strong colours to be used in a sensitive way.

Maiolicas originated in the Mediterranean where the warmer and drier climate made it possible to accept the porous body as practical. Good maiolica, wherever made, retains this freedom of the Mediterranean with its combination of richness and sensitivity, even though it may need to be harder fired to be accepted as a practical ware. The mug and wall figures by Adas Dworski, a Yugoslav living in Wales, exhibit these qualities.

HISTORY OF MAIOLICA. Tin-glazed wares had been made in many places around the Mediterranean long before the potters on the island of Maiorca (Mallorca) established a good trade in tiles and vases. Tin glazes were probably indigenous to Italy and Spain as a development from the lead glazes, but the Moorish conquest of Spain in the 8th century gave a boost to decoration. Lustred ware was introduced as a means of producing an alternative to precious metalware. See **Hispano-Moresque**. In the 15th century Italy imported Spanish pottery and especially the work from Maiorca. The name maiolica was given to these wares

and at first referred only to the lustred ware but later embraced all tin-glazed wares. It is in this broad sense that we use the term now.

It is interesting to note that exports from Italy tended to be called faience after Faenza. Later, when Italian potters established tin-glazed production in Delft in the mid-16th century, the exports were called delft. The methods employed were similar throughout but the feeling for colour and decorative rhythms of the Spanish wares were changed in Italy and the rest of Europe. The Classical Renaissance and Chinese influences led potters away from the Hispano-Moresque expression which had successfully blended mideastern decoration with gothic.

The large plates and vases made in Spain retained the freedom of the production pieces in their decoration. The brushstrokes themselves had decorative meaning irrespective of what they portrayed. In Italy the technique was subordinated to the subject depicted as the decorative method of Spain met the visual narrative of the Renaissance. The first fusions of these ideas were responsible for some fine productions of which the lustred work from Deruta in the early 16th century is the best. A large Deruta blue and gold plate is illustrated.

The over-emphasis on pictorial representation and the use of crude colour resulted in a loss of the decorative balance of the earlier wares. Only in the smaller and humbler productions did a sensitivity continue as with the small flask which is illustrated. This sensitivity fortunately continued and was extended into Europe and can be seen in the galleyware of Britain. See **Lambeth.**

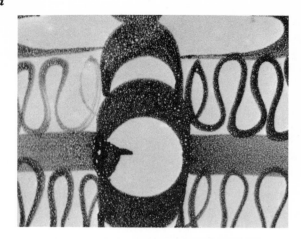

MAIOLICA METHODS. The maiolica method is open to many variations since its essential element is simply that colouring oxides are used to stain a glaze made white by tin oxide. The traditional method originated by Islamic potters and developed in the Mediterranean countries uses a malm-type clay which is thrown, hand-built and moulded. The ware is given a soft biscuit firing to enable the friable tin-opacified glaze to adhere. The unfired glaze surface is painted with metal oxides which sink into and stain the glaze during firing and produce an inglaze decoration. A subsequent lustre firing may be used. The temperatures involved approximate 900°C, 1000°C and 700°C (1652°F, 1832°F and 1292°F).

Variations have involved the use of red-burning clays which encourage the integration of iron from the body into the glaze on edges like rims and throwing rings; the use of slips and colours painted underneath the glaze; the use of extra transparent glazes sometimes fired with the tin glaze and sometimes fired subsequently along with some softer enamel-type colours; and the use of higher temperatures to give a stronger finished ware.

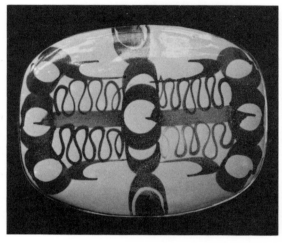

The historical maiolica, delft and galleyware used a clay of the true marl or malm type. These calcareous clays have a high coefficient of expansion and hence contraction upon cooling from 500°C (932°F) when the glaze has set. They therefore exert a squeeze on the glaze putting it into compression. Later expansion of the body with moisture takes up this compression with little or no crazing of the glaze. Some crazing of functional ware seems inevitable but it need not be excessive or disastrous.

Other clays do not possess this quality but a substitute body can be prepared from ball, china and red clays with some cristobalite to give the necessary compression.

The pleasant salmon pink colour of the maiolica body allows a glaze to be used which is not completely opaque. Not more than 10% of tin oxide, and often as little as 5%, is needed to opacify the glaze sufficiently to give a white. The pinkish body is just visible through this glaze which gives the quality of depth and allows the full suffusion of the glaze to be appreciated. In spite of the low tin oxide content, the surface of a maiolica glaze has often a slightly matt appearance which successfully emphasizes the essential two-dimensional aspect and integrates the minute texturings which occur at the surface as in a pointillist technique. See

photograph, which is a detail of the plate by Alan Caiger Smith also illustrated.

Lead oxide is necessary in the glaze to impart the gentle shine and to absorb the colour. Without lead oxide a harsh edge is given to the brushwork which does not suit the feeling of maiolica. Both lead and tin give elasticity to the glaze which helps the fit. A typical glaze recipe is:

lead bisilicate	70
china clay	20
tin oxide	10

With any maiolica glaze, the addition of potash by way of feldspar and boric oxide by way of a frit will help to spread the tin uniformly and produce a smoother white if the granular quality is not required. Small amounts (up to 5%) of zinc oxide and calcia, although not acting as strong fluxes alone at this range, are induced by the main flux to combine with the tin oxide. They help with the opacity and produce a more stable complex silicate, but zinc especially may modify the colours. Zirconia also helps opacity and in small amounts may even help to give a more brilliant shine.

Today many prepared colours are available which were not available to the early maiolica potters. Earlier potters often prepared their own which included a lead antimonate yellow and a manganese purple which were limited in their temperature ranges. Today's prepared colours have a wider range and are often extremely stable, which precludes the softening effect of suffusion and tempts the potter to use higher temperatures which also inhibit the delicate quality of the soft glaze.

Majolica. English majolica. A late 19th-century ware with shiny colourful glazes. It was produced as a contrast to the drabber wares of the earlier period. It is not to be confused with tin-glazed maiolica. The majolica body was cane clay which fired to a light straw colour. The ware was richly modelled to provide many highlights which showed the shiny glazes to advantage and with many pockets to collect the glazes.

Malachite. Copper carbonate ore. $CuCO_3 . Cu(OH)_2$. A weathered ore of copper which is easily identified by its bright emerald green colour. Small pieces up to half an inch across can often be found on the wash-out tips of old copper, zinc and lead mines. The pieces are easily crushed for use as glaze colourant or brushwork pigment. See **Copper ores.**

Malm. True marl. A clay of fairly recent geological deposition containing a high proportion of calcium compounds. These compounds are calcium sulphate and calcium carbonate, usually referred to as chalk. These could account for as much as 30% of the dry clay. See **Marl.**

Malms usually contain impurities of iron as carbonate, sulphate and sulphide. The iron is bleached by the calcium compounds so that the fired colour is often a yellowish buff. The raw colour can be ochre, brown, green or grey.

Well-weathered malms are plastic and have usually lost the more soluble sulphates. They are used as potting clays for the soft-fired earthenwares like maiolica. The calcium compounds give no fluxing action at the lower temperatures but give valuable anti-craze properties. Malms fired over 1100°C (2012°F) deform quickly and melt to a glass by 1250°C (2282°F). See **Calcia.**

The low plasticity malms are used for brickmaking.

Manganese carbonate. $MnCO_3$. The carbonate source of manganese oxides for bodies and glazes. It

occurs as the pink-coloured ore rhodochrosite. It decomposes upon heating to form manganous oxide (MnO) and carbon dioxide (CO_2). The manganous oxide immediately takes up free oxygen to become the dioxide (MnO_2). There is some advantage in using manganese carbonate for low-temperature glazes. It is bulkier for its staining power than manganese dioxide and therefore gives a more uniform spread of colour if this is required.

Manganese dioxide. Manganese (IV) oxide. MnO_2. A metal oxide used as a colourant for bodies and glazes. It is black and gives blacks, browns and purples. It sometimes occurs in clays but usually it is introduced as a black powder. Amounts up to 10% give brown slips. More than 15% fluxes stoneware slips sufficiently for them to be called vitrifying slips and slip glazes. Amounts up to 4% are readily dissolved in glazes. More than this is partially precipitated as a crystalline surface. Over 20% gives metallic surfaces. Manganese occurs with iron in many ores and is therefore a common constituent of early slips and glazes, e.g. European slipware and Eastern tenmoku. Manganese dioxide is responsible for the fernlike stains in moss agate. A similar effect in pottery is created in slip with tobacco and manganese dioxide. See **Mocha ware.**

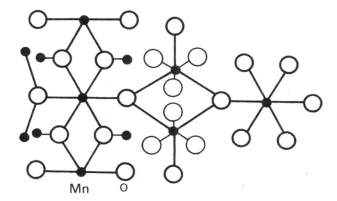

Mn   O

Manganese dioxide occurs in nature as the ore pyrolusite (MnO_2). This is the main source of the metal manganese which is used in the alloy ferromanganese, itself an additive to steel. Other manganese ores are: braunite, hausmannite, manganite, polianite, psilomelane, rhodochrosite, rhodonite, wad. The manganese ores originated in a similar way to iron ores and are often associated with them. The element manganese is a constituent of many igneous rocks. When these weather to clay, some of the manganese oxides are involved in the residual clays whilst manganese salts are carried away by water. The manganese in solution is precipitated as bog manganese, some of which is integrated with sandstones whilst some is metamorphosed into concentrated ores. The chief ore deposits are in west Africa, Cuba, Brazil, USSR and India. Manganese is often present in the ores of other metals where it partially replaces iron, aluminium, calcium, barium and magnesium. Manganese dioxide is also used in the manufacture of disinfectants, dry batteries and paint.

Manganese dioxide is an interesting oxide in its behaviour. It is introduced into bodies and glazes as the black powder MnO_2. In this form it is insoluble in water. In a ceramic fusion below 1080°C (1976°F), it is soluble in the alkaline content and as such behaves as an anti-flux or acid with some retarding effect upon the fusion. In this temperature range it gives a dry-looking black colour to bodies (5 to 10%) and purplish plum colours to transparent and semi-transparent glazes (up to 4%).

Manganese dioxide gives interesting coffee colours with tin oxide. Coarse manganese dioxide will give speckled effects in low-temperature glazes but above 1150°C (2102°F) the effect tends to be uniformly dispersed. The following glaze uses iron oxide to give a background beige against which the manganese dioxide gives an excellent coffee-coloured speckle at 1040°C (1904°F).

feldspar	10
china clay	5
900°C borax frit	65
tin oxide	10
red iron oxide	5
manganese dioxide	5 (unsieved)

A similar colour is obtainable at higher temperatures but the speckle is difficult to maintain. Where the manganese is dissolving too much it can be put unsieved into an engobe which is brushed onto the body. The speckle will burn through the glaze.

Above 1080°C (1976°F) the manganese dioxide liberates half its oxygen and becomes manganous oxide (MnO) as shown in the drawing. The change is inevitable and requires no effort at reduction on the potter's part. Manganous oxide is a green colour but this colour is never seen because immediately the oxide is formed it is involved in fusion with silica. Manganous

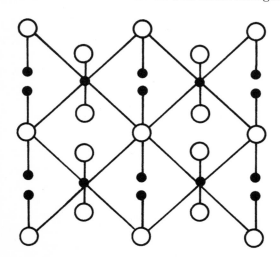

oxide, like other monoxides, is an active flux. The manganese dioxide's ceramic role is changed from that of an anti-flux to one of a flux by raising the temperature above 1080°C (1976°F). In combination with silica the manganous oxide gives violet colours. Amethyst is silica stained with manganous oxide. When alumina is also present the colour tends towards a brown. The brown is a bluish or purplish brown and pleasantly different from the brown obtained with iron oxide. Glazes high in alkali and low in alumina can be given a beautiful violet colour by 1% to 3% of manganese dioxide. The colour can be intensified by a very small amount of cobalt oxide (less than 0·5%).

Manganese dioxide was an important colourant in the Rockingham brown wares. With iron oxide in a transparent lead glaze it gives deep rich browns which have some crystalline striations and a reddish colour when seen in sunlight. The following recipe is for a Rockingham-type glaze which has all the qualities of the best Rockingham on buff and red clays at 1120°C (2048°F):

feldspar	28
china clay	14
flint	4
lead bisilicate	40
whiting	4
red iron oxide	3
manganese dioxide	7

The liberation of oxygen at 1080°C (1976°F) can cause trouble in glazes which are matured at this temperature. It will be noticed that the examples given avoid this temperature. The use of slips presents even more of a problem because the oxygen must travel the whole thickness of the glaze to escape. If one is firing to 1100°C (2012°F) with a glaze covering a slip containing manganese dioxide, one can expect oxygen bubbles in the glaze over the slip and they might spoil the glaze surface also. To avoid this one must fire lower than 1080°C (1976°F), or approximately 1110°C or 1120°C (2030°F or 2048°F) with slow maturing at the end, or use a different colouring in the slip. With the first alternative, the colour will never achieve the rich blacks possible with the higher temperature but some soft purplish greys are obtainable.

It is impractical to start with manganous oxide instead of the dioxide. Although stable enough to exist at room temperature, the manganous oxide will take up oxygen from the air in the early stages of warming up for the firing.

Alone, the manganous oxide is refractory but it melts easily with body interaction above 1150°C (2102°F). Manganese dioxide painted onto the body and fired unglazed produces its own glossy surface. A thick layer of manganese dioxide produces a fused black matt surface with very thick parts showing a coppery bronze colour which can be polished like a lustre. Therefore for firings above 1150°C (2102°F)

The crystalline striations as mentioned in this example and in the Rockingham-type glaze vary in crystal size according to glaze composition, rate of cooling and amount of oxide. The usual is a distinct grouping of crystals in the line of gravity. There also occurs a smokey lustrous surface of crystals, when the amount precipitated is very small in a glaze which is of the fully-matured transparent type, and a speckled metallic surface like a fine oil spot. All these effects are available at all temperatures.

Manganite. MnO(OH). A manganese ore and one of the sources of manganese dioxide.

Manganous oxide. Manganese monoxide. Manganese (II) oxide. MnO. The oxide of manganese which is stable above 1080°C (1976°F) and enters ceramic fusions as a flux and colourant.

Manganous oxide becomes manganese dioxide at temperatures below 1080°C by collecting oxygen from the atmosphere. It is therefore necessary to work with manganese dioxide as the raw material in glaze recipes etc and allow for the fact that the dioxide liberates oxygen to become the monoxide when the kiln reaches 1080°C. The change is inevitable and requires no effort at reduction on the potter's part.

one can use manganese dioxide as part of a slip or glaze up to 100%. The photographs show a bowl by Lucie Rie. The detail shows how manganese dioxide produces a thick lustrous metallic surface. In other words, whatever the amount it can produce satisfactory results. It can, of course, produce over-fluxed results that run down the pot. Slips containing over 15% manganese dioxide are often fused like glazes and can be used as once-fired slip glazes.

Manganous oxide is unaffected by reduction and does not assist iron and copper to give good colours in reduction. It is better to keep it for oxidized wares and it is at its best in slips and glazes for 1200°C (2192°F) and above. Here it does for oxidized glazes what iron oxide does for reduced and neutralized glazes: it gives pleasing and sometimes surprising results in most circumstances. Like iron oxide, it dissolves in stoneware glazes and more is able to dissolve when hot than cold. Therefore the difference is precipitated as crystals on the surface of the glaze during cooling. The amount which completely dissolves in stoneware glazes approximates 4%. The following recipe for 1200°C (2192°F) gives a good crystalline precipitation from the further 2% with the iron oxide:

mixed feldspar	46
china clay	14
flint	14
whiting	16
red iron oxide	4
manganese dioxide	6

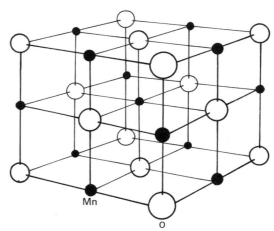

Thus bodies and glazes containing manganese oxides and ores tend to contain the dioxide if fired below 1080°C and if fired above 1080°C can only contain the monoxide. If the monoxide is required in a ceramic fusion below 1080°C it must be introduced already combined in some form of silicate or frit.

Manx stone. See **Cornish stone.**

Marble. $CaCO_3$. A metamorphosed limestone of fine texture. It is extremely hard but its dust could be used in glazes as a source of calcia. See **Limestone.**

Marbled ware. A marble is a variegated stain. It is achieved by partially blending two clays. Usually the clays are cream- and red-burning, and covered with a

transparent glaze which heightens the colour contrast.

The clays must be tempered with openers to make their shrinkages alike during drying and firing. They are blended by kneading or cutting and joining. The blend is usually thrown and later turned to take off the blurred surface and reveal the pattern in clean contrast.

Marbled ware was popular in the 18th century and a piece is shown under the heading of **Puzzle jug**. The illustration here shows the inside of a bowl by Derek Emms.

Marcasite. White iron pyrites. Ferric sulphide. FeS_2. An iron ore which is similar to iron pyrites but light in colour. It sometimes occurs in marls. It can be crushed after controlled 'weathering', when it has partially 'oxidized' to ferrous sulphate ($FeSO_4 . 7H_2O$). Its sulphur content still presents a hazard to its use as a colourant because the sulphur is slow to burn away during firing but some soft yellow colours can be produced in solution with lead glazes.

Marl. Specifically a natural clay containing iron oxide and a high proportion of calcium compounds. Marls are used as potting clays for low-fired earthenware and as brick clays. The high proportion of calcium compounds, often called chalk, make marls friable when dry. Other friable clays have come to be called marls although they contain no chalk, e.g. the Old Red Sandstone marls. Following this practice some plastic red clays having nothing to do with chalk or friability were also called marls, e.g. Etruria Marl in Stoke-on-Trent, England. The term marl is therefore a general one for iron-stained earthenware clays. To specify the original true marls the old name of malm is used.

Ignoring the Old Red Sandstone marls and the marls associated with Carboniferous strata like the Etruria marls, one can consider the true marls as a group of clays having similar properties. They were deposited during different geological periods and under different circumstances over about 150 million years but they all contain soluble salts and are asso-

ciated with calcium compounds. The marls used by British potters include the Keuper and Tea marls of the Triassic Period; the Oxford and Kimmeridge clays of the Jurassic System; and the Gault and Weald clays of the Cretaceous System.

The iron content is partially bleached by the calcia and often remains so during firing. Marls therefore fire to attractive ochres, buffs and pinks which are suitable backgrounds for tin glazes. The marls were used by the delftware potters.

Marls are used on a large scale for making general building bricks. They are not suitable for engineering bricks because they vitrify too quickly to be fired economically. For the same reason they cannot be used for stoneware. Instead they are used for earthenware where the high calcia content is an advantage.

For use as potting clays, the marls are weathered and changed from the short crumbly state to a practical plastic state. This weathering can be accentuated by thorough blunging and the removal of the water which contains the soluble salts. Even so, some of the calcareous compounds remain. Calcium carbonate will not be washed away and some marls contain as much as 30% calcium carbonate. This and other impurities act as fluxes above 1100°C (2012°F) which is why marls cannot be used as bodies at these temperatures: they quickly vitrify and deform. At temperatures around 1050°C (1922°F) the calcia is only partially involved in the fusion and gives to the body a high rate of contraction upon cooling. See **Calcia**. This is not the same as a high shrinkage rate during firing. The high contraction rate puts a compression on the glaze and therefore gives some insurance against crazing. See **Glaze fit**.

Martin brothers. The four Martin brothers, Wallace, Walter, Edwin and Charles were pioneers of the artist-potter movement in Britain. From 1873 to 1912 they produced salt-glazed stoneware in London and Southall, making full use of applied decoration and colouring oxides in combination with mottled glazes. Their production included architectural plaques, decorative vases and grotesque animals and birds. Their work is referred to as Martinique ware.

Massicot. Masticote. PbO. Yellow lead oxide. See **Litharge**.

Matting agents. Materials which are added to glazes to give a matt surface. Of the simple oxides the acidic ones are the easiest to control but they do raise the maturing range of the glaze. The alkaline oxides which are capable of creating matt effects have the opposite effect if present in too small an amount. To overcome these difficulties combinations are created and commercially marketed. Examples of the three types are given. Details will be found indexed under the oxide concerned. See also **Crystalline glazes**.

The acidic oxides which give matt results are:

titanium dioxide, up to 25%
rutile, up to 25% gives buff colour
tin oxide, 15 to 25%

Also included here because of their anti-flux properties:

alumina, 15 to 25%
red iron oxide, 8 to 25% gives dark brown

It is difficult to give precise amounts for alkaline oxides. The type and composition of the glaze is an important factor. The best amount can be established by a line blend by arranging the test amounts between 10% and 45%. The alkaline oxides which encourage matt crystallization are:

magnesia introduced by magnesium carbonate, talc
    or dolomite
calcia introduced by whiting
zinc oxide
baria introduced by barium carbonate
manganous oxide introduced by manganese dioxide
strontia introduced by strontium carbonate

Combined agents are made from the following recipes:

1.   china clay   50
            zinc oxide   50

The mixture is calcined between 600°C and 800°C (1112°F and 1472°F) and reground. The powder is added to glazes in amounts up to 30%.

2.   titanium dioxide 30
            tin oxide   30
            zinc oxide   30
            whiting   10

The minerals are mixed together and added to the glazes in amounts between 10% and 25%.

3.   titanium dioxide 40–30
            zinc oxide   30–40
            whiting   30

The minerals are mixed together and added to glazes in amounts up to 30%.

Maturing. Developing and improving. Clays are said to mature if they are stored in wet plastic condition. See **Ageing.** Glaze slops are usually allowed to stand for 24 hours after preparation. This is maturing. It encourages a full wetting of the materials. It is similar to the maturation of clays and, of course, often involves some clay.

Molten glazes are said to mature in the final stages of firing. This is usually considered as a length of time at one temperature. In contrast is the maturation of the body which takes place over a time and temperature range called the maturing range. See also **Glaze, chemistry** and **Grain size.**

Maturing range. The part of a firing, usually considered as between two temperatures, where the body reaches its correct strength and compactness through vitrification. Below this range the body is underfired, being too weak and porous. Above this range the body is overfired and is likely to be so dense and glassy that it is brittle when cool. Most overfired bodies also deform during firing by blistering and collapsing. This is the beginning of the eventual complete breakdown which results in a molten state.

The maturing range is different for every clay. Some red clays, which are rich in fluxes, mature in the range 950°C to 1050°C (1742°F to 1922°F). Some ball clays mature in the region of 1150°C to 1200°C (2102°F to 2192°F). It will be noticed that the range is not always the same length. Some fireclays have a very long maturing range from 1200°C to 1400°C (2192°F to 2552°F) whilst some special bodies may, by virtue of the active fluxes present, be matured in a range which allows no room for error from 1090°C to 1100°C (1994°F to 2012°F).

Medium. Liquid used to assist the application of colours to pottery. The medium has no part in the fired formula but burns out in the firing. Some media are: water, water with a gum such as arabic or tragacanth, wax emulsion, linseed oil, turpentine, stand oil, rape oil, aniseed oil.

Medium glaze. An intermediate glaze. One which matures in the region 1050°C to 1200°C (1922°F to 2192°F). See **Intermediate glaze.**

Meldon stone. See **Cornish stone.**

Mellor, John W. (1869–1938). The British ceramist noted for his study of the behaviour of ceramic minerals during fusion. He successfully completed and coordinated much of the work started by earlier continental ceramists, some of which concerned the solubility of lead oxide in glazes and the production of lead-free glazes. See **Low sol** and **Thorpe ratio.**

Melting point. The temperature which divides the solid state from the liquid state of a material. A crystalline compound has a definite melting point which is also the solidifying point. A glaze, on the other hand, has a melting point at the upper end of a melting range. It is not the same as its solidifying point which is at the lower end of the melting range. See also **Glaze, chemistry** and **Grain size.**

Melting occurs when the molecule to molecule bonds which are responsible for maintaining a solid state, are broken in response to the vibratory pressure of heat. The heat energy is used by the material to break the bonds. See **Heat.** Once a material has reached its melting point it remains at this temperature, irrespective of the temperature of the adjacent air or solid, and continues to absorb energy until all the solid has become liquid. Once the material has completely melted, the temperature of the liquid can be made to rise.

In a crystalline solid (mineral, oxide etc) there are many identical bonds regularly distributed. These bonds respond to heat in the same way and therefore break at the same time, hence the immediate melting point.

A glaze is an amorphous solid which is composed of many different minerals and oxides linked together by many and varied bonds. These bonds are broken at different temperatures and therefore there cannot be a single melting point. As the bonds are broken the viscosity of the glaze progressively decreases so that the glaze becomes first pliable and then a stiff liquid. When the point is reached at which the bonds between different minerals and oxides have all been broken, the glaze can be said to have melted. It will have reached a liquid state and be capable of flowing.

The melting points of potters' minerals are included in the **Tables** of this book.

Mensuration formulae.

Area of rectangle	= base × height
Area of triangle	= $\frac{1}{2}$(base × perpendicular height)
Area of circle	= πr^2
Circumference of circle	= $2\pi r$
Volume of cylinder	= πr^2 × perpendicular height
Surface of cylinder	= $2\pi r$ × (height + radius)

$$\pi = \frac{22}{7} = 3\cdot14159$$

Mesh. A fabric of interwoven threads producing theoretically square holes between them. Meshes are measured by the number of threads per linear inch and by the aperture size. When the number of threads is given, slightly different standards exist in each country, but an approximation can be made by considering the thread diameter as equal to the aperture width. Thus a 50's mesh has 50 threads per linear inch and of course 50 holes per linear inch. The threads and apertures being equal, the thread is therefore $\frac{1}{100}$ inch wide. The method is approximately true for mesh sizes numbered as threads per inch which the potter will use from 5's to 200's. These are his lawns or sieves.

Coarser meshes are measured by the length of the hole which is assumed to be square. These are riddles and start at $\frac{1}{10}$ inch which is the same as a 5's sieve, and go upwards to any size, although the potter will probably not use coarser than a $\frac{3}{8}$ inch. In riddles the wire threads are not the same as the width of the holes but are usually standard throughout a series at about $\frac{1}{10}$ inch diameter.

Thus the riddle size gives the diameter size of a particle that may pass through the mesh. To get the diameter size of particles that may pass through a sieve, multiply the sieve number by 2 and count as a fraction of an inch. For example, the particles that pass through a 100's mesh sieve are $\frac{1}{200}$ inch and smaller. This assumes spherical particles.

Meta. A term used in chemical nomenclature to indicate a sense of change. It is often used for a halfway sub-division in an equation and is also used to indicate simply 'with'. For example, metaboric acid is halfway between boric acid and boric oxide.

Metakaolin. The theoretical crystal which exists after firing clay. See **Ceramic change** and **Firing**.

$$Al_2O_3 . 2SiO_2 . 2H_2O \xrightarrow{600°C}$$
kaolinite (clay)

$$Al_2O_3 . 2SiO_2 \quad + \quad 2H_2O\uparrow$$
metakaolin (pot)   water vapour

Microcline. Potash feldspar. $K_2O . Al_2O_3 . 6SiO_2$. A feldspar which is chemically identical with orthoclase but has a different crystal structure. It occurs in granites and other acidic igneous rocks and is normally classed as orthoclase feldspar by the potter. See **Feldspar, types of**.

Mill. General term for grinding and mixing machines, e.g. pugmill, ballmill, grinding mill. On its own it usually means a grinding mill or pan. Like the word kiln, the original word was miln but it has lost the 'n' in most dialects and is now spelt mill.

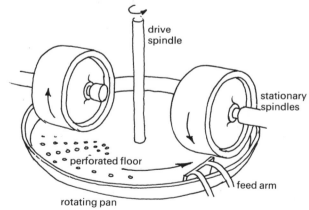

Mineral. A natural material which has a definable chemical formula in whole numbers and a definable molecular structure which gives it a distinct crystal formation. In its strictest sense a substance must be won from the earth by mining or quarrying to be a mineral and must be inorganic, although coal, oil and gas are exceptions.

In its wider sense in pottery, a mineral can also be prepared so that prepared oxides etc are accepted as minerals. The term has sometimes been extended to include raw materials like clay and cornish stone which are of variable composition and therefore cannot be given chemical formulae in whole numbers and do not form single crystal structures. It is better to refer to these variables as materials and reserve the term mineral for substances of predictable chemical composition.

Minerals are identified by general appearance, feel and colour; specific gravity; hardness; fracture and cleavage; and colour streak.

Mirror black. A Chinese glaze, which in Chinese is called black bronze, of the K'ang-hsi period (1662–1722). The colour is from iron and manganese oxides. The surface has a slight grain and is not an absolutely shiny mirror.

Mocha ware. A 19th-century English ware with dark tree-like motifs as decoration often on a pale blue ground. The ware is white earthenware, thrown and turned. The decoration is in coloured slips under a transparent glaze. The motif is produced by mixing manganese dioxide powder with tobacco juice. This stain is applied to the edge of the wet, freshly dipped or banded slip. The juice breaks a way through the slip in ever-dividing channels which are quickly filled and thus stained by the manganese dioxide. The effect is similar to moss agate which is manganese dioxide staining of cryptocrystalline quartz.

Modifiers. Modifying oxides. A general name describing all oxides other than the glass-forming oxides. In creating glazes, one considers that one starts with the all important glass-forming oxide silica. The silica is made to fuse at a convenient temperature by the use of alkaline fluxing oxides. The melt is stabilized by the use of amphoteric oxides and stained by colouring oxides. All these oxides, which are additional to the silica, are modifiers. However the term is used more specifically when it refers to oxides which are used to alter (modify) an existing standard glaze or colour. One then refers to the glaze and the modifiers and considers the new glaze to be the modified glaze. The term modified oxide arises in referring to a colouring oxide which has been altered in its colouring power by being mixed with, and in some cases fritted with, other oxides.

Mohammedan blue. Cobalt oxide modified with arsenious oxide gives a bright blue. The name is derived from cobalt ores with arsenic impurity which were imported into China in the Yuan dynasty. The usual impurity is manganese which gives the blue its more subdued colour and is sometimes referred to as Chinese native cobalt blue.

Mohs, Friedrich. The German mineralogist who originated the Scale of Hardness in the early 19th century.

Mohs' Scale of Hardness. A list of ten minerals arranged in order of their hardness and given numbers from 1 (soft) to 10 (hard). The minerals were chosen for their fairly universal availability and consistent structure and hence hardness. Some have a slight difference in hardness between an edge and a face of a crystal but for general field testing this can be ignored. It should be noted that the scale is not one of equal progression but only a convenient sequence.

1	Talc
2	Gypsum (rock salt)
(2·5	Finger nail)
3	Calcite
4	Fluorspar (fluorite)
5	Apatite
(5·5	Window glass and penknife blade)
6	Orthoclase feldspar
(6·5	Metal file)
7	Quartz
8	Topaz
9	Corundum (alumina)
10	Diamond

The scale is used to provide information about the hardness of substances. For example, dolomite is given the number H3·5 to 4. In fieldwork identification of a mineral or other material, the factors involved are: native colour, general appearance and feel; the colour of its streak when it is scratched across unglazed porcelain; its specific gravity; its fracture or cleavage; and its hardness. For example, the dogtooth spar of calcite is often mistaken for quartz. The crystals of these two minerals look similar but can be quickly differentiated by their hardness. Quartz (H7) will scratch window glass (H5·5). A penknife cannot cut into the quartz crystal. But the calcite crystal (H3) is much softer and can be scratched quite easily with a penknife (H5·5).

In Mohs' Scale the standard rule is that a mineral of one number is capable of scratching minerals of any lower number but not *vice versa*.

Molecule. The smallest part of a chemical compound that can exist independently whilst retaining all the properties of the compound in bulk form. In potting terms, a molecule cannot be seen. What is visible is a grain and particle, each composed of thousands of molecules. The molecule exists only as a theoretical unit in a discussion of ceramic fusions and in calculations of the unity formulae.

Molecular formulae are descriptions of molecules using chemical symbols to indicate the elements present and their relative proportions. In the descriptions of oxides and other compounds in this book, a formula for one molecule is included with the synonyms in the first line. For an explanation of these see **Formula, chemical**.

Mono. A term used in chemical nomenclature to indicate a combination with one atom or one molecule. For example, lead monoxide (PbO) has one atom of oxygen and lead monosilicate ($PbO.SiO_2$) has one molecule of silica.

Monoxide. In the monoxide molecule there is one (mono) atom of oxygen but there may be one or two atoms of the other element. For example, lead monoxide has one oxygen atom and one lead atom in each molecule and the chemical formula is written PbO; whereas sodium monoxide, commonly called soda, has two sodium atoms to each oxygen atom and the formula is written Na_2O. See also **Oxide**.

Montmorillonites. A group of silicates produced by the decomposition of igneous rocks. Their particles are extremely small flat hexagonal crystals and hence exhibit plasticity.

They are related to kaolinite and are often referred to as clays. The most important, from the potter's point of view, are bentonite and talc. Both exhibit the property of lubrication which arises from the flat particles. See **Bentonite**.

Mudstones. As the name suggests are stones made from mud. It is a name given to rocks which formed from deposits of mud and dust. Another term often used to describe them is argillaceous which implies the presence of some clay. However mudstones do not necessarily reconstitute into clays. Keuper marl is however an example of one that does. The presence of some directional cleavage, as in shales, is an indication of clay content. Crushed mudstones can be used in glazes. See also **Albany slip**.

Muffle. A thin-walled box to protect ware from direct contact with flames. It is like a saggar but is permanently part of the kiln structure. It is made from a refractory, such as fireclay, sillimanite or silicon carbide, and is as thin as possible to allow the heat from the flames outside to reach the ware inside. There is no direct heat transference from flame to ware, instead all the heating of the ware is by radiation and conduction.

A muffle lasts longer than a saggar because it is handled less. However it is only suitable for small kilns

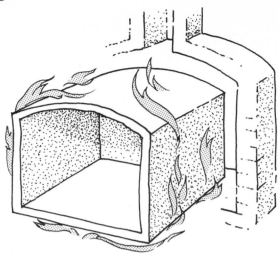

and is only necessary when direct flame contact is undesirable. Such conditions arise with some delicate colourings, onglaze enamels and some lustres. These colours are sometimes called muffle colours. Today's clean fuels, gas and electricity, have rendered a muffle kiln unnecessary. However, electric kilns are sometimes referred to as electric muffles.

A term semi-muffle is sometimes used for updraught kilns which have a high bag wall.

Mug. A drinking vessel for informal occasions. The examples shown are by Michael Casson, Sheila Casson, Haverfordwest Pottery, Glyn Hugo, Eric Stockl, Harry Stringer.

Mullite. $3Al_2O_3 . 2SiO_2$. An important alumino-silicate which is created within pottery bodies during firing. Mullite crystals are long needles which interlace to produce a strong body. Named after natural occurrence on the island of Mull.

Mullite is a product of vitrification. As the fluxed molten silica attacks the metakaolin crystal (originally the clay crystal), it removes silica into the melt. The remaining structure readjusts itself into an alumino-silicate of relatively higher alumina content, and one which does not yet melt. There are a few intermediate stages, but, from 1000°C (1832°F) upwards, mullite is an end-product of kaolinite crystal decomposition. The first stage is the ceramic change:

$$Al_2O_3 . 2SiO_2 . 2H_2O \xrightarrow{600°C}$$
kaolinite (clay)

$$Al_2O_3 . 2SiO_2 \quad + \quad 2H_2O\uparrow$$
metakaolin (pot) \quad water vapour

Further stages to mullite are:

$$Al_2O_3 . 2SiO_2 \longrightarrow Al_2O_3 . 1\tfrac{1}{2}SiO_2 + \tfrac{1}{2}SiO_2 \longrightarrow$$

$$Al_2O_3 . SiO_2 + SiO_2 \longrightarrow Al_2O_3 . \tfrac{2}{3}SiO_2 + 1\tfrac{1}{3}SiO_2$$

Fractions are used to give a better comparison with kaolinite. The last formula is, of course, mullite $(3Al_2O_3 . 2SiO_2)$.

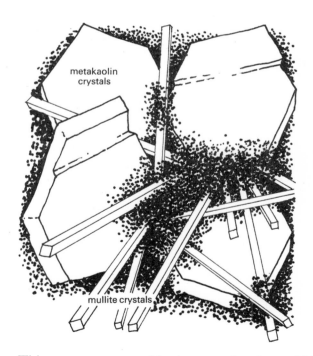

metakaolin crystals

mullite crystals

This rearrangement of lattice can take place within a body as it vitrifies. The resulting mullite crystals are even capable of growing outwards from their origin within the metakaolin crystal which is decomposing, thereby lacing together different particles and creating a structure of their own. Mullite crystals are long, square-sectioned needles which stiffen the vitrified mass and give strength to the final product. This is the valuable strength of stoneware and porcelain which is lacking in earthenware because insufficient meta-kaolin crystals are involved in the melt. The lesser strength of earthenware is maintained by the glass weld created at the point of contact between the metakaolin crystals etc. Mullite can form as low as 1000°C (1832°F) but its presence cannot be ensured without a firing above 1150°C (2102°F).

In glazes, the mullite is unable to grow as long needles because of the agitated state of the whole melt. Its place is found in short crystals or nuclei involved in the silica chains. These chains are stiffened by its presence. See **Alumina in glazes**. During cooling, these nuclei are starting points for the growth of crystals in crystalline glazes, especially glazes high in alumina like dolomite matts.

Mycenaean. The late Helladic civilization of the Greek mainland (1600 to 1100 BC). It was late Bronze Age in development. Mycenaean pottery was strongly influenced by late Minoan wares; in fact, it is likely that many of the potters came from Crete.

The wares were wheel-thrown, had a light-coloured ground and were painted with vitrifying slips. The slips were made from finely levigated red clay with additions of flux.

The best wares were probably the products of a division of labour between thrower and painter. The forms show a maturing style with increasing emphasis upon precision and use of tools. The painting of flowers and sea creatures has affinity with contemporary mural painting and at first continues the natural freshness of the best Minoan pieces. Later, there was a loss of identity with the source of inspiration and a stylized angularity appears in the drawing of figures and animals. The loss of natural freshness is partially balanced by an attractive humour in the figure-painting.

Both forms and painting become angular in the late period and develop naturally into the geometric style of the following Iron Age period.

N

Natch. See **Joggle**.

Natrium potash. Kalium soda. NaKO. See **Kalium soda**.

Natron. The natural form of hydrated sodium carbonate (washing soda) found as efflorescence around soda lakes. Varies from pure $Na_2CO_3.10H_2O$ to $Na_2CO_3.NaHCO_3.2-9H_2O$.

Neolithic pottery. The earliest known pottery. It was made during the Neolithic Period or New Stone Age. At this time the previously wandering hunters became the settled agriculturalists and stock breeders. This is the age of polished stone implements. In this settled existence pottery provided suitable cooking and storage vessels. It also provided the opportunity for decorative expression and therefore made comparatively speedy development. Within 500 years of the introduction of pottery-making, highly decorative vessels of expressive form were being produced and were an important means of artistic expression.

Clay was first used as a modelling material predating pottery by a few thousand years. Various dates have been given for the first pottery including a Japanese find dated as 9000 B.C. but the generally accepted date is 7000 B.C. for pottery made in Anatolia (Turkey). From here, pottery-making is said to have spread throughout the world reaching western Europe about 3000 B.C. and the Far East about 5000 B.C.

Nepheline. $K_2O.3Na_2O.4Al_2O_3.9SiO_2$. A feldspathoid mineral variable in colour from white to dark greenish brown. It melts in the range 1100°C to 1200°C (2012°F to 2192°F). Nepheline syenite is a transparent and colourless variety occurring in plutonic igneous rocks. It is given the formula $K_2O.3Na_2O.4Al_2O_3.8SiO_2$ and is a useful substitute for the normal feldspars in bodies and glazes because of its lower melting point. It is an excellent material for the introduction of soda.

Network structure. Network. The three-dimensional placing of fixed points on which atoms or molecules of a solid are positioned. If the network is regular as a repeating pattern it is called a lattice and results in a crystalline structure. If the network is not regular it is called a random network and in such cases the substance will be amorphous.

The diagrams show a lattice and a random network. They are calcia (CaO) and an imaginary glaze, respectively. Other examples are given under **Lattice structure, Random structure,** and some of the described minerals.

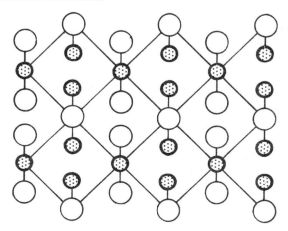

It is not necessary for the potter to study atomic structures and bonding. This is the work of the mineralogist who uses the information to identify specimens by their physical characters, and also of the chemist who tries to understand the combinations of atoms. It does however provide an allied interest for potters and explains why glazes mature when crystalline solids melt, why kaolinite particles are flat and result in plasticity and differential shrinkage of clay, and why some substances are physically harder than others.

Nickel oxide. NiO. NiO_2. Ni_2O_3. Ni_3O_4. A general name for compounds of nickel and oxygen which are used as colouring for glazes. Under most conditions the colour is not exciting, being greenish and brownish greys. However it is a useful modifier for the brighter colours like cobalt and copper oxides. It also produces pleasant greens and greys in combination with chromium oxide.

Nickel is a metal that occurs as ores in association with arsenic and sulphur. The main ores are nicolite ($NiAs$) and nickel glance ($NiAsS$) but all ores have iron, copper and cobalt as impurities. Canada is the major source. Nickel is used in alloys, notably stainless steel and nickel silver, and with chromium for resistance wire for kiln and other heating elements. The oxide is extracted from the ore by roasting.

There are three available forms of nickel oxide: the black and green nickelous oxide (NiO) and the black nickelic oxide (Ni_2O_3). Nickelcus oxide (NiO), sometimes called nickel monoxide, is the form which enters a ceramic fusion and this is the usual form which is marketed for potters. It is perfectly stable at room temperatures. It is available in a greenish grey form and a black form which are almost identical, being 99% nickel oxide. The trace oxides making up the other 1% influence the colour of the nickel in powder form but do not make any difference to the use of the nickel oxide as a glaze colourant. The oxide becomes unstable at temperatures above 1200°C (2192°F) and although dissolved in a glaze it tends to separate out of the melt causing a scum during the cooling.

Nickel oxide, like most other oxides, is capable of producing a full range of colours in carefully controlled experiments using exacting formulae. Colours range from citrus yellows to blues and red-violets. Some have been commercially developed as enamel colours, but for the individual potter using nickel oxide as a glaze stain it is likely to produce only drab colours in the green and brown range. It readily associates with silica and boric oxide long before the rest of the glaze has melted and therefore the opportunity to produce other colours in conjunction with alumina, potash, soda and even lead oxide is thwarted.

Nickel oxide is a strong colourant. The limit is about 3% in a glaze. The best colours are obtained with faint tinting using 1% or less in crystalline glazes. Nickel oxide is useful as a strong colourant to obtain black in conjunction with other colouring oxides as in the following colourant recipe:

nickel oxide	2
red iron oxide	5
cobalt oxide	5
manganese dioxide	2
chromium oxide	1

15 parts to every 100 parts of transparent glaze

Noggin. A very small drinking mug holding only a quarter of a pint (140 cc). Nog is a strong beer.

O

Ochre. Gall clay. An iron oxide ore and a ferruginous clay. The iron oxide ores are hydrated and semi-hydrated forms of iron oxide from $2Fe_2O_3 . 3H_2O$ to Fe_2O_3. They are crumbly earth ores. See **Limonite** and **Haematite**. When the term ochre is used for a clay it is reserved for fine clays with a very high iron oxide content and especially when these clays are used as a colouring. Ochre wash refers to its use as a slip brushed onto tiles, pots etc, often as only a thin basting from which the iron oxide burns decoratively into the clay or outwards into the glaze. Ochres are also used as colourings for slips, bodies and glazes. If no other colour is mentioned, such as red ochre or brown ochre, the word alone or the words raw ochre imply a yellow colour.

Ochres are the colour of iron oxide in different forms and all stabilize themselves as red iron oxide in an oxidized firing. Thus the term burnt ochre refers to the colour of red iron oxide, that is, terracotta colour.

The different forms of iron oxide found as ochres are ferric oxide giving the bright red colour, a mixture of ferric oxide and ferrous oxide giving browns and sometimes grey-browns, and ferric oxide in a bleached state and combined with water giving yellow. The red ochre is almost unchanged by firing. The deep brown and grey-brown ochres have some of the iron oxide in a reduced state. Oxygen has been taken away, possibly by organic action (bacteria and plant). On exposure to air such ochres begin to change to brown. The firing completes this process of reoxidation. Yellow ochre contains iron oxide which has been bleached by calcia and is combined with water. When fired, the calcia dissociates itself from the iron oxide to flux any free silica in the ochre itself or in body or glaze. The water evaporates. Thus the iron oxide changes to its red colour, or brown colour when suspended in glass. To keep the yellow colour of the ochre in a glaze, the free silica must be occupied with other fluxes. This is possible in a lime matt glaze where there is more than sufficient calcia present. See **Iron ores** and **Iron oxide**.

Oilspot. A decorative feature on stoneware glazes. The spots vary from pin-prick size to $\frac{1}{4}$ inch. They are caused by an excess of iron oxide crystals, possibly with other oxides such as those of cobalt and manganese. These crystals have pushed their way through the glaze from an under layer.

The effect is achieved by the use of two glazes or one glaze over a vitrifying slip. Both glazes contain iron oxide but the one underneath needs to be overloaded with iron oxide. The overloading amount varies according to the glaze composition, but can be as much as 30% of the recipe. The top glaze needs to fuse first so that when the underneath glaze fuses and bubbles it does so through an already molten glaze. The top glaze holds the craters containing the underneath glaze and when the whole smooths out the oil spots remain.

The oil spot decoration originated in Honan in northern China on tenmoku wares of the Sung dynasty. Many of these wares were copying southern Chinese wares from Fukien such as the famous Chien bowls. However the oil spot never occurred in the southern tenmokus. Our appreciation of oil spot and of all tenmokus derives from the Japanese admiration of them in connection with the tea ceremony.

Oligoclase. One of the plagioclase feldspars. It is mostly soda feldspar but contains up to 25% lime feldspar.

Once-fired. A description which is given to ware which is finished by a single firing as opposed to the use of two firings (biscuit and glaze).

Unglazed ware and salt-glazed ware are usually once-fired. Slipware, using a galena, clay and flint glaze, and stonewares using ash and clay slip glazes are also once-fired. Sanitary fireclay ware achieves unity of body and glaze by a number of thin layers of slip, engobe and glaze which again can be once-fired.

The advantages of once-firing are the saving in time and fuel, and the simplicity in the method of working which encourages a directness and spontaneity. The disadvantages are the disastrous effects of a single shattered piece on a kiln full of glazed ware, the difficulty of successfully biscuiting (oxidizing) a body which is covered by a glaze, and the difficulties of timing the making and glazing of the ware. See also **Through firing**.

Onglaze. O/G. Onglaze colour. Overglaze colour. Onglaze enamel. O/E. Ceramic colours applied on top of the fired glaze surface and given an extra firing. The firing is at a lower temperature than the glaze firing in order that the glaze is undisturbed whilst the onglaze colour fuses itself onto the original glaze surface. The temperature involved depends upon the hardness of the original glaze and is about 300°C (540°F) lower. Temperatures from 600°C to 1000°C (1112°F to 1832°F) have been used. The usual temperature for commercial colours is around 750°C (1382°F). A

special muffle kiln called the decorating kiln or enamel kiln is generally used.

The term onglaze colours is somewhat misleading because they are really soft-firing glazes, both opaque and transparent, which have been powerfully stained. The main fluxes are soda, potash, boric oxide and lead oxide. The colours are obtained by the same chemical combinations as other ceramic colours. For example, blues are still obtained from combinations with cobalt or vanadium oxides. But because lower temperatures are involved, a wider range of colours is possible. Some colour combinations which involve elements and compounds that volatilize at higher temperatures are stable at onglaze temperatures.

The colours are prepared by fritting and grinding. The colour is thus ready to melt and because it is finely ground it melts quickly and smoothly. It is not required to flow or be in agitated state in order to form the required colour and glass.

Onglaze colours are applied to the previously fired glaze by brush, spray gun, dusting onto a groundlay medium and by litho and engraved transfer. Oils and varnishes are usually used as carrying media but water can be used.

The disadvantages of onglaze colours are the extra firing required which must be in a clean gas atmosphere or preferably a ventilated muffle kiln; the toxic nature of some of the colours; and the poor resistance to abrasion and chemical attack which is provided by such a low-firing glaze.

It is not usual for individual potters to make their own onglaze colours. For one reason they are usually fritted and for another they are usually very finely ground. Both these points are necessary if a particular colour is required which is little affected by its surroundings and fuses quickly and smoothly in the firing. However there is no reason why a potter cannot use self-prepared soft glazes as enamels. Any convenient temperature can be used. A slightly extended firing will be necessary to fuse a coarser and unfritted colour and many of the colours which must be specially prepared will be impossible to obtain. Care should be taken

with regard to the possible toxic nature of these low-fired glazes.

The photograph is of a Persian minai bowl of the 13th century.

Oolite. Oolitic limestone. $CaCO_3$. A limestone which is composed of spherical particles. The coarse-grained oolite is called pisolite. See **Limestone**.

Opacifiers. Minerals which are included in glaze recipes for their property of opacification. Opacity is the result of light interference inside and at the surface of a glaze. This can occur in three ways: when light strikes opaque matter suspended in the glaze, when light is deflected by crystal facets and when it is deflected by matter of less than wave-length size.

The popular opacifier is one which does not readily dissolve in the molten glaze but remains as isolated oxide particles which are suspended in and thus cloud an otherwise transparent glaze. Tin oxide is the most dependable additive for a white opacification of this type. Others are antimony oxide, ceria and zirconia. The minerals mentioned are separately indexed for details of their use.

Crystalline opacity occurs when crystals form within and at the surface of a glaze during cooling. Crystal growth is encouraged by the inclusion in the recipe of titanium dioxide and/or zirconia. Also excess of alumina, calcia, magnesia, zinc oxide and baria is precipitated upon cooling and forms compound crystals. These oxides can also be responsible for interesting surface qualities. See **Crystalline glazes**.

Alumina and zirconia have a stiffening effect upon the fluidity of a molten glaze. This stiffness tends to trap minute bubbles which, if small, give a milky quality. If the bubbles are extremely fine so that they cannot be seen individually, even with a magnifying glass, the opacity is called colloidal. Some substances behave in a similar way to these colloidal bubbles. They subdivide and disperse through a molten glaze, but never fully melt. They are not necessarily opaque but interfere with the light waves because of their small

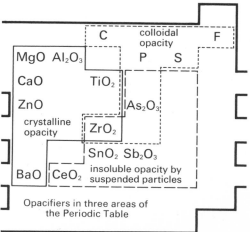

Opacifiers in three areas of the Periodic Table

size. The elements carbon, phosphorus, sulphur and fluorine can give colloidal opacity. Arsenic oxide and zirconia are also colloidal opacifiers. See **Colloid, glaze**.

The diagram shows part of the Periodic table and outlines three areas which include the three types of opacifier. It will be noted that zirconia is included in all three areas. Zirconium silicate is a prepared opacifier of great efficiency. See **Zirconium silicate**.

Open setting. Packing ware in a kiln without a muffle or saggars. The flames pass between and over the ware so that open setting must be carried out to accord with the chosen flame pattern.

Opener. Any material added to a clay to give it a character and quality. The first requirement of an opener is that it should assist with drying. The opener, by becoming a proportion of the body, cuts down the proportion of clay content to be dried. Porous openers provide ducts for the passage of the moisture drying out and thus the mass dries more uniformly. The opener therefore assists the uniform drying of ware and prevents warpage. Secondly an opener gives a working character to a body. Some clays are so smooth that without an opener they are difficult to handle on a wheel or by hand-building methods. An opener gives the necessary 'bite'. A third quality from an opener is the balance it gives to the fired quality of the clay. For example, the addition of a refractory grog to a body enables it to withstand a slightly higher temperature.

Openers are divided into ceramic and organic. Ceramic openers become part of the body during firing. They may still show as colour and texture and may play an important part in making the body withstand thermal shock in ovenware and raku. Ceramic openers are grog, pitchers, fireclay and sand. Organic openers give texture and working quality to the body but burn away during firing leaving a series of holes. This can be decorative and also useful in cooking ware. Organic openers are sawdust, husks, chopped straw etc, cow and sheep dung.

Orange peel. Pigskin. The texture of the surface of a glaze where there are many small craters resembling

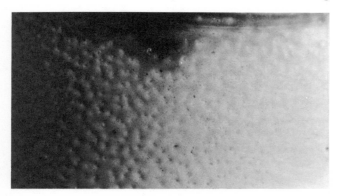

pin pricks. The craters are the remains of bubbles occurring during fusion. Because the glaze is stiff it does not flow together at the surface after a bubble has burst. Orange peel is often used to describe the texture of salt glaze and other glazes that are heavily pitted or textured. Pigskin is usually used to describe tenmokus that have a widely spaced pinholing.

Organic matter. Describes living matter. Organic chemistry is that which concerns carbon compounds. Carbon does not melt but it does readily oxidize (burn) to become a gas. Carbon compounds decompose in the kiln during firing and many paint colours and dyes are therefore useless as ceramic colours. But such colourings are very useful as stains for identifying raw materials, slips and glazes before they are fired. Organic matter such as wood and bone contain more than carbon, hydrogen and oxygen. Elements such as potassium, calcium and phosphorus are present so that organic matter, after burning, can be used in pottery as wood ashes in glazes and bone ashes in clays.

Ortho. A term used in chemical nomenclature to indicate the straight, correct, equal or normal balance of atoms or molecules within a crystal structure. Examples of its use are orthoclase feldspar, lead orthosilicate, sodium orthoborate. Some explanations of nomenclature are given under **Borate**.

Orthoclase. Potash feldspar. Pink feldspar. $K_2O . Al_2O_3 . 6SiO_2$. The commonest of the 12 types of feldspar. It is used as a flux in bodies and as a major constituent in glazes. It melts at approximately 1200°C (2192°F).

Orthoclase originates in molten magmas and separates upon cooling, occasionally creating masses of practically pure orthoclase which include large crystals. The photograph shows particularly well-formed crystals a couple of inches long. Often the crystals are smaller and integrated with other feldspars and silicates as in granite.

The molecular structure of orthoclase is based upon the oxygen tetrahedra which gives a hexagonal chain. One in four tetrahedra has an aluminium atom at its centre. The other three have silicon atoms. One chain directly fits upon another to form a honeycomb of boxes. The boxes form sites for potassium atoms in

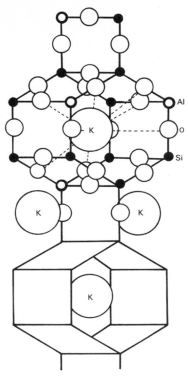

eight-fold co-ordination with the surrounding oxygen atoms which have unsatisfied valencies due to the lower valency of aluminium compared with silicon.

Orthoclase is a natural frit containing glass-former, flux and amphoteric stabilizer (silica, potash and alumina). It is not soluble and therefore is an important constituent for introducing potash into glazes and bodies without recourse to fritting. Alone, orthoclase begins to sinter around 1000°C (1832°F) and starts to melt at about 1150°C (2102°F). By 1200°C (2192°F) it has produced a very stiff glass which is rendered opaque by millions of tiny bubbles. See photograph. The high alumina content precludes the creation of a glass which will flow below 1350°C (2462°F). Thus orthoclase is a mineral which can be introduced into bodies in amounts up to 25% and will provide progressive densification over a wide temperature range. In glazes it is often the major constituent. Because of

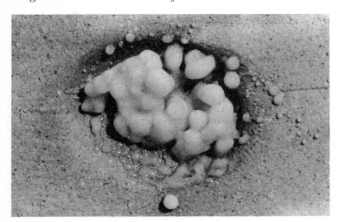

its stiff nature, extra silica is usually required and additional flux of a different composition. However its stiff character during fusion is invaluable. See **Alumina** and **Feldspar**.

Orthoclase, or indeed any feldspar, is so dependable as a glaze mineral that one can start with it as the basis for a glaze recipe. Orthoclase can be progressively fluxed with either a frit for low-temperature glazes or whiting and flint for high-temperature ones. See **Feldspathic glaze**. It is usual to include a small amount (5% to 10%) of a clay to aid slop suspension.

Orthoclase, albite and cornish stone are often interchangeable. They are not alike but the particular properties which they possess may not make obvious differences in complex recipes. Colour responses are similar and rarely give startlingly different results. The greatest difference will be found in the rates of expansion and contraction. In this field substitution is useful in the adjustment of glaze fit. See **Glaze fit**. For inclusion in glazes to be fired above 1200°C (2192°F), orthoclase is often preferable because the potash content is not subject to volatilization as is the soda content of albite and cornish stone. See also **Albite**.

Orthoclase is the pure mineral. This is only available as hand-picked specimens. The usual mineral available for potters is more correctly called potters' orthoclase or potash feldspar. This is not pure orthoclase structure but contains some, perhaps 20%, of other feldspars especially albite (soda feldspar).

Orton, Edward, (1863–1932). The American geologist and ceramic engineer who followed up the work which Hermann Seger had started in Germany. This work was the study of heat upon silicates and had resulted in the Seger cone. Edward Orton continued the research and extended the range of cones. By the end of the 19th century Orton cones were in commercial production at the Ceramic Engineering Department of the Ohio University, where Orton was the Director. Edward Orton's interest in education led to his being called the father of ceramic education. See **Cones**.

Orton Pyrometric Cones. Cones made by the Edward Orton Junior Ceramic Foundation of Ohio. See **Cones** and **Tables**.

Oven. Stoke-on-Trent, England, name for a kiln used for unglazed (bisc) firings.

Ovenware. Pottery used for oven cooking, and, in the case of casseroles, ramekins etc, used for serving the food at table. Function is of primary importance. The forms of ovenware must be carefully considered. The body and glaze must be capable of withstanding the thermal shocks and physical knocks involved. Ovenproof does not mean flameproof. Gas rings with direct flames and hotplates on electric cookers are hotter than oven atmospheres. Ovenware is not intended to withstand the shock of this extreme heat prolonged at one point only.

The forms of ovenware are traditional. They have evolved with cooking methods and are an integral part of the whole subject. It is not by chance that different foods are called dishes and the name casserole means both the pot and the food cooked in it. As a simplification one could say that there are plates and shallow dishes for pies, ramekins, eggbakers and other individual portion containers and the lidded oven pots and casseroles. Requirements common to all ovenware are stability, robustness, ease of handling and ease of cleaning.

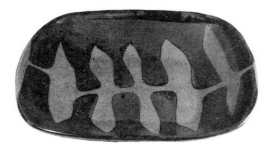

Stability must never be in doubt. One's general unease in the handling of a hot piece of pottery must not be increased by unsteadiness of the pot. Many oven shelves have uneven surfaces but there is no excuse for the potter to increase the cook's anxiety. The broad base, which is stable, presents a problem in making. A broad base warps more easily than a narrow one which has proportionately more pot above it to stabilize it. Adding a thick foot rim would stabilize a broad base but would increase the overall weight of the pot and would increase the risk of cracks from thermal shock.

Domestic ovens have become smaller. Shelf height is now a problem. The use of more selected foods rather than composite stews has led to a requirement for a wide shallow casserole. The globular stewpot or bean pot is less often suitable. The popularity of the shallow casserole has increased this century and it presents a challenge to the ovenware potter. See **Casserole**.

Hot and full cooking pots take knocks. Ovenware must be robust in form and the body and glaze physically strong. Robust does not mean clumsy. The traditional west African cooking pot is robust in form yet extremely light in weight. The form is globular which is the strongest form possible. At the same weight of pot, a flat base would be a decided weakness. Uniform thickness helps to give a pot its strength and at the same time decreases overall weight. By avoiding sharp corners one also increases a pot's robustness. The wide, shallow casserole previously discussed is unfortunately a weak form and it is likely to have the further weakness of a sharp angle between base and side.

Ovenware must be handled whilst hot. Delicate lug handles and small knobs on lids are impractical. Func-

tional design must be exaggerated in ovenware. The use of unglazed portions on stoneware is often an advantage because the gloved hand can more easily grip an unglazed piece. Glazed surfaces seem to become slippery when hot as they do when they are wet.

The foregoing points add up to good or bad design. The well-designed pot does its job. Its proportions and size are correct. The good form gives overall robustness to withstand thermal shock and physical knocks. Yet the weight is light enough for ease of handling and not too light so that it destroys confidence. The badly-designed pot may be three times the weight of the well-designed one but could be physically weaker and unable to cope with thermal shocks.

In every kitchen there are pots that seem to be in constant use. It is a worthwhile exercise to discover why. Analysis of historical pieces is also time well spent. If one approaches the subject enquiringly one can discover why a pot developed in the way it did over a few centuries. The oval cooking dish is a case in point. The oval shape is easier to handle in and out of an oven. If full of liquid it is less likely to spill when moved because the oval cuts across the swell at an angle. The manner in which oval dishes are thrown, cut across the base and compressed produces a break in the lines of stress spiralling the base. The clay, put onto the base to seal the cut, is compressed more than was the original base. This extra compression adds physical strength to the base. An oval dish will therefore last longer than its round counterpart before it finally cracks from the fatigue of thermal shocks. The example shown and the plate illustrated earlier are by Ray Finch.

Body and glaze present further problems. They are described in detail under **Thermal shock, Dunting** and **Shivering**. Thermal shock is the stress created within the pottery body by the sudden temperature changes which are experienced going into and coming out of the hot oven. The temperature difference between two parts of the same pot is responsible, through expansion, for a size difference between these two parts. There is also the phenomenon of different rates of expansion for body and glaze. These differences create stresses which may rupture the pot.

The temperature range which ovenware must span in use reaches 300°C (572°F). This includes the cristobalite dunting point. Cristobalite dunting is therefore an ever-present danger. It is probably impossible to exclude cristobalite completely from the body but every attempt should be made to do so. Some potters fire ovenware very quickly in order to give less time for the free silica to become cristobalite. See **Silica conversion**. One should think twice before refiring ovenware. Clay, slips and glazes, and in fact the whole workshop, should be free from industrial-type materials likely to contain cristobalite, e.g. a white earthenware body. The accidental introduction of even a small proportion of such material into the clay for ovenware can do untold damage because of cristobalite catalyst action upon other free silica.

But, ignoring the separate problem of cristobalite, the potter is faced with conflicting considerations. An open and porous body is physically weak. A partially vitrified body is stronger and there is a point at which a body reaches its maximum strength through vitrification. As a body becomes too glassy and begins to break down it becomes brittle and is less resilient to knocks. For normal tableware a potter would try to achieve the point of maximum strength in his wares. It is also the point of negligible porosity, which is conveniently practical. However, for ovenware one is faced with the problem of thermal shock. A body's resistance to thermal shock is almost the direct opposite of its physical strength. A body that is dense and physically strong has a low resistance to thermal shock. A weak body needs to be used thickly to be practical. Raku tea bowls are an example of this resistance to thermal shock. The raku body is porous and physically weak, and the pots are made correspondingly thicker.

The graph shows typical curves for porosity, physical strength and resistance to thermal shock. It

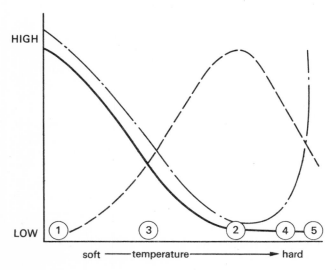

relates these to a temperature scale which can only be described as from soft fired to hard fired. Actual temperatures will be different for each body. It should be noted that this graph refers to strengths etc of the finished ware which has been to these temperatures. It does not relate to strengths during the firing. The three lines represent three different properties which are measured in different ways. However by the relationship of each line to the common factor of temperature certain conclusions can be drawn:

1. Soft-fired ware, although porous and physically weak, has a high resistance to thermal shock. Raku ware is an excellent example of this.

2. A higher temperature of firing produces a denser ware of negligible porosity. Physically the body is at its strongest but the resistance to thermal shock is very low. Providing the resistance was sufficient to withstand boiling water this would be the best condition for tableware.

3. The ideal for ovenware would lie between the extremes of 1 and 2 and would be dictated primarily by the establishment of sufficient resistance to the thermal shock to be experienced, commensurate with reasonable strength.

4. Bodies taken to the vitrification point become glassy and deform. They gain in resistance to thermal shock because most of their crystalline free silica is converted into fused silica. Fused silica expands at a much smaller rate than crystalline silica. However because they are glassy, they become brittle and thus lose their physical strength which was based upon a combination of physical hardness and resilience between the body particles.

5. For completeness, mention must be made of the extreme portion of the graph. Theoretically, the complete vitrification of the body, whereby it becomes a glass, would make the ware more resistant to thermal shock. Glass ovenware makes use of this fact. But pottery in this vitrified state would collapse in the firing. Porcelain comes near to this vitrified state and some, but not all, porcelains are ovenproof. Some potters have perfected this type of ovenware and some have even achieved a porcelain which is also flameproof. Most porcelains however are in a similar position to dense stonewares (2) in their relation to thermal shock. They can overcome most tableware shocks, e.g. hot tea in teacups, by being thinly potted.

Ovenware is a compromise of many factors. The compromise can only be found empirically. First the correct body must be created which is ovenproof. Some physical strength will have to be sacrificed here but some can be regained by increasing one's skill in the creation of well-designed pots. Too much reliance is often placed upon the strength of fired body and not enough on form. There is no place for speculative forms reminiscent of rococo tureens.

The best way to discover the ideal forms is to become a cook and use one's own ovenware.

Overburden. In digging clay or other raw material there is often a layer of soil, decomposed rock or glacial drift on top of the desired material. This has first to be removed before winning can proceed and this non-productive layer is called the overburden.

Overfiring. Firing higher than the required temperature and thus creating defects in the ware. An overfired biscuit has insufficient porosity for glazing. An overfired body warps and bloats. An overfired glaze often blisters by the volatilization of part of its composition. It also reaches a stage where its viscosity is too low to keep it on the pot.

Overfired earthenware glazes lose their character and become glossy and runny. In contrast, overfired stoneware glazes can be attractive. The stoneware body may bloat but in reaching its vitrification point it contributes greatly to the colour and character of the glaze through the body-glaze layer with inspiring results.

Oxford spar. A potash feldspar mined in the eastern United States.

Oxidation. In pottery this refers to the combination of oxygen with an element or compound. Such an action occurs in the firing at temperatures above red heat and if required is achieved by the introduction of excess air to the fire or by allowing pure air to track through the muffle. Small ports set low and high in electric kilns encourage this movement of air amongst the pots.

The important oxidations are those of carbon and sulphur which occur in bodies. The so-called burning out periods take place between 700°C and 1150°C (1292°F and 2102°F). See **Firing, biscuit**. A kiln atmosphere intended to achieve oxidation is called an oxidizing atmosphere. The opposite is a reducing atmosphere and one which hovers between the two is referred to as neutral.

Chemists include the removal of hydrogen and the loss of electrons as oxidation. Potters include the decomposition of carbonates, sulphates etc whereby the end product is an oxide which enters a ceramic fusion. For example:

$$CaCO_3 \longrightarrow CO_2\uparrow + CaO$$
$$2CaF_2 + O_2 \longrightarrow 2F_2\uparrow + 2CaO$$
$$2(FeSO_4.7H_2O) \longrightarrow$$
$$14H_2O\uparrow + SO_2\uparrow + SO_3\uparrow + Fe_2O_3$$
$$CuCO_3.Cu(OH)_2 \longrightarrow H_2O\uparrow + CO_2\uparrow + 2CuO$$

Some pottery materials require deliberate oxidation to rid them of injurious volatiles like sulphur and fluorine which often occur in muds and feldspathic rocks. Other materials, like tin oxide, are discoloured by lack of oxygen, whilst others, like lead oxide, are prevented from acting in their ceramic capacity thus causing blistering.

Oxide. A chemical combination of oxygen with another element. To the potter there are two types of oxide, the metal oxide and the non-metal oxide. The metal oxides are numerous and form the fluxes, colourings and opacifiers. The non-metal oxides are few and are the glass-formers and the volatiles. See the individual oxides and **Periodic table**.

The physical and chemical properties of an oxide will differ greatly both from oxygen and from the second element contained in the oxide structure. The combining power of oxygen and the second element may be predicted by a consideration of their valencies.

The different combinations the potter will meet with are: monoxide, where there is only one oxygen atom in the combination but one or two atoms of the other element (RO, R_2O); dioxide, where there are two oxygen atoms (RO_2); trioxide, where there are three oxygen atoms and one or two atoms of the other element (RO_3, R_2O_3). This latter combination (R_2O_3) is usually called sesquioxide; tetroxide, where there are four oxygen atoms and one or three atoms of the other element (RO_4, R_3O_4); pentoxide, where there are five oxygen atoms.

Another method of naming the oxide to imply the combination of elements is to alter the ending of the latin name of the element. This is used where there is more than one possible combination. ~ous means the combination with the least oxygen. ~ic means the combination with the most oxygen. If there is also a combination between these extremes a composite name is given, e.g. ferrous oxide FeO, ferroso-ferric oxide Fe_3O_4, ferric oxide Fe_2O_3.

A third method of describing the oxide is by using a different ending for the element name and omitting the word oxide. This is used where there is only one combination possible or only one stable combination likely to be met with. Thus, sodium oxide is called soda, potassium oxide is potash and potassa, calcium oxide is calcia, and we have magnesia, lithia, baria. Titanium dioxide becomes titania and we have zirconia, ceria and silica. Aluminium sesquioxide becomes alumina.

Some oxides may be described by more than one of the foregoing methods. Thus silicon dioxide, silicic oxide and silica are the same thing. Iron sesquioxide, iron trioxide and ferric oxide are the same and because these phrases are abstract in concept the potter would be more likely to use the visually descriptive name of red iron oxide for the same substance.

The rocks of the earth's crust are composed mostly of oxides with some carbonates, sulphides etc. The drawing shows proportionately an ultimate analysis of all the rocks. Silica (SiO_2) accounts for almost 60% and alumina (Al_2O_3) for 15%. All the other oxides and elements account for just over 25%.

COLOURING OXIDES. Metal oxides which impart colour to the fired ceramic, e.g. cobalt oxide gives blue. Generally speaking, the colouring power of a single common oxides of the Earth's crust

SiO$_2$		
Al$_2$O$_3$		
CaO		
MgO		
Na$_2$O		
FeO		
K$_2$O	Fe$_2$O$_3$	
	TiO$_2$	others

Oxide	Percentage	Colour
Antimony oxide	1	Yellow in soft lead glazes
Cerium oxide	3	Yellow with titania
Chromium oxide	1 (5)	Grey-green. Pink with tin oxide. Orange in soft lead glazes
Cobalt oxide	1 (10)	Blue. Pink with barium oxide
Copper oxide	5 (10)	Green. Turquoise in alkaline glazes
Iron oxide	12 (25)	Yellow, brown, black. Blue in high alkaline glazes
Manganese oxide	20 (100)	Brown. Purple in alkaline glazes
Nickel oxide	3	Grey-green and brown
Praseodymium oxide	5	Yellow-green with zirconia
Uranium oxide	15	Red and orange in lead glazes
Vanadium oxide	5	Yellow with tin oxide and zirconia

oxide depends upon the amount of vitrification that takes place around it. If it is dissolved in a glaze it will give a stronger colour than in a soft-fired body. To get equal colour strengths about 5 times the weight of colouring oxide is required in a body than in a glaze. The following list of colouring oxides gives percentages for colouring a glaze to full strength. The percentage in brackets is the limit that can be put into a glaze and this limit gives metallic, matt and crystalline surfaces, sometimes pleasant.

A colouring oxide acts as an additional flux or as an anti-flux in a body and glaze. The action can be predicted by the chemical formula. Monoxides like copper and cobalt will be fluxes. Acidic oxides like cerium and vanadium are anti-fluxes. Details are given under the separate oxides.

The composition of a body or glaze affects the colour achieved with a particular oxide. For example, copper oxide gives a green that is a yellowish apple green in a lead glaze, a brighter bluish green in a borax glaze, and a turquoise green in a high alkaline glaze.

Some colours are not very stable especially when they depend upon a combination of two oxides. The colouring oxide is therefore combined with others by calcination and grinding before adding to the glaze. These are known as modified oxides or oxide stains.

MODIFIED OXIDE. A metal oxide used for colouring which has been altered in strength or colour by the addition of other oxides. For example a strong blue glaze can result from the addition of merely 0·5% cobalt oxide. In small amounts this is difficult to weigh accurately and not easy to disperse through the glaze without specking. The cobalt oxide is therefore first modified by the addition of feldspar, flint, china clay and possibly alumina, zinc oxide or barium oxide. This separate recipe batch is fused together and re-ground. The modified cobalt oxide is not so powerful a stain, is more easily dispersed in the glaze and by control of the additions can be made into different types of blue stain such as mazarine blue and matt blue.

P

Paddle and anvil. A method of thinning and compressing the clay wall of a pot by beating it against an anvil with a paddle. The anvil is held inside the pot and the paddle is used on the outside. Alternatively, the paddle is used alternately inside and outside the pot as in the photograph. The paddle is usually a piece of wood but is sometimes a stone slab like a slate. The anvil is dome-shaped and is a pebble, a piece of wood or a piece of fired clay. Different clays require paddles and anvils of different absorbencies.

Paddle and anvil is a useful method to combine with pinching, coiling, slabbing and throwing. Compressing the clay wall strengthens it by reorganizing the alignment of the clay particles. See **Clay, physics**. The clay wall is also thinned so that this is an important forming process. Some potters start from a ball of clay, beat the anvil into it and then, by paddling the clay against the anvil, the whole pot form is produced. As the pot wall is thinned, the clay 'stretches'. To assist the clay to stretch without cracking, the surface is scratched with a comb. This makes the surface larger in area by providing furrows and ridges. The clay can be thinned until this surface is flattened with less risk of cracking than a smooth surface. The paddles and anvils are often pecked, pimpled, scored and ridged to assist this process.

Pan. Grinding pan. Grinding mill. Machine for grinding raw materials. Large mills are used for clay shales and grog. These have two heavy metal wheels up to 8 feet in diameter on a horizontal stationary spindle. The rollers rest on a circular floor which rotates and materials are directed under the rollers to be crushed. The circular floor is perforated and thus forms a first screening of the crushed material. Although essentially a dry process, some water is often sprinkled into the pan to reduce the amount of blown dust. See **Mill**.

Small pans are used for glaze materials which are ground in water to a slurry. The pan is usually stationary and the wheels go round. Also the pan is not perforated; the same material is ground until sufficiently fine. Sometimes stones, e.g. flint or limestone, are used instead of wheels and these are dragged or pushed around the pan.

Parian paste. A soft-paste porcelain used for unglazed figures. It is made from china clay 33%, cornish stone 66% and is fired to approximately 1200°C (2192°F).

Paris white. Whiting. Calcium carbonate. $CaCO_3$.

Particle size. Grain size. The term 'particle' is usually reserved for extremely fine grains in the order of 50 microns and less. This size will pass through a 300's mesh and includes those materials which are naturally colloidal, like clay; materials which are ground to a very fine state, like zircon opacifiers; and divided materials in partial suspension/solution in molten glazes, like the crystal nuclei which give rise to crystalline effects upon cooling.

The term 'grain' is conveniently used for pieces of a size larger than 50 microns. Grain sizes are usually measured in mesh numbers. Grains include glaze materials other than colloidal opacifiers and colourants, and all other pottery materials like grogs, sands and body fillers whose grains can be seen with the naked eye or the aid of a magnifying lens.

Particle size has relevance to two main points:

1. In glazes, the particle size is directly related to the time necessary to 'dissolve' the particle in molten glaze. Hence it is also related to whether any of the particle will remain as a crystal nucleus and create opacity and crystallization.

2. In bodies, the particle size of a clay is directly related to the plasticity, strength and shrinkage of the clay. See **Clay, physics**.

An instance of the importance of particle size follows. A similar consideration of grain size is given under **Grain size**.

Some pure ball clays compare very favourably with china clay when considered in terms of kaolinite content. Chemically these two can be almost alike. Physically however they differ in particle size and this means that they will give different results. Ball clay will shrink more than china clay in drying and in firing. In drying, it is the size of the gaps between the particles which is relevant, (see **Clay, physics**); in firing, it is the way in which a clay particle melts. China clay, with its larger particle size (which could be 50,000 times the bulk of a ball clay particle) presents a smaller surface area for its weight. It therefore resists the melting effects of temperature and interaction of fluxes for a longer period. In simple terms, a china clay particle can be 50,000 times the bulk of a ball clay particle, yet it presents a surface area of only 1500 times the size. It will therefore take it 33 times as long to melt. This is comparable to the relative melting times of crushed ice and ice cubes in domestic terms. The actual particle sizes involved are between 20 and 0·5 microns for china clay and between 1 and 0·02 microns for ball clay.

China clay has the justifiable reputation of being a refractory clay both in bodies and glazes, but ball clay has not. Ball clays often contain impurities which are given the credit for the vitrification which occurs with ball clays, but this is only part of the story.

In glazes, ball clays are often useful because they fuse more readily than china clay. Their larger drying shrinkage is also useful in slip glazes.

The comparison above rests upon the particle sizes of two clays. It should be remembered that the extremely fine particles involved are not always fully dispersed. They tend to form agglomerates of grain size.

Partridge feather. A finer version of the oil-spot tenmoku in which a host of fine bright specks of metallic lustre cover a dark brown or black glaze. The effect is associated with iron oxide but can involve other oxides such as manganese and cobalt.

It can be achieved by the use of an under-slip or glaze. This is overloaded with colouring oxide so that it promotes a metallic surface. It melts and bubbles through an already fused and fairly soft upper glaze. This allows the metallic glaze to form spots and circles but keeps them smaller than the oil-spot by being more liquid. See **Iron oxide in glazes**.

Paste. A prepared 'clay' for a special ware, usually of the porcellaneous type. A paste contains below 40% of clay content.

A clay is the natural raw material possibly refined but without additions. Blends of clays and clays with additions of sand etc are called bodies. A body is therefore a clay or clays prepared for specific use. Bodies which contain very little clay, e.g. porcelain and bone china bodies, are called pastes. Here the clay content is below 40% and the word paste seems a good one. It is descriptive of the texture of the material as one uses it. The words clay, body and paste are used advisedly throughout this book.

Pearl ash. Potash. Potassium carbonate. K_2CO_3. A highly-soluble potassium salt present in wood ash. It is used in glass-making and the preparation of frits. See **Potassium carbonate**.

Peeling. See **Shelling**.

Pegmatite. See **Cornish stone**.

Periodic kiln. An intermittent kiln allowed to cool completely between firings.

Periodic table. A classified arrangement of chemical elements which brings together those elements with similar properties. It was first demonstrated by Mendeleev in 1869 as his Periodic Law. The table has helped to predict previously unknown elements. Their properties and even their characteristics were known from the table before they were discovered.

The periodic table and the potter's periodic table, which is an adaptation of the original, help the potter to understand and in some cases predict the part a mineral will play in his ceramic. Once he has ascertained what the mineral contains chemically he can identify the constituents on the table. Because they are governed by the Periodic Law he is able to predict what their action will be.

To make the table, the elements are placed in the order of their atomic numbers. An element's atomic number is the number of its electrons. This puts the elements in an order which is the order of their atomic weights. There are a few exceptions but they do not affect the potter. The vertical columns of the table are called Groups and are numbered from O to VIII in Roman numerals. The horizontal rows are called Periods and are numbered from 0 to VI in Roman numerals. Roman numerals are used to avoid confusion with the atomic numbers which also appear on the table. A simplified table is given and includes the atomic number and the chemical symbol for each element. The names of the elements of immediate interest to the potter are given in full.

PERIODIC TABLE (general chemistry principles). From the table some general properties of the elements can be predicted. An understanding of these properties is useful in a general way and helps in understanding the more specific properties of the oxides in the potter's periodic table.

1. *Inert gases*. Vertical Group 0 contains the gases helium, neon, argon, krypton, xenon and radon. They are known as the inert gases because these elements have no combining capacity. They do not enter into compounds. They never form oxides and so are not used by the potter. For this reason they do not appear in the other periodic tables in this book.

2. *Valency*. Groups I to VIII contain elements which have the capacity to combine with other elements and thus produce compounds such as carbon dioxide, iron oxide and calcium chloride. This capacity to combine is controlled by the electrons of the atom and is called the atom's valency. It is the number of these same elec-

Periodic table of elements

	O	I	II	III	IV	V	VI	VII	VIII		
O								hydrogen 1　　　　H			
I	2 He	lithium 3　　　Li	beryllium 4　　　Be	boron 5　　　B	carbon 6　　　C	nitrogen 7　　　N	oxygen 8　　　O	fluorine 9　　　F			
II	10 Ne	sodium 11　　Na	magnesium 12　　Mg	aluminium 13　　Al	silicon 14　　Si	phosphorus 15　　P	sulphur 16　　S	chlorine 17　　Cl			
III A	18 A	potassium 19　　K	calcium 20　　Ca	21　　Sc	titanium 22　　Ti	vanadium 23　　V	chromium 24　　Cr	manganese 25　　Mn	iron 26　Fe	cobalt 27　Co	nickel 28　Ni
III B		copper 29　　Cu	zinc 30　　Zn	31　　Ga	germanium 32　　Ge	arsenic 33　　As	selenium 34　　Se	35　　Br			
IV A	36 Kr	37　　Rb	strontium 38　　Sr	39　　Y	zirconium 40　　Zr	41　　Nb	42　　Mo	43　　Tc	44　Ru	45　Rh	46　Pd
IV B		silver 47　　Ag	cadmium 48　　Cd	49　　In	tin 50　　Sn	antimony 51　　Sb	52　　Te	53　　I			
V A	54 Xe	55　　Cs	barium 56　　Ba	lanthanides 57 to 71	72　　Hf	73　　Ta	tungsten 74　　W	75　　Re	76　Os	77　Ir	platinum 78　Pt
V B		gold 79　　Au	80　　Hg	81　　Tl	lead 82　　Pb	bismuth 83　　Bi	84　　Po	85　　At			
VI	86 Rn	87　　Fr	88　　Ra	actinides 89 to 106							

trons that dictates where an element should be placed in the table. There is therefore a correlation between which Group an element is in and the way in which it combines.

Valency increases across the table in accordance with the number of the Group. Group I has elements that are monovalent. In Group II they are divalent. In Group III the valency is three. The maximum is seven in Group VII. Group VIII, being a transition Group leading back to Group I on the next row, has elements of different valencies. As if tapering towards the transition of Group VIII some elements of Groups V, VI and VII also have valencies of three, two and one.

Oxygen has a valency of two. Zinc is in Group II and also has a valency of two. Zinc and oxygen therefore combine on equal terms to produce zinc oxide (ZnO). Potassium has a valency of one and therefore two potassium atoms are required to combine with one oxygen atom. The result is potassium oxide (K_2O), more commonly called potash. In contrast, titanium in Group IV has a valency of four. One titanium atom requires two oxygen atoms, each with a valency of two, to balance it. The result is titanium dioxide (TiO_2).

3. *Density*. From left to right along any Period or from top to bottom down any Group there is an increase in atomic weight. It is natural therefore that we should find the heavy elements like lead and gold low down on the table and the light elements like hydrogen and lithium at the top.

4. *Acids and alkalis*. Compounds which include the elements numbers 9, 17, 35 and 53 (fluorine, chlorine, bromine and iodine) are strong acids. These four elements are each at a right-hand extremity of a Period. They are known as the halogens and the acids as the halogen acids, e.g. hydrochloric acid (HCl). In contrast, the elements numbers 3, 11 and 19 (lithium, sodium and potassium) form strong alkalis, e.g. sodium hydroxide (caustic soda). The right-hand side of the table at Group VII is therefore considered acidic. Moving to the left the acids formed are progressively less strong, e.g. sulphuric acid, nitric acid, carbonic acid and boric acid. From Group III the compounds become alkaline. Also from top to bottom the tendency is towards alkalinity. Thus compounds formed around the elements of the top right-hand corner tend to be acids. The alkalis are compounds formed around the elements on the left and in the lower part of the table.

5. *Metals and non-metals*. The elements can be simply divided into metals and non-metals. All the inert gases of Group O are obviously non-metals. The gases hydrogen, nitrogen, oxygen, fluorine and chlorine are also non-metals. The solids which border this area of gases in the right-hand top corner of the table are also non-metals. It will be seen that these are also the elements responsible for the acids.

In some periodic tables the double period (the horizontal portion) IIIA and IIIB is extended as one line only. Similarly IVA and IVB become one line and VA

Periodic table

IB	IIB	IIIB	IVB	VB	VIB	VIIB	O	IA	IIA	IIIA	IVA	VA	VIA	VIIA	VIII
						1 H	2 He	3	4						
		5 B	6 C	7 N	8 O	9 F	10 Ne	11	12						
		13	14 Si	15 P	16 S	17 Cl	18 A	19	20	21	22	23	24	25	26 27 28
29	30	31	32	33 AS	34 Se	35 Br	36 Kr	37	38	39	40	41	42	43	44 45 46
47	48	49	50	51	52 Te	53 I	54 Xe	55	56	57-71	72	73	74	75	76 77 78
79	80	81	82	83	84	85 At	86 Rn	87	88	89 etc					

(Non-metal Elements outlined block)

and VB become one line. This has the effect of bringing together the shorter B sections of these three Periods. And by allowing the Group O gases to follow the B sections all the non-metal elements can be brought together as a block without altering the sequence of atomic numbers. This block of non-metal elements is outlined.

All the other elements are metals. This division is suitable for potters but scientists prefer to have a third division for those elements that divide the two areas of the table and can show properties of both metals and non-metals. They are called metalloids and appear on both sides of the broken outline in the accompanying extended table.

PERIODIC TABLE FOR POTTERS. In this table are listed the oxides of some of the elements instead of the elements themselves. This is because it is the oxides that are combined in the fusion of a body or glaze. By including only the oxides which have ceramic use one obtains a general picture of the table from the potter's point of view. Oxides which behave similarly (have properties in common) come together in families in vertical Groups, horizontal Periods and areas. There are about 21 oxides which are in common use by the potter. About another 11 are in specialized use or exist as important impurities and a further 8 have been involved in experiments. Only 33 appear on the table. The table is analysed as a whole in consideration of its

Periodic table for potters

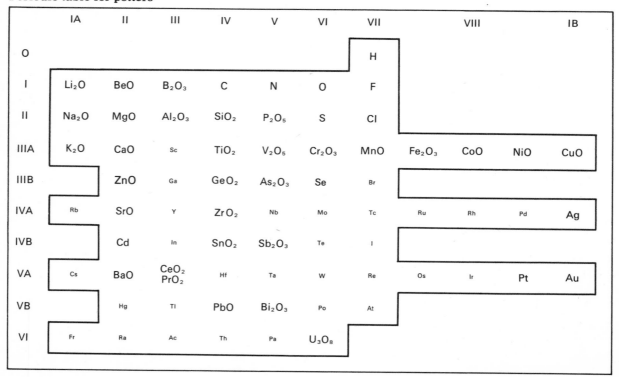

general principles and then analysed area by area in order to consider the different properties of the oxides of each area. Versatile oxides necessitate the overlapping of some areas but the principles outlined should make prediction of behaviour possible.

In order to facilitate the delineation of areas an arrangement is used which is sometimes found in Periodic Tables of Elements. It is to further extend the Periods which compose Group VIII. Copper, silver and gold (atomic numbers 29, 47, 79) which are in vertical Group I and horizontal Periods III, IV and V are given a separate Group IB. They therefore appear at the end of the extended Periods which compose Group VIII. The elements copper, silver and gold are still in correct sequence, e.g. (number 29) still follows nickel (number 28) and is before zinc (number 30).

POTTER'S PERIODIC TABLE (general principles). The general chemistry principles of the Periodic Table of Elements are relevant to the oxides of the potter's table. For example, it will be seen that the increasing valency of the elements from left to right across a Period gives oxides proportionately containing more oxygen. Period II is the best example in which the valency of each oxide corresponds to the number of the Group, e.g. Na_2O shows the monovalency of Group I elements and MgO shows the divalency of Group II elements.

	IA	II	III	IV	V	VI
II	Na_2O	MgO	Al_2O_3	SiO_2	P_2O_5	SO_3

However the one important principle of the potter's table of oxides is that there is a pattern to the acidic and alkaline oxides which thus form areas of the table. In compounding bodies, and more especially glazes, it is necessary to know the likely behaviour of each oxide present. An oxide's position in the periodic table in relation to another oxide is a direct clue as to whether it will behave as an acid or an alkali towards the second oxide.

The acidic area is the right-hand side at the top, (Periods O, I and II). The alkaline area is the part of the table furthest away from the acidic. This leaves a third area of in-between oxides. These are called amphoteric oxides and they have properties which are both acidic and alkaline. They are very important in bodies and

glazes as a link between the two major parts of acid and alkali. In some circumstances an amphoteric oxide would be considered acidic and sometimes considered alkaline. By reference to the table one can predict the behaviour of an oxide because of its proximity to, or conversely, its opposition to the other oxides under consideration.

A further description of the character of each oxide is given separately. Under the running heading of Periodic Table the families of oxides having similar properties are described.

ACIDIC AREA. This contains five non-metal elements which are gases, two non-metal solid elements and two non-metal oxides.

The gases are:

H	hydrogen
N	nitrogen
O	oxygen
F	fluorine
Cl	chlorine

The non-metal solids are:

C	carbon
S	sulphur

These seven are found in the compounds of many ceramic raw materials but they are rarely found in the final ceramic product. With the action of heat, the gases dissociate from their compounds. Carbon and sulphur combine with oxygen to form gases which again dissociate from the original compounds. In the majority of ceramic fusions these elements are unwanted so this decomposition of the material and expulsion of the gases is encouraged, e.g. by oxidation of a biscuit firing in the 700°C to 900°C range (1292°F to 1652°F). These elements often reform as new volatile compounds especially upon meeting the atmosphere outside the kiln. They form acids which corrode kiln structures, etch workshop windows etc. The seven elements form a block of non-metal volatiles on the periodic table.

Into the lower left corner of this block fit the two non-metal oxides of the acidic family. These are:

SiO_2	silica
P_2O_5	phosphorus pentoxide

They are both glass-forming oxides and of the two, silica is by far the more important. Thus silica is

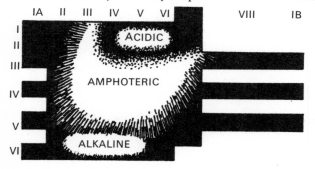

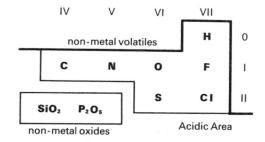

sometimes loosely referred to as the glass-former or the acidic oxide.

GLASS-FORMERS. Around the acidic oxides, silica and phosphorus pentoxide, and related to them is an area of oxides of different character but with one common property, that of forming a glass. See **Glass-former**. The diagram shows these oxides extracted from the periodic table but kept in their original positions to show the relationship of each to the acidic oxides.

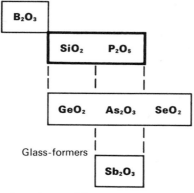

Glass-formers

The glass-forming oxides are:

B_2O_3 boric oxide
SiO_2 silica
P_2O_5 phosphorus pentoxide
GeO_2 germania
As_2O_3 arsenic oxide
SeO_2 selenium dioxide
Sb_2O_3 antimony oxide

Whilst involved in forming glasses, the elements are displaying non-metallic properties but, with the exception of silicon, phosphorus and oxygen, the elements concerned sometimes display metallic properties. Therefore these elements are given the in-between names of metalloids. Of these metalloid oxides the most important one is boric oxide.

Boric oxide assists and replaces silica in many glazes. Being a metalloid oxide it has a tendency to act as an alkali, that is as a flux, in addition to its role as an acid, that is as a glass-former. It is thus correctly called an amphoteric oxide. Its position on the periodic table is to the left of silica and therefore in relation to silica it will act as an alkali.

Germania and arsenic oxide are rarely isolated but are often present in glazes as trace substances. Antimony oxide gives yellow colours when related to lead oxide, otherwise it is difficult to melt and produces opacity. Selenium dioxide is unstable and rarely used.

ALKALINE OXIDES. The alkaline oxides are the fluxes. They are sometimes simply called the alkalis. They cause silica, which is the acid, to melt in bodies and glazes. Without this alkali/acid reaction it would be impossible to make glazes and dense pottery. These oxides are also known as the metal oxides although some

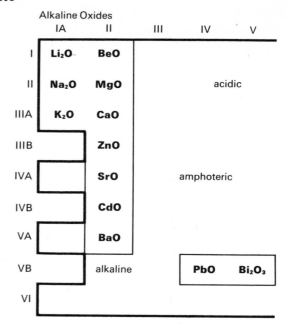

of the elements concerned are not familiar to us as metals. It is natural to accept lead, zinc and even magnesium as metals but in everyday life one does not meet the metals lithium, sodium, calcium, barium etc.

The important alkaline oxides are contained in the vertical Groups IA and II and the horizontal Period VB. The alkaline oxides are:

Li_2O lithia
Na_2O soda
K_2O potash
BeO beryllia
MgO magnesia
CaO calcia
ZnO zinc oxide
SrO strontia
CdO cadmium oxide
BaO baria
PbO lead oxide
Bi_2O_3 bismuth oxide

The colouring oxides of the transition area on horizontal Period IIIA are also active fluxes and are alkaline. They are:

MnO manganous oxide
FeO iron (ferrous) oxide
CoO cobalt oxide
NiO nickel oxide
CuO copper oxide

ALKALINE COLOURING OXIDES. The simplest colouring oxides are those which have self-colour when suspended in a glaze or give a colour when in solution in the glaze. The solution colour is the colour of the oxide/silica combination and is a dependable result. For example, cobalt oxide gives blue and copper oxide gives green.

218

The quality of the hue and in some cases the strength or staining power is altered by the presence of other alkaline and amphoteric oxides which in themselves have no colouring power. For example, zinc oxide in extremely small amounts often brightens colours but in large amounts tends to sully the colours; the presence of boric oxide often intensifies the sharper side of a colour.

These variations hint at the wider range of colours physically possible in combinations of colouring oxide and oxides other than silica. These combinations are possible in non-ceramic paint colours but difficult to stabilize in ceramic fusions. A few are used in ceramic stains but most are destroyed because the colouring oxide prefers a combination with silica.

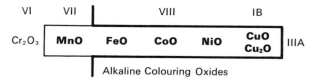

Alkaline Colouring Oxides

The family of predictable colouring oxides is stretched out on a limb of the periodic table in Period IIIA. It is called the transition metal oxide family or the metal oxide colouring family. The oxides involved are:

MnO	manganous oxide	(above 1080°C or 1976°F)
FeO	ferrous oxide	(reduced)
CoO	cobalt oxide	
NiO	nickel oxide	
CuO	cupric oxide	(oxidized)
Cu_2O	cuprous oxide	(reduced)

It will be noticed that the other colouring oxides which require special conditions are mostly nearby, starting with chromium oxide (Cr_2O_3) which is the strongest. They are amphoteric oxides.

AMPHOTERIC OXIDES. These oxides are between the acidic and the alkaline in their action and are found in the area between the acidic and the alkaline oxides on the periodic table. They are capable of acting as both acids and alkalis according to the situations in which they are placed. For example, boric oxide (B_2O_3) is capable of displaying properties of both acid and alkali at the same time by acting as a glass-former and a flux. Alumina (Al_2O_3) also displays properties of both acid and alkali, and in so doing provides a most important stabilizing link between the acids and the alkalis. The other amphoteric oxides tend to act as either acid or alkali but not both in any one situation.

The amphoteric oxides shown on the diagram occupy a large area of the periodic table. The area is large enough to overlap other areas described as alkaline oxides, colouring oxides, glass-formers and opacifiers. It includes those oxides usually accepted as amphoteric, that is, those with chemical formulae of the R_2O_3 type, and also many oxides of RO and RO_2 formulae. All

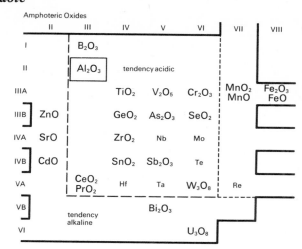

these oxides exhibit amphoteric properties in one way or another and having once become aware of this fact the potter can safely divide the oxides into three groups for it will be found that they are fairly consistent in their ceramic behaviour.

Alumina (Al_2O_3) behaves in such an individual way that it warrants a group to itself. In unity formulae it is well to always keep this oxide separate. The other oxides must therefore be put into columns of either alkali or acid.

Reasoning from the periodic table one expects those oxides which are close to the acidic area to act as acids and *vice versa*. This theory is borne out in practice and the dividing line is shown in the diagram of amphoteric oxides.

Amphoteric oxides tending to be alkaline in ceramic action are:

Bi_2O_3	bismuth oxide
CdO	cadmium oxide
FeO	black iron oxide
MnO	manganous oxide
SrO	strontia
U_3O_8	uranium oxide
ZnO	zinc oxide

Amphoteric oxides tending to be acidic in ceramic action are:

As_2O_3	arsenic oxide
B_2O_3	boric oxide
CeO_2	ceria
Cr_2O_3	chromium oxide
Fe_2O_3	red iron oxide
GeO_2	germania
MnO_2	manganese dioxide
PrO_2	praseodymium oxide
Sb_2O_3	antimony oxide
SeO_2	selenium oxide
SnO_2	stannic oxide
TiO_2	titania
V_2O_5	vanadium pentoxide
W_3O_8	tungsten oxide
ZrO_2	zirconia

By keeping to these groupings of the amphoteric oxides, unity formulae will be consistent and therefore comparative. The rule can be broken to get a different viewpoint on special glazes, e.g. zinc matts or iron rusts.

The alkaline list is the most crucial since this is brought to unity. An inaccuracy here upsets comparisons with other formulae regarding melting range and stiffness as read in the general ratios alkaline : acidic and alkaline : amphoteric. The more specific alumina : silica ratio is not upset by the choice of alkaline list.

In the diagram of the amphoteric oxides some of the rare elements are included. These elements have been used experimentally by ceramic chemists to produce colouring compounds. They are included for completeness and are:

Nb niobium (also called columbium Cb)
Mo molybdenum
Te tellurium
Hf hafnium
Ta tantalum
Re rhenium

The diagram also shows that there is a gap in the middle of the amphoteric oxides in Group III. These elements are rare and their compounds are apparently of no use to the potter.

AMPHOTERIC COLOURING OXIDES. The majority of the colours produced by amphoteric oxides are opaque. This contrasts with the colours produced by the alkaline colouring oxides which are transparent. Furthermore in contrast to an alkaline oxide, an amphoteric oxide does not always produce the same colour or indeed give a colour at all. In true amphoteric manner the presence and balance of other oxides are important.

Of the amphoteric colouring oxides only three can be said to always give colour. They are:

MnO_2 manganese dioxide
Fe_2O_3 ferric oxide
Cr_2O_3 chromium oxide

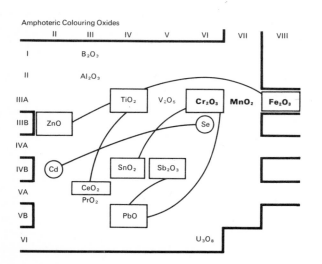

Their proximity to the alkaline colouring oxides is significant but they are amphoteric in character because their behaviour is dependent upon the balance of the remainder of the glaze, the temperature and the atmosphere.

Manganese dioxide gives excellent purples and plum colours in alkaline glazes up to 1080°C (1976°F). Above this temperature it becomes involved in the fusion as a monoxide. See **Manganese dioxide**.

Ferric oxide is affected in colour and intensity by the presence and amounts of boric oxide, alumina and titania. Boric oxide absorbs the ferric oxide thereby lessening its intensity. It also turns the ferric oxide black and, when crystalline, rust. Alumina turns the ferric oxide brown when without its presence it would be blue. Titania intensifies the staining power of ferric oxide.

Chromium oxide shows startling effects. Its usual colour is a grey-green but in the presence of sufficient lead oxide (PbO) its colour is an orange red. In the presence of stannic oxide (SnO_2), the colour of chromium oxide is a purply pink and in the presence of zinc oxide (ZnO) the colour is brown.

The remaining colouring oxides of the amphoteric area are only capable of producing colours under special conditions. For example, antimony oxide (Sb_2O_3) is an off-white opacifier but it produces a beautiful yellow when combined with lead oxide (PbO). Zinc oxide (ZnO) and titania (TiO_2) combine to give a pale yellow but are themselves colourless. The colours produced are those of the compounds lead antimonate and zinc titanate.

This is different from the mixing of two self-colouring oxides to produce a third colour. In such a case one can consider the developed colour as a simple mixture of two colours. In the periodic table the self-colouring oxides are all together in a block but lead antimonate, zinc titanate and the other amphoteric colour combinations have no single location. It is therefore difficult to relate them to other oxides and thus predict their behaviour.

Amphoteric colours are often exciting but being the result of many variables are not easily reproduced. Also, with the exception of the ferric oxide colours, they are fugitive and each has its upper temperature limit, some as low as 750°C (1382°F), whilst some spread their colouring to every suitable glaze in the kiln.

GLAZE OPACIFIERS. Opacity is the result of light interference inside or at the surface of the glaze. There are three different ways of achieving this and some oxides give opacity by a combination of effects. In the diagram these effects are considered as three areas of the periodic table and they involve oxides and individual elements.

The most important opacifiers are tin oxide, which does not dissolve but remains as particles which cloud the final glaze; titanium dioxide, which forms crystals

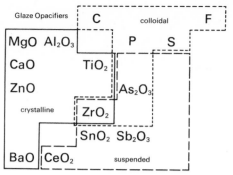

on cooling; and zirconia, which combines both these opacities with colloidal opacity. For further details see **Opacifiers**.

LUSTRES. The non-tarnishing metals, which are precious metals, come together as a horizontal family at the end of Period VA. They are:

Au gold
Ir iridium
Os osmium
Pt platinum

They are non-tarnishing because they do not readily oxidize.

Included as a precious metal is silver (Ag) and above silver in the vertical Group IB comes copper (Cu). Copper and silver tarnish by combining with oxygen in the air but like all this family of metals they are easy to reduce to pure metal state.

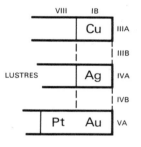

Platinum, gold and silver are used for precious metal lustres on pottery. Copper is also used for lustres. They can all be dissolved in acids and applied to pottery in liquid form. The acid is burnt away during the firing and the gases assist in keeping the metal reduced. See also **Lustres**.

Petalite. Lithium feldspar or feldspathoid. Li_2O. $Al_2O_3.8SiO_2$. A feldspathoid used in glazes to introduce lithia, alumina and silica. Ground petalite inevitably includes some soda and potash. It interacts readily with other feldspars and alkaline oxides producing fluid melts. Its range of maturity as a secondary stoneware flux is in the region 1200°C to 1350°C (2192°F to 2462°F).

Pure petalite, like spodumene, has a low expansion

rate and has been used in experimental flameproof stoneware bodies.

Petuntse. Chinese name for the equivalent of cornish stone. It is a variable feldspathic mineral and was used to fuse the plastic white clay, kaolin, in the making of porcelain. Petuntse is a corruption of the Chinese for 'white bricks' in which form it was transported from the quarry to the pottery. This is similar to the English origin of the term 'ball clays' which were transported in balls. See **Cornish stone**.

Phosphorite. $Ca_3(PO_4)_2$. A fossil deposit which is a source of phosphorus pentoxide and calcia for glazes. It contains some fluorine but the amount is variable and is not includable as a definite chemical composition.

Phosphorus pentoxide. Phosphoric oxide. P_2O_5. A glass-forming oxide which is present in many glazes as a trace constituent though it is not often deliberately introduced. In small amounts it gives colloidal opacity as in the Chinese chun glazes. See **Chun**. Large amounts give opacity, a dull surface and blistering. In bodies it gives vitrification without softening and is so used to give translucency to bone china.

Phosphorus pentoxide is often introduced into glazes via vegetable ashes and bone ash. The phosphorus, with the calcium, is an essential element in plant and animal growth. The amount of phosphorus involved in vegetable ashes may be small but sufficient to give a chun effect. With bone ash the amount of phosphorus can be calculated. See **Bone ash**.

Phosphorus also occurs combined with calcium in the rocks phosphorite ($Ca_3(PO_4)_2$) and apatite ($3Ca_3(PO_4)_2.Ca(Cl,F)_2$). These rocks are the origin of superphosphate fertilizers. Phosphorus pentoxide can be introduced into frits and glazes by the rocks and fertilizers. The lithium ore amblygonite has also been used to introduce phosphorus pentoxide. The rocks are not so useful as the vegetable and bone ashes because they contain unwanted trace elements like fluorine.

Phosphorus pentoxide shows as a bluish flush in glazes. The particles of phosphoric glazes are separate from the silicic glass though suspended in it. They are of colloidal size and therefore disperse the light. See **Colloid, glaze**.

In bodies, the phosphorus pentoxide produces a very stiff liquid which helps vitrification without allowing a fluid state. The calcia content of bone ash is checked from becoming an active flux by its involvement with the phosphorus pentoxide.

Isolated phosphorus pentoxide is a glass which is soluble in water. Like boric oxide it is also deliquescent and is therefore used as a desiccant. Phosphorus pentoxide cannot be considered in any way as a substitute for silica and does not enter the silica chain. If it were isolated it would vaporize at 300°C (572°F). In compounds it provides a viscous link in the structure at temperatures above 580°C (1076°F).

Phototrophy. The phenomenon of colour change caused by light. Normally glazes are physically unchanged by light although obviously their colourings are dependent upon the light which falls upon them. Glazes which contain rutile or titanium dioxide with a small amount of rutile, totalling 15%, however, darken in colour upon exposure to light. The dark colour fades again with the absence of light and the process can be repeated *ad infinitum*.

The amount of colour change is not noticeable except where a part of the glaze has been covered. For example a saucer will show a lighter circle where the cup has been placed. The image disappears in approximately a minute.

Pigskin. Orange peel. The texture of a glaze surface where it resembles pigskin or orange peel because it is covered with many small craters. Pigskin is usually used to describe tenmokus and glazes with widely-spaced pin pricks. Orange peel is used to describe irregular glaze surfaces especially salt glaze and heavily-pitted glazes.

Pilgrim flask. Pilgrim bottle. A bottle with thong-loop handles by which it can be carried. Pilgrim flasks exist in all shapes and sizes. Some are flat-sided whilst others are like a barrel on its side. They were made throughout Europe and Asia, and are associated with pilgrimages, sanctuaries and places of holy significance. They were used by the pilgrims as a means of carrying drinking water for the journey and also for bringing home holy water from a sanctuary. Small bottles with scenes depicting a saint or a religious emblem were often sold at shrines and contained the holy water of the shrine. See also **Costrel**.

Pinching. Forming a pot by the compressing action of fingers and thumb. The pot grows from a ball of plastic clay by pushing a hole in it and progressively

thinning the walls. The pot is slowly rotated in one hand as it is pinched with the other.

A soft plastic clay is required. Coarse clays can be used because there is no friction between clay and hands that would tear the hands. If coarse clays cannot be persuaded into pots, their workability for pinching can be improved by a generous addition of bentonite.

Beating compresses the clay and brings moisture to the surface. This strengthens the pot wall and returns the outer layer of clay to a more plastic state when it had started to dry. Some clays become very dry and require to be worked wet. With water, the pinching action becomes a stroking action and it is probable that throwing developed from this technique.

Large pinched pots are enlarged by further beating with a paddle and anvil. Two pots can be joined rim to rim to form a larger pot.

The idea is simple, and pinching is often used as an an introduction to pottery-making. The product is the direct result of the concentration and action of the maker. No tools intervene. Mastery of the technique promotes close observation of the clay's properties and the effects of the hands' actions. With development of skill one can make pots of great sensitivity, as shown in the photographs of pinched pots by Sheila Fournier and Tony George.

Pin-hole. A small smooth-edged hole in a glaze surface like a pin prick and a similar mark occurring as a defect on slip-cast ware. See **Casting slip, adjustment**.

The pin-hole in the glaze surface as illustrated here is the result of a burst bubble which has left a crater.

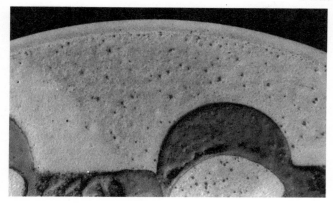

The crater has started to heal over but because of insufficient time has been unable to do more than round the edges of the crater. Horizontal surfaces are more prone to pin-holing than vertical ones because they lack the general glaze movement under gravity. Glazes intended for horizontal surfaces only, like tiles and plates, can afford to be more fluid than other glazes in order to overcome pin-holing.

Pin-holing sometimes occurs in re-fired glazes especially if the refiring is at a lower temperature than the original glaze temperature, e.g. on enamelled ware. This is caused by moisture in the ware which blisters the glaze as it escapes.

Pink. Pink in ceramics is usually achieved by the chrome-tin combination. Some pinkish lilac colours also occur with cobalt oxide and manganese oxide in high alkaline glazes. See **Chromium oxide** (chrome-tin pink). Pink lustre results from a very thin layer of gold lustre on a transparent glaze covering a white body or slip.

Pint weight. Slop weight. Ounces per pint. The weight of one pint of a clay or glaze suspension in water. It is a description of density and is expressed in ounces and is written as a number with 'oz pt'.

Care should be taken to ascertain whether the pint is Imperial (British) measure or US measure.

1 US pint = 0·83 Imperial pint
1 Imperial pint = 1·205 US pints

Thus a slip of 29 oz pt in Britain is of the same density as one rated 24·07 in the USA. See also **Formula, density**.

Pint weights of slips and glazes are noted in order to reproduce the same density in successive batches. However, note that the fluidity of the suspension can be altered by the phenomena of flocculation and defloc-culation whilst the density remains the same. Calculations involving the amounts of dry material and water in suspensions are made with Brongniart's formula. See **Formula, Brongniart's**.

For most slips and leadless glazes the average specific gravity of the materials is taken as 2·5. This

means that for Imperial pints the pint weight will lie between 20 oz pt (the weight of one pint of water) and 50 oz pt (the weight of one pint of solid dry clay). Equal bulks of water and clay give a pint weight of 35 oz pt. Equal weights of water and clay give a pint weight of 28·54 oz pt.

Pipe clay. A white clay found in small pockets often associated with fireclay. It is white, capable of being refined, and vitrifiable at around 1000°C (1832°F). It was used for making clay pipes.

Fireclays for making sewer pipes are also referred to as pipe clays.

Pipkin. A late medieval cooking pot, usually glazed inside only and with three legs on which it could stand securely in hot ashes. The straight tapering handle allowed the pipkin to be lifted in and out of the hot ashes by slotting over it a long stick or metal rod with a tubular end.

Pitcher. A large jug often with a relatively small top. It is intended for carrying and storing liquid rather than pouring and serving.

The examples are of the traditional Cornish pitcher glazed inside and over the rim only, and a slipware pitcher by Sidney Tustin.

Pitchers. Grog made from the same clay as that to which it is to be added. The word is rarely used in the singular. Pitchers are usually finely ground and are blended with the body to reduce shrinkage and increase workability rather than to give texture.

They are made from ground broken biscuit (soft pitchers) or bisc (hard pitchers). Occasionally glazed wasters are ground into pitchers but the glaze particles can cause unpredictable results. Because pitchers are of the same body as the ware, they do not alter the ultimate composition but are effective in the control of drying and firing shrinkages.

Hard pitchers are used in fine white earthenware. Soft pitchers are used in porcelain where they mature with the body.

Place. To pack ware into saggars. Earthenware and bone china for high-temperature bisque firings are placed in saggars surrounded by sand. The placing of plates in this way is known as nesting. The sand holds the ware in place during firing and thus restrains any tendency to warp.

Bone china is placed in powdered alumina because silica sand would be fused by the ware. White earthenware would be stained by alumina and is placed in a pure silica sand. The silica sand is smooth-grained but is coarser than the alumina used. If the sand is too fine it tends to fuse to a solid mass whereas a relatively coarse sand does not. Most individual potters, however, would call the industrial placing sand fine and many use it as an opener in stoneware bodies.

Plagioclase feldspar. Any one of the group of feldspars which has albite at one end and anorthite at the other. The group contains six feldspars which show progression from soda feldspar to lime feldspar.

Albite	$Na_2O . Al_2O_3 . 6SiO_2$
Oligoclase	
Andesine	
Labradorite	
Bytownite	
Anorthite	$CaO . Al_2O_3 . 2SiO_2$

Plaster of Paris (historical). Plaster was known to the Greeks and Romans and it is possible that its absorbent properties were used in bats for stiffening clay and in sprig moulds, but no evidence is available. The first references to the use of plaster by potters is in France of the early 18th century. Between 1745 and 1750 different potters, notably Ralph Daniel and Ralph Littler, both makers of salt-glazed figures, brought the method of making plaster moulds from Paris to improve their own productions in Staffordshire, England.

The name plaster of Paris remained, although plaster was soon produced not far away from Stoke-on-Trent at Burton-on-Trent. Potters had previously carved gypsum, the raw material for plaster, to make moulds for sprigs. They had also used alabaster, biscuit, copper, brass and wood. Plaster quickly replaced these because of the ease with which the impression could be taken from a master model.

The porosity of plaster enabled larger plates and pots to be press-moulded successfully and was the basis of the development of slip-casting. It is interesting to note that at the time of its introduction, the potters heralded plaster as a boon to the production of their salt-glazed whiteware. The salt-glazed ware had reached perfection in the struggle to outclass oriental and continental porcelain. Modelled decoration was crisp and pots were thin as a result of great pressure from metal moulds. Plaster was seen as a means of quicker and easier production. But plaster moulds wear quickly and there was soon a loss in crispness of detail and a resulting clumsiness in thickness of ware. The plaster moulds helped the rival creamware industry more because of its simpler approach with use of soft glazes and colour. Creamware overtook salt-glaze in popularity and plaster of Paris can be seen to be a major contributing factor.

Plaster of Paris (technical). Semi-hydrated calcium sulphate. Calcined hydrated calcium sulphate. $2CaSO_4 . H_2O$. Plaster of Paris is a white powder prepared from gypsum by driving off part of the water of crystallization.

$$2(CaSO_4 . 2H_2O) \longrightarrow 2CaSO_4 . H_2O + 3H_2O \uparrow$$
$$\text{gypsum} \qquad\qquad \text{plaster} \qquad \text{water}$$

To manufacture plaster of Paris the powdered gypsum is heated in steel pans. As the water escapes, the powder looks as if it is boiling. Plaster of Paris is sometimes called boiled plaster or boiled gypsum. If the gypsum is overheated it is called overburnt and is difficult to recrystallize. If it is completely calcined it is called dead plaster. Underburnt plaster quickly recrystallizes and so does plaster which has been able to absorb atmospheric moisture. By so doing it has begun to form the crystals which make it set.

To make plaster of Paris into a hard substance one adds the powder to water. After thorough mixing the plaster takes up sufficient water to form its crystals. That is, it takes back the water that was driven off in its manufacture and could be said to return to its gypsum state. Excess water, and there is always some, is removed from the set plaster by drying in a warm draught (25°C or 77°F).

The ratio of water to plaster affects the setting time, the final strength and the absorbency of the set plaster after it has dried. See chart. The weakest practical mixture is 100 parts of water to 110 parts of plaster by weight. The result is a light plaster with about 50% absorbency but it is not physically strong. The strongest mixture is 100 parts water to 140 parts plaster. This gives a strong heavy plaster with about 35% absorbency. These mixtures are called 110's mix and 140's mix. With the 110's mix there is about 7 minutes available between mixing and commencement of setting. With the 140's mix the time is about 4 minutes. The 140's mix is used for cases and any originals which need to remain intact during the parting process. A 130's mix is used for pressing moulds, casting moulds and jolley moulds where these moulds form the outside of the articles. A 120's mix is a general mix for hump moulds and absorbent bats where absorbency with reasonable strength is required.

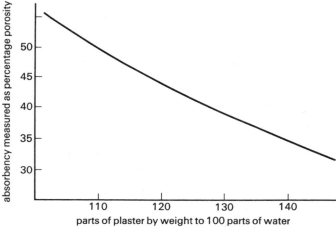

Some potters find difficulty in mixing plaster but no difficulty should be experienced if a careful routine is followed. First the measured amount of powdered plaster should be sifted through a 20's mesh and then sprinkled into the measured amount of water. The sprinkling is intended to give a thorough wetting to each particle. This is further ensured by allowing the mix to remain unstirred for one minute. Patience at this point is rewarded because a thorough wetting prevents the formation of lumps. This is also the reason for the sifting. When a stirring begins it must be thorough and continuous but frothing or entrapping of bubbles should be avoided.

From the commencement of stirring to the time setting begins, is the pouring time, and this varies with the mixture ratio. A fresh plaster in good condition should give 3 to 6 minutes of pouring time. An old

plaster which has had time to absorb moisture from the air may give only 1 minute. This time is further altered by retarders and accelerators. Some retarders are borax, gelatine, alum and sulphuric acid in the water, and lukewarm water (20°C–30°C) instead of cold. Accelerators are crystalline salts, e.g. potassium sulphate, chloride and nitrate, also hot water (above 40°C) and already-set plaster. The presence of only 1% of set plaster will cut down a pouring time of 5 minutes to 30 seconds. Cleanliness of mixing utensils is obviously essential or one may find one's hand set in the plaster as soon as stirring begins. Also it is necessary to store the plaster of Paris powder in a dry place, otherwise it becomes pre-set.

As the crystals form and interlock in the setting plaster an overall expansion takes place. This continues through the first 24 hours. It is only 0·4% but it is a useful aid to the parting of two blocks of plaster, such as a case and a mould. Heat is generated by the crystallization and reaches a maximum of 35°C (95°F) from water at room temperature. To reach maximum temperature during crystallization takes up to 30 minutes from mixing. The times on the chart are given as minutes after pouring. The point of maximum temperature can be taken as the point at which the plaster is strong enough to be moved. It is sufficiently accurate to judge this temperature by touch. The heat is also a useful aid to parting because it causes the set plaster to sweat. This softens a water-bound parting agent like soft soap thus enabling the parts to be more easily separated.

To calculate the amounts of water and plaster of Paris powder required, the following system can be adopted. The volume of the space to be filled is estimated or calculated by measurements. This volume multiplied by 5 and divided by 7 is the volume of water that will be required. The volume of water is taken as the unit from which the weight of plaster is calculated for 120's, 130's or 140's mix. A few examples are given:

225

	120's mix	130's mix	140's mix
per 100 cc	120 gm	130 gm	140 gm
per ½ UK pt	12 oz	13 oz	14 oz
per UK pt	24 oz	26 oz	28 oz
per ½ US pt	10 oz	11 oz	11½ oz
per US pint	20 oz	21½ oz	23 oz

In calculating the volume to be filled, the following formulae will be found useful:

To change cc to UK fl oz multiply by 0·035
To change UK fl oz to UK pints divide by 20
To change cc to US fl oz multiply by 0·034
To change US fl oz to US pints divide by 16
To change cubic inches to UK fl oz multiply by 0·58
To change cubic inches to US fl oz multiply by 0·55

Further capacity equivalents are given in the **Tables** of this book.

Chart of plaster mixes

Parts by weight Water	Plaster	Minutes pouring time	Further minutes setting	% absorbency	Use
100	110 }	6	13	50	patching moulds
91	100 }				
100	120 }	5½	18	45	absorbent bats; hump moulds
83	100 }				
100	130 }	5	20	40	casting moulds; jolley moulds; blocks
77	100 }				
100	140 }	3	18	35	cases
71	100 }				

Plastic clay. Clay in plastic state, that is, in a state in which it can be formed easily by moderate pressure and yet retain the new form without collapse. However, contrary to what the novice may wish, no clay is ready for use. All clays require some preparation by wedging and/or kneading immediately prior to use.

The term plastic clay is also used to imply a clay with high plasticity. The term long clay and fat clay are also used. The opposite is a short or lean clay.

Plasticity. The unique property held by clays which combines the strength of a solid with the fluidity of a liquid. Plasticity allows the solid to be reformed without rupturing and allows the new form achieved to remain without any attempt to return to the original form. That is, there is no elasticity involved.

Plasticity is an involved subject and it is not sur-

prising that no-one has yet given the complete definition. Many attempts have been made to measure plasticity. Their success has always been in a narrow field that required too many qualifying conditions. No measurement has been found that can apply to all potting circumstances. Yet every potter knows when he has a 'plastic' clay and when he has a 'short' clay. In working with a clay, its properties become evident. Clays have strength and a certain resistance, as well as plasticity. The three properties are summed up in the term 'workability'. The terms workability and plasticity are therefore used advisedly. Plasticity must include some strength but not necessarily all of the strength that is attributed to a clay.

If one has a clay that lacks plasticity, one can add this property by adding a clay of high plasticity. The resulting blend will be proportionate. Even 10% of a highly-plastic ball clay will make a noticeable difference in the workability. It is sufficient to knead the two clays together in a plastic state. It may also be necessary to add a little extra water.

Ten per cent of a light-coloured ball clay will have little effect upon the colour of a clay. It will, however, affect the general drying contraction and firing shrinkage. Plastic clays tend to have high wet-dry contraction and dry-fired shrinkage rates.

Another plastic material is bentonite. Though strictly not a clay, it is so called. A clay which is very low in plasticity can be made workable by 5% or 6% of bentonite. A usual amount added to many clays is 1% or 2%. This is a dry-weight measure of bentonite to the dry weight of the clay. However bentonite cannot be added as a powder to plastic clay. It must first be mixed with about twice its own weight of water. It then swells to a slippery mass rather like a greasy soap. This is added to the clay by slicing the clay with a wire, poking holes in the slices and sandwiching the bentonite before rekneading. The bentonite provides so much 'slide' that the process is not an easy one.

Of course, the ideal way is to start the improvement of plasticity at an earlier stage of preparation. To do this one needs to understand the major factors that contribute to plasticity. See also **Preparation of clay**.

PHYSICS OF PLASTICITY. Plasticity depends upon:
1. clay particle size
2. true clay content
3. moisture content
4. particle uniformity
5. plasticizers
6. strength of particle bond

These factors are now discussed in relation to the preparation of clay by the wet process, that is, rendering the clay to a slurry which is refined and dewatered to plastic state.

1. *Clay particle size.* The size of the clay particles has a direct bearing on plasticity. The smallest particle

226

sizes give the most plasticity. Even non-plastic materials like quartz and zircon exhibit plastic tendencies by mutual particle attraction if their particles are small enough. However their plasticity is nothing compared to that of clay.

The fineness of particle which gives plasticity is not a question of a mesh size. The clay particles are infinitely smaller than could be separated by sieving. The particles involved are of colloidal size and individually invisible to the naked eye. The largest size involved is in the region of 3 microns in diameter. A micron is one ten-thousandth of a centimetre. To give a comparison: the holes in a 100's mesh are each 130 microns across.

The 3-micron clay particle is that of a coarse clay. Such a clay is not very plastic, e.g. china clay.

In comparison, a ball clay has particles averaging 0·25 microns and bentonite 0·05 microns. Particles of this size are often packed together as large grains. To break down these grains into particles and thus achieve full plasticity it is necessary to soak the clay in water and age it or use a blunger, preferably of the high-speed type. The more water that is available at any stage of clay preparation, the more plastic the final clay is likely to be because the water penetrates between and divides the particles giving more particles of smaller size. See **Ageing, Weathering** and **Preparation of clay**.

2. *True clay content*. Whilst it is impossible to use a mesh to separate the different sizes of clay particles, it is perfectly possible to separate a lot of the non-clay particles from the clay particles by its use. Non-clay particles detract from plasticity since they exhibit very little or no plasticity themselves.

Pieces of shale and sands are the commonest non-plastic constituents of clays. These can be removed by a suitably-sized mesh. A test amount of very thin slip should be run through a series of sieves until the most efficient one is found. See **Preparation of clay** and **Analysis, mechanical**.

If the sand is too fine and sieving is impractical, the process of levigation can be used. This provides a very fine clay in the region of 90% true clay content. It involves a very watery suspension and a lot of settling. See **Levigation**.

The ball-clay miners used to assess the purity and hence plasticity of their clay by the bite test. If a small piece of clay is put between the teeth, the grittiness or smoothness of it can be assessed. With a little practice one can almost tell the grain size and amount of the non-plastic material. This does not truly test plasticity because a non-plastic clay like china clay is smooth, but it tests a clay's possibilities. It is a suitable test in ball clay pits where particle sizes are of a similar range and plastic potential depends upon the amount of impurities of quartz, mica and feldspar. Here one is trying to arrive at a rational analysis which states the proportions of true clay and non-clay content.

If a clay is purchased from a bulk supplier it may be possible to obtain a rational analysis and a mechanical analysis which will help to assess the clay's potential. See **Analysis**.

3. *Moisture content*. Plasticity is obviously linked with moisture content. A stiff clay becomes more plastic with increasing amounts of water. But there is an optimum point after which increasing amounts of water give too much fluidity. Obtaining the correct moisture content is important. The question of plasticity in casting slips is also related to moisture content. See **Preparation of clay**: control of moisture content, and **Water of plasticity**.

4. *Particle uniformity*. Consideration was given earlier to the mechanical analysis of clay, mainly with regard to removing unwanted non-clay material. Size uniformity of the clay content itself must also help to get closer packing of particles which will give extra strength. However it is worth mentioning that a clay can be so highly plastic that it lacks workability. Such a clay is sticky and very soft. It deforms easily with little initial resistance and lacks sufficient strength to support its own weight. This state of over-plasticity occasioned by a large proportion of extremely fine clay particles or by use of plasticizers can be mistaken for shortness by the inexperienced.

The optimum correction for this state can only be decided upon after consideration of a few trials each involving additions of different materials. China clay, a sharp sand and a sharp fine grog can be tried. All these provide friction between the particles, thereby adding strength. See **Preparation of clay**: control of particle size.

5. *Plasticizers*. Plasticizers encourage the slipperiness of existing clay particles or introduce highly-plastic particles to act as a lubricant for the clay and other materials.

A true plastic clay, like ball clay, has strength as well as plasticity. Plasticizers tend to improve plasticity but make little improvement on strength. This is perfectly acceptable for some forming processes like jigger and jolly, where a high strength is not required because the mould supports the clay. In fact, a weaker clay is less likely to tear, if well lubricated, because it deforms readily.

However it is less acceptable to have a plastic but weak clay for throwing and hand-building. Here a clay which is doctored by a plasticizer will probably require a fine sand of about 100's mesh size. The amount may be quite critical to give optimum strength without spoiling plasticity.

Bentonite is the most popular and by far the most effective plasticizer for clays. It is not a chemical but a variable mineral of the montmorillonite group. This group is closely related to the kaolinite group and therefore bentonite is often called a clay. Bentonite can be safely added to clays up to 2% of the total weight of the clay. About 6% is the limit. See **Bentonite**.

Other plasticizers which provide lubricating qualities are polymerized carbohydrate pastes and bacterial colloidal gels. See **Ageing**.

Also different clays respond in different ways to the presence of mild flocculants and deflocculants. It is possible that the presence of other non-clay material has a decided influence upon the result. The theory is simple, but only practical tests can provide evidence to support the exceedingly fine adjustments required. A flocculant will open the clay structure, thus accommodating more water and giving a wider workability range. There will be a slight stiffening which will help the clay to keep its form but the resulting green and dry ware will not be as strong. A deflocculant on the other hand, will give additional slipperiness to the particles by making them repel one another. The resulting green and dry ware will be densely packed and strong but there will be less strength at wet plastic stage.

6. *Strength of particle bond*. The strength of a clay is vital. There is obviously some strength from friction between clay and non-clay particles but there is also a strength derived from the structure created by the clay particles in plastic state.

The clay particles are flat hexagonal crystals. These crystals are lubricated with water and are able to slide past one another with ease. The flat faces of two adjacent crystals provide an excellent suction area when lubricated with water and this gives clay its strength, (fig. 1).

of a sand or grog but the shearing of bonds continues as a sequence of bond break-and-remake. On release of the pressure the bonds establish themselves strongly to hold the new form. This is the property of thixotropy and is important in clays which are thrown on the wheel into pots which are then lifted off. See **Workability**.

Crystals which are thin and flat present a large surface area for very small weight. They therefore respond to the mutual forces of attraction which, at the exceedingly small size of ball clay and bentonite particles, become increasingly larger forces proportionately. See **Forces of attraction**.

Clays with a correct balance of plasticity and strength will withstand the pull occasioned by their own weight in wide or tall free-standing clay structures (fig. 3). A clay with too much plasticity and insufficient strength collapses. It deforms by its own weight and uses its plasticity to enable it to do so (fig. 4). A clay with too little plasticity and too much strength also collapses. But it does so by tearing between the particles. Here the so-called strength was all in initial resistance to movement. Such clays feel dead to knead and often have a stodgy or bouncy feel to them. Their strength resists shear by compression or sideways displacement but cannot resist a tension tear. They cannot withstand that most crucial potter's test: the pulling of a handle (fig. 5).

The general strength of a clay is improved by bringing the particles closer together. The bonds and suction are increased even though the ability to slide, the true

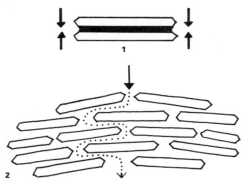

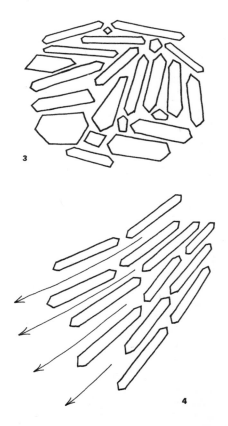

It is difficult to form a break across the crystals, at right angles to them, because of the brick-like structure which they form (fig. 2). Pulling the clay particles closer together by de-airing adds to their strength. See **De-airing**.

The plasticity of a clay lies with its capacity to allow its particles to slide past one another. There is a point at which the strength of the clay is overcome by pressure. This is called the yield point. The strength is a combination of physical abrasion and mutual attraction bonds between the particles. Once the strength is overcome, the plastic clay should deform with slight pressure. There may be a certain bite from the friction

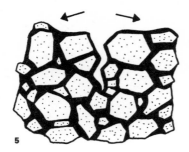

plasticity, is not increased. Ageing, wedging, pugging, especially de-aired pugging, helps in this way to improve overall workability and hence apparent plasticity.

Plumbic. Of lead or with lead from the latin *plumbum*, e.g. plumbic glaze contains lead. For information on lead glazes etc see **Lead oxide**.

Plumbous oxide. Lead oxide. Lead monoxide. PbO. The simplest and most stable oxide of lead which is an active glaze flux over a wide range of temperature. All lead compounds revert to plumbous oxide upon heating. The nearest raw lead oxide to plumbous oxide is litharge which also has the chemical formula PbO. Other names for litharge are yellow lead oxide and massicot.

For the use of plumbous oxide see **Lead oxide in glazes** where it is referred to as lead oxide.

Poison. A substance that injures the living organism when absorbed. The potter handles many potential poisons. Some are directly harmful if introduced into the lungs and digestive system, e.g. lead oxide, barium carbonate. Some substances are harmless until altered by heat when they liberate poisonous gases or decompose into poisonous substances. Most of the poisons are rendered sufficiently insoluble by complete involvement in ceramic fusions but underfired ware is suspect. Lead poisoning has received much publicity in the past (see **Lead poisoning**) but silicosis has been an equally dangerous hazard in some potteries.

Substances which should be treated with respect as direct poisons in raw state, on low-fired or underfired ware, and as concentrations in decoration are: red lead, litharge, white lead, galena, lead silicates, antimony oxide, arsenic oxide, barium carbonate, beryllia, cadmium and selenium compounds and colours, copper oxide and carbonate, chromium oxide, potassium dichromate, zinc oxide.

The previous list contains substances which can become poisonous by mishandling in the firing but there are substances that liberate poisonous gases during correct firing. These are the sulphides, chlorides, fluorides and to a lesser extent carbonates. For example, galena, cornish stone, crude feldspars and low-grade fireclays, fluorspar, gypsum, lepidolite, cryolite.

Some substances volatilize when overfired and produce poisonous fumes. They are the lead, antimony, cadmium and selenium compounds and the precious metals.

Lastly the silicates should be considered poisonous in dust form because of the danger of silicosis. Flint and quartz present the main hazard but all feldspars and clays, powdered cullet, cristobalite, bentonite, asbestos, or indeed any dust should be treated with respect.

Porcelain. A vitrified, white and translucent ware. A few wares fit this description. The one usually implied is that fired at 1300°C (2372°F) plus. In this, the body and the glaze mature together to create a very thick body-glaze layer which gives the whole piece an important strength. This ware is sometimes called hard-paste porcelain or *grand-feu*. There is also the soft-paste or *petit-feu* porcelain. Here the body and glaze mature together but at a lower temperature. To achieve translucency, the body contains a high proportion of glassy frit which requires very accurate firing. Wasters are consequently frequent.

China, both bone china and non-bone china, overcomes some of the difficulties of both hard- and soft-paste porcelains. The body of a china is fired to a translucent state as an unglazed bisc. It is prevented from warping by being embedded in alumina powder. See **Place**. The ware is given a soft-firing glaze.

A few pieces of the 18th-century white salt-glazed ware are also translucent and could be considered porcelain.

The name porcelain is said to have been coined by Marco Polo in the 13th century from *porcelino*. This was the name of the translucent cowrie shell which looked like a little pig or porcelino. He likened Chinese porcelain to this translucent white shell. The Chinese have always used the name Tz'u which is the same as stoneware.

An essential ingredient for the body of these high-fired porcelains was a plastic white-burning clay. The Chinese name was *kao ling* which survived in the English kaolin and china clay. The discovery of suitable clays in Europe in the 18th century enabled Western potters to emulate the Chinese success but European clays are not so plastic as the Chinese ones.

This has meant that pressing and slip-casting have been more frequently employed.

Potters have tried various body recipes to achieve a throwable porcelain body. But the addition of even a small amount of ball clay tends to darken the body. Some whiteness can be retrieved by hard reduction but this tends to encourage premature collapse. David Leach has successfully overcome the problem of plasticity by the use of bentonite. The bowl illustrated was fired at the remarkably low temperature of 1280°C (2336°F) with reduction.

The body recipe is:

china clay	55
potash feldspar	25
quartz	15
white bentonite	5

The glaze recipe is:

feldspar	25
china clay	25
flint	25
whiting	25

Porosity. The ability of a fired body to absorb water by capillary action. In a plastic clay the interstitial spaces between the clay and other mineral particles are filled with water (fig. 1). After the ceramic change at 600°C (1112°F) these spaces are empty. Clay fired at or just above 600°C becomes an extremely porous body (fig. 2). As the temperature increases above 600°C the feldspathoids and free silica are fluxed by the alkalis which are present. The resulting molten silicates begin

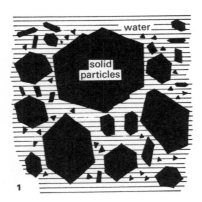

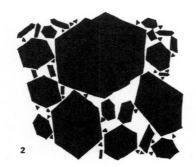

to fill the spaces and the whole mass shrinks as a result. Thus there is less space left and the body is less porous (fig. 3). The fluxing action continues until all the spaces are filled and the porosity is nil. This is complete vitrification. Beyond this point the body deforms and eventually melts.

If one is using the normal soft biscuit, the biscuit firing should be chosen to give the maximum strength, with maximum porosity. In practice this means between 900°C and 1000°C (1652°F and 1832°F). Above this it is difficult to get the glaze to adhere in a uniform layer. Below this the biscuit ware is so soft that it is easily damaged and large pieces cannot always survive the shock of dunting when cooling.

The porosity in earthenware is overcome by the use of the impervious glaze covering which of course should not be crazed. In stoneware the glaze is theoretically unnecessary and is for decorative and hygienic reasons. Crazing can be decorative in stoneware without trouble from porosity.

Although potters theoretically seek to get a porosity which is nil in their stoneware bodies, for practicality a very slight porosity is preferable. A porosity of 1% or 2% gives a much stronger body than one with no porosity at all. This is because the glassy nature of the latter is brittle and allows no chance of movement between the particles except by fracture. The graph shows typical porosity and strength curves for a stoneware clay when fired to different temperatures. By relating these two one can appreciate the relationship between porosity and ovenware. Ovenware based upon normal clays is usually porous between 5% and 10% in stonewares.

The normal test for porosity is to take a sample piece of fired body and whilst warm from the kiln to weigh it accurately. It is necessary to use a balance capable of weighing to within a hundredth of a gram. The test piece is put in boiling water for 5 minutes and left in the water as this is allowed to cool. When cold the test piece is taken out and dried, preferably with a damp sponge. This is better than a cloth which can leave fibres behind on the test piece. The test is then weighed again and the increase in weight is calculated as a percentage of the original dry weight.

$$\frac{\text{Wt after soaking minus wt dry}}{\text{weight dry}} \times \frac{100}{1} = \frac{\text{percentage}}{\text{porosity}}$$

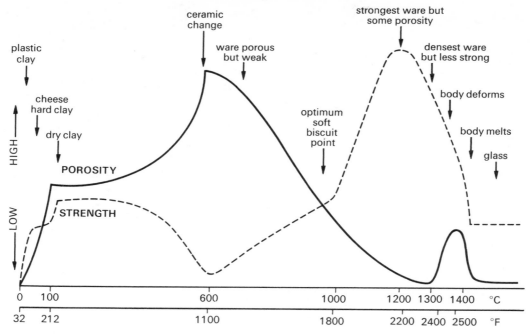

Posset cup. A 16th–18th-century large cup sometimes lidded. There is often a long spout or tube coming from the bottom and attached firmly to the inside or outside appearing near the rim as a spout from which the posset was sucked. Posset is hot milk curdled with wine or ale.

The photograph shows a late 17th-century slipware example made in Staffordshire, England. The spout is visible on the right and one of the two handles on the left.

Potash. Potassa. Potassium oxide. Kalium oxide. K_2O. One of the three strong alkaline fluxes for ceramic fusions. The others are lithia and soda. Potash is soluble in water but exists in feldspars in relatively insoluble form. Feldspars are used in glaze-making and most clays contain some potash in feldspathic combinations. Potash is introduced into frits by feldspar and potassium carbonate.

Potassium is a similar metal to sodium but it is not quite so reactive. See **Soda minerals**. The compounds of potassium are therefore not quite so soluble as those of sodium. The potassium feldspar (orthoclase, K_2O. $Al_2O_3 . 6SiO_2$) is relatively insoluble. In geological time the potash content can be dissolved and it is, with other feldspars, the source of china clay and indeed all clays. Feldspar is therefore a constituent of all clays with the exception of pure kaolinite.

Potash feldspar can therefore be introduced into clays and bodies. It provides a non-plastic shortening and a fusible content which gives hardness to the finished product. The potash is the flux which instigates the interactions which give the denser ware.

One cannot help comparing potash with soda, the slightly cheaper but slightly more active glaze flux. As if to compensate, potash begins its action a little earlier than does soda, at 750°C (1382°F). Its action is uniform throughout all glaze ranges and it does not suffer from

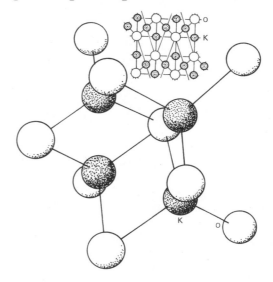

231

soda's defect of high-temperature volatility. See **Soda in glazes**. The resulting melt of a potash glass is not quite so fluid, but when set, it is more resistant to abrasion and to solubility attack than is soda glass.

However, potash cannot be used alone as a flux. Potash glass is brittle and as a glaze would be unstable and certainly crazed. Potash, like soda, is a valuable constituent in the manufacture of frits and glazes, including lead-free glazes, and in the making of hard glass. It encourages alkaline colour responses which again are similar to but not identical to those of soda. Because it is soluble, it is introduced into glazes by frits or as a second flux by way of feldspar. This use as a second flux cannot be overstressed. It brings to glazes an excellent, wide-ranging and predictable fluxing activity; it provides stability, adds brilliance and provides opportunity for balance of contraction rate. See **Glaze fit**.

The term potash is generally accepted as synonymous with potassium oxide. It is, however, correctly the name for potassium carbonate. The oxide's correct name of potassa is rarely used.

Potash feldspar. See **Orthoclase**.

Potassium carbonate. Pearl ash. True potash. K_2CO_3. A highly-soluble salt used in the preparation of frits and glass. During firing, decomposition takes place to give the flux potassium oxide and carbon dioxide:

$$K_2CO_3 \xrightarrow{900°C} K_2O + CO_2 \uparrow$$

Potassium carbonate is the true potash. It is so called because a solution of water and carbonate (lye) was evaporated in iron 'pots'. The carbonate was derived from the ashes of burnt vegetable matter. Wood ash when used for glazes will be found to contain soluble potassium carbonate. At least half of the potassium carbonate content of wood ash is soluble and if not washed from the wood ash before use in the glaze slop it will be found to dissolve in the glaze tub. If these glazes are stirred by hand one can feel the 'softness' of the water. In extreme cases the amount is sufficient to have a caustic effect and irritate sensitive skins and remove nail varnish.

This caustic action of wood ash solutions was used historically as a cleaning solution (lye) for textiles and is the origin of soft soaps.

Alone, the pure white crystals of potassium carbonate are deliquescent. They pick up water from the atmosphere and dissolve in it to become a solution.

Potassium dichromate. (Bichromate). $K_2Cr_2O_7$. A soluble crystalline material with a bright red-orange colour. It is used to introduce chromium oxide into low-temperature glazes. Because the chromium oxide is combined with the potash, it is more effectively dispersed in the glaze. It is possible to obtain a bright red colour with potassium dichromate in high lead glazes. See **Chromium oxide, chrome red**.

Care should be taken with potassium dichromate because it is soluble and poisonous.

Potassium minerals. The potter's main source of potash is orthoclase feldspar. Some other igneous minerals also contain potash, e.g. cornish stone and nepheline syenite. The decomposition of these rocks gives the soil in which plants grow and potassium has become essential to plant life. Therefore vegetable ashes contain potassium and are a source of potash for glazes. Feldspar is 10% to 15% potash. Wood ash is up to 15% potash but at least half of this is very soluble. Potassium carbonate is 68% potash which is all soluble and therefore potassium carbonate is used in making frits.

The term potash comes from the practice of burning wood to extract the potash. Potash is correctly potassium carbonate, the pot-ash which was dissolved from wood ashes and evaporated to crystals in iron 'pots'. Soda ash is the equivalent from burnt seaweed and salt-marsh plants. A correct term for potassium oxide is 'potassium' but it is rarely used and the more common potash is used throughout this book.

There is slightly more potassium than sodium in the earth's crust. This potassium is mostly in insoluble compounds like igneous rocks whereas the sodium is mostly in soluble salt deposits. A few soluble potassium salt deposits exist. They give:

sylvine	(KCl)
carnallite	($KCl.MgCl_2.6H_2O$)
kainite	($KCl.MgSO_4.3H_2O$)
potassium nitrate	(KNO_3)

Powder blue. Soufflé blue. Blue produced by cobalt oxide dusted on to or blown on to body or glaze. The action isolates the blue as specks on a white ground which gives a luminosity to the colour.

Praseodymium oxide. PrO_2. One of the lanthanide oxides in the amphoteric area of the periodic table. It is used in the production of yellow stains in combination with zircon. Such stains are not powerful but have wide temperature and glaze ranges.

Preheating. Process of warming-up prior to the firing of clay. What is apparently perfectly dry clay still contains water in the pores between the clay particles. This water turns to steam and escapes at temperatures over its boiling point, 100°C (212°F). Once this water is removed, a firing can proceed fairly rapidly but if this water has not been removed there is a grave risk of exploding the clay with a build-up of steam pressure. When pots are being fired in the sudden fierce heat of brushwood and grass bonfires this preheating is most important and is done by holding the pots over a small fire until hot. With pots set in a kiln the preheating is done by starting the firing very slowly. This period up to 120°C (248°F) is called the water-smoking period of kiln-firing.

Preparation of clay. Pockets of clay of perfect consistency and ideal composition for a particular product can be found. This proves that the preparation of clay for working is a natural process of events. All that the potter does is to simulate nature's ideas, accelerate them and emphasize one or another to produce the clay he requires. It is important to appreciate this and to try to work with nature rather than against it.

In a similar way one should consider working with clay so that one need not lift and move it more than necessary. An economical time-and-motion sequence for preparation and storage is important to release the potter for making pots. To this end, many potters buy prepared clays but they will also find that a knowledge of their purchases will help them to use their clays effectively.

A few clays are suitable for potting as dug from the ground. Some are potentially good clays but require preparation. It is all too easy to assume that the earliest potters used their clay 'as dug'. The exceedingly coarse nature of some of the bodies of Bronze Age pottery might lead one to think that no selection or preparation was carried out. However a closer study of primitive pottery proves this to be wrong. The pottery made now by people whose civilization is classified as Stone Age shows a remarkable understanding of the practical necessity of clay preparation, even if the technology is not understood. These people work with nature.

In the writings of some anthropologists, one can read of an amazement in the observation that a woman will take the trouble to remove sand from a clay only to add sand from another locality. It is hardly surprising that the potter could not explain dunting!

Clay preparation aims to produce an homogeneous material with sufficient workability for the job in hand. It is therefore necessary first to understand what demands will be made of the clay in one's chosen way of working. Having assessed the requirements, one can consider the preparation in four steps: the control of plasticity; the control of grain size; the control of moisture content; and preparation prior to forming. The first two may be taken in either order.

A typical preparation sequence to produce a throwing clay from a raw clay would be:

1. weathering ⎫
2. blunging   ⎬ plasticity
3. screening — grain size
4. settling   ⎫
5. dewatering ⎬ moisture content
6. wedging
7. storage   ⎭
8. preparation for the wheel

CONTROL OF PLASTICITY. One usually wishes to increase the plasticity of a clay. To this end one adds ball clay to one's own clay, or adds a plasticizer like bentonite. Ten to twenty per cent of ball clay will improve an otherwise dead clay. It will also lengthen the workability range. Two to four per cent of bentonite will give a similar feeling of plasticity but it will not have the same effect upon the workability range. See **Ball clay** and **Bentonite**.

These are additions to an existing clay but it is possible that more consideration of the earlier preparation of the clay could have rendered this doctoring unnecessary.

Plasticity can be related directly to particle size. The most plastic clays have the finest particles. See **Plasticity**. Some clays have naturally large particles. The particles themselves are large, orderly crystals. These clays are usually chemically pure kaolin and they are not very plastic, e.g. china clay and some fireclays. Other clays have fine particles which are compacted to form larger particles often called grains. These clays also are not very plastic, e.g. some fireclays and ground shales. However these clays have a high plastic potential if the particles forming the grains can be separated. Some clays have fine particles which are already separated. These clays are highly plastic, e.g. ball clays.

A clay particle is composed of thousands of clay molecules. These molecules link together to form strong sheets. The sheets are held together by comparatively weak links called hydroxyl bonds. A few hundred sheets form a tiny crystal. The tiny crystals are similarly held together to form the larger particles and so on. At the size easily visible to the naked eye these particles are often called grains.

In ordered kaolinite, the tiny clay crystals are so neatly packed together that they form what is virtually one large crystal. However in disordered kaolinite the tiny crystals are slightly distorted. They cannot fit together neatly and so their particles are formed of a more random packing of crystals. The bonds between these crystals and hence between particle and particle are weaker than in the ordered kaolinite. These hydroxyl bonds (O-H-O) are the first cousins of water (H_2O). Water is able to infiltrate the bonds in the disordered particle by becoming part of them until the bond is only loosely held across a chain of water. At this point physical force can shear the sides apart. The physical force is available in nature as rain or impact during transportation. This process which breaks up the grains into smaller particles is called weathering.

A clay in its first stages of disintegration may take a hundred or a thousand years to become weathered. Ordered kaolinite, requiring the first stage to disordered kaolinite before the weathering can have effect, will be millions of years before it becomes a fully plastic clay.

At the other end of the scale are clays that once were fully plastic but by pressure and drying have now become compacted again and consist of large grains. These grains are vulnerable to weathering so that a clay of this sort will show surprising disintegration after one year's weathering. These clays are rock-like fire-clays, marl shales etc. After millions of years in the earth as rocks they weather to plastic clays in a few years, the hardest taking perhaps twenty.

An important agent in disintegration is the frost. Water alone will slowly penetrate the clay grain that has plastic potential but frost greatly accelerates the process. Water expands as it freezes. Thereby the gap between the particles is widened and floods with water upon thawing. Once water has entered one end of a potential gap it drives a wedge inwards by the alternate actions of freezing and thawing. Following the frost, the particles are only loosely held by water bonds. Now the physical action of rain beating upon the clay is sufficient to move the particles apart.

Secondary clays that have been transported by water, ground and tossed about in rivers and finally allowed to rest below a lake, tend to be plastic. However if these clays have also dried out, been compressed or otherwise dehydrated, they will tend to have lost their plasticity. The particles will be packed tightly together to form large grains. From this one learns that, even on the smaller scale of the workshop, it is a retrograde step to allow intended plastic clay to dry out at any stage. For a clay to realise its full plastic potential, it requires water between the particles. Clays which are weathering should therefore be kept wet also if this is possible.

The foregoing has been described in detail to emphasise that an accurate assessment must be made of a clay's potential. Not all clays will improve by weathering: only those which have plastic potential. A study of the geological origin of the clay will help to identify the clay type. See also **Weathering**.

Weathering can be simulated by blunging. A whole winter's weathering can be achieved in 10 minutes of high-speed blunging. See **Blunge**. This literally forces the particles to collide with shattering impact. At this shock instant the water seepage is rapid. See drawing.

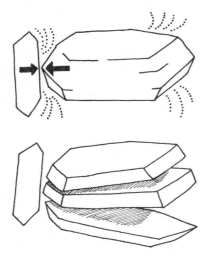

The standard slow-speed blunger or the hand blunger is best used as a follow-up to part the particles already loosened by open-air weathering.

Weathering also allows soluble salts to be washed away. It is true that blunging will also achieve this. However there is the point that during weathering an amount of chemical decomposition takes place. For most clays this decomposition and solution is desirable. The most common product is calcium sulphate which, if not washed away, causes scumming. See **Scum**. Chemical correctives can be added at the blunging stage to complete decomposition and precipitate the salts as harmless compounds.

After all this treatment, some clays may be found to be too plastic and sticky. These clays are difficult to handle but improve in workability by the addition of some non-plastic material. As a general rule, the fine non-plastics decrease the plasticity more than the coarse ones. It is sufficient to add grogs and sands at the kneading or pugging stage, but powders must be added at the blunging stage. See also **Filler**.

Powders, even wet powders, do not seem to mix thoroughly. They create agglomerate grains of their own if added to the clay at its plastic stage. Such powders are china clay and quartz flour. It may seem a nuisance to add these to the suspension, only to screen them and dewater them, but they do not seem to mix otherwise. It is of course pointless to add material of a size that will later be held back by a screen.

A further point on plasticity is mentioned later under storage. The physics of plasticity are dealt with under **Plasticity**.

CONTROL OF GRAIN SIZE. The foregoing weathering and blunging has been concerned with the improvement of plasticity. Blunging is also a preparatory step to the control of grain size which in itself has some effect on overall plasticity. A sandy clay is less plastic than the same clay with the sand removed. It may not be more workable but it will be more plastic. This presents a difficult problem which arises from the potter's use of the word plastic. He uses it to embrace the idea of workability. A clay which behaves itself well under all the conditions to which it is subjected is often called 'highly plastic' when it would be better to call it 'highly workable'.

A plastic clay, at its full potential, is a collection of plate-like particles. These particles are lubricated with water and electrostatic repulsion. Such a clay is too slippery for use and requires tempering with a non-plastic or low-plasticity material. A fine grog or a sand will theoretically position itself between the particles causing a friction where none existed before. This will stiffen the clay and give it a strength in its plastic state. The word 'theoretically' is used here because, in fact, the clay particles are much smaller than the sand.

Throwing clays often require some grog for this purpose. It ensures that as more water enters the clay, the clay particles do not slide too quickly past each other. The end result is that about 10% of fine grog (60's to dust) often improves the 'throwability' of a clay.

Large size grogs, however, present a different picture. They introduce large objects into the clay around which the clay particles must fasten in layers in an attempt to keep the mass plastic. If the grog is too large, and the size is relative to the clay particles, the clay takes on an awkwardness in its workability. It appears stiff and yet is soft. In throwing it feels stiff but softens suddenly. It lacks the in-between size of grain that would enable large objects and fine clay to flow as a whole. Strangely the addition of a medium/fine sand or grog can improve the workability of such a clay. This is a point to remember when introducing grogs for textural effect.

It is difficult to assess what needs to be added to a clay or taken from it except by trial and error. However one can obtain some idea of what a clay contains by a simple experiment. One requires a glass bottle that will hold about a pint. This is half-filled with water and about half a teaspoonful of the clay is added. It can be added in any convenient state, but the idea is to get it into suspension by vigorously shaking the bottle. When the clay is in suspension, the bottle can be almost filled with water and shaken again to mix the suspension. The bottle is then put at a slight angle. See drawing.

As the water comes to a standstill, the heavy material immediately settles and progressive sedimentation of different grain sizes follows. If there is sufficient plastic clay present to make a suitable potting clay, the mixture should remain completely cloudy for at least two hours. In fact it will take at least a day to completely settle.

The slight tilt on the bottle emphasises the sediments into identifiable layers against one side of the glass. If the test is carried out on a window sill the light shining through the bottle helps one to identify the particles. A magnifying glass can be used through the side of the bottle.

Bentonite can be added to a clay which has insuf-

ficient of the ultra-fine particles. This would be a clay that settled completely in 4 or 5 hours. Two per cent of bentonite is usually sufficient.

With a locally dug clay it is often necessary to take out unwanted material. This material may be large like twigs, roots, leaves and stones, or it may be small like sand or shale.

Large objects can be sorted by hand: a process used by primitive potters and one which does not take as long as one might think. If the clay is in plastic state, small pellets are broken off and squashed between finger and thumb. Large unwanted pieces are felt and removed. Some carbonaceous matter present as hair roots is often advantageous to plasticity. It will certainly help in the souring.

A larger problem is unwanted sand and shale. Weathered shales are often a nuisance in this respect, containing a lot of flat slatey pieces that do not reconstitute as clay.

The only way to get rid of this unwanted material is by turning the clay into a very thin slurry with water. In this state pieces of wood and carbonaceous matter often float and can be skimmed off. Very large and heavy material sinks and can be left behind in the container. Finer sand and shale is removed by screening.

An appropriate mesh size is chosen for the required final clay. A 60's mesh gives a good general potting clay. Some potters prefer finer clays and use an 80's or a 100's mesh, but take the suspension through a 20's or 40's mesh first. Too much coarse material might otherwise accumulate and tear the finer mesh. A brush should be used sparingly. There is no point in forcing material through the mesh because this is unlikely to be clay material. A brush can be used to keep the mesh clear. A vibrating screen is the best method. The use of a very thin or watery suspension helps to break the clay content into its finest particles. Overnight soaking before screening will help to reach plasticity potential and will help the suspension to flow through the mesh without clogging.

Some clays will not settle after this process. The addition of some acid to the water will increase the settling rate but fine clays, and these are the plastic clays, will always settle slowly. This is a good sign. Two or four days is not too long to wait for a good clay. The use of a test as previously described will give some indication of the mesh size to select and the time required for decanting the suspension from the first heavy sediment.

Clays, which contain unwanted material which is as fine as the wanted clay, can be refined by levigation. The process involves the use of the different densities of the clay and the unwanted material. The heavier material of higher density sinks in water quicker than the lighter material. See **Levigation**. On a large scale, timed settling and elutriation are also used. The process is sometimes necessary to remove sand specking from light-coloured clays. Porcelain bodies are sometimes refined in this way to get the maximum plasticity and purity.

CONTROL OF MOISTURE CONTENT. The correct moisture content for a plastic clay is a matter of personal choice. However, one could say that each clay has a moisture content amount at which its full plastic potential is realised. One should aim at knowing one's clay so intimately that this moisture content can be accurately achieved.

The plasticity of a clay and the fluidity of a slip are dependent upon the moisture content in relation to the behaviour of the clay particles and other material. A clay's behaviour depends upon its particle size and its electrostatic charges.

For slip-casting the electrostatic charges are emphasized in one direction in order that the particles can slide past one another. Also in large-scale preparation of plastic clay, the electrostatic charges are rebalanced. For small-scale preparation of clays it is sufficient if the potter realises that slight alkalinity or acidicy in the water of the clay can affect its plastic behaviour. For example, in the blending of two plastic clays from different sources, one is likely to find that one clay affects the other. The usual effect is that the slightly more acidic one opens up the other and creates spaces for more water. Two quite soft clays will then give a stiff blend which requires extra water to bring it to workable consistency. The phenomenon is dealt with under **Flocculation** and **Deflocculation**.

One should also be aware of the effects of the acidic and alkaline waters in the clay and as used for throwing. Alkaline clays soften quickly. Alkaline water feels slippery but softens clay quickly. Acidic clays are often 'thirsty' to throw with, stand up well and then collapse suddenly. Acidic water can even be responsible for 'tugging'.

Suspensions of clay etc and water, which are required to be constituted as plastic clays, are dewatered by settling and syphoning. They have been mixed with as much extra water as is convenient because this ensures a full wetting of the clay, eases screening and washes away solubles. After syphoning, the resulting thick slip is poured into drying troughs (see **Dewatering**), onto absorbent boards, onto a heated floor or just left in the open air to dry. Frequent attention is required to forestall any tendency to dry out too much at the edges.

On a large scale, which is anything requiring more than a hundredweight of plastic clay daily, a filter press is used. This is used instead of the settling process. A deflocculant gives extra fluidity for screening and the clay is returned to its stiffer and more permeable state by a flocculant. This thick slip is pumped under pressure or suction into a series of demountable boxes whose sides are made of a permeable, fine, strong cloth. The water passes through the cloths and the clay is held back to produce a 'cake'. See **Filter pressing**.

Most plastic clays are stored in a slightly over-wet condition. This assists ageing. Therefore plastic clay often requires a slight dewatering before use. It is achieved by wedging and kneading on a slightly absorbent bench. If the clay is too soft, it may be necessary to use a very absorbent plaster block or asbestos board to achieve correct moisture content. Alternatively arches of clay, left on a board outside in a breeze, quickly stiffen and can be wedged and kneaded. See illustration. Clay which has required much in the way of this late dewatering does not reach its maximum plasticity without a further rest in storage.

Clay that is too stiff can be remixed with water in a pugmill, a reconstitutor popularly called a dough mixer, or by hand. It is a laborious process by hand but can be done by cutting the clay into slabs, poking holes in the slabs and adding water or slurry before sandwiching. The lump is kneaded a little, wedged and kneaded again. Again, this clay will benefit from storage.

Clay which has dried out completely, as scrapped pots or the edges of clay which is dewatering, should be resoaked if possible. This is the only way to achieve full plastic potential.

PREPARATION PRIOR TO FORMING. The usual preparation is wedging followed by kneading. Wedging compresses and mixes the clay. Kneading prepares the specific amount required and makes it homogeneous. During this preparation the final moisture content is established. A porous bench is used if the clay is still slightly too wet. For throwing, many potters weigh out their clay and pat it into balls for use on the wheel. **Wedging** and **Kneading** are separately indexed.

Prepared. When used to describe clay this means that more than one clay or mineral has been blended together. The word 'body' is usually used rather than the term 'prepared clay'.

A prepared mineral or prepared oxide is one that has been chemically produced in contrast to one that is a selected and ground raw material. For example, red iron oxide can be crushed haematite or a prepared oxide precipitated from a ferriferous solution.

A prepared colour is one that has been manufactured from a number of ingredients, e.g. colouring oxides, alumino-silicates and fluxes. The ingredients are calcined or fritted and reground as a homogeneous powder ready for use.

Press-moulding. Forming pots by pressing plastic clay slabs onto and into absorbent plaster moulds. The clay slab is coaxed into place against the mould by the hands, sponges, leathers and rubber kidneys. As the clay stiffens, it retains the form of the mould and can be removed for fettling.

Hollow forms are sometimes made in piece moulds which are put together with a slab of clay in each piece. The slabs are joined together to form the pot before the mould is dismantled.

Large plates are often press-moulded because it is easier to make them in this way than to throw them. Non-circular plates and bowls must be moulded in some way. Also the method is useful for pre-forming pieces from which larger pieces are to be constructed.

The disadvantages of press-moulding when compared with throwing and free-forming is that the pot can only be as good as the mould allows. An increase in the potter's skill does not improve his work beyond the quality of the mould. Development can only take place when it includes new moulds of better design. Press-moulding is essentially a production method and unfortunately tends to slow down the development of expressive ideas.

PRESS-MOULDING CLAY. Clays for press-moulding need not be highly plastic. In fact, clays of low plasticity (short clays) often press well and have the merit of freeing themselves from the mould fairly quickly. Being relatively coarser than highly plastic clays, they are more open and the water can be drawn from the clay more quickly. There is also less water to be drawn from the clay before it stiffens and therefore there is less shrinkage. See **Water of plasticity** and **Drying**. The low shrinkage is important where contact with the mould could involve tightening onto the mould. The illustration shows a deep hump mould on which may be pressed dishes of short clays but not of more plastic clays. The plastic clay would grip the mould between the sides AA and probably split from the rim. A less plastic clay would free itself from the mould before this occurred.

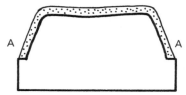

Primary clay. Residual clay. A clay found in its place of origin. The only common examples are china clay and bentonite. See **Clay, origin**. Clays which have been removed from their place of origin and deposited elsewhere are called secondary or sedimentary clays.

Proto-porcelain. Stoneware which was the forerunner of Chinese porcelain. The body was grey, the glaze was feldspathic and the ware must have been fired at least to 1200°C (2192°F). It developed contemporaneously with the lead glazes of the Han dynasty and probably superseded lead-glazed wares for general use during the T'ang dynasty, when it emerges as white stoneware or porcelain.

Pugmill. A machine for mixing and compressing a plastic clay. It mechanizes the handwork of wedging and kneading. Knives rotate on a central shaft and force the clay through a tapering barrel and out through a compressing nozzle. Individual potters use horizontal pugmills for small amounts and vertical pugmills for larger amounts. The one illustrated is made by Edwards and Jones Ltd of Stoke-on-Trent, England.

Pugging achieves some mixing of clay consistency but is more important for its effect upon compression. Compression improves the strength and thus workability of a clay. See also **Ageing, De-airing** and **Wedging**.

Pull. Draught. The energy exerted by the chimney on the kiln gases.

Puzzle jug. A popular tavern joke jug of the 17th to 19th centuries in Europe. The handle was hollow and the ale was drunk by sucking it up through one of the

spouts. To make the suction work, all the other holes, both obvious and secret, had to be covered. The example is in marbled ware. It is English and dated 1701.

Pygmy cups. Small ritual vessels only 2 or 3 inches in diameter of the Middle and Late Bronze Age. They are found in round cairn burials of 1400–1600 B.C. especially in western Britain. They are called pygmy because they are small. They were usually used along with the large overhanging rim urns and held a few small bones or accessory treasures, pendants, amulets etc. Being able to perform their accessory function easily they were not subject to the normal functional design found in the larger pieces. This allowed their makers the opportunity for experiment. No two are alike. There are globular ones, straight-sided ones, conical ones and open bowls. Decoration is impressed, incised and punctured. Their precise significance in the burial is still unknown.

Pyrite. Iron pyrites. Ferric sulphide. Fool's gold. FeS_2. An iron ore occurring in crystals which have a light yellow metallic shine. It occurs as impurity specking in fireclays and because it weathers very slowly and is harder than the clay it is impossible to grind it into a uniform colouring. The ore is too hard to grind for use as a pottery colourant.

The word pyrite comes from the Greek word for flame because it is possible to burn pyrite like coal. The particles in clay burn away part of their sulphur before 600°C (1112°F) but the remainder (ferrous sulphide, FeS) forms compact particles which are difficult to oxidize. Above 1200°C (2192°F) these particles melt, causing unpleasant blemishes on unglazed ware and sometimes erupting through a glaze in an unsightly way. It is possible with very small particles to achieve solution in the glaze as a decorative speckle.

Pyrite is also used as a general term for the other iron sulphide ores and for the copper and iron ore called copper pyrites.

Pyrolusite. MnO_2. The chief manganese ore and source of manganese dioxide.

Pyrometry. The measurement of temperature and heat-work.

Temperature is measured by pyrometers using a thermocouple and a galvanometer or a potentiometer. The thermocouple is two dissimilar metal wires joined at one end and introduced into the kiln. The heat generates a small voltage which is measured at the other ends of the wires and related to temperature. Pyrometers measure the temperature inside the kiln and can be linked to the kiln control to switch off, soak or control temperature rise and fall.

Heat-work is measured by pyroscopes. These are expendable objects made from carefully proportioned ceramic minerals. They are similar in composition to glazes and thus sinter, fuse and melt at predicted points as a result of temperature and the time subjected to the temperature. The temperature/time factor is called heat-work and is referred to as a temperature with the understood significance of a particular rise in temperature expressed in degrees per hour. Pyroscopes may be used as the visible check of heat-work during a firing and the kiln fired by means of these. Also they may be strategically placed for recovery after firing. The popular pyroscopes are cones, bars and rings.

Q

Quartz. Silica. SiO_2. The popular name for the mineral rocks specifically called milky quartz and crystal quartz. They are used as sources of silica for glazes and bodies and are introduced as a powder or as quartz sand. Quartz is also the technical term for the primary phase of silica. The two terms are separately described.

QUARTZ MINERAL. Milky quartz, sometimes called quartz rock, is an opaque white, greasy-looking and sharply angular rock. It occurs as veins through other rocks and being hard survives as white pebbles which are often included in conglomerate rocks. Crystal quartz has larger crystals which can be seen with the naked eye and whilst from a distance the quartz looks white, upon closer inspection the individual crystals are often perfectly clear and colourless. Large crystals over a foot in length are not unknown and those of an inch or so are quite common.

Both rock and crystal quartz are hard and are used as a measurement of hardness as number 7 on Mohs' scale. Quartz will therefore scratch window glass.

Disintegrated rocks have provided white sands, some of which are agglomerated as gritstone whilst others remain as beds of soft sand. The sand is quarried and marketed as quartz sand or silica sand. Some is ground to provide powdered quartz.

Quartz sand added to a clay or body acts as a grog. As a non-plastic material it opens a body and decreases the plasticity and shrinkage in the raw state. It gives visual texture and bite for workability especially for throwing. During firing it makes a body more refractory and during cooling increases a body's thermal contraction. Sand does not fuse but retains most of its crystalline structure in bodies thereby adding its high contraction rate to that of the body. See **Grain size** and **Glaze fit**.

Quartz sand is also used as a placing sand and as a source of silica in glass-making and frit manufacture.

Powdered quartz is used in glaze recipes. It is 100% silica (SiO_2) and therefore its addition to most recipes raises the glaze's melting point, increases the resistance to abrasion of the final glaze and improves its glassiness. See **Glass-former**.

Powdered quartz is occasionally added to stoneware and porcelain bodies to assist vitrification.

QUARTZ PHASE. Quartz is the technical term for the primary phase of silica. Other phases are cristobalite,

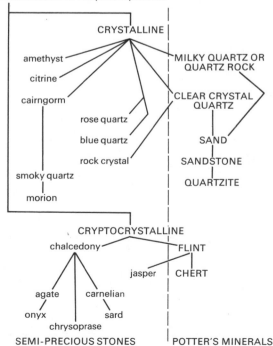

tridymite and silica glass. They are alike chemically but differ physically in their molecular structures.

Silica found as rock or sand is almost invariably of quartz phase. The other phases are extremely rare in nature and when required in ceramics are created by conversion from quartz phase.

The quartz phase of silica occurs in crystalline form as quartz rock or milky quartz, quartz crystals or crystal quartz, quartzite, sand and sandstone. It also occurs as the semi-precious stones rose quartz, blue quartz, citrine, amethyst, cairngorm and rock crystal. There exists also a cryptocrystalline form of quartz in which the crystals are too small to be discernible under the normal optical microscope. Natural forms of crypto-crystalline quartz are flint, chert and the semi-precious stones jasper and chalcedony. The colours of the semi-precious stones are due to impurities such as iron, manganese, nickel and rutile.

The quartz phase of silica is subdivided into two forms known as alpha quartz and beta quartz. Alpha quartz exists only at temperatures below 573°C (1063°F) and beta quartz only above this temperature. The difference is in the angle of the silica-oxygen-silica bond which changes at 573°C.

This change occurs every time crystalline quartz passes this temperature in either direction. It is called a reversible change or silica inversion. There is a decrease in size from beta to alpha and this may cause cracks called dunts in pottery bodies. See **Silica** and **Dunting**.

Quartz which has become part of a molten glass or

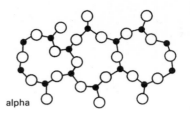

alpha

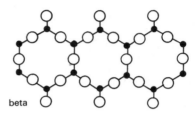

beta

glaze is no longer crystalline and does not become crystalline on cooling. This fused quartz is not subject to inversion and would strictly speaking no longer be the phase called quartz but would be called by the overall name of silica or the specific name silica glass.

Quartzite. Pure silica rock used as a refractory in some salt-glazed kilns. The rock is composed of a quartz sand naturally cemented by silica. A sandstone which has undergone metamorphism is also called a quartzite but is not necessarily a refractory.

R

R. Chemical symbol, which is not used for any of the elements and therefore can be used to denote an unknown element in a chemical formula. For example, R_2O_3 where R could be Fe or Al.

It is usual for potters to use R but also available and sometimes used are D, G, M and X.

Raddle. Reddle. Ruddle. Haematite. A red ochre with a high iron oxide content. Fe_2O_3.

This ochre is associated with iron ores and iron stones which produce reddish powders when disintegrated and crushed. It was considered the blood of the mother earth by primitive peoples and used by them to decorate pottery and themselves.

Radiation. Transference of heat through space by energy waves from the heat source outwards in all unhindered directions. The heat is absorbed when the waves meet cooler obstacles. In the kiln, radiation takes place from all hot objects, kiln wall, pots, electric elements, muffle, saggar. It takes place in still air and evens out the heat distribution differences. In moving air, convection replaces radiation. The wavelengths involved in radiation are between a tenth and a thousandth of a centimetre.

Radical. A group of atoms which preserves its identity although it passes from one compound to another. For example, when the carbonate identity (CO_3) moves from barium carbonate ($BaCO_3$) to calcium carbonate ($CaCO_3$).

$$CaCl_2 + BaCO_3 \longrightarrow BaCl_2 + CaCO_3$$

Barium carbonate is added to clays at slip stage when such clays show unsightly finger marks on the fired, unglazed ware. The finger marks are caused by the crystallization of soluble salts on the surface, being broken by handling.

Rainbow effect. Extremely thin layers of the metals silver, bismuth, copper and tin on the surface of glazes may produce lustres with rainbow or mother-of-pearl colouring. Some light usually passes through such a layer so that one sees the colour of the glaze and body beneath as well as the lustre. Light is reflected from both the top surface and the under surface of this metallic layer. Thus light reflected from the under surface travels a longer distance before reaching the eye. If this distance corresponds to a half wavelength of a particular colour the two sets of waves, one from the top and the other from the under surface, are travelling in opposition and cancel one another out so that the particular colour is not seen. The other colours of the spectrum are seen instead of white light. This phenomenon is called interference. Thus the slight variations of thickness of the thin metallic layer and the angle at which it is viewed present spectra or rainbow effects. The metallic layer itself does not need to be coloured. The effect is like that of oil on water which is an extremely thin transparent film. See also **Lustres**.

Raku. A Japanese word freely interpreted as 'enjoyment'. It was an ideograph engraved on a gold seal and given by the ruler Hideyoshi to Chojiro in 1598. Raku thereby became his family title. Chojiro is credited with being the first to produce, in 1580, a low-fired glazed pottery by a direct process which involved putting the pots into and taking them out of the red-hot kiln.

Long tongs are used for handling the pots as shown in the photograph. The firing takes up to an hour when the glazes have melted and the pots are removed to be replaced by another batch. The process gives the potter control of colourful expression as he subjects the pot and its glaze to oxidations and reductions during its

cooling. The openness of the body and the soft nature of the glaze enable extremely subtle variations of colour to be achieved.

Raku pots are made from a refractory clay which remains open and thus able to withstand the extreme thermal shocks imposed upon it. It is not hard-fired and therefore the pots are relatively fragile and porous until sealed by oil, tea or grease. Nevertheless, the body is an excellent thermal insulator and was accepted by the Japanese as ideal for tea bowls. Couple with this the intimate expressions of the variable colourings of raku which carry a narrative of the whole process and it is easy to see why raku gained its favour and was given its title of enjoyment.

Today potters extend the word enjoyment to cover the firing process which to be successful must include a total involvement of the potter with the happening so that continuity of development occurs in the expression as consecutive pots are processed.

RAKU CLAY. Taking the idea of total involvement to include an intimate understanding of the materials, raku offers an excellent opportunity to experiment with small amounts of local clay. Almost every clay can be made to work as a raku clay and two variable factors must be considered: additions to the clay and the temperature of the biscuit firing.

Additions are made to a clay to create a raku body which will withstand the stresses of thermal shock. The usual raku body is one in which the particles are only loosely fastened together giving an elasticity to the whole structure. This type of body is porous, under-fired in relation to a normally matured state, and often of coarse texture. Additions therefore make the body refractory, porous and often give a coarse texture. Fireclay and grog are popular openers.

Openers are not plastic and therefore it is necessary to start with a highly plastic clay if a workable body is to be produced. A ball clay and/or a highly plastic red clay are good starting points. A suitable raku body can be produced with ball clay in plastic state 66%, fireclay grog (dry weight) 33%. A grog between 40's and 100's is best.

A white or light-coloured body gives brighter colours to the glaze. A dark-coloured body gives interesting variations with reduction. Both can be given washes of coloured slips which, because of the coarseness and softness of the body, appear to have a translucent quality.

The second variable factor is the temperature of the biscuit firing. A popular temperature is 900°C (1652°F) but it depends upon the body, its refractoriness and the amount and type of volatiles which it contains. If the same body is tried as both a very soft and a hard biscuit it will be seen that the more delightful soft colourings occur on the softer ware. Porous bodies are susceptible to reduction and oxidation, and thus provide the opportunity to produce the most exciting colours. One

must accept that porous bodies are easily broken.

For the purpose of obtaining a stronger ware, a harder biscuit, up to 1200°C (2192°F) may be used. The body must be still flexible in order to withstand the thermal shock. See **Thermal shock**.

A biscuit firing is necessary to enable the ware to be handled and to prepare it for the thermal shocks of the glaze firing. Also, since the raku glaze melts over the same temperature range as the clay's burning-out period, it is necessary to clean the body previously by a biscuit firing. See **Firing, biscuit**. From 700°C (1292°F) the unwanted elements carbon, sulphur and fluorine are liberated from a clay in gases. If these were liberated during a glaze firing they would discolour and bubble the glaze.

The purist raku potter biscuits his raku pots only in the raku kiln during warming up but most potters prefer to control the biscuit firing more carefully and often use an electric kiln. The success of the effects following the glaze firing are thus more easily secured and this is sufficient justification. Some crank mixtures can be biscuited by placing directly into the hot raku kiln. This is done whilst the body is in plastic condition. The pores are thus kept open for the escape of steam from the interior.

RAKU COLOURINGS. First there is the colour of the body and slip coatings. Slips are more effective when brushed on rather than dipped. They also adhere better when brushed because of the coarseness of the body.

Secondly there are pigments which are painted on the body before glazing or over the glaze before firing. They are metal oxides or metal oxides modified by additions of glaze.

Thirdly there are the glazes themselves which are coloured by the popular oxides. Red iron oxide 2% gives a beautiful yellow. Increasing amounts up to 15% give rich browns and dark reds. Copper oxide 1% is sufficient to give a mid-green. Less than 0·5% of copper oxide is sufficient for reduced reds. Too much copper gives a brown colour in reduction. The lead sesquisilicate glaze given later is ideal for copper reds. The presence of boric oxide in the glaze encourages a lustre finish. The amount of copper compound can then be increased to as much as 7% depending upon the effect required and copper carbonate is often used to give a thorough dispersion of copper. Cobalt oxide 1% gives a strong blue which is rather harsh. It can be tempered with some manganese dioxide, 1% to 5%. Manganese dioxide itself gives various purply browns. See also **Lustres**.

RAKU FIRING. The raku kiln is often seen as a symbol of experimental involvement with heat and ceramics in contrast to the production kiln with its repetitious control. The kiln is usually a temporary affair built out-of-doors and fired by charcoal, coke, coal, wood, oil or gas although small electric kilns can be used.

Long-flame wood, oil or gas can be used in kilns with through flames impinging on the wares. Solid fuels like charcoal and coke which use direct contact for heat transference are used around a muffle which contains the ware. See drawings.

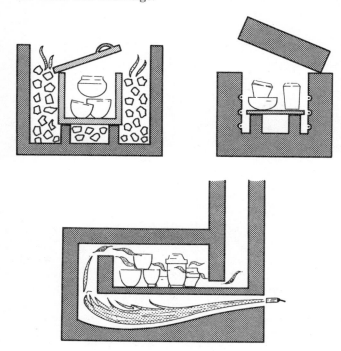

The ware is either previously biscuited or biscuited in the raku firing during its warming-up period. In the latter case the pieces are taken out hot by means of long tongs. When cool they are glazed, decorated, dried thoroughly and replaced in the red-hot kiln with the long tongs.

There is usually some heat loss at this point and the kiln is further baited to raise the temperature. The range used is between 750°C and 1000°C (1382°F and 1832°F). In 20 to 60 minutes the glazes have melted and the red-hot pots, now shining with melted glaze, are withdrawn with the long tongs. During the next few minutes as each piece of work cools it can be subjected to oxidation, to varying degrees and types of reduction and to differing rates of cooling, all of which bring their own particular effects to the various parts of the piece. For example, rapid cooling by sprinkled water gives areas of small crackle, reduction alters colours and gives lustres. Sawdust, chippings, wet straw, grass and leaves give different results as reduction materials. A usual ending to the processing is to dunk each piece in water to seal the results.

RAKU GLAZE. The traditional glaze given by Bernard Leach is:

white lead	66
quartz	30
china clay	4

This glaze can be recalculated to give a low solubility glaze thus:

lead bisilicate	90·5
quartz	4
china clay	5·5

This glaze is almost a eutectic mixture and will melt before 700°C (1292°F). It can thus be used in a kiln which reaches only the dull red heat of 750°C (1382°F).

The low clay content of this glaze makes it very friable on the ware so that pieces of the glaze are easily knocked off when a piece is being placed in the kiln. It is therefore necessary to add some binder to the glaze such as gum arabic or cellulose paste.

Most potters today try to build efficient raku kilns which will reach 900°C to 1000°C (1652°F to 1832°F) so that more clay can be added to the glaze. This makes a glaze slop which does not settle so quickly as the above and also produces a more stable glaze when fired because of the high alumina content. The comparable loss of shine is only very slight in this low solubility glaze:

lead sesquisilicate	83
ball clay	17

Leadless glazes can be prepared using commercially-made frits. Any soft frit melting at about 850°C (1,562°F) can be used in the following recipe:

frit	94
china clay	5
bentonite	1

Leadless glazes give the opportunity to get some of the high-alkaline colours by the use of alkaline frits. These frits tend to settle very quickly and set hard in the glaze tub. A liberal addition of bentonite, about 4% with calcium chloride, overcomes this. The calcium chloride addition can be liberal also to counteract the alkaline solubility of the frit.

Sometimes these glazes which are over 90% frit tend to be unstable when finished and subject to flaking or excessive crazing and chipping. The substitution of some lead bisilicate for up to 20% of the frit will im-

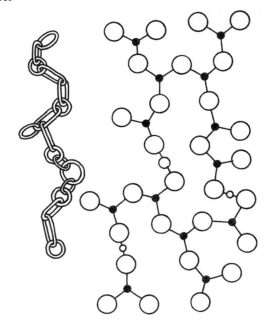

prove stability at the expense of some of the brighter colour effects.

When the higher temperatures are used it will be found that the glazes still remain molten during the cooling from 1000°C to the 700°C (1832°F to 1292°F) range. It is necessary to allow these glazes to set by leaving the work in the open air, or holding it in the tongs, before dunking or reducing in sawdust. Failure to do this results in a glaze surface spoilt by bubbling or physical contact.

The two raku pots are by Walter Keeler and Arthur Wiggett.

Ramekin. Ramequin. An 18th-century French cheese-cake. Also the small mould in which it was baked. Hence in modern potter's usage, a ramekin is any small deep bowl, often with a single side-handle, and often with a lid, used for both baking and serving individual portions. The one illustrated is by Colin Pearson.

Random structure. Random network. The three-dimensional placing of fixed points on which atoms or molecules are positioned in relation to one another. The random network does not follow a regular pattern but it must keep within a number of possibilities. Amorphous solids, and this includes glazes, are random structures. Glaze structures are usually imagined to be in chains, some of whose links are joined to other chains. The diagram shows this chain idea related to a structure.

Regular structures, which are also called lattices, give crystals. The difference between the random and the regular structures explains why a glaze and other amorphous substances have melting ranges whereas crystalline substances have melting points. The random chain breaks down slowly because some links are weaker than others. In the crystal the links (bonds) are equally strong throughout the substance, or more usually, there are a number of types of bond spread regularly throughout the substance. Each type has its own detachment temperature which results in a sudden collapse of the substance when one type of structure gives way throughout the substance. See also **Network structure**.

Range. The variation of temperature/time that a clay or glaze can withstand without being over or underfired.

Rare earths. Rare earth elements called lanthanons or lanthanides. A group of 15 rare metallic elements with properties resembling aluminium. So far only cerium and praseodymium have been used by individual potters although about 6 have commercial pottery value.

Ratio. The relationship between quantities expressed in the same form of measurement. For example, 6 grams and 2 grams are in the ratio of 6:2 or 3:1. Glaze ratio is a phrase used to describe the proportional amounts in the glaze of the alkaline, amphoteric and acidic compounds expressed in relative numbers of molecules. Glaze ratio has a direct relationship to melting temperature. See **Formula, (unity, in use)** and also **Thorpe ratio** which concerns lead solubility.

Raw. Uncooked, unfired, in original state. The term is loosely used to describe materials and processes, and can lead to confusion, especially with glazes and glaze materials. A number of definitions follow:

RAW CLAY. Clay as dug before it is processed by crushing or removal of stones. The phrase has been used by some potters to mean clay which has not been fired but the word clay alone implies this since when fired it is no longer clay.

RAW GLAZE. (*Noun*). A glaze compounded of materials that have not been previously fritted. The exception is wood ash which if considered strictly would be called a frit but which is always considered a raw material. The opposite of a raw glaze is a fritted glaze or one containing frits.

Raw glazes for stoneware are not difficult to compound because whiting, dolomite and wood ashes provide cheap fluxes. Below 1100°C (2012°F) the only cheap fluxes available are lead compounds, soda and borax. Lead has the disadvantage of being poisonous. Soda and borax need to be fritted because they are soluble in water. Raw glazes receive attention by potters because of three factors:

1. They use more readily available materials which require little preparation.

2. They are cheaper than glazes for which prepared frits are purchased.

3. In pioneering pottery away from commercial supplies of frits, the preparation of one's own frits in sufficient quantity can be very irksome. The pioneering spirit remains with many potters even within reach of a supply of frits so that there is some pride in scorning the prepared frit and using raw materials which potters feel are nearer to a native or indigenous way of working.

RAW GLAZING. RAW GLAZE. (*Verb*). In contrast to the above, this is the action of glazing raw, that is, on raw ware. This may be with a raw glaze but it could equally be done with a fritted glaze. The reasons which lead a potter to use a raw glaze, namely directness of approach and cheapness, also often lead him to glaze his wares at raw stage and thus cut out the extra firing to biscuit. The glaze and clay mature together, and since they start together, full integration of clay, slips and glazes for decorative effects is possible.

Raw glazing can be done on the dry ware, in which case the glaze is often one containing frits, other non-clay minerals and less than 10% clay. The glazing techniques are very similar to those used with biscuit. One advantage of this is that dry clay ware has a less variable porosity than biscuit ware from an uneven kiln and thus glaze thickness can be more accurately controlled.

Raw glazing can also be done at all other stages from soft through cheesehard to black-hard. Each has its own advantages in directness of approach or control of thickness. Glazes for these stages usually contain a high proportion of clay, 30% to 100%, and are thus vitrified or melted slips. They are often called slip glazes or in the cases where a fusible clay is used alone, clay glazes. They are applied to the pots as are slips by dipping and brushing and can thus be directly integrated with other slips and the body clay. Sgraffito through the slip glaze into the body is possible with very rich results as in the 11th- to 13th-century northern Chinese wares.

Besides the approach to working, the high proportion of clay in these glazes gives a characteristic matt surface not easily obtained by other means but slip glazes must be applied at exactly the right stage. This can be a disadvantage. A batch of pots must be brought to this stage together for economical glazing as a group. If they are glazed when too wet or too dry, the glaze may be too thin, too thick, may not adhere and thus crawl in firing, or even flake off before firing. Or the pot itself may crack. Glazes for dry ware give one a longer time in which the pots can be waiting but if the glazing is done too soon and the pots are not absolutely dry the glaze may well flake away.

General disadvantages of raw glazing are that for ware fired below 1100°C (2012°F) the glaze may melt so soon as to seal off the escape of gases from the clay. This would result in bubbled glazes and with clays nearing vitrification, bloating can also occur. The bubbling of glaze can often be overcome by slower firings and slight glaze modification. Quick firings in the early stages can also result in pieces exploding with steam build-up. Such explosions tend to send fragments into far too many pots where they stick because the ware is glazed. Explosions rarely happen to the work of the experienced potter but are frequent enough with students' work to make raw glazing hazardous in schools and colleges.

There has been some misunderstanding of the advantages and disadvantages of raw glazing amounting almost to a mystique, as if some new secret process were being introduced. This has been encouraged by some potters and potters' merchants but it should be remembered that in Europe a biscuit or bisque stage has been used for less than 300 years and is still not used by every potter. If one considers the reasons for introducing biscuiting, raw glazing is seen in more correct perspective.

RAW LEAD. Lead compounds, galena, litharge, white lead and red lead. These compounds are the source of lead oxide for glazes (see **Lead oxide**) but there are difficulties in their use.

Raw lead is poisonous when inhaled as dust or consumed as dust settled on food, food containers or cigarettes etc. The lead is said to be soluble in the gastric juices and is stored in the body and not discharged. It is therefore referred to as an accumulative poison and the symptoms and effects of lead poisoning may be delayed for a number of years until precipitated by some other bodily factors. The lead content in galena is much less soluble than that of the oxides and some people do not consider it a raw lead. It does contain soluble lead, however, as do all lead compounds. See **Lead poisoning**.

RAW MATERIALS. Any materials which the potter

uses. The name implies that he has not yet processed them. Although strictly speaking his raw materials should only include clay and minerals such as flint and feldspar, he may extend the term to cover wood ashes and grogs. The latter two have already been subjected to heat. The potter may even include lead silicates or other frits etc which are indeed raw to him in that he has not so far processed them himself. The fact that feldspar, cornish stone and quartz were formed by heat is always ignored since they are won as raw minerals.

RAW WARE. Pottery etc before it is fired.

Reaction. The effect two or more substances have on one another producing a change in the substances. For example, the combination of wood ash and clay to produce a glass at high temperatures. See also **Interaction**.

Readsorption. The intake of water from the air by the empty pores of dry clay.

Clay pores are filled with water when clay is in plastic state. Most of these pores drain during drying but the smallest pores retain their water by capillary tension. The size of pore which is able to retain its water is determined by the humidity of the air and the atmospheric pressure. The amount of water in air-dried clay therefore varies from day to day.

Not only do the pores dry out to this determined point but also those pores which were empty fill up to this point by taking water from the air. This is readsorption.

Clays can withstand these daily adjustments of water content without ill effect. However if clay is dried thoroughly and then allowed to readsorb moisture a slight expansion takes place which causes cracks with some clays in certain sections.

The clays most prone to readsorption cracking are prepared bodies which contain a large proportion of non-clay material. These have insufficient strength at this stage to withstand the tension exerted by the expansion.

The pot section which is vulnerable to readsorption cracking is the slowly tapered rim. The greatest expansion takes place where readsorption from both sides can meet. This is around the rim and thus the clay next to it in the pot is pulled into tension. If the clay is weak it may crack but the crack will be unseen until after the firing. In fact such a crack is difficult to see in biscuit but shows as a fine line of thicker glaze immediately after dipping. It usually opens more during the glaze firing to reveal a crack about $\frac{1}{2}$ inch in length at right angles to the rim.

Therefore if pots are dried on a kiln top they should be fired whilst they are still warm rather than after allowing them to cool completely, especially if conditions are humid.

The readsorption of moisture is in two stages. The first moisture to be readsorbed is attracted electrically to the clay particles. There is always a layer of water around each clay particle but its thickness varies from one to four molecules according to prevalent humidity. This variation accounts for the slight expansion on readsorption. The layer is known as the bound layer and is not completely removed by drying but is removed at red heat when the clay becomes pot. See **Ceramic change**.

In itself this layer accounts for the smaller part of the readsorbed moisture but it encourages the second stage of readsorption, which is the filling of the pores between the particles. Here pore water reforms by a process called capillary condensation. The surface tension of the water within such a small space is able to condense the water from the vapour in the air, not chemically as in the case of the water around the clay particles, but physically by tension.

The word should not be confused with reabsorption which is the capillary action of dry clay taking up liquid water as opposed to water vapour. Reabsorption is called soaking by potters but there is no simple potter's word for readsorption.

Recent. Geologically, the last period extending to the present day. It is part of the Quarternary or Pleistocene period which is the last million years and recent deposits are unsatisfactorily defined as those containing remains of flora and fauna still existing in the locality. To the potter, recent deposits are those he can see still being built. River and sea sands and the clays and muds of river and estuary are recent as opposed to deposits like the clay beds of glacial origin.

Reclamation. Reclaiming clay from turnings, broken unfired pots etc is easily done with most clays by softening the dry clay in water and drying out the resulting slops on plaster, asbestos bats or bricks with the possible aid of powdered clay or grog. This latter process is called dewatering.

Some very plastic clays are so fine that without an opener they resist the softening action of water by forming a waterproof skin. This happens especially with leatherhard clay. In such cases it is necessary to thoroughly dry the clay first. After this it can be more easily slaked. If the clay is exceedingly fine and of the highly plastic type, such as pure ball clay, it will be necessary either to dry it and repowder it before wetting or else bring it to a slip by blunging.

Some clays if reclaimed immediately after throwing appear to have become tired and less plastic. A resting period of a few days puts this right. Casting slips which have been allowed to dry should not be reclaimed because of the deflocculant balance.

Reconditioning. See **Reclamation, Kneading, Wedging**.

Rectangular down-draught kiln. An intermittent kiln of rectangular plan with firemouths along the longer sides. The roof is a flattish arch to which the flames rise to be drawn down through the ware by the pull of a tall chimney via under-floor flues. Small rectangular down-draught kilns have a fire at one side only and the exit flues at the other side.

Rectangular down-draught kilns are used for all types of ware and are more efficient than up-draught kilns. See **Down-draught kiln**.

Red. Red and orange are colours of wide interpretation in pottery. The rust reds and orange colours are called red in reference to clays. See **Red clay**. The colouring is from iron oxide which is the only practical deep stain for bodies.

For glazes there is a wider choice of red and orange stains. Iron oxide gives orange and reds at low temperatures in lead glazes. A bright colour requires complete oxidation. Accidental reduction, however slight, dulls the hue. Iron oxide also gives good rust colours at stoneware temperatures. See **Rust** and **Iron oxide**.

Chromium oxide gives reds in lead silicates and the combination is useful for producing pools of red glass on ceramic tiles. See **Chromium oxide** (chrome red and orange). There is also the crimson pink colour which results from the chromium oxide-tin oxide combination. See **Chromium oxide** (chrome-tin pink).

Bright red (sang-de-boeuf) glazes are obtained at temperatures above 1100°C (2012°F) by staining with copper oxide. The copper oxide is reduced during the firing to the cuprous oxide and colloidal copper states. See **Copper oxide in reduction**.

The brightest reds and oranges are dependent upon special conditions. The use of prepared stains helps to stabilize fugitive colours. Uranium oxide and lead silicate combinations have now been replaced by cadmium selenide stains. These require precise use to achieve brilliant colours and are mostly used in prepared on-glaze colours although stained glazes are also available. See **Cadmium** and **Selenium**.

Red clay. Red earthenware clay. The potter's name for brown clay. When fired to about 1000°C (1832°F) these clays burn to a deep orange colour, sometimes called flowerpot red. The red colour is due to 5% to 8% of iron oxide (Fe_2O_3) which is often heightened in its brightness as a red by the natural presence of some titanium dioxide (TiO_2). The titania may only be a trace amount below 1% but it has an effect upon the iron oxide during firing. Red clays vitrify below 1200°C (2192°F).

Some of these clays are quite a bright orange when dug, some are a deep rich brown, whilst others are a dull brown. The blackish clays which also burn to a similar red are more often called grey clays and terracotta clays. The yellow clays which burn to red are

referred to as ochres. Some red clays, and notably the English Staffordshire red clay from around Stoke-on-Trent, are sometimes erroneously called marls. A true marl is a pink-burning clay in which calcia has a bleaching effect upon the iron content.

Red clays are usually highly plastic clays. They have been ground fine and sorted into pockets of extremely fine clays by being deposited, removed and redeposited over the last few million years. The youngest deposits of less than a million years of age are probably re-deposits of previous deposits dating back 500 million years or more. The same process that ground the clays to fine state was also responsible for the addition of impurities of which the important ones are iron oxide and free silica. The free silica is sometimes in the form of quartz sand of large enough grain to be seen with the naked eye. This provides an excellent 'bite' to the clay for use on the potter's wheel.

The qualities of high plasticity, rich colour and workability endear this clay to potters today as they have to potters in the past. It is an ideal clay for fast throwing of plant pots; for providing the body for slip decorated ware, for modelling figures of the larger type like portrait busts and for making teapots. It is usually biscuit fired at around 950°C (1742°F) and glaze fired at around 1080°C (1976°F).

Red clays are ideal for blending with other clays. They possess sufficient character in colour and plasticity to assist poorer clays to become blends with excellent workability.

Red copper oxide. Cuprous oxide. Cu_2O. See **Reduction**.

Red-figure ware. The peak of Classical Greek pottery; it was decorated with red-brown figures on a black background. The red colour was a fine slip on the red body over which were painted the black background and the details on the figures. See **Attic pottery**.

Red heat. The temperature at which the pots in a kiln are seen to be glowing red hot. 700–750°C (1292–1382°F). See also **Incandescence**.

This phrase is usually used when the kiln is cooling. When the temperature of the pottery has dropped to red heat it is a sign that the crucial temperature of dunting is approaching and holes which would allow draughts into the kiln are sealed. It is also the temperature at which lead glazes begin to set. Above this temperature it was the practice amongst many slipware potters to allow clean air to enter the kiln through the raked-out firebox to brighten the shine of the glaze. Most stoneware potters clam up the kiln earlier than this in the 1000°C to 900°C (1832°F to 1652°F) range, clear red heat.

Red lead. Red lead oxide. Minium. Triplumbic tetroxide. Pb_3O_4. A bright scarlet powder which is one source of lead oxide (PbO) for raw lead glazes and preparation of lead frits. Red lead decomposes about 500°C (932°F) to become lead oxide (PbO) which is the flux entering the glaze fusion. Although a beautiful bright colour in its raw state, red lead has no colouring power at all in a glaze.

The red lead crystal is probably a combination of three crystals: two of the yellow lead oxide crystals (PbO) which have alkaline properties, and a brown lead dioxide crystal (PbO_2) which has acidic properties. The formula is sometimes written $2PbO.PbO_2$. The crystals can be separated by acid attack or alkali attack or by the action of heat which also liberates the extra oxygen atom from the combined crystal. This latter occurrence ensures that the potter will always get an alkaline flux in his glazes although the raw red lead is a neutral balance when added in the glaze batch.

Red lead is slightly heavier than litharge for the fluxing action it achieves. The conversion factor is 0·977 which means that 100 lbs of red lead converts into 97·7 lbs of lead oxide in fusion. In order to achieve 100 lbs of lead oxide in fusion one requires 102·4 lbs of red lead.

Red ochre. Raddle. Reddle. Fe_2O_3. The soft earthy variety of iron ore. It often contains some clay substance. See **Haematite**.

Reduction. The action of taking oxygen away from metal oxides. The potter uses reduction to coax different colours from the same metal oxide in his clay or glaze, such as black pots from a red clay or a metallic lustre from a white tin glaze. This he achieves by controlling the atmosphere surrounding his pots during the firing and/or cooling. By altering the atmosphere he alters the metal oxide he is using for his colouring.

Reduction is used during porcelain firings to assist the integration of body and glaze, and to counteract any tendency towards a cream colour in body or glaze caused by iron oxide.

Reduction of stoneware firings affects the iron oxide in the body making this an effective flux. Thus integration of body and glaze involves colour also, so that colour from the body burns into the glaze in a decorative unifying way. Reduced iron oxide in a glaze gives the colouring called celadon. See **Iron oxide in glazes** and **Celadon**.

Copper oxide gives a startling colour change when reduced. The oxidized copper oxide gives a green colour and the reduced copper oxide gives a red colour in glazes. See **Copper oxide in reduction**. It is also possible to completely deprive the copper of its oxygen to create a layer of metal on the glaze surface. Tin, silver, platinum, gold and bismuth are other practical metals for lustres. See **Lustres**.

Raku colourings often involve reduction. Here the reducing atmosphere is localized by the proximity of sawdust etc but the phenomenon is scientifically the same as when a kiln full of pots is reduced.

REDUCING ATMOSPHERE. The atmosphere inside a kiln either contains oxygen which it can give to the metal oxides or else is lacking in oxygen and takes some from the metal oxides. These are called respectively oxidizing and reducing atmospheres. A kiln atmosphere often fluctuates between oxidizing and reducing, and is called neutral. Sealed muffles and saggars tend to have neutral atmospheres.

To achieve reduction, carbon is introduced into the kiln atmosphere. This carbon, if hot enough, will combine with the oxygen in the atmosphere to form carbon dioxide. When nearly all the oxygen is used up, carbon monoxide is formed and to become carbon dioxide this takes oxygen from the metal oxides.

Electric and gas muffles are reduced by the introduction of gas, wood or other burnables at the correct time and temperature. See also **Silicon carbide**. Open set kilns are reduced by restricting the flow of secondary air into the combustion chamber. Solid fuels, fuel-oil and gas are thus only partially converted to carbon dioxide.

Smoke appears when there is incomplete combustion due to insufficient oxygen, but merely producing smoke does not guarantee reduction. To effect a change within the clay and glaze the carbon must be in a finely divided form and hot enough to form a gas with the oxygen. It is necessary to form carbon monoxide gas which is hungry for oxygen. A reducing kiln may be producing only a wisp of smoke at the chimney. The necessary reducing atmosphere is maintained inside the chamber by control of the pressure by damper.

REDUCTION AND COLOUR STRUCTURES. Colour is dependent upon reflected light. This light is reflected from three-dimensional patterns of interlinked atoms. A change in this network structure at the point at which the colouring oxide links with the silica may change the colour of the reflected light.

The network which a colouring oxide forms is affected by the number of oxygen atoms available for the construction and also by the metal atom's ability to attach itself to that number of oxygen atoms. This ability is called the metal's valency. Within the limits of the pottery process, only iron, copper and tin have alternative valencies giving alternative colours.

THE ORDER OF REDUCTION. Some oxides are held together by weaker bonds than others. There is an approximate order in which the metal oxides are willing to part with their oxygen atoms when subjected to reduction.

A slight reduction affects antimony oxide but it does not improve its colour. Antimony oxide is kept for oxidized glazes. Slight reduction next affects tin oxide. If the glaze has not melted the eventual glaze will be reduced to grey. If the glaze has already melted, only the surface is affected giving an iridescence on a white glaze. Thus tin oxide is suitable for reduction effects produced during cooling as with raku.

As reduction becomes heavier it affects lead, bismuth, copper, zinc, nickel, cobalt, iron and manganese oxides and lead silicate in that order.

Where lead oxide is required as a flux, it appears that bismuth and copper oxides cannot be reduced without affecting the lead oxide detrimentally. Fortunately lead oxide quickly reoxidizes and once involved in a silicate its position in the above list is at the end. Thus bismuth and copper oxides can be reduced in a lead glaze. Like tin oxide they can be reduced below 700°C (1292°F) a phenomenon made use of in raku.

Zinc, nickel, cobalt and manganese oxides are difficult to maintain in reduced state. Zinc oxide is lost by volatilization if it is reduced. See **Zinc oxide flux**. Iron oxide has a stable state as reduced iron oxide (FeO) and can be reduced above 700°C (1292°F). See **Iron oxide black**.

To reduce the oxides of aluminium, vanadium, titanium, cerium, barium, magnesium, chromium, calcium, sodium, potassium and silicon requires a very strong reduction beyond the capacity of pottery kilns. Their effective use in pottery is in fully oxidized state.

Refine. Usually refers to the processing of clays whereby unrequired materials, called impurities, are removed. Methods include dry and wet sieving, elutriation, levigation, settling and the use of magnets.

Refractive index. The number which indicates the ratio of the velocities of light outside and inside a material. As light enters a glaze its speed is reduced. The light rays therefore bend (are refracted) at the point of entry. The refractive indices of silicates used as frits and glazes lie between 1·4 and 1·8. Opacifiers have indices between 2·0 and 2·4. As light meets an opacifier it is therefore bent further or reflected from the surface. Both effects scatter the light. Opacifiers are not part of the general silicate structure but are isolated nuclei and particles which affect the light separately. See also **Colloid, glaze**.

Refractory. Resistant to high temperatures. The potter uses refractory materials for building his kiln. The materials therefore have to withstand not only high temperatures but constantly changing temperatures, uneven temperatures in close proximity and various gases. Industrially, refractory may mean temperatures of 1700°C (3092°F) but the individual potter would count clays and other materials as refractory if they withstood 1300°C (2372°F) without deformation.

Some common refractories and their uses by the individual potter are: fireclay for blending in with clay to make the mixture coarser, or to withstand higher temperature or thermal shock. Fireclay was the potter's

original refractory and is still very useful for making special expendable pieces of kiln furniture and for kiln patching and stopping. China clay is also a useful refractory for patching etc. Manufactured kiln shelves and furniture are made from sillimanite, alumina, zirconium silicate and silicon carbide. Each has its own advantages dependent upon the order of preference one puts on their properties, e.g. initial cost, strength, weight, purity when considering staining of ware, reaction to kiln gases such as reduction atmosphere or salt vapour.

Refractory cement, which with suitable aggregates makes refractory concrete, provides an easy way of casting awkwardly shaped kiln arches, flues etc, which cannot be made from standard bricks. Refractory cement is built around alumina and silica, whereas the usual cement is a combination of calcia and silica. Alumina and silica have melting points above 1700°C (3092°F) and do not overflux one another nor easily break down upon attack.

New materials developed for use in spacecraft are lightweight yet able to withstand high temperatures. They insulate with a very narrow thickness compared with conventional refractories. They are used in kiln insulation and are marketed under various trade names. Many are fibrous structures which are built around silicate chains, as is asbestos. They are not necessarily strong but for load-bearing structures are prepared as mixtures with other castables.

REFRACTORY COATING. A layer of refractory material used to insulate or to isolate a kiln wall from the effects of gases, or kiln shelving from the fluxing of bodies and glazes. It is usually administered as a thin slurry painted on the surface and called flint wash, zircon wash, alumina wash, bat wash etc. The choice of refractory depends upon the type of protection required.

Relative formula. Another name for Unity formula.

Relief decoration. A relief is achieved by modelling the surface of the clay, by adding pieces of clay (sprigging), by pushing the clay out from the other side (repoussé), and by using relief moulds. One photograph is of part of an 18th-century mould for a dish in

which the decoration shows as raised lines between which areas of slip were painted. See also **Applied ornament** and **Sprigging**. The other photograph is of a pot by Trevor Worton which includes relief decoration, applied and modelled.

Repetition throwing. The act of throwing repeat items on the potter's wheel. It is essentially a production method but has excellent value for all students. Whilst much depends upon the judgment of the eye for the silhouette and size of the rim, a great deal of judgment remains with the feel of the pot in the hands. This skill requires much practice with concentration upon what effect each pressure and movement is achieving. A good thrower realizes the necessity for each movement he makes and naturally comes to an economical use of his energy. This, rather than hurried movements, gives him his speed. The thrower uses lumps of prepared clay of the same weight to assist accuracy. This and the rhythmic use of economical movements gives repeat items. As a further check he often has a pointer, which is a stick with or without a rubber flexible tip or feather end, to define where the rim should come. He may also have other simple measuring sticks handy.

When the judgments by hand movements and sight are keen, then use can be made of repetition throwing on a stem. For this a large piece of clay is put on the wheel and partly centred by patting into a cone. Absolute centring is not necessary and in any case is difficult. What is necessary is sufficient centring to make the weight of the clay true enough to act as an even flywheel without throwing the spindle about. Then, by judgment, sufficient clay is centred at the top of the cone of clay and is thrown in the normal way. A necessity is the positive compressing of the base of the pot in a combined centring and opening process. Without this compression the clay in the base of the pot lacks equivalent density with the clay in the rest of the pot and tends to crack in firing.

A measuring stick or callipers may be used as a check on size, but movements and the eye are usually sufficient. Trimming by rib or other tool includes making a notch at the point where the pot is to be cut off. The cutting-off wire is placed or allowed to run in this notch for cutting off. The use of a twisted wire helps the two parts, pot and clay lump, to separate more easily and so does a peeling action when lifting the pot. It is difficult to cut a very thin base and most potters use some later turning. The clay lump is rarely used to the last bit but until its size is no longer convenient.

Repetition throwers are paid by the number of pots thrown. In some of the traditional rural potteries, especially those making plant pots, interesting methods of calculation have been used. Payment may be by the weight of clay thrown calculated as so many casts, cakes, lumps, slugs or pieces. These are the particular size of clay convenient for handling in the store and from the pug and vary from 20 lbs to 50 lbs. Other payment may be by the board, which is the plank upon which the pots are arranged in definite numbers according to size. Plant pots are often known by numbers such as 12's, 48's, 60's, which refer to the number of pots coming from one lump or cast of clay. It is interesting to note that the small plant pots were sold by the yard when stacked together in the store shed.

The use of an assistant, called a passer, greatly speeds up the output. The passer prepares and weighs the clay and lifts the pots from the wheel. The disadvantage in using a passer is that speed becomes more important than pot. Passing for oneself enables a continuous critical appraisal of each pot to be made as it is lifted from the wheel. The passer is often paid by the hour but given a small bonus by the thrower out of his own earnings.

Some approximate repetition throwing weights are given with measurements when thrown. They are approximate because they have been averaged from various sources but serve as an interesting guide. Plant pots: 40 lbs 18 inches, 20 lbs 15 inches, 10 lbs 12 inches, 5 lbs 10 inches, 2 lbs 7 inches, 1 lb $5\frac{1}{4}$ inches, 12 oz $4\frac{1}{2}$ inches, 10 oz 4 inches, 8 oz 3 inches. Bowls: 10 lbs 15 inches diam., 2 lbs 8 inches, $1\frac{1}{2}$ lbs 7 inches, 1 lb 6 inches, 12 oz 5 inches. Jars, vases, mugs, jugs etc: 30 lbs 25 inches high, 20 lbs 20 inches, 10 lbs 15 inches, $2-2\frac{1}{2}$ lbs $7\frac{1}{2}-8\frac{1}{2}$ inches quart, $1-1\frac{1}{4}$ lbs $5\frac{1}{2}-6$ inches pint, 12 oz 4–5 inches half-pint, 10 oz 4 inches, 6–7 oz $3\frac{1}{2}$ inches one-third pint.

For anyone learning to throw, whether intending to do repetition work or not, the skill of the repetition thrower is worth consideration and can be analysed under three points.

1. Use of thoroughly prepared clay weighed out to exactly the same weight. This means that mistakes on one piece can be corrected on the next and achievements are more easily consolidated.

2. Consideration of every movement the hands are making. Think of what they are achieving in terms of moving the clay. Repeat successful movements until they can be strung together in a rhythm.

3. Thinking positively towards creating a good pot with as little as possible thinking in terms of rescuing a bad pot. Getting rid of a bad pot and starting another good pot is quicker in the long run for both satisfactory production and learning.

To these three points of the repetition thrower could be added the idea of keeping to the same wheel and the same type of clay whilst learning.

Residual clay. Primary clay. Clays which are found in the place where they have decomposed to form clays. China clay, bentonite and a few fireclays can be called residual clays. All other clays have been removed and deposited elsewhere and are called secondary or sedimentary clays. See **Clay, origin**.

Resist. The action whereby a coloured decoration as slip or glaze is prevented from adhering to selected parts of the pot.

The simplest resist is paper. Newspaper is ideal. This is cut or torn to shape and attached to the pot at leatherhard or earlier stage by slip or wetting with a sponge. Subsequent dips or brushings of coloured slips therefore cannot adhere to the part protected by the newspaper. As the pot and slip begin to dry the newspaper comes loose and can easily be peeled away leaving a clean decoration.

To resist a glaze, e.g. on a foot rim, or to resist a second dip of glaze or a colouring brushed onto an unfired glaze surface, the most satisfactory is a wax resist. The area to be reserved is dipped in hot wax or has hot wax brushed on to it. The colour or glaze, being mixed with water, cannot adhere to the wax. Paraffin wax or candle wax alone are too quickly chilled and difficult to control. The addition of some paraffin oil (kerosene) and/or thin machine oil overcomes this.

The proportion required is a personal choice according to the job in hand. About equal parts of wax and oil make a good starting point. The wax and oil are melted together in a tin over a candle flame or low gas flame, electric ring etc, remembering that it is an inflammable mixture and can very easily catch fire when hot. If the mixture catches fire the flame should be smothered with a sheet of asbestos and the heat source removed.

Wax emulsions are marketed by potters' merchants. These are like the wax/water emulsions used in canvas waterproofing for tents. The water dries out leaving the wax as a resist or water repellent. Wax emulsion is useful on absorbent biscuit but hot wax is superior on unfired glaze. There is no need to remove the wax as it burns out completely in the firing.

To resist colours etc being applied over an already-fired glaze it is usual to use a water soluble resist. This is because the colours are mixed with oil. The resist is either a gum, such as gum arabic or dextrin, or a bulk such as paint pigment held by a water-soluble binder. The glaze surface is cleaned of grease by wiping with whiting. The resist is applied and allowed to dry. Over this an onglaze colour or a lustre is applied by groundlay, spraygun or brush, using an oil medium. This covers the resist also but when it has dried the pot is immersed in water or rinsed under a running tap. Gentle rubbing with a brush or cotton wool loosens the colour which is only adhering to the resist. The resist dissolves in the water and the colour above it is washed away.

Paper, wax and soluble resists most naturally give hard-edge definition to the colour contrast. This hard-edge style can be exploited and enhanced by the use of angular or pointed shapes. If a softening of the edge is required this can be done by coarse brushing of the colour in a 'dry brush' technique which allows some background to show through the brushed colour, or by the use of colours which bleed in the glaze, such as copper and manganese. A very delicate soft edge can be achieved if newspaper is torn rather than cut, and the slip it is resisting is used thinly. With wax resists, if the wax can be used thinly or the glaze can be thick, it is possible to get specks of the repelled colour adhering over the wax. These specks eventually burn onto the underneath surface especially with glazes and give a delightful speckled effect which successfully breaks the otherwise harsh contrast.

Rhodochrosite. Manganese ore. Manganese carbonate. $MnCO_3$. A transparent, lustrous, pink ore sometimes polished as a gemstone. It decomposes on heating to MnO and CO_2 and takes up oxygen to become manganese dioxide, MnO_2.

Rib. Any object or tool, such as a piece of slate, metal or wood, used in throwing pots on the wheel. Originally animals' ribs were used.

Rich clay. Very plastic clay. Fat clay. Long clay. Sticky clay.

Riddle. Coarse mesh used for separating dry materials into two sizes of particles: those that will pass through the riddle and those that will not. Its use is in sorting crushed dry clays, shales and soft rocks. A riddle is named by the size of its holes which are theoretically squares produced by interwoven wire warp and weft. Thus a $\frac{1}{4}$ inch riddle has holes $\frac{1}{4}$ inch × $\frac{1}{4}$ inch. It should be noted that shales and some grogs have particles which are flat and long and these could pass through a hole diagonally and lengthwise. Thus the material which passes a $\frac{1}{4}$-inch riddle can have pieces $\frac{5}{16}$ inch at least amongst it.

Riffles. Barriers set across channels down which a slurry is run to catch the heavier particles and thus separate by weight if not by size the sand etc from the clay. With clay processing one usually considers the sediment as impurity and this is thrown away, but in ore washings such as gold the sediment is what one is collecting and the impurities are washed away. See **Levigation**.

Rings. See **Buller's rings**.

RO formula. The unitary system invented by Prof Hermann Seger (1839–94) to assist in the analysis of the properties of different bodies and glazes. The system involves the grouping of ceramic oxides as RO, R_2O_3 and RO_2. For any one body or glaze the total number of molecules of one group is brought to one and the other two groups are then expressed in proportion. For bodies the R_2O_3 group is brought to unity and for glazes the RO group. See **Formula, unity**.

Following the use of unity formulae, RO, R_2O_3 and

RO_2 have become accepted shorthand expressions for monoxide, sesquioxide and dioxide in ceramic writings.

Rockingham. A pottery factory at Swinton near Rotherham, Yorkshire. From 1826 to 1842 a porcelain was made in an extremely lavish Rococo style. The high cost of production, especially the cost of applied gold, finally ruined the factory.

Prior to and during the production of porcelain, a general-purpose ware was made using a rich red clay and lead glazes stained with iron and manganese. Some of this ware was also decorated with gold.

The word Rockingham is now used in three ways: to describe items in extreme Rococo which in Rockingham reached its furthest taste, to describe rich red clays especially when highly plastic and used for teapots, and to describe shiny lead glazes stained dark brown by manganese and iron. See also **Manganese dioxide**.

Roll. A pronounced thickening of glaze used as a decorative feature, especially on bowls. Glazes for this treatment must be stiff and of the alumina type. Use is made of surface tension to collect the glaze at the lowest point of the glazed area. These glazes are applied thickly.

The edge of the glazed area must be horizontal when

252

set in the kiln so that an even roll is produced. If the edge is not horizontal the glaze collects at one side and overruns the unglazed area.

These glazes tend to have a low contraction on cooling and thus tend to be subjected to stress by the body. The thick roll therefore may often shiver or if very strong the body of the pot may be cracked. The crack occurs just above the roll in a horizontal ring.

Rolled inlay. Method of rolling pieces of coloured clay into the surface of a pot or clay slab from which a pot is to be made. This produces a strong colour contrast similar to sprigging but without the relief surface which a sprig makes. See also **Encaustic**.

Rolling. Glaze defect commonly called crawling.

Romano-British pottery. Civilian pottery produced under Roman occupation, probably under Roman direction and mostly for the military and Roman civilian use. The indigenous British wares in the form of burial urns continued through the occupation and after with little obvious influence from the occupation but the domestic ware is more difficult to trace as a continuous line.

Romano-British pottery owes something to the precision of Graeco-Roman tradition and often shows an almost mathematical consideration of form. It was obviously influenced by the Samian ware which was imported from Gaul, but it never copied the fully-oxidized red colour. Instead, the Romano-British ware always shows signs of reduction, sometimes of extreme reduction, and varies from pale greys and slate blue-greys to lustrous blacks.

Most of the ware is plain and wheel-thrown and very rarely is it glazed. The forms vary greatly, some being exceedingly free. Small feet are a typical feature on bottles, beakers and jars. The bottles swell to a fully round form before closing to the neck sometimes with rich throwing rings showing. The rims and handles are generous and show a feeling for plastic clay. Jars vary from very small to very large. The widest part is usually above half way giving a high shoulder and top-heavy appearance over the small base. The rims are flared.

Other wares from Eastern England are decorated with relief lines and dots in both the body clay and in a white clay apparently trailed onto the pots as a thick slip. These are called the Upchurch and Castor wares and are associated with the later Roman period after A.D. 200 when difficulties in trade with Gaul resulted in a dearth of Samian ware.

ROMANO-BRITISH KILN. The kiln used in Britain during and after the Roman occupation was a development of the simple trench fire. It was less sophisticated than one might expect of the Romans, yet it involves many features including those for slow water-smoking and reduction.

The kiln was a low beehive structure sunk into the ground with a dome which was remade over the closely packed pots for each firing. There was no chimney, only an exit hole in the dome, and the firemouth was a pit leading to a circular area with a central clay column supporting the chamber floor. By digging the kiln out of the clayey ground the kiln became a fired pot unit but was probably considered fairly expendable since more than one is usually found at one site. They also face different ways, perhaps to make use of different winds.

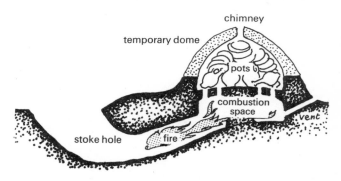

Recent experiments using kilns copied from the Roman ones, and with actual Roman kilns, have shown that the Romano-British kiln was capable of producing oxidized red ware as well as the common black and grey wares. Yet few reddish pieces have been found and this may be due to the potter's realization of the additional strength of the denser reduced body.

Roping. A slip-casting fault which is like a series of strings on the slip side of the cast. In vitreous and dense bodies the marks sometimes show on the outside (mould side) of the cast after firing. See **Casting slip, adjustment**.

A similar effect also occurs with glazes that are over-flocculated. This shows after firing as uneven ripples and looks similar to the 'stringing' effect of highly-fluxed ash glazes. See **Ashes**.

Roulette wheel. A small wheel with a handle or a spindle that can be held between finger and thumb. The circumference of the wheel is cut with notches etc so that when it is held to a pot on the wheel a relief pattern is imprinted round the pot. It was once a popular way of decorating cheap repetition articles and also of putting names around gingerbeer bottles, plant pots etc. It is a very simple yet very effective way of decorating.

Round down-draught kiln. An intermittent kiln of circular plan with flattish dome and four to twelve firemouths. The design is very efficient above 1000 cubic feet. Below this capacity a rectangular down-draught is preferred.

The photograph shows a round down-draught kiln which was used for salt-glaze drainpipes. The flames and vapour pass first upwards to the dome and then down between and through the pipes to escape by flues to the central chimney. Some kilns have underground flues to an isolated chimney.

Round up-draught kiln. An intermittent kiln of circular plan with one or more firemouths which heat the chamber through a pierced floor. There may or may not be a muffle or saggars. If shelves are used they are often pierced also. The flames travel upwards through the ware and heat is held in the chamber by a baffle ceiling. In large kilns this takes the form of a high honeycomb or pierced dome giving the beehive-shaped kiln. A chimney may be added to improve draught control and this may be incorporated in a complete outer skin wall for additional insulation as in the Stoke bottleneck kiln.

The round up-draught kiln is the simplest form of kiln. The Romano-British kiln was a round up-draught. By the late 18th century, refinements to this kiln had produced the Stoke bottleneck. With good fuel and good burners in attendance this was an excellent kiln if not as efficient as a good down-draught kiln. Temperatures of 1300°C (2372°F) were possible and some factories used their bottlenecks for the high temperature bisc long after using a continuous tunnel kiln for their glaze firings.

Rubbing stone. Rubbing stick. Originally a piece of fine-grained gritstone from the English Pennines used for the removal of blemishes by hand where the normal grinding wheel cannot reach. Now all sizes of sticks, discs, rectangular blocks and mouse-shaped stones are used. These are manufactured from silicon carbide, corundum and diamond-impregnated resin.

Ruby lustre. A copper lustre which is half-way between a complete metal and the red copper glaze. Its colour is a deep red tending to purple with lustrous shine. It has always been a popular colouring, being even richer in colour than the deepest gold lustres since it has the backing of the red glaze. It is effective as an all-over lustre on modelled surfaces and as brushwork.

There are three ways of producing a ruby lustre: one uses a copper compound in the glaze, another uses a copper compound painted onto the glaze and a third transfers the copper from a removable coating.

In the first method 2% to 8% of copper oxide or carbonate is mixed with the glaze. The amount is dependent upon the composition of the glaze. Adjustment of the amount is made upon the principle that too much copper compound produces a poor-quality red whilst insufficient gives a poor lustre. A good-quality red with some iridescence is called a rouge flambé. A full lustre with little or no red background is a copper lustre. The glaze must be soft, mature below 1000°C (1832°F) and contain some lead. It is fired oxidized to maturity and upon cooling is reduced either intermittently down to dull red heat, or more intensely in the 750°C to 600°C (1382°F to 1112°F) range or even given an extra reduction firing in this range. See **Copper lustre**.

The second method uses similar reduction techniques below 1000°C (1832°F) but the glaze can be harder, even fired as high as 1200°C (2192°F). The colouring is only at the surface and is therefore more easily reduced although the glaze is harder. Decoration is painted onto the unfired glaze with a pigment composed of glaze, copper compound and a very small proportion of iron oxide which reinforces the reduction. Varying amounts of reduction give variety of lustre from red to metallic.

In the third method a paste composed of clay and copper compound is painted onto the surface of the already-fired glaze. The glaze can be transparent over a white body or of the tin-opacified type. A low-temperature reduction firing in the region of 700°C (1292°F) transfers the colloidal copper into the glaze surface. See **Transmutation lustre**.

Ruckling. Another name for the glaze defect called crawling.

Run. (1) Glaze run. The amount by which a glaze moves under gravity during its fluid state in the firing.

The distance a glaze will move is dependent upon its thickness as well as its fluidity or viscosity. A thick glaze having more bulk and proportionately less friction on the body will move further than the same glaze applied thinly. The distance moved can often be seen where an iron fleck is dragged or other colouring streaks exist. Movement up to $\frac{1}{4}$ inch does little harm. The extra amount of glaze at the foot will usually be held there by its surface tension as a thickening or roll. More than $\frac{1}{4}$ inch of movement is unusual except for some of the very streaky art glazes. These glazes, popular in the 1920's and 30's, always required the pots to be supported on high stilts. The pots had to be severely ground at the base to restore a foot rim.

A shiny glaze needs to have been through a state in the firing during which it was very fluid. This allows the surface to smooth out completely after the disruptions of fusion.

Many other glazes have a very fluid state which causes excess run, sometimes called skating, and yet these glazes may be crystalline glazes or near-crystalline glazes. For example, stoneware wood ash and feldspar glazes, earthenware titanium matt glazes. In such cases it is an unnecessary risk to allow the glaze to run too much. The crystallization obliterates the colouring effects or the possible high shine which the long run could give. On the other hand a glaze which is so viscous that it cannot move at all tends to have an uninteresting surface which looks unmoved and dead.

The melting of the glaze and the speed with which it will melt over a given range is dependent upon the flux : silica ratio. The higher the temperature and/or the longer the time taken, the greater the proportion of silica which can be melted, varying from 1:2 to 1:7. But the run is governed by viscosity and this is dependent upon the alumina : silica ratio. The greater the proportion of alumina, the stiffer the molten glaze will be. Thus a glaze with no alumina at all will run very quickly once it has melted. It will also craze badly.

Since unity is always kept for the alumina when considering the alumina : silica ratio the appearance is that the silica amounts are being varied. In practice however it is the alumina amounts in the recipe that are being varied. For example, a very runny glaze might have a ratio of 1:20 but a very viscous glaze would have a ratio more like 1:6. This latter is the ratio of potash feldspar which does not succeed in becoming a runny glass at 1300°C (2372°F) although it begins to melt at 1160°C (2120°F).

To effect a change in the glaze recipe which is too runny the simplest way is to introduce alumina by way of china clay. China clay has an alumina : silica ratio of 1:2 so that it introduces a high proportion of alumina for its introduction of silica. Empirically it can be substituted in the glaze recipe for some of the flint or quartz content which is pure silica. If the glaze is too viscous, the reverse is true. Substitute flint for some of the china or ball clay. Some stoneware glazes can withstand as much as 30% of china clay in the recipe. However, in any glaze to go on biscuit, an amount of any raw clay over 10% might result in shrinkage cracks during drying and a viscous glaze which crawls away from the cracks in the firing.

Run. (2) Bleed. Blur. Describes the action of certain colours which when used as underglaze or similar decoration are partly dissolved by the glaze giving a diffused edge. Copper oxide, cobalt oxide and manganese oxide are typical examples.

The effect is partly due to the action of the glaze flux and partly to the fluxing action of the colourant. Lead oxide in a glaze is very active. Lead glazes move considerably during fusion and absorb silicates and colouring from the adjacent body. This accounts for the blurred edges under lead glazes especially those compounded with raw lead. However it does not account for the blurred edges under stiff glazes like feldspathic stoneware. Here the run is local to the colour. Copper oxide, cobalt oxide and manganese oxide are strong fluxes, which, even though combined with alumina, silica, etc as underglaze or other colourant, will actively attack the adjacent glaze and diffuse into it. High alkaline fluxes and frits, and also boric oxide encourage the running of colouring oxides.

Rust. Hydrated iron oxide. $2Fe_2O_3 . 3H_2O$. The surface coating which forms on iron when exposed to moisture and air. Rust sometimes refers to similar coatings on other metals, though tarnish is a more usual name. Iron rust and rusty pieces of flaking iron

are used by potters to produce iron speckling in bodies and glazes. See **Iron oxide**.

The rust colour in glazes is produced by iron oxide at the surface. In stoneware, this effect is called kaki by the Japanese. See also **Tessha** and **Tenmoku**. It can be achieved in three ways:

1. By overloading the glaze with iron oxide so that there is more than can be dissolved in the eventual solid glass. The extra iron oxide is precipitated during cooling and forms a coating at the surface. This method requires distinct oxidation in the firing and cooling. Even so the results are not a bright rust colour.

2. By hard firing with suitable clays which form a deep body-glaze layer resulting in a crystal formation through the glaze to the surface. The red colour of red iron oxide (Fe_2O_3) is due to its crystal structure. A thin glaze layer helps the crystals to reach the surface. This is first evident on rims of pots where rust patches break through a black glaze. See **Tessha**. Oxidation is essential. The use of clays with a high iron content increases the strength of colour and helps to form the crystal layer. The use of white clay or white slip as a buffer layer between the body and glaze helps to create a brighter colour. In methods 1 and 2 the presence of boric oxide assists the formation of a brighter colour. The two methods are often combined.

3. During the firing of glazes, which contain less than a saturation of iron oxide, the iron oxide in solution is not uniformly distributed. It tends to gravitate away from the glaze surface and towards the body, collecting in a concentrated layer. This leaves a comparatively clear layer of glaze above it. Some of the iron oxide can be persuaded to collect at the surface of the glaze by the use of a reduction atmosphere over the period when the glaze melts. This oxide is not red iron oxide (Fe_2O_3) but black iron oxide (FeO) and is said to come to the surface to gain oxygen to revert to the more stable form of Fe_2O_3.

At the molten stage, the iron oxide is in solution. It should be noted that there is not an excess amount when compared with the glaze as a whole. It is not the same as method 1. The iron oxide however is precipitated out of solution as separate crystals upon cooling because it has concentrated at the surface where it has produced a layer of glaze which is saturated. If this black iron oxide is further oxidized at this precipitation

stage it becomes red iron oxide, producing a bright rust crystal. Quick cooling keeps the crystals small and avoids a matt surface. This method forms the brightest rust colour because the crystals cover a volume of colourless glaze through which the light can reflect. See **Iron oxide in glazes**.

The photograph shows a close-up of the concentrations of iron oxide crystals at the surface known as segregation.

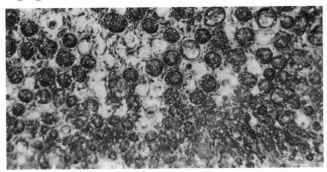

Rutile. TiO_2. Natural titanium dioxide with a small amount of iron which gives it a yellow colour. The yellow colour is retained when rutile is used in glazes, therefore some bright creams, yellows and oranges can be produced in association with tin oxide, cobalt oxide and red iron oxide.

Rutile is one of the three oxide ores of titanium. It is found associated with sandstones in Australasia. The other oxide ores are brookite and anatase. The three are chemically alike but identified by their different crystal structures. Rutile always contains impurities, mostly iron, and such is the colour-heightening power of titanium dioxide that only a trace is sufficient to give the rutile a yellow colour. Rutile containing much impurity is a dark brown, almost black.

Amounts of rutile, up to 10% in a glaze, give a broken colouring effect due to crystallization. In association with tin oxide a whole variety of streaked and mottled effects are obtainable. These effects in lead and low sol glazes, fired at approximately 1050°C (1922°F), were popular under the name of art glazes up to 1960.

Rutile readily produces a crystal structure in a glass on cooling and therefore opacity and a matt surface due to crystals can be produced by introducing up to 25% rutile in a glaze. See also **Crystalline glazes**.

Glazes containing 15% or more of rutile or rutile and titania are subject to phototrophy after firing. Phototrophy is the ability to change colour by the absorption of light. Such glazes darken with the light and grow pale with the lack of it. This process is reversible and continuous *ad infinitum*.

Rutile containing over 25% of iron, calculated as FeO, contains sufficient ferrous titanate ($FeTiO_3$) to be called by the ore name of ilmenite.

Rutile is a good electrical insulator and is used with very small amounts of plastic clay in the making of electrical condensers. See also **Titania**.

S

Saggar. A refractory box to protect ware from direct contact by flames and gases. Pots are packed in saggars which are then piled in bungs inside the kiln. See **Bung** and **Wad**.

Salt glaze. A glaze derived from salt, usually common salt, which is thrown onto the kiln fire. The salt decomposes and volatilizes, the most important product being soda which combines with alumina and silica from the hot pottery body to produce sodium aluminosilicate, i.e. glaze. The glaze varies from a light glossing of the surface to a twentieth of an inch in thickness depending upon the number of baitings and the amount of body which the volatile soda is able to flux. The volatile soda enters the pores of the body at a time when the body is still porous yet the alumina and silica are hot enough for immediate combination. The success of this simple process depends upon its use within definable limits.

Salt glazing probably originated in the Rhineland. Here, stoneware was developed during the 12th to 14th centuries and salt glazing appears to have been a part of this development. The Rhenish stoneware consisted largely of wine bottles, beer mugs and storage jars. This type of ware was made in Britain from the 17th century, notably by John Dwight at Fulham and later more imaginatively by the Martin brothers at the end of the 19th century.

Salt-glazed ware is still sometimes referred to as German salt glaze if it is brown and Dutch salt glaze if it is grey. The brown colour which is often a rich reddish-brown, is due to iron oxide in the clay. The grey colour is given by a small quantity of reduced iron oxide. The Dutch salt-glazed ware was often painted with cobalt oxide. This painting followed lines scratched in the soft clay and gave it the name of 'scratch-blue ware'. Cobalt oxide is the only colour that successfully integrates with the salt glaze. Painted iron oxide, if not integrated with the clay, tends to inhibit the formation of a good glaze.

Today few potters are using salt glaze and its industrial use for chemical containers and sewer pipes is rapidly decreasing. The examples shown are by Janet Hamer and Walter Keeler. Because salt glazing relies upon vapour to carry the glaze to the pot, the insides of all but the shallowest bowls remain unglazed. Insides of pots may be glazed with slip glazes prior to firing in the normal way. Slip glazes are popular be-

cause the whole process of salt glazing is a once-fired process. This is one of its attractive advantages.

The kiln used must be efficiently flued. Both up- and down-draught kilns can be used. For sewer pipes, a down-draught kiln is used and the pipes are stacked over some of the exit flues in the floor. The insides of the pipes are thus glazed along with the outsides.

For salt glazing to be effective, the salt must be quickly decomposed to create volatile soda. Salt is sodium chloride which melts at 800°C (1472°F). Thrown dry onto a kiln fire, the salt would melt into the fire before decomposing and some would be lost as it combined with the clinker. To achieve quick decomposition, water is added to the salt. This creates steam which decomposes the salt to produce soda and hydrochloric acid, both as gases.

$$2NaCl + H_2O \longrightarrow Na_2O\uparrow + 2HCl\uparrow$$
salt   water   soda   hydrochloric
                                acid

Soda is volatile at temperatures above 1200°C (2192°F). Glazes containing soda as the main flux are often bubbled by volatile soda if fired above 1200°C (2192°F). But the damp salt is able to decompose and volatilize above 1100°C (2012°F). Salt glazing is therefore carried out in a series of 3 or 4 baitings after 1100°C and the top firing temperature varies between 1180°C and 1250°C (2156°F and 2282°F).

The use of vaporized oil for kiln firing presented a problem to salt glazers. There was no open fire onto which the damp salt could be thrown. A solution to the problem was found in the use of salt and borax. This combination, already known to give more fluid and smoother glazes, can be handled as a dry granular material. As such it can be introduced into the combustion chamber by blown secondary air. See photograph. Borax is a combination of soda, boric oxide and water. The water assists the decomposition of the borax and also the salt. Up to 10% borax is used in the mixture. The equation is:

$$Na_2B_4O_7.10H_2O + 20NaCl \longrightarrow$$
borax   salt

$$11Na_2O + 2B_2O_3 + 20HCl$$
soda   boric   hydrochloric
             oxide   acid

Not all clays are fluxed by the soda because many contain insufficient free silica, e.g. china clays, ball clays and stoneware clays with alumina : silica molecular ratios approximating 1:2, 1:3 and 1:4. The best clays for salt glazing are fireclays which are high in silica. These have alumina : silica ratios of 1:5 and higher. Extra silica is sometimes added to clays as quartz sand but silica in isolation does not take a glaze. Some alumina is necessary.

A good salt glaze is very hard and chemical-resistant, hence its use for sewer pipes and acid containers. Alkalis from the body join the soda in the formation of the glaze. Small amounts of calcia and magnesia help to stabilize the glass. But alumina plays a more important part and is necessary if a glaze is to be formed at all. The simplest salt glaze is sodium alumino-silicate with a unity formula of:

$$Na_2O . 0.5 \text{ to } 1.0Al_2O_3 . 2.8 \text{ to } 5.5SiO_2$$

The alumina content is always high which accounts for the stiff nature of the glaze and its stability.

Samel. Half-burnt bricks, the result of being on the outside of a clamp.

Sand. Natural ground quartz. Sands vary in composition from pure silica to a mixture of silica, calcium compounds (shells), clay and soluble salts. There are often colouring impurities of iron and manganese, and traces of other minerals like titanium dioxide and zirconium silicate.

Pure silica sand is a source of silica for frits, glazes and glass. It is used for placing white earthenware in saggars and as a filler of both earthenware and stoneware. In earthenware, fine sand which will convert into cristobalite is often used. In stoneware either a very fine sand which fuses or a quartz sand which remains as quartz phase is used. See **Grain size**.

The less-pure sands are useful additions to clay often providing interesting speckle.

Sang-de-boeuf. Ox blood. Sacrificial red. A name

given to deep red and purplish glazes coloured by reduced copper oxide. See **Copper oxide in reduction**. The small bowl is by Derek Emms.

Sassoline. Sassolite. Italian mineral containing boric acid. See **Borax**.

Satin matt. Vellum matt. A low-temperature matt glaze on which the matt surface is caused by extremely fine crystals of zinc silicate, zinc titanate and possibly, lead titanate. Satin matts are produced by adding up to 18% of zinc oxide and 4% of titanium dioxide to soft runny glazes. Tin oxide and zirconium silicate are often added for extra opacity.

Satin matts rely upon the zinc oxide to remain isolated in the molten glaze but sufficiently loosened in molecular bonding to remake permanent bonds with titania and silica. The effect is lost if the zinc oxide acts as a flux and becomes involved in the melt. Satin matts are therefore restricted to temperatures below 1085°C (1985°F). They are usually fired below 1050°C (1922°F) with lead and boric oxides as the main fluxes. See also **Crystalline glazes** and **Zinc oxide**.

The molten glaze must be very fluid for the orientation of the zinc oxide and titania to take place. Satin matts are therefore runny glazes, often low in alumina content, and are restricted in practical use to horizontally fired surfaces like tiles and decorative plates. Their fine crystals provide a very smooth surface which does not mark and stain as do other crystalline glazes. The zinc and lead in crystalline compounds, however, make satin matts impractical for tableware on toxicity grounds.

The following is a recipe for a white satin matt used by Harry Fraser. It is fired at 1050°C (1922°F):

lead bisilicate	50
borax frit	20
zirconium silicate	12
titanium dioxide	3
tin oxide	3
zinc oxide	6
china clay	6

Saturation. The point at which the limit has been reached for dissolving one substance in another. A solution is a combination of a solvent and a solute. The solvent is usually liquid and keeps its identity as a liquid. The solute is often a solid which loses its identity as such. If more solute is present than is required for a fully-saturated solution, the excess remains undissolved.

In pottery, the term saturation usually refers to colouring oxides which are dissolved in glazes. The dissolved amounts give clean colours but the excess tend to give scummy or metallic colours. The saturation is different with each colourant and with each glaze but some typical amounts are:

iron oxide	8%
cobalt oxide	1%
nickel oxide	3%
copper oxide	3%
manganese oxide	5%

The concentration of the solution is dependent upon temperature. In glazes it is possible to dissolve more colourant when hot than cold. The difference between these two could be as much as a quarter of the colourant. This difference is precipitated out of solution as the glaze cools and is responsible for some interesting crystalline effects with iron and manganese oxides. See **Rust** and **Kaki**.

Sawdust firing. A simple system of firing in which pots are set in sawdust within a brick-built box with lid. The sawdust burns slowly achieving sufficient heat to turn the clay into pot. Pockets of oxidation and reduction are caused which produce interesting decoration especially on burnished red clays. See also **Jutland ware**.

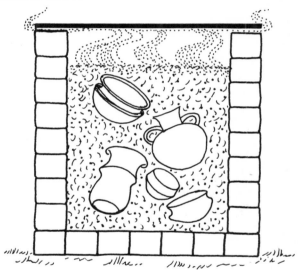

Scratch-blue. A method of decorating in which a deeply-scored line in soft clay is painted with cobalt

oxide. It was first used on salt-glazed ware in the 17th century and later copied on creamware. See **Salt glaze** and **Creamware**.

Screen. A framework across which is fastened an interwoven mesh or possibly a grid created by holes in a flat sheet of metal. A screen is used to separate materials by size; particles that will go through the holes and those that will not. Screening can be done wet or dry. A screen used for materials in suspension in water is also called a sieve. A coarse screen which is made from interwoven wire and is used for dry material only is also called a riddle. The terms screen and screening imply a continuous process and are therefore more common in industry than in the individual potter's workshop. However the term screening is sometimes used by the individual potter to mean the use of a middle-sized mesh between the fine sieve and the coarse riddle. This would be between 40's and 10's mesh for wet or dry work but might include coarser meshes in wet work.

Scum. The light-coloured marks which appear along edges and as finger prints on unglazed ware and biscuit. They are caused by the soluble salts in the clay which crystallize at the surface as the water evaporates. The salts may have entered the clay from the water supply. The crystals are broken in handling and leave remarkably clear finger prints which show only after firing.

Extra moisture is drawn to edges which catch the movement of air during drying. These edges therefore get an extra amount of the salt crystallization. During firing the salts become oxides and in a very soft biscuit are on the surface as a dust but with a harder biscuit or an unglazed stoneware they flux the body from the surface and cannot be removed. If the ware is to be glazed many glazes will absorb the excess oxide which is mostly calcia. However, thin layers of glaze on a fine body may not take properly on the rims and edges of handles. This is especially so on a medium to hard biscuit which is over-fluxed at these places.

The salts are of sodium, potassium, calcium, magnesium and iron. Some have entered the clay by its association with salt water or by the weathering of sulphides in proximity. The commonest mineral is calcium sulphate.

Some of the salts in the clay can be rendered harmless by the addition of 1% to 2% of barium carbonate. The barium carbonate is only slightly soluble and must be mixed thoroughly with the clay at a slurry stage. Blunging is preferable. Merely mixing with the clay is insufficient. The barium carbonate becomes 'soluble' in contact with the soluble salts with which it exchanges radicals. The new carbonate is precipitated as an insoluble powder or is a less soluble compound which cannot be carried to the surface of the clay by the water.

The barium salt does not cause scum. The equations are:

$$CaCl_2 + BaCO_3 \longrightarrow BaCl_2 + CaCO_3\downarrow$$

calcium chloride   barium carbonate   barium chloride   calcium carbonate

$$MgSO_4 + BaCO_3 \longrightarrow BaSO_4 + MgCO_3\downarrow$$

magnesium sulphate   barium carbonate   barium sulphate   magnesium carbonate

$$CaSO_4 + BaCO_3 \longrightarrow BaSO_4 + CaCO_3\downarrow$$

calcium sulphate   barium carbonate   barium sulphate   calcium carbonate

Soda and potash are also involved. They do not cause white scum but do cause over-fluxing. They cannot be precipitated because all their compounds are soluble. If the clay is worth the effort it can be 'washed' in plenty of water, settled and the excess water syphoned off.

There is also a biscuit scum caused by the use of soft coal from which sulphur combines with the body oxides in a slow or reduced firing. This must be brushed from the ware before glazing and the glaze firing needs to be slow and clean.

Secondary clay. Sedimentary clay. A clay which has been removed from its place of origin by natural forces and deposited elsewhere. A primary clay is one that is still in its place of origin. China clay is the obvious example of a primary clay, but most clays have been washed away by rain, carried in rivers and settled in lakes or the sea to form beds of plastic clay. Sometimes the clay beds have been subjected to pressure and heat to become mudstones, shales and even slates. During transportation, the clays are ground to fine particles, pick up the impurities including colour and are often sorted by levigation into fine and coarse clays. Secondary clays are therefore of many types: ball clay, red clay, stoneware clay, shales, marls, fireclays. See also **Clay, types** and **Disordered kaolinite**.

Sedimentation. Settling. The sinking of particles in a suspension. For example, the potter uses sedimentation to consolidate a slurry for reclamation as clay. The required clay settles and the water can be syphoned off the top.

The term is also used to describe the method of separating coarse, unwanted particles like sand from the finer, wanted particles of clay. The mixture is blunged, that is, thoroughly mixed with an excess of water. There must be an excess of water in order to make the slurry very fluid (thin). The slurry is allowed to stand still so that the heavier particles are no longer able to keep in suspension and settle out. After the desired effect of separation is achieved, (it is usually documented as a time), the required slurry is run off through a sieve and allowed to settle fully over a number of days before the water is syphoned or run off.

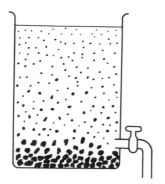

Sedimentation is a convenient method of washing and separating wood ash. It is also used commercially, for special clays, in which case large tanks are used and a deflocculant is first added to increase the suspension life of the clay and make the slurry more fluid for the passage of the unwanted sediment. When the wanted suspension has been run into a second tank, a flocculant is added to hasten the sedimentation of the clay.

Sedimentation uses the same physical idea as levigation to separate particles without screening, but levigation uses a constant motion past riffles.

Seger, Hermann A. (1839–94). The German ceramist who worked in other industries as a chemist before concentrating upon clay and heat treatment. He is known for his fundamental rules for overcoming crazing which followed his study of expansion rates and glaze fit; for his system of analysis, now called rational analysis, which describes clays in terms of pure kaolinite, feldspar and quartz; for his method of describing a glaze by the proportions of the constituent molecules, now called the unity formula method; and for his development of a method of gauging heat-work by pyrometric cones. All these systems originally carried his name (Seger rules, Seger analysis, Seger formula and Seger cones) but, with mid-20th century perfection of them, his name has been dropped from use, with the exception of the official Seger cone.

Seger cones. The range of pyrometric cones developed by Hermann Seger in 1885–6. The idea was adopted by other manufacturers in the 20th century and a bewildering range of different cones was produced. There are now three main types: Seger, Harrison and Orton. See **Cones**.

Seger cones are still produced by Chemisches Laboratorium fur Tonindustrie, Prof. Dr H. Seger and E. Cramer Kom-Ges, of Berlin and marketed throughout the British Isles and the Commonwealth countries by Wenger Ltd of Stoke-on-Trent, England.

Selenium. Se. A non-metal which under special conditions gives red colours. It is volatile and can only be used under controlled conditions at low temperatures. It is used to produce red glass but in pottery its greatest use is in onglaze colours.

The red colour develops when selenium is combined with cadmium to give cadmium selenide (CdSe). This is a dark maroon red which with cadmium sulphide becomes a bright red and orange. The colour must be fired quickly because it is volatile. It must also be reduced otherwise it will oxidize to cadmium oxide (CdO) and selenium dioxide (SeO_2) with loss of colour and volatilization.

Selenium dioxide is a glass-former but it has no place in glazes.

Sesquioxide. An oxide in which the combination of atoms which form the oxide molecule are in the ratio of 2 of the element to 3 of oxygen. For example, alumina is aluminium sesquioxide, there being two aluminium atoms to every three oxygen atoms in the alumina molecule. The chemical formula is written Al_2O_3. See also **Oxide**.

Sesquisilicate. A combination of a stated compound and silica which involves 3 molecules of silica to every 2 molecules of the other compound. The definition (and the molecular formula) is sometimes expressed as $1\frac{1}{2}$ times the other compound which is literally correct since 'sesqui' means 'and one-half added'.

The usual use of sesquisilicate is to describe the lead frit, lead sesquisilicate, which is given the molecular formula of either $PbO . 1\frac{1}{2}SiO_2$ or $2PbO . 3SiO_2$. See also **Silicate**.

Setters. Special refractories shaped to hold pots in the kiln. These may be for biscuit or glaze firing. Some pots require to be held firmly to prevent warpage. This is especially true in high-temperature bisc firings where setters are used in combination with sand or alumina. In some porcelain glaze firings setting rings are used to keep cup rims round, the rims being unglazed. The cups are fired upside down.

Setting. Kiln packing especially of repetition pieces and bricks.

Sgraffito. Sgraffiato. Scratched decoration especially when the scratched line or area reveals a different colour. The word comes from the Italian 'graffiare' to scratch and the adjective 'graffiato' is sometimes used in English for textured areas. Sgraffito refers to decoration which is in scratched lines and sgraffiato to decoration using areas which have been scratched. By general use however sgraffito embraces all types of scratched decoration including textured areas.

Sgraffito is such an obvious and direct method of patterning a surface that its qualities are often overlooked. There is a natural desire to mark a clean surface and the obvious way is to attack it and scratch it. This is seen in many primitive pots where the simple action of scratching has given a very successful decorative quality. The best examples of sgraffito make full use of the textured area in relation to the whole pot. The normal considerations of distribution and balance in area and line must be realized.

The technique is easier to acquire than using a brush, especially for those who normally write and draw with an inflexible tip. The feeling of sgraffito should be freedom and movement. Impressed and applied decoration in contrast are static.

Sgraffito can be of various types. The simplest is a scratching of the surface of the clay at leatherhard or white-hard stage. This reveals a different texture of clay. The scratched lines and areas will probably show as a coarser texture even if the surface is glazed. Such scratches can be emphasized by rubbing with metal oxides as in the photograph of a pebble pot by Bernard Rooke. Or the lines may show through a thick semi-

opaque glaze because the glaze is thicker on the lines. This effect can be made more marked by the use of a vitrifying slip. The slip may or may not be coloured differently from the body but it should contain sufficient soft flux to make the slip coating more dense than the body after biscuit firing. Thus the exposed body will be more porous and take to itself a thicker layer of glaze during glaze dipping.

With coloured slips the contrast becomes more marked and the removal of the slip at all stages from

freshly dipped to bone-dry gives distinctive effects. The photograph shows an 18th-century money box. Terms such as wet sgraffito, cheese-hard sgraffito and dry sgraffito have been used to define such methods. Finger-combing is an example of the directness of fresh slip sgraffito. At a leatherhard stage the slip can be attacked with many tools from single cutters such as pieces of wood and metal to multiple texturizers, such as hacksaw blades.

The use of a slip-glaze with stoneware opens up great possibilities because the contrast in colour and texture can be very effective. Because the body is incised the effect is very rich. Sgraffito is one of the best reasons for wanting a slip-glaze. Glazes on biscuit can also be sgraffitoed but the effect is not so rich. One can, however, gain a certain vitrification and colouring on the scratched surface by leaving a dusting of glaze there. Alternatively, another glaze over the top, possibly with further scratching, can give an infinite variety of decorative effects. The coffee pot by Michael Cardew shows the deep incision possible through a slip-glaze.

Shale. Flue. A clay in the form of small compressed flakes. The disc-like clay particles have orientated themselves at right angles to the pressure producing a cleavage. In this arrangement they can be packed more tightly and form hard, flat flakes up to an inch across.

Ordinary clay has its particles at all angles. Lumps of dry clay will break in any direction. Pressure put onto plastic and cheese-hard clay is resisted by a partial reshuffle of particles across the line of pressure. This occurs in clay kneading, centring on a wheel, throwing, and burnishing after turning. In clay deposits the pressure is great and continuous over millions of years, resulting in all the clay particles being lined up in the same direction. This produces shales. If heat is also present, the clay is partially 'fired' and the result is slate which exhibits cleavage along the lines of least resistance between the particles.

Shales, that is, clay shales, occur in all ages of rocks. The oldest ones are the Silurian shales of 420 million years ago. The Carboniferous System also has shales. Both the culm measures and the productive coal measures contain shales, some of which are fireclays.

These are over 280 million years old. The Tea marls of the Triassic Period of the New Red Sandstone System are also often shaley. These are about 200 million years old.

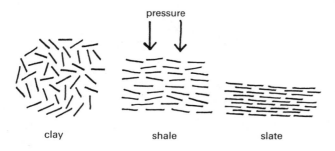

pressure

clay   shale   slate

All these shales will weather to clays. The process can be accelerated by crushing and blunging. Many shales can be converted into excellent potting clays by the addition of bentonite. Weathered shales are sometimes referred to as hungry clays.

Shape. The two-dimensional qualities of a pot or ceramic. These can be analysed as silhouette, outline, contrasts of colour and tone, proportions and angles. Shape is often used as a synonym for form but correctly shape should only be used in the consideration of a pot's silhouette, its comparative dimensions or proportions and its decoration. The confusion has arisen because of consideration of pots at a drawing board stage.

Shelling. Flaking. Peeling. A glaze or glaze and slip defect in which the glaze falls from the body in flakes. It often occurs where there is a slip on the body and mostly on low-fired ware or on porous bodies. It is caused by insufficient bond between glaze and body. This bond is lost when stress is placed on the article by handling or by normal expansions of the body and glaze.

The poor bond is the result of underfiring the glaze which melts itself but produces no body-glaze layer. Or, in the case of wares with slip covering, if the slip is put on the ware when the ware is too dry or possibly greasy it never properly adheres. After the glaze firing, the glaze is pulling at the slip, which parts its bond on the body. Shelling is usually in evidence on rims when the wares are taken from the kiln or in the period soon after. Complete shelling may take place in extreme cases.

Where there is sufficient bond between body and glaze, but flakes of glaze leave the ware, this action is called shivering and is described elsewhere. Shivering is characterized by the way the sliver of glaze shears off the pot, tearing part of the body with it.

Sherd. Shard. A piece of broken pottery. The term is often used archaeologically with the collective noun shraft.

Shivering. A glaze defect in which slivers of glaze shear away from the pot. It occurs especially on sharp outside edges, e.g. rims, the edges of handles, relief decoration and throwing marks. The flake of glaze has a very sharp edge and takes with it some of the body to which it was attached. It is known as a glaze defect although the fault often lies with the body. It is a result of poor glaze fit and is the opposite of crazing. It occurs more on stoneware than earthenware. In stoneware the body and glaze mature together and become integrated. If the glaze does not fit it takes with it part of the body. In earthenware and immature stonewares, the lack of this integrated body-glaze layer means that the glaze can leave the pot without tearing the body. This phenomenon is called shelling.

When a pot cools after firing, the glaze sets at approximately 500°C (932°F). From this temperature down to room temperature the body and the glaze lie side by side as two solids which should be bonded to each other. The body and the glaze each contract at a different rate. This puts the glaze on the finished pot either under tension or under compression by the body. Some compression is desirable as an insurance against crazing but too much compression results in shivering. It is impossible to know how much is too much until shivering occurs. Since the correct balance is a fine one and shivering when it occurs is dangerous with tableware and ovenware, some potters prefer not to have their glazes under compression at all. To be sure that there is no compression, they welcome a very slight crazing. According to the type of ware being made, one must steer a course between the two extremes of shivering and crazing. The problem is discussed under **Thermal shock**.

To overcome shivering, the glaze, or the body, or both must be altered in composition. The glaze must be made to contract more on cooling. This can be done by substituting other oxides of greater contraction rate for some of the fluxing oxides. The problem is discussed under **Glaze fit**. Shivering is typical of glazes of high clay content which are high in alumina, and also of alumina and magnesia matts. It will be seen from the table of expansion rates that these oxides are at the low expansion end of the scale.

Conversely the body may be made to contract less on cooling. The method is the opposite to that used for the glaze. However, most bodies do not contain fluxing oxides in the way that glazes do. The fluxes are part of raw materials and they cannot be isolated. One must therefore turn one's attention to the free silica in the body. Free silica exists in the body as crystalline quartz before firing. During firing, some of the crystalline quartz becomes involved in vitrification and becomes fused silica. As fused silica, it has a lower expansion rate than crystalline. A prolonged or higher firing will therefore result in more of the free silica becoming fused and the result will be that the eventual body will contract less on cooling than it did before.

However, one must not jump too quickly at this means of correcting shivering. Shivering usually occurs on stoneware where the body and the glaze mature together, and it is on the densest of stonewares, with the most vitrified bodies, that it occurs most. This is contrary to the correction theory just expounded because in practice the extra vitrification makes the body more brittle. It also decreases its physical strength. The stress between body and glaze, though lessened, may still exist and be sufficient to rupture the bond between glaze and body, ripping away the top layer of body embedded in the body-glaze layer. With a prolonged firing there is also the possibility that some of the crystalline quartz which is not fused may be converted into crystalline cristobalite. This would result in even greater body contraction than before. See **Silica conversion** and **Cristobalite**.

At this point one should not confuse the overall shrinkage from raw to fired ware with the contraction which takes place on cooling. The two are entirely separate and independent. A body that shrinks a great deal may still have a contraction rate that is low or high. Shrinkage is an irreversible process dependent upon vitrification. Contraction is the result of temperature fall and is reversible with heat.

Correction of body composition must therefore be sought in another way. Aluminous grog has a smaller contraction rate than silica sand, so if grog were used instead of sand the overall contraction would be less. If there is no additional sand in the body which can be replaced by grog it is possible that the addition of some grog may cause less contraction. It is not a certainty because some grogs contract more than some stoneware bodies. An aluminous grog should be tried. Even sillimanite and zircon have been used in extreme cases but these are expensive and an alteration of glaze is preferable.

If shivering occurs on some pots and not on others, one should note any temperature differences in their firings. One should also consider the forms themselves and the angles on which shivering occurs. Shivering often occurs on pots in which the clay became tired in throwing. Sandy bodies which have been oversponged on the rims, leaving them composed of sand rather than clay, are prone to shivering. A change in throwing habits and the use of a buffer slip may show immediate success but a change in the physical properties of the body and glaze should also take place.

Short clay. Lean clay. Clay which has little plasticity and strength. It is a relative term because clay can only be termed short when it has insufficient workability for the job in hand. A general standard amongst individual potters is that a clay should be capable of being thrown on a potter's wheel. This requires a high standard of workability. A simple test is the tie-a-knot test described under **Workability**. The short clay will show signs of tearing, if not complete rupture.

Short clays are often very difficult to knead. They have some capacity to slide; they have also a high resistance to pressure. That is, their yield point is high. They have a stodgy feel that is almost a bounce, like a bread dough. Many have such little strength that they sag under their own weight, especially as they become wet in throwing.

A natural clay which is short can have a plastic clay like ball clay blended with it. Alternatively a plasticizer can be added or more deliberate preparation may be required. See **Plasticity** and **Preparation of Clay**.

Shrinkage. Decrease in size due to drying and firing. Drying shrinkage is reversible with the return of water, but firing shrinkage is due to chemical and physical

changes in the clay and is permanent. See **Drying** and **Firing**. Shrinkage should not be confused with contraction, which is the opposite of expansion and is the result of temperature differences.

The photographs show the drying shrinkage of a patch of natural clay and the firing shrinkage of a red clay at the different centigrade temperatures of 850°, 1000°, 1130°, 1180° and 1250°C (or 1562°, 1832°, 2066°, 2156° and 2282°F). The chart compares the shrinkages of two clays and a prepared body. Note how the body which contains 20% non-plastic material has a low shrinkage during drying. This non-plastic material is however a densifying addition which increases the firing shrinkage up to the densification point at 1100°C (2012°F).

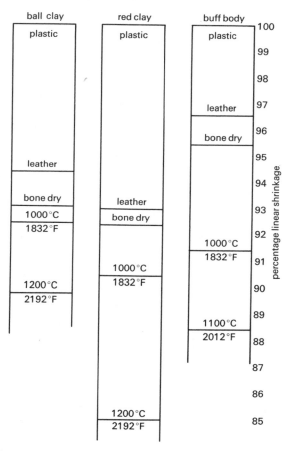

Siderite. Chalybite. Ferrous carbonate. $FeCO_3$. A low-yield iron ore formed when iron in solution replaces calcia in a limestone. To differentiate this from the high-yield ores, the siderite is often called an ironstone. Ironstones occur as replacement deposits which do not necessarily follow a strata. There are also partial replacements, referred to as ferruginous limestones, and crystals in shales called clay ironstones. The star shape of the cluster of crystals gives the ore its name, siderite: the stone of the stars. These ironstones can be empirically used as glaze colourants and fluxes. See **Iron oxide**.

Sieve. A frame or rim with a lawn or fine mesh across it used for separating by size the coarse material from fine, or unwanted from wanted etc. It is usual to sieve materials when they are suspended in water. In this form they are easier to handle. Industrially the word sieve is used in connection with test work and screen is used in production. The individual potter uses the word screen for coarser meshes and riddle for very coarse. Screening may be done wet or dry but riddling is done with dry materials.

The photograph shows an electric vibrating sieve in use.

Silica. Silicon dioxide. SiO_2. The glassy substance which is the most important constituent of pottery glazes and which is an integral part of clay and many potters' minerals. It occurs naturally as quartz rock, flint and sand. It also occurs in combination with other oxides in what are called silicates. An analysis of all the substances in the Earth's crust shows that 60% is silica.

Silica is a hard glassy substance which melts at 1710°C (3110°F) to a transparent glass. This temperature is too high for a potter's kiln and so some way of melting silica at a lower temperature is used in order to make a glaze. Fluxes are mixed with the silica. These have the effect of bringing down the melting temperature to within the range of the potter's kiln. The resulting melt is a mixture of silica and other oxides which link together on cooling to form a glass. Silica is the necessary constituent of this glass. There are many fluxes but only one silica. The only substance which gives similar results to silica is boric oxide. This is also a glass-former, but without silica it will not give a satisfactory glaze.

Clay is a combination of silica, alumina and water. The chemist calls clay hydrated alumino-silicate. The word silicate is a common one and explains that silica is present as an important constituent. Theoretically, pure clay is 47% silica but in practice it contains more silica than this. The extra silica is not integrated in clay particles but is present as sand or as extremely fine silica. This is called free silica and is important because it forms a glassy binding for the clay particles which gives strength to the finished pottery body.

Silica occurs naturally as quartz rock (also called milky quartz), quartzite, ganister, sandstone, sand, flint, chert and a number of semi-precious stones which are listed under **Quartz**. All these occurrences contain some impurities. Sand, sandstone, ganister and quartzite may contain 10% impurities in the form of iron oxide, calcia, feldspathoids and clay. Flint and chert contain up to 5% calcia. Quartz rock is the purest occurrence being 99% silica and only 1% impurity.

In a glaze the silicas from different sources would behave slightly differently because of the impurities. As a general rule, impurities help the silica to melt more easily. Impurities may also give some colouring. Quartz and flint are the popular silicas for glazes and are bought in powder form. Preparation of one's own silica is a difficult process because it is so physically hard. Quartz is crushed and ground. Flint is calcined and then ground. There is little difference between quartz and flint in a glaze because free silica in a glaze recipe rarely exceeds 20%. Flint should melt more easily than quartz but a mixture of the two will probably be found to melt more easily than either alone because of the phenomenon of interaction.

The addition of silica to a body makes the fired ware harder and more durable. Sand may also give a pleasing texture. Silica also alters the amount by which the body contracts in cooling after firing. This contraction is important for correct glaze fit. Silica is therefore added to a body for a number of reasons which must be balanced against one another. As a general rule, flint is to be preferred for earthenware because it converts to cristobalite more easily than quartz. Quartz or quartz sand are preferable for stoneware because they do not convert so easily to cristobalite.

The addition of silica to a body normally renders the body more refractory, that is, it will withstand a higher temperature because silica itself is refractory. However, there are some natural clays which are not refractory and yet contain a fairly high proportion of silica. This anomaly is explained by the fineness of some or all of the free silica. If the grain size is finer than a 600's mesh then the silica seems capable of fluxing itself.

Silica also occurs naturally in combination with other oxides in silicates such as feldspar, cornish stone, talc and wollastonite. It is also present in vegetation, being responsible for the sharp edges of grasses and the stinging needles on nettles. Vegetable ashes therefore contain silica. Some contain a very high proportion of silica but act as fluxes because of the phenomenon previously explained whereby extremely fine silica crystals or grains can flux themselves.

SILICA STRUCTURE. If four oxygen atoms are packed together as in fig. 1, there is a space inside them large enough to accommodate a silicon atom. The four oxygen atoms satisfy the valency and co-ordination requirements of the silicon as in fig. 2.

This triangular pyramid of four oxygen atoms around a silicon atom is the SiO_4 silica molecule and is referred to as the silica tetrahedron. It appears in many structural drawings as a solid tetrahedron, fig. 3, or as a simple square of oxygen atoms, fig. 4, or as a top view ignoring the apex oxygen, fig. 5.

Adjacent silica tetrahedra are joined together by a common oxygen atom as in fig. 6. In this way the valency of this oxygen atom is satisfied. When each

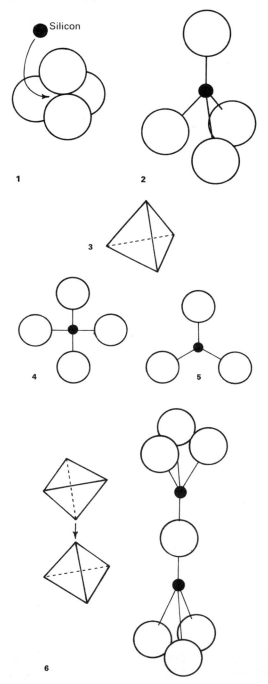

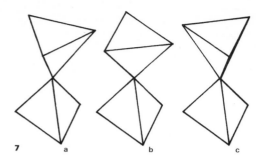

7   a   b   c

oxygen atom is bonded to two silica atoms and each silicon atom to four oxygen atoms, a series of interlinked chains is formed with twice as many oxygen atoms as silicon atoms. Thus the chemical formula overall is SiO_2.

When two tetrahedra are joined by their common oxygen there are three possible positions for the top triangular 'base' of the upper tetrahedron in relation to the 'base' of the lower one, fig. 7. The three different crystalline structures (a) quartz, (b) cristobalite and (c) tridymite result if the relationship which characterizes each pair is continued throughout a lattice. See **Crystal**. Inconsistency results in the amorphous phase of silica glass. Slight changes in the angle at the point where the tetrahedra join occur during the silica inversions as described later. Another method of describing the structures is given under **Cristobalite, physical**.

SILICA PHASES. The main types of silica are quartz, tridymite, cristobalite. The phases of silica are all chemically the same, having the formula SiO_2, but differ in the way in which the atoms are bonded together in the lattice structure. A silica phase is sub-divided into silica forms which are given identification by alpha, beta etc. Phases are sometimes called principal forms and are also called silica conversions because they are produced by converting one phase of silica into another. Some phases have no subdivisions and so are themselves called forms which could cause confusion. Fortunately, apart from silica glass, they are phases unknown to the individual potter.

SILICA

phases	*forms*
QUARTZ	∝ quartz β quartz
TRIDYMITE	∝ tridymite β tridymite
CRISTOBALITE	∝ cristobalite β cristobalite
SILICA GLASS	silica glass

SILICA FORMS. The subdivisions of the main types or phases of silica, e.g. alpha quartz, beta quartz, alpha cristobalite, beta cristobalite. Also types of silica which have no subdivisions are themselves called forms, e.g. silica gel, silica glass, silica W, keatite, compacted

vitreous silica, suprapiezo-vitreous silica, coesite, stishovite.

All silica forms are chemically identical, having the formula SiO_2. They are all composed of silica tetrahedra. See photograph, **Silica structure** and **Crystal**. The difference between one form and another is in the way these tetrahedra units are joined together. If they are joined together in a regular pattern a crystalline form results, e.g. alpha quartz. If they are joined in random manner an amorphous form results, e.g. silica glass. If they are joined together in an open network which leaves spaces in between, the form will be light in weight, e.g. silica W with a specific gravity of 1·98. If they are joined in a very compact manner the form will be heavy, e.g. stishovite with a specific gravity of 4·35. Alpha quartz has a specific gravity of 2·65 and is the commonest form of silica that the potter will meet. Indeed, although there are over twenty forms of silica the potter need concern himself with only five of them. These are alpha quartz, beta quartz, alpha cristobalite, beta cristobalite and silica glass. The differences between alpha and beta quartz and between alpha and beta cristobalite are the angles between the lattice bonds. The alpha form changes to the beta form upon heating. This is a rapid change and is called a silica inversion.

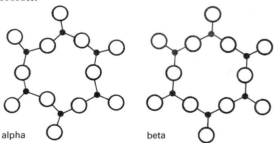

alpha   beta

SILICA CONVERSION. The action by which one type of silica is transformed into another type of silica. The types of silica are correctly called phases. The conversions of free silica of the quartz phase into free silica of the cristobalite phase or into silica glass are the only conversions that really matter to the individual potter.

Potters require cristobalite in their earthenware

bodies because of its silica inversion property which acts against the tendency of glazes to craze. Potters therefore attempt to convert the free silica in an earthenware body into cristobalite. They do this using temperature and time in what is commonly called soaking in the presence of other substances which assist. These other substances are called catalysts.

Potters convert the quartz phase of silica, which is crystalline, into the glassy phase, which is noncrystalline, in order to make glazes. Again they use both temperature and time with the assistance of other substances which in this case become intermixed with the new phase.

The commonest phase of silica is called quartz. This is a technical term used to describe silica which has a particular type of crystalline lattice. Quartz occurs naturally in quartz rock, sandstone, sand, flint and chert. If this quartz phase is heated, a change in the lattice structure begins to take place at 870°C (1598°F). This is a very slow change requiring days to complete and is called a conversion. The new phase is called disordered cristobalite. Further heating above 1470°C (2678°F) results in another slow conversion to the pure cristobalite phase. On cooling the new phases remain. Natural occurrence of cristobalite is extremely rare. This is because it usually cools under pressure within rocks and when under pressure it converts back to quartz which is a more compact or denser phase. Therefore quartz is the phase of silica which a potter is likely to have in his clay and glaze minerals.

The difference between one phase and another is the way in which the silica tetrahedra are joined to one another. There are many possibilities. Some produce fairly open networks, some produce very dense networks, some networks are regular and some networks are random. For a conversion to take place, the existing bonds between the silica tetrahedra must be loosened by heat or pressure or a combination of both and sufficient time allowed for the network to be rearranged.

Time is an important factor in all conversions. For example, at 1300°C (2372°F) it takes ten days to convert 100% quartz to 100% cristobalite. The time can be reduced by assisting the conversion with catalysts which do their work without changing their own states. The time would then be measured in hours rather than days. The first conversions to be discovered were dependent only upon temperature and time at atmospheric pressure and the new phases remained on cooling. Hence the term conversion has some hint of a one-way transformation. However, it has since been discovered that a conversion is reversible if the cooling occurs under pressure.

The potter may meet with another phase of silica called tridymite. Tridymite is a complex phase having two major subdivisions and nine minor subdivisions called forms. Quartz converts to tridymite between 870°C and 1470°C (1598°F and 2678°F) if suitable catalysts are present. It cannot exist indefinitely above 1470°C but at this temperature begins to convert into pure cristobalite. On cooling tridymite will remain as tridymite at atmospheric pressure. If under greater pressure, tridymite will convert back into quartz which is a denser phase. For this reason very little tridymite occurs naturally as a mineral. Tridymite has industrial application as silica bricks and in combination with cristobalite in earthenware bodies. The inversion properties of its nine forms combined with the inversions of cristobalite can give control of a tendency to craze, coupled with a higher resistance to thermal shock.

Tridymite and disordered cristobalite can obviously exist side by side at temperatures below 1470°C (2678°F). The same catalysts that assist the conversion of quartz to tridymite also act as catalysts for the conversion of both into disordered cristobalite. Therefore the easiest way is to consider these conversions from quartz into tridymite, disordered cristobalite and pure cristobalite as one and include these phases under the name cristobalite. This simplification is used throughout this book except for the explanation of tridymite inversions under **Silica inversions** and in the article on **Cristobalite**.

The potter is interested in conversions to cristobalite and to glass. In considering conversions a number of factors are involved.

1. Only the free silica of quartz phase which is in crystalline or cryptocrystalline state can be converted into cristobalite. Silica which is of an amorphous phase cannot be converted into cristobalite. This is because from the potter's point of view the silica has reached its ultimate state. The ultimate state is that which it would reach at its melting point of 1710°C (3110°F). When it reaches this state before this temperature by the action of fluxes it has passed the conversion stages. The quick cooling that pottery receives precludes the return to crystalline state possible in nature. Amorphous silica has no crystal structure and is present either as previously fused silica or as silica already involved in a liquid melt. Both quartz and cristobalite can be converted into fused silica, that is, silica glass.

2. Time is necessary for a conversion and therefore a conversion is not inevitable in a firing. This is in contrast to an inversion which is sudden and is unavoidable.

3. For the potter the lowest practical temperature for a quartz to cristobalite conversion is 1100°C (2012°F). At this temperature a long time is required. Three or four hours soaking at 1100°C would only convert a small proportion of the quartz to cristobalite. At higher temperatures proportionately less time is required.

4. The grain size affects the time required. Fine powdered quartz converts quicker than quartz sand at the lower temperatures.

5. The presence of suitable catalysts speeds the process of conversion. Calcia and magnesia are con-

sidered catalysts for the conversion of quartz to cristobalite. For conversion to tridymite the list is extended with potash, soda, alumina, iron oxide and combinations such as feldspar and cornish stone. For conversion to the glass phase the catalysts are called fluxes and the list includes all oxides, especially alkaline oxides.

6. A conversion is a progression. Once the conversion has started, the presence of some cristobalite stimulates the conversion of more quartz into cristobalite and the conversion goes ahead with increasing speed. Cristobalite itself is therefore an important agent or catalyst in the action and some potters add ground cristobalite to bodies to start conversion. The same can be said of conversion to the glass phase. Potters add previously fused silica to glazes and bodies in the form of frits.

Cristobalite is desirable in earthenware bodies as an anti-craze agent. See **Silica inversions** and **Cristobalite**. For this reason flint is added to earthenware bodies. Flint contains about 5% chalk as an impurity. The chalk becomes calcia in the calcination of flint and is an important catalyst in the conversion of the flint, which is the quartz phase of silica, into cristobalite during the firing. Ground rock quartz or sand would not convert so easily. Before the silica conversions were understood potters added talc to earthenware bodies as an anti-craze device. They had discovered this use of talc empirically. Talc is magnesium silicate and would itself convert and assist conversion of free silica to cristobalite during firing. Also magnesia in bodies works against the tendency to expand with moisture as explained under **Silica inversions**.

In stoneware bodies it is not desirable to have much cristobalite, if any. The more brittle nature of stoneware with its thicker glazes renders it more susceptible to cristobalite dunting. Therefore for stoneware bodies clean quartz sand is used in fireclays or ball clays. If red clay is added, the marl types, which are high in calcia, are to be avoided.

It will be seen that conversions are slow changes requiring time. The conversion of quartz to cristobalite is not inevitable. If the potter does not want cristobalite in the body he can reduce the amount of quartz converted to cristobalite by reducing the free silica present, by a quicker firing and cooling and by reducing the catalysts present. Thus the silica conversions from one phase to another can be avoided or at least controlled. In contrast, the silica inversions from one form to another within a phase cannot be avoided.

SILICA INVERSIONS. Minor changes in the lattice structures of silica. Inversions are responsible for sudden expansions and sudden contractions of pottery bodies which might result in cracks. Such cracks are known as dunts. Inversions can be used to control crazing of glazes especially on earthenware.

The inversion change takes place at an inversion point or temperature. At temperatures above the inversion point the lattice structure is strictly regular but at temperatures below the inversion point the lattice structure is irregular and could be described as collapsed or squashed. This means that at the inversion point a change in size occurs. An increasing temperature past the inversion point results in an increase in size of up to 3% volume. A decreasing temperature past the inversion point results in an equivalent decrease in size. An inversion is therefore a reversible change and will occur every time a silica passes its inversion point.

The two forms of silica, one below and one above the inversion point, are called alpha and beta respectively. Some phases of silica have more than one inversion point and thus more than two forms. The forms are called alpha, beta one, beta two etc.

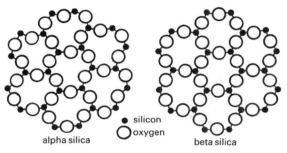

alpha silica · silicon ○ oxygen beta silica

Inversions only take place in crystalline silica where there is a large regular lattice of silicon and oxygen atoms. Once silica is fused in a molten glaze the silica network no longer exists as a large network. It is broken down into smaller units which move freely amongst other small units of other oxides. The different units form random chains or networks of oxides on cooling. The silica units do not have time or opportunity to re-establish contact with one another and so the original state of crystalline silica does not exist in the

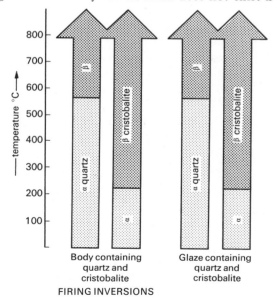

Body containing quartz and cristobalite

Glaze containing quartz and cristobalite

FIRING INVERSIONS

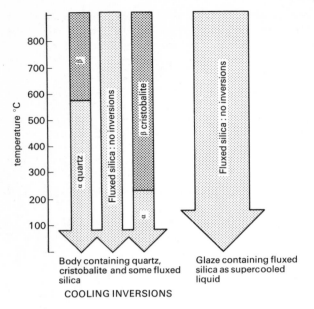

Body containing quartz, cristobalite and some fluxed silica

Glaze containing fluxed silica as supercooled liquid

COOLING INVERSIONS

are therefore subdivisions of the phase quartz. Quartz is a phase of the chemical silica.

The cristobalite inversion takes place between 220°C and 280°C (428°F and 536°F). It is a sudden change, unlike the quartz inversion which is a change with accelerating result from alpha to beta. Also unlike the quartz inversion it does not occur at an exact temperature but can occur at any temperature between 220°C and 280°C (428°F and 536°F). The cristobalite inversion is more important to potters in its cooling from beta to alpha and the temperature at which it changes is dependent upon the length and temperature of the firing from which it is cooling. The comparatively short firings used by the individual potter make the cristobalite lag to the lower end of the range of change before inverting so that it is usually below 230°C (446°F). A popular temperature is 226°C (439°F) and it is used throughout this book for simplicity.

The graph shows the reversible expansion of cristobalite when heated. It will be noted that if cristobalite is in the body then the whole pot will contract suddenly at this temperature. Ovenware has to withstand sudden cooling from a hot oven at possibly 290°C (554°F). In the making of ovenware the potter tries to exclude cristobalite. The problem is treated more fully under **Thermal shock**.

glaze. A glaze is therefore not subject to silica inversions. However, a body does contain crystalline silica, also called free silica, and this silica will invert and will therefore change its size.

Silica is the name of the chemical compound silicon dioxide. Silica can be subdivided into a number of different phases of which quartz and cristobalite are of concern to the potter. Phases of silica are chemically identical but are physically different and therefore behave differently. The inversion in the quartz phase takes place between 550°C and 575°C (1022°F and 1067°F) but is usually regarded as taking place at 573°C (1063°F). As the temperature rises the lattice straightens itself or regularizes itself as in the earlier diagram. It is always considered a sudden change but it is a change which starts at about 550°C (1022°F) and accelerates rapidly, reaching completion suddenly at 573°C (1063°F). The graph shows the reversible expansion of quartz when heated. Alpha and beta quartz

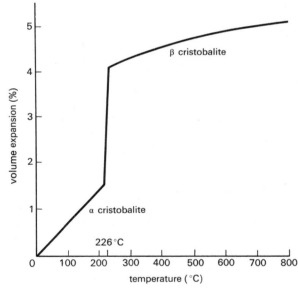

The inversion of tridymite will be mentioned for completeness. Its inversion gives further contrast to the previous two. The tridymite inversion takes place between 75°C and 200°C (167°F and 392°F) in nine stages. To further complicate things, these nine inversions are divided between two main phases of tridymite. Tridymite exists along with disordered cristobalite when quartz is converted with the help of catalysts as explained in **Silica conversion**.

Industrially, the balance of the phases of tridymite and the types of cristobalite existing in disordered cristobalite is controlled to give a series of small in-

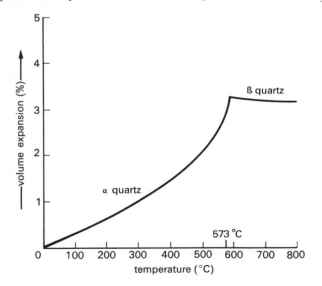

270

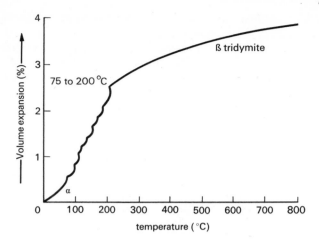

enough to contain the stress imposed by the cristobalite inversion. The opening of a kiln too soon, causing quick and unequal cooling, will result in dunting of stoneware if there is cristobalite in the body. The problem of cristobalite in stoneware is more fully dealt with under **Silica conversion**.

The cooling quartz inversion at 573°C (1063°F) is not likely to cause stress between body and glaze. At this temperature the glaze is still sufficiently plastic to allow itself to be compressed by the body when the body suddenly contracts. The cooling cristobalite inversion at 226°C (439°F) produces a stress between body and glaze because at this temperature the glaze is solid. The body contracts but the glaze cannot do so. The result is that the body tries to compress the glaze. If the stress is not too great this state is desirable for earthenware and tableware. It is not desirable for ovenware and is not necessary for true stoneware. This com-

versions rather than one large sudden inversion. The advantage of this is that the necessary overall contraction can be achieved in a smoother action than the sudden large contraction of a cristobalite inversion. The preparation of tridymite is beyond the scope of the individual potter, so for simplicity tridymite and disordered cristobalite are considered as simply cristobalite in this book. It is unlikely that much tridymite will exist in the pot bodies fired by the individual potter because conversion takes a long time. However he may introduce some under the name of cristobalite as a purchased powder.

The amount of free silica in different bodies varies between 5% and 50% of the body. During a firing, the volumetric change in size of this silica, as quartz and disordered cristobalite, will be between 3% and 4·5%. The overall volumetric change in size which it will create in a body cannot exceed 2·25%. Most of this will be part of a gradual expansion and contraction but part will be associated with the silica inversions. Quartz has a volumetric change in size of approximately 1% during inversion and cristobalite a size change of approximately 3%. In practice, this could mean a change in size of a pottery body in the order of 0·5% at the quartz inversion of a body containing 50% free quartz silica, and a size change in the order of 0·45% at the cristobalite inversion of a body containing 15% free cristobalite silica. Both these are extreme cases. Average bodies would give changes of 0·2% and 0·25% respectively. Even so this amount is sufficient to set up considerable stresses within the body itself and between the body and the glaze.

If the body is not strong enough to contain the stresses which are created within it then it ruptures. This is called dunting. Dunts to the body are usually caused by the quartz inversions at 573°C (1063°F) on cooling from a biscuit firing. If the biscuit is too soft and weak or the cooling too sudden then the body is not strong enough to contain the stress. Dunts may also be caused by the cristobalite inversion at 226°C (439°F) on cooling from a stoneware firing. Unglazed stoneware is sometimes brittle and in such cases may not be strong

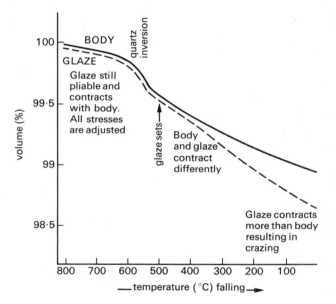

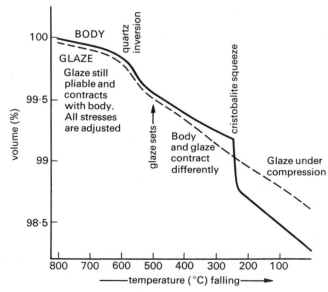

pression of the glaze means that it cannot craze. A glaze crazes when it is too small for the body which it is on. Such a stress between body and glaze is therefore the opposite of the state of glaze compression. Being brittle, the glaze cracks to accommodate the stress and the cracks are called crazes. Obviously a glaze under compression cannot craze.

Earthenware body is porous and although completely sealed by a layer of glaze it can still absorb moisture from the air through the covering glaze by a means as yet unexplained. The absorbed moisture makes the body expand. The glaze does not expand. If the two, body and glaze, were originally lying side by side without stress then the glaze would craze. However if there exists between body and glaze a stress of compression on the glaze, all that can happen when the body expands with moisture is an easing of the stress. If the stress was originally sufficient, crazing will not occur.

If the stress between body and glaze created by a cooling cristobalite inversion is too great the body may crack. Theoretically the glaze would be cracking the body by pulling it apart. As it cracks there is usually some sideways displacement and the glaze cracks also. This is called cristobalite dunting. Alternatively, if the body is strong the glaze may flake off in slivers which are sharp-edged and often take with them part of the body. This occurs mostly on rims, edges of handles and throwing ridges. This is called shivering. A glaze can withstand ten times as much stress in compression before it shivers as it can withstand in tension before it crazes.

Silica gel. A form of amorphous silica. The units of silica gel are the standard silica tetrahedra but they are not joined together in a regular lattice. Instead they attach themselves to one another in a random manner so that no crystal formation exists, therefore it is called amorphous.

Silica glass. Fused silica. Silica which has been melted and cooled again so quickly that the silica tetrahedra have not been able to establish a pattern of structure.

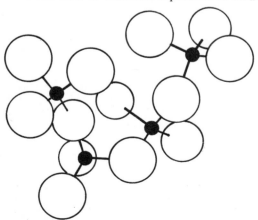

The silica is therefore amorphous, that is, non-crystalline. The tetrahedra units are attached to one another in random manner. If they had been able to attach themselves to one another in a pattern a crystalline structure would have followed and the silica would have become one of the crystalline forms.

Silica glass is sometimes called fused silica, or vitreous silica. Silica which is incorporated in a finished glaze or glass is sometimes referred to as fused silica because it has been unable to re-establish itself

as a silica crystal lattice. Silica glass and fused silica are sometimes erroneously called quartz glass and fused quartz. Quartz may have been the original mineral used but since quartz is the technical term for a crystalline phase of silica it cannot be also used for the non-crystalline silica glass.

Silica glass is not subject to inversions as are the crystalline phases. Its thermal expansion is very low compared with quartz and cristobalite. This shows markedly in the graph.

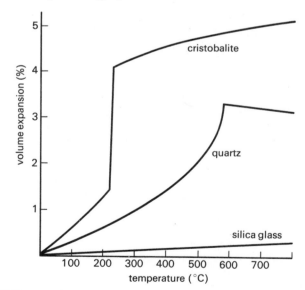

Silicate. A compound involving silica as an important part. Specifically the term implies that the ratio of silica to the other oxides is such that a crystal structure can be established. For example, kaolinite is hydrated alumino silicate ($Al_2O_3 . 2SiO_2 . 2H_2O$) and zircon is zirconium silicate ($ZrO_2 . SiO_2$).

In prepared silicates the crystal structure is unlikely

to be formed because of the glass-forming properties of silica. Hence lead bisilicate ($PbO.2SiO_2$) is an amorphous solid and not crystalline, although doubtless a crystal could be grown. When crystals have not grown it is impossible to classify it as a balanced compound on its physical appearance and yet many glasses which may not be strictly silicates are described as such. The term 'silicates' is therefore extended to include all glasses which are founded upon silica as an integral part of the substance. Thus all glazes and frits are occasionally referred to collectively as silicates.

Mineralogically there are many silicates which have found ceramic use. They include the groups called feldspars, micas, pyroxenes, amphiboles and zeolites.

Siliceous. Refers to minerals, especially clay, which contain a high proportion of free silica.

Silicon carbide. SiC. An artificial compound of silicon and carbon made from baked sand and coke. It is extremely hard, even harder than alumina and nearly as hard as diamond. It is therefore a useful abrasive both as a powder and as grindstones, and is sold under many trade names.

Silicon carbide is an electrical semi-conductor and is used to make kiln elements of the bar type. These are often tubular and mounted vertically in the kiln passing through the floor and roof to the terminals. Again different trade names are used.

Silicon carbide is a refractory and can withstand over 2000°C (3632°F). It is therefore used for kiln furniture for high-temperature work up to 1400°C (2552°F), and for reduction firings and salt glazing because it is not affected by these atmospheres. These shelves tend to be thick and absorb much heat and so are not economical in lower temperature oxidized firings.

Silicon carbide can be used as a local reducing agent.

SILICON CARBIDE REDUCTION. Since the 1930's in the USA, silicon carbide has been used as a local reducing agent by adding it to glazes and slips. By its use copper oxide can be induced to give reds and iron oxide can give celadon colourings. These effects are achieved in an oxidized firing and are therefore called local reduction. Only a selected part of the pot, e.g. the glaze, is reduced. Total reduction using a reducing atmosphere affects the whole pot and also the kiln furniture.

If silicon carbide is introduced into a glaze recipe it remains unchanged until about 1000°C (1832°F). Above this temperature it is attacked by a molten glaze which causes a breakdown or dissociation of the silicon and carbon. Each then seeks oxygen to become silica and carbon monoxide and dioxide respectively. The oxygen is taken from the surrounding glaze thereby reducing a part of it. The silica joins the glaze melt. The carbonaceous gases form bubbles in the glaze, rise to the surface, burst and escape.

If copper oxide is present in a glaze it is therefore not difficult to reduce it, from CuO to Cu_2O or even to the metal Cu. It readily gives up its oxygen when presented with oxygen-hungry silicon and carbon. An equal weight of silicon carbide to copper oxide will be sufficient, approximately 0·3% of each. Too much copper oxide, over 0·5%, gives a muddy colour. The difficulties are to keep the copper in the reduced red state and at the same time get rid of the gas bubbles.

The reduction will take place when the glaze melts. From that point to the end of the firing the glaze needs to be sealed and there needs to be present at least one stabilizer if re-oxidation is not to take place. For copper reds a useful stabilizer is tin oxide. One per cent of tin oxide is sufficient and this amount is practically dissolved by the glaze. Any excess reduced tin gives a pleasant lustrous surface. Theoretically, zinc and iron oxides will also act as stabilizers and the fluxes lead oxide, calcia and soda will assist in forming and keeping a clear colour. Each situation is different because there are more than the chemical factors of the glaze involved.

To get rid of the bubbles of carbon monoxide and dioxide a prolonged firing may be necessary with a potter's standard glazes. This gives too much opportunity for re-oxidation of the copper. To speed the liberation of the bubbles it may be necessary to alter the glaze recipe by cutting out some of the alumina. A glaze low in alumina is very fluid and will therefore liberate its bubbles and seal the surface easily. It may be too runny. Therefore a balance has to be found between the glaze that is too fluid but clears well and the glaze that is too stiff and traps the bubbles.

Silicosis. The sealing of the lung capillaries by lung tissue which surrounds inhaled silica particles. Free silica in the air as fine dust of less than 5 microns is able to enter the lungs with the air. Here it remains, is embedded by new lung tissue and causes the lung to choke up.

Silicosis is a potter's disease which must be guarded against by avoiding all forms of dust, especially of free silica. Asbestos dust similarly gives rise to asbestosis. See also **Poison**.

Sillimanite. Kyanite. Fibrolite. Andalusite. $Al_2O_3.SiO_2$. A hard and refractory mineral occurring in metamorphic rocks. Kyanite, the softest variety, is reconstituted as sillimanite kiln shelves, props etc.

Sinter. To fasten together by mutual adhesion without apparent fusion. The word comes from the German for cinder and this explains its link with a partial action (partly burnt or partly fused) and its use in metallurgy.

All ceramic materials, simple oxides or complex minerals, pass through a stage of sintering before melting. There is no liquid (molten) phase involved and yet the individual particles stick to each other. One could consider it a phenomenon of electrical friction involving some rearrangement of structure at the surfaces. The result is that materials which start as powders become solid at a temperature which is only half way to the melting point.

It is a difficult phenomenon to assess with the complex minerals of pottery but its action can be seen in clays which melt above 1200°C (2192°F) and yet have cohesion after being fired to only 600°C (1112°F). When the clay has been completely dehydrated at 600°C, the resulting pot would be theoretically a pile of dust with no cohesion and yet many historical primitive pots had only this low firing. Also, present-day primitive societies use a low firing to produce cooking pots. There is undoubtedly some incipient fusion of low-melting constituents, like fluxes, but the strength is due to sintering and thereby has an elasticity not associated with glassy vitrification. The elasticity enables these pots to be used for cooking directly on a fire.

It is probably this phenomenon of sintering that enables pots to be piled upon each other in a biscuit firing without crushing the ones beneath during the ceramic change.

Slabbing. Forming a pot from sheets of clay. The slabs (sheets) are wire cut, beaten out or rolled out. They are then cut and used in soft state or stiffer to construct the projected pot. Joints are usually scored and slurried.

Slabbed pots tend to be more angular and less organic than those formed by pinching, coiling and throwing. They can thus have a very dynamic character.

Slabs can also be used in a method similar to coiling. The form is beaten and sometimes turned. Beating helps to strengthen the clay sheet which is otherwise less strong than the wall of a thrown or coiled pot. Careful beating of joints should be undertaken with consideration of the clay structure. See **Clay, physics**.

The photographs show slab pots by Barbara Dordi and Anthony Jennings.

Slake. To disintegrate in water. Clays are said to slake if from their dry state they can be completely wetted by immersion in water. Such clays crumble as the water surrounds and separates the particles.

Some clays will not slake from the cheese-hard state but need to be thoroughly dried first. Some very fine clays, such as ball clays, will not slake at all but create a waterproof layer on the outside of the lumps with the first water absorbed.

Slaking is the simplest way of rendering raw clay down to a thin slurry for sieving and future preparation. Clays which will not slake must be ground exceedingly finely, e.g. airblown fineness or else blunged. Some clays even require a very vigorous machine blunging to separate the particles.

Slip. An homogeneous mixture of clay and water.

Slips are used for coating clays to give colour and a smooth textured surface. See **Slipware**. There is also a process for forming pots from slip. See **Slip casting**.

Although the simple mixture of clay and water is a slip there are often other ingredients. These are added for colouring and to make the slip fit the body during drying, firing and when finished, and to provide the necessary bonding with the body beneath and, if necessary, the glaze above.

The following are colouring oxides for slips with suggested minimum and maximum amounts to give pale and full strength colours. Combinations are possible. See individual oxides.

Chromium oxide	1–5%	grey-green
Cobalt oxide	1–5%	blue
Copper oxide	1–5%	green glazed, buff unglazed
Iron oxide	3–15%	cream to brown and black
Manganese dioxide	5–15%	browns
Nickel oxide	2–5%	grey-brown

Other additions to a slip can be feldspars etc for densification and strength, flint for hardness and whiteness, fluxes and frits for vitrification and bonding. A fusible slip containing perhaps 20% flux or 30% frit comes into other categories. See **Slip-glaze**, **Engobe** and **Buffer layer**. Additions of non-plastic material

274

reduce the stickiness of a slip and decrease the drying shrinkage.

It is usual to have a slip which is finer and richer than the body which it covers. Such a slip fits the body better at raw stage because it has good adhesion (stickiness) and a slightly higher drying shrinkage than the body. This should not be confused with firing shrinkage which is dependent upon vitrification.

Light-coloured slips are often based upon a rich ball clay and slips prepared from the body clay are passed through a 60's to 100's mesh. This takes out some of the grog and sand making the slip clay richer than the body.

Slip-casting. A pottery-forming process which uses moulds to give the forms and uses liquid clay (slip). The slip is poured into porous moulds which absorb some of the water from the slip. A layer of clay thus builds up against the wall of the mould to give a cast. When the excess slip is poured out, the clay forming the cast is left adhering to the mould, fig. 1. The cast is stiffened, removed from the mould, dried, fettled and fired in the usual way.

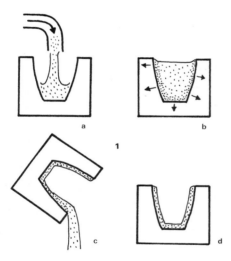

The moulds are usually plaster of Paris with a porosity of approximately 40%. This is achieved by a 130's mix, that is, 130 parts by weight of plaster to 100 parts by weight of water. Moulds are 'one-piece' for simple objects like short cylinders and tapering objects, fig. 2. The slight contraction of the cast as it dries assists freeing and removal.

However with increased complexity of form the number of mould pieces increases. Fig. 3 shows two alternatives for a 2-piece mould. Figures and animals may require 20- or 30-piece moulds. There is usually a 'head' or 'spare' (A in fig. 3) which is cast with the form and is trimmed away. It ensures a sufficient thickness at the required rim by providing a head of slip. This head gives a pressure inside the mould and obviates the necessity for a continual topping-up as the water soaks into the mould.

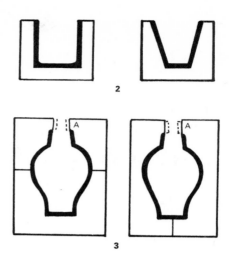

The moulds are filled with a special deflocculated slip. See **Casting slip.** A mould is filled in one operation and as quickly as possible as it rotates on a whirler. This ensures an equal distribution of slip to all corners of the mould. Sufficient time is then allowed for the required thickness of clay to build up. The slip sinks in the head of the mould as the water is absorbed so that at least one top-up is often necessary. When the build-up is of sufficient thickness the excess slip is poured out.

The mould is left inverted to drain until the cast has dimmed. Different moulds require different treatments but it will be found that most moulds drain better if left at a slight tilt. When the cast has dimmed, the spare is removed. This leaves a firm rim, fig. 3A.

The cast is removed when the clay is firm enough to stand. It is dried, fettled by scraping the seams, and quickly sponged with a fully wet sponge.

The 'pour-back' slip can be collected for re-use. It should be resieved through a 40's sieve without brushing. Slip should be stored in tall containers so that only a small surface area meets the air.

Freshly-mixed slip is best. Slip cannot be stored indefinitely but can be kept for about 20 days if the storage tank is non-corrosive and reasonably airtight. Wood or plastic containers are best. During storage a skin forms on the surface of the slip where it meets the air and unwanted foreign matter collects at the bottom. The skin must not be stirred into the slip because it contains carbon dioxide from the air. This acts as a flocculant which spoils the fluidity of the slip. Some potters put a layer of oil on the top of the slip to prevent this neutralization.

For the same reason, scraps of broken casts, trimmings etc should not be added to the slip. They have become partially flocculated by the air and by the calcium sulphate of the plaster of Paris. Bulk scraps can be reblunged but will require more deflocculant. The amount can only be established by trial. Reclaimed slip never seems to be as good as new slip.

Fig. 4 shows a tall storage tank which gives only a small area of slip at the surface. It shows the airtight

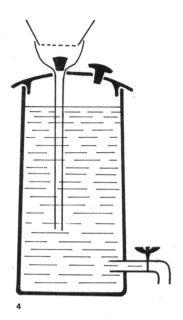

4

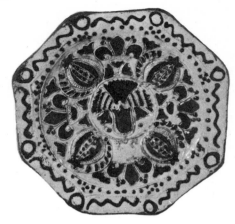

lid with stopper, return funnel with stopper and return sieve. The tube from the funnel is long so that returned slip does not become mixed with the skin. The run-off tap is above the sediment layer. It is necessary to ease the stopper in the lid when slip is run off.

There are a number of well-known hazards in slip-casting. The faults arising from the slip are dealt with under **Casting slip**. Preparation of the slip is also dealt with there.

Slip-glaze. A glaze that contains over 50% of clay and is applied as a slip to the raw ware. See **Albany slip**.

Slip stone. A small, slender abrasive stone used for removing blemishes on pots and for sharpening metal tools.

Slipware. Earthenware pottery decorated with coloured slips under a transparent lead glaze. The effect of the mellow shine of a lead glaze coupled with the richness of colour from the slips make slipware a justly popular ware. It developed as a rural or peasant ware in Europe and America reaching its peak in Staffordshire in the late 17th and 18th centuries. It is therefore often called English or Staffordshire slipware even though it was made in many more places and countries.

Slipware is domestic ware and was largely thrown but large oven plates were pressed. The body was red or buff and slips were made from this clay with added oxides of iron, copper and manganese. White slips were made from ball and china clays or the small deposits of pipeclays and white fireclays.

The making of slipware demands great skill and is time consuming. It naturally suffered in competition with increasing industrialization and production of simpler more sophisticated wares in the 19th century. Today's potters prefer to use their skill in the produc-

tion of a ware such as stoneware, which is more durable. Slipware is prone to chipping because of the many layers of slip and glaze inevitable on vulnerable rims etc.

Slipware employs the idea of coating a leatherhard clay with what is often a contrasting colour of slip either by dipping or pouring. The slip coating can then be decorated by finger-combing or when dry by sgraffito; or whilst the first slip is wet, other slips can be added and encouraged to sink into the ground slip in what is called slip trailing as shown in the photograph.

To obtain a good fit it is usual to make a slip a little richer than the body clay. Pure ball clay is often satisfactory but the addition of some frit will improve its fired adhesion to the body and integration with the glaze. A borax frit is an ideal addition because this encourages the bleeding of coloured slips into the glaze as the body-glaze layer is formed. This blurred outline of the slip softens the contrast and enriches the decorative qualities. Some pleasing colours can be obtained by using copper and cobalt oxides with up to 20% borax frit in the slip. Dark slips are usually made from the body clay by the addition of iron and manganese oxides. They should be sieved to take out some of the sand etc thus providing a smoother surface for the glaze.

Traditional slipware employed a raw lead glaze which gave a rich surface shine and partially dissolved the slips beneath, producing a softened effect. A low sol glaze is now to be preferred especially for tableware and whilst this can give the rich surface shine it does not produce the same integration with the slip. However the use of a borax frit in the slip, as mentioned earlier, will achieve this softening. A low sol glaze for 1080°C to 1100°C (1976°F to 2012°F) follows:

feldspar	12
china clay	10
flint	8
whiting	5
lead bisilicate	50
borax frit	15

If an amber glaze is required, a red body clay should be used instead of the china clay. It should be noted that although this is a low sol glaze the stability can be upset by heavily stained slips.

Slop. An homogeneous mixture of glaze materials and water. A slop is the most convenient form in which to handle glaze materials. It is applied to the ware by dipping, spraying or brushing. The water soaks into the ware and then dries out. The glaze materials are left in a layer on the surface ready for the firing.

The thickness of the layer, especially from dipping, is dependent upon the porosity of the ware and the density of the slop. Densities are measured by weight per pint of slop. See **Formula, density**.

The usual method of preparing a slop is to measure the water first into the mixing container and follow this with the weighed amounts of powder. The powders are thus able to soak before being blunged and sieved. A convenient mesh size is 100's to 120's with coarser sizes for ash glazes and finer for uniform colours and slops for spraying.

Some glaze materials require to be ground and these are put into a ball mill or jar mill.

Glaze materials are heavier than water and settle to the bottom of the glaze tub. Slops made from uniform materials, like completely fritted glazes, tend to do this more than those made from a variety of materials and those including clay. See **Suspender**.

Slop pint. The volume of slop that contains 20 oz of dry material. A pint of water weighs 20 oz and therefore a pint is associated with 20 oz as a pound is associated with 16 oz.

A slop pint is not the same as a pint of slop which would contain less than 20 oz of dry material. At say 30 oz pint weight a feldspar slop might contain only 16 oz of dry material per pint of slop. It would thus be necessary to have $1\frac{1}{4}$ pints to get 20 oz of dry material and the $1\frac{1}{4}$ pints would be called the slop pint.

It is more accurate to measure the glaze constituents in slop form than to weigh so-called dry materials which inevitably contain varying amounts of moisture. Thus a glaze may be compounded of so many pints of flint slop, feldspar slop etc each at different convenient slop weights. The accuracy depends upon knowing the specific gravity of each material and the use of Brongniart's formula or the accurate drying and weighing of test amounts.

The individual potter is likely to make less mistakes by carefully storing his materials in a dry place where new stock can dry out to an average moisture content before use, and then weighing dry.

Slop weight. Pint weight. Weight of the volume of slop. It is usually given as ounces per pint and is an indication of the thickness of glaze one will get on the ware. Most potters work with glazes at 29 or 30 oz pt or 32 oz pt for lead glazes. It can only be a guide, especially with glazes of high clay content which are subject to deflocculation by the soluble alkalis released by wood ash, feldspar etc. However, the pint weight is useful in calculating the dry content of a slop or slip by Brongniart's formula.

Slug. A length of clay from a pugmill. A slug is a measured length containing a known amount of clay. It can be any convenient size and enough for one pot or more.

Slum. Fireclay containing a large amount of fine coal which makes it necessary to fire the clay very slowly although the coal does help the firing if sufficient oxygen can be introduced.

Slurry. An uneven mixture of clay or glaze and water. If the slurry were more evenly mixed and sieved so that it were in homogeneous state, it would be called slip or slop.

Smithsonite. Zinc carbonate. $ZnCO_3$. A zinc mineral which is decomposed to zinc oxide and carbon dioxide by heating to 300°C (572°F).

Smoked glaze. Glaze defect especially on light-coloured glazes whereby they look smokey or discoloured. It is caused by over-reduction or by the trapping of carbon in the glaze.

Smoked lustre. A transmutation lustre.

Snake skin. See **Lizard skin**.

Snakes. Rolls or strips of refractory clay such as wad clay, used to temporarily seal bungs of saggars.

Soda. Sodium oxide. Natrium oxide. Na_2O. One of the three strong alkaline oxides providing active fluxes in ceramic fusions. The other two are lithia and potash. See **Periodic table**.

Soda is an active flux from 800°C (1472°F) upwards and creates glazes which give exciting colour responses. The more notable responses are a blue from copper oxide and purples from cobalt and manganese oxides.

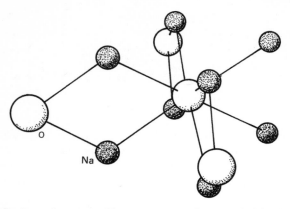

Soda and most sodium compounds are soluble. Soda is therefore introduced into glazes in the form of frits, and soda feldspar. Soda is rarely used in bodies except where it has been introduced primarily as a deflocculant for casting slips. See **Deflocculation**.

SODA IN GLAZES. Soda is important on four counts: colour responses; fluxing action; contraction rate; solubility.

Soda encourages bright and exciting colour responses from the colouring oxides. For example copper oxide gives turquoise blue, cobalt and manganese oxides give mauve and iron oxide gives blue. Some of these colours are fickle and their ranges are limited but all are sufficiently exciting to make their pursuit hopeful. See also **Alkaline glazes**.

To get the colour response, the glaze must be highly alkaline and this usually means high in soda. Lithia and potash give similar but not identical results. At least two-thirds of the flux needs to be soda and this presents its own problems of crazing and solubility. Alumina must be kept very low, which presents the problem of over fluidity and instability. The only way is to work empirically from an existing colour which can be obtained by the use of the soluble materials, home-made frits or commercial frits. This test will need to be progressively improved to a glaze which is an acceptable compromise between colour and stability.

Soda is an active flux for all temperatures, its action beginning at approximately 800°C (1472°F). It is at the lower temperatures that soda is most useful in the making of lead-free glazes, assisted by boric oxide, potash and lithia. Soda is combined with boric oxide in the mineral borax and therefore is often included in boron frits.

From 1100°C (2012°F) upwards there are other fluxes available which can be used in combination with soda. Calcia is the most popular but baria is used where a more alkaline flux is required.

Soda becomes unstable at temperatures above 1200°C (2192°F). Some soda will volatilize from high soda glazes at these temperatures, although the glazes may have matured. However, complex glazes with at least equal amounts of three other fluxes suitably engage the soda. The property of soda to volatilize is used in the creation of salt glaze. Here wet salt, or salt and borax, is thrown into the firebox where it volatilizes. The resulting glaze deposited on the pots is a sodium alumino-silicate. See **Salt glaze**.

Simple combinations of soda and silica give freely-flowing but brittle glazes. They can be used in hollows on tiles that are fired horizontally. Flint can be fluxed with soda ash or washing soda. The ingredients are dry-ground together and the powder is packed into the hollows. These glazes give exciting colour responses as mentioned above. However they are very unstable and have insufficient resistance to weathering and abrasion. The soda remains soluble and will even be attacked by a damp atmosphere. Acids dissolve them. The extreme example of their quality is water-glass. This is a sodium silicate and it is completely soluble in water.

To stabilize these dry-powder glazes it is necessary to add some alumina by feldspar or china clay, and to increase the number of fluxes. Calcia is successfully used in glass-making. More than minor alterations will dull the colour effect.

It will have been noted that the high alkaline glazes are prone to crazing. Soda has the highest coefficient of expansion of all the glaze constituent oxides. Its inclusion in a glaze means that it will bring to the glaze a high rate of expansion proportionate to the amount present. A glaze depending mostly on soda for fluxing is therefore certain to craze. The high expansion, and hence contraction, rate of the glaze will be greater than the rate of the body. Soda also creates rather brittle glazes which naturally cannot withstand the tension and therefore rupture. Elasticity is given to glazes by lead oxide and, to a lesser extent, by boric oxide and calcia. Boric oxide and calcia provide excellent counter-action to the crazing caused by soda. See **Glaze fit**.

The solubility of simple soda-silica glazes has already been mentioned. Even the soda contents of the minerals albite and nepheline syenite are partially soluble. Soda is the most soluble of all the potter's oxides and therefore cannot be used alone in clay bodies and glaze slops. Instead, soda is first rendered insoluble by a process called fritting. In fritting, the soda is first melted with alumina, silica and other fluxes to produce a glass. This glass is ground to a convenient powder. See **Frit**. There also exist three natural minerals that contain soda and sodium in almost insoluble form. They are cryolite, nepheline and albite. Cryolite is used mostly in vitreous enamels but albite and nepheline syenite are widely used in bodies and glazes. Albite and nepheline syenite are of igneous origin and can be considered to be natural frits.

Soda is present in most glazes and contributes its extreme properties of active fluxing and high contraction without which the balancing of satisfactory glazes would be very difficult.

Soda ash. Sodium carbonate. Na_2CO_3. Originally the ashes of burnt sea plants. See **Barilla** and **Kelp**. Now the term is synonymous with sodium carbonate, although this is produced from sodium chloride (NaCl) rock salt by the Solvay process.

Soda feldspar. See **Albite**.

Sodalite. Sodium alumino-silicate and chloride. $3(Na_2O.Al_2O_3.2SiO_2).2NaCl$. A soda feldspathoid which is one of the mineral constituents of nepheline syenite and other alkaline (basic) igneous rocks.

Sodium carbonate. Soda ash. Sal soda. Na_2CO_3. The chief source of soda for glazes. It is highly soluble and therefore can only be used in frits. It is used in combination with sodium silicate as a deflocculant for casting slips. See **Deflocculation**.

Until the discovery of the LeBlanc and Solvay processes at the end of the 18th and middle of the 19th centuries, sodium carbonate for glass-making was produced by burning seaweed and salt-marsh plants. Hence the name soda ash. The processes now employed use rock salt and sea water.

Sodium chloride. Common salt. Rock salt. NaCl. The most abundant natural compound of sodium. It is indirectly the source of most of the soda used in glazes, the sodium chloride being converted into sodium carbonate for inclusion in frits. Sodium chloride is used with water, or with borax, in salt glazing. See **Salt glaze**. The fusion of a small pile of salt on a tile was once used as an indication of temperature in the kiln. The melting temperature is 800°C (1472°F).

Sodium minerals. The element sodium is a metal which is very reactive and quickly combines with adjacent elements to form compounds. Sodium is therefore never found as a native ore but occurs in a number of natural materials. Sodium is essential to animal life and to sea-plant life. Sodium compounds occur widely but by far the most common is sodium chloride which occurs in the sea and salt lakes and as rock salt. Household compounds are sodium chloride (NaCl) common salt, hydrated sodium carbonate ($Na_2CO_3.10H_2O$) washing soda; sodium bicarbonate ($NaHCO_3$) baking soda; and borax ($Na_2B_4O_7.10H_2O$).

Soda for glass- and glaze-making is derived from the following, which are separately indexed:

sodium carbonate	Na_2CO_3
	(soda ash)
borax	$Na_2B_4O_7.10H_2O$
albite	$Na_2O.Al_2O_3.6SiO_2$
	(soda feldspar)
nepheline syenite	$K_2O.3Na_2O.4Al_2O_3.8SiO_2$
sodium chloride	NaCl
	(common salt)
sodium nitrate	$NaNO_3$
sodalite	$3(Na_2O.Al_2O_3.2SiO_2).2NaCl$
ulexite	$NaCaB_5O_9.8H_2O$
cryolite	Na_3AlF_6

barilla and kelp: ashes from burnt sea plants

There are over twenty sodium compounds which could be used in frit-making, but some are uneconomical. The simpler compounds are processed from rock salt by the Solvay process, the cheapest and most convenient compound being sodium carbonate. Borax, which introduces boric oxide is also popular.

Soda is the most soluble of all the oxides that the potter uses. Potash and lithia are close seconds but occur in non-soluble minerals. The so-called non-soluble soda minerals are likely to lose some of their soda into solution. The most convenient minerals are albite and nepheline syenite.

Sodium nitrate. Soda nitre. Chile saltpetre. $NaNO_3$. A highly-soluble sodium salt which is used in fritting for its oxidizing properties. As a source of soda it is too expensive.

Sodium silicate. Sodium metasilicate. Water-glass. Na_2SiO_3 or $Na_2O.SiO_2$. Soda and silica combined in approximately equal proportions. It is soluble in water and is used as a clay deflocculant in casting slips. See **Deflocculation**.

Sodium silicate is usually bought as a concentrated solution whose density is expressed in degrees Twaddell (°TW). It is in this form that it is introduced into casting slips. This stiff solution has given it the name of water-glass. The dry form is brittle, glassy and crystalline.

Sodium silicate is prepared from sodium carbonate and quartz. As water-glass, its composition can be varied but that used for deflocculation is usually calculated as the anhydrous formula given above. Water-glass is used as a glue, an egg preservative, a fireproofer and a binder and hardener in concretes and artificial stones.

Water-glasses have melting points between 1000°C and 1100°C (1832°F and 2012°F) and can be used with clay to make paste glazes. The method is not particularly satisfactory and is more expensive than using soda ash or washing soda.

Sodium silicate is difficult to store. It combines with carbon dioxide in the air to give sodium carbonate and silicic acid. Its deflocculating power is then altered.

Soft. Low temperature. In describing glazes the term means 600°C to 1050°C (1112°F to 1922°F). Soft fluxes are those which can be used for these glazes and include soda, potash, lead oxide and boric oxide. Soft glazes are physically soft and are easily scratched.

Soft as a relative term means at a lower temperature

not necessarily referring to below 1050°C. See also **Hard (2)**.

Soft soap. Soft soap, as opposed to hard soap, is used as the parting medium in plaster mould-making. When prepared it is a liquid which can be painted on to the first piece to fill the pores. Excess is wiped away with a damp sponge before the plaster is poured on.

Soft soap is potash soap; hard soap is soda soap. Detergents have replaced soft soap for household and most commercial uses but some is still sold for hair conditioning. When purchased it is of the consistency of soft butter and is prepared for the mould-maker's use by dissolving it in an equal amount of warm water. It can then be stored ready for use. It should not be boiled.

A passable substitute is soda soap which has been dissolved by soaking in warm water. Also some of the liquid detergents are effective parting media.

Solid solution. A term used to describe glazes implying that the now solid state is really more than one substance and was achieved by a mixture and/or combination of substances in a liquid state.

Solubility. Measurement of a substance's capacity to go into solution. The word is often used when referring to fired glazes and their capacity to withstand the dissolving action of food acids, drinks etc. See **Lead poisoning** and **Low sol**.

Soluble materials. Most raw materials contain some soluble matter as soda, potash, sulphates and phosphates. Small amounts cause no harm but large amounts can be the cause of scumming, non-uniform fluxing and unwanted flashing of glaze onto unglazed surfaces. Soluble materials also cause cementing of glaze slops in the bottom of tubs.

Unwanted solubles can be removed by washing or the addition of chemicals which combine with the solubles to produce insoluble precipitates.

Sour. Age. To improve the plasticity of clay by damp storage. Many clays begin to smell, some in an overpowering way. The introduction of some of this very sour clay into fresh plastic clay will assist the souring of the fresh clay.

The action is bacteriological. The organic growth is able to penetrate between the clay particles and open these spaces for the water of plasticity to follow. The bacteria can be encouraged by the use of a suitable disinfectant or introduced as yeast. Alone, water will not divide the clay particles without the vigorous action of a centrifugal blunger.

If sufficient space is not available for souring of all clay then clay for special purposes, such as handles, is soured. Clay which has been thoroughly wet, as is wheel-trough scrap, is suitable.

There is usually some temporary discolouration of soured clay due to the organic growth which uses oxygen and reduces the oxide content of the clay. The clay regains its colour on contact with the air and with firing. The blue colour associated with red and cream plastic clays is an indication that souring is taking place. Clay which is intended to be sour must not be allowed to dry out otherwise its especial property gained over months of souring is lost.

All clays improve their plasticity with keeping, especially over the first few days after making up from dry. This however is not souring but the natural balancing out of the water distribution in the clay. Weathering, which uses the action of frost, also improves plasticity. However souring seems able to improve on weathering because it divides particles which water alone cannot penetrate. See also **Ageing**.

Spall. To crack with temperature change. The word is usually reserved for kiln brickwork where it is considered the result of the wide difference in temperature between the hot face and the interior of the brick coupled with silica inversions. The resulting expansion and contraction and the inability to adjust because of the rigidity of brickwork results in cracks both into the depth of the brick and across the brick shearing away flakes.

The term spall is not applied to pottery. Pottery is thinner than brickwork so the temperature differences through a pot are small and any difference in expansion can be absorbed. Pottery cracks are more commonly the result of silica inversions and therefore are called dunts. Indefinable cracks are said to be the result of thermal shock which is an all-embracing term covering both spalling and dunting.

Spar. A miner's term for crystalline rocks which break easily along lines of cleavage. They are rocks containing large crystals which are comparatively soft, like feldspars at hardness H 6 and fluorspar at hardness H 4.

Specific gravity. SG. Specific gravity is expressed as a number for each substance. It is best considered as the number of times by which the substance is heavier than the same volume of water. For example, the specific gravity of china clay is 2·5 which means that it is two-and-a-half times as heavy as water. It will therefore sink in water.

In practice the potter can regard the SG as being the weight in grams of one cubic centimetre of the substance and consider this weight the same as density or relative density. The scientist is more exact than this and states that the comparative volume of water must be at 4°C and the temperature of the substance must also be stated.

Specific gravity is used in calculating the amounts of water and substance required to make a suspension of a particular thickness or weight per pint. Conversely if the weight per pint and the volume of a suspension is known, the dry weight it contains can be calculated by Brongniart's formula using the specific gravity of the substance. See **Formula, Brongniart's**.

A list of specific gravities for different substances is given in the **Tables**. Examples using specific gravities are worked in **Calculations, percentage and batch recipe**, and **Formula, density**.

$$SG \times 20 \cdot 042 = oz \; pt \; UK$$
$$SG \times 16 \cdot 705 = oz \; pt \; US$$

Specific heat. A measurement of the quantity of heat required to warm a substance. Each substance has a different specific heat. For potters it is sufficient to realize that soft fired, open textured and porous bodies have a high specific heat. Fine textured and dense bodies have a lower specific heat. This means that porous bodies are slower to warm up and are therefore better heat insulators. They are also slower to cool down. This fact is useful in making teapots and explains why red earthenware teapots infuse the tea better than porcelain ones. The fact is also useful and interesting in making tureens, casseroles, hot water bottles etc.

Spinel. A mineral having the composition $RO \cdot R_2O_3$. It is a compound of an alkaline oxide and an amphoteric oxide which is acting as the acid. Natural spinels are magnesium aluminate ($MgO \cdot Al_2O_3$) and beryllium aluminate ($BeO \cdot Al_2O_3$) with some replacements by other metals. Many other spinels have been artificially produced and provide stable colourants for bodies and glazes. The following are examples:

$CoO \cdot Al_2O_3$	blue
$CrO \cdot Al_2O_3$	pink
$MnO \cdot Al_2O_3$	pink
$ZnO \cdot Al_2O_3$	green
$CdO \cdot Cr_2O_3$	green
$NiO \cdot Cr_2O_3$	green
$FeO \cdot Cr_2O_3$	brown

There are also combinations called spinel-type combinations which form in glazes, e.g. lead antimonate yellow, chrome-tin pink and calcium borate opacity.

Spluttering. Sputtering. A glaze defect in which small pieces of glaze fall from the ware during fusion and are found fused to the shelf after the firing. The glaze layer sometimes heals over but sometimes crawls.

Spluttering is caused by a loose glaze layer which fails to adhere during fusion. This can occur with wet ware in a glaze firing and with glazes containing colemanite which releases its water content around 800°C (1472°F). See **Wet ware** and **Colemanite**.

Spodumene. Lithium feldspar or feldspathoid.

$Li_2O \cdot Al_2O_3 \cdot 4SiO_2$. A natural material of the feldspathic type occurring as isolated crystals in granites. Selected specimens can be given the ideal formula above. It is used in bodies and glazes to introduce lithia, alumina and silica. Ground spodumene inevitably contains some potash and soda.

Pure spodumene has a low expansion rate compared with other feldspars and has been used in experimental flameproof stoneware bodies. Lithia has a lower expansion rate than most of the other alkalis and spodumene contains sufficient alumina to involve free silica in mullitic and other non-dunting fusions.

In glazes, the spodumene introduces an extra alkali with some potash and soda. By interaction, small amounts have beneficial effects in lowering the fusion range, increasing gloss and improving stability. However spodumene alone is high in alumina (28%) and is therefore comparatively refractory for use as a feldspathic material. Alone it matures very slowly in the 1250°C to 1400°C range (2282°F to 2552°F).

Spoil. Removable bricks at the base of a kiln chimney. In conjunction with the damper, the spoil affects the quality of the chimney's draw. If the kiln is fired by vaporized oil under pressure, the spoil is used to control chamber pressure, oxidation and reduction. The spoil is also the place where a small fire is made at the beginning of a firing to start the drawing action of the chimney.

Spout. A projection on a pot to assist pouring. Spouts are of two types, the open or jug type and the closed tubular type used on the teapot.

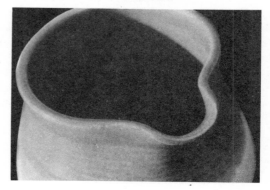

Jug spouts may be pulled or squeezed from the pot body or added as separately-formed pieces:

1. Snip spout or lip, knocked or tapped from coarse clay or clay of low plasticity.
2. Squeezed spout from fine clay of low plasticity.
3. Pulled spout from plastic clay.
4. Parrot beak modelled from coarse clay.
5. Monk's hood, pressed or cast.
6. Thrown and cut spout, luted into position.

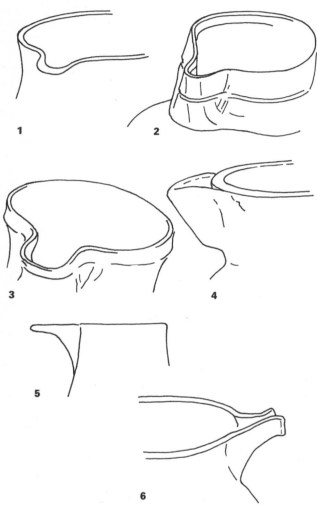

The different types have evolved for different thicknesses of liquid to be poured and to suit the pot to be poured from. Some spouts are for generous pouring, others for controlled dropping of small amounts. The clay also influences the type of spout that can be produced.

General principles are that there should be a single flow-line from the belly of the jug out and over the lip. The sides of the spout should throw the liquid into the spout. The lip of the spout should cut the flow effectively and preferably without a drip. A thin section or sharp edge to the tip is the most effective non-drip finish but this is vulnerable in pottery and a compromise has to be made with a thicker section. The effect of the sharper edge can be partially gained by the sudden curl over of the spout end.

The spout is the giving part of the jug. It should look generous, even extrovert; never mean or introvert. Jugs suffer by under-emphasis rather than over-emphasis of their spouts. The photographs show two different methods of pulling a spout. The usual pulling of a spout using two hands is followed by the thinning of the lip. The thinning and raising of a lip with one hand is followed by a further shaping using two hands. Pictures of whole jugs are given under **Jug**.

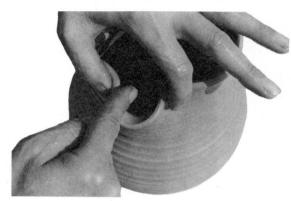

The tubular spout is used for teapots and coffee pots. It is made separately by throwing, pressing or casting and is luted into position whilst still softer than the body of the pot. For the coffee pot a hole is cut in the pot wall and the spout fitted over it. For the teapot the wall is perforated to become a strainer. The holes should be pierced or drilled at the same angle as the flow of liquid through the spout. The wall thickness may be shaved down to make less resistance in the holes. In this way they are less likely to be blocked by the glaze and later the tea leaves. Some potters cut the holes with a tapering spike which leaves them wider on the outside which again counters blockage. The holes should not be too small. About $\frac{3}{16}$ inch is popular. It is impossible to hold back every tea leaf but the composite action of restricted flow helps to keep the tea leaves in the pot.

The cross-sectional area of all the holes should be larger than the area across the exit of the spout. This gives the pressure within the spout to thrust the tea out over the rim. For this reason teapot and coffee pot spouts should taper noticeably towards the exit. The taper may become less at the end where the spout becomes a directional pipe (fig. 7). A short spout, whilst providing thrust by taper, gives no direction to the flow (fig. 8). The resulting ideal has concave sides in which the underneath line of the spout joins the body of the pot to form a smooth line of flow (fig. 9). It is important to remember that it is the inside of the spout that should be considered as the taper. The inside of the spout should also be smooth and without throwing ridges which would impede the flow.

The end of the spout is often cut diagonally (fig. 10). This brings the end nearer to a horizontal so that the lower lip, over which the liquid pours, protrudes further. A smoother flow is thereby achieved because there is no drag on the upper part as the liquid is released. Directional flow is also improved because the slight out-turning of the rim, as shown in the photograph, is used effectively at A, whilst the part B is cut away. If B were left it would slow down the rate of flow and disperse the liquid multi-directionally. The cutting-off edge can be separately modelled or carved to effect a cleaner non-drip end.

Long spouts if wheel-thrown will twist in firing especially if fired to a vitrified state. Seen from the exit end, a spout will twist in a clockwise direction if it was thrown on a wheel turning anti-clockwise. The amount varies with throwing technique, clay and firing but can be as much as 45°. The whole spout will also pull itself across the pot like the hand of a clock. This is only noticeable on long coffee pot spouts and the amount is small.

The angle of attachment for a spout depends upon the body of the pot. The spout should use the body of the pot as its first direction of flow and continue this movement through itself. Approximately 45° is a popular angle and a good general starting point for consideration. The top of the spout should come at least above the upper level of the liquid if not above the level of the rim of the pot.

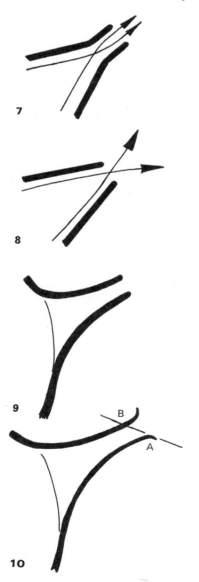

7

8

9

B

A

10

Sprigging. Adding more clay on to the main pot form. Taken literally, handles are sprigs but common usage gives the name to decorative features more than functional parts.

The sprigs may be in the same clay as the body or in clay of a contrasting colour. They may be freely modelled after being applied to the pot or they may be previously pressed in a mould and applied with enough pressure to make them adhere without deforming the detail.

Some means of softening the two surfaces to be joined must be used. With fine clays and preformed sprigs, water is sufficient. With coarser clays, slurry or slip is better and this probably led to the use of coloured slips and differently coloured sprigging clay. The

Mug by Alan Caiger Smith; 18th-century Italian flask.

method is very direct and gives scope for both colour contrasts and modelled forms. If different clays are used some adjustment of shrinkage by the addition of a fine ball clay to create more shrinkage, or of fine grog to reduce shrinkage, may be necessary.

The photograph shows a 19th-century salt-glazed jug from Lambeth. The sprigging is in fairly high relief. See also **Lambeth, Applied ornament, Relief decoration** and **Elers brothers**.

Springing. The defect of incorrectly joined handles which part from the pot at one end. See **Crack S**.

Stabilizer. A modifying oxide added to a glaze, frit or colour to stabilize the colour or the oxides. For example in the making of lead frits, small amounts of alumina, titania and calcia are included and these dramatically reduce the solubility of the lead content. See **Low sol**. The intermediate or amphoteric oxides are also generally referred to as glaze stabilizers.

Staffordshire cones. The earlier name for Harrison Pyrometric Cones. See **Cones**.

Stannic oxide. SnO_2. The stable white oxide of tin. It is used as an opacifier in glazes. See **Tin oxide**.

It would be correct to use the name stannic oxide for the oxide involved in a glaze and to refer to the mineral as tin oxide. However potters usually avoid the chemical phrase and refer to tin oxide or white tin oxide.

Stanniferous painting. Painting on an unfired tin glaze as in maiolica ware. See **Maiolica**.

Stannous oxide. SnO. The grey or black oxide of tin. The normal oxide of tin is the white dioxide (SnO_2). The white is an opacifier giving white glazes and acting as an anti-flux but reducing atmospheres before and during fusion result in the black tin monoxide. One could expect this to act as an alkaline, that is, a flux and it will do so above 1200°C (2192°F) and become partially dissolved. However its action appears slight or slow compared with other fluxes and the reduced tin oxide (stannous oxide) more often clouds a glaze with an unattractive grey. Very heavy reduction of tin oxide, as by raku, can give some excellent metallic tin lustres. See **Tin lustre**.

Steger's bending bar. A method of measuring the stress between body and glaze. A thin bar of clay is biscuited, then glazed. It is fired with one end fixed and the other end free in space. As the glaze sets in cooling the difference in contraction between body and glaze bends the bar and is measured whilst bending is in progress. The idea can be used with thin test tiles to discover what sort of stress exists between body and glaze.

Stibium oxide. Sb_2O_3. See **Antimony oxide**.

Stiff glazes. Glazes with little or no run. Some glazes, like pale celadons, are effective only when thickly applied. Such glazes need to be stiffer than average and this is achieved by a high alumina content. The alumina : silica ratio is between 1 : 6 and 1 : 8. Feldspar and china clay are important ingredients and therefore feldspathic glazes are stiff glazes. See **Feldspathic glaze** and **Alumina in glazes**.

Stiff glazes are characterized by a semi-opacity due to suspended fine bubbles and sometimes crystals. They have a high surface tension and are not so shiny as runny glazes. See also **Run**.

Stokes's law. The law which declares that if particles

of a substance are suspended in a liquid the particles will settle in order of their decreasing size. Therefore in a mixture of clay and water the sedimentation of the largest particles takes place first and the finest particles sediment last. The finest particles, if smaller than 10^{-4} cm in diameter, will be of colloidal size and may never settle and these are controlled by a movement called Brownian movement. Stokes's law explains the natural sorting of clay sediments in lakes and is made use of in levigation of clay.

Stone. See **Cornish stone**.

Stoneware. A hard, strong and vitrified ware, usually fired above 1200°C (2192°F), in which the body and glaze mature at the same time and form an integrated body-glaze layer. The quality of the glaze owes much to the establishment of this layer and it is therefore the glaze quality which determines a ware's acceptance as stoneware. This quality shows as an integration of the colours of body and glaze, mottlings and soft edges to colour variations. The glaze surface is hard.

Under **Earthenware**, the division between earthenware and stoneware is given as depending upon the porosity of the body. Whilst this criterion is often taken for deciding what is earthenware, it is rarely taken as the criterion for stoneware. There are many porous

stonewares with well-integrated body-glaze layers in which much of the quality of the glaze is derived from the body beneath. Their porosity does not invalidate their claim to be stonewares. See **Porosity, Hard** and **Vitrification**.

The following are stonewares:

Stoneware : body and glaze integrated in a firing above 1200°C (2192°F); body of less than 5% porosity.

Ovenware : body and glaze integrated; body up to 10% porosity.

Red stoneware : Non-porous body or less than 2% porosity; firing temperature between 1100°C and 1250°C (2012°F and 2282°F).

Salt-glazed wares : body and glaze integrated; low porosity; physically hard.

Porcelain is a special type of stoneware which has a white, completely vitrified and often translucent body. See **Porcelain**.

China uses a porcelain body with a soft (earthenware) glaze. See **China**.

STONEWARE CLAY. Clay suitable for making the dense ware called stoneware. It must be plastic with a good workability range. It must have a long vitrification period with an almost dense end-product that is strong but not brittle. It should have an interesting colour, take glazes well and possibly not break down in reduction.

Most stoneware pottery is thrown, for which a high degree of plasticity is required. Good plasticity is often accompanied by a long workability range which allows turning and the adding of handles etc.

In the firing, the clay needs to vitrify slowly so that whatever the product it can mature without distortion. Potters who make stoneware tableware aim to get an end-product which is theoretically vitrified and therefore is non-porous. This takes the body near to its point of deformation. With most clays this vitrification also gives a brittleness or rather a lack of resilience. It is preferable that the body shall have an absorbency of 1% or even 2%. In this state it has resilience and can withstand physical knocks. Below 1% absorbency, most stoneware clays decrease in strength to the point of vitrification where they may be only half as strong as at 1% absorbency.

This connection between strength and absorbency/vitrification cannot be related to porcelain which is quite different. In porcelain the body is homogeneous; it does not contain variously-sized particles of sand, grog etc. The body therefore becomes of equal vitrification and the glaze is of similar composition to the body and integrated with it. The combined body and glaze unit is very strong. In stoneware, whilst some integration takes place, there is always a stress between body and glaze that must be considered. The ideal stoneware clay is therefore one which can be accurately fired to required porosity.

Many stoneware potters use reduction to gain more

integration of body and glaze for reasons of strength and colour response. Good stoneware clays should respond favourably to reduction and give added colour interest. All clays vitrify more quickly under reduction and some may become too brittle to be practical for stoneware.

A stoneware clay should be interesting in natural fired colour. The base of a pot will always be unglazed in stoneware and the body will show. It is a poor clay that must be given a wash of oxide to cover its colour. Lastly stoneware clays should take glazes well. This seems obvious but not all clays do this. The siliceous clays often take glazes better than the aluminous ones because they integrate well in the early stages of firing.

Natural stoneware clays exist and have been used for industrial stoneware for 150 years. They are usually a type of ball clay which contains colouring impurities. Normal ball clays can be used for stoneware. They are usually too fine and long, and need to be shortened by grog, sand and other clays. Ball clays are also rather insipid in colour.

Heavy clay industrial stoneware uses fireclay. These fireclays are often classified as low grade because they contain many impurities but, if weathered well, they make excellent stoneware clays. If the impurities are potash and other fluxes with some finely-divided iron oxide, the clay will make a stoneware clay. It may be necessary to blend it with ball clay for plasticity and/or to add some bentonite for plasticity. A very short fireclay may require 5% of bentonite but 2% is more usual.

Stouker. A person who fixes handles and other modelled decorations.

Strain. The condition of a ceramic body that has been subjected to stress. It can be measured as a linear displacement or a percentage distortion from the ideal.

Stress. The force exerted between two parts of a ceramic body. It can be measured as energy. There is always some stress between body and glaze, and between one part of a pot and another, e.g. foot rim and sides. Stress results in strain which is the effect upon the body and is measured as a distortion.

All pots contain stresses. Sometimes the stresses are such that if a pot is dropped it bounces. In this case the stresses created by the collision are in opposition to and are counteracted by the existing stresses. On the other hand a pot is sometimes given a slight knock that results in the shattering of the piece. In this case the existing stresses were finally overloaded. Pots do not always crack where we would expect because we are unaware of the existence of the stresses.

Strontia. Strontium oxide. SrO. A useful glaze flux for all temperatures, once it has been incorporated in a frit. If introduced into a glaze batch as strontium carbonate its fluxing action is limited to temperatures

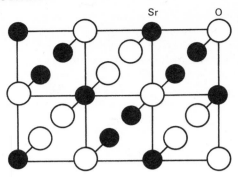

above 1090°C (1994°F). It is similar in effect to calcia and zinc oxide.

Strontium occurs in the minerals celestine ($SrSO_4$) and strontianite ($SrCO_3$). The metal strontium can be isolated and melts at 757°C (1395°F) but the oxide is a refractory, melting at 2430°C (4406°F).

The fluxing action of the oxide is effective from around 650°C (1202°F) upwards to any pottery temperature and it is unaffected by reduction. To be effective at the lower temperatures, however, it must be incorporated in a frit. When strontia is introduced into a glaze by means of the insoluble strontium carbonate, its fluxing action is not realized until 1090°C (1994°F). In this way it is similar to calcia.

The action of strontia is often compared with that of calcia. The thermal expansion and the fluxing powers are approximately the same, although the interaction power of strontia is more akin to that of zinc oxide. Like both calcia and zinc oxide, it requires interaction to be effective as a flux, and also like them an excess precipitates a crystalline matt surface.

For the individual potter who uses raw glazes, strontia is a useful additional flux to give interaction in the middle temperature range, 1100°C to 1200°C (2012°F to 2192°F). Although little used, strontia is not a new flux. It has been used since the late 19th century when it was tried as a substitute for lead oxide. The glaze experiments were successful and lead-free and zinc-free non-poisonous glazes were produced. Strontium compounds are not poisonous. However the price of strontium minerals precluded their use and strontium carbonate is still about four times the cost of whiting, so there is no point in such a substitution. However, as a replacement for lead oxide on a molecular basis it will be found to be of approximately the same price and here strontia is worth consideration for glazes containing small amounts of lead oxide.

Strontianite. Strontium carbonate. $SrCO_3$. Insoluble strontium mineral associated with lead ores in limestone replacement lodes. It is a source of strontia for frits and glazes. Strontianite is named after the village of Strontian in Scotland, where it was first discovered.

Strontium carbonate. $SrCO_3$. Source of strontium

oxide in glazes. The oxide form is soluble in water therefore the carbonate is used in a glaze batch. If the strontium carbonate is prepared from the crushed ore it usually contains some calcium carbonate. Strontium carbonate decomposes by 1075°C (1967°F) to give the oxide:

$$SrCO_3 \xrightarrow{1075°C} SrO + CO_2\uparrow$$

Super-cooled liquid. Undercooled liquid. A technical term meaning that a liquid has been cooled below its freezing point without crystallization.

A glaze is a super-cooled liquid because it cools so quickly that there is usually no time for crystals to grow. If a glaze were cooled very slowly, various crystals would grow and separate themselves from the liquid, e.g. calcium silicate, orthoclase, quartz. After such a slow cooling the glaze would be a complete mass of crystals, as is granite, and would not be a glass. Because a glaze cools quickly it sets without this opportunity and is therefore scientifically regarded as a liquid although it has set to a solid state.

The terms solid solution and amorphous solid are also used to describe a glaze. Both are linked with the conception of a glaze as a liquid which is so viscous as to present the appearance of a solid. Therefore a glaze which is reheated has no melting point. Instead its viscosity is slowly decreased until it is sufficiently fluid to flow.

Surface tension. The apparent pull which the surface of a liquid has whereby it tries to contain the liquid. It is imagined as a tight skin which is always trying to compress the liquid, or as a skin which is stretched by the liquid which it contains. Thus a free or unattached volume of liquid forms itself into a sphere: the volume surrounded by the smallest possible surface area. In reality surface tension is caused by the attraction of the component molecules of the liquid whereby they group themselves into the most compact mass. There is in reality no skin under tension at the surface. This is an apparent phenomenon resulting from the internal stresses. However the so-called surface tension can be measured and laboratory measurements are made of the surface tensions of molten glazes.

The term comes into the potter's vocabulary in relation to molten glazes. A glaze with a low surface tension quickly creeps into narrow crevices or porous surfaces. This phenomenon is called 'wetting' and is similar to the action of a thin liquid like petrol which can wet a material upon which water would stand as globules. Water has a higher surface tension than petrol.

A glaze with a high surface tension does not 'wet' the pottery body but if at all loose tends to curl back or consolidate itself in globules. This phenomenon is called 'crawling'.

Stiff or viscous glazes tend to have high surface tensions. Runny or fluid glazes tend to have low surface tensions.

The surface tension of a glaze is directed by its chemical composition. Some constituent oxides make a glaze of low surface tension. An example is potash (K_2O) which is also an active flux and creates fluid glazes. Some oxides make a glaze of high surface tension. An example is alumina (Al_2O_3) which also increases a glaze's viscosity. If the glaze oxides are put into a table in the order of their action upon surface tension it will be found that potash is at one end and alumina at the other. The oxides between them are in approximately the same order as their action on viscosity. To give a comparison, a table of oxide action on viscosity at approximately 1050°C (1922°F) is also given. It is extracted from the fuller table given under **Viscosity**. On both tables, silica is included in its correct place and is taken as the standard with which the others are compared.

	HIGH SURFACE TENSION		HIGH VISCOSITY
↑ increases surface tension	Alumina		
	Magnesia		
	Zirconia		Alumina ↑
	Calcia		Zirconia
	Tin oxide		Tin oxide
	Zinc oxide		Baria increases viscosity
	Strontia		Titania
	Baria		
	SILICA		SILICA
↓ lowers surface tension	Titania		Magnesia
	Boric oxide		Calcia
	Lithia		Strontia
	Lead oxide		Zinc oxide
	Soda		Boric oxide increases fluidity
	Potash		Lead oxide
	LOW SURFACE TENSION		Lithia
			Soda
			Potash ↓
			LOW VISCOSITY

The two tables do not match exactly which means that minor adjustments made to one state do not necessarily affect the other. However their relationship is strong because they depend upon the same actions. These actions are the breaking and making of bonds between oxide molecules especially between an oxide and silica in the creation of linked chains. In a molten glaze the bonds are continually being broken and remade in new combinations.

A rise in temperature brings into action more fluxes and increases the ease with which bonds are broken, thus increasing fluidity. It also lowers the surface tension slightly.

Small amounts of additional oxides interfere with the creation of regularized patterns which have a stiffening effect. They thereby increase fluidity quite markedly but they lower the surface tension only slightly.

A reducing atmosphere often increases fluidity by creating greater interaction with the body and turning iron oxide into a flux. It has no effect upon surface tension.

Lastly, it should be stated that surface tension of the molten glaze is not related to the physical thickness of the glaze layer. It is true that the high surface tension shows most in thick glazes where it can cause crawling; and that a thinner layer of glaze may overcome the problem of crawling; it does not however alter the surface tension but gives less opportunity for a rupturing of the glaze layer.

Suspender. An addition to a glaze slop to keep the materials in suspension. Popular suspenders are bentonite with calcium chloride and polymer adhesives. See **Flocculation**.

Polymer adhesives help to bind a friable glaze to the ware before firing as well as providing slop suspension. Many other adhesives like gelatine, cellulose pastes and resin gums, temporarily thicken a glaze slop and keep it in suspension. However the most popular suspender is 1% bentonite which is flocculated by the addition of calcium chloride to the water.

Syenite. An igneous rock with less than 10% free silica (quartz). Above this amount of quartz the rock is called a granite. See **Nepheline**.

Symbol. See **Chemical symbol**.

T

Tables. See **Appendix of Tables**, pp. 327–48.

Talc. Magnesium silicate. French chalk. Steatite. Soapstone. $3MgO.4SiO_2.H_2O$. An insoluble mineral and convenient source of magnesia for bodies and glazes. See **Magnesia**.

Talc is an idealized mineral which in nature has a variable formula of proportions and nearly always contains some calcium, iron and aluminium. Steatite and soapstone are attempts to name two varieties.

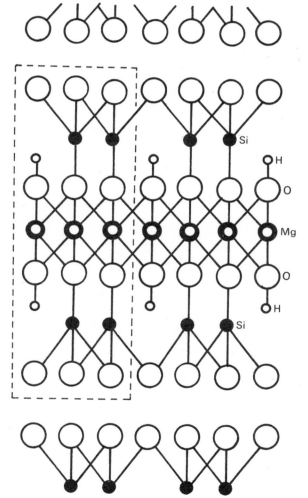

Before the action of magnesia as a catalyst was understood, it was discovered empirically that talc restrained the tendency of the glaze to craze if it were added to the earthenware body. The required action is not that of a flux although some fusion must take place in high temperature bisc firings. Rather it depends upon there being some free silica available which does not fuse. This free silica is often deliberately introduced into the body as powdered quartz. During the bisc firing, some is converted from quartz phase to cristobalite phase by the catalystic action of the magnesia and it remains crystalline. The cristobalite has a high rate of contraction and the body thereby exerts a squeeze upon the glaze which acts against any tendency to craze. See **Silica conversion** and **Cristobalite**.

Talc is also added to stoneware bodies to increase resistance to thermal shock. At first this appears contradictory to the idea of using it to increase cristobalite. The explanation lies in the composition of the body. The cristobalite earthenware body contains a large proportion of free silica. In some cases as much as 50% of the body will be free silica. Shockproof stoneware bodies must contain as little as possible free silica. They are composed of kaolinite and other aluminous clays. The talc provides a flux which itself is low in expansion rate. This flux involves the free silica left from mullite formation and the silica introduced in the talc. The process is intended to use magnesia as a flux and not as a catalyst. The free silica is thus involved in a melt which, because it is with magnesia, is a viscous melt and one not so destructive to pottery forms as fluid flux/silica melts. By becoming molten, the silica, whether quartz or cristobalite, loses its crystalline nature and is rendered of low thermal expansion. See **Table of thermal expansion and contraction** on p. 336.

These talc/clay shockproof bodies are called cordierite bodies. Cordierite is a magnesium and iron silicate mineral. The idealized formula attempted by reconstruction in cordierite bodies is $2MgO.2Al_2O_3.5SiO_2$. Some cordierite ware is flameproof which is an extreme test for a pottery body. Cordierite bodies are also used for electrical insulators for high frequencies.

Cordierite bodies have a narrow firing range because there is a necessity to involve the free silica before distorting the ware. They are also difficult to cover with a satisfactory glaze because of their low expansion rates.

Talc in glazes provides unattached magnesia and silica. It is a useful mineral for glazes maturing above 1000°C (1832°F) because it decomposes at 900°C (1652°F) into free magnesia, free silica and water. It can be used to produce opaque and matt glazes as described under **Magnesian matts**. Its popular use is in stoneware glazes, where, after becoming involved in a liquid phase, it reforms as enstatite upon cooling. See **Enstatite**.

289

Tea-dust. Describes the decorative surface of glazes where a matt, very fine speckle covers what appears to be a more shiny glaze underneath. As with many of these overall textural effects the origin was Chinese. The term is sometimes limited to effects produced in the original manner using a matt enamel which is dusted onto the glaze. The original colour varied from a mustard yellow to a sage green. However the description also fits many effects resulting from over-loading glazes with metal oxides especially when such glazes are over other glazes or vitrifying slips. There is a variant of tenmoku which has been described as tea-dust.

The following is a tea-dust glaze for 1200°C (2192°F). It is black with brown dust on top.

potash feldspar	50
china clay	15
flint	5
whiting	15
red iron oxide	5
manganese dioxide	5
cobalt oxide	5

Tea marl. A red and green shale of the Triassic Period. It is only soft and can be reconstituted as a clay by crushing and blunging. It produces a red-burning clay. See **Marl**.

Teapot. A pot for infusing and serving tea. It is usually a lidded pot of compact form with a spout and handle. The teapot originated in China in the 14th century and was developed from the kettle previously used. It came to Europe in the 17th century as an import with the tea. At first tea was regarded as a medicine and teapots were small, some only a few inches in diameter. Cheaper tea grown in India and Ceylon during the days of the British Empire resulted in tea becoming the popular drink of 19th-century Britain. Teapots became larger. Some held as much as two gallons and had two spouts. Two-spouted pots either fill two separate cups or have two spouts side by side to fill one cup more quickly.

The development of the teapot, as it is made by individual potters today, can be considered British or even English. The teapot is a symbol of friendliness. First the society ladies of 18th-century England held their afternoon tea parties. Later, in the 19th century, tea was the alternative stimulant to beer for the working classes. Today the relaxing and confidential aura of tea-drinking remains but it has lost the precious atmosphere which was reflected in the decorative effects of chinoiserie and rococo. The individual potter is able to make teapots which capture this friendliness by the successful integration of the different parts and the harmony of body and glaze. His teapot has developed over 300 years from the Elers pieces of the 17th century which copied Chinese red stoneware. Astbury, Whieldon and Wedgwood each gave some character to the development so that by the 19th century a truly English teapot had developed. An over-decorated and fashionable style in stoneware and porcelain teapots fortunately never became the main development. The simpler, popular ware was more functional but mention should be made of the excellent forms of a few of the porcelain teapots, notably from Worcester. In the 20th century, Oriental influence, this time Japanese, added to the character. It can be seen in the use of Oriental-type stoneware and the cane handle but the overall character remains western.

The examples shown are respectively by Michael Casson, Sheila Casson, Leighton Clark, Crowan Pottery, Janet Hamer, David Leach, William Marshall, Eric Stockl, Geoffrey Whiting, Trevor Worton.

The functional points of a teapot are simple, but the satisfactory combination of these points is a challenge to the potter's skill and imagination, especially when some elegance or aesthetic interest is required of this teatable focal point. The pot must hold sufficient tea, usually four to six cupsful, keep it hot whilst the tea infuses, be stable and easily lifted and accurately manoeuvred to pour the tea into the cups. It must, to some degree, strain the tea by holding back the tea

291

leaves in the pot and yet it must be capable of being easily cleaned.

Capacity is usually reckoned in cupsful. A small teapot holding two cupsful is a half-pint one. A theoretical form to be considered for the body of the pot is a sphere. This is adjusted in consideration of other factors. The sphere is the form that gives the greatest capacity for a given surface area. This is advantageous as regards the weight of the pot which has to be lifted and controlled. It also gives less surface for heat loss. Boiling water is used to infuse the tea and it is advantageous to keep the tea as hot as possible for the five minutes required for infusion.

A form broader than high gives a larger cross-section for the movement of the tea during this process. The broader form is also more stable. To keep the tea hot during infusion, earthenware is considered better than stoneware or porcelain. Traditionally, red earthenware (which is lower fired and hence more porous and the better insulator) is preferred to white earthenware. Tea connoisseurs declare that they can taste the difference in tea made in a red earthenware pot. It is interesting to note that the raku tea bowl, which is a good insulator, acts as both teapot for infusing and the cup for drinking.

The popular broad body for the pot presents a pleasing rhythm from which may spring the spout and handle. The spout should describe in outline, or indicate in general feeling, the action of the tea as it flows. Analysis of handles, spouts and lids is given separately under these headings.

TEAPOT CLAY. Any red clay which has the combination of properties necessary for making teapots: plasticity for throwing, a long enough working range to allow spouting and handling before drying and when fired, to be sufficiently hard to stand up to everyday use, be a good insulator to hold in the heat and be a rich brown colour under a clear glaze. The North Staffordshire red clay is traditionally a teapot clay.

Technique. The individual way in which each potter carries out a process. Technique is allied to skill. It is developed by establishing a personal relationship with the work and is often the result of repeated progressive actions. Technique cannot be taught or learnt, it can only be acquired. What is taught is a method or a process.

Temper. An addition to clay which improves workability, e.g. sand and grog. Temper will also affect the fired result but its introduction is essentially to assist forming and uniform drying. See also **Grog**, **Workability**, **Preparation of clay** (control of grain size), **Filler** and **Grain size**.

Temperature. A means of describing heat. Temperature is measured in degrees Centigrade (°C) or degrees Fahrenheit (°F). These are the two common scales used

by potters. Five Centigrade degrees equal nine Fahrenheit degrees, but, whereas Centigrade is based upon 0° as the freezing point and 100° as the boiling point of water, on the Fahrenheit scale the freezing point is 32°.

$$100°C \text{ per hour} = 180°F \text{ per hour}$$

Tables of temperature equivalents and incandescence are included in the **Tables** of this book. Centigrade is used as standard throughout this book. See also **Heat**, **Celsius** and **Kelvin**.

TEMPERATURE CONVERSION FORMULAE.

$$\text{Degrees Fahrenheit} = (°C \times \tfrac{9}{5}) + 32$$
$$\text{Degrees Centigrade} = (°F - 32) \times \tfrac{5}{9}$$

Tenmoku. Temmoku. A stoneware glaze which is deeply stained by iron oxide. Tenmokus are usually dark brown and black with some rust patches, but occasionally they are yellow, green or purple. Good tenmokus have an expressive depth and variation of colour. This is achieved by the use of a glaze that has some flow. It fills hollows, gives thickness variation on the pot's form and by the use of the correct amount of iron oxide gives an interesting balance of solute and precipitate. The photograph is of a jug by Sheila Casson. See **Iron oxide in glazes**.

Tenmokus are either slip glazes made from ferruginous clay and wood ash etc or feldspathic type glazes, fluxed with wood ash or limestone, to which 4% to 12% of iron oxide has been added. The Far Eastern

tenmokus were traditionally fired and cooled quickly and were oxidized. Western counterparts have more often been given some reduction to get a more blue-black colour in the dark parts. Any stoneware glaze which is deeply stained by iron oxide could acceptably be called a tenmoku. Specifically, tenmokus are restricted to shiny glazes of the black or dark brown type and the other matt and mottled effects are given separate names. Calcia is a suitable flux for reduced tenmokus but oxidized tenmokus require soda, potash, boric oxide and lead in order to achieve a clean colour. See **Calcia**.

TENMOKU (VARIATIONS). The connoisseur makes many sub-divisions of the tenmoku family of wares. The three main types are called tenmoku, tessha and kaki. Tenmokus are the black and dark brown glazes with a tendency to 'break to rust' on the rims and sharp edges. If the rust-coloured parts spread over more of the glaze causing rust patches, it would be called tessha and if the rust colour covered most of the surface it would be a kaki glaze. The kaki is sometimes given the name persimmon if it is especially bright in colour and shine. The duller kakis are simply called rusts.

Crystallization gives more matt effects amongst which one has been called tea-dust. This is self explanatary and the colour varies from mustard green to black. All the connoisseur names are descriptive. Pig-skin is a semi-matt glaze with a dimpled surface. Oil-spot tenmoku has a series of lustrous spots up to $\frac{1}{4}$ inch across which vary with metallic sheen as do oil spots on water. Partridge feather is similar but with smaller bright spots. Hare's fur is of two types: one is like the soft smokey grey under-fur and streaks the dark tenmoku's surface; the other is like the light coloured tips of the hairs against the darker fur.

TENMOKU (ORIGIN). In China from the Han Dynasty through the T'ang Dynasty (1st to 10th centuries) a development took place involving brown glazed wares. During the Sung Dynasty (A.D. 960 to 1279) the perfection of firing allowed a thicker glaze layer and a more mature glaze. The result was the dark brown stoneware glaze.

The finest examples of this period are the Chien bowls. These are rice and tea bowls rarely wider than 5 inches in diameter and varying from black to rust with many variations of the smokey hare's fur variety. The glaze was either a clay and ash slip or a straight clay slip glaze, which was put on raw ware and once-fired in an oxidizing atmosphere. The idea of the rich dark glaze with its infinite possibilities caught the imagination of many potters, though not the imperial court, and the idea spread.

To the north east of Chien in the Province of Fuchien is a group of mountains called T'ien-mu Shan. Japanese Zen Buddhist monks visiting the monastery there used the Chien tea bowls and later took them back to Japan where they were excitedly admired. Later trade used a nearby port for export and the wares be-

came known as T'ien-mu or Tenmoku. These bowls and further developments in Japan were the source of contemplative delight until the development of raku in the 16th century.

Tenorite. Copper oxide ore. CuO. A black, soft ore resulting from the oxidized weathering of other ores. See **Copper ores**.

Tension. Stretch. The act of being pulled to increase size. Glazes are in tension before they craze. The crazing accommodates the stress of tension which existed.

Terracotta. Earthenware modelling both glazed and unglazed. The word comes from the Italian and means simply fired earth though the word is often used to describe the orange-brown colour of red-burning clay.

Terracotta clay is usually grey or buff which fires to red but red clays are often referred to as terracotta and terracottas have been modelled in cream-burning clays also so the description is quite broad.

The best use of terracotta is in the intimate piece of work where the sensitive quality of direct expression in clay can be used. Some of the finest examples of terracotta are the least pretentious and were made as toys, domestic ornaments and burial offerings. Terracottas have been made throughout the world at pottery centres, being associated more with pottery than with sculpture. Examples are of a 19th-century cottage ornament, a lion, and contemporary work, cathedral and madonna by Adas Dworski. When terracotta is used for architectural work it is in the personal detail that it is most successful. It was effectively used in 19th-century

Britain with unglazed pieces and in Renaissance Italy with high-relief plaques with coloured glazes.

Tessha. A variation of the tenmoku glaze in which the rust parts spread in patches over about half the surface. The rust colour is due to the crystallization of the red oxide upon cooling. See **Iron oxide in glazes**.

Tetroxide. An oxide involving four atoms of oxygen with one or three atoms of another element in each molecule. See also **Oxide**.

Theoretical formula. A chemical formula used in calculations because it is simpler than using a chemical analysis. The theoretical formula ignores important 'impurities'. For example flint, which could be 95% silica and 5% calcium carbonate, is given a theoretical formula of SiO_2 as if it were 100% silica. Other common examples of theoretical formulae are:

china clay	$Al_2O_3 . 2SiO_2 . 2H_2O$
potash feldspar	$K_2O . Al_2O_3 . 6SiO_2$
soda feldspar	$Na_2O . Al_2O_3 . 6SiO_2$
dolomite	$CaCO_3 . MgCO_3$

Thermal shock. The stress created within a ceramic object by temperature change. Thermal shock is responsible for the occurrence of cracks and is an overall term.

Its normal use refers to sudden changes of temperature such as happen to ovenware. If there is a large difference in temperature between two parts of the same piece of ceramic there is obviously a size difference due to expansion/contraction. This is the cause of the stress.

The ways in which some cracks occur have been given separate names and are called dunting and spalling. Dunting is the result of stress caused by silica (quartz and cristobalite) inversions. These inversions create marked changes in size of the silica and affect the size of the ceramic body containing them. Stresses which are not absorbed result in cracks which are called dunts. Spalling is cracking of kiln brickwork and is the result of both silica inversions and the normal thermal shock. **Dunting** and **Spall** are separate items in this book.

A ceramic body is a poor conductor of heat. When boiling water is poured into a teapot there is a time lag before the heat reaches the outside. In the section of the side of the pot, the inside is expanding with the heat of the boiling water before the outside. Stress is obviously created during this time-lag which may weaken some of the mechanical bonds of the body. When repeated a hundred times, a crack may appear which grows until it is noticeable. The crack may not happen suddenly but it is the result of thermal shock. A crack of this type may start parallel to the surfaces of the pottery body, that is, within the wall of a pot between inside and outside. However it soon angles itself to the surface at a point where the pot wall is thinner. Cracks in teapots often occur around the sectional unevenness of the foot rim. If the thickness is uniform it may be possible to absorb this transient stress an unlimited number of times.

With ovenware the heat or cold may suddenly envelop one side of the pot as it is placed into or withdrawn from the oven. The temperature difference is in this case across the whole pot as well as possibly through the thickness of the pot wall. This thermal shock can create sufficient stress to rupture the pot between the hotter and the colder halves. The actual amounts involved could be as much as 0.25% linear increase as the pot enters a hot oven. This is $\frac{1}{40}$ inch across a 10 inch plate. This amount is sufficient to rupture a pot whose body has insufficient elasticity to absorb the temporary differential.

As with the example of the teapot, ovenware in the form of casseroles and pie dishes may sustain ruptures through thermal shock which are not immediately apparent. If the body is very dense it is likely that a through crack will result, probably very quickly and with an alarming noise. If the body is not dense, the cracking may be slower and one may hear cracking as it takes place. It may be quite slow, lasting a minute or more, as the strain is relieved a part at a time.

A glassy, vitrified part may crack but the crack cannot continue through the body because it is stopped by a space. The stress then builds up against the next glassy part which then cracks as far as the next space. This continues until the stress is eased and the natural elasticity of the body can absorb the remaining stress. An open porous body can therefore absorb a thermal shock better than a dense vitrified body but this does not mean that it has not cracked partially.

The periodic extension of a crack can often happen in a casserole. Sometimes one may hear it take place but fail to see the minute crack. Each time the casserole is used the crack is extended a little. All this is unknown to its owner until the remaining unruptured part gives way. An examination of the crack will often show that it has existed for a long time as can be seen by the way grease and water have entered the crack and discoloured the body.

It is generally known that an open porous body is a better insulator than a dense body. For example, kiln insulation bricks are light and porous. The trapped air provides excellent heat insulation. It follows that a vitrified body and a glaze are better conductors of heat than an open porous body. Conversely a coarse open body or similarly a fine but porous body will retain its heat when a dense or vitrified body, and certainly a glaze, will have lost its heat. The porosity acting as insulation makes the porous body slow to warm up and and slow to cool down.

When pottery is used in the oven the first part of a pot to warm through is the glaze. This will occur quickly. The second part is the body and this will occur more slowly if the body is porous. When the glaze is warm, but not the body, there exists a stress between the two. The glaze is too big for the body and is under what is called a state of compression forced on it by the body. Most glazes are able to withstand this compression. Ones which cannot do so flake off at sharp corners on rims and handles. The phenomenon is called shivering. The stress must be quite extreme for this to occur. It is unlikely to happen on sound ware. Tell-tale signs will previously have occurred with ware prone to shivering. Such signs would be minor shivering, shelling and inexplicable plate cracks on overfired ware.

The sharp slivers of glaze are a menace with ovenware. It can also happen that if the glaze is very thick inside a wide cooking dish the glaze exerts sufficient pressure to rupture the body and this will take with it the glaze in a sudden shattering of the pot. Pots have been known to shatter suddenly into four or five pieces.

When the body also warms thoroughly it will catch up with the expansion of the glaze. In fact it will overtake it. Many bodies have greater thermal expansion and contraction rates than the glazes which cover them. If the rates are very different, the glaze will now come under tension from the body. The glaze will be too small for the body. Even the most elastic lead glaze has a limit to the amount of tension it can withstand. With any glaze it is only about one-tenth of the stress that it can withstand in the opposite direction under compression. The result is that the glaze ruptures. The body remains intact but the glaze cracks in what is known as crazing. If the stress is not sufficient to cause crazing in the oven it may well become sufficient when the piece of pottery is taken from the oven. At this point the glaze meets the colder air first. Being a relatively good conductor it quickly gives out its heat and in so doing it contracts. The porous body conserves its heat and remains expanded. Few glazes can withstand this treatment which is why ovenware is so frequently crazed.

It should also be remembered that ovenware is often left to soak in water. The porous body takes water into the pores and the body expands as a result. This too puts a tension on the glaze which can cause the crazing to spread.

Some potters like to see a small amount of crazing on their unused ovenware. This is especially true of their stoneware. Although this crazing will get worse with use it is an indication that the glaze is not starting under compression at room temperature. Crazing is considered preferable to shattering and shivering.

Thermal shock is the stress which may or may not result in a crack, in shivering or in crazing. It is bound to exist and cannot be entirely removed. The stress occurs between contiguous parts of ceramic bodies when pots are suddenly warmed or cooled in the kiln or in the oven or when used for hot liquids. Thick pots are more prone to the effects of thermal shock than thin ones. Glazed pots are more prone than unglazed ones. Thick glazes are more prone than thin glazes. Further application of thermal shock theory to pottery-making is discussed under **Ovenware**. A relationship between vitrification and strength is made under **Vitrification**. The cause of cracks is dealt with under **Cracks** and the theory of dunting which is related to thermal shock is dealt with under **Dunting**.

Thermoscope. Pyroscope.

Thermotrophy. The phenomenon of colour change by heat. Apart from the fact that ceramic bodies and glazes are glowing red at temperatures above 600°C (1112°F), they are also undergoing reversible colour changes in the range from room temperature to 600°C (1112°F). On cooling from firing, bodies and glazes do not achieve their final colour until the temperature has fallen below 80°C (176°F). If a kiln is opened when it is hot the difference is sometimes quite startling. Some bodies appear much lighter than their final colour and some glazes appear darker. Glazes containing titania, especially with tin oxide, appear a yellow buff colour which eventually fades to a pure white at room temperature.

Thivier's earth. A red ochreous sand.

Thixotropy. The property of slips to change fluidity by being left undisturbed; the slip at rest becomes more viscous. Also the property of plastic clays to resist initial pressure. See **Workability**.

All clay suspensions (slips) have this property which is the result of the establishment of mutual attraction bonds between the particles. Thixotropy begins to build up as soon as the slip comes to rest. It usually passes unnoticed but some slips and glaze slops containing clays show pronounced thixotropy if left unstirred for a few days. On first restirring one is tempted to add more water but a thorough stirring returns the suspension to its original fluidity and no extra water is required.

Thixotropy should not be confused with the maturation of a newly-made slip whereby the clay particles are split into smaller pieces by the penetration of water. This naturally produces a more viscous slip. See **Fluidity of slip and glaze suspensions**.

The slip or glaze suspension which exhibits noticeable thixotropy is often one in which a small amount of soluble alkalis has been released into the water. Magnesium oxide and carbonate, some soft alkaline frits and most wood ashes can be responsible for the phenomenon described above.

Large amounts of alkali in the slip usually destroy the property of thixotropy. Therefore in the preparation of casting slips a balance between fluidity and thixotropy must be achieved. Thixotropy is a valuable property in a casting slip because it enables the newly-formed cast to keep its form without distortion whilst it is still wet in the mould. Too high a thixotropy however would mean that the mould could not be drained after filling because the slip would 'set'.

The two popular deflocculants for casting slips are sodium carbonate and sodium silicate. They both give slips of high fluidity but sodium carbonate has little effect upon a clay's natural thixotropy whereas sodium silicate destroys it. The required thixotropy in the casting slip is therefore achieved by a balanced combination of the two deflocculants.

Flocculated glaze slops are usually thixotropic. The flocculation of the clay particles which causes a higher viscosity also increases the thixotropy. It is a valuable property because it enables a thick layer of glaze to remain steady on the newly-glazed pot prior to being set down for drying. The property is especially valuable on non-porous bisc. Over-flocculated glazes sometimes exhibit too much thixotropy. The fault shows as a glaze which will not smooth out immediately after dipping although it is still wet. The fault is usually evident in the unstirred glaze slop also. It can be corrected by a tiny amount of sodium silicate.

Thorpe, Sir Thomas E. (1845–1925). The British chemist noted for his Directorship of the Government Laboratories at which research into the solubility of lead in frits and glazes was carried out. This research led to predictions upon safety limits for frits and glazes dependent upon a base:acid ratio.

Thorpe stated that solubility does not depend upon the amount of lead in the glaze but upon its involvement in a lead silicate and that the other oxides help or hinder this involvement. This conception of lead solubility was revolutionary. From his observations he suggested a ratio for use when compounding frits and glazes. See **Thorpe ratio**.

Since the first use of the Thorpe ratio in the late 1890's, research has shown that small additions of different oxides can have marked effect upon the solubility and insolubility of the lead content of a glaze. Thorpe realized that this could be so but had not the time to establish the full facts which now invalidate the accuracy of his ratio. However, at the time of its inception, the ratio was an important step in attempts to control lead solubility. It remains an excellent starting point for an understanding of the subject. See **Low sol**.

Thorpe ratio. The alkali:acid ratio which gives an indication of a fired glaze's solubility without recourse to testing. See **Low sol**.

The ratio was originally one of percentage amounts of alkaline oxides (bases) and acidic oxides. All oxides were recalculated as if they were either lead oxide or silica and the result was expressed as

$$\frac{\text{base } \%}{\text{acid } \%}$$

giving a number for each glaze. Thorpe maintained that this number must be lower than 1·45 if the glaze was to be stable (insoluble). Theoretical lead bisilicate gives $\frac{65}{35} = 1·85$ and lead monosilicate $\frac{79}{21} = 3·76$.

In attempting to simplify the problem, Thorpe was unable to explore the widely differing functions of the amphoteric oxides and included them with the bases. He thereby erred on the side of caution in respect of alumina which is an important stabilizer. However the conception of the simple ratio was an important step in the 1890's when there were hundreds of cases of lead poisoning each year in the British pottery industry and the use of frits based upon this ratio was advocated.

John Mellor later correlated different European researches into lead solubility and reassessed the Thorpe ratio. Instead of percentages he employed molecular equivalents. Lead bisilicate ($PbO.2SiO_2$) therefore became $\frac{1}{2} = 0·5$ and lead monosilicate ($PbO.SiO_2$) became $\frac{1}{1} = 1$. It was suggested that 0·5 was the highest safe limit for this ratio, that is, the acidic oxides should more than double the alkaline oxides in a glaze's unity formula.

However, as Felix Singer pointed out, the place of the amphoteric oxides was still not resolved. Alumina (Al_2O_3) increases resistance to acid attack, that is, it decreases the lead solubility whilst boric oxide (B_2O_3) increases the lead solubility. Therefore there is no simple ratio possible and the Thorpe ratio remains only a starting point for consideration and solubility must be verified by practical tests.

Through firing. A glaze firing of raw ware. The firing has to go through a biscuit stage first and therefore the normal precautions of both biscuit firing and glaze firing are combined resulting in a longer firing.

All clays are suitable for through firing but one precaution is necessary. A clay which contains a large amount of volatile material, carbon and sulphur, requires a complete oxidation of these before the glaze melts. This is not possible with a soft glaze which starts to fuse at the same temperature as the volatiles burn out.

The body is thus sealed and the volatiles will cause blistering and bloating. The traditional lead-glazed wares were often slipped and glazed on one side only for this reason. Only at a few pottery centres were clays available which could be completely sealed and it was at these centres that the most decorative slipwares were made.

Stoneware is suited to through firing because it requires integration of body and glaze. The same precaution at burning out is necessary for although the glaze has not melted it has often hardened. Also the body reaches a state of vitrification at the end of the firing in which volatiles can cause bloating. See **Black core**.

Glazes for through firing can be applied to the bone-dry ware or to the leatherhard ware. The latter usually contain a large amount of clay and are called slip glazes. Salt glaze is a through fired glaze.

Any glaze can be applied to raw ware. Exceptions to the method of through firing lie with the body and the compatability of body and glaze. Some clays cannot withstand the shock of being glazed at bone-dry stage and crack with unequal expansion. Others blister as water soaks into the clay and air is expelled. The blisters often occur where slip has been applied or the clay has been previously wetted.

Adjustments to body and glaze may be necessary in order to get a good fit before firing. Glazes for dry ware should be low in clay content (less than 20%) whereas glazes for leatherhard ware need at least 50% clay. Good fit before firing does not guarantee good fit after firing.

Recently the term through firing has been extended to include the firing of wet plastic clay. Some coarse clays can be fired from wet state, even being placed into a raku kiln in this state. The coarse clay allows the passage of steam and the continuous passage of steam precludes the sealing of the pores which occurs at the surface of slowly dried clay.

Throwing. The action of making pots on a quickly rotating wheel using only the hands and for lubrication, water. It is one of the most exciting, expressive and impressive skills in pottery-making. The process involves centring a spinning lump of plastic clay upon the wheel-head. When the piece is running true, it is opened in the centre, an inside base is formed and the walls of the pot are lifted from the remainder of the clay by a series of upward movements involving the balanced pressure of fingers inside and outside the pot. The wheel-head usually rotates in an anti-clockwise direction which seems to suit most right-handed potters, but some potters, notably in the Far East, use a clockwise direction. The wheel-head is usually horizontal but ones at an angle have been used for throwing large bowls and upside down ones have been used for large pots where the clay's own weight helps to extend the clay.

Throwing probably developed from the use of a simple turntable, which was made to rotate freely, and the use of a wet pinching process with water for lubrication. The Egyptians are credited with the first use of the potter's wheel about 3000 B.C. The people of the eastern Mediterranean used the potter's wheel during their Bronze Age, but elsewhere in the world, the use of the potter's wheel seems to have been an Iron Age innovation at the same time as the use of wheeled carts.

Throwing is a faster method of making pots than any other hand method. It contains all the elements of a great skill: the potter is in direct contact with his material. This reliance on personal skill is its attraction for the individual potter today but industry has almost dispensed with it and instead has turned the process sideways into a mechanized jigger-jolley system with complete loss of individual expression.

Throwing is important therefore, not because it is a fast method of production but because it is a means of expression. Although each pot can be sufficiently like the last to be called a repeat item, each one is a restatement of an idea and is therefore different. The opportunity for making a gradual improvement in the idea sets throwing above processes which use moulds. Pots made with moulds are limited by the mould and are often conceived in flat profile. Thrown pots are conceived in their three-dimensional existence and are capable of continual development. The best thrown work has a fluidity that speaks of the process of rhythmic manipulation of spinning clay. Photographs of Michael Casson and David Leach.

THROWING CLAY. Throwing seems to demand of the clay a higher standard of workability, based primarily on plasticity, than does any other forming method. The hand-building processes, which require a well-behaved clay, seem to be capable of more flexibility of technique to cope with peculiarities.

Throwing clay must be plastic—capable of being formed quickly. It must be thixotropic—capable of holding the new form when pressure is released. It must be strong—capable of being pulled and worked without breaking. It must also have friction against the hands so that it can be gripped and lifted. This property is often called 'bite' to differentiate it from the general drag of a short clay which inhibits its sliding through the hands. There is a balance here of two opposing properties which is equated with the potter's skill.

The property of bite is further discussed under **Clay preparation, control of grain size**. Here is mentioned the fact that a highly plastic clay which is too slippery can often be improved in workability by the addition of a sharp sand or grog. The addition adds bite for throwing and also a resistance to shear which helps the clay to stand up on the wheel.

Within these strict demands there is still room for the personal preference of the potter. Some potters prefer the soapy feel of a clay with little perceptible bite, whilst others like a strong texture to run through the fingers. Some like the dense heaviness of a de-aired clay, whilst others like the softer texture of hand-prepared clay.

Tiger skin. A variety of salt glaze as shown here or any other glaze which shows this texturing. It is caused by close crawling or beading which has been sealed in this case by subsequent salt glazing.

The effect is sometimes called leopard skin but the name tiger skin arose in the 18th century when all the leopard family were included as tigers.

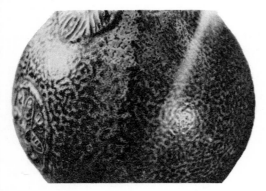

Tin ash. A mixture of tin oxide and lead oxide. It is a brown colour but gives white opacity to glazes when the lead oxide fluxes the silicates and the tin oxide remains as suspended particles.

Tin ash was the glaze constituent for the Hispano-Moresque wares and later tin-glazed wares until the 20th century. Lead and tin ores or their metals were roasted together to produce the oxides. There is obvious danger from lead fumes which prohibits the process today.

In consideration of early glaze recipes which contain tin ash one should realize that the proportions of the oxides vary from 50:50 to 85:15, lead oxide:tin oxide.

Tin-glaze. Tin-enamel. See **Maiolica** and **Delft**.

Tin lustre. An iridescent lustre on the surface of a glaze produced by complete reduction of tin oxide.

Tin oxide in glazes normally produces a white opacity which is sullied by reduction. However if a heavy, but quick, reduction is effected, as it can be by the raku method, an iridescence is produced on the surface whilst maintaining the white glaze underneath.

The following raku glaze is effective on a pink body which blushes pleasantly through the glaze and contrasts with it by reducing to black where unglazed:

lead monosilicate	78
ball clay	16
tin oxide	6

Tin oxide. White tin oxide. Tin dioxide. Stannic oxide.

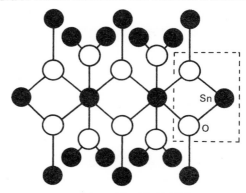

SnO_2. The normal or fully-oxidized state of the metal tin. It is purchased as a white powder which is very light in weight. Amounts up to a maximum of 15% give increasing opacity and whiteness as the oxide is suspended in a glaze. It has been used as a glaze opacifier for at least 600 years. The photograph shows a contemporary Spanish piece.

Tin is a metal with a low melting point. It occurs as cassiterite or tin stone, which is the crude ore form of the dioxide. The ore is roasted to oxidize the impurities and is then reduced with carbon to extract the metal. The ore contains arsenic, bismuth, copper, iron and zinc, some of them as sulphides. The tin metal has the lowest melting point and can therefore be extracted by a controlled heat of 232°C (450°F). Tin was one of the earliest metals to be smelted and along with copper gave the alloy bronze. Tin stone and tin pyrites are widely found in the world, but the largest economical deposits are in south-east Asia, west Africa and South America.

There are two types of tin oxide. They are the white dioxide (SnO_2) and the black monoxide (SnO): stannic and stannous oxides. Both are stable at room temperatures. The white can be reduced to the black at temperatures above 200°C (392°F). The black is easily reoxidized at temperatures above 700°C (1292°F). Both oxides give opacity to glazes. Both oxides are practically inert below 1150°C (2102°F) being finely divided particles in suspension in the glaze and giving opacity by having a refractive index different from the surrounding glass. Both oxides melt at approximately 1150°C (2102°F) when they begin to dissolve in the glaze. The white tin oxide acts as an acid or anti-flux thereby stiffening the melt and dissolving slowly. The black tin oxide acts as a flux and is quicker to dissolve in the glaze.

The black tin oxide gives unpleasant grey cloudiness to a glaze. Opacity is practically lost in high temperature reduction and sometimes reoxidized black tin oxide gives an unpleasant light grey scum on cooling. It is obvious that to use tin oxide in reduction firings is a very expensive way of producing an unpleasant effect. It is included here for completeness because it may be discovered accidentally.

The white tin oxide gives a pleasing creamy white opacity. The amount required varies according to the glaze composition and the temperature. The effect of some is lost at the higher temperatures. Between 5% and 10% is usually sufficient to turn an otherwise transparent glaze into an opaque one. Some glazes might require as much as 15% but this would be a limit and amounts of tin oxide over 8% have a noticeable anti-fluxing effect upon a glaze. Tin oxide increases the glaze's viscosity resulting in pinholing and, as an extreme, in crawling and mattness.

Tin oxide is still the most popular white opacifier in spite of its high price. It holds this place because it gives a more pleasant opacity than its cheaper rivals. It

is also more dependable because it always gives a white opacity and clean colours when stained. A possible drawback is its power of picking up pink flashes if chromium oxide is present in other glazes in the same kiln. See **Chromium oxide** (chrome-tin pink).

Rival opacifiers which are used because of their relative cheapness give excellent whiteness and opacity but under controlled circumstances. Zirconia and zirconium silicate are popular. The white can be whiter than tin oxide but the quality is glassy. Calcium phosphate sometimes turns grey and even brown. Cerium oxide is limited to low temperatures; similarly antimony oxide, which also dissolves in some glazes and gives yellows with lead silicates. Titanium dioxide picks up colour from the body and accentuates colour from any iron present giving creams.

The following glaze for 1050°C (2102°F) uses tin oxide to give a soft creamy white:

cornish stone	12
china clay	10
lead bisilicate	70
tin oxide	8

Tincal. Himalayan borax. See **Borax**.

Tired clay. Clay that has lost its strength by being overworked. The strength of a clay is related to, but is not the same as, its plasticity. The two factors are part of a clay's workability. See **Workability**.

Plastic clay has strength even though it is soft. It can support its own weight in extended circumstances like wide bowls and tall pots. Clay can also be pushed and pulled into new shapes without breaking. This displays a combination of plasticity, strength and flexibility as described under Workability.

Plasticity is a measure of the clay's capacity to allow its particles to slide past one another yet keep in contact. The particles are held together partially by the suction that is encouraged by the water between them. It is rather like a pile of wet playing cards which will slide across one another yet stick together. If air enters between the particles, then the clay is more easily ruptured. A tired clay is like this. The plasticity potential is still the same. The particles will slide past one another as before but they can also be separated, and with less force.

Clay becomes tired when it has been overworked. Throwing on the wheel tires the clay as well as the potter. Thrown clay, rekneaded, is not as workable if used immediately. Clay mixed in a dough mixer has been knocked about so much that it is tired. Some pugmills also create this state although most of them work against tiredness.

The cure for tiredness is a rest. Sometimes a short rest of a day or two is sufficient but usually a longer rest called ageing and souring is needed. Rested clays regain their strength and previously thrown clays often seem to have improved in plasticity. Clays which have been constituted from powder by the dough mixing method will certainly be improved by throwing and resting.

There is no rule about how long a clay should rest except the longer the better. A couple of months is the usual time. It should be resting, of course, in its plastic state and preferably with slightly more moisture content than is eventually envisaged. It is always easier to slightly dewater a clay by kneading than to increase the moisture content. Also during the resting period there is hope that the clay will improve in plasticity by sub-division of particles. This will require extra water to fill the new spaces. Wrapping the clay in close-fitting polythene sheets is ideal for the resting.

The rest which improves the strength of the clay consolidates the particles. De-airing the clay by the use of a vacuum pugmill is said to be equivalent to two months rest. However, what de-airing does not do is to encourage the bacteriological growth. This takes time and produces a colloidal gel between the clay particles. This gel increases plasticity. It is called souring and is descriptive of the smell which such clays have. See also **Preparation of clay**.

Titanates. Compounds involving titania, e.g. lead titanate ($PbO.TiO_2$), zinc titanate ($ZnO.TiO_2$), calcium titanate ($CaO.TiO_2$) also called perowskite, ferrous titanate ($FeO.TiO_2$) also called ilmenite.

Titania. Titanium dioxide. White titanium oxide. TiO_2. An opacifying oxide which creates crystals within the glaze. In amounts between 5% and 10% of a glaze the titania gives a pleasant opacity with crystalline soft matt surface. The crystals are very small and cannot be seen separately. Titania glazes have the power to transmute colour from the body beneath. The colour is incorporated with the crystals and a small amount is enlivened by the light reflected through the crystals.

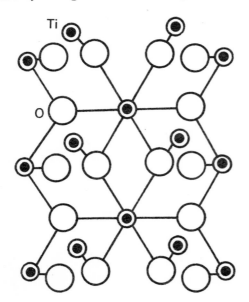

The name titania is used for the chemical oxide which enters the fusion of the glaze. The name titanium dioxide is used for the powdered material which is part of the glaze batch and results in titania in the molten glaze.

Titania is widely distributed in nature in small and large pockets of ores and titanite sands. It also occurs within the structure of many silicates in partial replacement of silica. It accounts for over 1% of the earth's crust. The metal titanium is exceedingly difficult to isolate because it quickly combines with other elements. For example, titania can be reduced to a monoxide but no further and it quickly regains its full complement of oxides upon cooling. The metal titanium is used in alloys. It is extracted from the oxide ores anatase, rutile and brookite, and from the titaniferous iron ore, ilmenite. The white titanium dioxide is used as a paint pigment and in ceramics.

Titania readily disperses in glazes during fusion but its nuclei are sources of recrystallization as titanates during cooling. Its action is as an acid. It hardens the glaze making it more refractory and has a slight stiffening effect on low-temperature glazes. Small amounts, that is, below 1%, can be completely dissolved. From 1% upwards the recrystallization gives opacity, first as a bluish-white flush, then from approximately 5% a complete opacity. At this amount there is also a matting of the surface. Although 10 to 15% is a usual maximum as much as 25% can be absorbed by some lead glazes. See also **Crystalline glazes**.

Titania which is dissolved in a glaze gives a stabilizing effect to the glass structure. It is valuable in lead frits where it lessens the solubility of the lead. The amount is only small, perhaps only 0.1% of the final glaze, but it is sufficient to intensify and stabilize a colour also. Titania acts in three ways on colours. In small amounts it intensifies the colour making it brighter, e.g. iron oxide can be induced to give bright yellows and oranges. Moderate amounts of titania (2% to 6%) break up the colouring effect by a mottle. Larger amounts tend to subdue colours but give interesting sparkles to the surface.

Glazes containing titania with some rutile are subject to the phenomenon of phototrophy. This is the change of colour by the action of light. The amount is only slight. See **Phototrophy**. These glazes are also subject to thermotrophy which is the change of colour by the action of heat. Glazes which are white at room temperature are a yellow colour at temperatures above 150°C (302°F). The colour difference is quite noticeable and can be startling if the kiln is opened when hot. It can also be a disconcerting phenomenon on ovenware.

Titanite. Sphene. Calcium silicon titanate. $CaO.SiO_2.TiO_2$. Calcium titanium silicate. $OCaTi(SiO_4)$. A crystalline mineral which separates from glazes and produces crystalline effects including matt surfaces.

Toft dishes. Large slipware dishes made during the late 17th and early 18th centuries in Staffordshire. They were made by some 16 different potters of whom Thomas Toft was the outstanding master and over 30 of his dishes are known.

These dishes are deep plates 15 inches to 22 inches across and are richly decorated with figures and animals, scenes and pseudo portraits. Much of the work is heraldic and symbolically royalist. The wide rim gives opportunity for the potter to produce a decorative border. Thomas Toft was especially good at producing a closely criss-crossed yet free border which is called a Toft border.

The dishes were first thrown and turned. Then a layer of white slip was used to cover the red clay. Onto this the outlines were trailed in dark slip and the filling-in done with buff slip. Finally, white was piped onto the outlines as a series of dots, giving a richness and movement to the dark line. The glaze was galena dusted onto the wet slip through a coarse cloth bag. The plates were fired on edge resting on the rim, which often shows signs of warping. The glaze also has run down in the firing dragging some of the colour from the dark lines which further enhances their richness.

Top hat kiln. An intermittent kiln for which the ware is set on a refractory base and the open-based kiln is lowered over the top. The kiln is fired by electricity through overhead cables. The advantages of a top hat kiln are economy of use on alternate bases which can be more easily set in the round.

Tourmaline. A variable mineral associated with quartz and granites. It is often present in cornish stones. Tourmaline is a crystalline borosilicate of aluminium with magnesium, sodium and sufficient traces of iron to render most crystals black.

Transfer decoration. An indirect method of applying repeat on-glaze and underglaze decorations. The motif is printed in ceramic colours onto paper or flexible plastic material and transferred from this to the pottery surface. See also **Liverpool**.

Transmutation. The act of changing a glaze's colour. Most potters are aware of how one pot with a glaze containing chromium oxide can colour all the tin-glazed pots in the kiln with pink. Also to a lesser extent copper oxide will spread from one pot onto adjacent pots producing greenish flashes or spots, especially with lead glazes. These are usually unintentional transmutations but there are two intentional transmutations of colour in what are called transmutation glazes and transmutation lustres.

TRANSMUTATION GLAZE. A glaze which is opaque but which is capable of picking up the colour from the body or slip beneath it and pulling this colour into the glaze. In this way a decoration on the body becomes a decoration in the glaze. The colouring oxides are drawn into the glaze by the presence of 5% to 15% of titanium dioxide. Iron, manganese, copper and cobalt oxides all transmute effectively.

Three example recipes are given for different temperatures:
For 1100°C (2012°F):

feldspar	10
flint	5
lead bisilicate	50
whiting	10
zinc oxide	15
titanium dioxide	10

For 1200°C (2192°F):

cornish stone	40
ball clay	10
lead bisilicate	20
whiting	10
zinc oxide	10
titanium dioxide	10

For 1250°C (2282°F):

feldspar	50
china clay	15
flint	10
whiting	20
titanium dioxide	5

TRANSMUTATION LUSTRE. A lustred surface created on a glaze by transferring metal from an applied paste.

The paste is applied to the already-fired surface and given a special firing at a low temperature in a reduction atmosphere. After firing, the coating is cleaned away to reveal the lustre which has been absorbed by the glaze surface.

Both lead and lead-free glazes will take a transmutation lustre. The important point is that whilst its structure must be activated during the extra firing in order to absorb the extra lustre, the glaze must not soften or else its surface will be spoilt by the paste. Tin opacified glazes of the 1000°C to 1050°C range (1832°F to 1922°F) are usual. A small percentage of titanium dioxide in the glaze assists the capture of the metal.

The composition of the paste depends upon the quality of the lustre to be produced. For solid all-over lustres, a calcined clay with 5% to 30% copper oxide is mixed to a paste with an adhesive. It is brushed onto the glaze in a thick layer. The calcined clay is usually china clay but any non-vitrified clay will do providing it is fine enough to make a paste, is free from fusible matter and has previously been fired a couple of hundred degrees above the temperature at which it is now to be used. For this reason it is called a refractory coating but the term refractory is only relative. The amount of copper oxide varies according to the colouring required and the take-up capacity of the glaze.

Where lustre is to be painted onto the glaze surface in decorative brush strokes, a thinner slop is prepared which often contains a raw clay. The Hispano-Moresque lustres of the 14th century were of this type, hence the alternative name of Arabian lustre. An ochreous clay was often used, deflocculated slightly with gum arabic, which eased the painting and assisted adhesion and reduction. The carbonates and other volatiles of the raw clay also assisted intimate reduction and the iron oxide helped to hold the effects of the reduction thus sealing it at the surface. A silver salt was added with the copper compound to produce the particularly fine lustre often called gold lustre though no gold was ever used.

The plate illustrated is by Alan Caiger Smith who uses this traditional method of painting with an ochre slip containing copper and silver sulphides.

The firing must be to a temperature lower than the softening point of the glaze, but high enough to effect reduction of the copper compounds and the active capture of the copper by the glaze surface. In practice

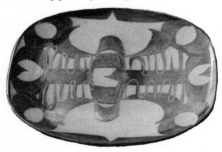

this limits the firing to between 600°C and 700°C (1112°F and 1292°F). Reduction is effected at the top temperature or during the cooling, the intensity being regulated according to the type of lustre required: rouge flambé, ruby lustre or metallic. The effects are judged by the fish-outs.

The refractory coating is washed or rubbed off after the firing. Dry rubbing of thin coatings burnishes the surface which improves the lustre.

Transparent glaze. A glaze in which all the oxides have been involved in the melt and formed irregular chains, there being no crystallization or particles to obstruct the passage of light. Being balanced in flux and glass-former, it is fully fused, flows evenly and has a smooth shiny surface. The transparent glaze recipe is usually simple to understand, there being a main flux like lead oxide or calcia with alumino-silicates like clay and feldspar.

If a transparent glaze is stained by oxides which act as fluxes it will remain transparent. Additions of amphoteric and acidic oxides tend to give opacity. See **Periodic table**.

A transparent glaze recipe is often used as the basis for a range of glazes. Additions are made of tin oxide, colouring oxides etc. Adjustments to simple recipes like the following are straightforward because each material is acting in its most obvious way.

For raku 1000°C (1832°F):

china clay	5
flint	5
lead bisilicate	90

For earthenware 1100°C (2012°F):

feldspar	10
china clay	10
flint	10
lead bisilicate	65
whiting	5

For 1200°C (2192°F):

potash feldspar	20
china clay	10
flint	15
lead bisilicate	40
whiting	15

For stoneware 1250°C (2282°F):

potash feldspar	50
china clay	15
flint	15
whiting	20

For porcelain 1280°C (2336°F):

potash feldspar	25
china clay	25
flint	25
whiting	25

Trial rings. See **Buller's rings**.

Tridymite. Silica. SiO_2. One of the primary phases of silica. It exists in disordered cristobalite where its unique nine sub-divisions, called forms, 'invert' at different temperatures, thereby smoothing the otherwise sudden size change of pure cristobalite.

Tridymite is introduced into pottery bodies along with cristobalite to produce craze-resistant wares which are also resistant to thermal shock. It is also used in industrial silica refractories. See **Silica conversion** and **Silica inversions**.

Trioxide. An oxide involving three atoms of oxygen in each molecule. The other element may be represented by one or two atoms. In the latter case the oxide would also be known as a sesquioxide. For example SO_3 and Al_2O_3. See **Sesquioxide** and **Oxide**.

Trolley kiln. Trolley hearth kiln. An intermittent kiln for which the ware is stacked on a trolley or bogey which runs on rails into the kiln. The advantages are the ease with which setting and drawing can be done around the trolley; and in the use of two or more trolleys so that the kiln structure can be kept in more economical use. Trolley kilns are usually fired by gas or electricity and are between 10 and 100 cubic feet capacity.

Tunnel kiln. See **Continuous kiln**.

Turning. Trimming. Skimming. Shaving. Removing unwanted clay to achieve a particular form, thin a pot wall or create a foot rim, etc. It is usually done on thrown ware and at the leatherhard stage. The unwanted clay is removed in a series of long shavings. The tools are wire loops and sharp blades of metal, wood and plastic.

The throwing wheel is often used for turning and the pot is centred and stuck to the wheel-head by wetting and suction assisted if necessary by pieces of clay. Inverted narrow-necked pots are held in a chuck or chum. Simple cylindrical and cup forms are often turned on a horizontal spindle (lathe) by sealing the rim to a mandrel.

The tools need to be kept sharp. A file, stone, emery and glass paper are used. Clay is a very abrasive material and quickly blunts the tools. Some short clays are difficult to turn and tend to crumble rather than allow themselves to be cleanly cut. They are easier to turn if the wheel is rotated for turning in the opposite way to that used for throwing.

TURNING TOOLS. Wire loops and sharp stiff blades capable of cutting thin slices of leatherhard clay. The blade must be stiff enough to cut the shaving of clay without flexing itself. The wire loop must be strong enough to push its way through the clay.

Mild steel is the most popular material for blade tools. Stainless steel is also used but does not take as keen an edge and is thus less suitable for fine clays like porcelain, fine stoneware and fine earthenware. Spring steel, soft mild steel and spring wire can be used for loop tools which are useful for turning soft and coarse clays. Cheap alloy spoons, sharpened by filing the back side towards the edge, are useful for the insides of bowls, etc. A file or a rubbing stone is used to sharpen metal tools.

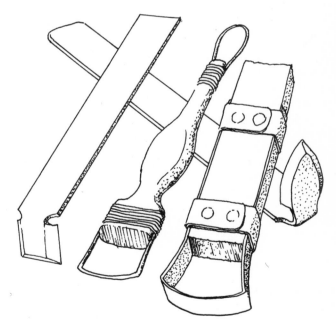

Wooden tools are made from hard dry bamboo or boxwood. They are sharpened with a plane, knife and glass-paper. Similarly, hard plastic sheeting can be sawn to shape and sharpened with glass-paper. These tools are used for the softer clays.

For turning on a horizontal lathe, straight chisel-type metal tools are used. They are sometimes cut to a particular shape for the repetition work of turning foot rims or decorative rings.

Twaddell. Twaddle. °TW. Degrees Twaddell. Units

used to measure the specific gravities of solutions and suspensions. This scale provides an expansion of normal SG numbers which for potter's solutions and suspensions would fall between 1 and 2 and therefore always involve either fractions or decimals. The portion in excess of 1 is multiplied by 200. This has the effect of making the specific gravity of water 0°TW and potters' suspensions in the range up to 200°TW. 200°TW would be equivalent to a slip of 40 oz pt UK or 33 oz pt US. The scale is named after William Twaddell who made the first hydrometer (Twaddell shot) with this scale.

The formulae concerned are:

$$\text{Degrees Twaddell} = 200 \times (\text{SG} - 1)$$

$$\text{Specific Gravity} = 1 + \frac{°\text{TW}}{200}$$

$$\text{Weight of one UK pt in oz} = \left(1 + \frac{°\text{TW}}{200}\right) \times 20$$

$$°\text{TW} = 200 \times \left(\frac{\text{oz pt UK}}{20} - 1\right)$$

$$°\text{TW} = 200 \times \left(\frac{\text{oz pt US}}{16 \cdot 7} - 1\right)$$

See also **Formula, density**.

Tyg. A 16th- to 19th-century drinking mug, often with more than one handle and in extreme cases as many as twelve. Tygs were usually made in a dark-coloured clay, were sometimes decorated with sprigs and glazed with an iron-stained lead glaze.

Tz'u-chou. A collection of stoneware kilns in northern China famous for decorated pottery, especially bottles and jars. Its best production was during the 7th to 12th centuries (T'ang and Sung dynasties). The name is used quite generally for all Chinese wares of the Tz'u-chou type whether they are from these kilns or not.

U

Ulexite. $NaCaB_5O_9.8H_2O$ or $Na_2O.2CaO.5B_2O_3.16H_2O$. A mineral containing boric oxide, soda and calcia. It occurs with borax and colemanite in California and with gypsum in Chile. It is also called boronatrocalcite and natroborocalcite, and is in hydrated form. It is used as a source of flux and glass-former in empirical frits.

Underclay. Glum. Hustle. Fireclay from the seam directly under the coal seam. It is sometimes mined with the coal.

Underclay is often softer than other fireclays and for pottery purposes requires less weathering to bring to plastic state. When blunged, sieved and settled, an underclay often makes a good ovenware body. See also **Fireclay**.

Underfired. Fired at a temperature lower than the intended or with insufficient heat-work and showing defects because of this. The defects are:

1. The biscuit is too porous and takes too much glaze from dipping. See **Porosity**.

2. Bisc has no chance to mature in the softer glaze firing and the final ware will probably craze. See **Crazing**.

3. Where body and glaze mature together there is insufficient integration to give full strength to the ware. The glaze may also craze or shell. See **Body-glaze layer**.

4. Underfired glazes are often dull and lifeless with a 'dry' surface which is lighter in colour than anticipated. Transparent and shiny glazes tend to craze because they have not integrated with the body. See also **Fosted**.

Underglaze. U/G. Ceramic colours applied usually on a biscuit and covered with a transparent glaze.

The quality of underglaze is the intensity of colour established by the thickness of the glaze. Its advantage over onglaze decoration is its permanence, it being as permanent as the covering glaze.

Underglaze colours are modified oxides which gain their full colour with the 'wetting' action of the covering glaze. They usually contain a small amount of glaze, referred to as flux, which binds them to the body and integrates them with the glaze above. The glaze must not absorb too much colour or blur the outline. Raw lead glazes are not suitable but fritted lead and other low sol glazes are. Glazes with a high proportion of boric oxide also tend to blur the decoration.

The colours are prepared in different ways according

to the strength and stability of the colouring oxide. The process involves the fusion of the oxides which establish the colour and then possibly calcination of all the ingredients followed by grinding. The colours are mixed with an oil or varnish for application to biscuit or with a gum to raw ware. They are applied by brush, transfer, spray etc. Biscuit ware is given a low firing in the region of 700°C to 800°C (1292°F to 1472°F) to harden on the colour and burn out the oil.

Underglaze colours are prepared to withstand specified temperatures. They are stable colours and similar to prepared glaze and slip stains etc, and therefore many can be used for inglaze decoration, maiolica painting and glaze staining.

Unity formula. See **Formula, unity**.

Unomi. A Japanese teabowl. Although playing little part as a ceremonial object in the western world, the unomi still provides the opportunity to make a single statement through a simple functional form. The examples are by Kenneth Jones, David Leach and Kenneth Quick.

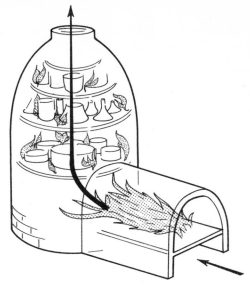

This type of statement is linked with the attitudes of the whole tea ceremony and contemplative Buddhism. See **Zen**. The ceramic message in a teabowl can be traced back to 10th-century China. See **Tenmoku, origin**. The appreciation of the unomi in stoneware and raku, as we now understand it in the west, is traceable to the perception of Rikiu Sen, the 16th-century Japanese tea master.

Up-draught kiln. A kiln in which the hot gases pass upwards through the ware. It is the simplest form of kiln and does not require a chimney. There is sufficient draw in the chamber itself to pull in air at the firemouth, through the fire, combustion space and into the chamber from whence the exit is through holes in the cover. By the late 18th century the up-draught kiln had been perfected as the Stoke bottleneck making possible a temperature of 1300°C (2372°F).

Uranium oxide. U_3O_8. A colouring oxide which gives yellows, oranges and reds under specific conditions. It is often used to modify other colours in the yellow and green range.

The oxide is purchased as a spent oxide which has only a low radio-activity. Amounts up to 15% are used. A red colour is possible in lead silicate glazes which are low in alumina, and free from boric oxide. The effect is similar to chrome red but withstands 1050°C (1922°F). Yellow is a more usual colour in glazes which are oxidized. Reduction sullies the colour. Green colours are prepared by the use of the trioxide:

$$UO_2 + UO_3 = U_2O_5 + UO_3 = U_3O_8$$

The result is an amphoteric oxide which sometimes dissolves in the glaze as in the case of lead oxide glazes and sometimes remains suspended as opacity.

V

Vacuumed clay. Clay which has been subjected to a vacuum. In this state, the air bubbles in the clay explode and are removed. The clay particles are brought into closer contact resulting in an increase in strength. See **De-airing**.

Valency. Valence. The theoretical combining power of an atom. The valency of hydrogen is 1. The valency of oxygen is 2. Two hydrogen atoms are therefore required to combine with one oxygen atom. In symbols this is written as H_2O and the compound is water.

The valency of barium is 2. It therefore combines on equal terms with oxygen to produce barium oxide (BaO). The valency of aluminium is 3. In order to write

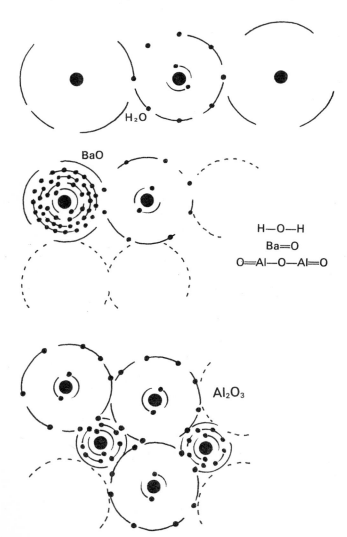

$$H—O—H$$
$$Ba=O$$
$$O=Al—O—Al=O$$

the symbol for alumina (aluminium oxide), it is necessary to think in terms of two atoms of aluminium with a total valency of 6. To combine with this valency of 6, three oxygen atoms, each of valency 2, are required. The chemical symbol for alumina is therefore written Al_2O_3 which keeps the theoretical atoms in whole numbers. The valency bond number is 6 which is the lowest common multiple of 2 and 3.

A list of the elements found in pottery materials with their valencies is given in the **Tables** in this book.

An atom's valency depends upon the number of electrons in the outer layer of the atom. These electrons are available for transferring or sharing with other atoms to form bonds. Also the size of the atom determines how many other atoms of a different size can be packed around it in the creation of bonds. The potential of an atom in this respect is called its co-ordination number. It is not necessary for the potter to understand all the aspects of atomic theory which affect valency. It is sufficient if he appreciates their existence and can comprehend the common oxides within the more complex substances which are his raw materials. See also **Atom, Formula, structural** and **Lattice structure**.

Vanadium oxide. Vanadium pentoxide. V_2O_5. Vanadium trioxide V_2O_3. A rare metal oxide which gives a weak yellow colour in ceramic fusions. It has stronger staining power when prepared as a stain with tin oxide, zirconia or zircon.

Vanadium oxide occurs as an ore in the United States and South Africa. Vanadium metal is used in steels to improve shock resistance.

Vanadium pentoxide (V_2O_5) is acidic but vanadium trioxide (V_2O_3) can exist which is alkaline. The stable state is the pentoxide which can be used as a yellow glaze colourant in amounts up to 10%. The glaze needs to be well fused and glassy before the vanadium oxide is satisfactorily absorbed. Lead glazes are ideal but the colour is never strong and is not as rich as the yellow obtainable from antimony oxide in a lead glaze. The advantage of vanadium oxide is that it can be used at higher temperatures than antimony oxide.

Vanadium stains. Two prepared stains are available: yellow and blue. They are both recent developments which make use of vanadium trioxide as a flux at high temperatures. In the yellow stain the vanadium oxide is combined with tin oxide or zirconia. The yellow is a stronger stain than vanadium oxide alone and is much easier to use.

In the blue stain the vanadium oxide is combined with zircon (zirconium silicate). Like the yellow, this is a stable colour for all temperatures but these stains do tend to be refractory and not easy to dissolve. They are often fritted with soft glasses to render them more usable though this weakens the colouring power slightly.

Vaporization. With the action of heat some body and glaze constituents change from solid or liquid (melted) state to gaseous state. If they then come into contact with suitable compounds some liquify again and form new compounds. Thus chromium oxide, copper oxide and sometimes cobalt oxide are found to have transferred themselves to new surfaces. Also lead oxide, soda and boric oxide will be seen to transfer themselves to unglazed surfaces like kiln furniture where they flux the silicates and produce a thin glaze.

Some substances remain as vapours and escape from the kiln. See **Volatiles** and **Fumes**.

VAPORIZATION OF LEAD. Raw lead glazes tend to vaporize above 1000°C (1832°F) with a loss of as much as 10% of the lead oxide content. White lead is especially prone to vaporization.

Saggars were once common for lead glazed wares. The insides of these became flashed with the lead. New saggars were said to suck the glaze and were often given a wash of lead glaze inside to counteract this. It is possible to make use of this in reverse and to flash a gloss onto a ware. This is useful with delicate modelling where a glaze of any thickness would tend to obliterate the detail. It is not necessary to seal the saggar lid and it may be preferable not to do so if white lead is used. Lead in frits does not vaporize easily which is fortunate for most uses but lead monosilicate can be made to flash modelling in close proximity to the saggar wall. The lead oxide eats into the saggar to produce a glaze which runs down and collects in the bottom of the saggar. The saggar must therefore be a good one. The modelling must be protected from this pool of glass on very sharp stilts or spurs supported on fireclay arching.

Vapour glazing. Lead oxide, soda and boric oxide can be used for vapour glazing because they will volatilize from a melt and reliquify upon suitable surfaces. See **Vaporization of lead**. Soda and boric oxide are used in salt glazing. See **Salt glaze**.

Vehicle. Any medium used to assist in applying colour or glaze. The vehicle has no part in the fired formula but burns out in the firing.

Vellum matt. See **Satin matt**.

Vent. A small circular or square sectional opening through the kiln wall or door by which the kiln chamber is ventilated. It is usual to have two vents, one placed low down and the other high up, in order to achieve a track of air into and out of the chamber. When necessary, a vent is closed by a bung, stopper or flap. The usual spy-hole serves as a vent in many small kilns.

Vents are opened and closed as part of the adjustment of kiln atmosphere to oxidation and reduction.

Viscosity. The stiffness of a liquid created by the friction amongst its particles and molecules. The term viscosity can be applied to clay slips and glaze slops, and also to molten glazes. Viscous slips are thick and pour with difficulty. Viscous glazes do not move, or move very little, in the firing. The reciprocal of viscosity is fluidity.

It is normal ceramic practice to consider molten glazes in terms of viscosity. A runny glaze will have a low viscosity. A stiff glaze will have a high viscosity. The unit of measurement for viscosity is the poise. A runny glaze of low viscosity might have a rating in the order of 1000 poise. A very stiff glaze of high viscosity would have a rating in the order of 100,000 poise.

Slips, slops and other liquid suspensions are usually considered in terms of fluidity. A runny suspension will have a high fluidity. Glazes and suspensions are dealt with here in consideration of viscosity. They are separately dealt with in consideration of their fluidity under the heading of **Fluidity**.

VISCOSITY OF CLAY AND GLAZE SUSPENSIONS. The viscosity of a slip is a measure of its internal friction. In stirring a slip or other suspension one moves a part of the whole. This part attempts to drag with it the adjacent parts. If the slip is very fluid there is minimal friction and the adjacent parts are said to have a high velocity difference. On the other hand if the slip is very viscous there is a high degree of friction and the velocity difference is kept low. The measurement of the forces required to overcome different frictions and achieve a standard velocity difference between adjacent parts gives values by which different viscosities can be compared.

It is normal practice to talk of suspensions in terms of fluidity. The values of viscosity are translated into values of fluidity by the following formula:

$$\frac{1}{\text{viscosity (poise)}} = \text{fluidity (rhe)}$$

Therefore a viscous slip with a high viscosity value of 500 poise becomes a slip of low fluidity with a value of 0·002 rhe. A runny slip of low viscosity with a value of 10 poise becomes a slip of high fluidity with a value of 0·1 rhe.

The subject is treated more fully under **Fluidity**.

VISCOSITY OF MOLTEN GLAZES. The viscosity of a glaze is measured when the glaze is maturing. It is at this point that it is important to know how it behaves. It is necessary to have movement in a glaze in order that it can mature since maturation is the smoothing out of the glaze after the bubblings of the melting reactions. The glaze must therefore be liquid at this stage but it may be a stiff liquid (of high viscosity) or it may be a very runny liquid (of low viscosity). In order to be a glaze it must, however, have this liquid phase. If there is no liquid phase it cannot be considered a glaze. It would then be like a slip or a body which, however vitreous (glassy), remains a solid and retains its form. Glazes have no form of their own but take the form of the object they cover. They cannot exist alone.

If the glaze is on a horizontal surface when it matures, it must smooth out by finding its own level. This is rather like a lot of lumps of ice which, when they melt to water, run together to form a flat-surfaced pool. Glazes on tiles or contained on shallow plates can be less viscous than other glazes. They are not able to run away, but equally it is more difficult for them to flow together. There are two factors involved: one is gravity which encourages the layer to be flat surfaced and the other is surface tension which encourages a smooth surface around the bulk of the layer. See **Surface tension**.

A glaze on a vertical surface needs to be more viscous than a glaze on a horizontal surface, otherwise it will run down and off the surface under the pull of gravity. Fortunately the more viscous glaze will still be able to mature and smooth out because the amount of actual movement involved will probably exceed that obtained on a horizontal surface. The ideal glaze for the vertical surface has therefore a higher viscosity than the one for a horizontal surface. This difference is encountered when one tries to use the same glaze on horizontal surfaces like plates and vertical surfaces like coffee pots. It presents a problem familiar to makers of tableware which can only be solved ideally by having different glazes for the different pieces.

The theory of glaze viscosity is explained thus: when part of a liquid moves, as for example when the outer layer of a molten glaze moves downwards with the pull of gravity, it can do so only by breaking its contact with the next adjoining layer within the glaze. The breaking of this grip is called shear. If friction is very high between adjacent molecules then it is impossible for the stress created by gravity to shear the layers. Movement cannot then take place. A glaze like this would be considered to be of extremely high viscosity. On the other hand if there is very little friction it is possible for the outer layer to slide downwards and to drag with it the next layer, and the next, etc. The innermost layer is unable to slide because it is held by the friction of the solid body. It is usual to consider the action as one of layers shearing, with each layer moving a similar amount to the next. The outer one therefore moves the furthest. This action is diagrammatized in fig. 1.

A glaze which is applied thickly can therefore move further than the same glaze applied thinly but the vis-

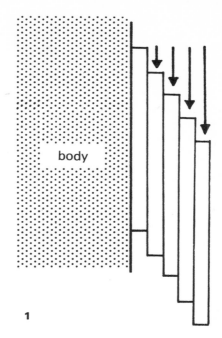

1

cosity of the glaze remains the same. Thus on a vertical surface there are three factors involved in the maturation and production of a smooth surface: gravity pulling against viscosity giving a speed of movement, surface tension, and glaze thickness influencing the amount of movement.

The amount of movement can be seen in many glazes as short pulled lines of colour. An average amount of movement is about $\frac{1}{10}''$ and this is desirable to smooth over the glaze surface. Glazes of a higher viscosity are required over underglaze colours which have a tendency to be 'pulled' by the glaze. Some decorative glazes which rely upon movement to give their effect can be measured in inches of movement. They are of low viscosity and are applied thickly.

Glazes of high viscosity have strong or numerous bonds across neighbouring layers of glaze. In diagrammatical form this is seen as the difference between the glaze of high viscosity, fig. 2 and low viscosity, fig. 3.

It is impossible to distort the structure at fig. 2. It can only flow by the breaking and remaking of the bonds down the dotted arrow.

The structure at fig. 3 is more vulnerable. There are fewer bonds to break and the structure can also be distorted as at fig. 4.

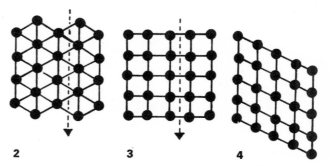

2　　　　**3**　　　　**4**

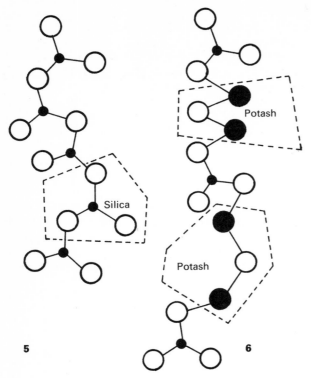

5   6

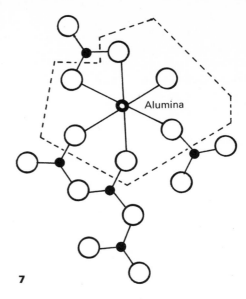

7

These examples are purely diagrammatic but serve to show the factors involved. Molten glazes are a series of flexible chains, considered as silica chains, fig. 5, whose links are joined together in long lengths and also across from chain to chain. Monovalent oxides like potash provide very flexible links. The flexibility of a chain and also its place of shear is at the oxygen atom. The potash molecule freed from its own structure and introduced into the silica chain is obviously capable of great flexibility, fig. 6. Compare this with the alumina molecule where aluminium is in six-fold co-ordination with oxygen. When alumina is introduced into the silica chain it creates a more rigid structure than existed before, fig. 7.

Potash and alumina are at opposite ends of the scale in their influence upon viscosity. Potash creates fluid melts of low viscosity. Alumina introduced into a melt creates a stiffening so that the melt is of high viscosity.

The other glaze oxides lie between these two extremes. Their influences on the viscosity of the melt are partly governed by their fluxing actions since flow is a property of fusion. The influences are also partly governed by the type of bonds produced. The oxides can be put in an order of influence upon viscosity for each temperature range. This is shown in the table.

Notes on the table of oxide influence upon viscosity.

Zone A. The oxides on the far left promote the least viscosity. That is, their presence lowers the viscosity of the melt. Each oxide is subject to the law of eutectic mixtures which relates to melting points and thus to viscosity at a given temperature. The number of fluxes present has effect upon viscosity by the law of interaction.

Zone B. The oxides on the left promote less viscosity than those on the right. Each oxide is also subject to the law of eutectic mixtures whereby there is an optimum result beyond which greater amounts of oxide act in the opposite direction and raise the viscosity. The number of fluxes present has effect upon viscosity by the law of interaction.

Neutral zone. The oxides here have little effect upon

Table of oxide influence upon viscosity

←———————— *Viscosity lowered* ————————   ———————— *Viscosity raised* ————————→

Zone A					Zone B						Neutral zone		Zone C									
K_2O	Li_2O	B_2O_3	NaKO	Na_2O	BaO	SrO	CaO	ZnO	MgO	PbO	TiO_2	SiO_2	SnO_2	ZrO_2	Al_2O_3				*over 1250°C*	*over 2280°F*			
K_2O	Li_2O	Na_2O	B_2O_3	NaKO	BaO	SrO	CaO	ZnO	PbO	MgO	TiO_2	SiO_2	SnO_2	ZrO_2	Al_2O_3				*1200–1250°C*	*2190–2280°F*			
K_2O	Na_2O	Li_2O	NaKO	PbO	B_2O_3	SrO	CaO	ZnO	BaO	MgO	TiO_2	SiO_2	SnO_2	ZrO_2	Al_2O_3				*1150–1200°C*	*2100–2190°F*			
	K_2O	Na_2O	NaKO	PbO	B_2O_3	SrO	ZnO	CaO	BaO	MgO	TiO_2	SiO_2	SnO$_2$	ZrO_2	Al_2O_3				*1100–1150°C*	*2010–2100°F*			
1050–1100°C	K_2O	Na_2O	NaKO	Li_2O	PbO	B_2O_3	ZnO	SrO	CaO	MgO	SiO_2	TiO_2	BaO	SnO$_2$	ZrO_2	Al_2O_3				*1920–2010°F*			
1000–1050°C	K_2O	NaKO	Na_2O	Li_2O	PbO	B_2O_3	ZnO	SrO	CaO	MgO	SiO_2	TiO_2	BaO	SnO$_2$	ZrO_2	Al_2O_3				*1830–1920°F*			
950–1000°C	*1740–1830°F*		NaKO	K_2O	Na_2O	Li_2O	PbO	B_2O_3	ZnO	MgO	SiO_2	TiO_2	BaO	SrO	CaO	SnO$_2$	ZrO_2	Al_2O_3					
below 950°C	*below 1740°F*		NaKO	K_2O	Na_2O	PbO	B_2O_3	Li_2O	SiO_2	ZnO	TiO_2	MgO	BaO	SrO	CaO	SnO$_2$	ZrO_2	Al_2O_3					

310

viscosity and can be included in reasonable amounts without apparent change of viscosity. Silica is included as a mid-way guide. Its amount in a melt obviously affects viscosity and it is taken here as the central norm by which the viscosity is judged.

Zone C. Apart from a slight effect from interaction, all the oxides in this zone raise the viscosity. Alumina at the far right creates the most viscous glaze melt.

N.B. Other factors to be considered in the balancing of a glaze by alteration of oxides by substitution or addition are: surface tension and rate of thermal expansion/contraction.

Vitrifiable clay. Clay which has a long maturing range and can therefore be fired successfully up to its vitrification point without deformation. This is necessary for the making of stoneware.

The slow maturation is dependent upon the presence of suitable fluxes and anti-fluxes. The suitable fluxes are potash and soda whose action starts at around 500°C (932°F) and progresses consistently. About 2% to 5% is sufficient. Unsuitable fluxes are calcia, magnesia etc which have short active periods of fluxing.

There is really only one suitable anti-flux and that is alumina. An alumina content of around 30% will satisfactorily check a tendency to fuse too quickly.

Stoneware clays, most ball clays and the least refractory fireclays could be called vitrifiable clays. Some red clays can also be vitrified but most have a tendency to bloat before densification is reached. Porcelain body is a prepared vitrifiable clay.

Vitrification. The furthest stage to which a body can be taken without deformation. At the vitrification point in

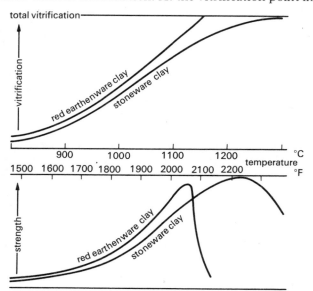

the firing, a body is usually in a malleable state. That is, it could be deformed by pressure but a pot keeps its form because of the strength of its structure. However more heat-work in the form of higher temperature or prolonged temperature would result in deformation by the pot's own weight and the bloating of the body.

Vitrification is the result of the fluxing of the feldspathoids and free silica in the body. This molten silicate flows into the interstices between the clay particles and attacks and begins to flux them by interaction. See **Firing, biscuit** for diagrams. When the whole has cooled, the original clay particles are welded together by a glassy matrix which almost fills all the interstitial spaces. A vitrified body is usually accepted as having a small porosity. When a body has reached the point of being absolutely non-porous it is also so glassy that it fractures more easily.

The graphs show a typical relationship between fired strength and vitrification. Stoneware clays are capable of coming to this point slowly. This is called maturing. Earthenware clays tend to be ones which reach the end point suddenly so that one has to accept a fair amount of porosity. See **Breakdown**.

Volatiles. Elements and compounds which vaporize during firing. The temperature at which each volatilizes depends upon its involvement at the time so the temperatures given are necessarily approximate and represent the lower end of the range. See also **Vaporization**.

Complete loss			
water	H_2O	100°C	212°F
nitrogen	N	200°C	392°F
chlorine	Cl	200°C	392°F
hydroxyl group	OH	500°C	932°F
carbon oxides	CO, CO_2	700°C	1292°F
sulphur oxides	SO_2, SO_3	900°C	1652°F
fluorine	F	1000°C	1832°F

Measurable or noticeable loss			
zinc oxide	ZnO	950°C	1742°F
lead oxide	PbO	1000°C	1832°F
copper oxide	CuO	1000°C	1832°F
chromium oxide	Cr_2O_3	1050°C	1922°F
soda	Na_2O	1100°C	2012°F
boric oxide	B_2O_3	1150°C	2102°F

Slight loss			
cobalt oxide	CoO	1100°C	2012°F
barium oxide	BaO	1200°C	2192°F
manganous oxide	MnO	1200°C	2192°F
potash	K_2O	1200°C	2192°F

W

Wad (1) Manganese dioxide ore often containing cobalt oxide. See **Asbolite**. The name is sometimes used for other ores which occur in the form of clusters of cylinders.

Wad (2) Wadding. A strip or lump of refractory clay used to seal saggars in bungs, support shelves etc. Wad clay is highly refractory and so remains friable and does not fuse to the fireclay shelves, supports etc but can be chipped away after firing.

WAD BOX. Dod box. A cylindrical box with a plunger which extrudes plastic clay through a tapered nozzle or die. It is used for making wads or snakes for setting saggars etc. See also **Dod box**.

The drawings show the principle of the wad box and the model manufactured by William Boulton Ltd.

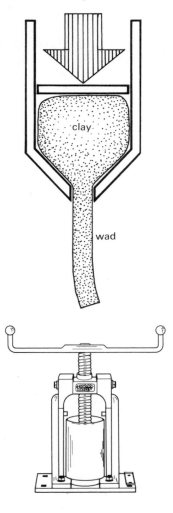

Washing soda. Natron. Hydrated sodium carbonate. Soda crystals. $Na_2CO_3.10H_2O$. Soluble sodium salt used as a source of soda for frit and glaze making. Commercial frit manufacturers use the anhydrous sodium carbonate. Small amounts of dry-powder glaze can be made experimentally for filling hollows on tiles etc which are fired horizontally. See **Soda in glazes**.

The molecule of washing soda is about six times the weight of silica. This should be borne in mind when making dry-powder glazes. A glaze to melt at about 1000°C (1832°F) will have equal molecules of soda and silica and can be made with about six times as much washing soda as flint. Equal weights give a glaze with one molecule of soda to every six of silica and this melts at approximately 1200°C (2192°F). These glazes require stabilizing with some clay or feldspar.

Water. H_2O. Most potters appreciate water's importance in providing the lubricant for the clay particles. What is not generally appreciated is that the potter rarely uses distilled or pure water. Spring water and tap water contain dissolved ingredients which help or hinder the potter. Mostly the result is unnoticed but sometimes a water may contain sufficient calcia to cause scumming. This will show on the unglazed parts of the fired ware. Alternatively, the water may contain salts which soften the clay and even improve a clay's plasticity. Some commercial water softeners have this deflocculatory effect. Some potters save the water syphoned from one glaze for mixing with the next. Others settle the throwing water from the wheel and re-use it. Re-used water of this sort can be felt to be sticky or slippery when wet fingers are rubbed together. It is worthwhile considering if there is any particular advantage in re-using water, other than economy, before always using fresh.

Water is analysed in its various functions in clay and as water in glazes and slips. Some other minerals contain water between the chemical structure, e.g. chert and flint, or as part of their chemical structure, e.g. borax and colemanite.

WATER IN CLAY. Water can account for as much as 40% of the weight of plastic clay. This 40% would be made up of about 20% lubricant, 10% to fill the pores between the particles of clay and 10% chemically combined within the clay particles. These three different functions which water performs give rise to a host of names describing the water and the processes involved in its addition or removal. They are here headed: water

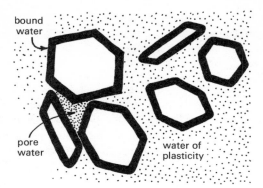

bound water

pore water

water of plasticity

of plasticity, pore water and bound water. See also **Drying**.

Water of plasticity. Lubricant water. Separate water. This water provides the lubrication for the clay particles and enables them to slide past one another. The quality of plasticity of a clay is dependent upon the size and shape of these clay particles and the amount of other material, e.g. sand, which is present and cannot be plasticized. There is an optimum amount of water of plasticity for each clay. Beyond this amount the clay is too soft and sticky for use.

Highly plastic clays (such as ball clays) require more water than low plasticity clays (such as fireclays) to bring them to the plastic state. As much as 30% of the weight of a plastic clay can be water of plasticity. An average clay has 20% but in low plasticity bodies which contain non-plastic materials, like flint and feldspar, the water can be as low as 10%. Apart from the non-plastic materials present, the size of the clay particles is all-important. The most plastic clays have smaller sized particles. These present more surface area per given weight of clay than do large particles. Therefore there is a greater surface area to be surrounded by water in fine clays. This is apparent if one thinks of starting with one large piece which, when broken in two, presents two additional surfaces for the same bulk weight. This reasoning is true down to the exceedingly small particle size of clay where one could put 250 000 particles end to end in an inch. It is helpful to realize the range of particle size. The smallest clay particle from a highly plastic clay would fit about 8000 times into the bulk of a clay particle from a low-plasticity clay.

Clays which require a lot of water of plasticity naturally take longer to dry. They also contain a large bulk of water, which accounts for a considerable shrinkage from plastic to dry state. The water of plasticity can be added quite simply and calculated in pints per hundredweight. It can be removed quite simply by evaporation.

Pore water. Water of formation. Equilibrium moisture content (EMC). Atmospheric water. Water which is locked inside the pores of dry clay. It is held there by capillary action, by the surface tension of the water layer around each particle (this layer being attached to

the hydroxyl groups of the clay), and by the imprisoning nature of the surrounding particles. It is water in the sense that it was mixed with the water of plasticity at the plastic stage whereas the bound water is in the form of hydroxyl (OH) groups.

Pore water could account for 12% of the weight of apparently dry clay. The amount varies with the moisture content of the surrounding air, as explained under **Readsorption**. Clay which has been dried in the sun on a warm day will contain very little pore water but always contains some.

Pore water is not completely removed until the clay has reached a temperature higher than the boiling point of water and remained there for some time to dispel the water as steam. The point at which the clay is theoretically bone dry is 120°C (248°F). The early part of a firing is always taken slowly in order to dispel the pore water safely without rupturing the ware. This is called the water-smoking period.

Bound water. Chemically combined water. The water of crystallization, combination, constitution, composition or hydration. Water which is part of the chemical structure of the compound, e.g. in gypsum, copper sulphate and kaolinite. The term usually arises with reference to clay to differentiate between the bound water and the plasticity and pore waters. The water of plasticity dries out from the clay in the atmosphere. The pore water is driven off by heat up to 120°C (248°F) but the bound water remains as part of the clay compound ($Al_2O_3 . 2SiO_2 . 2H_2O$) until red heat, 600°C (1112°F).

Bound water accounts for up to 14% of the weight of dry clay and can be seen escaping as water vapour from muffle kilns at red heat. It leaves the clay with little danger of steam pressure rupturing the ware. It is able to do this because the process is a slow one starting at about 450°C (842°F), increasing to 600°C (1112°F) and trailing off to 700°C (1292°F). Also, as the process starts, the clay becomes comparatively open. The pores become clear passages leading out to the interior.

When the bound water has gone, the clay is no longer clay but pot, that is, fired body. This is the ceramic change. The process is also called dehydration, dehydroxylation, anhydration, decomposition and sometimes, casually, burning off. The last water to escape is in the form of hydroxyl groups attached to the alumina or gibbsite layer and would theoretically be called the water of constitution. See **Double layer theory**.

WATER IN GLAZES AND SLIPS. The water which is used to make a slop or slip is either a very weak acid or a mildly alkaline solution. The difference is slight and can occur with the water itself or from containers and materials. The effects are quite noticeable and should be understood by the potter in case they occur accidently. The deliberate occasions are given below.

For casting slips the water is an alkaline solution.

This deflocculates the clay particles and produces a fluid slip. See **Deflocculation**. The phenomenon also occurs with slip-glazes containing wood ash. See **Wood ash**.

For glaze slops the water is made slightly acidic by the inclusion of calcium chloride. This flocculates the clay content which hinders sedimentation. When required, slips for clay decoration are flocculated slightly to make them dry more quickly. See **Calcium chloride, Flocculation** and **Bentonite**.

Water-glass. Sodium silicate. Various combinations of soda and silica from $Na_2O . SiO_2$ to $Na_2O . 4SiO_2$ which are soluble in water. They can be used in simple glazes.

Water-glass is used commercially as a glue and concrete hardener. The metasilicate is used as a deflocculant in casting slips. See **Deflocculation** and **Sodium silicate**.

Water smoking. Pre-heating. The drying of clay during the early stages of firing. The water-smoking period must be taken slowly and is usually considered as from room temperature to 120°C (248°F). It is popular to take two hours over this period. With primitive firing methods which involve quick firings in open bonfires, the water smoking is done previously over hot charcoal and is called pre-heating.

All air-dried clay contains some atmospheric water held in the pores by adsorption and capillary action. This water is converted to steam at 100°C (212°F), the boiling point of water. It can be seen as water vapour escaping from vents and cracks in the kiln, and it can be felt by the hand in the warm wet air coming from a chimney or vent. When the water-smoking period is over, the vent air will be dry and hot.

During damp weather the water held in the pores of air-dried clay could be as much as 4% of the weight of the clay but 1% as a general amount. Compared with an amount of water like 25% water of plasticity, this 1% seems small. Even so, this represents a large volume of steam. Water expands rapidly when converted into steam and because the pores are formed from closely-held clay particles, the escape passages are small. Pottery which is burnished will also have its surface pores sealed.

If unable to escape, the steam builds up pressure until it blows itself free. Probably every potter has experienced this at some time. The resulting debris is often a shattered pile of flakes, reminiscent of the frost-shattered detritus on the summits of mountains.

The amount of water held in dry clay is dependent upon the humidity of the atmosphere and the type of clay. As a general rule, finer clays, like ball clays, have smaller pores and therefore hold more water against the action of normal drying. See **Drying**.

Watkin's recorders. Small pellets of compounded glaze minerals which are used to measure heat-work in a similar way to cones. They are graded for different time/temperatures and a suitable series is placed in dents on a refractory block. This is withdrawn and examined at intervals. The beginnings of fusion can be noted and other effects deducted from recorders as is done with glaze fishouts. The measurement done by Watkin's recorders is nearer to temperature than the heat-work measurement done by other pyroscopes. They are based upon, and are often used in conjunction with, salts that melt at definite temperatures rather than the interaction of minerals as fluxes and silicates like cones and bars.

Wax resist. Wax, either melted or as an emulsion, which is applied to pottery to prevent colour, glaze etc from adhering at that point. See **Resist**. Teapot by Crowan Pottery; plate by Frank Hamer.

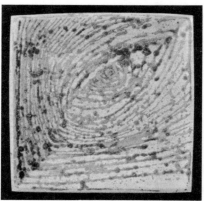

Weald clay. Wealdon clay. Clays found in the south-east of England associated with the chalks of the Cretaceous System. See **Marl**.

Weathering. The action on clays left in the open air whereby they disintegrate and improve in plasticity. The action is one that is continuous in nature and is partially responsible for the creation of clay from igneous rock and fully responsible for the removal of primary clays to become secondary clays.

Weathering achieves the sub-division of the clay grains or large particles into clay crystals or small particles. The finer the particles, the more plastic will be the clay. Rain, wind and frost are involved; and they can act most quickly upon clays which were once plastic but have lost plasticity by compression and drying, e.g. a shale. Even a shale which produces a clay of poor plasticity when it is crushed and reconstituted, will have much more plasticity after one winter's weathering. After 10 or 20 years of weathering the shale can reach its original potential and achieve the plasticity it had before it was compressed.

Clays with large, orderly crystals are difficult to weather. Such clays are the kaolins. Here it is a case of dividing a large crystal and this is more difficult than making a division between crystals which were held together to form grains. The sub-division of a crystal is a slow process and only possible along lines of weakness in the structure. Such a weakness occurs where some isomorphous substitution of aluminium and silicon has taken place. See **Disordered kaolinite**.

The quicker processes of weathering which take 10 to 100 years can be simulated and accelerated by blunging and with the use of chemical additives, but the slower processes which involve substitutions cannot be simulated. In short, fireclays, shales and some mudstones can be made plastic by natural or simulated weathering but china clays require a few million years of weathering to make them plastic.

There is therefore a limit in the improvement in plasticity that can reasonably be expected of any clay in a potter's lifetime. This limit is the clay's potential. The action of weathering is not magic. It cannot create plasticity where there is no potential. Shales and rock fireclays have a high potential. The potential of china clay is too remote. It is impossible to weather a sand into a clay because it has no potential at all.

Loams contain clay but they also contain a high proportion of sand. Their plasticity potential is low. This is shown in that loam soils have not weathered to plastic clays. In a similar way it is pointless to try to further weather a surface clay. Even though recognizable as a clay, if it has been exposed for a number of years and still shows insufficient plasticity, it probably has little potential. This is probably due to its low content of plastic clay and/or its high content of kaolinitic clay of large crystal size.

Some prepared bodies come into this category. They are sold as 'clays' for specialized use. This use does not require a high plasticity and therefore the body contains only a small amount of plastic clay. However the potential of this plastic clay has been realized in the preparation of the body. One cannot expect weathering to improve the plasticity of such a body.

Weathering also helps to decompose iron pyrites.

The resulting iron sulphate is washed away. Other soluble salts are also washed away by weathering. For weathering a clay is spread out on a concrete base or in troughs in an exposed place. About a 4-inch thickness is considered the limit that the action can penetrate. In suitable clay pits it may be possible yearly to build up a pile of clay in 4-inch layers until the stack has had sufficient weathering.

Weathering and plasticizing are also dealt with under **Preparation of clay**.

Wedging. A hand process of preparing plastic clay which involves mixing and compressing the clay. It is so-called because it packs or thrusts the clay into itself.

A plastic clay must be homogeneous for use. Sometimes the clay required is a mixture of two clays or the clay has been de-watered from a slurry by the use of drying troughs. These clays are not homogeneous. They are composed of harder parts and softer parts. These parts of different consistency must be thoroughly mixed and the air bubbles which are trapped in the clay must be expelled. The process whereby this is achieved is called wedging. It is a general conditioning of the clay and is a process replaced by pugging when working in large amounts. Wedging is often done before ageing or storage. It is followed, either immediately or after storage, by kneading. Kneading achieves the same end except that it does not compress the clay as much. It is also usually concerned with a piece of clay of particular size for the work in hand.

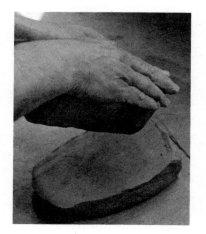

In wedging, a conveniently-sized lump of clay is thrown down onto the wedging bench. This is a stoutly-built, strong table about 27 inches high. The lump of clay is thrown down to form a wedge shape with the wide end towards the potter. This end half is cut off with a wire, lifted, turned over and brought down to meet the other half with force. The whole lump is lifted, knocked onto the bench to regain its lump shape and thrown down to start the process again. The process is repeated fifty times or so until the clay is thoroughly mixed and compressed. Air bubbles are expelled where they lie close to a cut.

The compression of the clay, including the removal of air bubbles, improves the clay's workability. See **Workability**. Some potters use wedging as an initial mixing process and employ kneading for most of the conditioning of the clay. Some wedge only and some knead only: it depends upon the potter, his strength and the condition and type of clay.

Wedgwood, Josiah. Born in 1730 into a family of potters in Burslem, England, he became the most famous potter in the world and died in 1795 leaving an important, thriving business. Wedgwood was one of the first industrial potters to organize division of labour for greater production. He was an excellent businessman, had an inventive mind, was a tireless experimenter, and unlike many potters he knew his limitations.

Wedgwood made many friends and these helped him to overcome his deficiencies in taste and education. Thomas Bentley, his partner, was especially helpful and looked after the neo-classical wares whilst Josiah concentrated on functional ware and perfecting the many ideas current at the time.

Wedgwood's most famous wares are his cream-coloured earthenware, renamed Queen's Ware when Queen Charlotte ordered tea and coffee sets in 1765, Black Basalt or Egyptian Ware made from a black stoneware, Red Stoneware, and Jasper Ware with its finely-modelled white sprigging on a coloured background. See **Creamware**.

Wet ware. Ware put into a glaze firing without prior drying. Biscuit ware absorbs water from the slop as glaze is applied. The early stage of the glaze firing removes this water as vapour. If this is done too quickly, the steam might loosen the glaze layer sufficiently to cause crawling, or even result in pieces of glaze falling from the ware. This would happen when the glaze started to melt and move. Faults arising from this loosening of glazes are termed wet-ware faults.

Wheel. Potter's wheel. A rotating disc on which pots are formed. It is motivated by outside power, electricity, etc, or by foot or hand with the help of a flywheel. Its purpose is to turn the clay whilst the hands form the pot. The action of the hands is thus applied symmetrically. Where the rotation is produced by foot, mechanical power etc the hands are left free to manipulate the clay. Production is thereby increased.

The wheel-head is usually horizontal but some are at an angle or even horizontal but upside down. These require a different throwing technique but once controlled are a benefit for throwing some forms because the lifting action is assisted by gravity. Wheel-heads at an angle are used for bowls. Wheel-heads upside down are used for large tall forms.

Egypt is credited with being the place of origin of the potter's wheel. It was here that the turntable shaft was lengthened about 3000 B.C. and a flywheel added. The flywheel was kicked and later was moved by pulling the edge with the left hand whilst forming the clay with the right. This led to the anti-clockwise motion for the potter's wheel which is almost universal. Only in parts of Japan and in parts of India was a clockwise motion used.

The clockwise wheel evolved from the use of a flywheel as wheel-head which was motivated by a hand-held stick located in notches near the edge. Holding the stick at its top end in the left hand and locating the other end in a notch the right hand is used to pull the stick towards one. When the wheel is turning sufficiently one can begin throwing. The wheel has to be given periodic impetus during the throwing of a pot.

Most potters learn to throw anti-clockwise and if a power wheel is used it is unlikely to be reversible. However, some experience with throwing clockwise is beneficial because it makes one analyse one's actions thoroughly. Also some clays, notably those containing only a small amount of naturally plastic clay, e.g. special bodies like porcelain, sometimes tire of being turned one way only. Some tear if the leatherhard trimming (turning) is done with the same wheel direction as the throwing. In such cases throwing is done anti-clockwise and turning is done clockwise. Also after throwing many potters reverse the wheel direction and burnish the leatherhard clay surface. For this a kick wheel, which is easily reversed, is essential. See also **Throwing** and **Turning**. The photograph is of the Podmore and Sons' 'Plus Seven' wheel.

Whieldon, Thomas. A mid-18th century Staffordshire potter, famous for his marbled ware and tortoiseshell ware. Marbled ware was made by mixing together differently coloured clays. The half-mixed clay was thrown and then turned to remove the slurry and reveal the variegations. Tortoiseshell ware was a cream earthenware with a mottled glaze produced by dabbing the surface with a sponge soaked in cobalt, copper or manganese-coloured glaze. Josiah Wedgwood was partner to Whieldon before setting up his own pottery. See **Creamware**.

Whirler (1). A heavy turntable used in press-moulding. It is usually cast in plaster of Paris onto an armatured spindle. Because it is heavy the whirler will revolve slowly and steadily. This is essential for accurate press-moulding. To allow both hands to be free to work the whirler is turned by the stomach. Press-moulders are suitably proportioned for this work.

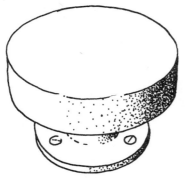

Whirler (2). A faulty plate, saucer etc which will spin round on a central part instead of standing firmly on its foot rim. It is the opposite of a humper.

Thrown plates and dishes tend to become whirlers and, whether turned or unturned, the pull is accentua-ted by the drying of the rims before the wells. It is often necessary to forcibly depress the bases of over-turned plates as they dry. The use of extra grog in the clay for plate-making also helps to overcome the fault.

White. White is achieved in pottery by the use of minerals which are themselves without colourant.

In clays, the usual colourant is iron oxide, traces of which give cream-coloured bodies. The iron stain can be given a bluish tinge by reduction. This is often done with white porcelain. Alternatively it can be given an over-riding bluish tinge by the addition of cobalt oxide. This method is used in earthenware.

White glazes are opaque glazes using tin oxide, titanium dioxide, zinc oxide and zirconium dioxide opacifiers. See **Opacifiers**.

White lead. Basic lead carbonate. Sometimes unnecessarily called white lead carbonate and erroneously white lead oxide. $2PbCO_3.Pb(OH)_2$. A dense white powder used in paints and as a source of lead oxide for glazes. Although it is used for opaque white paints it gives no opacification in glazes but is a very active flux for transparent glazes for all temperatures up to 1200°C (2192°F). See **Lead oxide**.

White lead decomposes upon heating and provides lead oxide, carbon dioxide and water. The carbon dioxide and water escape as gases.

$$2PbCO_3.Pb(OH)_2 \longrightarrow 3PbO + 2CO_2\uparrow + H_2O\uparrow$$

White lead therefore loses some of its weight during firing. The conversion factor is 0·863. This means that 100 lbs of white lead provides 86·3 lbs of lead oxide (PbO) to enter a glaze fusion. If 100 lbs of lead oxide are required to enter fusion, 115·8 lbs of white lead are required.

Because white lead is bulkier than other raw lead compounds it remains in suspension better in glaze slops.

White-hard clay. White-dry clay. Clay from which the water of plasticity has evaporated at the surface. The term is used even with coloured clays because there is a whiteness about the sharp edges where drying begins. At this stage the outside of the clay is dry but the inside is still damp. White-hard clay is not completely dry and is not theoretically ready for firing. A simple test is to put the clay to the cheek. If it feels cold it is not dry. Dry clay is at air temperature.

It should be remembered that the term dry used here is relative. The air itself contains moisture and the clay will contain an equal amount of moisture. This is called the equilibrium moisture content (EMC). Because of the atmospheric moisture in the pores of the clay the first part of a firing must take place slowly. This is called water smoking. See **Water** and **Drying**.

Whiting. Calcium carbonate. Paris white. $CaCO_3$.

Source of calcia for bodies and glazes. Potter's whiting is usually precipitated and is therefore as near to the pure chemical as it is possible to get. For its action during firing see **Calcia**.

Other sources of whiting are crushed limestone, crushed chalk and ground seashells. Musselwhite is whiting made from mussel shells. They contain some chromium compounds which sometimes discolour tin glazes.

Wicket. The entry hole into the kiln chamber whereby the ware is set and drawn. The wicket is bricked in and clammed over for firing except for spy-holes or holes for fishout tests.

Willemite. Wilhelmite. Zinc silicate. Zn_2SiO_4 or $2ZnO.SiO_2$. A crystalline zinc mineral with translucent properties. Similar crystals are formed during the cooling of zinc matt glazes. See **Zinc oxide crystallizer** and **Crystalline glazes**.

Win. The process of digging or mining a material, especially clay, and transporting it to be processed. Winning is divided into the two operations, getting and transporting.

Wind. Press-moulder's name for air bubbles.

Window dip. The action of dipping a pot sideways into slip or glaze. The best effect is on a swelling form where the 'window' is a complete shape which does not meet the pot rim or foot. The advantage of a window dip is that the window shape has affinity with the form of the pot and makes a good area for a panel decoration.

Witherite. Barium carbonate. $BaCO_3$. A white crystalline mineral associated with lead ores. It is one source of barium oxide for glazes and is also used as an agent for de-scumming clays. See **Barium carbonate**.

Wollastonite. Calcium silicate. $CaSiO_3$ or $CaO.SiO_2$. The natural mineral which combines calcia and silica,

and a source of these for glazes. It occurs in such metamorphic rocks as granitized calcareous sandstones. The true mineral is not so difficult to grind but it is still more expensive than using calcium carbonate and silica.

The wollastonite crystal forms in glazes during cooling providing there is a high proportion of calcia and a high proportion of free silica. The crystals give opacity and a matt surface. See **Lime matt** and **Crystalline glazes**.

There is more than one explanation of the way in which the silica chain accommodates itself to the sixfold calcium cation. The diagram shows one of the simplest explanations in which a silica chain is linked by isolated cations. Other chains would be accommodated back and front.

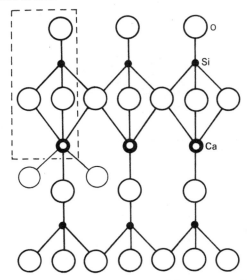

Wood ash. The inorganic residue after the combustion of the organic structure of wood. The term is popularly extended to include other vegetable ashes, e.g. grass, reed and straw. Wood ash contains up to 50% alkaline fluxes: potash, magnesia and calcia. The remainder is silica and phosphorus pentoxide which are glass-formers and alumina which is the important amphoteric oxide. A wood ash is therefore similar to a glaze, and could be called a natural glaze frit. A few wood ashes will make a glaze alone but mostly they are useful constituents and have been so for centuries. See also **Ashes**.

Historically wood ashes were used as the main flux in Oriental stoneware and porcelain glazes. Wood ash was readily available because the kilns were wood fired. The quality of glaze achieved encourages world-wide use of wood ash even when kilns are fired by other fuels.

Wood ashes vary enormously. They are by far the most variable material that a potter uses. The ashes can be as different, chemically, as chalk and granite. They not only act as glaze fluxes but introduce colour, usually very subtle colour with reduction, and produce crystalline opacity with interesting flecking. The photo-

graph is of a bottle by Katharine Pleydell-Bouverie.

Wood ashes rarely act as practical fluxes below 1150°C (2102°F) because of the calcium compounds present. Amounts added to existing glazes usually provide interesting opacification, colour and crystallization. Above 1150°C (2102°F) wood ashes act as fluxes and amounts over 30% of a glaze will give crystalline opacity also. These statements are necessarily broad, for each ash, even two batches from the same species of tree, will behave uniquely. However the principles explained under **Eutectic mixture** apply and many ash glazes crystallize because they contain more than the eutectic amount of flux.

Wood ash is incorporated into a batch by weight as are the other ingredients. The following recipes for 1250°C (2282°F) show amounts varying from 18% to 40%.

Off-white crystalline slip-glaze for porcelain:

potash feldspar	15
porcelain clay	62
beech ash	18
whiting	5

Olive celadon slip-glaze for stoneware:

potash feldspar	30
ball clay	15
red clay	20
wood ash	25
whiting	10

Semi-transparent to go on biscuit:

potash feldspar	50
china clay	10
quartz	10
wood ash	30

Crystalline to go on biscuit:

potash feldspar	40
china clay	20
wood ash	40

Wood ashes contain soluble compounds: potash, carbonates, sulphates and chlorides. These dissolve in the water of the glaze slop and can be detected as a soft feel to the water and in extreme cases as a caustic burning of the skin. These compounds soak into the pottery body during glazing and a small amount remains there to flux the body and increase the body-glaze layer. The rest returns to the surface of the glaze during drying and crystallizes there. During firing these compounds provide extra fluxing.

The effect can be advantageous or a nuisance. Certainly with slip-glazes the solubles deflocculate the clay causing the slop to be thin and slippery. It is then impossible to obtain a sufficiently thick layer on the pot. The addition of calcium chloride or vinegar corrects the deflocculation but the resulting acidic balance of the water only encourages more alkali to dissolve. The slop must be re-balanced each time it is used.

Some, but never all, of the soluble compounds can be removed from the ash by washing. To do this the ash is mixed thoroughly with plenty of water, allowed to settle and the water syphoned off. At this mixing stage, unburnt material and charcoal can be removed because it tends to float. The process of washing, settling and syphoning is repeated until the water is clean and tasteless. The wood ash is sieved through a 6's to 10's mesh progressing to a 60's. This is about the finest practical because wood ash quickly clogs a mesh. Some potters prefer coarse ash because it brings texture to the glaze.

The washed ash is finally settled and dried for use as a glaze constituent. Because it clogs a mesh it is often added to the slop after the other constituents have been sieved.

If wood ash is to be used unwashed it is usually dry-sieved through a coarse sieve and added to the other constituents after they had been sieved. Some potters wash their wood ash after weighing it. There is obviously a loss of weight by this method but ash glazes are variables and often require adjustment by the addition of whiting or silica to the batch after the first test firing.

Workability. The character of a clay that is a combination of strength, plasticity and thixotropy. It is difficult to analyse because the three properties overlap in the qualities they bring to the clay.

To achieve maximum workability for a clay, it is necessary to understand how the three properties are to be promoted. It is also necessary to know which ones to promote in order to give correct workability for the particular job in hand.

A clay of good workability stands up well to the stress of stretching, as in throwing, pressing and the pulling of handles. This demands a combination of strength and plasticity. A good clay also has the capacity to allow itself to be deformed by a reasonably slight pressure. This is the property of plasticity. Covered by the term thixotropy is the capacity to provide the necessary strength and plasticity when needed. A good clay is often required to have a resistance to shear that is high at a given moment, rather than one that is high over a continuous movement. It is a question of particle

319

attraction rather than frictional drag. This is a similar property to inertia. A clay for throwing and hand-building must reasonably support its own weight. The three properties are described in more detail under **Plasticity, Thixotropy** and **Preparation of clay**. The lack of workability is described under **Short clay**.

The usual potter's tests for workability are a simple deformation test and a tie-a-knot test. In deformation testing, one pushes a piece of clay with the thumb or finger and notes how much initial resistance there is. Also one notes whether the clay went in the way intended and whether it held the intended form. Some poor clays have too much initial resistance and feel hard and bouncy. Some have no resistance and stick to the fingers as one takes off the pressure, thus spoiling the intended form. Others tear instead of sliding in the shear.

In the tie-a-knot test, a piece of clay is rolled between the palms to give a strip about the thickness of a pencil. This strip is tied in a knot. A good clay will accept this exercise without rupture. The poor clay will rupture if it does not actually break.

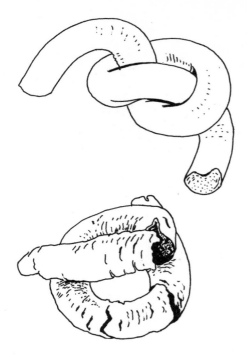

WORKABILITY RANGE. The variation of water content that a plastic clay can stand and still remain plastic. If too little water is present the clay is too stiff to work and if too much water is present the clay becomes too wet and sticky. Red clays and ball clays which have very fine clay particles have better, that is wider, workability ranges than the coarser clays such as fireclay and china clay. The use of plasticizers such as bentonite whilst increasing working plasticity do not necessarily increase the workability range. See also **Plasticity**.

Wreathing. A slip-casting fault showing as a rippled surface on the slip side of the cast. See **Casting slip, adjustment**.

Y

Yellow. Yellow colours are produced in different ways in pottery. Each way is individual and works only within limits which are often narrow.

The most positive yellow stain is antimony oxide in a lead glaze. Iron oxide also gives yellows when bleached in a lime matt glaze or restricted by titania. Vanadium pentoxide gives yellow in combination with tin oxide or zirconia as a prepared stain. See **Antimony oxide, Iron oxide** and **Vanadium stains**. Occasionally, bodies containing traces of copper oxide produce bright yellows under lead glazes. Consistency is impossible to establish.

Yellow ochre. Limonite. $2Fe_2O_3.3H_2O$. A soft crumbly variety of iron ore. It sometimes contains some clay and limestone. See **Limonite**.

Z

Zen. One of the two important schools of Japanese Buddhist·thought developed from about A.D. 1200. The other school is Shin. Zen ignores the rituals, objects of devotion and scriptures of other Buddhist schools and concentrates upon freeing the mind of material worries in the path towards Satori (Enlightenment). The acceptance of a direct and immediate approach to spiritualization allows an unbiased acceptance and awareness of good in all its forms. The direct impersonal expression of clay and the various colouring effects of raku and stoneware are thus acceptable for what they are without reservations of what they might have been. Zen Buddhism is responsible for much of the Western World's understanding of the subtle qualities of Oriental pottery.

Zeta potential. The measurement of the ability of a colloidal clay particle to repel similar particles by electrostatic charge. The potential is measured in millivolts and is mostly dependent upon the distance between the two layers on the outside of the clay particle. See **Double layer theory**.

The outer layer is composed of positive charges and if this layer is at a sufficient distance from the clay particle, then no two particles will ever physically meet. In-

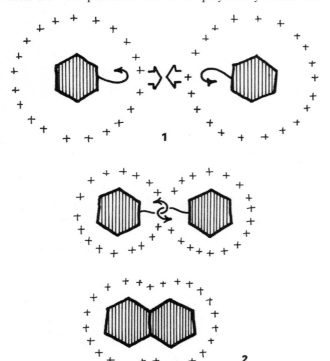

stead, they will repel each other before the forces of attraction can pull them together and form a bond, fig. 1.

If the so-called 'stand-off distance' of the outer layer is small, the zeta potential will be low. The clay particles are able to link their unsatisfied bonds through the layer and form one large particle, fig. 2. Here the mutual forces of attraction of the two particles overcomes the repulsive force of the outer layers. See **Forces of attraction**.

The zeta potential is considered when making casting slips. The stand-off distance is increased by introducing suitable cations which prefer a large stand-off distance. These substitute themselves for the existing cations of the outer layer. The result is a dispersed or deflocculated state whereby the particles do not stick together but slide past one another, constantly repelling each other. This gives fluidity to the suspension in spite of its high clay content.

Zettlitz clay. Czechoslovakian kaolin from Karlsbad. This was the clay used by Dr Hermann Seger in his tests on refractoriness. It became cone number 35 with the later estimated temperature of 1770°C (3218°F).

Zinc blende. Blende. Sphalerite. Black Jack. Zinc sulphide. ZnS. The main ore of zinc. It occurs in limestones and is often associated with lead sulphide.

Zinc oxide. ZnO. A useful auxiliary flux for oxidized glazes. It is introduced as a clean white powder which gives some opacity in the final glaze and encourages crystal growth if present in large amount. It also has a reputation as an anti-craze. In simple shiny feldspathic glazes a small amount of zinc oxide heightens the colours given by copper and cobalt oxides but in more complex glazes and with other colouring oxides, zinc oxide gives muddy colours. It was thoroughly investigated in the 19th century as an alternative flux to lead oxide. This was the first attempt to overcome lead poisoning in the pottery industry. It resulted in the Bristol glaze named after Bristol in England but now only used commercially in the USA. Though not so poisonous as lead oxide, all zinc compounds are poisonous and should be handled accordingly.

Zinc ores occur with copper, tin and lead in igneous rocks and in replacement lodes in limestone sediments. Zinc metal melts at 419°C (786°F). Coatings of zinc are put on to iron to prevent rusting. This is the galvanized iron which is often used for clay storage bins. Damp causes it to tarnish to carbonate but it is reasonably serviceable for clay, with a life of about 15 years. However, slips and glaze slops tend to attack the coating with detriment to bin and contents. This is accentuated with suspensions which are slightly alkaline or acidic, e.g. casting slips and flocculated glazes. Zinc is used with copper in brass. It is also used in paints and rubber. The common ores are zinc blende, smithsonite, zincite, willemite and hemimorphite.

Zinc oxide is used in glazes as a flux, as a general stabilizer and hardener, as an opacifier, as a crystallizer and as an anti-craze. It is not soluble in water and is therefore a useful glaze material although its use can bring difficulties. Its action in small amounts seems always to be beneficial but there is an optimum point for each glaze after which increased amounts give unpredictable results. Some glazes which rely heavily on zinc oxide for fluxing and opacity are fickle and difficult to fire with consistent results.

Zinc oxide has a beneficial effect upon the creation of stable silicates. In the lower temperature glazes, the zinc ion can enter the lattice without loosening it as would a flux (except for exciting other fluxes by interaction). Glazes of simple formula, relying upon a high proportion of a single flux, are obviously affected most.

The zinc oxide also introduces valuable anti-craze properties. It is often substituted for other fluxes of high contraction rate, e.g. soda, potash and calcia. It is second only to boric oxide in the 1100°C to 1200°C range (2012°F to 2192°F). See **Glaze fit**. It should be used with due consideration of its other properties regarding opacity and colour response.

There are advantages in the addition to a recipe of zinc oxide but there are also some possible disadvantages apart from its relatively high cost. Zinc oxide can cause crawling and discolouration.

Raw zinc oxide has a high initial shrinkage in the early stages of firing. This is before fusion takes place. This shrinkage can cause cracks in the glaze which are the source of scars when the glaze melts. Zinc oxide glazes have fairly high surface tensions and are therefore prone to crawling. To eradicate the initial shrinkage, the zinc oxide should be calcined before use in a glaze batch. Zinc oxide is unusual in that it does little to lower surface tension yet much to lower viscosity in the molten glaze. See **Viscosity of glazes** and **Surface tension**.

With soda, potash and calcia, the zinc oxide gives clean colours with cobalt and copper oxides. With other fluxes and with other colouring oxides it gives mottled effects which are pleasing but the colours are dull with a muddy opacity. Even a small amount of zinc oxide in a glaze will upset many prepared colours used as stains and underglaze decoration.

ZINC OXIDE FLUX. As a flux, its action can be divided into below 1085°C (1985°F) and above. Above 1085°C it is active as a flux providing it is not reduced by the kiln atmosphere. Even slight reduction is sufficient to extract the oxygen which results in the loss of the zinc also. See later. Its usual use is in the 1150°C to 1250°C range (2102°F to 2282°F) but there is no limit to the temperature at which it can be used. It was at one time considered only as a substitute for lead oxide but it has wider applications as an auxiliary flux that justify its use in spite of its high price. However it cannot be used as the only flux in a glaze. In this way it is similar to calcia. Alone it will not produce a silicate melt below about 1350°C (2462°F) but in the presence of assisting fluxes, e.g. calcia, soda and potash, it is very active. It is usual not to exceed 0·3 equivalents of zinc oxide unless crystalline effects are required. It gives a smooth-looking glaze of soft, silky shine and even small additions to a glaze will appreciably alter the glaze surface towards this character.

Below 1085°C (1985°F) the zinc oxide is not an active flux. Yet again it is useful in small amounts because in very small amounts, e.g. up to 1% of a recipe, it seems to have strong interactive influences which result in increased fusion. It can be useful in this way to improve sluggish glazes if its other properties are also desirable. A small amount of boron frit is a more common additive however.

Zinc oxide, although an active flux, is quite refractory with a melting point of 1800°C (3272°F). This means that there is no upper temperature limit to its use in glazes. Yet, strangely for such a refractory oxide, it is easily reduced to the metal at temperatures above 950°C (1742°F). Unfortunately there is no advantage in this since the metal alone melts at 419°C (786°F) and boils at 925°C (1697°F). Any reduction therefore at 950°C or above, having taken away the oxygen, leaves a boiling metal. The boiling metal volatilizes and is lost. The volatile zinc will condense in the atmosphere of workshop or outside as a poisonous dust. Zinc oxide should therefore be used only in fully oxidized firings.

ZINC OXIDE OPACIFIER. The effectiveness of zinc oxide as an opacifier depends upon the whiteness of its crystal and upon the whiteness of the crystal structures that it encourages. Zinc oxide is unusual, in that, whilst acting as a flux, it can retain its crystal identity and some of its opacity. Other fluxes, although equally white powders in raw state, become involved completely (dissolved) in the ceramic fusions they engender. Zinc oxide has some amphoteric properties which are seen here because it is acting as both a flux, like calcia, and an anti-flux, like tin oxide. It can fulfil this role in glazes with alkaline fluxes like soda, potash and calcia but if the stronger amphoteric flux boric oxide is present, the zinc oxide is forced into the position of being a flux only. It is then fully involved in fusion and loses its opacity.

Thus zinc oxide can be used as a flux with pleasing opalescent character. Its reflective property as an opacifier is not as high as other opacifiers but it will be seen that opacity can be increased in a glaze without loss of shine. In fact it is possible to increase the shine and the opacity by the introduction of zinc oxide. This is an advantage compared with the other opacifiers which only act as anti-fluxes and therefore dull the glaze surface.

The following recipe is an opaque white stoneware glaze for 1250°C (2282°F). The zinc oxide acts here as both flux and opacifier.

feldspar	50
china clay	15
flint	10
whiting	10
zinc oxide	10
tin oxide	5

As with its use for a flux, zinc oxide is a beneficial addition to opaque glazes in small amounts where it improves surface shine and adds to the opacity created by other opacifiers. At temperatures below 1085°C (1985°F), it acts as a beneficial filler and opacifier which partially enters fusion giving anti-craze effect and general stability.

ZINC OXIDE CRYSTALLIZER. The crystalline effects from zinc oxide can be divided into those with small crystals, described later as matts, and those with large crystals. The large crystals, looking like frost patterns up to three inches across, are produced by zinc oxide and silica. These glazes are usually fired in the 1150°C to 1250°C range (2102°F to 2282°F) and cooled very slowly from 1000°C to 500°C (1832°F to 932°F). The cooling over this period may last a few days.

During cooling, the zinc oxide seeks the free silica to form zinc silicate crystals of willemite ($2ZnO . SiO_2$). It will be seen that little free silica is actually required. There is only one molecule of silica to every two of zinc oxide. Yet for these large crystals to form it is necessary for the glaze to be very fluid. This means a minimum of stiffeners, especially alumina. Zinc crystalline glazes therefore contain a minimum of china clay and are runny glazes high in free silica although the free silica is not required for the crystals. See also **Crystalline glazes**.

Consideration of these facts can be made in the molecular formula. The alumina equivalent must not exceed one-fifth of the fluxes excluding zinc oxide. The silica equivalent must be at least a total of two products: zinc oxide equivalent times one and alumina equivalent times ten. Successful glazes have been made without alumina. In such cases titania or zirconia are introduced to give some viscosity and crystal nuclei.

Small crystals give a matt surface. A matt glaze can be produced by the introduction of a separately prepared spinel of zinc aluminate. If the zinc oxide is introduced raw into a glaze, however, it will seek to crystallize with the free silica as in the crystalline glazes previously described.

Small willemite crystals form readily, encouraged by the fact that the zinc oxide retains its crystal identity in the glaze. In fluid glazes which contain boric oxide,

a small amount of titania will act as a catalyst by providing nuclei from which crystals can grow. It is not necessary to slow down the cooling rate. Most kilns cool sufficiently slowly to allow these crystals to form. See **Satin matt**. Neither is it necessary to limit the amount of alumina present unless the particularly smooth satin finish is required. Most glazes are still sufficiently fluid in the 1050°C to 900°C range (1922°F to 1652°F) when these small crystals form and there will be sufficient free silica for the willemite. A high alumina content will inhibit only the growth of large crystals. Small crystals will give matts and can form in high alumina glazes. In fact, a matting agent can be prepared from zinc oxide and china clay of equal weights. The mixture is calcined at 650°C (1202°F) and reground. It can be added to earthenware glazes in amounts up to 25% of the recipe.

The following recipe is for a crystalline matt glaze to be fired at 1100°C (2012°F):

feldspar	10
flint	5
whiting	10
lead bisilicate	50
zinc oxide	15
titanium dioxide	10

It is a decorative glaze with transmutation properties arising from the titania. In order to get full fusion and yet allow crystals to grow, a high proportion of lead bisilicate is used. This makes it a rather fluid glaze which runs down the pot in the firing. Bulbous pots with narrow feet require a much thinner application on the lower half, otherwise a thick layer produces the best results. The titanium dioxide is present to increase the number of crystals. If a slow cooling glaze with very large crystals is required, the titanium dioxide should be reduced and the flint increased.

Zincite. Red zinc oxide. ZnO. A zinc oxide ore which is orange in colour due to manganese impurity.

Zirconia. Zirconium oxide or dioxide. ZrO_2. An opacifier which is similar in properties to tin oxide. Amounts of up to 15% can be added to transparent glazes to give increasing opacity and whiteness. Zir-

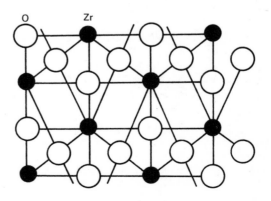

conia is highly refractory and can be used at all temperatures.

Zirconium is a metal with a high melting point. It is used in alloys. It occurs in the silicate mineral zircon which is also cut as a gemstone. The marketed oxide of zirconium is usually called zirconium oxide. It is also called zirconium dioxide which is strictly correct and the term zirconia should correctly be reserved for the theoretically pure chemical that is involved in the glaze fusion. Zirconium oxide is used in paints and ceramics as a white opacifier. It is also used as a refractory acidic stabilizer in frits, especially frits involving colours.

Zirconium oxide is often introduced into glazes as a substitute opacifier for the more expensive tin oxide. The effects are similar and therefore the substitution can be weight for weight. Most potters find that complete substitution gives a glaze of different quality which is not as pleasing as the original. The whiteness from zirconia is more dead-white and harsh. It lacks the soft quality of tin oxide which gives a creamy white or a bluey milk white. The advantages of zirconia as an opacifier over tin oxide are that it is not influenced adversely by reduction and is not subject to chromium flashing. It is also cheaper. Substitution by zirconia for half of the tin oxide content in a glaze gives a satisfactory white glaze with only a little loss of quality and often some gain in a soft surface shine.

Different qualities of opacity and surface texture can result from the use of different fluxes. Although zirconia does not fully enter the fusion but remains suspended, it responds to the different fluxes. Lead oxide gives a pleasing pastel softness in the following glaze which can be used as a maiolica. It is an unusual glaze in that it does not contain any clay. It is for 1100°C (2012°F):

feldspar	33
flint	6
lead bisilicate	50
zirconium oxide	11

Zirconium oxide is prepared from the mineral zirconium silicate. The silicate is therefore cheaper and introduces more zirconia for an equivalent sum of money It also disperses the zirconia more widely in the glaze, an effect which renders a better opacity. This dispersion is improved by the use of a critical particle size around 0·2 microns. Zirconium silicate is marketed as an opacifier ground to this size and coated with dispersal media to prevent coagulation. There are various trade names.

Zirconium silicate. Zircon. $ZrO_2 . SiO_2$. A mineral associated with igneous rocks. It is highly refractory

and harder than quartz. Large crystals which are colourless can be cut as gemstones. The sparkle is second only to diamond. In ceramics it is used to introduce zirconia and silica into glazes and bodies. See **Zirconia**.

It is often easier to disperse zirconia in a glaze by using the silicate rather than the oxide. Amounts are easily related to recipes which use zirconia by considering the silicate as $\frac{2}{3}$ zirconia and $\frac{1}{3}$ silica. Adjustments will be necessary in the silica of the recipe. For example, the following is a semi-opaque zirconia glaze for 1250°C (2282°F) rewritten for zirconium silicate:

feldspar	36	feldspar	36
china clay	9	china clay	9
flint	26	flint	23
whiting	23	whiting	23
zirconium oxide	6	zirconium silicate	9

When zirconium silicate is used it is sometimes found that there is too much silica present. The best whites often form where there is little free silica. To overcome this some zirconium oxide is used in conjunction with the zirconium silicate. Alternatively, extra alumina is introduced to occupy the free silica.

If zirconium silicate is found to be too refractory in glazes then a little zinc oxide is added to increase fusion without loss of opacity.

Zirconium silicate is highly refractory with a melting point of 2550°C (4622°F). It makes an excellent bat wash when mixed with 10% of china clay. It is also strong and is used for making kiln shelves and other furniture. Its physical hardness enables sintered pellets to be used as grinding media in ball mills etc. The photograph shows Podmore and Sons' vibro-energy mills which use zirconium silicate grinding media for grinding zirconium silicate opacifiers to sub-micron size.

APPENDIX OF TABLES

Standard abbreviations

At No	Atomic number	cm	centimetre(s)
AW	Atomic weight	cub	cubic
BS	British Standard	cwt	hundredweight(s) avoirdupois
°C	Degrees centigrade or Celsius	fl oz	fluid ounce(s)
CF	Conversion factor	ft	foot (feet)
D	Density	gall	gallon(s)
EMC	Equilibrium moisture content	gm	gram(s) also written g
°F	Degrees Fahrenheit	imp	imperial measure (UK)
H	Hardness on Mohs' Scale	in	inch(es)
I/G	Inglaze colour	kg	kilo(s) or kilogram(s)
°K	Degrees Kelvin	l	litre(s)
MF	Molecular formula	lb	pound(s) avoirdupois
MP	Melting point	m	metre(s)
MW	Molecular weight	ml	millilitre(s) (synonymous with cc)
O/E	Onglaze enamel		
O/G	Onglaze colour	mm	millimetre(s)
SG	Specific gravity	oz	ounce(s) avoirdupois
°TW	Degrees Twaddell	oz pt	ounces per pint (correctly weight of one pint in ounces)
U/G	Underglaze colour		
UK	United Kingdom (imperial capacity measure)	pt	pint(s)
		qt	quart(s)
US/USA	United States of America (capacity measure)	wt	weight
		yd	yard(s)
avdp	avoirdupois		
cc	cubic centimetre(s) also written cm³ (synonymous with ml)		

Atomic weights of common elements

Al	27·0	Mg	24·3
B	10·8	Mn	54·9
Ba	137·3	N	14·0
C	12·0	Na	23·0
Ca	40·1	Ni	58·7
Cl	35·5	O	16·0
Co	58·9	P	31·0
Cr	52·0	Pb	207·2
Cu	63·5	S	32·1
F	19·0	Si	28·1
Fe	55·8	Sn	118·7
H	1·0	Ti	47·9
K	39·1	Zn	65·4
Li	6·9	Zr	91·2

Simplified ultimate analyses of some common materials

Where two analyses are given they show the possible range.
Amounts below 0·4% are marked t for trace. Seven
glazes are included for comparison.

Material	SiO_2	TiO_2	Al_2O_3	Fe_2O_3	B_2O_3	CaO	MgO	K_2O	Na_2O	Li_2O	loss
Clays:											
Albany slip	57	1	15	6		6	3	2	1		9
Ball clay	47	1	33	1		t	t	2	t		16
	70	1	19	1		t	t	2	t		7
Boulder clay	67		23	3		3		2			2
China clay	46	t	38	1		1	t	1	t		13
	47		39								14
Fireclay	44		39	2		1	t				14
	71	1	19	1		1	t	t	t		7
Malm	44		15	6		15	2	1			17
	77		11	1		5		2			4
Red clay	56		24	6		1	3	1			9
	60	1	20	9		1	1	1	t		7
Stoneware clay	44		38	3		t	t	t	t		15
	68	1	22	t		1	t	2	1		5
Feldspars:											
Potash feldspar	65		18					17			
	68		18	t		1	t	10	3		t
Soda feldspar	66		21			1		3	9		t
	69		19						12		
Lime feldspar	43		37			20					
Mixed feldspar	64		20	t		2	t	9	5		t
	67		19	t		t	t	7	7		
Plagioclase feldspars:											
Oligoclase	66		22			2			10		
Andesine	62		24			5			9		
Labradorite	57		27			9			7		
Bytownite	51		31			14			4		
Feldspathoids:											
Basalt	49	2	14	11		8	10	1	2		3
Cornish stone	71	t	17	t		2	t	7	2		1
	79	t	12	t		t	t	4	4		1
Granite	70		18			1		9	1		1
Lepidolite	48		29	t		t	t	17	1	3	2
	54		25	t		t	t	8	2	5	6
Nepheline syenite	53		29	2		t	t	7	7		2
	56		25	t		1	1	9	8		t
Petalite	76		16	t		1	1	1	1	4	
	78		18	t		t	t	t	t	4	
Spodumene	63		28	1		t	t	1	1	6	t
	64		29	t		t	t	t	t	7	t
Other materials:											
Colemanite	5		t	t	44	26	t				25
					51	27					22
Dolomite	1		1	t		29	19	t	t	t	50
	4		t	t		33	22				41
Talc	52	t	7	2		t	31				8
	63						32				5
Wollastonite	50	1	1	1		47	t				

Material	SiO_2	TiO_2	Al_2O_3	Fe_2O_3	B_2O_3	CaO	MgO	K_2O	Na_2O	P_2O_5	loss
Wood Ash	33		22	2		11	5	9		13	5
	78		9	3		4	2	2		1	1

Material	SiO_2	TiO_2	Al_2O_3	Fe_2O_3	B_2O_3	CaO	MgO	K_2O	Na_2O	PbO	loss
Glasses:											
Cullet	71	2			3	8	2	1	13		
	74	0			0	5	2	1	18		
Lead monosilicate	21									79	
Lead bisilicate	35									65	
Lead sesquisilicate	31									69	
Leadless 1000°C	44		10		22	15		6	3		
1100°C	54		11		15	13		7			
1200°C	66		13		4	11	1	5			
1300°C	71		14		2	8	1	4			
Plumbic 900°C	46		3		6	5				40	
1000°C	50		7		7	5		2	3	26	
1100°C	51		8		9	4		4	4	20	

Table of Harrison pyrometric cones

(Harrison Mayer Ltd, Meir,
Stoke-on-Trent, England)

Cone no.	Squatting temperatures when heated at 240°C/hr (432°F/hr) °C	°F to nearest 5°	Cone no.	Squatting temperatures when heated at 240°C/hr (432°F/hr) °C	°F to nearest 5°
022	600	1110	02A	1070	1960
022A	625	1155	01	1080	1975
021	650	1200	01A	1090	1995
020	670	1240	1	1100	2010
019	690	1275	1A	1110	2030
018	710	1310	2	1120	2050
017	730	1345	2A	1130	2065
016	750	1380	3	1140	2085
015	790	1455	3A	1150	2100
014	815	1500	4	1160	2120
013	835	1535	4A	1170	2140
012	855	1570	5	1180	2155
011	880	1615	5A	1190	2175
010	900	1650	6	1200	2190
09	920	1690	6A	1215	2220
08	940	1725	7	1230	2245
08A	950	1740	7A	1240	2265
07	960	1760	8	1250	2280
07A	970	1780	8A	1260	2300
06	980	1795	8B	1270	2320
06A	990	1815	9	1280	2335
05	1000	1830	9A	1290	2355
05A	1010	1850	10	1300	2370
04	1020	1870	10A	1310	2390
04A	1030	1885	11	1320	2410
03	1040	1905	12	1350	2460
03A	1050	1920	13	1380	2515
02	1060	1940	14	1410	2570

Table of Harrison pyrometric cones
(Harrison Mayer Ltd, Meir, Stoke-on-Trent, England)
Computer numbers
Six-digital computer numbers are replacing the cone
numbering system including A and B. Potters familiar
with the old numbers will see that they are incorporated in
the last four numbers. Thus cone 012 for 855°C becomes
340120 and cone 8 for 1250°C becomes 341080.

Standard cone no.	Small cone no.	Degrees °C	Standard cone no.	Small cone no.	Degrees °C	Standard cone no.	Small cone no.	Degrees °C
340220	342220	600	340075	342075	970	341045	343045	1170
340225	342225	625	340060	342060	980	341050	343050	1180
340210	342210	650	340065	342065	990	341055	343055	1190
340200	342200	670	340050	342050	1000	341060	343060	1200
340190	342190	690	340055	342055	1010	341065	343065	1215
340180	342180	710	340040	342040	1020	341070	343070	1230
340170	342170	730	340045	342045	1030	341075	343075	1240
340160	342160	750	340030	342030	1040	341080	343080	1250
340165	342165	760	340035	342035	1050	341085	343085	1260
340150	342150	790	340020	342020	1060	341087	343087	1270
340155	342155	800	340025	342025	1070	341090	343090	1280
340140	342140	815	340010	342010	1080	341095	343095	1290
340130	342130	835	340015	342015	1090	341100	343100	1300
340120	342120	855	341010	343010	1100	341105	343105	1310
340110	342110	880	341015	343015	1110	341110	343110	1320
340100	342100	900	341020	343020	1120	341120	343120	1350
340090	342090	920	341025	343025	1130	341130	343130	1380
340080	342080	940	341030	343030	1140	341140	343140	1410
340085	342085	950	341035	343035	1150	341150	343150	1435
340070	342070	960	341040	343040	1160	341160	343160	1460
						341170	343170	1480
						341180	343180	1500

Table of Orton pyrometric cones
(The Edward Orton Jr Ceramic Foundation,
Columbus, Ohio)

Cone no.	Large cones; squatting temperatures when heated at: 60°C/hr	108°F/hr	150°C/hr	270°F/hr	Cone no.	Large cones; squatting temperatures when heated at: 60°C/hr	108°F/hr	150°C/hr	270°F/hr
022	585	1085	600	1112	04	1050	1922	1060	1940
021	602	1116	614	1137	03	1086	1987	1101	2014
020	625	1157	635	1175	02	1101	2014	1120	2048
019	668	1234	683	1261	01	1117	2043	1137	2079
018	696	1285	717	1323	1	1136	2077	1154	2109
017	727	1341	747	1377	2	1142	2088	1162	2124
016	764	1407	792	1458	3	1152	2106	1168	2134
015	790	1454	804	1479	4	1168	2134	1186	2167
014	834	1533	838	1540	5	1177	2151	1196	2185
013	869	1596	852	1566	6	1201	2194	1222	2232
012	866	1591	884	1623	7	1215	2219	1240	2264
011	886	1627	894	1641	8	1236	2257	1263	2305
010	887	1629	894	1641	9	1260	2300	1280	2336
09	915	1679	923	1693	10	1285	2345	1305	2381
08	945	1733	955	1751	11	1294	2361	1315	2399
07	973	1783	984	1803	12	1306	2383	1326	2419
06	991	1816	999	1830	13	1321	2410	1346	2455
05	1031	1888	1046	1915	14	1388	2530	1366	2491

Cone no.	300°C/hr	540°F/hr	Cone no.	300°C/hr	540°F/hr	Cone no.	300°C/hr	540°F/hr
	Small cones; squatting temperatures when heated at:			*Small cones; squatting temperatures when heated at:*			*Small cones; squatting temperatures when heated at:*	
022	630	1165	010	919	1686	3	1196	2185
021	643	1189	09	955	1751	4	1209	2208
020	666	1231	08	983	1801	5	1221	2230
019	723	1333	07	1008	1846	6	1255	2291
018	752	1386	06	1023	1873	7	1264	2307
017	784	1443	05	1062	1944	8	1300	2372
016	825	1517	04	1098	2008	9	1317	2403
015	843	1549	03	1131	2068	10	1330	2426
014	870	1596	02	1148	2098	11	1336	2437
013	880	1615	01	1178	2152	12	1355	2471
012	900	1650	1	1179	2154			
011	915	1680	2	1179	2154			

Table of Seger pyrometric cones
(Wenger Ltd, Stoke-on-Trent, England)

Cone no.	°C	°F	Cone no.	°C	°F	Cone no.	°C	°F
	Large cones; squatting temperatures when heated at 150°C/hr (270°F/hr)			*Large cones; squatting temperatures when heated at 150°C/hr (270°F/hr)*			*Large cones; squatting temperatures when heated at 150°C/hr (270°F/hr)*	
022	595	1103	010a	920	1688	3a	1170	2138
021	640	1184	09a	935	1715	4a	1195	2183
020	660	1220	08a	955	1751	5a	1215	2219
019	685	1265	07a	970	1778	6a	1240	2264
018	705	1301	06a	990	1814	7	1260	2300
017	730	1346	05a	1000	1832	8	1280	2336
016	755	1391	04a	1025	1877	9	1300	2372
015a	780	1436	03a	1055	1931	10	1320	2408
014a	805	1481	02a	1085	1985	11	1340	2444
013a	835	1535	01a	1105	2021	12	1360	2480
012a	860	1580	1a	1125	2057	13	1380	2516
011a	900	1652	2a	1150	2102	14	1400	2552

Cone no.	°C	°F	Cone no.	°C	°F	Cone no.	°C	°F
	Small cones; squatting temperatures when heated at 150°C/hr (270°F/hr)			*Small cones; squatting temperatures when heated at 150°C/hr (270°F/hr)*			*Small cones; squatting temperatures when heated at 150°C/hr (270°F/hr)*	
022	605	1121	010a	925	1697	3a	1185	2165
021	650	1202	09a	940	1724	4a	1220	2228
020	675	1247	08a	965	1769	5a	1230	2246
019	695	1283	07a	975	1787	6a	1260	2300
018	715	1319	06a	995	1823	7	1270	2318
017	735	1355	05a	1010	1850	8	1295	2363
016	760	1400	04a	1055	1931	9	1315	2399
015a	785	1445	03a	1070	1958	10	1330	2426
014a	815	1499	02a	1100	2012	11	1350	2462
013a	845	1553	01a	1125	2057	12	1375	2507
012a	890	1634	1a	1145	2093	13	1395	2543
011a	900	1652	2a	1165	2129	14	1410	2570

Conversion scales

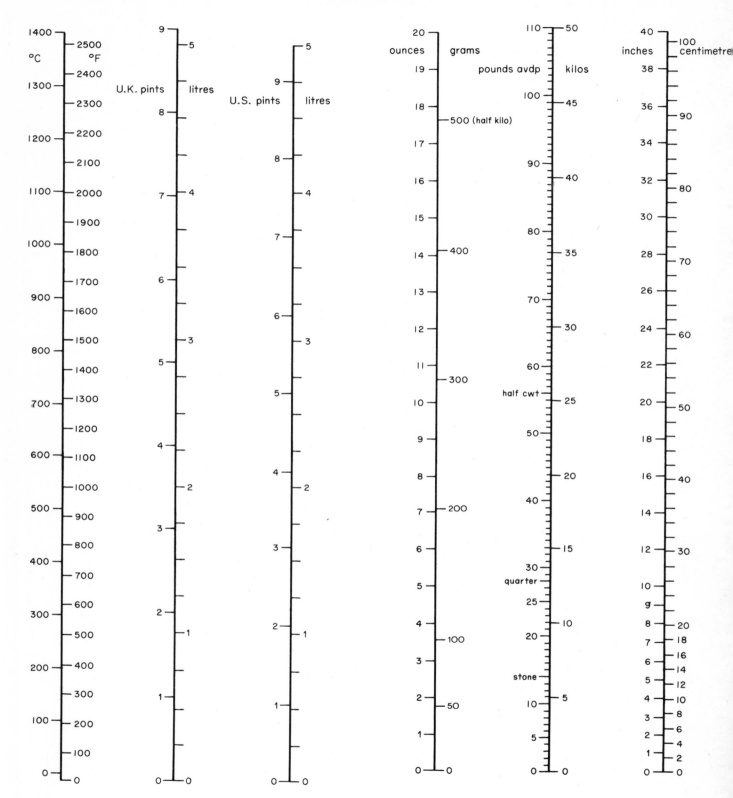

Tables concerning densities and contents of suspensions

See **Formula, Brongniart's**

Slips and stoneware glazes
(Metric measures)
(Dry materials averaging SG 2·5)

Density gm 100 cc	Contents		Approx percentages dry – water	cc water per 100 gm dry material
	gm	cc		
140	66·7	73·3	48 – 52	109
145	75	70	52 – 48	93
150	83·3	66·7	56 – 44	80
155	91·7	63·3	59 – 41	69
160	100	60	63 – 37	60

Slips and stoneware glazes
(UK measures)
(SG 2·5)

oz pt UK	Contents		Approx percentages dry – water	Approx pints per 100 oz of dry material for usual suspensions
	oz dry	fl oz water		
25	8·3	16·7	33 – 67	
26	10	16	39 – 61	
27	11·7	15·3	43 – 57	
28	13·3	14·7	48 – 52	5·5
29	15	14	52 – 48	4·7
30	16·7	13·3	56 – 44	4
31	18·3	12·7	59 – 41	3·5
32	20	12	63 – 37	
33	21·7	11·3	66 – 34	
34	23·3	10·7	69 – 31	

Low sol glazes
(UK measures)
(SG 3·0)

oz pt UK	Contents		Approx percentages dry – water	Approx pints per 100 oz of dry material for usual suspensions
	oz dry	fl oz water		
25	7·5	17·5	30 – 70	
26	9	17	35 – 65	
27	10·5	16·5	39 – 61	
28	12	16	43 – 57	
29	13·5	15·5	47 – 53	
30	15	15	50 – 50	5
31	16·5	14·5	53 – 47	4·4
32	18	14	56 – 44	3·9
33	19·5	13·5	59 – 41	3·5

Plumbic glazes
(UK measures)
(SG 4·0)

oz pt UK	Contents		Approx percentages dry – water	Approx pints per 100 oz of dry material for usual suspensions
	oz dry	fl oz water		
27	9·3	17·7	34 – 66	
28	10·7	17·3	38 – 62	
29	12	17	41 – 59	
30	13·3	16·7	44 – 56	
31	14·7	16·3	47 – 53	
32	16	16	50 – 50	5
33	17·3	15·7	52 – 48	4·5
34	18·7	15·3	55 – 45	4·1
35	20	15	57 – 43	3·75

Slips and stoneware glazes
(US measures)
(SG 2·5)

oz pt US	Contents		Approx percentages dry – water	Approx US pints per 100 oz of dry material
	oz dry	oz water (fl oz)		
23	10·5	12·5 (12)	46 – 54	
24	12·2	11·8 (11·3)	51 – 49	5·8
25	13·8	11·2 (10·8)	55 – 45	4·9
26	15·5	10·5 (10)	60 – 40	4
27	17·2	9·8 (9·4)	64 – 36	

Low sol glazes
(US measures)
(SG 3·0)

oz pt US	Contents		Approx percentages dry – water	Approx US pints per 100 oz of dry material
	oz dry	oz water (fl oz)		
25	12·5	12·5 (12)	50 – 50	6
26	14	12 (11·5)	54 – 46	5·1
27	15·5	11·5 (11)	60 – 40	4·4
28	17	11 (10·5)	65 – 35	3·9

Plumbic glazes
(US measures)
(SG 4·0)

oz pt US	Contents		Approx percentages dry – water	Approx US pints per 100 oz of dry material
	oz dry	oz water (fl oz)		
27	13·7	13·3 (12·8)	51 – 49	5·8
28	15·1	12·9 (12·4)	54 – 46	5·1
29	16·4	12·6 (12·1)	57 – 43	4·6
30	17·7	12·3 (11·8)	59 – 41	4·2

Table of elements

Element	Symbol	AW	Valency	Element	Symbol	AW	Valency
Aluminium	Al	27·0	3	Magnesium	Mg	24·3	2
Antimony	Sb	121·8	3	Manganese	Mn	54·9	2, 3 and 4
Arsenic	As	74·9	3	Nickel	Ni	58·7	2 and 4
Barium	Ba	137·3	2	Nitrogen	N	14·0	3
Beryllium	Be	9·0	2	Oxygen	O	16·0	2
Bismuth	Bi	209·0	3	Phosphorus	P	31·0	3 and 5
Boron	B	10·8	3	Platinum	Pt	195·1	—
Cadmium	Cd	112·4	2	Potassium	K	39·1	1
Calcium	Ca	40·1	2	Praseodymium	Pr	140·9	4
Carbon	C	12·0	2 and 4	Selenium	Se	79·0	—
Cerium	Ce	140·1	4	Silicon	Si	28·1	4
Chlorine	Cl	35·5	1	Silver	Ag	107·9	—
Chromium	Cr	52·0	3	Sodium	Na	23·0	1
Cobalt	Co	58·9	2 and 3	Strontium	Sr	87·6	2
Copper	Cu	63·5	1 and 2	Sulphur	S	32·1	2 and 4
Fluorine	F	19·0	1	Tin	Sn	118·7	4
Germanium	Ge	72·6	4	Titanium	Ti	47·9	4
Gold	Au	197·0	—	Uranium	U	238·0	3, 4 and 5
Hydrogen	H	1·0	1	Vanadium	V	50·9	2, 3, 4, and 5
Iron	Fe	55·8	2 and 3	Zinc	Zn	65·4	2
Lead	Pb	207·2	2 and 4	Zirconium	Zr	91·2	4
Lithium	Li	6·9	1				

List of capacity equivalents

See also **Formula**

Note that there are two systems involving fluid ounces, pints and gallons: the imperial measure used in the United Kingdom (referred to as UK measure) and the US measure used in the United States of America. All the other measures in ounces and pounds avoirdupois, inches and feet, and the metric system are universal. The cubic yards, feet and inches are reserved for measurement of solids but are useful in calculating the capacity of pots.

1 cubic metre	=	1 stere	1 cc	=	0·06102 cub in	1 US gall	=	3·7853 litres
	=	1000 litres		=	0·0352 UK fl oz		=	0·8327 UK gall
1 litre	=	1000 cc (ml)		=	0·0338 US fl oz		=	231 cub in
1 cc	=	1000 cubic mm				1 US pt	=	0·4732 litre
			1 cub ft	=	28·317 litres		=	473·2 cc
1 cub yd	=	27 cub ft		=	6·237 UK gall		=	0·8327 UK pt
1 cub ft	=	1728 cub in		=	7·481 US gall		=	16·6528 UK fl oz
			1 cub in	=	16·387 cc		=	28·875 cub in
1 UK gall	=	4 UK qt		=	0·5768 UK fl oz	1 US fl oz	=	29·573 cc
	=	8 UK pt		=	0·5539 US fl oz		=	1·0408 UK fl oz
1 UK pt	=	20 UK fl oz					=	1·805 cub in
			1 UK gall	=	4·5461 litres			
1 US gall	=	8 US pt		=	0·1603 cub ft	wt of 1 UK pt of water	=	20·042 oz
1 US pt	=	16 US fl oz		=	1·201 US gall	wt of 1 US pt of water	=	16·705 oz
			1 UK pt	=	0·5683 litre			
1 litre	=	0·2199 UK gall		=	568·3 cc			
	=	1·7598 UK pt		=	1·201 US pt			
	=	35·196 UK fl oz		=	19·22 US fl oz			
	=	0·2642 US gall		=	34·677 cub in			
	=	2·1132 US pt	1 UK fl oz	=	28·412 cc			
	=	33·8112 US fl oz		=	0·961 US fl oz			
	=	61·025 cub in		=	1·734 cub in			

Pint weight equivalents

See Formula, density

oz pt UK	oz pt US	SG	°TW
22	18·3	1·10	20
22·8	19	1·14	28
23	19·2	1·15	30
24	20	1·20	40
25	20·8	1·25	50
25·2	21	1·26	52
26	21·7	1·30	60
26·4	22	1·32	64
27	22·5	1·35	70
27·6	23	1·38	76
28	23·3	1·40	80
28·8	24	1·44	88
29	24·2	1·45	90
30	25	1·50	100
31	25·8	1·55	110
31·2	26	1·56	112
32	26·7	1·60	120
32·4	27	1·62	124
33	27·5	1·65	130
33·6	28	1·68	136
34	28·3	1·70	140
34·8	29	1·74	148
35	29·2	1·75	150
36	30	1·80	160
37	30·8	1·85	170

List of length equivalents

1 metre	=	100 centimetres
1 centimetre	=	10 millimetres
1 yard	=	3 feet
	=	36 inches
1 foot	=	12 inches
1 inch	=	0·0833 feet
1 metre	=	1·0936 yards
	=	3·2808 feet
	=	39·3696 inches
1 centimetre	=	0·3937 inches
1 yard	=	0·9144 metre
1 foot	=	30·48 centimetres
1 inch	=	2·54 centimetres

To convert from inches into centimetres multiply by 2·54
To convert from centimetres to inches multiply by 0·3937

Capacity factors

To convert from :	into :	multiply by :
UK pints	US pints	1·201
UK pints	litres	0·5683
UK fl oz	cc	28·412
US pints	UK pints	0·8327
US pints	litres	0·4732
US fl oz	cc	29·573
litres	UK pints	1·7598
litres	US pints	2·1132

List of weight equivalents

1 tonne	=	1000 kg
1 kg	=	1000 gm
1 gm	=	0·001 kg

gross or long measure (UK)

1 ton	=	20 cwt
	=	2240 lb
1 cwt	=	112 lb
1 lb	=	16 oz
1 oz	=	0·0625 lb

net or short measure (US)

1 ton	=	20 cwt
	=	2000 lb
1 cwt	=	100 lb

1 tonne	=	2204·61 lb
	=	0·9842 ton
1 kg	=	2·2046 lb
1 gm	=	0·0353 oz

1 gross cwt	=	50·803 kg
1 net cwt	=	45·359 kg
1 lb	=	453·6 gm
	=	0·4536 kg
1 oz	=	28·35 gm

Density factors

See also Formula, density

To convert from :	into :	multiply by :
oz pt UK	oz pt US	0·8327
oz pt UK	gm/cc	0·0499
oz pt US	oz pt UK	1·201
oz pt US	gm/cc	0·0599
gm/cc	oz pt UK	20·042
gm/cc	oz pt US	16·705

Dry weight factors

To convert from :	into :	multiply by :
ounces	grams	28·35
pounds	kilograms	0·4536
gross cwts (UK)	kilograms	50·803
net cwts (US)	kilograms	45·36
grams	ounces	0·0353
kilograms	pounds	2·2046
kilograms	gross cwts (UK)	0·0196
kilograms	net cwts (US)	0·0221

Table of oxide effect on surface tension

See Surface tension

HIGH SURFACE TENSION

Alumina
Magnesia
Zirconia
Calcia
Tin oxide
Zinc oxide
Strontia
Baria
Silica
Titania
Boric oxide
Lithia
Lead oxide
Soda
Potash

LOW SURFACE TENSION

Table of acceptable limits for unity formulae of glazes

	R_2O_3	R_2O_3 with B_2O_3	RO_2
Lead glazes			
900°–1000°C 1652°–1832°F	0·1 to 0·3	to 1·0	1·5 to 3·0
1000°–1100°C 1832°–2012°F	0·1 to 0·35	to 1·0	1·7 to 3·2
1100°–1200°C 2012°–2192°F	0·2 to 0·4	to 1·0	2·0 to 3·2
Leadless glazes			
900°–1000°C 1652°–1832°F	0·1 to 0·4	to 2·4	1·0 to 3·0
1000°–1100°C 1832°–2012°F	0·2 to 0·5	to 1·5	2·0 to 3·5
1100°–1200°C 2012°–2192°F	0·3 to 0·6	to 1·0	2·0 to 4·0
1200°–1300°C 2192°–2372°F	0·4 to 0·7	to 1·0	1·5 to 3·0 (crystalline) 3·0 to 7·0 (full fusion)

Table of thermal expansion and contraction
(approximately proportionate)

For use of table see Glaze fit

HIGH EXPANSION

Na_2O
(If the list were proportionate there would be a gap here
equal to the list from B_2O_3 to CuO)
K_2O
SiO_2 crystalline cristobalite $\alpha\beta$ includes inversion
(If the list were proportionate there would be a gap here
equal to the list from B_2O_3 to PbO)
CaO SrO
ThO_2
Cr_2O_3
BaO BeO
CoO
SiO_2 crystalline quartz α no inversion
PbO NiO Fe_2O_3 TiO_2 CeO_2
Typical lead glass
Sb_2O_3
Typical soda glass
Typical white earthenware body
Li_2O P_2O_5 As_2O_3
ZnO
Typical earthenware glaze
Typical stoneware body
CuO MnO
Typical grog
MgO
Porcelain body
Top-quality firebrick
Sillimanite
SnO_2 ZrO_2
Al_2O_3
SiO_2 fused in bodies or glazes
B_2O_3

LOW EXPANSION

Mohs' Scale of hardness

For use see Mohs' Scale

SOFT

1 Talc
2 Gypsum
3 Calcite
4 Fluorspar
5 Apatite
6 Orthoclase
7 Quartz
8 Topaz
9 Corundum
10 Diamond

HARD

Effective ranges of glaze oxides

See individual indices for details

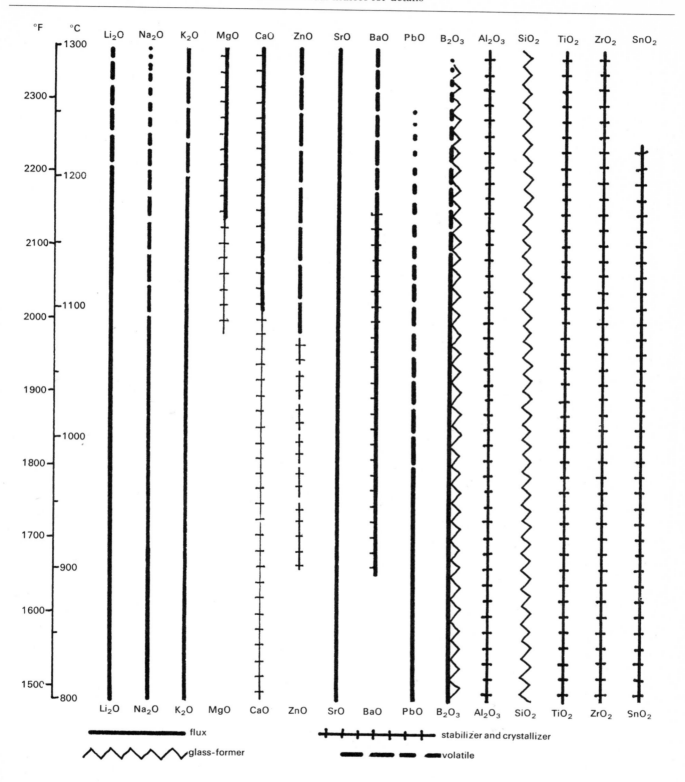

flux

glass-former

stabilizer and crystallizer

volatile

337

Table of mineral constants

MP and D = Melting temperatures and decomposition temperatures which give some indication of behaviour but are often lowered by interaction. The relevant articles must be read in conjunction with this table.
* = Variables—typical examples given.

Name	Chemical formula	MW	SG	H	MP °C	MP °F	CF	Oxides entering fusion
Alabaster	$CaSO_4.2H_2O$	172·2	2·3	3	D 1450	D 2642	0·326	CaO
Albite (soda feldspar)	$Na_2O.Al_2O_3.6SiO_2$	524·6	2·6	6·5	1170	2138	0·118 0·194 0·688	Na_2O Al_2O_3 SiO_2
Alumina	Al_2O_3	102·0	3·8	9	2050	3722	1·0	Al_2O_3
Amblygonite	$Li.AlF.PO_4$	147·9	3·0	6	D 1100	D 2012	0·101 0·245 0·480	Li_2O Al_2O_3 P_2O_5
Anatase	TiO_2	79·9	3·8	6·5	1560	2840	1·0	TiO_2
Andalusite	$Al_2O_3.SiO_2$	162·1	3·2	7·5	1380	2516	0·629 0·371	Al_2O_3 SiO_2
Andesine (plagioclase feldspar)	$0·6Na_2O\ Al_2O_3.4·4SiO_2$* $0·4CaO$	426·1	2·7	6·5	1350	2462	0·087 0·053 0·239 0·621	Na_2O CaO Al_2O_3 SiO_2
Anhydrite (calcium sulphate)	$CaSO_4$	136·2	2·9	3·5	D 1450	D 2642	0·412	CaO
Anorthite (lime feldspar)	$CaO.Al_2O_3.2SiO_2$	278·3	2·8	6·5	1550	2822	0·202 0·366 0·432	CaO Al_2O_3 SiO_2
Anorthoclase (mixed feldspar)	$NaKO.Al_2O_3.6SiO_2$	540·7	2·6	6·5	1190	2174	0·144 0·189 0·667	NaKO Al_2O_3 SiO_2
Antimonate of lead	$Pb_3(SbO_4)_2$	993·2			800	1472	0·664 0·294	PbO Sb_2O_3
Antimony oxide	Sb_2O_3	291·6	5·5		650	1202	1·0	Sb_2O_3
Apatite	$CaF_2.3Ca_3(PO_4)_2$	1009·0	3·2	5	D 1300	D 2372	0·556 0·422	CaO P_2O_5
Aragonite	$CaCO_3$	100·1	2·9	4	D 825	D 1517	0·561	CaO
Azurite	$2CuCO_3.Cu(OH)_2$	344·5	3·7	4	D 500	D 932	0·689	CuO
Baria (baryta)	BaO	153·3	5·0		1923	3493	1·0	BaO
Barium carbonate	$BaCO_3$	197·3	4·4		D 1450 reduced— D 900	D 2642 D 1652	0·777	BaO
Barytes (barium sulphate)	$BaSO_4$	233·4	4·5	3·5	D 1350	D 2462	0·657	BaO
Barytocalcite	$BaCO_3.CaCO_3$*	297·4			D 900	D 1652	0·515 0·189	BaO CaO
Bauxite	$Al_2O_3.2H_2O$	138·0	2·5	3	D 300	D 572	0·739	Al_2O_3
Bentonite	$Al_2O_3.4SiO_2.H_2O$*	360·4			D 600	D 1112	0·283 0·667	Al_2O_3 SiO_2
Beryllia	BeO	25·0	3·0		2500	4532	1·0	BeO

Name	Chemical formula	MW	SG	H	MP °C	MP °F	CF	Oxides entering fusion
Bismuth oxide	Bi_2O_3	466.0	9.0		850	1562	1.0	Bi_2O_3
Bone ash	$Ca_3(PO_4)_2$*	310.3	3.1		1670	3038	0.542 0.458	CaO P_2O_5
Boracite	$6MgO.MgCl_2.8B_2O_3$*	893.9	2.9	7	D 900	D 1652	0.316 0.623	MgO B_2O_3
Borax	$Na_2B_4O_7.10H_2O$	381.2	2.5	2	D 350	D 662	0.163 0.365	Na_2O B_2O_3
Boric acid	$B(OH)_3$	61.8	1.5		D 200	D 392	0.563	B_2O_3
Boric oxide	B_2O_3	69.6	1.8		700	1292	1.0	B_2O_3
Brookite	TiO_2	79.9			1830	3326	1.0	TiO_2
Bytownite (plagioclase feldspar)	$0.8CaO \quad Al_2O_3.2.8SiO_2$* $0.2Na_2O$	327.6	2.7	6.5	1500	2732	0.137 0.038 0.311 0.514	CaO Na_2O Al_2O_3 SiO_2
Calcia	CaO	56.1	3.3		2570	4658	1.0	CaO
Calcite	$CaCO_3$	100.1	2.7	3	D 825	D 1517	0.561	CaO
Calcium borate	$Ca(BO_2)_2$	125.7			1100	2012	0.446 0.554	CaO B_2O_3
Calcium carbonate	$CaCO_3$	100.1	2.8	3	D 825	D 1517	0.561	CaO
Calcium chloride	$CaCl_2$	111.1	2.15		D 780	D 1436	0.505	CaO
Calcium fluoride	CaF_2	78.1	3.2		D 1360	D 2480	0.718	CaO
Calcium phosphate	$Ca_3(PO_4)_2$	310.3	3.2		1730	3146	0.542 0.458	CaO P_2O_5
Calcium sulphate	$CaSO_4$	136.2	2.9	3.5	D 1450	D 2642	0.412	CaO
Cassiterite	SnO_2	150.7	6.7	7	1150	2102	1.0	SnO_2
Celestine	$SrSO_4$	183.7	3.9	3.5	D 1300	D 2372	0.564	SrO
Celsian (barium feldspar)	$BaO.Al_2O_3.2SiO_2$	375.5	3.4	6.5	1500	2732	0.408 0.272 0.320	BaO Al_2O_3 SiO_2
Ceria	CeO_2	172.1	7.3		1950	3542	1.0	CeO_2
Chalk	$CaCO_3$	100.1	2.7	2.5	D 825	D 1517	0.561	CaO
China clay	$Al_2O_3.2SiO_2.2H_2O$*	258.2	2.5	2.0	D 600	D 1112	0.395 0.466	Al_2O_3 SiO_2
Chromite	$FeO.Cr_2O_3$	223.8	4.4	5.5	2000	3632	0.357 0.679	Fe_2O_3 Cr_2O_3
Chromium oxide	Cr_2O_3	152.0	5.2		2265	4109	1.0	Cr_2O_3
Cobalt carbonate	$CoCO_3$	118.9	4.0		D 800	D 1472	0.630	CoO
Cobalt oxide	CoO	74.9	5.7		1805	3281	1.0	CoO
Cobalt oxide	Co_3O_4	240.7	6.0		D 900	D 1652	0.934	CoO
Colemanite	$2CaO.3B_2O_3.5H_2O$*	411.0	2.3	4.5	D 800	D 1472	0.273 0.508	CaO B_2O_3
Copper carbonate	$CuCO_3$	123.5	5.0		D 500	D 932	0.644	CuO
Copper carbonate basic	$CuCO_3.Cu(OH)_2$	221.0	4.0		D 500	D 932	0.719	CuO
Copper oxide black (cupric oxide)	CuO	79.5	6.4		1148	2098	1.0	CuO

Name	Chemical formula	MW	SG	H	MP °C	MP °F	CF	Oxides entering fusion
Copper oxide red (cuprous oxide)	Cu_2O	143·0	6·0		1230	2246	1·112	CuO
Copper sulphate	$CuSO_4.5H_2O$	249·6	2·3		D 650	D 1202	0·319	CuO
Cristobalite	SiO_2	60·1	2·3		1710	3110	1·0	SiO_2
Crocus martis	$FeSO_4$	151·9			D 1200	D 2192	1·051	Fe_2O_3
Cryolite	Na_3AlF_6	210·0	3·0	2·5	D 1000	D 1832	0·443 0·243 0·543	Na_2O Al_2O_3 F_2
Cuprite	Cu_2O	143·0	5·8	4·0	1230	2246	1·112	CuO
Diaspore	$Al_2O_3.H_2O$	120·0	2·9	3·5	D 350	D 662	0·850	Al_2O_3
Diopside	$CaMg(SiO_3)_2$	216·6	3·3		1392	2538	0·259 0·186 0·555	CaO MgO SiO_2
Dolomite	$CaMg(CO_3)_2$	184·4	2·8	4	D 1000	D 1832	0·304 0·219	CaO MgO
Enstatite	$MgSiO_3$	100·4			1550	2822	0·401 0·599	MgO SiO_2
Epsom salts	$MgSO_4.7H_2O$	246·4	1·7		D 1127	D 2061	0·163	MgO
Feldspar barium (celsian)	$BaO.Al_2O_3.2SiO_2$	375·5	3·4	6·5	1500	2732	0·408 0·272 0·320	BaO Al_2O_3 SiO_2
Feldspar lime (anorthite)	$CaO.Al_2O_3.2SiO_2$	278·3	2·8	6·5	1550	2822	0·202 0·366 0·432	CaO Al_2O_3 SiO_2
Feldspar mixed (anorthoclase)	$NaKO.Al_2O_3.6SiO_2$	540·7	2·6	6;5	1190	2174	0·144 0·189 0·667	NaKO Al_2O_3 SiO_2
Feldspar plagioclase (see Andesine, Bytownite, Labradorite, Oligoclase, Hyalophane under this table)								
Feldspar potash (orthoclase)	$K_2O.Al_2O_3.6SiO_2$	556·8	2·5	6	1200	2192	0·169 0·183 0·648	K_2O Al_2O_3 SiO_2
Feldspar soda (albite)	$Na_2O.Al_2O_3.6SiO_2$	524·6	2·6	6·5	1170	2138	0·118 0·194 0·688	Na_2O Al_2O_3 SiO_2
Ferric oxide	Fe_2O_3	159·6	5·3		1565	2849	1·0	Fe_2O_3
Ferrosic oxide	Fe_3O_4	231·4	5·2		D 1538	D 2800	1·035	Fe_2O_3
Ferrous carbonate	$FeCO_3$	115·8	3·8		D 450	D 842	0·689	Fe_2O_3
Ferrous oxide	FeO	71·8	5·7		1420	2588	1·111	Fe_2O_3
Ferrous sulphate	$FeSO_4.7H_2O$	277·9	1·9		D 1200	D 2192	0·287	Fe_2O_3
Ferrous titanate	$FeTiO_3$	151·7	4·8	6	1365	2489	0·526 0·527	Fe_2O_3 TiO_2
Flint	SiO_2	60·1	2·6	7	1600	2912	0·970 0·030	SiO_2 CaO
Fluorspar	CaF_2	78·1	3·2	4	D 1330	D 2426	0·718	CaO
Galena	PbS	239·3	7·5	2·5	D 1210	D 2210	0·933	PbO
Germania	GeO_2	104·6	4·3		1115	2039	1·0	GeO_2
Gibbsite	$Al(OH)_3$	78·0	2·4	3	D 300	D 572	0·654	Al_2O_3
Gypsum	$CaSO_4.2H_2O$	172·2	2·3	2	D 1450	D 2642	0·412	CaO

Name	Chemical formula	MW	SG	H	MP °C	MP °F	CF	Oxides entering fusion
Haematite	Fe_2O_3	159·6	4·9	6·5	1457	2655	0·99	Fe_2O_3
Hemimorphite	$2ZnO.SiO_2.H_2O$*	240·9	3·4	5	D 200	D 392	0·676 0·249	ZnO SiO_2
Hyalophane (barium feldspar)	$K_2O.BaO.2Al_2O_3.8SiO_2$*	932·3	2·6	6	1350	2462	0·101 0·164 0·219 0·516	K_2O BaO Al_2O_3 SiO_2
Ilmenite	$FeTiO_3$*	151·7	4·8	6	1365	2489	0·526 0·527	Fe_2O_3 TiO_2
Iron carbonate	$FeCO_3$	115·8	3·8		D 450	D 842	0·689	Fe_2O_3
Iron chromate	$FeCrO_3$	155·8	5·0		1700	3092	0·512 0·488	Fe_2O_3 Cr_2O_3
Iron oxide black	FeO	71·8	5·7		1420	2588	1·111 reduced— 1·0	Fe_2O_3 FeO
Iron oxide red	Fe_2O_3	159·6	5·3		1565	2849	1·0	Fe_2O_3
Iron pyrites	FeS_2	120·0	4·9	6·5	D 510	D 950	0·665	Fe_2O_3
Iron spangles	Fe_3O_4	231·4	5·2		D 1538	D 2800	1·035	Fe_2O_3
Kalium soda	NaKO	78·1			700	1292	1·0	NaKO
Kaolinite	$Al_2Si_2O_5(OH)_4$	258·2	2·6	2·5	D 600	D 1112	0·395 0·466	Al_2O_3 SiO_2
Kyanite	$Al_2O_3.SiO_2$	162·1	3·6	4/7	1350	2462	0·629 0·371	Al_2O_3 SiO_2
Labradorite (plagioclase feldspar)	$0.6CaO$ $Al_2O_3.3.6SiO_2$* $0.4Na_2O$	376·9	2·7	6	1400	2552	0·089 0·066 0·271 0·574	CaO Na_2O Al_2O_3 SiO_2
Lead bisilicate	$PbO.2SiO_2$	343·4	4·5		900	1652	0·649 0·351	PbO SiO_2
Lead carbonate (cerussite)	$PbCO_3$	267·2	6·6	3·4	D 315	D 599	0·835	PbO
Lead carbonate basic	$2PbCO_3.Pb(OH)_2$	775·6	6·5		D 315	D 599	0·863	PbO
Lead monosilicate	$PbO.SiO_2$	283·3			800	1472	0·788 0·212	PbO SiO_2
Lead orthosilicate	$2PbO.SiO_2$	506·5			750	1382	0·881 0·119	PbO SiO_2
Lead oxide red (minium)	Pb_3O_4	685·6	9·1		D 500	D 932	0·977	PbO
Lead oxide yellow (litharge)	PbO	223·2	9·3		880	1616	1·0	PbO
Lead sesquisilicate	$2PbO.3SiO_2$	626·7			850	1562	0·712 0·288	PbO SiO_2
Lead titanate	$PbTiO_3$	303·1			1000	1832	0·736 0·264	PbO TiO_2
Lepidolite	$Li_2F_2.Al_2O_3.3SiO_2$*	334·1	2·8	3	D 1200	D 2192	0·089 0·305 0·539	Li_2O Al_2O_3 SiO_2
Leucite	$KAlSi_2O_6$	218·3	2·5	6	1350	2462	0·216 0·234 0·550	K_2O Al_2O_3 SiO_2

Name	Chemical formula	MW	SG	H	MP °C	MP °F	CF	Oxides entering fusion
Limestone	$CaCO_3$	100·1	2·6	3·5	D 825	D 1517	0·561	CaO
Limonite	$2Fe_2O_3.3H_2O$	373·2	3·8	5·5	D 200	D 392	0·855	Fe_2O_3
Lithia	Li_2O	29·8	2·0		1700	3092	1·0	Li_2O
Lithium carbonate	Li_2CO_3	73·8	2·1		D 1310	D 2390	0·404	Li_2O
Magnesia (periclase)	MgO	40·3	3·5		2800	5072	1·0	MgO
Magnesium carbonate (magnesite)	$MgCO_3$	84·3	3·0	4·5	D 350	D 662	0·478	MgO
Magnesium carbonate light	$3MgCO_3.Mg(OH)_2.3H_2O$	365·2			D 410	D 770	0·441	MgO
Magnesium sulphate	$MgSO_4$	120·4	2·7		D 1127	D 2061	0·335	MgO
Magnetite	Fe_3O_4	231·4	5·1	6·5	D 1538	D 2800	1·035	Fe_2O_3
Malachite	$CuCO_3.Cu(OH)_2$	221·0	3·9	4	D 500	D 932	0·719	CuO
Manganese carbonate	$MnCO_3$	114·9	3·6		D 300	D 572	0·615	MnO
Manganese dioxide (pyrolusite)	MnO_2	86·9	4·9		D 1080	D 1976	below 1080°C 1·0 MnO_2 above 1080°C 0·816 MnO	
Manganite	$MnO(OH)$	87·9	4·3	4	D 200	D 392	0·807	MnO
Manganous oxide	MnO	70·9	5·3		1650	3002	1·0	MnO
Marcasite	FeS_2	120·0	4·7	6·5	D 510	D 950	0·665	Fe_2O_3
Metakaolin	$Al_2O_3.2SiO_2$	222·2			1770	3218	0·459 0·541	Al_2O_3 SiO_2
Microcline (potash feldspar)	$K_2O.Al_2O_3.6SiO_2$	556·8	2·5	6	1200	2192	0·169 0·183 0·648	K_2O Al_2O_3 SiO_2
Mullite	$3Al_2O_3.2SiO_2$	426·2	3·2		1810	3190	0·718 0·282	Al_2O_3 SiO_2
Natrium potash	$NaKO$	78·1			700	1292	1·0	$NaKO$
Natron	$Na_2CO_3.10H_2O*$	286·0	1·4	1·5	D 860	D 1580	0·217	Na_2O
Nepheline	$K_2O.3Na_2O.4Al_2O_3.9SiO_2$	1229·1	2·6	6	1200	2192	0·077 0·151 0·332 0·440	K_2O Na_2O Al_2O_3 SiO_2
Nepheline syenite	$K_2O.3Na_2O.4Al_2O_3.8SiO_2$	1169·0	2·6	6	1200	2192	0·081 0·159 0·349 0·411	K_2O Na_2O Al_2O_3 SiO_2
Nickel oxide	NiO	74·7	6·7		1990	3614	1·0	NiO
Oligoclase (plagioclase feldspar)	$0.8Na_2O\ Al_2O_3.5.2SiO_2*$ $0.2CaO$	475·3	2·7	6·5	1250	2282	0·104 0·024 0·215 0·657	Na_2O CaO Al_2O_3 SiO_2
Oolite	$CaCO_3$	100·1	2·7	3	D 825	D 1517	0·561	CaO
Orthoclase (potash feldspar)	$K_2O.Al_2O_3.6SiO_2$	556·8	2·5	6	1200	2192	0·169 0·183 0·648	K_2O Al_2O_3 SiO_2
Petalite (lithium feldspathoid)	$Li_2O.Al_2O_3.8SiO_2$	612·6	2·4	6·5	1300	2372	0·049 0·166 0·785	Li_2O Al_2O_3 SiO_2

Name	Chemical formula	MW	SG	H	MP °C	MP °F	CF	Oxides entering fusion
Phosphorite	$Ca_3(PO_4)_2$	310·3	3·2	5	1730	3146	0·542 0·458	CaO P_2O_5
Phosphorus pentoxide	P_2O_5	142·0	2·4		580	1076	1·0	P_2O_5
Plaster of Paris	$2CaSO_4.H_2O$	290·4			D 1450	D 2642	0·386	CaO
Plumbous oxide	PbO	223·2	9·3		880	1616	1·0	PbO
Potash	K_2O	94·2	2·32		700	1291	1·0	K_2O
Potassium carbonate	K_2CO_3	138·2	2·4		D 895	D 1643	0·682	K_2O
Potassium dichromate	$K_2Cr_2O_7$	294·2	2·7		D 500	D 932	0·320 0·517	K_2O Cr_2O_3
Potassium permanganate	$KMnO_4$	158·0	2·7		D 240	D 464	0·298 0·449	K_2O MnO
Praseodymium oxide	PrO_2	172·9					1·0	PrO_2
Pyrite	FeS_2	120·0	4·9	6·5	D 510	D 950	0·665	Fe_2O_3
Pyrolusite	MnO_2	86·9	4·9	2·5	D 1080	D 1976	0·816	MnO
Quartz	SiO_2	60·1	2·7	7	1710	3110	1·0	SiO_2
Red ochre	Fe_2O_3	159·6	3·5	2	1565	2849	1·0	Fe_2O_3
Rutile	TiO_2	79·9	4·3	6·5	1825	3317	1·0	TiO_2
Siderite	$FeCO_3$	115·8	3·8	4·5	D 450	D 842	0·689	Fe_2O_3
Silica	SiO_2	60·1	2·7	7	1710	3110	1·0	SiO_2
Silicon carbide	SiC	40·1	3·2	9·8	D 2700	D 4892	1·499	SiO_2
Sillimanite	$Al_2O_3.SiO_2$	162·1	3·2	7	1545	2813	0·629 0·371	Al_2O_3 SiO_2
Smithsonite	$ZnCO_3$	125·4	4·3	5	D 300	D 572	0·649	ZnO
Soda	Na_2O	62·0	2·3		900	1652	1·0	Na_2O
Sodalite (soda feldspathoid)	$3NaAlSiO_4.NaCl$	484·8	2·2	6	1200	2192	0·256 0·316 0·372	Na_2O Al_2O_3 SiO_2
Sodium carbonate (soda ash)	Na_2CO_3	106·0	2·5		D 860	D 1580	0·585	Na_2O
Sodium chloride	NaCl	58·5	2·17		D 800	D 1472	0·529	Na_2O
Sodium silicate (waterglass)	Na_2SiO_3	122·2	2·4		1100	2012	0·508 0·492	Na_2O SiO_2
Spodumene (lithium feldspathoid)	$Li_2O.Al_2O_3.4SiO_2$	372·2	3·1	6·5	1400	2552	0·080 0·274 0·646	Li_2O Al_2O_3 SiO_2
Stannic oxide (tin oxide)	SnO_2	150·7	6·8		1150	2102	1·0	SnO_2
					oxidizes—			
Stannous oxide	SnO	134·7	6·5		700	1291	1·119	SnO_2
Strontia	SrO	103·6	4·7		2430	4406	1·0	SrO
Strontianite (strontium carbonate)	$SrCO_3$	147·6	3·6	4	D 1075	D 1967	0·702	SrO
Talc	$3MgO.4SiO_2.H_2O$	379·3	2·7	1	D 900	D 1652	0·319 0·634	MgO SiO_2
Tin oxide (stannic oxide)	SnO_2	150·7	6·8		1150	2102	1·0	SnO_2

Name	Chemical formula	MW	SG	H	MP °C	MP °F	CF	Oxides entering fusion
Titanite (sphene)	$CaO . TiO_2 . SiO_2$	196·1	3·5	5·5	1385	2525	0·286 0·407 0·307	CaO TiO_2 SiO_2
Titanium dioxide (titania)	TiO_2	79·9	4·2	6·5	1830	3326	1·0	TiO_2
Tridymite	SiO_2	60·1	2·3	7	1700	3092	1·0	SiO_2
Ulexite	$NaCaB_5O_9 . 8H_2O$	405·1	1·65	1	D 300	D 572	0·077 0·138 0·429	Na_2O CaO B_2O_3
Uranium oxide	U_3O_8	842·0	7·3		2176	3949	1·0	U_3O_8
Vanadium oxide	V_2O_5	181·8	3·4		690	1274	1·0	V_2O_5
Washing soda	$Na_2CO_3 . 10H_2O$	286·0	1·5		D 860	D 1580	0·217	Na_2O
Whiting	$CaCO_3$	100·1	2·8	3	D 825	D 1517	0·561	CaO
Willemite	Zn_2SiO_4	222·9	4	5	1200	2192	0·730 0·270	ZnO SiO_2
Witherite	$BaCO_3$	197·3	4·3	3·7	D 1450 reduced— D 900	D 2642 D 1652	0·777	BaO
Wollastonite	$CaSiO_3$	116·2	2·8	5	1545	2813	0·483 0·517	CaO SiO_2
Yellow ochre	$2Fe_2O_3 . 3H_2O*$	373·2	3·5	5	D 200	D 392	0·855	Fe_2O_3
Zinc blende	ZnS	97·5	4·1	4·0	D 1020	D 1868	0·835	ZnO
Zinc oxide (zincite)	ZnO	81·4	5·7	4·5	1970	3578	1·0	ZnO
Zirconia	ZrO_2	123·2	5·5		2700	4892	1·0	ZrO_2
Zirconium silicate (zircon)	$ZrSiO_4$	183·3	4·5	7·5	2550	4622	0·672 0·328	ZrO_2 SiO_2

Table of incandescence

See **Temperature** and **Incandescence**

°C	°F	Kiln interior glow: muffle and other kilns firing and cooling	Kiln interior glow: electric kilns firing only	°C	°F	Kiln interior glow: muffle and other kilns firing and cooling	Kiln interior glow: electric kilns firing only
1400	2552	blue-white		650	1202		
1350	2462			600	1112	first visible red	dull red
1300	2372	white	white	550	1022	black	
1250	2282	yellow	yellow-white	500	932		first visible red
1200	2192	bright orange	light yellow	450	842		black
1150	2102			400	752		
1100	2012	orange	bright orange	350	662		
1050	1922	bright red	orange	300	572	hottest domestic oven	
1000	1832		bright red	250	482		
950	1742			200	392		
900	1652	deep red		150	302		
850	1562			100	212		
800	1472		deep red	50	122		
750	1382			0	32		
700	1292	dull red					

Conversion of temperatures

See also **Centigrade, Celsius, Fahrenheit, Kelvin** and **Calculations**

$$°C = \frac{(°F - 32) \times 5}{9} \qquad °F = \frac{9(°K - 273)}{5} + 32$$

$$°C = °K - 273 \qquad\qquad °K = °C + 273$$

$$°F = \frac{°C \times 9}{5} + 32 \qquad °K = \frac{5(°F - 32)}{9} + 273$$

List of temperature equivalents

See **Temperature**

°C	°F	°C	°F	°C	°F	°C	°F	°C	°F	°C	°F
2000	3632	1280	2336	1180	2156	1090	1994	850	1562	450	842
1900	3452	1270	2318	1177	2150	1080	1976	816	1500	400	752
1800	3272	1260	2300	1170	2138	1070	1958	800	1472	350	662
1700	3092	1250	2282	1160	2120	1060	1940	760	1400	300	572
1600	2912	1240	2264	1150	2102	1050	1922	750	1382	250	482
1500	2732	1232	2250	1149	2100	1038	1900	704	1300	200	392
1400	2552	1230	2246	1140	2084	1000	1832	700	1292	120	248
1350	2462	1220	2228	1130	2066	982	1800	650	1202	100	212
1316	2400	1210	2210	1120	2048	950	1742	600	1112	0	32
1300	2372	1204	2200	1110	2030	927	1700	573	1063		
1290	2354	1200	2192	1100	2012	900	1652	550	1022		
1288	2350	1190	2174	1093	2000	871	1600	500	932		

Valency table

See **Valency**

	Valency 1 (monovalent)		Valency 2 (divalent)		Valency 3 (trivalent)		Valency 4 (tetravalent)		Valency 5	
Metals	Copper(ous)	Cu	Copper(ic)	Cu	Aluminium	Al	Cerium	Ce		
	Lithium	Li	Cobalt(ous)	Co	Cobalt(ic)	Co	Tin	Sn		
	Potassium	K	Manganese(ous)	Mn	Manganese(ic)	Mn	Manganese	Mn		
	Sodium	Na	Iron(ous)	Fe	Iron(ic)	Fe	Titanium	Ti		
			Nickel	Ni	Arsenic	As	Nickel (rare)	Ni		
			Lead(ous)	Pb	Antimony	Sb	Lead(ic)	Pb		
			Vanadium	V	Vanadium (basic)	V	Vanadium	V	Vanadium (acidic)	V
			Beryllium	Be	Uranium	U	Uranium	U	Uranium	U
			Barium	Ba	Boron	B	Zirconium	Zr		
			Calcium	Ca	Chromium	Cr	Praseodymium	Pr		
			Magnesium	Mg						
			Strontium	Sr						
			Zinc	Zn						
Non-metals	Chlorine	Cl	Oxygen	O	Nitrogen	N	Silicon	Si	Phosphorus	P
	Fluorine	F	Sulphur	S	Phosphorus	P	Sulphur	S		
	Hydrogen	H	Carbon	C	Bismuth	Bi	Carbon	C		
Radicals	Hydroxide	OH	Carbonate	CO_3	Phosphate	PO_4				
	Nitrate	NO_3	Sulphate	SO_4	Arsenate	AsO_4				
	Chlorate	ClO_3	Sulphite	SO_3						
	Bicarbonate	HCO_3								

Percentage reckoner

Place straight edge on number on left-hand scale and total number on middle scale.
Read the percentage on right-hand scale.

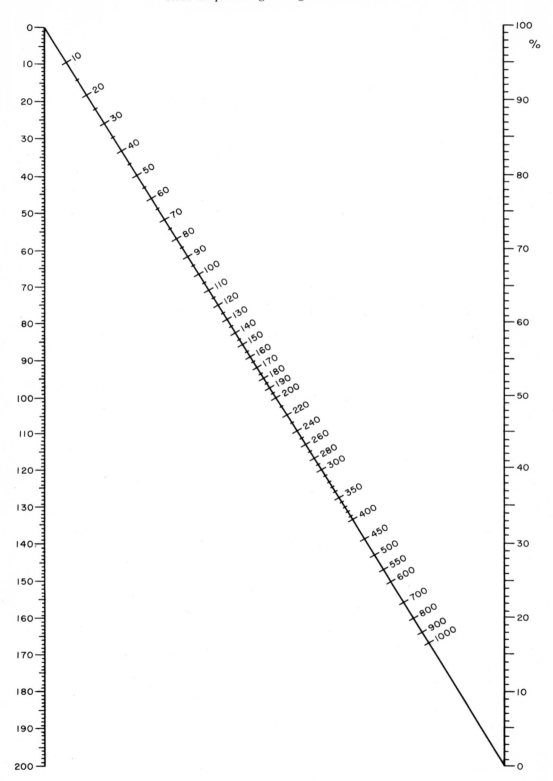

Atomic to visible particle sizes compared with wavelengths of electromagnetic radiation

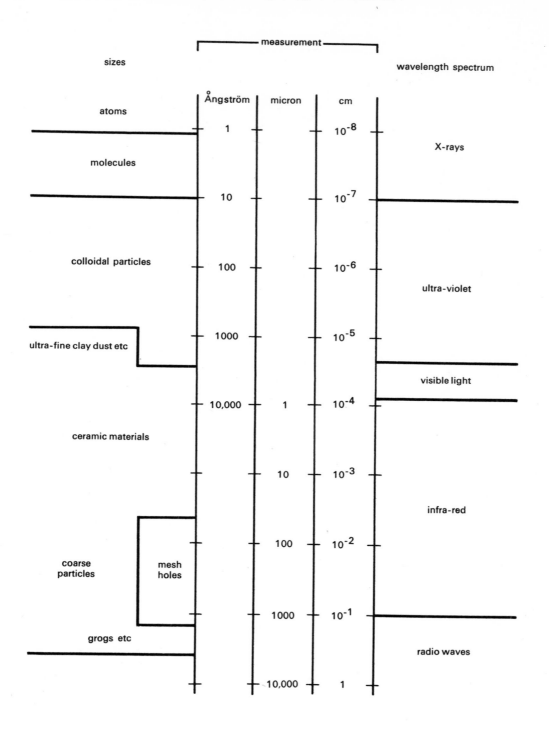

Periodic table of elements

For use see **Periodic table**, p. 215

	O	I	II	III	IV	V	VI	VII	VIII		
O								hydrogen 1 H			
I	2 He	lithium 3 Li	beryllium 4 Be	boron 5 B	carbon 6 C	nitrogen 7 N	oxygen 8 O	fluorine 9 F			
II	10 Ne	sodium 11 Na	magnesium 12 Mg	aluminium 13 Al	silicon 14 Si	phosphorus 15 P	sulphur 16 S	chlorine 17 Cl			
A III B	18 A	potassium 19 K	calcium 20 Ca	21 Sc	titanium 22 Ti	vanadium 23 V	chromium 24 Cr	manganese 25 Mn	iron 26 Fe	cobalt 27 Co	nickel 28 Ni
		copper 29 Cu	zinc 30 Zn	31 Ga	germanium 32 Ge	arsenic 33 As	selenium 34 Se	35 Br			
A IV B	36 Kr	37 Rb	strontium 38 Sr	39 Y	zirconium 40 Zr	41 Nb	42 Mo	43 Tc	44 Ru	45 Rh	46 Pd
		silver 47 Ag	cadmium 48 Cd	49 In	tin 50 Sn	antimony 51 Sb	52 Te	53 I			
A V B	54 Xe	55 Cs	barium 56 Ba	lanthanides 57 to 71	72 Hf	73 Ta	tungsten 74 W	75 Re	76 Os	77 Ir	platinum 78 Pt
		gold 79 Au	80 Hg	81 Tl	lead 82 Pb	bismuth 83 Bi	84 Po	85 At			
VI	86 Rn	87 Fr	88 Ra	actinides 89 to 106							

Potter's periodic table

For use see **Periodic table**, p. 216

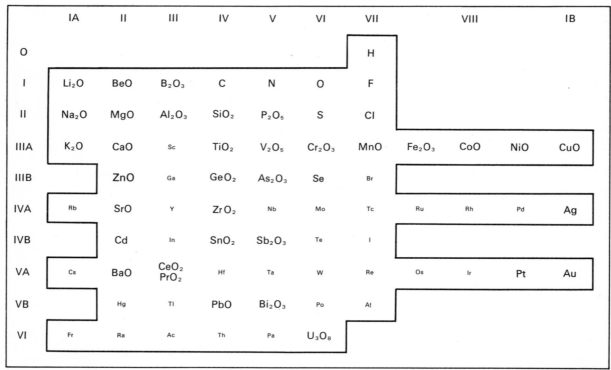

348

BIBLIOGRAPHY

Books on ceramics

M. Cardew: *Pioneer Pottery* (Longmans, Green 1969; St Martin 1971)

A. E. Dodd: *Dictionary of Ceramics* (George Newnes 1967; Littlefield 1964)

M. Fieldhouse: *Pottery* (Foyle 1952)

R. W. Ford: *Drying* (Institute of Ceramics textbook, Maclaren & Sons 1964)

W. F. Ford: *The Effect of Heat on Ceramics* (Institute of Ceramics textbook, Maclaren & Sons 1967)

H. Fraser: *Kilns and Kiln Firing for the Craft Potter* (Pitman 1969)

D. Green: *Understanding Pottery Glazes* (Faber & Faber 1963; Watson-Guptill 1973)

J. B. Kenny: *Ceramic Design* (Pitman 1967; Chilton 1963)

B. Leach: *A Potter's Book* (Faber & Faber 1949; Transatlantic 1973)

F. Moore: *Rheology of Ceramic Systems* (Institute of Ceramics textbook, Maclaren & Sons 1965)

G. C. Nelson: *Ceramics, a Potter's Handbook* (Holt, Rinehart & Winston 1971)

C. W. Parmelee: *Ceramic Glazes* (Industrial Publications 1951; Cahners 1973)

D. Rhodes: *Stoneware and Porcelain* (Pitman 1960; Chilton 1959)

D. Rhodes: *Clay and Glazes for the Potter* (Pitman 1962; Chilton 1959)

D. Rhodes: *Kilns* (Pitman 1969; Chilton 1968)

A. B. Searle: *The Clayworker's Handbook* (Charles Griffin 1953)

A. B. Searle: *The Glazer's Book* (Technical Press 1948)

A. B. Searle: *Refractories for Furnaces* (Crosby Lockwood & Sons 1948)

K. Shaw: *Ceramic Colours and Pottery Decoration* (Maclaren & Sons 1968)

K. Shaw: *Ceramic Glazes* (Elsevier 1971)

F. Singer: *Low Solubility Glazes* (Borax Consolidated Ltd 1948)

F. Singer and W. L. German: *Ceramic Glazes* (Borax Consolidated Ltd 1964)

F. Singer and S. S. Singer: *Industrial Ceramics* (Chapman & Hall 1971; Halsted Press 1963)

Scientific books

W. E. Addison: *Structural Principles in Inorganic Compounds* (Longmans 1968)

G. Maitland and G. Slinn: *Ceramist's Handbook* (Podmore 1973)

I. N. Quick: *Introductory College Chemistry* (Macmillan 1965)

E. B. Uvarov and D. R. Chapman, revised by A. Isaacs: *A Dictionary of Science* (Penguin Books 1964)

A. F. Wells: *Structural Inorganic Chemistry* (Clarendon Press, Oxford 1963)

Books on minerals and raw materials

G. W. Himus and G. S. Sweeting: *The Elements of Field Geology* (University Tutorial Press 1965)

P. Lake and R. H. Rastall: *Textbook of Geology* (5th edn) (Edward Arnold 1964)

F. Rutley, edited by H. H. Read: *Elements of Mineralogy* (26th rev. edn) (Murby 1970)

W. Ryan: *Properties of Ceramic Raw Material* (Pergamon Press 1968)

W. E. Worrall: *Clays* (Maclaren; Transatlantic, 1968)

W. E. Worrall: *Raw Materials* (Institute of Ceramics textbook, Maclaren & Sons 1964)

H. S. Zim and P. R. Shaffer: *Rocks and Minerals* (Paul Hamlyn 1965; Western Publications 1957)

Books on historical ceramics

R. J. Charleston (Ed.): *World Ceramics* (Hamlyn 1968)

F. H. Garner: *English Delftware* (Faber & Faber 1948; International Publications Service 1972)

G. St G. M. Gompertz: *Chinese Celadon Wares* (Faber & Faber 1958; Praeger 1969)

B. Gray: *Early Chinese Pottery and Porcelain* (Faber & Faber 1953)

H. Hodges: *Pottery* (Hamlyn 1972)

A. Lane: *Early Islamic Pottery* (Faber & Faber 1947)

A. Lane: *Greek Pottery* (Faber & Faber 1948; International Publications Service 1971)

B. Rackham: *Medieval English Pottery* (Faber & Faber 1947)

Periodicals

Ceramic Arts and Crafts (Livonia, Michigan)

Ceramic Review (Craftsmen Potters Association of Great Britain, London)

Ceramics Monthly (Professional Publications, Columbus, Ohio)

Craft Horizons (The American Crafts Council, New York)

New Zealand Potter (PO Box 12–162, Wellington, New Zealand)

Pottery in Australia (Potters' Society of Australia, Turramurra, New South Wales)

Pottery Quarterly (Northfield Studio, Tring, Herts, England)

Studio Potter (Warner, New Hampshire)